Annotated PCT

Annotated PCT

Edited by

Malte Köllner

Wolters Kluwer

Published by:
Kluwer Law International B.V.
PO Box 316
2400 AH Alphen aan den Rijn
The Netherlands
E-mail: lrs-sales@wolterskluwer.com
Website: www.wolterskluwer.com/en/solutions/kluwerlawinternational

Sold and distributed by:
Wolters Kluwer Legal & Regulatory U.S.
920 Links Avenue
Landisville, PA 17538
United States of America
Email: customer.service@wolterskluwer.com

Printed on acid-free paper.

ISBN 978-94-035-0388-2

e-Book: ISBN 978-94-035-0398-1
web-PDF: ISBN 978-94-035-0408-7

© 2025 Malte Köllner

Acknowledgement:
Cover image source: https://www.wipo.int/pct/en/pct_contracting_states.html

All rights are reserved, including those for text and data mining, AI training, and similar technologies. No part of this publication may be reproduced, stored in a retrieval system, or transmitted in any form or by any means, electronic, mechanical, photocopying, recording, or otherwise, without written permission from the publisher. Permission to use this content must be obtained from the copyright owner.

Contributors

Dr Malte Köllner

Malte Köllner is a European and German patent attorney. He holds a law degree and a PhD in physics. He has authored and co-authored numerous publications on intellectual property, among others the German language *PCT-Handbuch*. He is editor-in-chief of *Mitteilungen der deutschen Patentanwälte*, the Scientific Journal of the German Chamber of Patent Attorneys, which is the leading journal on patent law in German-speaking countries. Malte is a regular lecturer on intellectual property.

He is responsible for: Art. 1–14, Art. 22–30, Art. 38–49, R. 1–32, R. 48–52, R. 76–80, R. 82–83, R. 89*bis*, R. 90–96, Schedule of Fees, Fee Reduction, Annexes, Introduction to the PCT.

Barbara Heidecke

Barbara Heidecke is a lawyer. She studied law in Osnabrück, Germany and Leiden, The Netherlands. She worked as a corporate counsel for a large international corporation, after which she joined an intellectual property firm. She has been co-author of more than 16 editions of the German language *PCT-Handbuch*.

She is responsible for: Art. 1–14, Art. 22–30, Art. 38–49, R. 1–32, R. 48–52, R. 76–80, R. 82–83, R. 89*bis*, R. 90–96, Schedule of Fees, Fee Reduction, Annexes, Introduction to the PCT.

Dr Thomas Henninger

Thomas Henninger is a lawyer and holds a PhD in comparative law from the University of Geneva. He did his bar exam in Munich, Germany. He has practiced intellectual property as a legal attorney in the private sector and worked as an assistant at the University of Geneva, Switzerland. Thomas joined WIPO in 2009, where he is currently Senior Legal Information Officer in the PCT Legal and User Relations Division, responsible for managing legal information resources. He regularly gives PCT training seminars.

He is responsible for: Art. 50–69, R. 81, R. 84–89, R. 89*ter*, PCT Legal Framework and Resources.

Piotr Wierzejewski

Piotr Wierzejewski has been with the EPO since 2003. As a computer scientist, he initially served as a patent examiner specializing in computer-implemented inventions. Over the years, he has established himself as an expert in patent procedures, contributing significantly to the substantive content of the EPO Examination Guidelines and the creation of the Guidelines for Search and Examination at the EPO as a PCT Authority. Currently, Piotr coordinates the EPO's international cooperation with the USPTO and CIPO, as well as with major international user associations, to enhance the global patent system.

He is responsible for: Art. 15–21, Art. 31–37, R. 33–47, R. 53–75.

Preface

This book is a commentary on the PCT and results from a fusion of the books *PCT Strategy and Practice* (Kluwer Law International BV, 2021) and *PCT-Handbuch* (17th edition, Carl Heymanns Verlag, 2023). 1

Unlike most laws, there is practically no case law on the PCT. There is also no appeal body that can be called upon – with the exception of questions relating to unity of invention. As a result, all contentious issues have been decided by the Contracting States and codified in the text of the Regulations under the PCT or in other legal provisions. 2

The multiplicity of legal texts has made the legal framework of the PCT complex and at times confusing, which is why many people find working with the PCT challenging and unfamiliar, and might avoid it sometimes as a result. This is regrettable, as the international patent application under the PCT is of enormous and increasing practical importance, since in the majority of cases the priority application is followed by an international application under the PCT. 3

This book, therefore, is meant as a helping hand for users of the Patent Cooperation Treaty. The logical structure of the book should make it relatively easy to locate the desired information. 4

Hierarchically organized, detailed tables of contents and an extensive alphabetical index guide the user quickly to the Rule they are looking for, which contains the information. 5

The legal text is accompanied by explanations and cross-references to Articles and Rules that are related to the provision at hand. They refer, for example, to Rules in which time limits, grace periods, surcharges and the like are codified. The references are generally formulated in condensed form. They use abbreviations and are limited to the essentials, e.g. the title of the cited Rule. Details can be found in the cited Articles/Rules themselves. 6

Readers interested in a more general context, background and strategy will find the information mainly in the introductions to the Articles/Rules. Readers who are looking for more specific information and details or who want to quickly find further related Articles/Rules may find what they are looking for with the help of the keyword-like notes and references directly under the Articles and Rules. 7

The book provides expert guidance on how to carry out the procedures from filing a single international patent application to starting prosecution before a plurality 8 of national Offices. The options available to the applicant at the various stages are clearly set out, including factors to consider in making a choice between them.

9 A special feature of the PCT is the variety of its legal sources, both at an international and at a national level. The book gives an overview of the sources and the way they link to form the legal basis for a complete procedure. Each statement in the book is provided with a reference to its legal basis, thereby allowing the reader to deepen any open question if necessary. The legal sources, such as international and national law, can be quickly accessed by links embedded in the text. Readers of the paper book are given guidance on how to find the sources on the Internet.

10 The book is intended both for experienced practitioners and for trainees preparing for examinations, such as the European Qualifying Examination. Practitioners, patent attorneys, and paralegals will find a wealth of guidance for daily practice, including citations from the Practical Advice of the PCT Newsletter published by International Bureau of the World Intellectual Property Organization (WIPO).

11 This book does not replace the so-called PCT Applicant's Guide. Details of the various national/regional requirements are only mentioned if they are particularly important.

12 The team of authors includes legal experts from WIPO, the European Patent Office (EPO) and the patent practice. Hence, inside knowledge from the legal departments of Intellectual Property Offices and experience of users of the PCT are at the basis of the book. The views expressed in parts of the book written by employees of WIPO and the EPO do not necessarily reflect the views of WIPO and the EPO.

13 For better readability, the masculine form is used for personal pronouns. The relevant terms generally apply to all genders and the use does not imply any value judgment.

14 In spite of all due care taken while writing the book, the authors do not accept any responsibility for errors and consequences of any actions based on such errors. Comments on inaccuracies or suggestions for improvement are welcomed. Please send them to Anja Kramer at anja.kramer@wolterskluwer.com.

Malte Köllner
Barbara Heidecke
Thomas Henninger
Piotr Wierzejewski
November 11, 2024

History of the Book

The present book is based on the two books *PCT Strategy and Practice* (Kluwer Law International, 2021) by Derk Visser et al. and *PCT-Handbuch* (17th edition, Carl Heymanns Verlag, 2023) by Malte Köllner and Barbara Heidecke. The first book, *PCT Strategy and Practice*, is based on the PCT chapter in the 2019 edition of the book *Visser's Annotated European Patent Convention* by Derk Visser et al (Kluwer Law International, 2020). 1

The in-depth explanations of legal principles from *PCT Strategy and Practice* are used in the present book as an introduction to the various Articles and Rules of the PCT. The cross references between legal provisions from *PCT-Handbuch* have been included immediately below the Articles and Rules. 2

The index is based on the WIPO PCT Legal Text Index (for details see Index). 3

The book therefore provides a comprehensive commentary on the PCT, containing both the full legal text of the PCT, in-depth explanations of legal principles, cross references and interrelations between legal provisions, and an extensive index. 4

The team of authors hopes that the *Annotated PCT* offers the reader added value. 5

Instructions for Use

Text Shaded in Gray

The official legal text of the PCT Treaty and the Regulations under the PCT is shaded with a gray background. A considerable number of Articles and Rules refer to other Articles and Rules. If not expressly mentioned in the legal provision itself, it is not always easy to remember the situations regulated in these cited Articles/ Rules. Therefore, the authors sometimes insert very brief comments for quick understanding of what the cited Rules pertain to. These very brief comments are put into brackets and written in italics in a lighter font to clearly distinguish them from the legal text. Where the official text contains such comments in brackets (see e.g. Art. 1(1)), these official parts of the Regulations under the PCT are not printed in italics. 1

Text Shaded in Light Gray

The text shaded in light gray contains cross-references to related articles and rules and other legal sources. 2

Text with White Background

The text with a white background contains the explanations by the authors. 3

Overviews at the End of the Book

The book contains some overviews in the Annex. These summarize different topics that are best summarized in tabular form, such as the list of Contracting States. 4

Index

In order to provide the reader with the quickest possible access to information, a very extensive alphabetical index has been added. The alphabetical index has been based on the WIPO PCT Legal Text Index, but with some additions. 5

Miscellaneous

6 The references to sources of information are included in the running text to allow the reader to check the legal basis of the statement preceding the reference. A reference after the last period of a paragraph refers to the entire paragraph.

7 Candidates for the European Qualifying Examination are reminded that the Examination Board expects that the legal basis they give in part D1 of the examination is taken from a specific group of documents. References to other documents will not attract full marks. Several sources cited in this book are not among the group of documents, in particular, the Euro-PCT Guide. The Euro-PCT Guide may still be useful for candidates in that it includes in its margin references to documents in the allowed group.

Updates

8 This book contains legal changes up to August, 2024. Since legal provisions change frequently, the reader is advised to check critical issues before applying them to an actual case. An overview of recent and future amendments to the PCT Regulations can be found in PCT Highlights https://www.wipo.int/pct/en/highlights/. For example, Uruguay will become bound by the PCT on January 7, 2025. Amendments to national provisions relevant to the PCT are most easily checked in the documents on national procedure accessible through the PCT Applicant's Guide, which is updated weekly. Generally, the application of amended Rules is based on the international filing date; any special features with regard to transitional provisions are indicated in the Articles/Rules concerned.

PCT Legal Framework and Resources

The Patent Cooperation Treaty is an international agreement defining a broad framework for many aspects of filing, searching and examination of patent applications. Its Contracting States have agreed to accept the international filing date and the form and content of an international application having the effect of a national application but they have not limited their freedom to grant patents, to an International Authority (Art. 11(3), 27). In contrast, the Contracting States of the European Patent Convention (EPC), also an international agreement, have ceded such powers and acts of sovereignty to the European Patent Office. 1

Legal Sources

The legal provisions of the PCT are laid down in the 'Patent Cooperation Treaty' comprising Articles and in the 'Regulations under the Patent Cooperation Treaty' comprising Rules. Since the PCT has no instance for appeal to interpret, further develop or fill in holes in the provisions, the Rules of the PCT have to cover all situations that might occur and are therefore very detailed. Moreover, some provisions are rather complicated because of exceptions that the PCT had to permit the Contracting States in view of national peculiarities and issues left open in the PCT to be implemented under national law. An example of the exceptions is Art. 64, permitting a Contracting State to declare that it is not bound by certain provisions of the PCT. An example of a left open issue is the allowed methods for filing documents with an International Authority. A complete view of a procedure before an International Authority can thus only be obtained by combining the relevant provisions of the PCT with implementations under the national law applied by the particular Office. 2

The Rules are usually amended every year, while Articles are amended only occasionally (see annotations to Art. 60). The amendments usually come into force in January or July (https://www.wipo.int/treaties/en/ShowResults.jsp?country_id = ALL&start_year = ANY&end_year = ANY&search_what = N&treaty_id = 6). 3

The PCT framework defines executive functions for treating international applications, which may be granted to national Offices of a PCT Contracting State. Such national Offices may act under the PCT as receiving Office, ISA and IPEA. The International Bureau of WIPO and the national Offices have signed agreements for the work of the national Offices as ISA and IPEA (https://www.wipo.int/pct/en/access/isa_ipea_agreements.html). 4

5 The Articles and Rules of the PCT are supplemented by Administrative Instructions (AIs) (https://www.wipo.int/pct/en/texts/ai/ai_index.html) for the use of the International Authorities. The legal sources are, in hierarchical order, Articles of the Treaty, Rules of the Regulations and Sections of the Administrative Instructions. The Administrative Instructions contain Annexes, such as the PCT Forms (Annex A) and the important Annex F, containing the Standard for Electronic Filing and Processing.

Semi-Legal Guidelines

6 These formal legal sources are complemented by the Guidelines, first for receiving Offices (RO Guidelines) and second for International Search and Preliminary Examination (ISPE Guidelines). These semi-legal guidelines shall provide for a common practice in applying the legal texts. There might, however, be some divergent practice in application of the guidelines by the various Offices.

Contracting State-Specific Legal Texts

7 As already illustrated above with the possibility of reservations in Art. 64 – besides these five common legal and semi-legal sources, the PCT system provides for Contracting State-specific legal provisions, in the form of reservations, declarations, notifications and incompatibilities with the Treaty, the Regulations and the Administrative Instructions, as well as, for Agreements between the International Bureau and the International Authorities, such as the ISA/IPEA Agreements. All these country-specific legal and practical adaptions are chronologically published and recorded in the Official Notices (PCT Gazette).

Comprehensive and Up-to-Date PCT Applicant's Guide

8 The PCT Applicant's Guide (also abbreviated 'Guide' by the International Bureau) (AG) aims at providing practical information on the PCT for applicants, and also to a certain extent to Offices. While the legal and semi-legal sources are organized hierarchically and the Official Notices chronologically, the PCT Applicant's Guide aims at providing a comprehensive and always up-to-date Guide. It contains a general part comprising all legal provisions that are common, and a country- and Office-specific part in the Annexes. It thus includes the 'Introduction to the International Phase' (AG-IP) (https://www.wipo.int/pct/en/guide/ipindex.html or in PDF format https://www.wipo.int/export/sites/www/pct/guide/en/gdvol1/pdf/gdvol1.pdf) and the 'Introduction to the National Phase' (AG-NP) (https://www.wipo.int/pct/en/guide/ipindex.html or in PDF format https://www.wipo.int/export/sites/www/pct/guide/en/gdvol1/pdf/gdvol1.pdf), two guides for applicants giving a useful overview of the procedures under PCT in the international phase before the receiving Office, ISA and IPEA and in the national phase before the designated and elected Offices. The PCT Applicant's Guide (www.wipo.int/pct/en/guide/index.html) also provides in an Annex for each national Office and general information and specific procedures and details for the International Bureau, such as methods for filing, often based on national law, where the national Office or International Bureau acts as receiving

Office, ISA or IPEA. WIPO updates the PCT Applicant's Guide weekly and includes practical information for applicants on how to use the PCT system.

All Legal Resources

Hence, the legal framework of the PCT is made up of the following major building blocks in order of descending legal weight. A link to most documents mentioned below can be found here: https://www.wipo.int/pct/en/. 9

- Patent Cooperation Treaty (https://wipolex.wipo.int/en/treaties/textdetails/12635) – the Articles of the PCT, the highest level in the legal hierarchy;
- Regulations under the PCT (https://wipolex.wipo.int/en/treaties/textdetails/19780) – the Rules of the PCT, implementing the Articles;
- PCT Administrative Instructions (https://www.wipo.int/pct/en/texts/ai/ai_index.html) – supplementing the Articles and Rules with details for specific issues;
- PCT Forms www.wipo.int/pct/en/forms/ – as Part of the Administrative Instructions;
- PCT Reservations, Declarations, Notifications and Incompatibilities (https://www.wipo.int/pct/en/texts/reservations/res_incomp.html) – list of legally binding declarations and exceptions concerning the PCT and issued by national/regional Offices;
- ISA and IPEA Agreements (https://www.wipo.int/pct/en/access/isa_ipea_agreements.html) – agreements between the International Bureau of WIPO and national Offices about their functioning as ISAs and IPEAs under the PCT;
- Guidelines for Authorities and Offices (https://www.wipo.int/pct/en/texts/gdlines.html), divided into PCT RO Guidelines and PCT ISPE Guidelines – instructions assisting receiving Offices, ISAs, and IPEAs to carry out their duties under the PCT;
- PCT Gazette, which includes the Official Notices (https://www.wipo.int/pct/en/official_notices/index.html) – the official, weekly WIPO publication of incremental updates of the PCT system, such as changes of legal provisions, fees, conditions, exceptions;
- PATENTSCOPE (https://patentscope.wipo.int/search/en/structuredSearch.jsf, https://www.wipo.int/patentscope/en/news/pctdb/2006/news_0004.html) – a searchable database with data and documents relating to specific international applications;
- PCT Applicant's Guide (AG) (https://www.wipo.int/pct/en/guide/) – a practical guide for applicants containing an introduction to the procedures under the PCT in the international phase (AG-IP) and national phase (AG-NP) and a large number of Annexes with weekly updated information of each Contracting State/organization;
- PCT Assembly documents and reports (www.wipo.int/meetings/en/topic.jsp?group_id=135) (www.wipo.int/pct/en/meetings/assemblies/reports.html) – a collection of all preparatory documents for the PCT Assembly and a record of the decisions taken by the Assembly. These reports also contain

agreed interpretative statements of legal nature made by the Assembly, (e.g. 2017 PCT Assembly Understanding);
- PCT Working Group documents: (www.wipo.int/pct-wg/en/index.html) – a collection of documents and recommendations made by the PCT Working Group to the PCT Assembly. For any predecessor meeting, refer to the annotations under Art. 53;
- PCT Newsletter (https://www.wipo.int/pct/en/newslett/) – a monthly WIPO publication containing all information published in the Official Notices but in a more user-friendly manner and, in addition, Practical Advice and other relevant updates for users of the PCT.

10 Certain ISAs and IPEAs issue Office-specific guidelines informing applicants about applicable procedures and requirements of the Office issuing them.

11 EPO:
- Guidelines for Search and Examination at the EPO as PCT Authority (https://www.epo.org/law-practice/legal-texts/guidelines-pct.html) – instructions for the EPO acting as ISA and IPEA on the practice and procedure to be followed in handling international applications;
- Euro-PCT Guide: PCT procedure before the EPO (https://www.epo.org/applying/international/guide-for-applicants.html) – guide for applicants of international applications with an emphasis on the PCT procedure before the EPO.

12 USPTO:
- Manual of Patent Examining Procedure Chapter 1800 (https://www.uspto.gov/web/offices/pac/mpep/mpep-1800.html)

13 IP Australia:
- Manual of Practice and Procedure (http://manuals.ipaustralia.gov.au/patents/Patent_Examiners_Manual.htm)

14 Canadian Patent Office:
- Manual of Patent Office Practice (https://www.ic.gc.ca/eic/site/cipointernet-internetopic.nsf/eng/h_wr00720.html)

15 Historical information can be found in:
- Washington Diplomatic Conference: www.wipo.int/pct/en/texts/washington.html
- History of the Regulations: www.wipo.int/export/sites/www/pct/en/docs/texts/pct-regulations-history.pdf
- Official Notices: www.wipo.int/pct/en/official_notices/index.html

16 Statistical information and case studies are available:
- PCT Yearly Review: www.wipo.int/pct/en/activity/index.html
- IP Statistics Data Center: www.wipo.int/ipstats/en/index.html
- IP Advantage on PCT: www.wipo.int/pct/en/inventions/case_studies.html

Notations and Abbreviations

Articles and Rules of the PCT are usually cited in the book without the addition 'PCT'; where confusion could arise 'PCT' is added. Citations from other legal sources always indicate the origin (e.g. Art. 81 EPC). 1

Where a situation is relevant to both Chapter I and Chapter II of the PCT, a reference is given in the form (Art. 22(1) [Art. 39(1)]), where the first reference relates to Chapter I and the reference in square brackets to Chapter II. 2

For abbreviations related to names of States and organizations see the codes in the List of Territories or https://www.wipo.int/export/sites/www/standards/en/pdf/03-03-01.pdf. 3

The book uses the following abbreviations for terms and references to other legal sources: 4

AG-IP Annex X	PCT Applicant's Guide – International Phase, Annex https://www.wipo.int/pct/en/guide/index.html with information of a PCT Contracting State, where X is: B (general information); C (receiving Office); D (ISA); SISA; E (IPEA); or L (deposits of biological material)
AG-IP Annex B(EP)	PCT Applicant's Guide, Annex B for the European Patent Office
AG-IP 5.038	PCT Applicant's Guide, Introduction to the International Phase https://pctlegal.wipo.int/eGuide/view-doc.xhtml?doc-code = pctip&doc-lang = en&doc-type = guide, paragraph 5.038
AG-NP Annex	PCT Applicant's Guide – National Phase, Annex (National Chapter) https://www.wipo.int/pct/en/guide/index.html with information on a PCT Contracting State as designated and elected Office

AG-NP Annex (US)	PCT Applicant's Guide – National Phase, Annex with information on the USPTO as designated and elected Office
AG-NP 4.010	PCT Applicant's Guide, Introduction to the National Phase paragraph 4.010 https://pctlegal.wipo.int/eGuide/view-doc.xhtml?doc-code = pctnp&doc-lang = en&doc-type = guide
AIs	PCT Administrative Instructions https://www.wipo.int/pct/en/texts/index.html
AIs 216	Section 216 of the PCT Administrative Instructions
Art.	Article or Articles
Art. 8	Article 8 of the PCT https://www.wipo.int/pct/en/texts/articles/atoc.html
Art. 150 EPC	Article 150 of the EPC https://www.epo.org/en/legal/epc/2020/convention.html
BlPMZ	Blatt für Patent-, Muster- und Zeichenwesen (German periodical) https://www.dpma.de/english/our_office/publications/blatt_fuer_pmz/index.html
BOT	British Overseas Territory
CCD	Common Citation Document
cf.	compare
Ch.	Chapter
CON	Commonwealth of Nations
CRep	common representative
DAS	Document Access Service
Dem.	demand (Form IPEA/401)
DG	Director General
DO	designated Office
DO/FR	The French Patent Office acting as designated Office under the PCT
DPMA	German Patent Office
ed.	edition
E-filing	electronic filing
e.g.	for example
EO	elected Office

EPC	European Patent Convention https://www.epo.org/en/legal/epc
ePCT	WIPO's online portal for filing and managing PCT applications
EPO	European Patent Office (not European Patent Organization)
etc.	and so forth
et seq.	and the following
Euro-PCT Guide 2.4.002	Euro-PCT Guide https://www.epo.org/en/legal/guide-europct point 2.4.002
fax	facsimile
Fees	if used without further information in the Index it means Schedule of Fees
FN	footnote
G	decision of the Enlarged Board of Appeal (EPO)
Gaz.	PCT Gazette
GL Exam EPO A-II, 1.7	Guidelines for Examination in the EPO, https://www.epo.org/en/legal/guidelines-epc point A-II, 1.7
IB	International Bureau
IDS	information disclosure statement
i.e.	that is
IFD	international filing date
IGO	intergovernmental organization
IntPatÜbkG	Act on International Patent Conventions
Introd.	Introduction
IPC	International Patent Classification
IPE	international preliminary examination
IPEA	International Preliminary Examining Authority
IPER	international preliminary examination report
IPRP	International Preliminary Report on Patentability
IPRP I	International Preliminary Report on Patentability prepared by the ISA
IPRP II	International Preliminary Report on Patentability prepared by the IPEA
IS	international search

ISA	International Searching Authority
ISA/EP	The European Patent Office, in its capacity as International Searching Authority under the PCT
ISPE Guidelines	PCT International Search and Preliminary Examination Guidelines https://www.wipo.int/pct/en/texts/gdlines.html
ISR	international search report
J	decision of the Legal Board of Appeal (EPO)
mn.	margin number
n.	note
NGO	non-governmental organization
No.	number
Nos	numbers
OCT	overseas countries and territories
OEE	Office of Earlier Examination (PPH)
OJ EPO 2020 A10	Official Journal of the EPO https://www.epo.org/law-practice/legal-texts/official-journal.html Article 10 of the year 2020
OJ EPO 2010 p. 498	Official Journal of the EPO page 498 of the year 2010
OLE	Office of Later Examination (PPH)
OMR	outermost regions
p.	page
PACE	Program for accelerated prosecution of European patent applications
para.	paragraph
paras	paragraphs
Paris Convention	Paris Convention for the Protection of Industrial Property https://www.wipo.int/treaties/en/ip/paris/
PatG	German Patent Act https://www.dpma.de/english/our_office/law/index.html
PatV	German Patent Ordinance https://www.dpma.de/english/our_office/law/index.html
PCT	Patent Cooperation Treaty
PCTa	international patent application

PCT EPO Guidelines	Guidelines for Search and Examination at the European Patent Office as PCT Authority, https://www.epo.org/en/legal/guidelines-pct
PCT/WG/11/21	PCT Working Group publication 11/21
PLT	Patent Law Treaty
pp.	pages
PPH	Patent Prosecution Highway
Pract. Adv. NL 10/1998	Practical Advice in PCT Newsletter No. 10 of the year 1998, accessible via keyword search https://www.wipo.int/pct/en/newslett/practical_advice/search.jsp and in the Archive of Newsletters https://www.wipo.int/pct/en/newslett/year.jsp
R.	Rule or Rules
R. 32	Rule 32 of the Regulations under the PCT https://www.wipo.int/export/sites/www/pct/en/docs/texts/pct-regs.pdf
R. 81 EPC	Rule 81 of the Implementing Regulations to the EPC https://www.epo.org/en/legal/epc/2020/regulations.html
RC	record copy
Reg.	Regulations under the PCT
RFees 2(1)	Rules relating to Fees of the EPC https://www.epo.org/en/legal/epc/2020/rfees.html of the EPC, Article 2(1)
RO	receiving Office
RO Guidelines	PCT Receiving Office Guidelines https://www.wipo.int/pct/en/texts/gdlines.html
Req.	request (Form RO/101)
S.	sentencc
SC	search copy
Sec.	Section
SISA	International Searching Authority specified for supplementary search
SISR	supplementary international search report
SL	sequence listing
Stand.	WIPO Standard
TPO	third party observation
Treaty	in the Index it means Patent Cooperation Treaty (often used in contrast to the Regulations)

USPTO	United States Patent and Trademark Office
W	decision of a Technical Board of Appeal in PCT protection procedure (EPO)
WIPO	World Intellectual Property Organization
WO-ISA	Written Opinion of the ISA
WTO	World Trade Organization
§	Section of a German law or ordinance

Table of Contents

Introduction to the PCT

1. Historical Background

In the late 1950s, several Member States of the European Economic Community started negotiations on the unification of patent law in Europe. The internationalization of industry and commerce with their cross-border connections had increased the demand for patent protection in more than one State. The unification sought to reduce the laboriousness and ever-increasing complexity of international patent protection within Europe. In 1965, work on the European patent system came to a standstill because several issues could not be resolved. This led the government of the United States to encourage the World Intellectual Property Organization (WIPO) in Geneva, a specialized agency of the United Nations, to take up the task of simplifying patent protection on a world-wide scale (*The First Twenty-Five Years of the Patent Cooperation Treaty (PCT) 1970–1995*, pp. 11, 12. https://tind.wipo.int/record/28756). 1

The envisaged world-wide system would permit applicants to get patent protection in any Member State of the system by filing a single international application. The differences between patent legislations all over the world precluded the creation of a unified patent system comprising every stage from filing to grant and maintenance of patents. Therefore, the system would concentrate on filing, search, publication and an optional, non-binding examination report (Van Empel, *The Granting of European Patents*, Sijthoff-Leyden, 1975, point 16). These stages would be carried out on the international application in the international phase of the procedure. After the international phase, the international application would separate into a series of national patent applications for each of the States or regions for which protection was desired. During the national phase (the term 'national phase' must be construed as 'national or regional phase'; the same applies to 'national Office' and 'national patent application'), each national Office would subject the international application to a grant procedure according to the same law that governs their national patent applications (https://www.wipo.int/pct/en/faqs/faqs.html, no.1). 2

After a relatively short period of preparatory work, the Patent Cooperation Treaty (PCT) was signed by twenty States on June 19, 1970 in Washington D.C., at the end of a diplomatic conference. By December 31, 1970, the last day the Treaty was open for signature (Art. 67(2) PCT), fifteen more States had signed the Treaty. The PCT entered into force on January 24, 1978 and the first international application was filed on June 1, 1978 (Art. 63 PCT). (https://tind.wipo.int/record/28756, pp. 133, 153) 3

4 The PCT is an open treaty in that any Signatory Country to the Paris Convention may accede (Art. 62(1) PCT). In March 2024, the PCT is in force for 157 of the 177 Member States of the Paris Convention. The list of PCT Contracting States is regularly published by WIPO (https://www.wipo.int/pct/en/pct_contracting_states.html) and every year by the European Patent Office (EPO) in the fourth issue of its Official Journal.

2. Aim and Purpose of the PCT

5 According to its Preamble, the PCT essentially has the following aims:

- simplifying and rendering more economical the obtaining of protection for inventions in several countries;
- improving public access to patent information;
- assisting the economic development of developing countries by improving the national patent systems and facilitating access to modern technology.

6 To achieve the aims, the States party to the PCT constitute a Union for cooperation in the filing, searching and examination of applications for the protection of inventions, and for rendering special technical services (Art. 1(1)). One such service is the technical assistance for Contracting States in developing their patent systems (Art. 51), in line with the third aim mentioned above.

7 The first aim is understandable in view of the situation before the entry into force of the PCT. An applicant could only obtain patent protection in several countries by filing a separate patent application with the filing Office of each of these countries. Each filing Office applied its own national law, resulting, amongst other things, in different formal requirements to be observed before each Office, such as compulsory use of prescribed forms, layout of the application, payments and time limits. After filing, each Office carried out its own formal examination and, depending on national law, its own search and substantive examination.

8 Under the PCT system, an applicant who wants patent protection in several countries need only file a single international application with a so-called receiving Office (RO). The countries where the applicant desires protection are designated in the international application. The applicant has to comply only with the formal requirements of the PCT to secure his rights for all designated States. The first 30 or so months of the life of the international application are called the international phase, in which the international application follows a single, unitary procedure. During this procedure, an International Searching Authority (ISA) carries out a search and the International Bureau (IB) publishes the application. The publication achieves the above-mentioned second aim of improving public access to patent information. The applicant may then choose whether or not an International Preliminary Examining Authority (IPEA) should carry out a substantive examination of the international application, still in the international phase. Under the PCT, no decision to grant a patent is taken.

9 At the end of the international phase, the international application enters the national phase in each of the countries where the applicant desires protection. The unitary procedure in the international phase is now changed into several national procedures

running in parallel. On entry, the applicant has to comply with the different formal requirements of the national Office of each country. However, a national Office may not require the use of specific prescribed forms and must accept the form and content of the application as approved in the international phase. The cost of entering the national phase before each national Office is comparable to the cost of filing a direct national application with the Office.

An advantage of the PCT route is that the relatively high cost of entering the national phase before several Offices can be deferred to the end of the 30-month international phase. Another benefit is that by that time the development of the market may be clearer than on the date of filing of the international application and therefore applicants have a first opinion on the patentability of their invention, which may help applicants in deciding in which countries to continue the prosecution of their inventions. 10

In the national phase, each national Office may carry out a further search and a substantive examination. Use of the results of the international search and any international preliminary examination (IPE) saves the national Offices work and may result in fee reductions for the applicant. If the application meets the national requirements for patentability, the national Office will grant a patent on the international application with the same effect as a patent granted on a direct national application. 11

Regional patent systems have a similar purpose as the PCT. An advantage of regional systems is that, in contrast to the PCT, they usually have a procedure that includes the grant of a patent. A disadvantage is that the number of countries bound by such systems is low in comparison to the PCT system. See No. 4.2 below for the relation between a regional patent system and the PCT. 12

3. Organization

The PCT is administered by WIPO, a specialized agency of the United Nations. The Assembly, formed by one delegate from each Contracting State, maintains and develops the Union of Contracting States and the implementation of the PCT (Art. 53(1), (2)). The International Bureau of WIPO carries out the administrative tasks concerning the Union of Contracting States (Art. 55(1)). The PCT Working Group (https://www.wipo.int/pct-wg/en/index.html) decides on substantive recommendations for changes to the PCT system to be adopted by the PCT Assembly (https://www.wipo.int/meetings/en/topic.jsp?group_id=135). The budget of the Union is financed mainly from fees and charges for services rendered by the International Bureau (Art. 57(3)). 13

The procedure in the international phase is carried out before International Authorities, i.e. before the receiving Office, ISA, Supplementary International Search Authority (SISA) and the IPEA. The International Bureau is an International Authority and many national and regional Offices, i.e. the (inter)governmental authorities of the Contracting States entrusted with the granting of patents, may act as International Authorities. More than 120 national and regional Offices carry out functions under the PCT, thereby acting as International Authorities. The vast majority of these Offices act as receiving Offices, which carry out the formal check on filing of an 14 international application. More than 20 Offices act as ISAs, which carry out the search of the international application, and also act as IPEAs, which carry out the substantive examination of the international application.

15 Where national Offices act under the PCT, the prevailing law they apply is the PCT, where necessary supplemented by national law. The PCT Applicant's Guide contains a table indicating the various roles that national or regional Offices can fulfill under the PCT (https://www.wipo.int/pct/en/guide/index.html). The PCT determines which one of the several possible national Offices will carry out specific parts of the procedure in the international phase of a particular international application. For every procedure, the PCT prescribes which Office the applicant must communicate with. After the international phase, all national Offices act as so-called designated Office (DO) or elected Office (EO). The latter applies if an IPE (Chapter II) has been carried out. (Art. 2(xiii), (xiv); No. 6.2.2 below)

16 As part of its administrative tasks under Art. 55(1), the International Bureau acts in the international phase as a central hub for coordination, for example, by transmitting information between Offices on the one hand and between applicant and Offices on the other hand. The International Bureau also publishes the international applications (Art. 21), acts as a receiving Office (R. 19.1(a)(iii)), records bibliographic changes (R. 92*bis*), provides access to its files (R. 94.1) and can receive fees (see, for example, R. 14.1(b); 45*bis*.3(b)).

4. PCT and International Agreements

4.1 PCT and Paris Convention

17 The Paris Convention of 1883 is an agreement between countries for mutual recognition of industrial property rights. It has as its general purpose that nationals of Signatory Countries enjoy in the other States the same treatment in the field of industrial property as the nationals of the other States enjoy. It secures the right of priority of a first filing in one State for subsequent applications in other States.

18 Art. 19 of the Paris Convention allows its Signatory Countries to conclude special agreements between themselves for the protection of industrial property. The Paris Convention takes precedence over laws of the Countries and over such special agreements. The PCT is a special agreement within the framework of Art. 19 Paris Convention (See the Guide to the application of the Paris Convention (https://www.wipo.int/edocs/pubdocs/en/intproperty/611/wipo_pub_611.pdf), especially pp. 12 and 193).

4.2 PCT and Regional Patent Treaties

19 A regional patent treaty is an agreement between several States that provides a single procedure for certain parts of the procedures for grant and maintenance of patents valid in these States. They may use different systems, for example, providing for a unitary regional patent with legal effect in the Contracting States or a system that requires validation in the Contracting States or even enables extension of the regional

Figure 1. PCT Between Paris Convention and Regional/National Law

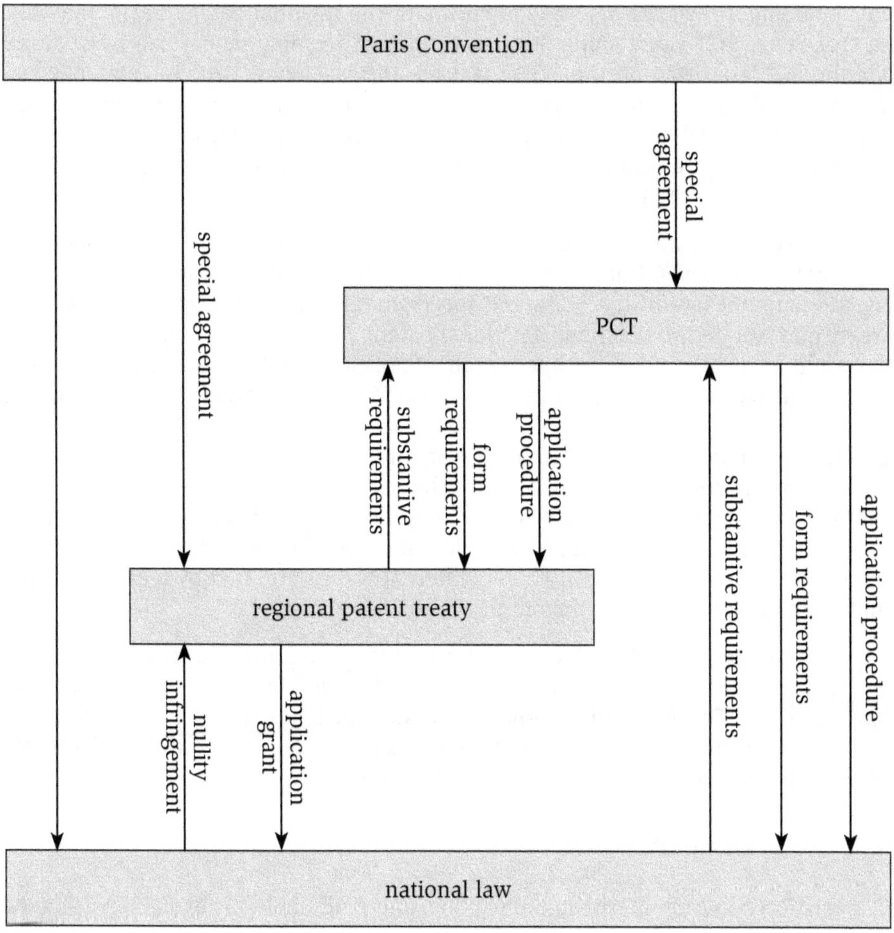

The drawing is reproduced with consent of the FernUniversität in Hagen, Germany, for which the authors provided study material.

patents to non-Contracting States. Information about the regional organizations (EPO, ARIPO, OAPI, GCC, EAPO) and regional Offices set up by the regional patent treaties can be found on the WIPO website (https://www.wipo.int/patents/en/topics/worksharing/regional-patentoffices.html). A regional patent treaty may also be a special agreement in the sense of Art. 19 Paris Convention, open only for Signatory Countries of the Paris Convention. A patent can be 'in or for a State', where 'in' means a national patent granted by a national Office and 'for' means a regional patent granted by a regional Office (AG-IP 5.001).

20 A regional patent treaty may be combined with the PCT system under Art. 45 PCT. It gives an applicant of an international application the right to designate a State for obtaining a regional patent granted under the regional patent treaty and valid in that State. PCT Contracting States for which a regional patent can be obtained via the PCT are listed on the WIPO website (https://www.wipo.int/pct/en/texts/reg_des.html). Advantages of the combination of a regional patent and the PCT are set out in No. 7 below. Note that a GCC regional patent (Gulf Cooperation Council, a cooperation of Arab Gulf States) cannot be obtained via the PCT because the GCC is party neither to the PCT nor to the Paris Convention.

21 There are different ways of obtaining a patent via the PCT route in or for a State that is party both to the PCT and to a regional treaty. The available ways are determined by the national law of the State and the regional treaty. For example, a regional treaty may not permit obtaining a national patent via PCT (OAPI), in which case the State can be designated in the international application only for a regional patent. A regional treaty may allow obtaining both a regional and a national patent (EAPO), so the State can be designated in the international application for both a regional and/or a national patent. Where a regional treaty allows obtaining both a national and a regional patent for a State (EPO, ARIPO), the national law of such a State may close off the national route; in such a case, the State can be designated in the international application only for a regional patent. See the WIPO website (https://www.wipo.int/pct/en/texts/reg_des.html) for the different ways permitted by regional treaties and national law to obtain a patent in a State.

22 The provisions of the PCT treat an application for a national and regional patent in the same way, which is evident from Art. 2(iii) – (vi). Likewise, a national Office and a regional Office are equivalent (Art. 2(xii)), as is also clear from the frequent use of the formulation 'in or for a State' in PCT provisions, where 'in' relates to a national Office and 'for' relates to a regional Office.

4.3 PCT and EPC

23 The relation between international, regional and national law is explained using the European patent system as an example.

24 The European Patent Convention (EPC) is according to its Preamble a special agreement under Art. 19 of the Paris Convention. Therefore, the EPC and its interpretation may not contravene the provisions of the Paris Convention (Art. 19 Paris Convention). The European Patent Organization (Art.4 EPC), established by the EPC, is a grant union intended to grant patents for its Contracting States by a single procedure (Singer/Stauder/Luginbühl, *EPÜ*, 8th edition 2019, Art. 2, Note 5–8). Patent litigation is not covered by the EPC; litigation is governed by national law of the Contracting States, except where provisions of the EPC prevail over national law, such as the grounds for revocation (Art. 138 EPC).

25 The European Patent Organization is not part of the European Union, and the Contracting States of the European Patent Organisation (https://www.epo.org/about-us/foundation/member-states.html) are not the same as the Member States of the European Union (https://europa.eu/european-union/about-eu/countries_en).

All Contracting States to the EPC are party to the PCT. From the perspective of the PCT, the EPC is a regional patent treaty under Art. 45 PCT (Preamble EPC), i.e. a PCT applicant can obtain a European patent effective in one or more Contracting States of the EPC by filing an international application. 26

The task of the European Patent Organization to grant patents is carried out by the EPO, an organ of the Organization. The EPC provides the legal framework for the EPO to grant European patents. 27

The EPO can also act as an International Authority and process international applications. It can perform any task under the PCT as receiving Office, ISA, SISA, and IPEA in the international phase and can act as designated Office and elected Office in the regional phase. The EPO carries out these tasks in applying the provisions of the PCT supplemented by several provisions of the EPC. Art. 150–153 EPC and R. 157–165 EPC enable the EPO to operate under the PCT and provide the legal basis for the transition of the international application from the international to the regional phase. Additional rules for the EPO as ISA and IPEA are laid down in an agreement (https://www.wipo.int/pct/en/access/isa_ipea_agreements.html) between the European Patent Organization and the International Bureau of WIPO (Art. 16(3)(b); Art. 32(3)). 28

In principle, the Articles and Rules of the PCT apply directly to the EPO when processing an international application, both in the international phase and in the regional phase. In case of conflict between provisions of the PCT and EPC, the provisions of the PCT take precedence over those of the EPC (Art. 150(2) EPC) and national law (for example, Art. III 1(3) German Act on International Patent Conventions). The PCT provides a few exceptions, where the EPO may use regional law instead of the PCT, for example, in Art. 27 PCT and Art. 64 PCT. In the international phase, the EPO applies the PCT for both procedural and substantive issues, supplemented by a few procedural provisions of the EPC, for example, Art. 75, 151, R. 157–158 EPC. An international application for which the EPO is a designated or elected Office is called a Euro-PCT application. The entry of such an application into the European phase is governed by Art. 22 and 39 PCT, supplemented by R. 159–165 EPC; several conflicts between provisions of the PCT and EPC during the entry are solved by giving priority to the PCT provisions. 29

The EPO as designated Office or elected Office may not use requirements of the EPC as to form and content of the international application in addition to those of the PCT (Art. 27(1) PCT). Hence, an international application complying with the PCT requirements regarding form and content may not be objected to because of different requirements of the EPC. The EPO acting as designated/elected Office applies the substantive requirements for patentability of the EPC, as allowed by Art. 27(5) PCT. The EPO as designated/elected Office also applies the procedural provisions of the EPC because the PCT contains hardly any procedural provision for the national phase. 30

The EPO brochure Euro-PCT Guide (https://www.epo.org/applying/international/guide-for-applicants.html) gives an overview of the procedures before the EPO as International Authority and as designated/elected Office. 31

5. Legal Framework of PCT

32 See 'PCT Legal Framework and Resources' in this book.

6. Overview of Procedure

6.1 International and National Phase

33 The procedure from filing an international application to grant of one or more national patents is divided into the international phase and the national phase. Roughly speaking, the international phase is governed by the PCT and the national phase is governed by national law (see No. 5 above for details).

34 The international phase starts with the filing of the international application and includes the international search, the international publication and, optionally, the IPE. The international application is processed in the international phase as a single, unitary patent application and, hence, has the same description, claims, drawings and priority claims for all designated States.

35 On entry into the national phase, the international application converts into separate applications on which the national Offices will decide under national law whether or not to grant a patent.

36 The international phase postpones the start of the national phase and gives the applicant time to decide as to whether and where protection for his invention is desired.

6.2 International Phase

37 The international phase starts automatically on filing of an international application with a receiving Office. Within the international phase, the procedure is divided into Chapter I (Art. 3–30; R. 3–52) on the search and publication and Chapter II (Art. 31–42; R. 53–78) on the IPE. Chapters I and II of the PCT contain the provisions that govern the procedure for search and publication, and for IPE, respectively.

38 The international phase for any particular State ends when the international application enters into the national phase before the national Office of that State. Each national Office has set a time limit for entering the national phase, which is usually 30 or 31 months after the priority date. Where an international application does not enter the national phase, the international phase ends at the expiry of the said time limit. Since the applicant may decide to enter the national phase before different Offices at different times, the international application may simultaneously be in the international phase for some States and in the national phase for others (AG-IP 3.005).

6.2.1 Chapter I PCT

39 The Chapter I procedure is carried out in the first part of the international phase and comprises three stages.

Figure 2. Procedure in the International and National Phase Where the PCT Application Claims Priority from a National Application

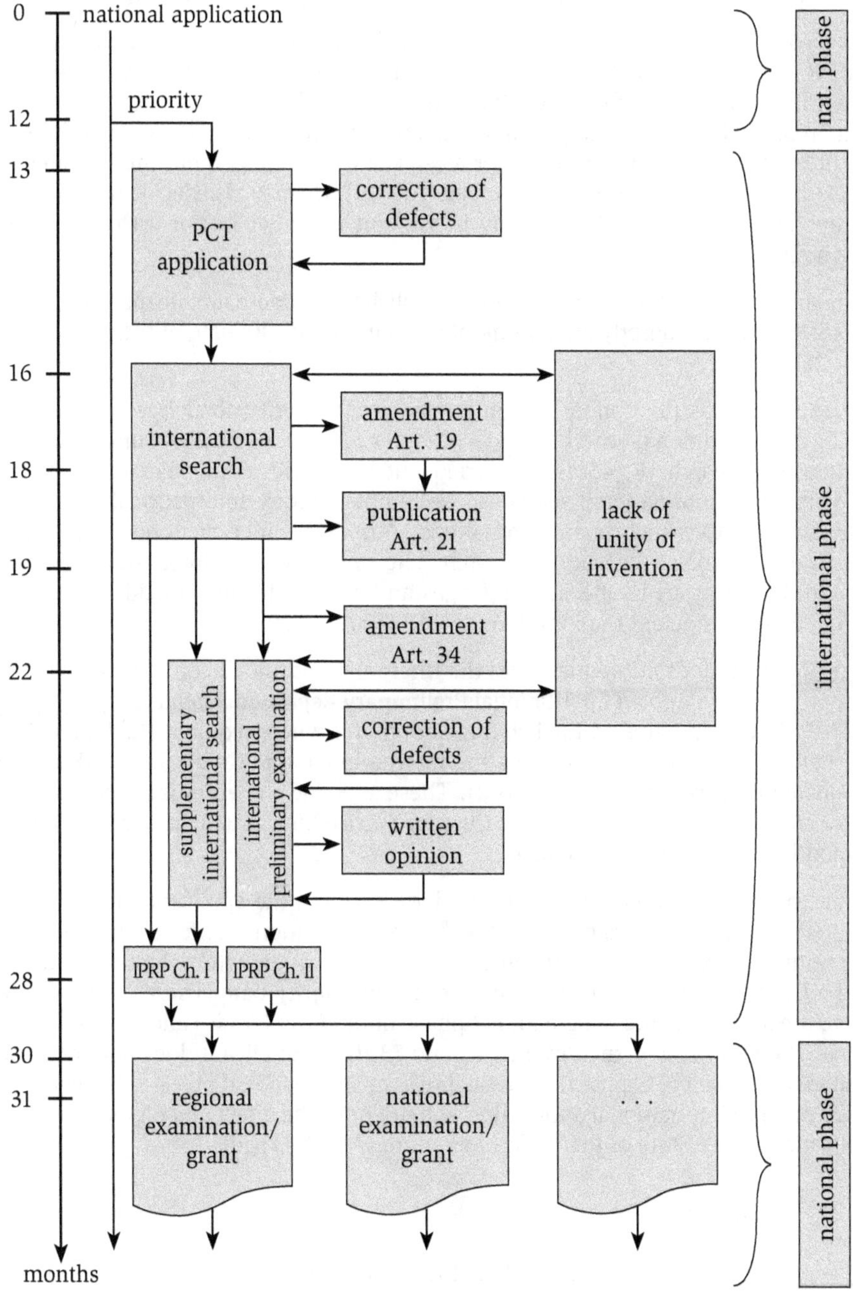

The drawing is reproduced with consent of the FernUniversität in Hagen, Germany, for which the authors provided study material.

40 The first stage is the filing of the international application and its processing by the receiving Office, which includes the accordance of an international filing date, followed by a check on formal requirements and payment of fees (Art. 3–14).

41 The second stage is the establishment by an ISA of an international search report (ISR, R. 43) together with a written opinion on the novelty, inventive step, and industrial applicability of the invention (Art. 15–18). The search report and written opinion of the ISA give the applicant a first impression of his chances of obtaining a patent on the claimed invention. After receipt of the ISR, the applicant may amend the claims before the International Bureau (Art. 19). He may also decide to withdraw the application (R. 90*bis*.1), possibly in view of prejudicial prior art cited in the search report.

42 In the third stage the International Bureau publishes the international application and the search report promptly after 18 months from the priority date of the application (Art. 21).

43 The applicant has the option – upon payment of the prescribed fees – to request one or more additional searches under Chapter I. Such a so-called supplementary international search (R. 45*bis*) is carried out by an ISA competent to carry out supplementary international searches, the Supplementary International Searching Authority (SISA), which is an International Authority different from the ISA that carried out the main international search. The supplementary international search aims to find prior art in specific languages and specific technical fields where the SISA is more competent than the ISA. (AG-IP 8.001–8.009)

44 If the applicant does not request IPE, the International Bureau converts the written opinion of the ISA into an International Preliminary Report on Patentability (Chapter I) (IPRP I), and prepares an English translation of it where required (R. 44*bis*). The International Bureau communicates the international application and IPRP to the designated Offices (Art. 20; R. 44*bis*.2). These acts and the entry into the national phase are usually the last acts of the Chapter I procedure, usually carried out about 30 months from the priority date.

45 At the end of the international phase under Chapter I, the applicant can enter the national phase. The applicant must do so before each national Office where he wants to continue the prosecution of the international application within the time limit set by the Office, usually 30 or 31 months from the priority date. The national Office where the applicant enters the national phase under Chapter I is called a designated Office. The entry is governed by Art. 22 and 23. If the applicant does not enter the national phase before expiry of the time limit, the international phase will end at the expiry and the international application will not have the effect of a regular national application in the State of that Office any more (Art. 24(1)(iii)).

6.2.2 Chapter II PCT

46 The applicant has the option under Art. 31 to file a so-called demand, i.e. a request for an IPEA to subject the international application to an IPE governed by the provisions in Chapter II of the PCT (Art. 31–42; R. 70). A valid filing of the demand ends the

Chapter I procedure and starts the Chapter II procedure. If no demand is filed, the Chapter I procedure continues until entry into the national phase or until expiry of the time limit for entry into the national phase.

The procedure under Chapter II offers the possibility to amend the claims and other parts of the international application – if need be – and to discuss novelty and inventive step with an examiner by submitting amendments and arguments (Art. 34(2)(b); R. 66.4; Pract. Adv. NL 5/2010, https://www.wipo.int/pct/en/newslett/practical_advice/pa_052010.html). The applicant has typically six months to discuss the merits of the invention with the examiner, namely from filing the demand (typically 22 months from the priority date, R. 54*bis*) to the establishment of the report on patentability (28 months from the priority date, R. 69.2). 47

The IPEA conducts in general a top-up search, R. 66.1*ter*) to find documents that have become available after the date on which the ISR was established. 48

At the end of the Chapter II procedure, the IPEA will prepare the IPRP under Chapter II, the IPRP II, according to Art. 35 and R. 70. The Report provides a preliminary opinion on novelty, inventive step, and industrial applicability of the invention. The Report is not binding on a designated Office when deciding on the grant of a patent (Art. 33(1)). It gives the applicant a second opinion of the patentability of the invention, on which he may decide whether or not to enter the national phase of one or more Offices. The International Bureau makes the IPRP II available to the national Offices. Some elected Offices take over the findings of the IPRP II. (AG-IP 10.083) 49

The international phase under Chapter II ends at the same time as under Chapter I, i.e. usually 30 or 31 months after the priority date, depending on the national Office. The applicant must enter the national phase for each national Office where he wants to continue the prosecution of the international application within a time limit set by the Office, usually 30 or 31 months from the priority date. The national Office where the applicant enters the national phase under Chapter II will take the IPRP II into account and is called an elected Office (EO). The entry is governed by Art. 39–40. If the applicant does not enter the national phase before expiry of the time limit, the international application will not have the effect of a regular national application in the State of that Office (Art. 39(2)). 50

Until 2002, the time limit for entry into the national phase was 20 or 21 months under Chapter I and 30 or 31 months under Chapter II. The extra 10 months under Chapter II were used for carrying out the IPE. Many applicants regarded Chapter II as an extension, albeit an expensive one, of the international phase and filed a demand just for the extension, not for the preliminary examination. Since 2002, the time limit for national entry is the same under Chapters I and II for most designated Offices, which relieves the IPEAs from carrying out examinations in which applicants are not interested. As a consequence, the number of filed demands decreased from approx. 81,000 in 2001 to approx. 15,000 in 2012 and has remained stable at that level. Only about 3 % of the applicants make a demand (PCT Yearly Review 2024, p. 87). Since the change in 2002 resulted in far fewer preliminary examination reports, WIPO has introduced a written opinion to be established together with the search report (R. 43*bis*) to ensure that national Offices that do not examine patent applications and 51 national Offices less competent in certain technical fields still receive together with the international application an opinion on novelty, inventive step, and industrial applicability. Two Contracting States, LU and TZ, still require entry into the national phase within 20/21 months if no demand has been filed (see https://www.wipo.int/pct/en/texts/reservations/res_incomp.html under Art. 22(1). See also AG-IP, National Chapter for LU and TZ).

6.3 National Phase

52 In order to enter the national phase, the applicant has to carry out several acts before each of the national (or regional) Offices where he wants to continue prosecution. The acts may include paying fees and filing translations. The time limit for entering the national phase is usually 30 or 31 months from the priority date, depending on the designated Office or EO. In the national phase, the designated Office carries out a formal and a substantive examination, which may include a supplementary search. National Offices may only require that certain additional formal requirements, which do not relate to the form and content of the international application, must be met, such as submitting documents relating to the identity of the inventor or entitlement to grant of the applicant. These requirements can be met during the national phase (AG-NP 5.001). Failure to meet certain requirements in the international phase may often be corrected in the national phase (see, for example, Art. 24, 25, 26, 48(2)).

53 The applicant may decide to enter the national phase for certain States before expiry of the time limit of 30 or 31 months from priority. In such a case, the international application can be simultaneously in the national phase for these States and still in the international phase for other States. Any action taken in respect of the application still in the international phase has no effect on the procedure of an application that has already entered the national phase.

7. Advantages of PCT

54 Use of the PCT compared to use of only national and regional treaties has the following advantages for an applicant:

- The applicant needs to file only one application for obtaining protection in several States or regions instead of one application for each State or region. The PCT has rather strict formal requirements for the international application, such as for the drawings. However, once they are complied with, any designated Office must accept the application and may not impose additional formal requirements (Art. 27(1)). On the other hand, if deficiencies are not remedied in due time during the international phase, the international application will be considered withdrawn for all designated States (Art. 14), terminating the existence of the international application. The applicant then has to apply for a review procedure before each designated Office and use a remedy in the national phase to revive the international application with effect for each individual State (Art. 24(2); Art. 25).
  The final decision as to whether or not to obtain a patent in a State can be taken at a relatively late moment in the procedure, i.e. near the end of the

international phase. If the PCT route were not used, the decision should be taken within 12 months from the priority date. When using the PCT, the decision can be taken within 30 or 31 months from the priority date. At that time, the applicant already has the ISR and, if requested, the IPRP, giving him a good assessment of the value of his application and his chances of obtaining a patent. The longer time available for making the decision also places the applicant in a better position to assess the technical and economic value of his application in view of market developments and to choose the States where he desires protection. The ISR together with, if requested, the IPRP II provide for a stronger patent also in countries with a registration system or with less-trained patent Office personnel.

- A further advantage of the PCT route is that the initial costs are relatively low compared to the costs of filing in several States. The late entry into the national phase therefore defers a substantial part of the costs of a patent family to a later moment in time. The costs of national phase entry are relatively high if a plurality of countries is chosen because of the fees to be paid to each national and regional Office and the translations of the application to be made. The fees to be paid to the national Offices on entry are in general equal to the fees when filing directly with a national Office, not using the PCT route. Some Offices have discounts for official fees to be paid for applications entering via the PCT route.
- Not only are the costs postponed to 30/31 months from the priority date, instead of 12 months from the priority date, but also the considerable formalities hassle of entering the national phase in several countries is postponed.
- In some States it is possible to use PCT examination results to accelerate the prosecution of the national examination (see annotations to Art. 22).
- Another advantage of the PCT is that – in most cases – the application with effect for many countries can be filed in a language that is familiar to the applicant.
- In the case of unfavorable results during the international search or preliminary examination, the applicant can decide not to proceed further and save the considerable costs of national phase entry in the various States altogether. Without these international search and preliminary examination results, the fees for national filings would most likely have been spent in vain.
- The more countries are desired for patent protection for a particular invention, the more a PCT application makes sense, as discounts and the possibility of taking over search and examination results from the international phase into the national phase will reduce the overall costs of the patent family.

8. Decisions before Filing

Before filing an application, the applicant should decide whether or not the first filing should be a priority application (or a provisional application where available) and whether to file an international application or a national or regional application. An overview of decisions to be taken can be found in a WIPO presentation of 2013 55 on the international phase (https://www.wipo.int/export/sites/www/pct/en/pct_strategies/4_06_2013.pdf).

56 A priority application, which can be filed free of charge with most patent Offices, has the advantage that the 20-year patent term starts on the date a subsequent priority claiming application is filed – typically one year after the priority filing. The total lifetime of the application/patent can thus be extended to 21 years after the first filing.

57 The applicant should also decide whether the first filing should be a national, regional or international application. The choice may depend on the cost of the options, on the familiarity of the patent attorney with the options, and on the applicant's right to act without representation before the Offices involved. Depending on the nature of the invention and the nationality and residence of the applicant, national law may force an applicant to file nationally because of national security provisions.

58 Where no fees are paid for the priority application, the applicant will not receive a search report before the subsequent priority claiming application is filed and, therefore, has to decide on further prosecution without an assessment of the chances of success of the application.

59 When the fees for the priority application are paid, the applicant will receive a search and, if requested, an examination report, normally before he has to decide on further prosecution. The search report of an international application is available nine months after filing. If the subsequent priority-claiming application is prosecuted before the Office that searched the first filing, the search fee paid for the priority application may be refunded in part or in full.

60 The applicant has to decide whether the subsequent priority-claiming filing should be an international application or a bundle of regional and national applications. The decision may depend on whether or not the applicant desires to defer the costs of filing and the applicant already knows the countries where protection is desired. When filing an international application, the applicant obtains the advantages mentioned above in No. 7.

61 Instead of filing a priority application, an applicant may file an international application without claiming priority. A disadvantage of this way of filing is that the maximum lifetime of the application/patent is 20 instead of 21 years. An advantage is that the applicant receives a search report within nine months from filing, allowing him to decide whether or not to continue the prosecution. A filing without claiming priority has the additional advantage that the grant of a patent can be accelerated by early entry into the national phase, which may be beneficial if a quick enforcement of the patent is envisaged.

62 The applicant should take into account in which Contracting States protection can be obtained via a PCT or a regional application. The PCT or a regional treaty may not apply to all territories of a State, in particular if a territory is overseas or has a special status (see List of Territories and OJ EPO 2014 A33 §10–11 and its Annex). On the other hand, some States allow an extension or validation of a granted regional patent to their territory, even though the State that allows extension or validation is not a member of a regional patent and not in the same geographical region. For example,

it is possible to obtain a European patent in Cambodia or Morocco. Furthermore, many States that are part of the British Overseas Territories or Commonwealth of Nations allow a re-registration for their State of a national patent granted in the United Kingdom (GB) or of a European patent validated in GB (OJ EPO 2018 A97; UKIPO website www.gov.uk/government/publications/extension-of-uk-intellectual-property-rights-abroad). It should also be considered that there are disputed territories where the law of another State is applied or enforcement of rights might be difficult.

Annotations to Art. 10 and Pract. Adv. NL 3/2019 (https://www.wipo.int/pct/en/newslett/practical_advice/pa_032019.html) give further arguments for the decision where to file an international application. See Introduction to Art. 31 and Pract. Adv. NL 5/2010 (https://www.wipo.int/pct/en/newslett/practical_advice/pa_052010.html) for factors to consider when deciding whether or not to make a demand for IPE. 63

9. Definitions

The PCT uses several terms in its Articles and Rules that have a special meaning. 64
The following definitions are relevant to the interpretation of many provisions. A definition of a term with a reference to the PCT is used both in the PCT and in this book. A definition without a reference to the PCT or another WIPO document is used only in this book.

- An 'application' means an application for the protection of an invention in the form of a patent, inventor's certificate, utility certificate, utility model, patent or certificate of addition, inventor's certificate of addition, or utility certificate of addition (Art. 2(i); see also Art. 43).
- An 'international application' means an application filed under the PCT (Art. 2(vii)).
- A 'national application' means an application for a national patent (Art. 2(vi)). A 'regional application' means an application for a regional patent (Art. 2(v)). A reference to a 'national application' must be construed as a reference to a national and a regional application (Art. 2(vi)).
- A 'regional patent' means a patent granted by a national or intergovernmental authority having the power to grant patents effective in more than one State (Art. 2(iv)). A reference to a 'patent' must be construed as a reference to a national and a regional patent (Art. 2(viii)).
- A 'national Office' means the government authority of a PCT Contracting State entrusted with the granting of patents (Art. 2(xii)). A 'regional Office' is an intergovernmental authority which several States have entrusted with the granting of regional patents (Art. 2(xii)). A reference to a 'national Office' must be construed as a reference also to a regional Office (Art. 2(xii)).
- An International Authority is an authority acting under the PCT, i.e. the International Bureau, receiving Office, ISA and IPEA (see AG-IP https://www.wipo.int/export/sites/www/pct/guide/en/gdvol1/pdf/gdvol1.pdf, search for 'International Authority' in the index of the document).
- The 'priority date' of an international application claiming priority is the filing date of an earlier application whose priority is claimed (Art. 2(xi)(a)). Where the international application contains several priority claims,

the 'priority date' is the filing date of the earliest application whose priority is claimed (Art. 2(xi)(b)). Where the international application does not contain a priority claim, the 'priority date' is the international filing date of the application (Art. 2(xi)(c)).

- A 'request' means a part of the international application containing bibliographic data and a petition that the international application be processed according to the PCT (Art. 4(1)).
- A 'demand' means a request for an IPE (Art. 31). The demand should not be confused with the request.
- A 'designated Office' means the national Office of or acting for the State designated by the applicant under Chapter I of the PCT (Art. 2(xiii)). An 'elected Office' means the national Office of or acting for the State elected by the applicant under Chapter II of the PCT (Art. 2(xiv)). A reference to a designated Office must be construed as a reference also to an elected Office, unless the context indicates differently; for example, a designated Office in the context of Chapter I does not refer to an elected Office. The PCT uses a similar definition of 'designated Office', although it does not state so explicitly. For example, Art. 25–27 clearly apply to both designated Offices and elected Offices, but the provisions mention only 'designated Office'.
- Representation is used as a generic term in AG-IP 11.001 that includes agent and common representative. An 'agent' means a person having the right to practice before the national or regional Office where the international application is being processed and who may be appointed by the applicant to represent him before that Office acting under the PCT (R. 2.2 and R. 90.1). An 'agent' is a 'professional representative' in EPC terminology. A reference to an 'applicant' must be construed as meaning also the agent of the applicant, except where the context indicates differently, for example, where a provision refers to the residence or nationality of the applicant (R. 2.1).
- A 'common representative' means an applicant representing all applicants of an international application that has two or more applicants (R. 2.2*bis*). A 'common agent' is an agent representing all applicants (R. 90.2(a)).
- The 'home copy' is the copy of the international application that remains with the receiving Office. The 'record copy' is the copy of the international application transmitted by the receiving Office to the International Bureau and the 'search copy' is the copy of the international application transmitted by the receiving Office to the ISA. The record copy is considered the true copy of the international application for the PCT procedure (Art. 12(1), (2)).

Patent Cooperation Treaty (PCT)

Done at Washington on June 19, 1970,

amended on September 28, 1979,

modified on February 3, 1984, and on October 3, 2001

Table of Contents of Articles

Some important Rules are listed within the Table of Contents of Articles to help the reader get started quickly.

The Contracting States,

Desiring to make a contribution to the progress of science and technology,

Desiring to perfect the legal protection of inventions,

Desiring to simplify and render more economical the obtaining of protection for inventions where protection is sought in several countries,

Desiring to facilitate and accelerate access by the public to the technical information contained in documents describing new inventions,

Desiring to foster and accelerate the economic development of developing countries through the adoption of measures designed to increase the efficiency of their legal systems, whether national or regional, instituted for the protection of inventions by providing easily accessible information on the availability of technological solutions applicable to their special needs and by facilitating access to the ever expanding volume of modern technology,

Convinced that cooperation among nations will greatly facilitate the attainment of these aims,

Have concluded the present Treaty.

Introductory Provisions

Article 1
Establishment of a Union

(1)

The States party to this Treaty (hereinafter called "the Contracting States") constitute a Union for cooperation in the filing, searching, and examination, of applications for the protection of inventions, and for rendering special technical services. The Union shall be known as the International Patent Cooperation Union.

Art. 9, R. 18	Entitlement of the applicant to file PCTa depending on the Contracting State
Art. 10, R. 19	Competent receiving Office
Art. 45	Regional patent treaties
Art. 168 EPC	Territorial field of application

Which territory belongs to a State party is determined by its constitution and general international law. In the case of treaties, it is possible that the scope of application only includes certain territories of a Contracting State on the basis of declarations by Contracting States. It is also possible that the effect of the PCT or a regional patent convention may be extended to territories outside the territory of a Member State by national, regional or international law. Furthermore, different Contracting States can unite to form a single legal territory with regard to patent law (as happened in the case of CH and LI). In the Annex to this book, there is a list of territories of the world that cannot be easily allocated, with information on the patent law applicable in each case. 1

The territorial scope of the PCT is not always identical with the entirety of the territories of an EPC State. Some EPC Contracting States have declared that the PCT and/or the EPC apply or do not apply to certain territories. For information on whether a PCT applicant can obtain protection via a validated European patent, see the Annex to OJ 2014 A33 and AG-NP (EP). If the application of the EPC is excluded for a certain territory, only a Paris Convention national patent application or entry into the national phase under the PCT can be considered. The latter is excluded if a State has generally closed entry into the national phase and only regional patent protection remains. However, re-registration of a European patent may be possible for some territories not accessible via PCT-EP (see in the Annex to this book). 2

(2)

No provision of this Treaty shall be interpreted as diminishing the rights under the Paris Convention for the Protection of Industrial Property of any national or resident of any country party to that Convention.

Article 2
Definitions

For the purposes of this Treaty and the Regulations and unless expressly stated otherwise:

(i) "application" means an application for the protection of an invention; references to an "application" shall be construed as references to applications for patents for inventions, inventors' certificates, utility certificates, utility models, patents or certificates of addition, inventors' certificates of addition, and utility certificates of addition;

Art. 43	Seeking certain kinds of protection
Art. 44	Seeking two kinds of protection at national level
R. 6.5	Utility models; no designs are taken into account.

(ii) references to a "patent" shall be construed as references to patents for inventions, inventors' certificates, utility certificates, utility models, patents or certificates of addition, inventors' certificates of addition, and utility certificates of addition;

(iii) "national patent" means a patent granted by a national authority;

(iv) "regional patent" means a patent granted by a national or an intergovernmental authority having the power to grant patents effective in more than one State;

Art. 45	Regional patent treaties (for example EPO)

(v) "regional application" means an application for a regional patent;

(vi) references to a "national application" shall be construed as references to applications for national patents and regional patents, other than applications filed under this Treaty;

(vii) "international application" means an application filed under this Treaty;

(viii) references to an "application" shall be construed as references to international applications and national applications;

(ix) references to a "patent" shall be construed as references to national patents and regional patents;

(x) references to "national law" shall be construed as references to the national law of a Contracting State or, where a regional application or a regional patent is involved, to the treaty providing for the filing of regional applications or the granting of regional patents;

(xi) "priority date," for the purposes of computing time limits, means:

Art. 8	Claiming priority	
R. 4.10	Priority claim	
R. 17	The priority document	
	R. 17.1	Obligation to submit copy of earlier national or international application
	R. 17.2	Availability of copies

(a) where the international application contains a priority claim under Article 8, the filing date of the application whose priority is so claimed;

(b) where the international application contains several priority claims under Article 8, the filing date of the earliest application whose priority is so claimed;

1 The oldest priority date determines the running of the time limits.

(c) where the international application does not contain any priority claim under Article 8, the international filing date of such application;

(xii) "national Office" means the government authority of a Contracting State entrusted with the granting of patents; references to a "national Office" shall be construed as referring also to any intergovernmental authority which several States have entrusted with the task of granting regional patents, provided that at least one of those States is a Contracting State, and provided that the said States have authorized that authority to assume the obligations and exercise the powers which this Treaty and the Regulations provide for in respect of national Offices;

(xiii) "designated Office" means the national Office of or acting for the State designated by the applicant under Chapter I of this Treaty;

Art. 4(3)	Designation
	If it is planned to continue an international application in the national or regional phase before an Office, the Office which is to deal with the PCTa thereafter, i.e. in the national or regional phase, is referred to as the 'designated Office' or 'elected Office'. The term

	'designated Office' (DO) is used when the regional or national phase is to be initiated following Chapter I, i.e. without filing the request for IPE under Art. 31 (demand). The term 'elected Office' is used when the demand for IPE is filed and only then the national or regional phase is to be initiated. See also Euro-PCT Guide 1.7.004.
Art. 153(2) EPC	A PCTa with EPO as designated or elected Office is considered a European patent application.

(xiv) "elected Office" means the national Office of or acting for the State elected by the applicant under Chapter II of this Treaty;

AIs 107	Designation of international authorities, designated and elected Offices

See (xiii) for the difference between designated and elected Office (Art. 153(2) EPC). 2

(xv) "receiving Office" means the national Office or the intergovernmental organization with which the international application has been filed;

(xvi) "Union" means the International Patent Cooperation Union;

Art. 1	Establishment of a Union

(xvii) "Assembly" means the Assembly of the Union;

Art. 53	Assembly
Art. 58(2)	The Assembly may amend the Regulations.
R. 88	Amendment of the Regulations

(xviii) "Organization" means the World Intellectual Property Organization;

(xix) "International Bureau" means the International Bureau of the Organization and, as long as it subsists, the United International Bureaux for the Protection of Intellectual Property (BIRPI);

(xx) "Director General" means the Director General of the Organization and, as long as BIRPI subsists, the Director of BIRPI.

R. 1	Abbreviated expressions	
	R. 1.1	Meaning of Abbreviated Expressions
R. 2	Interpretation of Certain Words	
	R. 2.1	'Applicant'
	R. 2.2	'Agent'

R. 2.2*bis*	'Common representative'
R. 2.3	'Signature'
R. 2.4	'Priority period'

Chapter I: International Application and International Search

For general information regarding Chapter I see the 'Introduction to the PCT', Ch. 6.2.1 in this book. 1

Article 3
The International Application

INTRODUCTION

1. General Aspects of Filing an International Application

An international application or PCT application (PCTa) is an application filed under the PCT (Art. 2(vii)). The international application must be filed with a receiving Office (Art. 10) in a language accepted by that Office (Art. 3(4)(i); R. 12.1). The international application has to comply with certain physical requirements, as set out in R. 3 to 11, which are similar to the EPC requirements. Certain States allow deviations from the formal requirements under their national laws (see, for example, R. 6.3(c); R. 6.4; R. 11.5). The international application must also comply with the requirement of unity of invention (Art. 3(4)(iii); R. 13) and is subject to the payment of fees (Art. 3(4)(iv); R. 14, 15 and 16). The description of the international application must disclose the invention in a way sufficiently clear and complete for a person skilled in the art to carry it out (Art. 5). 2

If the form and contents of an international application comply with the requirements of the PCT, it may not be rejected in a national procedure because of different national requirements (Art. 27(1)). However, national law may be more favorable for applicants than the PCT as to form and content of an international application (Art. 27(4)). 3

The permitted methods of filing an international application are determined by each receiving Office and are set out in AG-IP Annex B and C. An overview of methods of filing is given in Art. 10 and at the beginning of Chapter F of the Regulations. The receiving Office checks whether the international application complies with the physical requirements as set out in Art. 11. The receiving Office allows correction of non-compliance with these requirements (see Art. 14). 4

Any correspondence submitted by the applicant to the International Authorities after filing the international application itself is governed by R. 92 and requires a letter signed by the applicant. Any letter from the applicant to the International Bureau must be in English, French or, if filed via ePCT, in the language of publication (R. 92.2(d)). 5

The requirements for the different elements of the international application are described in the following paragraphs. 6

2. Elements of the International Application

7 An international application must contain

- a request (Art. 4);
- a description (Art. 5);
- one or more claims (Art. 6);
- where required one or more drawings (Art. 7); and
- an abstract (R. 8) according to Art. 3(2).

8 Art. 11 specifies the elements which are necessary for according an international filing date, namely an indication that it is intended as an international application, including a designation of a Contracting State (Art. 4) and the name of the applicant (Art. 9), a description and at least one claim (see Art. 11). Drawings have to be filed only in case they are necessary for the understanding of the invention. Although the international application must include an abstract, its presence is not required for an international filing date; it can be submitted later.

9 Provisions on incorporation by reference in the PCT allow, under certain circumstances, inclusion of accidentally omitted description, drawings and claims pages that are contained in a priority document (Art. 8), without affecting the international filing date (see Art. 11, R. 20).

10 Obvious mistakes in the elements may be rectified by following the procedure of R. 91. Non-compliance of the elements with the physical requirements of R. 11 may be corrected as set out in Art. 14(1)(a)(v), (b).

11 Changes other than the correction of obvious mistakes are considered amendments (R. 66.5). The claims may be amended after issuance of the ISR or if a demand is filed (Art. 19 and 34). The description and drawings may be amended only if a demand is filed (Art. 34). Each designated Office must permit amendments in the national phase (Art. 28(1) and Art. 41; see also Art. 22). Since the possibilities for correction of defects are different for the different elements of the international application, they will be dealt with separately.

12 On filing, the description, claims and drawings may be replaced by a reference to a priority application, from which the receiving Office will copy them (see R. 20).

3. Language

3.1 Languages Accepted by Receiving Offices

13 The international application must be filed with a receiving Office in a language prescribed by the receiving Office (Art. 3(4)(i); R. 12.1(a)). Some receiving Offices allow the applicant to choose between two or more languages. Every receiving Office accepts at least one language which is both a language accepted by the competent ISA and a language of publication (R. 12.1(b)). When using this language, an applicant need not provide a translation either for international search or for international publication.

AG-IP Annex C indicates the accepted language(s) for each receiving Office. It also indicates the competent ISA(s). AG-IP Annex D contains the languages accepted by the different ISAs. Publication languages are currently Arabic, Chinese, English, French, German, Japanese, Korean, Portuguese, Russian, and Spanish (R. 48.3(a)). Slightly less than half of all international applications are filed in English (https://www.wipo.int/edocs/pubdocs/en/wipo-pub-901-2023-en-patent-cooperation-treaty-yearly-review-2023.pdf, p. 63). RO/IB accepts any language (AG-IP Annex C(IB)). Most receiving Offices also accept international applications in one of the official languages of the State concerned. 14

All elements of the international application (description and claims) are normally in the same language. For the accordance of an international filing date, it is sufficient that the description (and the language-dependent free text in the sequence listing) and the claims are in a language accepted by the receiving Office (Art. 11(1)(ii); R. 20.1(c); AG-IP 5.013). The request must be filed in a language which is both a language accepted by the receiving Office and a language of publication (R. 12.1(c)). This means that the languages of the request and the description/claims may be different, for example, a request in English and description and claims in Dutch. 15

The receiving Office or the ISA may require a translation of the international application for the purpose of search or publication (R. 12.3 or 12.4). The International Bureau will also forward any such translation later to any SISA (R. 45*bis*.4(e)(iv)). If the applicant files a supplementary international search request and the international application is filed in a language which is not accepted by the SISA and any translations filed under R. 12.3 or 12.4 that could be transmitted by the International Bureau are not accepted either, the applicant must furnish a translation of the international application into a language accepted by the SISA (R. 45*bis*.1(c)(i)). 16

RO/EP accepts only French, German and English as languages of the international application (R. 157(2) EPC). It does not accept other official languages of EPC Contracting States admissible under Art. 14(2) EPC. For example, an international application in Swedish filed with RO/EP will be transmitted to RO/IB under R. 19.4(a)(ii). 17

All receiving Offices of EPC Contracting States have specified the EPO as the competent ISA (Art. 152 EPC; AG-IP Annex C(EP)). ISA/EP carries out international searches in English, French and German. Searches in Dutch are also possible, if the international application is filed in Dutch with RO/NL ISA/IPEA (Agreement EP-IB, Annex A(ii), www.wipo.int/export/sites/www/pct/en/texts/agreements/ag_ep.pdf). Historically, many of the examiners in The Hague branch of the EPO are familiar with the language (OJ EPO 1979 p. 137). The receiving Office of any EPC Contracting State will accept at least one of the languages English, French and German. 18

The acceptable official languages of the receiving Office of an EPC Contracting State need not be the same as the official languages admissible under Art. 14(4) EPC and need not to be the same as the official languages of that State. 19

3.2 *Unacceptable Language*

20 If a national Office as receiving Office does not accept the language of the international application, it will transmit the international application to the International Bureau under R. 19.4. The International Bureau will act as receiving Office and will regard as date of receipt the date on which the national Office received the international application. RO/IB accepts any language (see Art. 10, R. 19). In this case, the applicant will have to pay a new set of fees to RO/IB, the non-competent receiving Office will refund the fees except the transmittal fee (AG-IP 6.034), and the applicant is responsible for transmitting any priority document to RO/IB (see Art. 8).

3.3 *Translations*

21 The PCT distinguishes the following cases where the applicant must provide a translation of the international application in the international phase (AG-IP 6.013–6.020):

- the language of filing is not a language accepted by the ISA (or SISA) (R. 12.3); and
- the language of the ISA is not a language of publication (R. 12.4).

3.3.1 Language Not Accepted by ISA

22 Where the language of the international application is not accepted by the ISA selected in the request, the applicant must furnish to the receiving Office a translation within one month of receipt of the international application by the receiving Office (R. 12.3(a)). If the applicant furnishes the translation late, the receiving Office may request payment of a late furnishing fee equal to 25% of the international filing fee (R. 12.3(e)).

23 The translation must be in a language that is all of the following:

- a language accepted by the ISA,
- a language of publication and
- a language accepted by the receiving Office.

24 If the international application is filed in a language of publication, the last condition is not required and the language of the translation need not be a language accepted by the receiving Office under R. 12.3(a). The above translation requirement does not apply to the request (R. 12.3(b)). It applies to and any sequence listing part of the description that is language-dependent free text (R. 12.3(a-*bis*)). See annotations to Art. 4 for the language of the request.

25 If the translation has not yet been provided by the time the receiving Office notifies the applicant of the international filing date under R. 20.2(c), the receiving Office will invite the applicant to furnish the translation within one month from the date of receipt of the international application (R. 12.3(c)(i)). A later submission of the translation is possible, subject to the payment of a late furnishing fee where applicable (R. 12.3(c)(ii) and R. 12.3(e)). The time limit for late submission is one month from the date of the invitation or two months from the date of receipt of the international

application by the receiving Office, whichever expires later. If the applicant does not furnish the translation and any payment on invitation, the international application will be considered withdrawn and the receiving Office will so declare (R. 12.3(d)). A translation and payment received before the receiving Office issues the said declaration and before the expiry of 15 months from the priority date will be considered as received in time (R. 12.3(d)).

Hence, it is recommended to provide the translation swiftly, in particular if it is already after the expiry of the time limit. 26

3.3.2 Language Accepted by ISA but Not Language of Publication

Some ISAs will carry out searches in a language other than a language of publication. In the case that the language of the search is not a language of publication the applicant must file, with the receiving Office and within 14 months from the priority date, a translation of the application in a language of publication acceptable to the receiving Office (R. 12.4(a)). If not complied with, even after an invitation similar to the one in the previous paragraph, including any late furnishing fee (R. 12.4(c)–(e)), the application will be considered withdrawn (R. 12.4(d)). A translation and payment received before the receiving Office issues the said declaration and before the expiry of 17 months from the priority date will be considered as received in time (R. 12.4(d)). 27

3.3.3 Parts of International Application in Different Languages

Where the abstract or any text matter of the drawings is filed in a language different from the language of the description and the claims, the receiving Office will invite the applicant to furnish a translation into the language in which the application is to be published (Art. 3(4)(i); R. 26.3*ter*(a)). 28

Where the description is filed in a language different from the language of the claims, or parts of the description or parts of the claims are filed in a language which is different from the language of the remainder of this element, and where all such languages are accepted by the receiving Office under R. 12.1(a), the receiving Office will invite the applicant according to R. 26*ter*(e) since July 1, 2024 to furnish a translation such that the description and claims are in a single language which is all of the following: 29

(i) one of the languages contained in the description or claims as filed;
(ii) a language accepted by the ISA that is to carry out the international search; and
(iii) the language in which the international application is to be published.

The receiving Office will not issue an invitation to furnish a translation in cases where a translation of the international application is already required for the purpose of the international search or where the abstract and text matter is in the language in which the application is to be published (R. 26.3*ter*(a)). The procedure for the correction is set out in the annotations to Art. 14. 30

31 In some technical fields, such as telecommunications, computer and automotive technology, certain expressions, which usually stem from the English language, are used equivalent to words in the national language. A translation is often not desirable because it would render the disclosure of the international application more unclear than if the expression remained in English as filed. In case the receiving Office objects to those words, the applicant may file a statement explaining the special character of those expressions. Most receiving Offices, including the International Bureau, will accept such a statement.

32 Where the request is not in a language which is both a language accepted by the receiving Office and a language of publication (R. 12.1(c)), the receiving Office will invite the applicant to file a translation in a publication language (R. 26.3*ter*(c); see annotations to Art. 14 for the procedure).

3.3.4 International Application Not in Official Language of Contracting State

33 Some Contracting States that accept international applications filed in languages other than the official language of that State may require, for reasons of national security (Art. 27(8)), that an international application filed by a national or resident be accompanied by a translation into the official language. See AG-IP Annex C.

3.4 Incorrect Translation

34 An incorrect translation of an international application may give rise to the scope of a patent granted on an international application that exceeds the scope of the international application in its original language. In such a case, the Contracting State concerned may retroactively limit the scope of the patent (Art. 46).

4. Fees

35 The international application is subject to the payment of fees (Art. 3(4)(iv)). On filing of an international application, three fees become due to the receiving Office:

- the transmittal fee;
- the international filing fee (including a sheet fee if the international application has more than 30 sheets, see Schedule of Fees); and
- the international search fee.

36 Currently, the PCT does not foresee claims fees, although proposals have been discussed in the PCT Working Group. Where national law requires claims fees, they will become due only on entry into the national phase (see annotation to Art. 22). While the majority of designated Offices base their claims fees on the number of claims present on entry into the national phase, a few designated Offices will base the claims fee on the number of claims in the international phase (see AG-NP e.g. (DE)).

37 The amounts of some fees are fixed in Swiss Francs, as set out in the Schedule of Fees, included in the Annex to the PCT Regulations as mentioned in R. 96. The

amounts of other fees are fixed by the national Offices. An overview of all fees to be paid to a receiving Office are given in AG-IP Annex C for each receiving Office.

4.1 Method of Payment

Fee payments must be made directly to the Office specified in the PCT that is to collect the particular fee, as indicated in the following paragraphs. Payments must be effected in the currency or one of the currencies prescribed by that Office (see R. 15.2(b)–(d); R. 16.1(b)–(e); R. 57.2(b)–(d); R. 58.1(c)). The PCT has no provisions for permitted methods of payment and for determining what is regarded as the date of payment, for example, the value date of the payment or the date of the bank statement containing the payment. These aspects of payment in the international phase follow the rules and practices of the respective Office. The AG-IP originally provided only information on the amounts of the fees, but since 2024 (refer to circular C.PCT 1659) methods of payment at the different Offices and Authorities in their different PCT functions will be progressively introduced in the Guide. A brief indication of the payment methods for Offices participating in ePCT is also provided on the webpage Office Profiles (https://pct.wipo.int/ePCTExternal/pages/OfficeProfile.xhtml). 38

Thus, payments to RO/EP, ISA/EP, SISA/EP and IPEA/EP are subject to the provisions set out in the Rules relating to Fees (see Rfees1(b)) and the Arrangement for Deposit Accounts, the most important of which are: date of payment (Rfees7(1)), the fail-safe provision (Rfees7(3); however, the provisions are not applicable to payments from outside an EPC Contracting State), and payment by debit order (ADA.5.1). The automatic debiting procedure is available both in the international phase and in the regional phase before the EPO (https://www.epo.org/law-practice/legal-texts/official-journal/2019/etc/se4/p10.html, ADA.5.1.1 and (e); GL Exam EPO A-X, 4.3, PCT EPO Guidelines A-III, 3). The methods of payment are use of a deposit account, bank transfer or credit card (OJ EPO 2024 A37 with further references). A debit order for paying one or more fees from a debit account to the EPO must be filed electronically (ADA.5.1.1). 39

All payments to the International Bureau can be made by eWallet, bank payment online (secured by SOFORT), debiting a current account at WIPO. Credit card payments, PayPal, bank, or postal transfers are also accepted, but not payment by cheque (http://www.wipo.int/pct/en/fees/). 40

4.2 Transmittal fee

Almost every receiving Office charges a transmittal fee for its own benefit as payment for checking the international application and transmittal of the record copy and search copy to the International Bureau and ISA, respectively (R. 14.1(a)). The amount as fixed by each receiving Office (R. 14.1(b)) can be found in AG-IP Annex C. The requirement to pay a transmittal fee to RO/EP is laid down in R. 157(4) EPC and the amount due is fixed in Rfees2(1)18. 41

The time limit for paying the transmittal fee is one month from the date of receipt of the international application by the receiving Office, i.e. not from the international 42 filing date (R. 14.1(c); AG-IP 5.191). Therefore, a shift of the international filing date, for example due to a later submission of a missing element or part (R. 20.5), does not change the time limit for payment of the fee, which is still calculated from the original date of receipt. However, a transmittal of the international application to RO/IB under R. 19.4 because the receiving Office is not competent does change the time limit and the date RO/IB receives the international application triggers the one-month time limit (R. 19.4(c)).

4.3 *International Filing Fee*

43 The applicant must pay an international filing fee to the receiving Office for the benefit of the International Bureau (R. 15.1) for services provided by the International Bureau including publication of the international application, translations where applicable, and communication with the applicant and various designated Offices, the ISA, the SISA, and the IPEA. The international filing fee consists of a fixed amount and an additional amount for each sheet of the application in excess of 30 (Schedule of Fees 1).

44 Since the international filing fee must be paid before the formalities check of Art. 14(1)(a) and any resulting correction, the additional amount for the pages exceeding 30 sheets is calculated on the basis of the documents as filed. RO/IB may accept international applications with pages in slightly smaller print (for physical requirements see R. 11), which reduces the additional amount; an electronically generated request has fewer pages than a printed request form, resulting in a lower fee. Further, declarations can be duly filed after the international filing date, thus reducing the page count and possibly the additional amount.

45 Schedule of Fees 4 and 5 and AG-IP Annex C indicate possible reductions of the international filing fee for each receiving Office for electronic filings and a reduction of 90% for applicants filing as natural persons in their own rights from low and middle-income countries (see http://www.wipo.int/pct/en/fees/ for the list of countries, including several Middle and South European countries).

46 The time limit for paying the international filing fee is the same as for the transmittal fee, i.e. one month from the date of receipt of the international application by the receiving Office (R. 15.3; see annotations to Art. 3).

4.4 *International Search Fee*

47 All ISAs require that the applicant pay an international search fee for their own benefit for carrying out the international search, establishing the ISR (R. 16.1(a)), and the written opinion of the ISA (WO/ISA) (R. 43*bis*). This fee is collected by the receiving Office (R. 16.1(b)).

48 The amount of the international search fee is fixed by each ISA (inferable from R. 16.1(b)) and indicated in AG-IP Annex D. The time limit for payment is the same as for the transmittal and international filing fee, i.e. one month from the date of receipt of the international application by the receiving Office (R. 16.1(f)).

The EPC does not provide a legal basis for ISA/EP to levy a search fee, not even in R. 158 EPC, but only indirectly via Art. 51(1) EPC and Rfees2(1)2 referring to R. 16.1 PCT and fixing the amount of the fee, or via Art. 152 EPC and the ISA/IPEA Agreement EP-IB (www.wipo.int/export/sites/www/pct/en/texts/agreements/ag_ep.pdf, Annex D-I). The fee for carrying out the international search should cover the actual cost of the search and is, therefore, higher than the search fee for a European search, the cost of which is partly paid for by renewal fees. 49

4.5 Non-payment and Remedy

If the applicant has not paid the (full amount of the) transmittal fee, international filing fee and international search fee within one month from the date the receiving Office received the international application (R. 14.1(c); R. 15.3; R. 16.1(f)), the receiving Office will invite the applicant to pay the outstanding amount within one month from the date of the invitation (R. 16*bis*.1(a)). A receiving Office may subject the payment in response to the invitation to the payment of a late payment fee for its own benefit (R. 16*bis*.2; see AG-IP Annex C for each receiving Office). RO/EP does charge such a late payment fee (OJ EPO 1992 p. 383; Euro-PCT Guide 2.24.023). 50

Any payment received by the receiving Office after one month from the date of receipt of the international application but before the receiving Office issues an invitation is considered to have been received before expiry of that time limit (R. 16*bis*.1(d)). 51

If the applicant does not duly pay the fees, including, where applicable, the late payment fee, within one month from the invitation, the international application is considered withdrawn under Art. 14(3)(a) and R. 16*bis*.1(c). The receiving Office will so declare and proceed as provided in R. 29 and set out in the annotations to Art. 14 (R. 16*bis*.1(c)(i), (ii)). Any payment received by the receiving Office after the time limit of one month from the invitation but before making the declaration that the application is deemed withdrawn is considered to have been received before expiry of that time limit (R. 16*bis*.1(e)). 52

If an applicant wants to make sure that an international application is not published, he should actively and timely withdraw the application because a withdrawal by non-payment depends on a decision of the receiving Office or International Bureau and the decision may be taken too late to prevent publication (see introduction to Art. 37). 53

Agents should alert applicants that following international publication they may receive fraudulent requests for payment unrelated to the processing of the PCT application (www.wipo.int/pct/en/warning/pct_warning.html). 54

4.6 Refunds

The international filing fee and the international search fee will be refunded according to R. 15.4 and R. 16.2 if no international filing date is accorded or the international application is not treated as such because of national security prescriptions (see annotations to Art. 10). The international filing fee is also refunded if the international 55 application is withdrawn or considered withdrawn before the transmittal of the record copy to the International Bureau (R. 15.4(ii)).

56 A receiving Office will refund the international filing fee and the international search fee to the applicant where the receiving Office is not competent and the applicant has instead to pay the applicable fees to RO/IB (see annotations to Art. 10; AG-IP 6.035).

57 The international search fee is also refunded if the international application is withdrawn or considered withdrawn before the transmittal of the search copy to the ISA (R. 16.2(ii)). Most ISAs are more lenient than required under R. 16.2(ii), in that they refund the entire international search fee if the international application is withdrawn or considered withdrawn under Art. 14(1), (3), or (4) after the transmittal of the search copy but before the start of the international search (AG-IP Annex D).

58 Since the amount of refund in case of withdrawal is usually dependent on the timing before the transmittal of the record and search copy by the receiving Office, it is recommended to address such withdrawal in this case to the receiving Office and not the International Bureau; otherwise, the International Bureau might only act on the withdrawal after the transmittal.

59 Non-establishment of an ISR under Art. 17(2) does not give entitlement to a refund of the international search fee because this case is not mentioned in R. 16.2 as a ground for refund. In order to conclude that an ISR cannot be established, the ISA will have to carry out a search.

60 The PCT has no provision for refund of the transmittal fee (see AG-IP 5.197).

4.6.1 Partial Refunds

61 An ISA must make a partial refund of the international search fee if its search can be based on an earlier search carried out on an earlier application the priority of which is claimed (R. 16.3) or on an international-type search or other search to which reference is made in the request (R. 41.1; R. 4.12). Most ISAs provide for such a partial refund; the conditions are set out in AG-IP Annex D. For that purpose, the applicant can check a box in the request for taking into account results of an earlier search under R. 4.12 (see annotations to Art. 3).

4.6.2 EPO Refunds

62 The ISA/EP will refund the entire international search fee under the conditions of R. 16.2 and, in particular, if the international application is withdrawn or considered withdrawn before the start of the international search (ISA/IPEA Agreement EP-IB, www.wipo.int/export/sites/www/pct/en/texts/agreements/ag_ep.pdf, Annex D-II(2)).

63 The international search fee will be refunded wholly or partially if the EPO can base its ISR on an earlier search already made by the EPO on an application whose priority is claimed for the international application (R. 16.3 and R. 41). The refund requires a valid priority claim (Euro-PCT Guide 3.1.027).

The rate of a partial refund depends on the extent to which the EPO benefits from the earlier search and the type of earlier search. The criteria for the refund rate are similar to those for refunds of European search fees and are set out in OJ EPO 2024 A7 and in AG-IP Annex D(EP). The extent to which the EPO benefits from the earlier search is determined by the degree of similarity between the claims searched and the claims to be searched, as set out in OJ EPO 2009 p.99. The earlier search may be one of several different types, including a European search on a European patent application, an international (supplementary) search on an international application, an international-type search or a search on a national application made by the EPO on behalf of a national Office (OJ EPO 2024 A7). 64

5. PCT Direct Letter

An applicant filing an international application claiming priority from an earlier application already searched by the EPO and selecting the EPO as ISA may submit a PCT Direct letter together with the international application, irrespective of the receiving Office used. The PCT Direct letter contains informal comments and any amendments aimed at overcoming objections raised in the search opinion established by the EPO for the priority application (OJ EPO 2015 A51 and OJ EPO 2017 A21 for formal details of PCT Direct letters). 65

The PCT Direct letter may include explanations, new arguments, or amendments with their basis in the application. If the claims and/or the description of the international application differ from those of the earlier application, applicants should preferably include a marked-up copy indicating the differences. The EPO as ISA will take the comments into account. 66

Since the introduction of the PCT Direct service by the EPO in 2014, it was adopted by other national Offices. A receiving Office will transmit free of charge any PCT Direct letter submitted to it to the selected ISA to be taken into account by the ISA. 67

The PCT Direct letter provides an extra opportunity for the applicant to exchange views on patentability with the examining authorities (Pract. Adv. NL 11/2017 www.wipo.int/pct/en/newslett/practical_advice/pa_112017.html). 68

6. Reference to Genetic Resources and Associated Traditional Knowledge

Currently, there is no provision in the PCT system to provide for the disclosure of genetic resources or associated traditional knowledge. However, the new Treaty on Intellectual Property, Genetic Resources and Associated Traditional Knowledge as adopted in May 2024, once it enters into force in the future, agree in footnote 4 that 'with a view towards providing an opportunity for applicants who file an international application under the PCT designating a PCT Contracting State which, under its applicable national law, requires the disclosure of genetic resources and traditional knowledge associated with genetic resources, to comply with any formality requirements related to such disclosure requirement either upon filing of the international 69 application, with effect for all such Contracting States, or subsequently, upon entry into the national phase before an Office of any such Contracting State.'

Article 3
The International Application

(1)

Applications for the protection of inventions in any of the Contracting States may be filed as international applications under this Treaty.

R. 92.4	Use of telegraph, teleprinter, fax machine, etc. for filing
EPO as receiving Office	Euro-PCT Guide Chapters 1 and 2

(2)

An international application shall contain, as specified in this Treaty and the Regulations, a request, a description, one or more claims, one or more drawings (where required), and an abstract.

Art. 4, R. 4	Request
Art. 5, R. 5	Description
Art. 6, R. 6	Claims
Art. 7, R. 7	Drawings
R. 8	Abstract

(3)

The abstract merely serves the purpose of technical information and cannot be taken into account for any other purpose, particularly not for the purpose of interpreting the scope of the protection sought.

(4)

The international application shall:

(i) be in a prescribed language;

R. 12	Prescribed language is decisive for the filing date (see Art. 11(1)(ii) and Introduction to Art. 3 No. 3)
R. 19.4(a)(ii)	Possibility of remedy in case of inadmissible language
R. 26.3*ter*	Mixed languages used in abstract, drawings, description, claims

(ii) comply with the prescribed physical requirements;

R. 11	Physical requirements	

(iii) comply with the prescribed requirement of unity of invention;

Art. 17, R. 13	Unity of invention	
R. 40	Lack of unity of invention (international search)	
	R. 40.1	Invitation to pay additional fees; time limit
	R. 40.2	Additional fees
R. 68	Lack of unity of invention (IPE)	
	R. 68.1	No invitation to restrict or pay
	R. 68.2	Invitation to restrict or pay
	R. 68.3	Additional fees
	R. 68.4	Procedure in the case of insufficient restriction of the claims
	R. 68.5	Main invention

(iv) be subject to the payment of the prescribed fees.

Art. 14(3)	Legal consequence of non-payment of fees is the fiction of withdrawal of the application	
R. 4.9	Designation of States; kinds of protection; national and regional patents	
R. 15	The international filing fee	
	R. 15.1	International filing fee
	R. 15.2	Amount; transfer
	R. 15.3	Time limit for payment; amount payable
	R. 15.4	Refund
R. 16*bis*	Extension of time limits for payment of fees	
R. 13*ter*.1	Fee for the late furnishing of sequence listings R. 5.2	
R. 27.1	List of fees under Art. 14(3) – International filing fee (R. 15) (Art. 4(2), R. 15.1, R. 15.3, R. 16*bis*) – Transmittal fee (R. 14) – Search fee (R. 16) – late payment fee (R. 16*bis*.2)	

70 DE: In the absence of explicit provisions in the PCT and the Regulations, the provisions of the PatKostG and PatKostZV also apply to fees charged by the DPMA as receiving Office for the benefit of the International Bureau or the ISA (BPatG, decision of July 8, 2004–10 W (pat) 56/03) in BlPMZ 2005, p. 80 et seq). This concerns in particular the calculation of time limits.

Article 4
The Request

INTRODUCTION

1. General Aspects of the Request for International Application

1 The request is part of the international application and must contain a petition to the effect that the international application be processed according to the PCT (Art. 4(1)(i); R. 4.1(a)(i), preferably worded according to R. 4.2, this wording is pre-printed in the request Form PCT/RO/101 (https://www.wipo.int/pct/en/forms/index.html) and included automatically when using electronic filing means. The request must also contain data on the applicant and, if applicable, on the agent, data on inventor(s), and the title of the invention (Art. 4(1)(i)–(iv), R. 4.1). Filing of the request constitutes designation of all Contracting States bound by the PCT on the international filing date (R. 4.9(a)).

2 The request can be made using the editable Form PCT/RO/101. If the international application is filed on paper, the request form can be submitted either on paper or as a computer print-out (R. 3.1; AG-IP 5.015). Copies of the printed form are available free of charge from the receiving Offices and the International Bureau (R. 3.2). If the applicant files the international application fully electronically, the request form will be automatically generated from the data entered, which may result in lower fees due to a reduced total number of sheets (see annotations to Art. 3).

3 The request must contain a checklist indicating the content of the application documents (R. 3.3). The request may contain declarations to simplify fulfilling certain national requirements of designated Offices (R. 4.17). A later correction of or addition to these declarations is possible (R. 26*ter*; AG-IP 6.045;-6.050; see annotations to Art. 4).

4 The language of the request must be both a language accepted by the receiving Office and a language of publication (R. 12.1(c); see annotations to Art. 3 and R. 12). The requirements for other items in the request, such as the data on the applicant, any agent, the inventor, and the signature, are set out in the following sections (see also R. 4).

5 The WIPO website contains an example of a completed request form (https://www.wipo.int/pct/en/forms/) including explanatory notes.

2. Designation of Contracting States

On filing an international application, all Contracting States bound by the PCT on the international filing date are designated automatically (Art. 4(1)(ii) and R. 4.9(a)(i)), for every kind of protection available for the States (R. 4.9(a)(ii)), including both national and regional patent protection (R. 4.9(a)(iii)). The request may indicate different applicants for different States (R. 4.5(d), see also annotations to Art. 9). Since 2004 no fee need be paid for the designations; the abolishment of the payment of designation fees has made Art. 4(2) meaningless (R. 27.1(b)). An international application accorded a filing date will have the effect of a regular national application in the designated State with a filing date equal to the international filing date (Art. 11(3)). 6

2.1 Special Designations

2.1.1 Designation of Grant of National Patent Interpreted as Grant of Regional Patent

National law of a Contracting State may provide that the designation of that State for the grant of a national patent in the request will be treated as an indication of the wish to obtain a regional patent for that State (Art. 4(1)(ii); Art. 45(2)). AG-IP Annex B indicates in such cases for each Contracting State the competent regional authority that will act as designated Office. For example, a designation in an international application of The Netherlands for the grant of a Dutch patent will be treated as an indication to obtain a European patent for The Netherlands with the DO/EP. 7

2.1.2 Newly Acceded States and Disintegrated States

A State newly acceded to the PCT can be designated in an international application on or after the date the State is bound by the PCT (R. 4.9(a)(i)). The newly acceded State may be a successor State of a Contracting State that has split into several independent States. The effect of an international application filed during a certain period following the disintegration of a Contracting State will be extended to its successor States, provided they become PCT Contracting States. The International Bureau will publish information on the extension (R. 32; AG-IP 11.089–11.093). Examples of disintegrated States are Yugoslavia, Czechoslovakia and the Soviet Union. 8

2.1.3 National and Regional Designations under EPC

The EPO will act as designated Office for those EPC Contracting States for which the PCT is in force, which are designated in the international application and for which the applicant wishes to obtain a European patent (Art. 153(1)(a) EPC). All current EPC Contracting States are also PCT Contracting States. Some EPC Contracting States have made use of Art. 45(2) PCT to close the national route because they prefer the well-examined European patents over their own less-examined or un-examined registered patents. (For States see annotations to Art. 45; AG-IP Annex B; Euro-PCT 9

Guide 2.12.007.) An indication of the applicant's wish to obtain a national patent in such a State is interpreted as the wish to obtain a European patent for that State (Art. 4(1)(ii); AG-IP 5.052).

2.1.4 Extensions under EPC

10 The effects of a European patent may be extended to a State having an extension agreement or validation agreement with the EPO. The extension and validation are governed by national law, which effectively makes use of the EPO for the grant of national patents (AG-IP 4.026; www.epo.org/about-us/foundation/extension-states.html, www.epo.org/about-us/foundation/validation-states.html). The extension and validation system can only be used when both the EPO and the extension and validation State are designated in the international application. See also annotations to Art. 45.

2.1.5 Designation of US

11 As of September 16, 2012, it is no longer required that an inventor of a US application also be designated as applicant. However, the inventor must furnish an oath or a declaration upon national phase entry into the US that he is an original inventor and has authorized the filing of the application (R. 51*bis*.1(a)(iv)), unless a PCT declaration of inventorship under R. 4.17(iv) is filed together with the international application (see annotations to Art. 4).

12 Some applicants often file in parallel a US application and an international application that does not enter the national phase in the US. This strategy allows the US application to be adapted to the US style of drafting and avoids the international application becoming part of any litigation relating to the US patent.

2.2 Kinds of Protection when Designating a Contracting State

13 A designation of a Contracting State is treated as an indication of the wish to obtain a patent in the State, unless the applicant asks for another kind of protection (Art. 4(3)). The PCT permits an applicant to apply for any kind of protection of inventions available for a State (Art. 2(i), Art. 3(1)). Kinds of protection other than patents are utility models, petty patents or similar titles (Art. 43). A State permitting such other kinds of protection may also allow that the international application is for the grant of two different kinds of protection in respect of that State (Art. 44; AG-IP 5.055–5.056). AG-IP Annex B indicates for each Contracting State the kinds of protection available via the national and regional route. For example, DE national: patent and utility model; DE regional patent EP. A table with an overview of the types of protection available via the PCT in PCT Contracting States can be found on the WIPO website (www.wipo.int/pct/en/texts/typesprotection.html).

14 The designation of a State in the request form is an indication that the international application is for the grant of every kind of protection available in that State (R. 4.9(a)(ii)). The specification of the kind of protection desired in a State is deferred until

entry into the national phase of the State (R. 49*bis*.1 and 49*bis*.2). However, if the kind of protection sought is a title of addition, such as a patent of addition, or a continuation or a continuation-in-part of an earlier application, the applicant must indicate this for the designated State in the request of the international application and identify the earlier application where appropriate (R. 4.11(a)(i) and (ii)); such indications can be also added or corrected after filing of the international application (R. 26*quater*; see annotations to Art. 4).

Any designated State in which the grant of a utility model is sought may apply national law instead of the PCT provisions in respect of the layout of the claims and unity of invention, provided the applicant is given at least two months after entering the national phase to adapt his application accordingly (R. 6.5; R. 13.5). 15

2.3 *Exception to All-Inclusive Designation System*

Under national law of some States, the filing of an international application that designates such a State and that claims the priority of an earlier national application filed in that State is regarded as self-designation and will have the result that the earlier national application ceases to have effect for that State, with the same consequences as the withdrawal of the earlier application. An applicant that desires to maintain the said effect of the priority application should exclude that State from the automatic and all-inclusive designation (R. 4.9(b)). An applicant may exclude the designations of Germany, Japan, and South Korea by marking a check-box in the request to avoid an undesired loss of the national priority application (AG-IP 5.053). 16

Alternatively, the designation of the States may be excluded after filing of the international application by withdrawing the designation under R. 90*bis*.2. The notice of withdrawal must be filed with the International Bureau for DE before entry into the national phase, for JP before 16 months and for KR before 15 months from the priority date (AG-IP Annexes B (DE), (JP) and (KR); see annotations to Art. 4). The exclusion of Germany from the international application relates only to the designation DE for a national patent obtained via the German national phase and not to the designation EP for a regional patent obtained via the EP regional phase and granted for Germany. 17

Since the designation of Germany for a European patent is not regarded as a self-designation and the self-designation leads only to a loss of effect of the priority application if the international application is filed with RO/DE, an applicant who desires to maintain the effect of the priority application need neither exclude nor withdraw the automatic designation EP in the international application nor the designation DE before RO/EP (Euro-PCT Guide 2.12.006). 18

2.4 *Withdrawal of Designation*

The applicant may withdraw the designation of any State up to 30 months from the priority date (R. 90*bis*.2(a)). Where a State is designated both nationally and regionally, the withdrawal of the designation of that State is taken to mean the withdrawal of the national designation only, unless otherwise indicated (R. 90*bis*.2(b)). 19

A withdrawal of all designations is treated as a withdrawal of the international application (R. 90*bis*.2(c)). Withdrawal is free of charge (AG-IP 11.050). Note that withdrawal under R. 90*bis*.2 is a different act compared to exclusion as allowed for certain States under R. 4.9(b) (see annotations to Art. 4).

20 The withdrawal can be effected by sending a notice signed by all applicants (or common agent or duly appointed common representative) for the designation concerned to the International Bureau, or, if a demand is filed, to the IPEA (R. 90*bis*.2(d); R. 90*bis*.5). The designation will not be included in the publication of the international application if the notice of its withdrawal has reached the International Bureau before the technical preparations for the international publication have been completed (R. 90*bis*.2(e)). The technical preparations are generally completed by the 15th calendar day prior to the date of publication (AG-IP 9.013). Hence, the last moment for submitting changes that will be taken into account for publication is midnight (CET) at the end of Tuesday, 15 calendar days before publication (usually on a Thursday; see Pract. Adv. NL 06/2014, www.wipo.int/pct/en/newslett/practical_advice/pa_062014.html). The scheduled publication date is available in ePCT with strong authentication.

21 Withdrawal of a designation is generally not recommended, since any withdrawal is irrevocable and the same effect can be achieved by not entering into the respective national phase. The only exception where withdrawal is useful is the case set out in the annotations to Art. 4.

3. Representation

22 The PCT does not generally require that applicants are represented by agents in the international phase. However, each receiving Office may apply national law to require the applicant to be represented by an agent (Art. 27(7)). AG-IP Annex C indicates for each receiving Office whether or not the applicant must be represented by an agent. Some receiving Offices do not require the applicant to appoint an agent, for example, International Bureau and US. Most receiving Offices do not require appointment of an agent for applicants that are residents of the State concerned, for example, DE and EP. If the applicant is represented, the request must so indicate and provide the data of the agent (Art. 4(1)(iii); R. 4.7).

23 The receiving Office also specifies who may act as an agent (see AG-IP Annex C for each receiving Office). Most receiving Offices only accept agents qualified to practice before the national Office acting as receiving Office. Therefore, a US patent attorney cannot act as an agent before RO/EP. Some receiving Offices allow any person to act as an agent (see, for example, AG-IP Annex C(SE)). If an agent is not authorized to act before a specific receiving Office, he will be registered as 'address for correspondence'. In such a case, a signature of the applicant is required for each submission (Pract. Adv. NL 04/2015 https://www.wipo.int/pct/en/newslett/practical_advice/pa_042015.html).

24 An agent having the right to practice before the national Office with which the international application was filed may also practice before the International Bureau, ISA and IPEA in respect of that application (Art. 49; R. 83). More information on

representation before an ISA and before an IPEA is given in annotations to Art. 49, and before a designated Office is given in annotations to Art. 22. General information about representation is given in the annotations to Art. 27(7) and about signing a document by an agent in the annotations to Art. 4.

3.1 *Representation before EPO*

RO/EP does not require the appointment of an agent if the applicant has a residence or principal place of business in one of the EPC Contracting States. 25

However, RO/EP does require the appointment of an agent if the applicant is a national of an EPC Contracting State but has neither residence nor a place of business in one of those States (Art. 133(2) EPC via Art. 27(7) PCT; AG-IP Annex C(EP)). In principle, such an applicant may only initiate the processing and file an international application with RO/EP without an agent (Art. 27(7) PCT in combination with Art. 133(2) EPC) but has to carry out all further acts through an agent. In practice, the EPO also accepts all further acts of such a national before the receiving Office. In addition, a national patent attorney (not being a European patent attorney) can act in the international phase before the EPO if the international application is filed at the national Office (Art. 49; R. 83). 26

The use of the term 'other person' in Art. 49 PCT is the legal basis for representation by an employee of an applicant resident in an EPC Contracting State (cf. Art. 133(3) EPC). 27

4. Title of the Invention

An international application must contain a title (Art. 4(1)(iv)). The title must be stated in the request (R. 4.1(a)(ii)) and at the beginning of the description (R. 5.1(a)), and should be short (preferably from two to seven words when in English or translated into English) and precise (R. 4.3). 28

A missing title is regarded as a defect (Art. 14(1)(a)(iii)). The receiving Office will invite the applicant to furnish the title, failure of which could result in the international application being considered withdrawn by the receiving Office (Art. 14(1)(b)). The receiving Office notifies the ISA that it has invited the applicant to correct the defect; the ISA will proceed with the international search, but stops if it is notified that the application is considered withdrawn (R. 37.1). The ISA will establish a title itself if the title is missing and it has not received a notification that the receiving Office has invited the applicant to correct the defect, or if the title is too long or not precise (R. 37.2). The ISR states either the approval by the ISA of the title or the title as established by the ISA (R. 44.2). 29

5. Inventor

The name and address of the inventor(s) can be provided in the request. AG-IP Annex B indicates for each Contracting State whether the information of the inventor must be given in the request when the State is designated (Art. 4(1)(v); Art. 4(4); 30

R. 4.1(a)(iv); R. 4.6(a)) or may be supplied in separate notices to each designated Office during the national phase (R. 4.1(c)(i); see, for example, R. 163(1) EPC). The inventor must be designated on filing the international application if at least one Contracting State where protection is desired requires that the name is furnished at the time of filing the international application. If an inventor is indicated, an address has to be provided (R. 4.6(a)). In case of privacy concerns, it is recommended to provide the work address of the inventor.

31 Since the information on the inventor is generally required in the national phase, it is recommended always to include it in the request, unless special reasons prevent this (AG-IP 5.036). Moreover, it may be difficult to collect the information on the inventors for furnishing to the designated Offices about 30 months after the priority date.

32 When providing the information on an inventor who is not an applicant in the request form, the PCT does not require a declaration concerning the entitlement of the applicant to file the patent application; the inclusion of such a declaration in the request is optional (R. 4.17 'may contain'; for further recommendations when to use declarations, see annotations to Art. 4).

33 The EPC allows information on the inventor to be provided on entry into the European phase (R. 163(1) EPC). If the information on an inventor who is not an applicant has already been provided on filing of the international application, without the said declaration of entitlement, the EPO as designated Office does not require the declaration, called 'statement' in R. 19(1) EPC (implied by GL Exam EPO E-IX, 2.3.4). However, other designated Offices will require further evidence of entitlement, unless a declaration under R. 4.17(ii) had been included (R. 51*bis*.1(iii)), and it is therefore recommended to make use of the optional declaration.

5.1 Inventor as Applicant

34 A person can be identified in the request Form PCT/RO/101 as (AG-IP 5.035; see also annotations to Art. 4):

- applicant only;
- inventor only; or
- applicant and inventor.

35 The request may indicate different inventors for different States where national laws of the designated States are not the same in respect of designation of inventors (R. 4.6(c); AG-IP 5.038–5.039).

36 National law determines whether a designated Office may request the applicant to furnish evidence of the identity of the inventor. In general, a designated Office may not request furnishing such evidence if a declaration as to the identity of the inventor has been filed in the international phase of the PCT or the identity is indicated in the request (R. 4.17(i); R. 51*bis*.1(a)(i); R. 51*bis*.2(i)) or in a declaration or oath of inventorship (R. 4.17(iv); R. 51*bis*.1(a)(iv); R. 51*bis*.2(iv)). See annotations to Art. 4 on filing declarations.

5.2 Changes Concerning Inventor

Changes in the person, name or address of the inventor will, on request of the receiving Office or the applicant, be recorded by the International Bureau (R. 92*bis*.1(a)(ii)) free of charge (AG-IP 11.018). See annotations to Art. 9 for the time limits for filing any such request. The PCT has no provision similar to R. 21(1) EPC that an inventor must give his consent to be removed from the international application; such a request need only be signed by the applicant as a normal letter under R. 92.1 (AG-IP 11.018). If the inventor dies before the international application is filed, the request must indicate that he is deceased (AG-IP 11.025). If the inventor dies during the international phase, no action need be taken (AG-IP 11.026). 37

6. Signature

The applicant must sign the request (R. 4.15). An agent may sign the request on behalf of the applicant, provided he is duly appointed in a power of attorney signed by the applicant (R. 90.4). Where the receiving Office requires the furnishing of a power of attorney (AG-IP Annex C) and it is erroneous or missing, the signature is considered missing until the power of attorney is submitted (AG-IP 5.089). Where an international application is filed with a receiving Office that has waived the requirement of filing a separate power of attorney, for example, RO/EP or RO/IB (see table on waivers under www.wipo.int/pct/en/texts/waivers.html), the application may be signed by an agent and no signature of an applicant is required. Note that R. 90*bis*.5 is not subject to 'waiver' situations, so a notice of withdrawal must be signed by all applicants or an agent duly appointed by all applicants. 38

The name and role of the person signing on behalf of a legal entity must be clearly indicated next to the signature (AG-IP 5.090). The signature is understood to mean a seal where the national law of the receiving Office requires use of a seal instead of a signature (R. 2.3). 39

6.1 Missing Signature

Absence of a signature of an applicant or agent is a defect under Art. 14(1)(a)(i) and R. 26.2*bis*(a)). The receiving Office will invite the applicant to furnish the signature. Failure to do so will result in the international application being considered withdrawn (Art. 14(1)(b); R. 29). 40

In the case of several applicants, a signature of one of the applicants is sufficient for the receiving Office (R. 26.2*bis*(a)). Any missing second or further signature is not regarded as a defect under Art. 14 and can be furnished in the national phase (R. 51*bis*.1(a)(vi)). See annotations to Art. 9 for more detail. 41

7. Declarations

The applicant may include in the request certain declarations relating to national requirements, briefly called 'declarations' (R. 4.17). Declarations can also be added or corrected after filing within 16 months from the priority date (R. 26*ter*). 42

43 A declaration enables the applicant to comply with some of the national requirements of the designated Offices referred to in R. 51*bis*.1 already during the international phase. Declarations may be filed as to:

- the identity of the inventor (R. 4.17(i); it need not be filed if the identity of the inventor is otherwise indicated in the request (AIs 211(b)));
- the applicant's entitlement to apply for and be granted a patent (R. 4.17(ii));
- the applicant's entitlement to claim priority of an earlier application (R. 4.17(iii));
- a declaration of inventorship (R. 4.17(iv)); and
- non-prejudicial disclosures or exceptions to lack of novelty (R. 4.17(v)).

44 Any transfer of rights for the declarations under R. 4.17(ii) and (iii) needs to take place before the international filing date.

45 Only the declaration of inventorship (R. 4.17(iv)), relevant for the US national phase, must be signed by all inventors on the same declaration or on copies thereof; it is possible to obtain the signatures of the inventors by using the 'external signature' function in ePCT (AG-IP 5.074–5.083; Pract. Adv. NL 10/2019, www.wipo.int/pct/en/newslett/practical_advice/pa_102019.html).

46 Any declaration should be entered in the request using a standardized wording. The standardized wording of each declaration is given in AIs 211–215 and will be automatically created when using the electronic filing means. Any declaration using the standardized wording generally prevents designated Offices from requesting further documents or evidence during the national phase (R. 51*bis*.2 and AG-IP 5.078).

47 Though declarations are not mandatory, their use is recommended, since a simple declaration filed together with the international application avoids having to furnish further documents in the national phase before each designated Office.

8. Earlier Search Results

48 The applicant may indicate in the request that the ISA take into account the results of an earlier search (R. 4.12), resulting potentially in a refund of the international search fee (AG-IP 5.073; see annotations to Art. 3). Even without such a request for taking into account earlier search results, since 2017 receiving Offices will transmit any earlier search or classification result available to them to the ISA (R. 23*bis*.2; R. 41.2), unless the receiving Office has made one of the two types of notification of incompatibility of R. 23*bis*.2(a) with national law, leaving the applicant the choice of 'opting in' or 'opting out' of such procedure to be indicated in the request (R. 23*bis*.2(b) or (e); see Pract. Adv. NL 02/2018, www.wipo.int/pct/en/newslett/practical_advice/pa_022018.html and PCT Reservations, www.wipo.int/pct/en/texts/reservations/res_incomp.html under R. 23*bis*.2(b) and (e)). Corresponding boxes are contained in the request form.

Article 4
The Request

(1)

The request shall contain:

(i) a petition to the effect that the international application be processed according to this Treaty;

Art. 11(1)(iii)(a)	Possible legal consequences in the event of defects: loss of the filing date	
Art. 14	Notification of defects	
R. 3	The request (form)	
	R. 3.1	Form of request
	R. 3.2	Availability of forms
	R. 3.3	Check list
	R. 3.4	Particulars
R. 4	The request (contents)	
	R. 4.1	Mandatory and optional contents; Signature
	R. 4.2	Petition
Art. 8, R. 4.10	Priority claim	
R. 4.11	Reference to a continuation or continuation-in-part, or parent application or parent patent	
R. 4.11(a)(i)	Patent of addition, certificate of addition, inventor's certificate of addition or utility certificate of addition	
R. 4.11(a)(ii)	Application for a continuation or a continuation-in-part of an earlier application	
R. 4.12	Taking into account results of earlier search	
R. 4.14*bis*	Choice of ISA	
R. 4.15	Signature	
R. 4.16	Transliteration or translation of certain words	
R. 4.17	Declarations relating to national requirements referred to in R. 51*bis*.1(a)(i)–(vii)	
R. 4.18	Incorporation by reference of an earlier application	
R. 4.19	Additional matter	

(ii) the designation of the Contracting State or States in which protection for the invention is desired on the basis of the international application ("designated States"); if for any designated State a regional patent is available and the applicant wishes to obtain a regional patent rather than a

national patent, the request shall so indicate; if, under a treaty concerning a regional patent, the applicant cannot limit his application to certain of the States party to that treaty, designation of one of those States and the indication of the wish to obtain the regional patent shall be treated as designation of all the States party to that treaty; if, under the national law of the designated State, the designation of that State has the effect of an application for a regional patent, the designation of the said State shall be treated as an indication of the wish to obtain the regional patent;

Art. 45	Regional patents: EPO, ARIPO, OAPI, Eurasian patent
R. 4.9	Designation of States; kind of protection; national and regional patents
Art. 45	Regional patent treaties
Art. 153 EPC	EPO as designated Office
J 30/90 EPC	EPO is designated Office only for those States for which the EPC and the PCT were in force on the international filing date (Art. 4(1)(ii) PCT in conjunction with Art. 153(1) EPC). Art. 153(1) EPC)
Art. 153(1) EPC, Art. 45(2) PCT	For regional patent treaties, extension and validation, see annotations to Art. 45.
GL Exam EPO A-III, 12.1	For an extension of European patent applications and European patents to non-Contracting States of the EPC for which an extension agreement has entered into force, a national designation in the PCTa is necessary for the desired extension States. A request for extension shall be deemed to have been filed for any European application filed after the entry into force of the respective extension agreement, subject to payment of an extension fee. Extension can be requested for the following States: Extension can be requested for Bosnia and Herzegovina (BA). Due to the accession of ME to the EPC, the agreement existing since March 1, 2010 is valid until September 31, 2022 (OJ 2022 A78). For previous applications, a comparable effect may result from the agreement with YU (OJ 2007 407) (OJ 2010 p. 10). Due to agreements between EPO and non-members, validation is possible in Tunisia (TN), Morocco (MA), Republic of Moldova (MD), Cambodia (KH), Georgia (GE) since January 15, 2024.

(iii) the name of and other prescribed data concerning the applicant and the agent (if any);

R. 4.4	Names and addresses
R. 4.5	Applicant, R. 4.5(d) different designations for different applicants
R. 4.7	Agent

R. 4.8	Common representative

(iv) the title of the invention;

R. 4.3	Title of the invention

(v) the name of and other prescribed data concerning the inventor where the national law of at least one of the designated States requires that these indications be furnished at the time of filing a national application. Otherwise, the said indications may be furnished either in the request or in separate notices addressed to each designated Office whose national law requires the furnishing of the said indications but allows that they be furnished at a time later than that of the filing of a national application.

R. 4.1(a)(iv) and (c)(i)	Information on the inventor: For reasons of data protection, it is also possible to use a professional address of the inventor in the international phase. In the national phase, however, the national regulations are prevailing. It is easier to avoid using details of the private address from the outset than to remove or change them subsequently (PCT Newsletter 10/2020, p. 14).
R. 4.6	Inventor
Art. 4(4)	Failure to indicate data concerning the inventor

(2)

Every designation shall be subject to the payment of the prescribed fee within the prescribed time limit.

The designation fee has been abandoned as of January 1, 2004. The text concerning the former designation fee has, however, been preserved in Art. 4(2).

R. 4.9(a)(i)	All Member States are automatically designated.
R. 4.9(a)(ii)	All kinds of protection are automatically requested.
R. 4.9(a) (iii)	All regional patents are automatically requested.
R. 4.9(b), AG-IP 5.053	Exemption from designation of DE, JP, KR
R. 90*bis*.2	Withdrawal of designations

(3)

Unless the applicant asks for any of the other kinds of protection referred to in Article 43, designation shall mean that the desired protection consists of the grant of a patent by or for the designated State. For the purposes of this paragraph, Article 2(ii) shall not apply.

(4)

Failure to indicate in the request the name and other prescribed data concerning the inventor shall have no consequence in any designated State whose national law requires the furnishing of the said indications but allows that they be furnished at a time later than that of the filing of a national application. Failure to furnish the said indications in a separate notice shall have no consequence in any designated State whose national law does not require the furnishing of the said indications.

Art. 90(5) EPC, R. 60 EPC (until December 12, 2007 thematically regulated in Art. 91(5) EPC).

The inventor designation must be filed 16 months after the priority date. If the time limits have already expired, the inventor designation may be filed subsequently (Art. 27(2)(ii), R. 51*bis*.1(a)(i) PCT (national requirements) in conjunction with R. 163 EPC).

If the US is designated as the designated or elected Office, the name and address of the inventor may be mentioned in the application or submitted subsequently. If the information is not available even after entry into the national phase in the US, the USPTO requests the submission of the inventor's data (AG-IP Annex B (US)).

Article 5
The Description

The description shall disclose the invention in a manner sufficiently clear and complete for the invention to be carried out by a person skilled in the art.

R. 5	The description	
	R. 5.1	Manner of the description
	R. 5.2	Sequence disclosure
R. 13*ter*	Nucleotide and/or amino acid sequence listings (procedure before ISA, IPEA)	
	R. 13*ter*.1	Fee for late furnishing of sequence listings
R. 9	Expressions, etc., not to be used	
	R. 9.1	Definition
	R. 9.2	Noting of lack of compliance
	R. 9.3	Reference to Art. 21(6) international publication
R. 10	Terminology and signs	
	R. 10.1	Terminology and signs
	R. 10.2	Consistency
R. 11	Physical requirements of the international application	
	R. 11.1	Number of copies
	R. 11.2	Fitness for reproduction
	R. 11.3	Material to be used
	R. 11.4	Separate sheets, etc.
	R. 11.5	Size of sheets
	R. 11.6	Margins
	R. 11.7	Numbering of sheets
	R. 11.8	Numbering of lines
	R. 11.9	Writing of text matter
	R. 11.10	Drawings, formulae, and tables, in text matter

	R. 11.11	Words in drawings
	R. 11.12	Alterations, etc.
	R. 11.13	Special requirements for drawings
	R. 11.14	Later documents
R. 12.1	Languages accepted for the filing of international applications	

1 The description must disclose the invention in a manner sufficiently clear and complete for the invention to be carried out by a person skilled in the art (Art. 5). The best mode for carrying out the invention must be indicated in the description if at least one of the designated Offices so requires (R. 5.1(a)(v); AG-IP 5.096). The parts of the description and their order are prescribed by R. 5.1. The international application may not contain any matter contrary to morality or public order, or disparaging statements or irrelevant matter (Art. 21(6); R. 9). The physical requirements, numbering of pages and lines, presentation of formulae and tables are set out in R. 11. The international application must contain a description in order to be accorded an international filing date (Art. 11(1)(iii)(d)). Since the receiving Office does only a formal examination, a part which on the face of it appears to be a description is sufficient. See annotations to Art. 11 and R. 20 for the procedure to correct a missing or erroneous description.

2 Where the international application discloses a nucleotide or amino acid sequence, the application documents must include a sequence listing complying with the WIPO standard as part of the description (see R. 5.2; AG-IP 5.099–5.104; Euro-PCT Guide 2.24). The sequence listing could also be furnished after filing, for search purposes only (see R. 13*ter*; AG-IP 7.005, 7.011), but it is recommended to file it as part of the description in order to avoid any issues in the national phase before certain designated Offices (Pract. Adv. NL 12/2015 www.wipo.int/pct/en/newslett/practical_advice/pa_122015.html). Applicants are advised to file sequence listings in the latest version of the required WIPO Standard in the electronic form since WIPO Standard ST.26 requires XML format for sequence listings in international applications since 2022 (AG-IP 7.099 et seq.). For details concerning ST.26, see annotations to R. 5.2.

3 The requirements for the electronic form accepted by Offices can be found in Annex F. Any receiving Office that does not accept XML format will transmit the PCTa to the International Bureau under R. 19.4. Applicants are discouraged from sending the sequence listing separately in electronic form and the main body of the PCTa on paper (AG-IP 5.100). For the case that a separate electronic file appears to be a disclosure of sequences in a format other than XML, see AG-IP 5.102.

4 For the procedure concerning sequence listings before the ISA, IPEA, designated Office and elected Office see R. 13*ter*. If the description refers to biological material and its deposit see R. 13*bis*.

Article 6
The Claims

The claim or claims shall define the matter for which protection is sought. Claims shall be clear and concise. They shall be fully supported by the description.

R. 6	The claims	
	R. 6.1	Number and numbering of claims
	R. 6.2	References to other parts of the international application
	R. 6.3	Manner of claiming
	R. 6.4	Dependent claims
	R. 6.5	Utility models
R. 11	Physical requirements of the international application	
R. 12.1	Languages accepted for the filing of international applications	

The claim or claims must define the matter for which protection is sought and must be clear, concise and fully supported by the description (Art. 6). The claim drafting directives in R. 6, relating to numbering, dependencies, two-part form, references to the description, and reference signs, are not mandatory. However, when drafted according to these Rules, claims must be accepted by all designated Offices. In the national phase, a designated Office may require adaptation of the claims to national law. 1

Where an ISA under its national law does not allow multiple dependent claims to serve as a basis for another multiple dependent claim, it need not establish a search report (R. 6.4(a); Art. 17(2)(a)(ii), (b)). Where the international application contains several dependent claims, some designated Offices may require amendment of the claims on entry into the national phase (AG-IP 5.113). The ISA checks compliance of the claims with the requirement of unity of invention (Art. 3(4)(iii); Art. 17(3)(a)). 2

The international application must contain at least one claim for the accordance of an international filing date (Art. 11(1)(iii)(e)). It is sufficient that the part on the face of it appears to be a claim. See annotations to Art. 11 and R. 20 for the procedure to correct missing claims. 3

Article 7
The Drawings

(1)

Subject to the provisions of paragraph (2)(ii), drawings shall be required when they are necessary for the understanding of the invention.

(2)

Where, without being necessary for the understanding of the invention, the nature of the invention admits of illustration by drawings:

(i) the applicant may include such drawings in the international application when filed,

(ii) any designated Office may require that the applicant file such drawings with it within the prescribed time limit.

Art. 14(2)	Consequences of missing drawings	
	R. 7	The drawings
	R. 7.1	Flow sheets and diagrams
	R. 7.2	Time limit for furnishing missing drawings at least two months from invitation
R. 11	Physical requirements of the international application	
	R. 11.11	Words in drawings
	R. 11.13	Special requirements for drawings
R. 26.3*ter*, R. 26.5	Incorrect language in the drawings is a defect within the meaning of Art. 14	
R. 20.5	Missing parts	
20.5*bis*	Erroneously filed elements and parts	

1. General Aspects of the Drawings

1 An international application may contain one or more drawings where required (Art. 3(2)). Drawings are required when they are necessary for the understanding of the invention (Art. 7(1)). A designated Office may require that the applicant files

drawings not necessary for understanding the invention but for its illustration (Art. 7(2); R. 7.2). Particular physical requirements for drawings are given in R. 11.10, R. 11.11 and R. 11.13; see also AG-IP 5.128–5.163. Drawings may not contain text matter, except one word or a few words when absolutely indispensable (R. 11.11; AG-IP 5.156). Non-compliance with the requirements can be corrected under Art. 14(1)(b); R. 26. Obvious mistakes may also be corrected (R. 91).

Note that even single words in drawings might require translations in the national 2
phase.

2. Informal Drawings

In contrast with most national laws, the PCT does not provide for the possibility to 3
submit informal drawings and easily replace them after filing by formal drawings (see annotations to Art. 14). It is, therefore, strongly recommended to submit formal drawings at the time of filing the international application.

3. Color and grayscale drawings

The PCT makes no provision for color or grayscale drawings, including photographs. 4
Although they do not comply with the requirements of R. 11.13(a), color drawing and photographs received may be retained by the receiving Office and/or International Bureau. Whether designated Offices accept color drawings is laid out in the PCT Applicant's Guide – National Phase for the individual Contracting States. Photographs may exceptionally be submitted where a drawing does not present what is to be shown. The International Bureau will convert all color drawings or photographs into black and white for international publication purposes, which may cause a loss of details (AG-IP 5.159). Most electronic filing means, such as ePCT, contain a preview function to see how scanned photographs or color drawings are rendered in black and white for publication and will also show a warning if initial drawings are not in black and white. If, however, the international application containing a photograph is filed by fax, and the photograph is not transmitted properly, the photograph will be considered a missing drawing, the correction of which may result in re-dating of the international application (AG-IP 11.070). Some receiving Offices transmit to the International Bureau a copy of the electronically filed application documents in their original format as filed. In such a case the International Bureau will make it available on PATENTSCOPE (including color) and the published international application will include on the front page a notice that the color drawings are available on PATENTSCOPE. The color drawings can accordingly be consulted in the national phase by Offices where color drawings are accepted. See, for example, decision T1544/08 of the EPO as designated Office that accepted color drawings in an international application.

In case the applicant wants to file an international application with color drawings, it 5
is recommended to select both a receiving Office and a method of filing that permit the transmittal of the color drawings as filed to the International Bureau and also permits previewing the rendering of the drawings for international publication in

black and white. Using ePCT at RO/IB for filing provides for these functions (Pract. Adv. NL 04/2019 www.wipo.int/pct/en/newslett/practical_advice/pa_042019.html).

4. Missing Drawings

6 Where the receiving Office finds that a drawing is missing, i.e. a drawing is referred to in the international application but not included in it, it will invite the applicant to furnish the missing drawing within two months from the invitation (Art. 14(2); R. 20.5(a)). Where no invitation is sent and the applicant notes that a drawing is missing, the missing drawing may be sent to the receiving Office within two months from receipt of the international application (R. 20.7(a)(ii)). The time limit is not extendable (AG-IP 6.037). If the drawing is duly filed, the international filing date will be the date on which the drawing is received by the receiving Office (Art. 14(2)), unless it is possible to incorporate the missing drawing by reference to a priority application (R. 20.6). The applicant may file a written notice confirming incorporation by reference of the missing drawings to maintain the original international filing date (see annotations to Art. 14 and R. 20.5(a)(ii)). Where no incorporation by reference is possible, the international filing date can only be maintained by disregarding any late-filed drawings and considering any reference to the missing drawings non-existent (Art. 14(2); AG-IP 6.025). Note that re-dating may cause a loss of priority and include extra prior art.

7 If the receiving Office has not sent an invitation to furnish the missing drawing within two months from receipt of the application, the applicant may check with the receiving Office if it is willing to issue such an invitation, which will trigger a new time limit of two months.

Article 8
Claiming Priority

INTRODUCTION

1. General Aspects of Priority Claims

An international application may claim priority from one or more earlier applications filed in or for any country party to the Paris Convention (Art. 8(1)) or in or for any Member of the World Trade Organization that is not party to the Paris Convention (R. 4.10(a); see AG-IP 5.057, 5.060). The priority period is 12 months (Art. 4C(1) Paris Convention; R. 2.4(a)). Under R. 26*bis*.3, restoration of the right to priority, under certain conditions, is allowed if the international application is filed after expiry of the priority period, but within two months from the expiry (see No. 6 below). 1

The PCT applies the priority rules of the Stockholm Act (1967) of the Paris Convention (Art. 8(2)(a) PCT). Since the Paris Convention relates to external priority only, the PCT has added Art. 8(2)(b), which allows internal priority, i.e. the international application claiming the priority of an earlier application filed in or for a State may contain the designation of that State. The effect of the internal priority in that State is governed by national law (Art. 8(2)(b)). The EPC also allows internal priority (Art. 87(1) EPC). 2

Since the international application has, in each designated State, the effect of a regular national application (Art. 11(3), (4)), it may be used as a basis for a priority claim in a later application. A valid priority claim has the effects provided by Art. 4 of the Paris Convention (Art. 8(2)(a)), in particular, the effect that the filing date of the earlier application is regarded as the filing date of the priority claiming application (see Art. 2(xi)(a) and (b)). 3

The formal validity of the priority claim is important for the PCT procedure because it establishes the priority date for computing time limits under the PCT (Art. 2(xi)). The receiving Office and International Bureau will check certain formalities of the priority claim and may in case of defects declare it 'considered void' (R. 26*bis*; see No. 4.2 below). The substantive validity of the priority claim is not determined during the international phase, although the priority is taken into consideration for establishing the written opinion of the ISA (R. 33.1; AG-IP 7.003) and the IPRP (R. 64.1(b)). 4

2. Formal Requirements for Claiming Priority

5 A claim to the priority of an earlier application must indicate the filing date of the earlier application, its number, the country in which it was filed for an earlier national application, the regional Office for an earlier regional application, or the receiving Office for an earlier international application (R. 4.10(a)(i)–(v)). National law determines whether a designated Office may request the applicant to furnish evidence of his entitlement to claim the priority (R. 4.17(iii); R. 51*bis*.1(a)(iii); R. 51*bis*.2(iii)).

6 The entitlement is based on Art. 4A(1) of the Paris Convention, which states that a person who has duly filed an application for a patent or his successor in title has a right of priority. Designated Offices have different interpretations of this Article, which may result in a loss of priority of the international application in the national phase.

7 The EPO requires that the applicant claiming the priority from a previous application must be the applicant of the previous application or the successor in title to the applicant who filed the previous application. A transfer of the priority right to a successor in title must have taken place before the filing date of the international application. If a previous application was filed by several applicants, all the applicants for the previous application must be applicants for the international application or have transferred their rights to the applicant, or (at least) one of the applicants, of the international application. A deficiency in the entitlement cannot be remedied in the European phase (AG-NP EP.29), but implicit transfer of the priority right might be presumed under suitable conditions (see decision G 1/22 and G 2/22). See, for example, decision T844/18 of the EPO Boards of Appeal, where the priority claim of a Euro-PCT application was based on earlier US applications and the priority right was lost before the EPO as designated Office because the above requirements were not met.

8 A priority claim is preferably made in the request on filing the international application (R. 4.1(b)(i); R. 4.10(a)), although a priority claim may be added after filing under certain conditions (see No. 4 below).

3. Furnishing of Priority Document

9 The applicant is obliged to furnish a copy of the earlier application certified by the issuing authority (the ‘priority document’) for each priority claimed in the international application (R. 17.1). The applicant has three different ways to provide the priority document under R. 17.1(a), (b) and (b-*bis*) as set out below. If the priority document is not provided in due time, the applicant must provide it upon entry into the national phase of each designated Office within a certain time limit. Otherwise, the designated Office may disregard the priority claim (R. 17.1(c)).

10 In principle, the applicant must submit a certified copy of the priority document to the receiving Office or International Bureau within 16 months of the priority date (R. 17.1(a)). The certified copy of the priority document is usually issued on paper by the authority where the earlier application was filed, against payment of a fee. In practice, some Offices issue a priority document as an electronic, digitally signed

PDF. The priority document will be regarded as received in time if received by the International Bureau before the date of the international publication (R. 17.1(a)).

Where the earlier application was filed with the receiving Office, the applicant need not submit the priority document but can instead request the receiving Office to prepare and transmit the priority document to the International Bureau (R. 17.1(b)). The request may be made either in the request form (R. 4.1(c)(ii)) or be submitted by separate letter. The request must be filed within 16 months from the priority date and may be subject to the payment of a fee for the benefit of the receiving Office (R. 17.1(b)). Both RO/EP and RO/US require such a fee for the transmittal of the priority document to the International Bureau (AG-IP Annex C(EP), (US)). 11

Where the priority document is made available to the International Bureau from a digital library prior to the date of publication of the international application, the applicant need not submit a certified copy of the earlier application but can instead request the International Bureau to retrieve the priority document from the digital library (R. 17.1(b-*bis*)). The digital library in the PCT system is the WIPO Digital Access Service (DAS). When filing an earlier application with an Office of earlier filing that participates in DAS (www.wipo.int/das/en/participating_offices/search.jsp?territory_id = &depositing_id = 2388&accessing_id), the applicant can make the copies of that earlier application available electronically through DAS by indicating so on filing or by sending a letter to the Office of earlier filing. In response the Office of earlier filing will send the applicant the access code of the priority document. On filing the priority claiming international application, the applicant may submit the access code and request (free of charge) the International Bureau to retrieve the priority document from the digital library (R. 17.1(b-*bis*)); Pract. Adv. NL 12/2010 www.wipo.int/pct/en/newslett/practical_advice/pa_122010.html and 11/2019 www.wipo.int/pct/en/newslett/practical_advice/pa_112019.html; OJ EPO 2018 A78). The access code and request may also be submitted via ePCT or in a letter to the International Bureau before international publication. 12

Many patent Offices, including the EPO, participate in DAS. The EPO automatically generates a DAS access code for each European application and PCT application filed with it and sends the code to the applicant (OJ EPO 2019 A27). Other Offices require the applicant to request an access code when filing an application (Pract. Adv. NL 11/2019 www.wipo.int/pct/en/newslett/practical_advice/pa_112019.html). See annotations to R. 17.1(b-*bis*) and (d). 13

Even if the Office of earlier filing is late in providing the access code, it is the applicant's responsibility to provide the access code to the International Bureau before international publication. Therefore, the applicant should contact the Office of earlier filing well in advance and should regularly check the receipt of the access code and the retrieval at the International Bureau. It is recommended to submit the access code to the International Bureau using ePCT with strong authentication, allowing real-time validation of the access code and the International Bureau to obtain the priority document (Pract. Adv. NL 12/2019 www.wipo.int/pct/en/newslett/practical_advice/pa_122019.html). 14

15 If the applicant complies with R. 17.1(a), (b) or (b-*bis*) and the International Bureau has timely received the priority document, no designated Office may ask the applicant to submit a further copy (R. 17.2(a); AG-IP 5.070; GL Exam EPO E-IX, 2.3.5, F-VI,2.1).

16 The EPO furnishes a certified copy of a European application on request and upon payment of an administrative fee (R. 54 EPC; Rfees3(1)). Note that the national Offices of certain States do not always furnish certified copies in time, making excuse procedures necessary before each designated Office.

17 If the applicant has not submitted the priority document or the request to the receiving Office or International Bureau in due time (R. 17), the applicant may still provide a priority document to the International Bureau before the end of the international phase, which will be added to the documents on PATENTSCOPE and may be accepted at some designated Offices. However, if the priority document is not duly filed during the international phase, any designated Office may disregard the related priority claim, provided it gives the applicant an opportunity to furnish the priority document within a certain time limit in the national phase (R. 17.1(c)). The EPO as designated Office invites the applicant to furnish it upon entry into the regional phase (R. 163(2) EPC), failure of which will result in the loss of the priority claim under R. 163(6) EPC. Upon entry of the European phase, the EPO also includes priority documents in the file upon request of the applicant using DAS; alternatively, it includes free of charge a European patent application or a PCTa filed with EPO as receiving Office, if DAS cannot be used or is not requested (GL Exam EPO A-II, 6.7; OJ EPO 2021 A83, OJ EPO 2019 A27).

18 The International Bureau will forward copies of the priority document to each designated Office at the request of that Office (R. 17.2(a)), either via PCT-EDI data transfer, DVD-R, ePCT or simply making the documents publicly available on PATENTSCOPE (for details of distribution at each Office see Office Profiles https://pct.wipo.int/ePCTExternal/pages/OfficeProfile.xhtml).

19 It is one of the PCT's procedural and financial advantages that the applicant need only file a single priority document and does not have to provide certified copies for each designated Office.

4. Correction or Addition of Priority Claim

20 The applicant may correct any item of a priority claim or add a missing priority claim of his own volition by submitting a notice to the receiving Office or International Bureau (R. 26*bis*.1(a)). Adding a priority claim to an international application filed without a priority claim is also possible (R. 26*bis*.1(a)).

4.1 Correction or Addition of Priority Claim of Applicant's Own Motion

21 An applicant may voluntarily file a notice of correction or addition of a priority claim within 16 months from the priority date or 16 months from the priority date as changed by the correction, whichever expires first (R. 26*bis*.1(a)). Nevertheless, the notice may be filed at least up to four months from the international filing date (R. 26*bis*.1(a)).

The four-month period is relevant for applications where the uncorrected priority date is more than 12 months before the filing date. The reason why the periods were determined in that way is so that any corrected or added priority claim is received in time to be included in the publication of the international application. The correction and addition of a priority claim are free of charge (AG-IP 6.053). Where the correction changes the priority date, any time limit calculated from the priority date that has not already expired will be recalculated from the changed priority date (R. 26*bis*.1(c)). A correction received after the expiry of the time limit but before the priority claim is declared 'considered void' and, not later than one month after the expiry, is still considered received in due time (R. 26*bis*.2(b). An applicant may, within 30 months from the priority date, request the International Bureau to publish a late correction and addition, subject to payment of a special fee (R. 26*bis*.2(e)).

An applicant may add a priority claim to an international application that would result in a new priority date more than 12 months prior to the international filing date, provided the time limit for restoration of two months from the expiry of the priority period has not yet expired. Note that the priority period will be extended if it expires on a day the receiving Office is closed (R. 80.5, IPO Closed Dates). The 2-month period for restoration will consequently start at a later date. The applicant must request restoration of priority before the receiving Office or before the designated Offices (see No. 6 below; Pract. Adv. NL 02/2010 www.wipo.int/pct/en/newslett/practical_advice/pa_122019.html). Any such priority claim will remain in the application and serve as the basis for calculating time limits during the international phase whether or not the request for restoration of priority is granted (R. 26*bis*.2(c)(iii) and Pract. Adv. NL 09/2011 www.wipo.int/pct/en/newslett/practical_advice/pa_092011.html). 22

A priority claim of a Euro-PCT application may be corrected even after publication of the international application, provided the interests of third parties are not adversely affected, which is the case when the mistake is apparent on the face of the published application (R. 52(3) EPC; J2/92). A priority claim may even be corrected or added within the time limit of 26 months from the priority date as a 'rectification of an obvious mistake', but only if the corrected or added priority claim does not change the original priority date (R. 91.1(g)(iv); R. 91.2; AG-IP 11.037). Since priority claims may only be rectified if both the mistake and the correction are obvious (R. 91.1(c)) and if the correction does not change the (earliest) priority date (R. 91.1(g)(iv), such corrections are rare in practice. 23

4.2 Correction of Priority Claim on Invitation by Office

The validity of a priority claim is not substantively checked in the international phase. This follows from the definition of the priority date in Art. 2(xi), which defines the priority date 'for the purpose of computing time limits'. The receiving Office, or if it fails to do so the International Bureau, carries out a formality check (R. 26*bis*.2(a); AG-IP 6.041–6.044) and determines whether: 24

(i) the international application has an international filing date later than the expiry of the priority period but within two months, and no request for restoration of priority under R. 26*bis*.3 has been submitted;

(ii) the priority claim does not comply with the requirements of R. 4.10 (AG-IP 5.060), for example,

a. the earlier application is not filed in a country party to the Paris Convention or Member of the World Trade Organization;

b. the required details of the date and country or Office of filing have not been provided (Art. 8(2)(a), referring to the Paris Convention, in particular Art. 4A(1) and 4C(1); 4D(1), 4D(4)); or

(iii) any indication in the priority claim is inconsistent with the corresponding indication in the priority document, such as the number of the earlier application or the filing date.

25 The receiving Office or International Bureau will invite the applicant to correct any defect within the 16- or four-month time limit mentioned in R. 26*bis*.1(a) (R. 26*bis*.2). If the international filing date is after but within two months of the expiry of the priority period, the receiving Office will notify the applicant that restoration of priority may be possible (R. 26*bis*.2(a); see No. 6 below). Failure to submit a correction in due time results in the priority claim being considered not to have been made, i.e. void, for the purpose of the PCT procedures and the receiving Office or International Bureau will so declare (R. 26*bis*.2(b)). If the receiving Office or International Bureau receives a request for correction of a priority claim before the priority claim has been declared void and within one month of the R. 26*bis*.1(a) time limit, the request will be considered as timely received (R. 26*bis*.2(b)). The International Bureau will publish information on a priority claim being considered void together with the application (free of charge) (R. 26*bis*.2(d)).

26 If an applicant attempts to correct or add a priority claim after the time limit of R. 26*bis*.1(a) has expired, the International Bureau may publish information concerning the matter if the applicant so requests and pays a special fee (R. 26*bis*.2(e)). The priority claim will not be considered void only because the number of the earlier application is missing, because an indication in the priority claim is not the same as the corresponding indication in the priority document, or because the international application has an international filing date outside, but within two months of the end of the priority period (R. 4.10(a)(ii); R. 26*bis*.2(c)(i)–(iii); Art. 4D(5) Paris Convention).

27 An applicant may further provide proof before a designated Office in the national phase that the determination of a priority claim being considered void by the receiving Office or International Bureau was erroneous; if satisfied, the Office must rectify the error if such an error is rectifiable under national law had it been made by the designated Office itself and treat the application as if the priority claim had not been considered void (R. 82*ter*.1(a)).

5. Withdrawal of Priority Claim

The applicant may withdraw any priority claim of an international application within the international phase, usually to postpone publication of the international application or to have more time for entering the national phase. The notice of withdrawal must be submitted prior to expiry of 30 months from the priority date (R. 90*bis*.3(a) and (b)). The withdrawal is free of charge (AG-IP 11.056). The withdrawal becomes effective on receipt of a notice addressed by the applicant or agent, at his option, to the International Bureau, the receiving Office, or the IPEA if a demand is filed (R. 90*bis*.3(c)). Where the withdrawal changes the priority date, any time limit computed from the priority date and not already expired will be recomputed from the changed priority date (R. 90*bis*.3(d)). The notice must be signed by all applicants or by a duly-appointed agent or common representative (R. 90*bis*.5). If the notice is received by the International Bureau after the completion of the technical preparations for publication, the international publication will still be published on the date as computed from the original priority date (R. 90*bis*.3(e)). **28**

6. Restoration of Right of Priority

The priority provisions in the PCT allow restoration of a priority claim in an international application if the international application is filed after expiry of the priority period but within two months from that expiry (R. 26*bis*.2–3; R. 49*ter*; AG-IP 5.062–5.066). The provisions align the PCT with Art. 13 of the PLT (https://wipolex.wipo.int/en/text/288996). **29**

6.1 Requesting Restoration

A request for restoration may be filed with the receiving Office (R. 26*bis*.3) during the international phase or with a designated Office during the national phase (R. 49*ter*.2) or with both. The PCT provisions given below apply to the receiving Office, many of which are mirrored in R. 49*ter*.2 for designated Offices. **30**

6.2 Formal Requirements of Request for Restoration

The following conditions must be satisfied if a request for restoration of priority is to succeed: **31**

- a request for restoration of priority must be filed within two months from expiry of the priority period (R. 26*bis*.3(b)(i), 3(e)); for requests filed with designated Offices see below;
- the request must state the reasons for failing to file the international application within the priority period (R. 26*bis*.3(b)(ii)), preferably accompanied by a supporting declaration or other evidence (R. 26*bis*.3(b)(iii)), and, if required, within a time limit reasonable under the circumstances (R. 26*bis*.3(f));

- the request must satisfy one of the criteria for restoration applied by the Office, i.e. either the 'unintentional' or the 'due care' criterion, or both for those Offices applying both criteria;
- payment of a fee, if required and as fixed by the Office, within a period of two months from the said expiry, with an additional extension of up to two months at the option of the Office (R. 26*bis*.3(d));
- the priority claim in question must have been made at the time of filing the international application or added within two months of expiry of the priority period (R. 26*bis*.3(c); R. 26*bis*.1(a)).

32 See Pract. Adv. NL 02/2010 (www.wipo.int/pct/en/newslett/practical_advice/pa_022010.html) for advice on how to add a priority claim not falling within the 12-month priority period and Pract. Adv. NL 09/2015 (https://www.wipo.int/pct/en/newslett/practical_advice/pa_092015.html) for requesting restoration of priority.

33 If the request for restoration is filed with a designated Office under R. 49*ter*.2, instead of or in addition to requesting restoration in the international phase with the receiving Office, this must be done within one month from expiry of the time limit for entering the national phase under Art. 22 or, if a request for early processing has been filed, one month from receipt of the request by the designated Office (R. 49*ter*.2(b)(i)).

34 The advantage of requesting restoration in the international phase is, that with a single request the applicant can cover all designated Offices, except those with notifications of incompatibilities; however, if the time limit for requesting restoration in the international phase is missed or the request is refused or partially refused by the receiving Office, the applicant has a second chance before each designated Office.

6.3 *Substantive Decision by Offices on Restoration*

35 An Office has a choice of applying two different criteria when deciding whether to restore the right of priority to an international application and may apply one, the other, or both (R. 26*bis*.3(a)). The table on restoration (www.wipo.int/pct/en/texts/restoration.html) shows the criteria receiving Offices and designated Offices apply. The criteria are that the failure occurred in spite of 'due care' required by the circumstances having been taken (R. 26*bis*.3(a)(i)), or that the failure was 'unintentional' (R. 26*bis*.3(a)(ii)), the latter being the less stringent criterion. For the latter criterion, a statement indicating that the failure to comply with the priority period was not intentional should generally be sufficient, although a receiving Office may require that the statement is submitted in the form of a declaration. A receiving Office may require a declaration and/or supporting evidence for the 'due care' criterion. Generally, 'due care' requires that the applicant/agent proves that all measures have been taken which a reasonably prudent applicant/agent would have taken under the concrete circumstances of the case.

36 The PCT RO Guidelines 166G (www.wipo.int/pct/en/texts/ro/ro166a_166t.html#_166g) contain useful guidance on how factual circumstances might be decided by receiving Offices. It is recommended to study the guidance in detail either to prevent errors often made by applicants and agents, or to be prepared in requesting restoration; see also Pract. Adv. NL 09/2015 (www.wipo.int/pct/en/newslett/

practical_advice/pa_092015.html) for advice on how to provide declarations and evidence on restoration and Pract. Adv. NL 02/2020 (www.wipo.int/pct/en/newslett/practical_advice/pa_022020.html) for advice on how to meet the requirements under the 'due care' criterion.

A receiving Office may not refuse a request for restoration of priority without giving the applicant the opportunity to make observations on the intended refusal within a time limit which is reasonable under the circumstances (R. 26*bis*.3(g); R. 49*ter*.2(e)). 37

6.4 *Effect of Decision on Restoration*

If a receiving Office does not accept the restoration of a priority claim, the calculation of time limits in the international phase will nevertheless be carried out as though the priority claim were valid. This occurs because a designated Office might subsequently allow the restoration (under R. 49*ter*.2) and then the national phase entry would still have been performed correctly with respect to the 'too early' priority date (R. 26*bis*.2(c)(iii); Pract. Adv. NL 09/2011 www.wipo.int/pct/en/newslett/practical_advice/pa_092011.html). 38

Restoration of priority granted by a receiving Office based on the 'due care' criterion will in general bind all designated Offices (R. 49*ter*.1(a)), but a refusal by a receiving Office does not bind designated Offices (R. 49*ter*.1(e)). Restoration of priority granted by a receiving Office based on the 'unintentional' criterion is only effective for designated Offices that apply that criterion (R. 49*ter*.1(b)). Nevertheless, a designated Office may review a restoration of priority granted by a receiving Office under certain limited circumstances (R. 49*ter*.1(c), (d)), similar to a refusal to grant a restoration of priority by a receiving Office (R. 49*ter*.1(f)). 39

If an applicant has missed the 12-month priority period for filing his international application and has a choice of receiving Offices (for example, EP, International Bureau) in which the international application may be filed, the applicant should consider whether the designated Offices in which he wants to enter the national phase will recognize a restoration of priority granted by each of the available receiving Offices (Pract. Adv. NL 09/2011 www.wipo.int/pct/en/newslett/practical_advice/pa_092011.html). 40

6.5 *Notification of Incompatibilities with National Law*

Some Offices have declared that the provisions for restoration of the right of priority are incompatible with their national law (R. 26*bis*.3(j); R. 49*ter*.1(g); R. 49*ter*.2(h)). See the list of reservations (www.wipo.int/pct/en/texts/reservations/res_incomp.html) and the table on restoration (www.wipo.int/pct/en/texts/restoration.html) on the WIPO website for details of any such declarations and any other element of restoration as applied by Offices. If a receiving Office has made a declaration of incompatibility under R. 26*bis*.3(j) that it does not accept requests for restoration of priority, the applicant can request that the receiving Office forward the international application to RO/IB (R. 19.4(a)(iii)). The International Bureau has made no declaration of incompatibility under R. 26*bis*.3(j) and allows requests for restoration to be 41 based on both criteria; it does not charge a fee. Once the international application has been forwarded to RO/IB, the applicant can then request RO/IB to restore the right of priority (Pract. Adv. NL 09/2011 www.wipo.int/pct/en/newslett/practical_advice/pa_092011.html).

Article 8
Claiming Priority

(1)

The international application may contain a declaration, as prescribed in the Regulations, claiming the priority of one or more earlier applications filed in or for any country party to the Paris Convention for the Protection of Industrial Property.

42 The membership of territories in the Paris Convention or WTO can be seen in the List of Territories in the Annexes to this book.

Art. 2(xi)(b)	Several priority claims	
Art. 11	The filing date and effects of the international application	
R. 4.10	Priority claim. Since January 1, 2000 an applicant can claim the priority of an earlier application filed in or for any WTO Member State. See also further comments to R. 4.10. The WTO Member States are listed in the List of Territories in the Annexes to this book.	
R. 17	Priority document	
	R. 17.1	Obligation to submit a copy of an earlier national or international application
	R. 17.2	Availability of copies
R. 26*bis*	Correction or addition of a priority claim	
R. 26*bis*.3	Restoration of right of priority by receiving Office in case of expiry of the priority period	
R. 49*ter*.2	Effect of restoration of right of priority by receiving Office; restoration of right of priority by designated Office	
R. 66.7	Copy and translation of earlier applications whose priority is claimed (priority document) for IPE	
R. 76.4	Time limit for translation of priority document	
R. 90*bis*.3	Withdrawal of priority claims	

(2)

(a) Subject to the provisions of subparagraph (b), the conditions for, and the effect of, any priority claim declared under paragraph (1) shall be as provided in Article 4 of the Stockholm Act of the Paris Convention for the Protection of Industrial Property.

Art. 4 C. Paris Convention	The priority periods of the PCT are derived from the Paris Convention.
Art. 87 EPC	EPO recognizes priority establishing effect of US provisional patent application (OJ EPO 1996 p. 81).

(b) The international application for which the priority of one or more earlier applications filed in or for a Contracting State is claimed may contain the designation of that State. Where, in the international application, the priority of one or more national applications filed in or for a designated State is claimed, or where the priority of an international application having designated only one State is claimed, the conditions for, and the effect of, the priority claim in that State shall be governed by the national law of that State.

Art. 8(b)	The first sentence refers to the so-called internal priority
R. 4.9	Designation of States, internal priority, effect of withdrawal
§ 40 PatG	Priority of an earlier domestic patent application (internal priority) with the effect of deemed withdrawal https://www.dpma.de/english/patents/application/index.html, https://www.gesetze-im-internet.de/englisch_patg/englisch_patg.html

Article 9
The Applicant

(1)

Any resident or national of a Contracting State may file an international application.

Art. 1	Definition of Contracting State For the application of treaties on the territory of a State see annotations to Art. 1.
Art. 9	The entitlement initially refers only to the right to file a PCTa. However, throughout the PCT, applicant refers to the holder of the right. The entitlement to file would not exist if an inventor had already assigned the rights to the invention at the time of filing to his employer, who has no entitlement to file (OJ EPO 2014 A33).
R. 18.1	Resident or national of PCT Contracting State
R. 18.3, R. 19.2	If there are two or more applicants, the right to file an international application shall exist if at least one of them is entitled to file an international application according to Art. 9
Art. 9(3)	It is possible to name different applicants for different designated States.
AG int. P. No. 11.018C	It is possible to transfer the PCTa after filing to a national of a non-Contracting State. The PCTa remains effective.
Art. 8	When claiming the priority right of an earlier application, it is sufficient if one of several PCT applicants is the applicant of the earlier application or his successor in title (OJ EPO 2014 A33, and EPO G1/22 and G2/22).
R. 18.4	Information on requirements under national law as to applicants

(2)

The Assembly may decide to allow the residents and the nationals of any country party to the Paris Convention for the Protection of Industrial Property which is not party to this Treaty to file international applications.

The Assembly has not yet decided on this matter. 1

R. 19.1(c)	Prescribed receiving Office for non-PCT members (currently not applied)

(3)

The concepts of residence and nationality, and the application of those concepts in cases where there are several applicants or where the applicants are not the same for all the designated States, are defined in the Regulations.

R. 18.1	Residence and nationality

For statements of WIPO concerning Art. 9 see PCT/A/VI/15, p. 5 para. 30 (https://www.wipo.int/edocs/mdocs/govbody/en/pct_a_vii/pct_a_vii_15.pdf). 2

Article 10
The Receiving Office

INTRODUCTION

1. General Aspects on the Competent Receiving Office

1 The applicant must file the international application with a competent receiving Office (Art. 10). Applicants may choose between the receiving Office of or acting for the State of which they are residents and/or nationals and RO/IB (R. 19.1(a)). If there are two or more applicants, the receiving Office must be competent for at least one of the applicants (R. 19.2(i)). AG-IP Annex B gives for each Contracting State which receiving Offices are competent for nationals and residents of that State.

2 A PCT Contracting State appoints at least one receiving Office, which is often its national Office. Additionally, a State may appoint an intergovernmental organization such as the EPO to act as receiving Office for that State. It is also possible to transfer all receiving Office activities to such an organization or the national Office of another State (R. 19.1(b)). Some States have transferred all receiving Office activities to the International Bureau (AG-IP Annex C(IB)). Where a State has appointed more than one receiving Office, an applicant can choose with which receiving Office to file the international application (R. 19.1(a)).

3 Most EPC Contracting States give their residents and nationals the choice to file international applications with their national Office, the EPO or the International Bureau. The national Offices of a few EPC Contracting States (BE, MC, SM) do not act as receiving Office and, therefore, do not give their residents and nationals the option to file with their national Offices (OJ EPO 2018 A17; A105). More than 50% of all PCT applications from EPC Contracting States are filed with RO/EP. An advantage of using a national Office of an EPC Contracting State instead of RO/EP is that the international application may be filed in a language other than English, German or French. Since usually a translation for search purposes has to be provided within one month, it should be noted that filing in a language other than English, German or French only makes sense if the chosen ISA also carries out searches in that language. An example of an ISA that searches in languages other than English, German and French is ISA/EP, which will search in Dutch if the international application is filed with RO/NL (OJ EPO 2018 A24). Otherwise, the advantage of using a national Office is reduced to the additional time for providing a translation into English, German

or French. Note that even if no translation is necessary for search purposes, often a translation has to be provided for publication in one of the ten PCT publication languages (R. 12.4; 48.3(a)).

Where an international application and a national application of which it claims priority are both filed with the same Office, the transmittal of the required certified copy of the priority document to the International Bureau can simply be effected by clicking a box in the PCT request (R. 17.1(b)). 4

AG-IP Annex B also indicates whether applicants who are residents and/or nationals of that State must file with the national Office of the State for reason of national security as allowed by Art. 27(8) PCT, thereby limiting the choice of receiving Office mentioned in R. 19.1. However, national security provisions of many States only apply to first filings; a subsequent filing claiming the priority of the first filing may be filed with any competent receiving Office. More information on national security of the Contracting States is provided on the WIPO website (http://www.wipo.int/pct/en/texts/nat_sec.html). Where national security so requires, the national Office will not treat the international application as such but will subject it to national law and will not transmit the record copy to the International Bureau (R. 22.1). RO/IB does not check compliance with national security provisions, which remains the applicant's responsibility (AG-IP 6.010; Pract. Adv. NL 06/2014 https://www.wipo.int/pct/en/newslett/practical_advice/pa_062014.html). 5

2. International Bureau as Receiving Office

Applicants of all PCT Contracting States also have the option of filing with RO/IB (R. 19.1(a)(iii)). If there are two or more applicants, at least one applicant must be a resident or national of a Contracting State (R. 19.2(ii)). If the applicants are of different nationalities and residence, RO/IB offers a wider choice of ISAs than many national Offices (R. 35.3). 6

The International Bureau accepts electronic filing, such as the recommended ePCT. Filing by fax is also possible, albeit only in emergency situations and subject to confirmation within 14 days from filing (AG-IP Annex B(IB); R. 92.4(d)). Other electronic filing options are EPO Online Filing, as well as filing on CD-R or DVD-R (AG-IP Annex C(IB)). Furthermore, the ePCT Business Continuity Service (FAQs) can be used if any of the conventional online filing systems fails (PCT Newsletter No. 10/2023, p. 2 (https://www.wipo.int/pct/en/faqs/epct-continuity-service-faq.html,https://pctcs.wipo.int/ePCTFiling/)). 7

The International Bureau accepts any language (AG-IP Annex C), including languages of non-PCT States. Pract. Adv. NL 03/2019 (https://www.wipo.int/pct/en/newslett/practical_advice/pa_032019.html) gives strategic considerations when to file with RO/IB. 8

3. EPO as Receiving Office

9 RO/EP is competent for applicants who are residents and/or nationals of a Contracting State to both the PCT and the EPC (Art. 151 EPC; R. 157(1) EPC; OJ EPO 2014 A33).

10 RO/EP is regarded as a national Office acting for the EPC Contracting States according to R. 19.1(b) PCT, where 'national Office' is construed as referring to an intergovernmental authority in the sense of Art. 2(xii) PCT.

11 Applicants choosing RO/EP must file directly with the EPO (Art. 151 EPC; R. 157(1) EPC), i.e. with one of the EPO filing Offices in Munich, The Hague or Berlin (see Art. 75(1) EPC; R. 35(1) EPC; Euro-PCT Guide 2.2.014). Under the PCT, national Offices do not act as a mailbox for RO/EP under Art. 75(1)(b) EPC and R. 35(1) EPC. Since Art. 151 EPC and R. 157(1) EPC declare Art. 75(2) EPC, relating to national security provisions, to be applicable to international applications (as allowed by Art. 27(8) PCT), the applicant is obliged to file his international application with a national Office only where the national law so prescribes for reasons of national security (see AG-IP Annex B for the provisions of each EPC Contracting State). Most States allow a resident to file an international application directly with the EPO if the application claims the priority of an earlier application filed in that State. See R. 157(3)–(4) EPC for the transmittal of the international application by the national Office to RO/EP. Such direct filing enables RO/EP to transmit the record copy of the international application quickly to the International Bureau and the search copy to ISA/EP (Art. 12 PCT; R. 21 and 22) after the accordance of an international filing date and the formalities examination.

12 An international application is preferably filed with the EPO in electronic form (OJ EPO 2018 A45 Art. 2(1)), using, for example ePCT or mail (Euro-PCT Guide 2.2). For means of communications see Introduction in Part F of the Regulations.

4. Non-competent Receiving Office

13 A national Office may find itself not competent to act as receiving Office for an international application it has received due to the applicant's residence/nationality or because the international application was filed in a language not accepted by the Office (R. 12.1(a)). In that case, the International Bureau becomes the receiving Office, the national Office will be considered to have acted on behalf of RO/IB and will forward the international application to RO/IB. The date the national Office received the international application is deemed to be the date of receipt of the international application at RO/IB (R. 19.4(a),(b)). Fees already paid to the non-competent national Office will be refunded and the applicant will have to pay the transmittal fee (for the benefit of RO/IB), the international filing fee (for the benefit of the International Bureau), and the international search fee (for the benefit of the ISA) to RO/IB) (AG-IP 6.034). The time limits for paying these fees start running on the date RO/IB actually received the international application (R. 19.4(c)). See Pract. Adv. NL 04/2013 (https://www.wipo.int/pct/en/newslett/practical_advice/pa_042013.html) for more detailed information.

The non-competent national Office may subject the transmittal of the international application to the payment of a fee, for its own benefit and equal to the transmittal fee of that Office (R. 19.4(b); AG-IP 6.034; see AG-IP Annex C for the amount levied by each receiving Office). RO/EP currently does not charge the fee. Where a receiving Office does charge the fee, it will invite the applicant to pay within 15 days from the invitation, unless the fee was paid up front. If the fee is not paid, the receiving Office informs the applicant that no filing date is accorded and the application is not treated as an international application (R. 20.4; Art. 11(1)(ii); PCT RO Guidelines 275 www.wipo.int/pct/en/texts/ro/ro274_277.html). 14

Applicants can extend the time available for filing an international application by filing with a receiving Office in a different time zone in a westerly direction. They may file with a non-competent receiving Office and use the above procedure or use a further applicant entitled to file with that receiving Office, if necessary (see annotations to Art. 9). For example, an applicant or agent residing in a State in the Middle-European time zone may gain one hour by filing by fax or electronically with the UK Intellectual Property Office (UKIPO), or six hours by filing directly via ePCT with the United States Patent and Trademark Office (USPTO). Likewise, applicants can benefit from different receiving Offices being closed for business on different days. The dates when many Offices are closed have been published on the WIPO website (www.wipo.int/pct/dc/closeddates/faces/page/index.xhtml). 15

Even if an international application is filed with a non-competent Office for the above reasons, the date and time of receipt at the non-competent Office, including relevant closed dates, will be retained for determining the international filing date after transmittal to RO/IB (R. 19.4). Such strategy should only be used in emergency situations, since the relevant Art. 4C(3) Paris Convention is ultimately applied by the designated Offices and, while it is perfectly acceptable for RO/IB, its applicability with each designated Office cannot be guaranteed. 16

5. Methods of Filing

The permitted methods of filing an international application are determined by the receiving Office and are set out in AG-IP Annex B and C for each receiving Office. For an overview of permitted methods of filing with Offices participating in ePCT, see the web portal Office Profiles (https://pct.wipo.int/ePCTExternal/pages/OfficeProfile.xhtml) and annotations to Annex F of the Administrative Instructions (https://www.wipo.int/pct/en/texts/ai/annex_f.html). Additionally, all receiving Offices accept filing on paper, through delivery by hand and by mail (R. 89*bis*.1(a); AG-IP 6.003). Many receiving Offices still accept filing by fax, often subject to confirmation by a paper copy within 14 days (R. 92.4(d); AG-IP 11.069). Each receiving Office may determine the number of copies to be filed, if filed on paper (R. 11.1, see AG-IP Annex C for each receiving Office). 17

Applicants are advised to familiarize themselves with alternative means of filing, also with other receiving Offices, in case the preferred filing methods fail and a contingency is needed urgently. For Communication in general, see annotations under Part F of the Regulations. 18

5.1 *Electronic Filing (Refer Also to Annotations under R. 89*bis*)*

19 The PCT allows filing of an international application in electronic form or by electronic means (R. 89*bis*). Presently, more than 99% of all international applications are filed fully electronically. A national Office may allow applicants to accompany international applications filed on paper by a copy in electronic form (R. 89*ter*.1). Filing by e-mail is generally not allowed; see AG-IP Annex B for receiving Offices that do accept filing by e-mail under R. 92.4. Even where a receiving Office exceptionally permits so, filing an international application by e-mail is not recommended (see also Pract. Adv. NL 12/2001 www.wipo.int/pct/en/newslett/practical_advice/pa_122001.html). The international filing fee may be reduced for electronic filings and further reduced if the request is prepared in character-coded format, for example, using ePCT online filing (R. 96.1, Schedule of Fees 4; AG-IP 5.189). If the request and the international body of the application (description, claims, and abstract) are filed in character-coded format (XML), the highest reduction applies. XML has further advantages and is highly recommended (PCT Newsletter 12/2023, p. 7). Some electronic filing means, such as ePCT, provide for conversion from Microsoft Word™ docx files into character-coded format.

20 The majority of receiving Offices, including the International Bureau acting as receiving Office, accept electronic filing via the modern web-based ePCT filing system. Some receiving Offices operate their own electronic filing software; see, for example, for RO/EP the Euro-PCT Guide 2.2. In general, electronic filing can be used for filing international applications as well as corresponding subsequent documents. Some receiving Offices also offer the possibility to pay fees within those systems. Web-based electronic filing systems have the advantage of pre-checking data before submission to avoid formal errors; ePCT has the most up-to-date automated validation system. Further information on ePCT can be found on the WIPO website (https://pct.wipo.int/ePCTExternal/pages/landing.xhtml).

21 ePCT at RO/IB allows the applicant to make corrections after filing on the same day until midnight, without affecting the international filing date ('same day corrections'; see Pract. Adv. NL 07-08/2019 www.wipo.int/pct/en/newslett/practical_advice/pa_072019.html).

5.2 *Pre-conversion of Files*

22 When an international application is filed electronically, the applicant or the filing system converts the international application from the format in which it was drafted, for example, the format of text processing software such as Microsoft Word™, to a format accepted for electronic filing, for example, machine-readable XML or PDF. As errors may occur during such conversion, some receiving Offices accept files in specified pre-conversion formats and the filing system will allow uploading of such pre-conversion files together with the international application. In the international phase, the applicant may request the receiving Office to correct a conversion error by referring to the pre-conversion file uploaded on the international filing date (see AIs 706 and 710).

AG-IP Annex C gives the options for filing documents in pre-conversion format available for each receiving Office. There is an overview of the Offices at https://www.wipo.int/pct/en/texts/preconversion-format.html, https://www.wipo.int/edocs/pctndocs/en/2024/pct_news_2024_1.pdf. 23

The EPO accepts documents in pre-conversion format, which means that RO/EP follows a practice similar to the one in the regional procedure for EP applications. RO/IB, and receiving Offices using ePCT generally also allow for uploading of pre-conversion files.

Article 10
The Receiving Office

The international application shall be filed with the prescribed receiving Office, which will check and process it as provided in this Treaty and the Regulations.

R. 19.1	Competent receiving Office
R. 19.1(b), Art. 151, R. 157 EPC	The EPO is competent receiving Office if the applicant is resident in a PCT and EPC Member State.
Art. 11	Decisive for the determination of the competent receiving Office are the data on nationality, seat, or residence of the applicant on the filing date determined according to Art. 11 PCT, irrelevant are data on the inventor (OJ EPO 2014 A33).
R. 19.2, R. 18.3	If there are two or more applicants, at least one must be entitled within the meaning of the PCT.
R. 19.4(a)(i), (b)	If the receiving Office is not competent, the PCTa is transmitted to the International Bureau.
R. 20	Receipt of the international application
R. 26	Checking by, and correcting before, the receiving Office of certain elements of the international application
R. 21	Preparation of copies
R. 22	Transmittal of the record copy and translation
R. 23	Transmittal of the search copy, translation and sequence listing
R. 23*bis*	Transmittal of documents between Offices and Authorities relating to earlier search or classification
Art. 27(7)	Where an applicant is not a national of an EPC Member State, an agent must be appointed to act for that person.
Art. 49	The right to practice before the international authorities

Article 11
Filing Date and Effects of the International Application

INTRODUCTION

1. General Aspects of Check of Requirements and Accordance of International Filing Date

1 The receiving Office performs the following procedural steps upon receipt of an international application:

- a check of the requirements for according an international filing date and, if required, a correction procedure (Art. 11; R. 20);
- check of formal requirements, such as fees, language, form and content, and, if required, a correction procedure (Art. 14; R. 26); and
- transmittal of copies of the international application (Art. 12; R. 22).

2. Requirements for According an International Filing Date

2 A receiving Office will accord as the international filing date the date of receipt of the international application, provided the receiving Office has found that, according to Art. 11(1), at the time of receipt:

(i) the applicant is allowed to file an international application with the receiving Office because of residency or nationality (see annotations to Art. 10);
(ii) the international application is in a language prescribed by the receiving Office (Art. 3(4)(i); R. 12.1);
(iii) the application contains at least the following elements:
  (a) an indication that it is intended as an international application (R. 4.2; see annotations to Art. 4);
  (b) the designation of at least one Contracting State (R. 4.9; see annotations to Art. 4);
  (c) the name of the applicant (R. 4.5; see annotations to Art. 9);
  (d) a part which on the face of it appears to be a description (Art. 3(2); see annotations to Art. 5);

(e) a part which on the face of it appears to be a claim or claims (Art. 3(2); see annotations to Art. 6).

The following defects do not affect the accordance of the international filing date: 3

- non-payment of fees (R. 16*bis*; AG-IP 6.009; see annotations to Art. 14(3)(a);
- missing signature;
- missing title or abstract;
- non-compliance with the physical requirements such as number of copies, paper and print quality, margins, numbering (R. 11; see annotations to Art. 14);
- incomplete, erroneous, or missing declarations (R. 4.17; R. 26*ter*; AIs 216, 419);
- obvious mistakes (R. 91);
- competence of the receiving Office (R. 19.4).

The obligation in Art. 11 (1) (ii) that the international application must be in a language 4 prescribed by the receiving Office is no longer a filing date requirement, since R. 19.4 was introduced (see annotation No. 3 below Art. 11 (2)).

3. Check of Requirements by Receiving Office and Correction of Defects

If the international application does not comply with the requirements in Art. 11 (1) 5 (i) and (iii), the receiving Office will not accord an international filing date and will invite the applicant to file the required corrections (Art. 11 (2) (a); R. 20.3) within two months of the invitation (R. 20.7(a) (i)). The period is not extendable (AG-IP 6.037).

Where applicants themselves note a defect in the filed application, they may send 6 a correction to the receiving Office within two months from the date they filed the international application (R. 20.7(a)(ii)). After filing an international application using ePCT, 'same day corrections' are available up until midnight in the time zone of the receiving Office. This may save the international filing date (Pract. Adv. NL 7-8/2019, https://www.wipo.int/pct/en/newslett/practical_advice/pa_072019.html).

If the application is corrected in due time, the date of receipt of the correction will be 7 accorded as the international filing date (Art. 11 (2) (b); R. 20.3(b) (i)). As an exception, the corrected international application may retain the original international filing date in specific circumstances. The following sections set out the correction possibilities for each requirement and any effect of the correction on the international filing date.

4. International Filing Date

If the requirements are fulfilled on the day of receipt of the international application, 8 the international filing date will be the date on which the receiving Office receives the international application (Art. 11 (1)). Note that the date on which the receiving Office receives the international application counts as the international filing date and not the date the applicant dispatches the application (Art. 11 (1); see also annotations to Art. 47 and to R. 80).

9 Where the sheets of the international application are not received on the same day, the date of receipt will be the date on which all of the requirements of Art. 11(1) are fulfilled (R. 20.5(b); R. 20.5(c)), or incorporated by reference (R. 20.5(d) and R. 20.6). If the international application has been duly corrected, the international filing date will be the date of receipt of the required correction (Art. 11(2)(b)) or the date on which one or more elements of the international application were first received by the receiving Office, depending on the circumstances.

10 The receiving Office will stamp a copy of the international application, which becomes the record copy (R. 20.2(b)), and which is considered the true copy of the international application for the purposes of the international procedure (Art. 12(2)). The receiving Office notifies the applicant and the International Bureau promptly of the filing date (R. 20.2(c)), in practice within two months from filing (see also AIs 101, 301, 308, 324).

11 Payment of fees is not required for the accordance of an international filing date (AG-IP 6.009) but is necessary to avoid future negative consequences for the international application (see annotations to Art. 14(1)(a)).

12 If the receiving Office has accorded an international filing date and discovers within four months from filing that any of the items (i) and (iii) of Art. 11(1) was not complied with, the receiving Office will declare the application to be considered withdrawn (Art. 14(4); R. 30.1), and the applicant and the International Bureau will be notified (R. 29.1(ii)). If the International Bureau or ISA discovers such non-compliance, they will draw the receiving Office's attention to it (R. 29.3). The receiving Office will notify the applicant before the declaration under Art. 14(4) is made and give him an opportunity to comment within two months (R. 29.4(a)) and/or confirm that a missing element is incorporated by reference (R. 29.4(b); R. 20.6(a); R. 4.18; AG-IP 6.012).

13 An applicant may prove in the national phase before a designated or elected Office that the international filing date is incorrect or is erroneously considered void due to an error made by the receiving Office or International Bureau; if satisfied, the Office must rectify the error if such an error is rectifiable under national law had it been made by the Office itself, and treat the application as though the error had not been made (R. 82*ter*.1(a)).

5. Effect of Accorded Filing Date

14 An international application which is accorded an international filing date will have the effect of a regular national application in each designated State (Art. 11(3)) and will be equivalent to a regular national application within the meaning of the Paris Convention (Art. 11(4)). The equivalence has the effect that the international application may serve as a priority application for a subsequent national, regional or other international application.

15 In spite of the fact that the international application is equivalent to a regular national application in a designated State, the designated Office of the State is forbidden to start processing the application of their own motion within 30/31 months from the priority date (Art. 23(1); Art. 40(1), see also annotations to Art. 22). A designated

Office may start processing after expiry of the 30/31 months or earlier provided the applicant duly enters the national phase before expiry of the 30/31-month time limit and files an express request with the designated Office to start processing early under Art. 23(2).

6. Application Not Treated as International Application

If the international application does not comply with all requirements (i) and (iii) in No. 2 above (minimum requirements for accordance of an international filing date) and the receiving Office does not receive the requested correction in due time or the correction is insufficient, the receiving Office will not accord an international filing date (R. 20.4(i)). The receiving Office notifies the applicant and the International Bureau that the application will not be treated as an international application (R. 20.4(i), (ii)) and forwards a copy of the application to the International Bureau (R. 20.4(iv)). If the applicant considers the finding of the receiving Office incorrect, he may apply for a review under Art. 25 before each designated Office after entry into the national phase. See annotations to Art. 24 and Art. 22 for possible remedies under national law of the loss of rights if the international application is not accorded an international filing date. 16

If the receiving Office later discovers, or on the basis of the applicant's reply realizes, that it has erred in sending the invitation to correct and that the requirements for according an international filing date were fulfilled when the application was received, it will accord the international filing date and continue with the formalities check (R. 20.3(c); R. 82*ter*.1). 17

7. National Security Provisions

Each receiving Office may apply national security provisions to an international application it has received (Art. 27(8); annotations to Art. 10). It may decide not to treat the application as an international application and not transmit a copy to the International Bureau and ISA where the content of the international application is relevant for national security. If the receiving Office decides not to transmit the copies after it has accorded an international filing date, it must inform the International Bureau. 18

The International Bureau acting as receiving Office will not check compliance with national security provisions for an international application filed with it; such compliance is the applicant's responsibility (AG-IP 6.010). Information about the security provisions of each Contracting State is provided on the national security page of the WIPO website and in AG-IP Annex B (https://www.wipo.int/pct/en/texts/nat_sec.html). 19

Article 11
Filing Date and Effects of the International Application

(1)

The receiving Office shall accord as the international filing date the date of receipt of the international application, provided that that Office has found that, at the time of receipt:

Art. 14(4)	Finding of certain defects in the international application after the accordance of the international filing date	
R. 20	International filing date, see overview in the Introduction to R. 20 referring to missing parts or elements	
	R. 20.1	Determination under Art. 11(1)
	R. 20.2	Positive determination under Art. 11(1)
	R. 20.3	Defects under Art. 11(1)
	R. 20.4	Negative determination under Art. 11(1)
	R. 20.5	Missing parts
	R. 20.5*bis*	Erroneously filed elements and parts
	R. 20.6	Confirmation of incorporation by reference of elements and parts
	R. 20.7	Time limit
	R. 20.8	Incompatibility with national laws
AIs 301	Notification of receipt of the purported international application	

(i) the applicant does not obviously lack, for reasons of residence or nationality, the right to file an international application with the receiving Office,

Art. 9, R. 18	The applicant	
Art. 10	The receiving Office	
R. 19	The competence of the receiving Office	
	R. 19.4	In case of transmittal to the International Bureau, the International Bureau shall act as receiving Office.
	R. 19.4(a)(i)	Remedy by transmitting to the International Bureau
AIs 329	Correction of indications concerning the residence or nationality of the applicant	

20 No international filing date will be accorded if the applicant is not allowed to file an international application with a receiving Office because of residence or nationality (Art. 11(1)(i)). R. 19.4 provides that a filing date will still be accorded if the applicant is a resident or national of a PCT Contracting State. In such a case the receiving

Office will forward the international application to the International Bureau, which becomes receiving Office without loss of filing date, provided any fee under R. 19.4 is paid (see annotations to Art. 10).

However, if the applicant is not a resident or national of a PCT Contracting State, for example, a resident and national of Argentina, Art. 11(1)(i) does apply, and no international filing date will be accorded (see annotations to Art. 9). The receiving Office will invite the applicant to correct. The applicant should submit a correction of his nationality or residence and corroborative evidence, which the receiving Office will regard as a request for correction of a defect. If the receiving Office accepts the correction, the international filing date will be the date of receipt of the application, not that of the correction (see however AG-IP 6.036). 21

(ii) the international application is in the prescribed language,

R. 12	Language	
	R. 12.3	Language for the international search
	R. 12.3(a)	Time limit for translation one month from international filing date
	R. 12.3(c)	Additional time limit for submitting the translation
R. 20.1(c)	At least claims and description must be in the same language	
R. 26.3*ter*	Mixed languages used in abstract, drawings, description, claims can be remedied	
Art. 14, R. 20.1(c), (d)	Defects	
R. 19.4	Remedy	

The filing date requirement that the international application must be in the prescribed language has been superseded by the Rules. An international application filed in a language not prescribed by the receiving Office will still be accorded as international filing date the date the receiving Office received the application (R. 19.4(c)). The receiving Office will forward the international application to the International Bureau, which accepts all languages and which becomes the receiving Office (R. 19.4(b); annotations to Art. 10; AG-IP, Annex C(IB)). 22

(iii) the international application contains at least the following elements:

(a) an indication that it is intended as an international application,

If the filed documents do not contain an indication that they are intended as an international application (Art. 11(1)(ii)(a)), the receiving Office will invite the applicant to correct the defect (R. 20.3(a)(i)). If corrected in due time, the date of receipt of the correction becomes the international filing date (R. 20.3(b)(i)) (AG-IP 6.025). 23

(b) the designation of at least one Contracting State,

R. 4.9(a)(i)	Automatic designation of PCT Contracting States including validation and extension States. Possibility of exemption see below
R. 4.9(a)(ii)	All kinds of protection are automatically requested
R. 4.9(a) (iii)	All regional patents are automatically requested
R. 4.9(b), AG-IP 5.053	Exclusions from designation of DE, JP, KR
R. 90*bis*.2	Withdrawal of designations

24 The requirement to designate at least one Contracting State is complied with if the prescribed request form is used because all PCT Contracting States are automatically designated in the request on filing an international application (R. 4.9(a)(i)), including extension and validation States (see annotations to Art. 4).

(c) the name of the applicant, as prescribed,

R. 20.1(b)	Identifiability and remedy of defects of the indicated name
R. 89*bis*	Electronic filing

25 For the accordance of an international filing date, it is sufficient that the name of the applicant is indicated in a way which allows the identity of the applicant to be established (R. 20.1(b)). If the indication does not comply with this requirement, the receiving Office will invite the applicant to correct the name of the applicant (R. 20.3(a)(i)). If corrected in due time, the date of receipt of the correction becomes the international filing date (R. 20.3(b)(i); AG-IP 6.025). Accordance of an international filing date does not require that the applicant can be contacted, whereas the PLT does (Art. 5(1)(ii) PLT). The PLT aims to simplify and harmonize some formality requirements with respect to national and regional applications and patents. It applies to international applications only in the national and regional phase (Art. 2, 3 PLT; for further information see https://www.wipo.int/treaties/en/ip/plt/ and https://www.wipo.int/edocs/pubdocs/en/patents/450/wipo_pub_l450plt.pdf).

A missing address is a formal defect under the PCT (see annotations to Art. 14).

(d) a part which on the face of it appears to be a description,

26 Art. 11(1)(iii)(d) requires that an international application includes a part which on the face of it appears to be a description. Drawings are not required. However, if the description mentions drawings which are missing, this is treated as a deficiency under Art. 14(2) and R. 20.3(a)(ii) (see annotations to Art. 7 and annotations to R. 20). An international application filed without description will nonetheless be accorded an international filing date, if the international application is filed by reference to an earlier application incorporating the description of that application into the international application (R. 20.6(b); Art. 5(7) PLT; see annotations to R. 20).

(e) a part which on the face of it appears to be a claim or claims.

The accordance of an international filing date requires the presence of at least one claim or, as stated in Art. 11(1)(iii)(e), a part which on the face of it appears to be a claim. 27

This requirement is in contrast to Art. 5(1) PLT, which requires the presence of a description for the accordance of a filing date, but not the presence of a claim or claims. 28

An international application filed without claims will nevertheless be accorded an international filing date, if the international application is filed by reference to an earlier application incorporating one or more claims of the earlier application into the international application (R. 20.6(b); see annotations to R. 20). 29

An element or part missing from the international application as filed may be added after the day on which the first documents were filed. The addition may, where possible, refer to an earlier application that contains the entire element or part or by filing the missing part. Such a reference results in the missing element or part being incorporated by reference in the international application. Depending on the circumstances, the international application with the missing element or part supplemented may retain its original international filing date or may be re-dated. 30

An 'element' for the purpose of supplementing the application as filed is the entire description or all of the claims (R. 4.18 referring to Art. 11(1)(iii)(d) and (e)). A 'part' is a part of the description, a part of the claims or a part or all of the drawings (R. 4.18 and R. 20.5(a)). Note that a missing element will affect the accordance of the international filing date; a missing part will not. 31

The PCT distinguishes two cases further explained in the annotations to R. 20. 32

(2)

(a) If the receiving Office finds that the international application did not, at the time of receipt, fulfill the requirements listed in paragraph (1), it shall, as provided in the Regulations, invite the applicant to file the required correction.

R. 20.3(a)	Invitation to correct defects
R. 20.7, R. 26.2	Time limit is two months, non-extendable
R. 20.4	If the applicant does not comply with the invitation, the application is not treated as an international application.
R. 16.2(i), R. 15.6(i)	Refund of fees is possible
Art. 14	Certain defects
Art. 14(2)	Subsequently submitted drawings

(b) If the applicant complies with the invitation, as provided in the Regulations, the receiving Office shall accord as the international filing date the date of receipt of the required correction.

(3)

Subject to Article 64(4), any international application fulfilling the requirements listed in items (i) to (iii) of paragraph (1) and accorded an international filing date shall have the effect of a regular national application in each designated State as of the international filing date, which date shall be considered to be the actual filing date in each designated State.

R. 20.3(b)	Re-dating of the filing date. The filing date is maintained in case of incorporation by reference according to R. 4.18, R. 20.6.
Art. 24(1)	Consequences of incorrect application
Art. 64(4)(a)	Effect as national deposit. However, there was a reservation in the US under Art. 64(4)(a) (Hilmer doctrine). To avoid the problems resulting from the Hilmer doctrine, an early entry into the national phase under Art. 23(2) (suspension) or filing and publication of the application in English made sense. However, the America Invents Act abolished the Hilmer doctrine. 'The new prior art law, as well as the grace period law, applies to all U.S. applications as of the filing date of March 16, 2013. The new law also applies to U.S. applications that at any time have at least one claim whose subject matter has an effective filing date after March 16. 35 U.S.C. 102 and 103 in effect on March 16, 2013, will apply to any application that ever contains a claim that has an effective filing date on or after 16, 2013.' (VPP Newsletter No. 3/2012, p. 140)
Art. 29	Effects of the international publication
Art. 153(2) EPC	International publication is equivalent to European application
Art. 76(1), R. 36 EPC	The legal fiction of Art. 11(3) PCT says something about the effect of an international application, but nothing about the question of whether a procedure is pending before an Office. For a divisional application – at least before the EPO or the DPMA – not only an application with effect in the relevant territory is required, but also proceedings pending before the relevant Office. J 18/09 says that the requirements of Art. 22 PCT must be fulfilled (OJ EPO 2011 p. 480 supplemented by communication of February 21, 2013, OJ EPO 2013 p. 156). See also EPO decision T 1316/20 or BPatG 7 W (pat) 5/19 'Ohrhörer' (the latter, however, in connection with European patent applications and Art. 66 EPC). According to these interpretations, no divisional application can be based on a PCTa.

(4)

Any international application fulfilling the requirements listed in items (i) to (iii) of paragraph (1) shall be equivalent to a regular national filing within the meaning of the Paris Convention for the Protection of Industrial Property.

R. 4.10	The PCT application as the basis of a priority claim

Article 12
Transmittal of the International Application to the International Bureau and the International Searching Authority

INTRODUCTION

General Aspects of Transmission of Copies

When the receiving Office has accorded the international application an international filing date and national security prescriptions do not thwart such action, the receiving Office will transmit one copy of the application (called 'record copy') to the International Bureau (Art. 12(1); R. 22.1(a)). The record copy is considered to be the authentic text of the international application, the 'true copy' (Art. 12(2)). This procedure underscores the PCT's dedication to preserving an unambiguous and authoritative document for ongoing reference throughout the patenting process. Where the applicant has made a translation for the search or publication (see Art. 3), the receiving Office will also transmit this translation to the International Bureau (R. 22.1(h)). See Art. 21 for the procedure of publication. 1

The receiving Office will keep one copy, called 'home copy' (Art. 12(1)). At the latest on the same day as it sends the record copy to the International Bureau, the receiving Office will send a copy of the international application (called 'search copy') to the ISA, or, where the ISA requires a translation of the international application (Art. 3), a copy of the request and the translation (considered to be the 'search copy') (Art. 12(1); R. 23.1(a), (b)). However, if the search fee has not yet been paid, the search copy will only be transmitted after payment of the search fee (R. 23.1). The ISA notifies the International Bureau, receiving Office and applicant of the receipt of the search copy (R. 25.1). 2

(1)

One copy of the international application shall be kept by the receiving Office ("home copy"), one copy ("record copy") shall be transmitted to the International Bureau, and another copy ("search copy") shall be transmitted to the competent

International Searching Authority referred to in Article 16, as provided in the Regulations.

R. 21	Preparation of copies
R. 22	Transmittal of the record copy to the International Bureau
R. 24	Receipt of the record copy by the International Bureau
R. 23	Transmittal of the record copy, translation and sequence listing to the ISA
R. 23*bis*	Transmittal of documents relating to earlier search between Offices
R. 25	Receipt of search copy by the ISA

(2)

The record copy shall be considered the true copy of the international application.

AIs 305	Identifying the copies of the PCTa
AIs 401	Marking of the sheets of the record copy
AIs 416	Correction of request in record dopy

(3)

The international application shall be considered withdrawn if the record copy has not been received by the International Bureau within the prescribed time limit.

R. 22.3	**Time limit** for receipt of the record copy by the International Bureau: As a rule, receipt takes place at the latest within a little more than 17 months from the priority date. This period can be understood from the following: Usually, the receiving Office sends the record copy to the International Bureau immediately after receipt (Art. 12(1)). In case the record copy did not reach the International Bureau within 14 months from the priority date, the International Bureau sends a corresponding communication to the receiving Office (R. 22.3(c)). The receiving Office then has another three months to transmit the record copy to the International Bureau (R. 22.3). In practice, international applications are not withdrawn if the receiving Office does not transmit the record copy since national security is still pending; for more details refer to agreed statements under R. 22.3.

Article 13
Availability of Copy of the International Application to Designated Offices

(1)

Any designated Office may ask the International Bureau to transmit to it a copy of the international application prior to the communication provided for in Article 20, and the International Bureau shall transmit such copy to the designated Office as soon as possible after the expiration of one year from the priority date.

(2)

(a) The applicant may, at any time, transmit a copy of his international application to any designated Office.

(b) The applicant may, at any time, ask the International Bureau to transmit a copy of his international application to any designated Office, and the International Bureau shall transmit such copy to the designated Office as soon as possible.

(c) Any national Office may notify the International Bureau that it does not wish to receive copies as provided for in subparagraph (b), in which case that subparagraph shall not be applicable in respect of that Office.

R. 31	Copies required under Art. 13	
	R. 31.1	Request for copies
	R. 31.2	Preparation of copies
R. 93*bis*	Electronic download instead of transmission, transmission only on request, at a specific time and in electronic form	

Article 14 Certain Defects in the International Application

INTRODUCTION

1 Once the receiving Office has accorded an international filing date, it checks the international application for the following defects (Art. 14(1)(a)):

(i) no signature (R. 4.15; R. 26.2*bis*(a); R. 51*bis*.1(a)(vi); see annotations to Art. 4);
(ii) missing indications concerning the applicant (R. 4.4; R. 4.5; R. 26.2*bis*(b); R. 51*bis*.1(a)(vii); see annotations to Art. 9);
(iii) no title (R. 4.3; R. 37; see annotations to Art. 4);
(iv) no abstract (R. 8; R. 38);
(v) non-compliance of the international application and, where applicable, its translation with the physical requirements (R. 9, 10, 11).

2 Art. 14(2) and (3) mention the further defects of missing drawings and missing fees. These defects have rules for correction that differ from the rules for correction of defects under Art. 14(1)(a). See annotations to Art. 14(3) for missing fees and annotations to Art. 14(2) for missing drawings.

3 The receiving Office also checks whether the abstract, any text matter of the drawings or the request is in a language accepted by the receiving Office (R. 26.3*ter*(a); R. 26.3*ter*(c); R. 12.1; see annotations to Art. 3).

4 If the receiving Office finds any of the defects under Art. 14(1)(a), it invites the applicant, preferably within one month from receipt of the international application (R. 26.1), to submit corrections (Art. 14(1)(b)), accompanied by observations if the applicant so wishes (R. 26.1) following the procedure of R. 26 (for the time limit and its extension see the next but one paragraph).

5 Corrections must generally be filed in the form of one or more replacement sheets incorporating the correction and accompanied by a letter explaining the differences between the replacement sheets and the original sheets they replace. A correction in the request does not require a replacement sheet but may be stated in the letter (R. 26.4; AG-IP 6.052). Any correction can be performed free of charge (AG-IP 6.053).

A correction must be furnished to the receiving Office (R. 26.4) within two months from the date of the invitation to correct (R. 26.2). The correction must be in the language in which the international application is filed, unless the correction is in a furnished translation, in which case the correction must be in the language of the translation (R. 12.2(c)). The receiving Office may extend the period *ex officio* or at the applicant's request and free of charge at any time before a decision is taken, even after expiration of the two-month period (R. 26.2; AG-IP 6.037, 6.053). 6

Each receiving Office may adopt its own procedure for correction of defects under Art. 14(1) (AG-IP 6.037). The EPO is relatively strict, whereas the International Bureau is very lenient. In practice, the International Bureau as receiving Office sends several reminders at one-month intervals after the invitation and extends the period *ex officio* till after receipt of the correction, so that the correction can be considered as having been received timely. 7

After receipt of any correction of defects, the receiving Office takes a decision under R. 26.5. If the correction is filed in due time and is sufficient, the international application will be corrected and retains its international filing date (AG-IP 6.032). Failure to furnish the required correction in time results in the international application being considered withdrawn (Art. 14(1)(b)). The effect of the deemed withdrawal is set out in annotations to Art. 24. 8

Once the International Bureau has received a copy of the international application (annotations to Art. 10), it may also check the international application for defects (AG-IP 6.051). If the International Bureau notes any defects referred to in Art. 14(1)(a)(i), (ii) or (v), it will bring this to the attention of the receiving Office (R. 28.1(a)). Subsequently, the receiving Office will carry out the correction procedure according to R. 26 unless the receiving Office disagrees with the International Bureau on the correction (R. 28.1(b)). 9

(1)

(a) The receiving Office shall check whether the international application contains any of the following defects, that is to say:

Art. 24	Consequence of missed time limit	
R. 9	Expressions, etc., not to be used	
R. 26	Checking by, and correcting before, the receiving Office of certain elements of the international application	
	R. 26.1	Invitation under Art. 14(1)(b) to correct certain defects
	R. 26.2	Time limit for correction
	R. 26.2*bis*	Signature, indication of one of several applicants
	R. 26.4	Procedure
	R. 26.5	Decision of the receiving Office
R. 43.6*bis*	Consideration of rectifications of obvious mistakes by ISA	

R. 66.1(d-*bis*), R. 70.2(e)	Consideration of the rectification of obvious mistakes by IPEA
R. 70.16	Rectification of obvious mistakes as an annex to the IPRP II
R. 91.1	Rectification of obvious mistakes in documents for example referring to a priority claim
R. 91.2	Requests for rectification
R. 91.3	Authorization and effect of rectifications
AIs 325 and 413	Corrections of defects under R. 26.4 and rectification of obvious mistakes under R. 91
AIs 217	Corrections concerning expressions not to be used under R. 9.2.
AIs 335	Procedures relating to sequence listings

(i) it is not signed as provided in the Regulations;

Art. 14(1)(b)	Invitation to correct defects, R. 26
R. 2.3	Signature
R. 4.1(d)	Signature of the applicant
R. 4.15	All applicants shall sign
R. 26.2*bis*(a)	Allows the signature of only one applicant
R. 90*bis*.5	A withdrawal of the PCTa must be signed by all applicants
R. 4.15(b)	Specific signing requirements for the US before September 16, 2012
R. 90.3	Agent and representative
Art. 49, R. 90.4	The absence of a power of attorney is considered to be the absence of a signature. The requirement of an additional power of attorney may be waived in accordance with R. 90.4(d), (e).
R. 51*bis*.1(a)(vi)	Invitation by designated Office to furnish missing signatures
AIs 316	Procedure where international application lacks signature
R. 60.1(a)*ter*	Corresponding formal requirements for application under Chapter II

10 If the request of the international application is not signed as required by R. 4.15, the receiving Office will invite the applicant to correct the defect within two months (Art. 14(1)(a)(i); R. 26.1 and 2; AG-IP 6.032). If the signature is not submitted in due time, the international application will be considered withdrawn (Art. 14(1)(b)).

11 If there are several applicants, it is sufficient that one of them signs the application (R. 26.2*bis*(a)), in spite of the requirement in R. 4.15 that all applicants must sign (AG-IP 5.088). It is irrelevant whether or not the signatory is entitled to file an international application, as long as one of the applicants is entitled to file an international application (Reischle, 'Ausführliche Darstellung der ab 1. Januar 2004 geltenden Änderungen der PCT-Ausführungsordnung', *Mitteilungen der deutschen Patentanwälte* 2004, p. 533). In the national phase, a designated Office may invite

to furnish the missing signatures of the other applicants (R. 51*bis*.1(a)(vi); AG-IP 5.088; see annotations to Art. 9).

(ii) it does not contain the prescribed indications concerning the applicant;

R. 4.5	Applicant
R. 26.2*bis*(b)	Missing indications in respect of one of several applicants is not a formal defect
R. 60.1(a-*bis*)	Missing indications in respect of one of several applicants is not a formal defect of the demand according to Chapter II
AIs 329	Correction of indications concerning the applicant's residence or nationality

(iii) it does not contain a title;

R. 37.1	Lack of title of the invention
R. 37.2	Establishment of title of the invention

(iv) it does not contain an abstract;

R. 8	Abstract
R. 38.1	Missing or defective abstract
R. 38.2	Establishment of abstract
R. 38.3	Modification of abstract

(v) it does not comply to the extent provided in the Regulations with the prescribed physical requirements.

The receiving Office checks whether the international application and, where applicable, its translation complies with the physical requirements (R. 9, 10, 11). It will do so only to the extent that compliance therewith is necessary for a reasonably uniform international publication and a satisfactory reproduction (R. 26.3(a), (b); R. 26.3*bis*). Color and grayscale drawings may not reproduce satisfactorily when printed in black and white in the international application (see annotations to Art. 7). If the receiving Office regards that compliance is insufficient, it will invite the applicant to correct the defect as set out in annotations to Art. 14. If not remedied, it is at the receiving Office's discretion to decide whether the international application should be considered withdrawn for lack of compliance with physical requirements (R. 26.5). In practice, such withdrawals are extremely rare (Pract. Adv. NL 03/2016, https://www.wipo.int/pct/en/newslett/practical_advice/pa_032016.html). 12

R. 9	Expressions, etc., not to be used
R. 10	Terminology and signs
R. 11	Physical requirements of the international application
R. 26.3	Checking of physical requirements under Art. 14(1)(a)(v) (defects) in the context of international publication

(b) If the receiving Office finds any of the said defects, it shall invite the applicant to correct the international application within the prescribed time limit, failing which that application shall be considered withdrawn and the receiving Office shall so declare.

R. 28	Defects noted by the International Bureau
R. 26.1	Invitation under Art. 14(1)(b) to correct defects (time limit for the applicant)
R. 26.2	The time limit for the correction is two months from the request (extendable).
R. 26.3*bis*	Invitation under Art. 14(1)(b) to correct defects under R. 11 (form of the international application)
R. 26.3*ter*	Invitation to correct defects under Art. 3(4)(i) (language); procedure if mixed languages are used in abstract, drawings, description, claims
R. 26.5	Decision on withdrawal
R. 29	Applications considered withdrawn may be remedied at national level. Revival at national level is described in detail at Art. 25. A review under Art. 25 is carried out by the designated Ofices.
Art. 24(2), Art. 48(2)	Possibilities of maintenance and effect in the event of exceeding the time limit: one possibility before the EPO is further processing under Art. 121, R. 135 EPC in conjunction with R. 51.3 (time limit for payment), R. 51.1 (time limit for filing a request), Art. 25(1)(a) and (2) (review). R. 51.3 (time limit for payment), R. 51.1 (time limit for filing a request), Art. 25(1)(a) and (2) (review). Reinstatement is another possibility. Further guidance can be found in the Euro-PCT Guide 5.14.001 et seq. (R. 159(2) EPC).
Art. 25	Remedy
AIs 414	Notification to IPEA where the international application is considered withdrawn
AIs 312	Notification to decision not to issue declaration that the international application is considered withdrawn

(2)

If the international application refers to drawings which, in fact, are not included in that application, the receiving Office shall notify the applicant accordingly and he may furnish them within the prescribed time limit and, if he does, the international filing date shall be the date on which the drawings are received

by the receiving Office. Otherwise, any reference to the said drawings shall be considered non-existent.

R. 20.5	Missing drawings: incorporation by reference, original filing date is maintained
R. 20.5*bis*	Erroneously filed elements and parts

1. Missing Drawings

If one or more drawings are missing from the international application as filed, the applicant has the following three options: 13

- The applicant furnishes the missing drawings late. As a consequence, the international filing date is changed to the date of receipt of the missing drawings (Art. 14(2), first sentence).
- The applicant can, where possible, incorporate the missing drawings in the international application by referring to an earlier application that completely contains the drawings and from which priority is claimed. He must also meet the requirements of R. 20.5(a). If they are met, the original international filing date will be maintained (R. 20.5(d); see also general annotations to R. 20).
- Where re-dating is undesirable and incorporation by reference is not possible, the applicant may decide not to supplement the missing drawings. As a consequence, any reference in the international application to those drawings will be considered non-existent (Art. 14(2), second sentence).

Note that the consequences of missing drawings are different from the consequences of other defects mentioned in Art. 14. Instead of the international application being deemed withdrawn (annotations to Art. 24), references in the application to the drawings are considered non-existent (Art. 14(2)). 14

2. Informal Drawings

If formal drawings complying with the requirements of R. 11 are not yet available at the intended date of filing, it is recommended to file an application with informal drawings rather than to miss the 12-month priority period. The applicant must make sure that the drawings are of sufficient quality to be published, which he can check online with the preview function included in ePCT Filing (Pract. Adv. NL 04/2019, https://www.wipo.int/pct/en/newslett/practical_advice/pa_042019.html). 15

Replacing them with formal drawings later under PCT may be demanding; some Offices do not accept it; other Offices make it rather difficult (AG-IP 11.038). The EPO as receiving Office is relatively lenient (Official Journal of the EPO 1987 p. 123 and GL Exam EPO A-IX, 10). A receiving Office is unlikely to consider the application withdrawn because of defects in the drawings as filed, provided these defects still allow international publication (R. 26.5). 16

17 If the receiving Office does not accept a replacement in the form of a correction under R. 26 because it might add new matter, the international application will be published with the informal drawings. In such a case, it is possible to make a demand for IPE and submit the formal drawings as amendments under Art. 34(2)(b), which do not need to satisfy the 'nothing else could have been intended' requirement for rectification of an obvious mistake under R. 91.1(c). These formal drawings will not be part of the international application but will be available for designated Offices in an Annex to the IPRP. The last possibility to correct the drawings is to submit the formal drawings with each designated Office as an amendment during the national phase. See Pract. Adv. NL 05/2019 for details (https://www.wipo.int/pct/en/newslett/practical_advice/pa_052019.html).

(3)

(a) If the receiving Office finds that, within the prescribed time limits, the fees prescribed under Article 3(4)(iv) have not been paid, or no fee prescribed under Article 4(2) has been paid in respect of any of the designated States, the international application shall be considered withdrawn and the receiving Office shall so declare.

Art. 3(4)(iv), R. 27.1(a)	Prescribed fees
R. 14	Transmittal fee
R. 15.1	International filing fee
R. 15.3	Time limit for international filing fee
R. 16	Search fee
R. 16*bis*	Extension of time limits for payment of fees
R. 16*bis*.2	Late payment fee

18 If the receiving Office finds that the fees prescribed by R. 27.1(a) have not been paid or only in part within the prescribed time limits, it invites the applicant to pay any missing fees within one month (R. 16*bis*.1). The fees as prescribed by R. 27.1(a) are:

- the transmittal fee (R. 14; see annotations to Art. 3);
- the international filing fee (R. 15.1; see annotations to Art. 3);
- the search fee (R. 16; see annotations to Art. 3);
- and, where required, the late payment fee (R. 16*bis*.2).

19 A receiving Office may impose a late payment fee as laid down in R. 16*bis*.2. If the fees are still not paid by expiry of the one-month time limit, the international application will be considered withdrawn, and the receiving Office will so declare (Art. 14(3)(a)).

20 The period for correction of a missing or underpaid fee under R. 16*bis*.1(a) of one month is not extendable (AG-IP 6.037). Any payment received by the receiving Office before sending the invitation for correction is considered to have been received before expiration of the time limit under R. 14.1(c), 15.3 or 16.1(f), as the case may

be (R. 16*bis*.1(d)). In addition, any payment received by the receiving Office before issuing a declaration that the international application is considered withdrawn (Art. 14(3)) is considered to have been received in time (R. 16*bis*.1(e)). If the time limit expires imminently, it is recommended to pay fees online using ePCT and avoid making payments by cheque (Pract. Adv. NL 05/2015 (https://www.wipo.int/edocs/pctndocs/en/2015/pct_news_2015_5.pdf). The RO/IB does not accept payments by cheque (https://www.wipo.int/pct/en/filing/filing.html).

(b) If the receiving Office finds that the fee prescribed under Article 4(2) has been paid in respect of one or more (but less than all) designated States within the prescribed time limit, the designation of those States in respect of which it has not been paid within the prescribed time limit shall be considered withdrawn and the receiving Office shall so declare.

Art. 4(2)	Former fee for designation has been abolished
Art. 24(1)(ii)	Consequence: Loss of effect in designated states
R. 29	International applications considered withdrawn
AIs 414	Notification to IPEA where the international application is considered withdrawn
AIs 312	Notification to decision not to issue declaration that the international application is considered withdrawn

(4)

If, after having accorded an international filing date to the international application, the receiving Office finds, within the prescribed time limit, that any of the requirements listed in items (i) to (iii) of Article 11(1) *(minimum requirements for the accordance of a filing date)* **was not complied with at that date, the said application shall be considered withdrawn and the receiving Office shall so declare.**

R. 29	International applications considered withdrawn	
	R. 29.4	Notification of intent to make declaration under Art. 14(4). The applicant has two months to reply and is invited to confirm the incorporation
R. 30.1	The time limit under Art. 14(4) is four months from the international filing date	
AIs 414	Notification to IPEA where the international application is considered withdrawn	

Article 15
The International Search

INTRODUCTION

1 Every international application will be the subject of an international search during the international phase (Art. 15(1)). The search is carried out by an ISA, whose task includes the establishment of an ISR (Art. 16(1)) or a declaration of non-establishment of ISR (Art. 17(2)(a)). Currently, there are 24 ISAs operating under the PCT. Every ISA also acts as IPEA. Any national Office or intergovernmental organization satisfying the requirements relating to manpower, patent documentation, and quality management (ISPE Guidelines Ch. 21, https://www.wipo.int/pct/en/texts/ispe/index.html) can be appointed as ISA by the Assembly. Its operations are further governed by an agreement between such an Office or organization and the International Bureau (Art. 16(3)(a)–(c); R. 36). A list of all national/regional Offices that act as ISA and IPEA, including the Agreements between the individual Offices or organizations and the International Bureau of WIPO, can be found on the WIPO website (https://www.wipo.int/pct/en/access/isa_ipea_agreements.html). European ISAs include the EPO as well as the national Offices of AT, ES, FI, SE, TR, XN (the Nordic Patent Institute) and XV (the Visegrad Patent Institute) (AG-IP Annex D).

(1)

Each international application shall be the subject of international search.

Art. 17(1)	Procedure before the ISA
Art. 17(3)	Unity of invention in international search
R. 35	International search carried out by the ISA
R. 45*bis*.9	Supplementary international search carried out by the ISA as SISA. Depending on which authority carried out the international search, there may be fee reductions for the supplementary European search in the regional phase before the EPO (Art. 153(7) EPC).
R. 66.1*ter*	Supplementary search carried out by the IPEA

(2)

The objective of the international search is to discover relevant prior art.

Art. 17(2) Unsearchable subject matter

The purpose of the international search is to discover relevant prior art by consulting at least the documentation specified in R. 34 (Art. 15(4)). The search will be done in the technical field of the invention to which the international application relates and in fields with analogous arts (R. 33.2). Prior art is everything available to the public anywhere in the world by means of written disclosure prior to the international filing date (R. 33.1(a)). The ISR will separately mention any disclosures made in a form other than writing, such as an oral disclosure, use, or exhibition, or if they are referred to in a written disclosure that became public on or after the international filing date (R. 33.1(b)). 2

Prior art documentation taken into account during international search must be publicly available before the international filing date (R. 33.1(a)) or, where a priority has been validly claimed, before the priority date (ISPE Ch. 11, https://www.wipo.int/pct/en/texts/ispe/index.html). Prior art published between the priority date and the international filing date will be specially mentioned in the ISR (R. 33.1(c)). Prior rights with respect to the international filing date (not the priority date) of the international application will also be specially mentioned in the search report (R. 33.1(c)). 3

Whether a public disclosure made by the applicant before the priority date will be regarded as prior art by a designated Office depends on the national law of that Office (Art. 27(5), second sentence). The EPC does not have a general period of grace but applies a six-month period for disclosure due to evident abuse or for display at an international exhibition (Art. 55(1) EPC). 4

(3)

International search shall be made on the basis of the claims, with due regard to the description and the drawings (if any).

According to Art. 15(3), the international search is based on the claims of the international application. R. 6 provides details on these claims. The description (R. 5) and the drawings (R. 7), if present, are also considered during the search. The process of the international search is further complemented by Art. 15(2) and R. 33, which focus on the scope and methodology of the search against prior art. 5

(4)

The International Searching Authority referred to in Article 16 shall endeavor to discover as much of the relevant prior art as its facilities permit, and shall, in any case, consult the documentation specified in the Regulations.

R. 33, 33.1	Relevant prior art for the international search
R. 33.2	Fields to be covered by the international search
R. 33.3	Orientation of the international search
R. 34	Minimum Documentation
AIs 801 et seq.	TPOs concerning the prior art. See also PCT EPO Guidelines E-II and Introduction to Art. 33.

(5)

(a) If the national law of the Contracting State so permits, the applicant who files a national application with the national Office of or acting for such State may, subject to the conditions provided for in such law, request that a search similar to an international search ("international-type search") be carried out on such application.

6 An international-type search is a search similar to an international search carried out at the request of the applicant on a national application filed with a national Office (Art. 15(5)(a)). For example, the EPO offers an international-type search.

(b) If the national law of the Contracting State so permits, the national Office of or acting for such State may subject any national application filed with it to an international-type search.

(c) The international-type search shall be carried out by the International Searching Authority referred to in Article 16 which would be competent for an international search if the national application were an international application and were filed with the Office referred to in subparagraphs (a) and (b). If the national application is in a language which the International Searching Authority considers it is not equipped to handle, the international-type search shall be carried out on a translation prepared by the applicant in a language prescribed for international applications and which the International Searching Authority has undertaken to accept for international applications. The national application and the translation, when required, shall be presented in the form prescribed for international applications.

7 The international-type search is carried out by the ISA that would have been competent if the national application were an international application filed with the same national Office as receiving Office (Art. 15(5)(c)). A reason for having an international-type search carried out is to have an assessment of the patentability prospects of an invention in a national application which is to be used as priority document for an international application.

8 For TPOs under PCT, see Introduction to Art. 33.

Article 16
The International Searching Authority

(1)

International search shall be carried out by an International Searching Authority, which may be either a national Office or an intergovernmental organization, such as the International Patent Institute, whose tasks include the establishing of documentary search reports on prior art with respect to inventions which are the subject of applications.

Annex C of the PCT Applicant's Guide lists competent ISAs (and IPEAs) designated by the respective receiving Office. In DE, for example, this is the EPO. Applicants from some non-European countries may also choose the EPO as ISA (e.g. JP and US). Filing Offices which had not designated the EPO on January 1, 2023 are AE, AU, CA, DM, KP, KR, PG (Euro-PCT Guide 3.1.008). 1

The choice of receiving Office and ISA may have an impact on the competent IPEA, as its scope of competence may be limited to certain ISAs in the agreements with WIPO. The EPO acts as IPEA only if the ISA was the EPO or the industrial property office of an EPC Contracting State, i.e. AT, FI, ES, XN, XV, TR or SE (AG-IP Annex E (EP)). The EPO has not limited its competence as ISA and IPEA to receiving Offices from EPC Member States (Euro-PCT Guide 3.1.006 and 4.1.014). 2

Since January 1, 2015, US nationals or residents who have filed a PCT with the US receiving Office or the International Bureau may select the EPO as ISA or IPEA irrespective of the technical field in which the application is classified (OJ 2014 A117; PCT Gazette November 20, 2014). Previously, there were restrictions in this respect. Where the subject matter relates to business methods but involves technical means, the EPO will draw up a search report for the parts relating to more than pure business methods, irrespective of the nationality or residence of the applicant (Euro-PCT Guide paras 3.1.010, 3.3.006, 4.1.019). See also the comments on R. 39.1 and Art. 17 (lack of unity). This corresponds to previous practice established by case law and will now also apply to applications from the US. For the background to the amendment, see http://documents.epo.org/projects/babylon/eponet.nsf/0/fe9b7f7048bf6529c1257d7900469114/$FILE/No_more_limitations_to_PCT_work_en.PDF. 3

Art. 17	Search procedure, subject matter
Art. 32	The Authority entrusted with the IPE
R. 35	Competent ISA
R. 35.1	When only *one* ISA is competent
R. 35.2	When *several* ISAs are competent
R. 35.3	When the International Bureau is receiving Office under R. 19.1(a)(iii)

(2)

If, pending the establishment of a single International Searching Authority, there are several International Searching Authorities, each receiving Office shall, in accordance with the provisions of the applicable agreement referred to in paragraph (3)(b), specify the International Searching Authority or Authorities competent for the searching of international applications filed with such Office.

4 Every receiving Office (except the International Bureau, according to R. 35.3(c)) specifies which ISA or ISAs are competent to carry out the international search for international applications filed with the said receiving Office (Art. 16(2); R. 35.1; R. 35.2). The choice of ISA may be based on various factors, including linguistic capabilities and the presumed quality and coverage of the searches. AG-IP Annex C indicates the ISA(s) competent for each receiving Office. Some national Offices acting as receiving Office also act as ISA, for example, the EPO and the USPTO. Applicants must indicate their choice of ISA in the request (R. 4.1(b)(iv)).

(3)

(a) International Searching Authorities shall be appointed by the Assembly. Any national Office and any intergovernmental organization satisfying the requirements referred to in subparagraph (c) may be appointed as International Searching Authority.

(b) Appointment shall be conditional on the consent of the national Office or intergovernmental organization to be appointed and the conclusion of an agreement, subject to approval by the Assembly, between such Office or organization and the International Bureau. The agreement shall specify the rights and obligations of the parties, in particular, the formal undertaking by the said Office or organization to apply and observe all the common rules of international search.

5 The agreements can be found at https://www.wipo.int/pct/en/access/isa_ipea_agreements.html.

(c) The Regulations prescribe the minimum requirements, particularly as to manpower and documentation, which any Office or organization must satisfy before it can be appointed and must continue to satisfy while it remains appointed.

(d) Appointment shall be for a fixed period of time and may be extended for further periods.

(e) Before the Assembly makes a decision on the appointment of any national Office or intergovernmental organization, or on the extension of its appointment, or before it allows any such appointment to lapse, the Assembly shall hear the interested Office or organization and seek the advice of the Committee for Technical Cooperation referred to in Article 56 once that Committee has been established.

R. 45*bis*.9	ISA as SISA
R. 66.1*ter*	Top-up searches conducted by IPEA

ACCELERATION OF PROSECUTION USING PPH

1. Introduction

Several patent Offices have signed bilateral or multilateral agreements to promote work-sharing between the Offices and permit accelerated prosecution of applications in the national phase. This system of cooperation is known as the 'Patent Prosecution Highway' (PPH). The principles of PPH are set out at https://www.jpo.go.jp/e/toppage/pph-portal/pph.html and www.wipo.int/pct/en/filing/pct_pph.html. 6

The basic idea of PPH is that if one Office, the so-called Office of earlier examination (OEE), has determined that a set of claims is patentable, this set of claims can be presented to another Office, called the Office of later examination (OLE), in a PPH request, indicating that this set of claims has been considered patentable by the OEE. The OLE can reduce its search and examination workload and improve its examination quality by using the work results of the OEE. The decision whether to grant a patent remains the responsibility of the OLE. The intended benefits for the applicant are a faster grant, a higher grant rate, and lower cost because of fewer Office actions. 7

The so-called PCT-PPH is intended for sharing work results from search and examination carried out by ISAs and IPEAs with Offices in the national phases. The IP5 Offices (CNIPA, EPO, JPO, KIPO, USPTO) – among others – participate in the PCT-PPH. The EPO acting as ISA or IPEA in the international phase and as elected or designated Office in the regional phase is not regarded as another Office in the sense of the PPH agreements (Singer/Stauder/Luginbühl, *EPÜ*, 8th edition, 2019, Art. 153 Note 220). Thus, a PCT-PPH request can only be filed with the EPO if the EPO did not act as ISA or IPEA in the international phase. 8

The most important requirements for filing a PCT-PPH request is that an ISA or IPEA considers a set of claims to comply with the requirements of novelty, inventive step, and industrial applicability. Another requirement is that the substantive examination before the OLE may not yet have started (see, for example, OJ EPO 2022 A115). A PPH request is generally free of charge. However, it does require the preparation and filing of various documents. To alleviate the task of the applicant, several Offices 9 will, at the applicant's request, themselves retrieve the documents from a digital document library. See, for example, EPO form 1009, allowing the EPO to retrieve documents via DAS or PATENTSCOPE.

2. PPH Statistics

10 The PPH portal, administered by the JPO (https://www.jpo.go.jp/e/toppage/pph-portal/statistics.html), shows statistical data on the effectiveness of PPH for several Offices (refer also to PCT-PPH statistics in the PCT Yearly Review 2024, p. 89).

11 A brief analysis of the statistics on the PPH portal demonstrate that a PPH request leads in general to an accelerated examination and can be used for this purpose. It does, however, not lead to a significant reduction in the number of Office actions during prosecution and, therefore, a more cost-effective way to grant.

12 The recognition by an OEE that a set of claims complies with the requirements of novelty, inventive step, and industrial applicability is a positive sign concerning the quality of the claims. A patent application with a PPH request is therefore likely to enjoy a more favorable attitude of a patent examiner (Rieck/Köllner, Mitteilungen der deutschen Patentanwälte 2013, 525).

13 An applicant can request acceleration of processing before many PPH Offices, either by a PPH request or by any other existing means of requesting accelerated prosecution. The choice may depend on cost.

14 Since a request for acceleration at the USPTO is expensive, it is recommended to use the free PPH request – where available – for acceleration, in spite of the effort needed to prepare it.

15 When the EPO as OLE receives a PPH request for a European application, it processes the examination in an accelerated manner while at the same time allowing the examiner to exploit available work results from the OEE. The examiner is under no obligation to take over the results. The conditions for the acceleration are the same as those applicable to the PACE program. Both PACE and PPH are free of charge; a PPH request, however, puts some burden on the applicant. Therefore, in many cases at the EPO, a PACE request is recommended compared to a PPH request.

3. Efficient Prosecution in Latin America Using PCT and PPH

16 Some Latin American countries have accrued significant patent examination backlogs. The patent prosecution in such countries can be sped up using PCT, PPH and PPH-PROSUR (http://prosur.org/en/). See the practical advice in PCT Newsletter 01/2017 (https://www.wipo.int/pct/en/newslett/practical_advice/pa_012017.html).

17 PPH-PROSUR is a multilateral agreement (see translation of May 6, 2016 MOU, https://www.wipo.int/scp/en/meetings/session_25/comments_received/Argentina_2.pdf) between the eight IP Offices of the Latin American countries AR, BR, CL, CO, EC, PY, PE, UY within the framework of PPH. Under the multilateral agreement, a request for PPH processing submitted to an IP Office of a PROSUR country can be based on

the positive result of national examination work previously carried out by the Office of another PROSUR country or of international search or examination work carried out by the Brazilian or Chilean patent Office in its capacity as ISA and/or IPEA. Hence, an international search and/or examination carried out by the Brazilian or Chilean patent Office as International Authority can be used to lever an accelerated prosecution in the other PROSUR countries.

The work of other ISAs of countries not being party to PROSUR may also be used as a basis for accelerated examination in the PROSUR countries, although less directly. For example, an applicant has used the EPO as ISA during the international phase. The EPO currently has a PCT-PPH agreement in place with the national Office of Colombia (OJ EPO 2022 A 88). Thus, on the basis of a positive assessment by the EPO of the claims in an international application, the applicant may request PCT-PPH accelerated processing in the Columbian national phase. If the Columbian patent Office considers that one or more claims are patentable during its substantive examination in the national phase, the examination will be accelerated on request in the other PROSUR countries in accordance with the PPH-PROSUR Agreement. 18

Proceeding in this manner should significantly shorten the time to receive a decision on the patentability of a patent application, even in countries with significant backlogs. 19

It should be noted that this indirect strategy also allows the applicant to seek accelerated processing in countries which are currently not PCT Contracting States, such as Argentina, Paraguay and Uruguay. Uruguay will become bound on January 7, 2025. 20

Another way to accelerate processing is to use a grant, for example, in one of the IP5 jurisdictions (CN, EP, JP, KR, US), and file a PPH request in Brazil to accelerate examination, as Brazil has bilateral PPH agreements in place with each of the IP5 patent Offices. A grant in Brazil can then be used to lever an accelerated prosecution in other Latin American countries using PPH-PROSUR. There are similar PPH agreements in place between other Latin American patent Offices and some of the IP5 patent Offices, but not all combinations are available. Details can be found, for example, on the JPO website (https://www.jpo.go.jp/e/toppage/pph-portal/network.html). 21

4. Strategic Choice of ISA or IPEA in Connection with PPH

Where the applicant can choose between several ISAs or IPEAs, a strategic choice in combination with a PPH request may help to speed up patent prosecution (see Pract. Adv. NL 02/2011 (https://www.wipo.int/pct/en/newslett/practical_advice/pa_022011.html). 22

For example, a national and resident of India has the Indian patent Office as the competent receiving Office, which gives the applicant a wide choice of ISAs and IPEAs, namely: AT, AU, CN, EP, IN, JP, SE, US. 23

The rows of the following table list the Offices that can act as ISA and IPEA for an international application filed with the Indian receiving Office. The columns list the designated Offices of several countries that have a PPH agreement with these Offices 24 (https://www.wipo.int/pct/en/filing/pct_pph.html) and where the applicant can file a PPH request, provided the assessment of the ISA or the IPEA is positive.

DO / ISA/IPEA	AU	CN	EP	JP	KR	RU	US	...
AT	GPPH*			GPPH	GPPH	GPPH	GPPH	...
AU		PCT-PPH	PCT-PPH	GPPH	GPPH	GPPH	GPPH	...
CNIPA						PCT-PPH		...
EPO	PCT-PPH					PCT-PPH		...
IN								...
SE	GPPH	PCT-PPH		GPPH	GPPH	GPPH	GPPH	...
USPTO	GPPH			GPPH	GPPH	GPPH		...

* GPPH = Global Patent Prosecution Highway including PCT work products

25 The table shows that the best choice of ISA/IPEA for accelerating patent prosecution in the largest number of countries (among those listed in the table) would be Australia. IN has no suitable PPH agreements in place and the choice of IN as ISA or IPEA would be unsuitable for the desired goal.

26 Bear in mind, however, that the following issues must also be considered when choosing an ISA/IPEA, namely:

- the fee charged by the ISA or IPEA for carrying out an international search or preliminary examination, taking into account any possible fee reductions or refunds (for details about the fees payable at the various ISAs and IPEAs, as well as any applicable reductions or refunds, see AG-IP Annex D and E at https://www.wipo.int/pct/en/guide/index.html);
- any fee exemptions, reductions, or refunds of fees that are available for examination in the national phase where specific ISAs and IPEAs have carried out the international search and preliminary examination (see AG-IP Annex, the National Chapter Summaries in the PCT Applicant's Guide at https://www.wipo.int/pct/en/guide/index.html);
- the language of filing of the international application. If the international application is filed in a language which is not accepted by the chosen ISA/IPEA, the applicant will incur translation costs. Note that the ISAs and IPEAs mentioned in the table will all carry out search and preliminary examination in English and that an international application filed in English does not need any translation in the international phase;
- specific subject matter an ISA or IPEA is not required to search or examine under PCT R. 39.1 or 67.1. More information for each Office acting as ISA and IPEA in this regard can be found in the Agreements between each Office and the International Bureau of WIPO in relation to the functioning of the Office as ISA and IPEA under the PCT (https://www.wipo.int/pct/en/access/isa_ipea_agreements.html).

27 An applicant must be aware of the fact that all PCT-PPH programs are currently operating as pilot programs. Although it is expected that the pilot programs will be

successful and will therefore be either extended or fully implemented, there is no guarantee that for an international application filed now, a PPH program between any two specific Offices will still be in operation by the time of national phase entry.

Article 17
Procedure before the International Searching Authority

(1)

Procedure before the International Searching Authority shall be governed by the provisions of this Treaty, the Regulations, and the agreement which the International Bureau shall conclude, subject to this Treaty and the Regulations, with the said Authority.

R. 43	The ISR
R. 43*bis*	Written opinion of the ISA (since April 1, 2005 for declaration under Art. 17(2)(a))
R. 42	Time limit for drawing up the ISR. Typically, the time limit is 16 months from the priority date.
R. 16.1	Search fee
R. 16.2	Refund of the search fee
R. 12.3	There are more search languages than languages in which the application is published (R. 48.3).
	Translation for the purposes of the international search. The time limit for filing the translation is one month from application date (R. 12.3(a)). Extension of time limit: R. 12.3(c) and R. 12.3(d) S.2
R. 45	Translation of the ISR
R. 33	Relevant prior art for the international search (to be distinguished from the prior art mentioned in R. 64, which refers to the relevant prior art for the preliminary examination)
R. 37	ISA's role in establishing missing or defective title
R. 38	ISA's role in establishing missing or defective abstract
R. 41	Taking into account results of earlier search
R. 16.3	Partial refund of the search fee
R. 20.5*bis*(d)	Basis in case of erroneously filed elements and parts
R. 40*bis*.1	Additional fees in case of missing parts or corrected elements

R. 44	Transmittal of the ISR, written opinion, etc. (time limit for request for IPE R. 54*bis*)
R. 44*bis*	IPRP by the ISA
G 1/89	PCT Guidelines for Conducting International Preliminary Examination of WIPO is binding upon the EPO when acting as an ISA or IPEA
G 2/89	ISA prepares a preliminary opinion on novelty and inventive step without binding effect for examination proceedings
AIs 420	Copy of the international application, the ISR, and the SISR for the authority in charge of the IPE

(2)

(a) If the International Searching Authority considers

(i) that the international application relates to a subject matter which the International Searching Authority is not required, under the Regulations, to search, and in the particular case decides not to search, or

R. 39.1	Non-searchable, non-technical, or not industrially applicable subject matter
Art. 152 EPC	R. 158(1) EPC, EPO as ISA: OJ EPO 1999 p. 300. The searches for the US have been restricted. Accordingly, no searches were carried out for inventions relating to biotechnology and business methods (OJ EPO 2002 p. 52). Applicability of the limitation to parallel European direct application and request for regional phase (OJ EPO 2002 pp. 52). Repeal with regard to biotechnology from January 1, 2004 (OJ EPO 2003 p. 633). Extended with regard to business methods until March 1, 2009 (OJ EPO 2005 p. 149, OJ EPO 10/2006 p. 555). Amendment by IPC since January 1, 2006: G 06F17/60 corresponds to G06Q, G06Q 10/00, 30/00, 40/00, 50/00, 90/00, 99/00 (OJ EPO 2006 p. 149). Business methods in accordance with the aforementioned IPCs are still not researched. Although the restriction on the competence of the ISA with regard to business methods has been deleted from the WIPO-EPO Agreement since January 1, 2015, the Communication on business methods in OJ EPO 2007 p. 592 continues to apply according to the EPO Communication (OJ EPO 2014 A117), see annotations to Art. 16(2).
EPO	Exception in the case that the EPO would examine it as a European patent application (Annex C to the WIPO/EPO Agreement, see annotations to Art. 16(3)(b))
R. 45*bis*.5(e)	Limitation of scope of supplementary international search
R. 45*bis*.9(c)	Limitation of scope of supplementary international search by SISA

(ii) that the description, the claims, or the drawings, fail to comply with the prescribed requirements to such an extent that a meaningful search could not be carried out,

the said Authority shall so declare and shall notify the applicant and the International Bureau that no international search report will be established.

R. 42	The time limit for the declaration under Art. 17(2)(a) (non-searchable subject matter) is three months.
Art. 34(4)(a)(i)	in conjunction with R. 67: no IPE of subject matter that is excluded from patentability
R. 66.1(e)	Claims for which no ISR is established cannot be the subject of IPE. If deficiencies are remedied, a search is possible in the regional phase before the EPO in the course of examination (PCT EPO Guidelines C-IV 4.2).
EPO	If the EPO as ISA has filed a standardized non-search declaration under Art. 17(2), R. 39 and has not carried out a subsequent search in the European phase, the search fee will not be refunded. There is no legal basis for a refund in this case, neither in the PCT nor in the WIPO-EPO Agreement or in a decision of the EPO (T 0506/08). There is also no possibility of appeal (T 0506/08). There is no provision providing for a review by the IPEA of the ISA's decision on non-search or for an appeal against it PCT EPO Guidelines C-IV 4.2.
Art. 152, 153(6) EPC	Declaration of non-searchable subject matter replaces European search report
EPO	As ISA: in case of ambiguities, it informally invites clarification at its discretion and, if necessary, issues an incomplete or no search report if no clarification is provided (PCT EPO Guidelines B-VIII 3.3)

(b) If any of the situations referred to in subparagraph (a) is found to exist in connection with certain claims only, the international search report shall so indicate in respect of such claims, whereas, for the other claims, the said report shall be established as provided in Article 18.

1 An ISA is not required to search subject matter that is excluded from patenting because it is non-technical, for example, scientific or mathematical theories, schemes, rules or methods of doing business, mere presentation of information, and computer programs to the extent that the ISA is not equipped to search prior art concerning such subject matter. It is neither required to search subject matter that is excluded for other reasons, for example, plant or animal varieties or essentially biological processes (other than microbiological processes) and their products, methods for treatment of the human or animal body, as well as diagnostic methods (Art. 17(2)(a)(i); R. 39.1(i)–(vi)).

Most ISAs do indeed not search such subject matter. However, they may make an exception for subject matter which is searched under national law (AG-IP Annex C for each ISA). Detailed information on the subject matter that an ISA does search in spite of R. 39.1 is not provided in the PCT Applicant's Guide, nor in the ISA and IPEA agreements between a national Office and WIPO. The options an ISA has for excluding and including subject matter from the search are set out in the ISPE Ch. 9 and Appendix (https://www.wipo.int/pct/en/texts/ispe/9_02_15.html). Some information on the options chosen by an ISA may be found in documents published by the national Office acting as ISA. The EPO has published the information in the Euro-PCT Guide. The EPO as ISA restricts the search in the same way as it does for European applications (Euro-PCT Guide 3.3.005). For example, the EPO as ISA does search computer programs, provided they have technical character (Euro-PCT Guide, Annex I, point A9.15, option 2). 2

The ISA need not extend its search to subject matter of the international application that is too unclear for carrying out a meaningful search (Art. 17(2)(a)(ii)). Nevertheless, some ISAs do extend their search to non-searchable matter as a courtesy to the applicant. 3

If no meaningful search can be carried out for the whole international application, the ISA will issue a so-called declaration of non-establishment of ISR (often briefly referred to as 'declaration') and transmit it to the International Bureau and the applicant (Art. 17(2)(a); R. 44.1). The international search fee will not be refunded in such cases, as the ISA did spend time on the international search. The entry into national or regional phases is not affected by a declaration (Art. 22(2)). 4

If only certain claims relate to subject matter not searched, this will be indicated in the ISR, whereas for the other claims the results of the search will be stated (Art. 17(2)(b)). If the national law of the national Office acting as ISA does not allow a several dependent claim to refer to another several dependent claim, such a dependency may result in unsearched claims and, consequently, an indication under Art. 17(2)(b) in the ISR (R. 6.4(a)). 5

The outcome of the international search does not have any influence on the validity of the international application, the processing of which continues in respect of all claims (AG-IP 7.021). Nevertheless, a designated Office may consider unsearched parts as withdrawn, unless the applicant pays a special fee to the national Office (Art. 17(3)(b)). 6

Upon entry into the national phase, most designated Offices re-assess whether the claims fulfill the requirement of unity of invention in accordance with their national law. 7

(3)

(a) If the International Searching Authority considers that the international application does not comply with the requirement of unity of invention as set forth in the Regulations, it shall invite the applicant to pay additional fees. The International Searching Authority shall establish the international search report on those parts of the international application which relate to the invention

first mentioned in the claims ("main invention") and, provided the required additional fees have been paid within the prescribed time limit, on those parts of the international application which relate to inventions in respect of which the said fees were paid.

8 PCT applications cannot be divided. Only additional fees for search or examination can be paid. Divisional applications are only possible in the national/regional phase.

R. 40.1, 40.2(a)	Invitation to pay additional fees in case of non-unity of invention	
R. 158(1) EPC	Additional international search fee	
R. 40	Lack of unity of invention (international search)	
R. 45*bis*.1(d) R. 45*bis*.5(b)	Lack of unity of invention (supplementary international search)	
Art. 34(3)(a), R. 68	Lack of unity of invention (IPE)	
Art. 3(4)(iii)	Unity of invention	
R. 13	Unity of invention	
	R. 13.1	Requirement (of unity)
	R. 13.2	Cases in which the requirement of unity of invention is deemed to be fulfilled. In short: where the characterizing features are identical. Very detailed examples can be found in the PCT AIs Annex B.
	R. 13.3	Determination of unity of invention irrespective of the wording of the claims
	R. 13.4	Dependent claims are unitary
	R. 13.5	Utility models
W 52/92	For the determination of non-unity *a priori* (before the search), the problem is to be determined on the basis of the description and the prior art assessed therein from the applicant's point of view	
W 8/87	According to R. 13.1, lack of unity can be established *a posteriori* (after the search), i.e. after examination of the common characterizing features	
G 2/89	Lack of unity may be established *a priori* or *a posteriori* – with an invitation to pay a further fee	
OJ EPO 2017 A20, PCT/WG/10/14	The applicant receives a *preliminary opinion* on the patentability of the invention (or unitary group of inventions) first mentioned in the claims together with the invitation to pay additional fees and the results of the partial search for information purposes. A reply to this is not required. It remains possible to react after receipt of the final ISR and the WO-ISA (see annotations to R. 43*bis*.1(c). The preliminary opinion is publicly accessible via online file inspection.	

G 1/89	The EPO may request an additional search fee as ISA under Art. 17(3)(a) PCT if it considers the application to be non-unitary *a posteriori*. The relevant communication under R. 40.1 PCT must contain, in addition to the list of inventions defined in the new independent claims (resulting from the combination of the dropped main or secondary claim) and the invitation to pay further search fees under Art. 17(3)(a) PCT, the reasons for the finding of lack of unity (established case law). An invitation to pay which does not contain these reasons is not legally binding with regard to the lack of unity established *a posteriori* (established case law, e.g. W 8/87, W 15/00). The invitation under Art. 17(3)(a) PCT to pay additional fees is only legally effective if the lack of unity is sufficiently substantiated. According to R. 40.1(i), the reasons for lack of unity must be stated in the invitation.
W 21/03	The fee may only be charged in 'clear cases'
W 6/96	Any doubts regarding the question of unity of invention are to be handled to the advantage of the applicant
R. 40.2(a)	The ISA determines the amount of the additional fee
R. 40.2(b)	The ISA is entitled to the additional fee
R. 40.1(ii) in conjunction with Art. 17(3)(a)	The *time limit* for paying additional fees is one month from the date of the invitation. From November 1, 2014, applicants can pay extra search fees in the regional phase for non-unity issues identified during the international phase, regardless of the ISA's identity. If a time limit is missed, further processing under R. 135(2) EPC from November 1, 2014, is available.
W 3/93	For the time limit under R. 40.1(ii) (payment of additional fees), *re-establishment* is allowed, although Art. 48(2) does not refer to the ISA, i.e. re-establishment in the PCT without initiation of the national phase under Art. 25(2)
R. 40.1(iii), 40.2(c)	A (reasoned) protest against the invitation is possible, along with the simultaneous payment of the required additional fee – under protest
W 16/92	The protest statement by the applicant according to R. 40.2(c) must contain comprehensible reasons. Mere assertion of unity of the application is not sufficient to prevent the protest from being dismissed as inadmissible
R. 40.2(e) S. 2	If the protest fee is not paid on time, the protest is deemed not to have been filed. There is no grace period. The additional search fee will not be refunded. Instead, the additional search will be carried out.
AIs 403	Transmission of the protest against the payment of an additional fee and decision thereon in case of lack of unity of invention by International Bureau to designated Office and elected Office on request of the applicant

9 Since the EPC 2000 took effect on December 13, 2007, international applications filed from this date follow a one-step procedure, initially introduced in the March 1, 2005 communication (OJ EPO 2005 p. 225), which was later replaced (Special Edition No. 3 OJ EPO 2007 p. 142) and updated (OJ EPO 5/2010 p. 320). Notably, these updates solely affect the EPO's application as SISA and do not alter the process when the EPO serves as ISA and IPEA (OJ EPO 5/2010 p. 322). The decision of June 9, 2015 (OJ EPO 2015 A59), which specifically revises the composition of the review panel, supersedes the aforementioned provisions.

PROTEST PROCEDURE

10 The review panel set up on the basis of the decision (see also the term 'review panel' in R. 40.2(c) S.2) is the sole instance for reviewing a protest. If additional fees are paid under protest and the protest fee is duly paid, the protest will be submitted to the review panel for decision.

1. If the review panel finds that the protest was fully justified, the additional fees and the protest fee shall be refunded.
2. If the review panel finds that the protest was only partially justified, the corresponding additional fees, but not the protest fee, will be refunded.

W 20/01	If an applicant has paid the additional fees late under protest, the protest must still be taken into account if the ISA has carried out the additional search as if the additional fees had been paid on time
G 1/89	The protest procedure is the same as for the normal search and examination under the EPC by the EPO
R. 40.2(c) S. 2	The protest is examined by a review panel
R. 40.2(c) S. 2, second half-sentence	The additional search fee may be refunded
	If the protest was only partially justified, only the excess search fee paid will be refunded, but not the protest fee (Euro-PCT Guide 3.3.022).
R. 40.2(e), S. 3	Refund of the protest fee if the protest was fully justified (see one-step procedure above).
W 4/93	Stating new reasons and evidence for non-unity of invention on the occasion of the notification of the review result is inadmissible. A deficiency in the statement of grounds for non-unity of invention in the request for payment of additional fees is not remedied by new reasons in the notification of the result of the review of the protest. The review is to be carried out solely on the basis of the reasons contained in the invitation to pay additional fees.

W 11/93	The review panel cannot examine of its own motion whether lack of unity exists for reasons other than those stated in the invitation. There is no entitlement to oral proceedings. An informal hearing under R. 66.6 PCT is generally not expedient.
W 3/02	The suspension of grant proceedings under R. 14 EPC (vindication) after entry into the regional phase before the EPO does not extend to protest proceedings pending before the Board of Appeal
R. 40.2(c) S. 3	The protest and the decision on it are forwarded to the designated Office upon request
R. 40.2(c) S. 4	Submit translation of protest and decision with Art. 22 to designated Offices. However, only a few Offices insist on this

(b) The national law of any designated State may provide that, where the national Office of that State finds the invitation, referred to in subparagraph (a), of the International Searching Authority justified and where the applicant has not paid all additional fees, those parts of the international application which consequently have not been searched shall, as far as effects in that State are concerned, be considered withdrawn unless a special fee is paid by the applicant to the national Office of that State.

The absence of an ISR or parts thereof has no effect on the validity of PCTa. This can be concluded from Art. 22(1) and (2) (time limit: 30 months from the priority date), Art. 15(2) (determination of the prior art), and Art. 27(5) (national requirements). Weaker consequences are outlined, for instance, in R. 164 of the EPC. 11

Article 18
The International Search Report

(1)

The international search report shall be established within the prescribed time limit and in the prescribed form.

R. 42	Time limit three months from receipt of the search copy or nine months from priority	

(2)

The international search report shall, as soon as it has been established, be transmitted by the International Searching Authority to the applicant and the International Bureau.

R. 43	The ISR	
R. 43.1	Identifications	
	R. 43.2	Dates in the ISR
	R. 43.3	Classification
	R. 43.4	Language
	R. 43.5	List of cited prior art documents
	R. 43.6	Technical fields searched
	R. 43.6*bis*	Consideration of rectifications of obvious mistakes
	R. 43.7	Remarks concerning unity of invention
	R. 43.8	Authorized officer
	R. 43.9	Additional matter
	R. 43.10	Form
R. 43*bis*.1	Written opinion of the ISA	
R. 40*bis*	Additional fees in case of missing parts or correct elements and parts included in the PCTa or considered to have been contained in the PCTa under R. 20.5 or 20.5*bis*	

R. 44	Transmittal of the ISR, written opinion, etc.
R. 44*bis*	IPRP by the ISA (IPRP Ch. I)
R. 62*bis*	Translation for the IPEA of the written opinion of the ISA
Art. 152, 153(6) EPC	ISR replaces European search report

(3)

The international search report or the declaration referred to in Article 17(2)(a) shall be translated as provided in the Regulations. The translations shall be prepared by or under the responsibility of the International Bureau.

Art. 17(2)	Non-establishment of the ISR because of subject matter or deficient documents
R. 45	Translation of the ISR into English

Article 19
Amendment of the Claims before the International Bureau

INTRODUCTION

1 Shortly after filing the international application, claims missing from the application may be added if they are completely contained in a claimed priority application (R. 20.5; R. 20.6; see annotations to Art. 11). Adding a missing part could be regarded as a correction instead of an amendment (however, see AG-IP 5.110).

2 The international search will be carried out on the unamended international application, since the first opportunity to amend the claims of the international application is only after the applicant has received the ISR (Art. 19(1)). However, before the search, any formal errors in the international application may already have been corrected under Art. 11(2) and Art. 14(1)(b), and any obvious mistakes rectified under R. 91.

3 The applicant has an opportunity to amend the claims of the international application under Art. 19(1) in response to the ISR. The applicant may file a brief statement (500 words maximum) explaining the claim amendments (Art. 19(1); R. 46.4). In addition, a letter accompanying the replacement sheets must be filed explaining the differences between the replaced sheets and the replacement sheets (R. 46.5; AG-IP 9.005). Amendments to the claims under Art. 19 are not allowed where the ISA has declared under Art. 17(2)(a) that no ISR will be established (AG-IP 9.004).

4 There is a further opportunity to file amendments during the preliminary examination before the IPEA, provided the applicant has filed a demand (Chapter II of PCT). This opportunity allows the applicant to amend the description, claims, and drawings under Art. 34(2)(b). Claim amendments under Art. 34(2)(b) may be in addition to or instead of the amendments under Art. 19(1) (AG-IP 9.011). If filed in time, the preliminary examination will be carried out on the amended international application. See annotations to Art. 34 for further details.

5 Whereas under Art. 19 amendments may be filed only once, in the procedure under Chapter II, Art. 34 amendments may be filed several times. While amendments under Art. 19 must be sent to the International Bureau (Art. 19(1)), amendments under Art. 34 must be sent to the IPEA (Art. 34(2)(a)). Under Art. 19 only claims can be amended but under Art. 34 claims, description, and drawings may be amended.

Amendments under Art. 19 will be published with the international application or thereafter (R. 48.2(f), (h)) with the effect that any preliminary protection will be based on the international application including such amendments.

The preliminary protection might be relevant in view of the national law of certain States and might be a reason to file amendments under Art. 19, even though later another possibility of filing amendments is given (Art. 29; Art. 2; AG-IP 9.011, 9.024). 6

Amendments under Art. 34 will not be published in the sense of Art. 21, R. 48 but are open to file inspection. Amendments under Art. 19 are confidential until publication of the international application (or separate publication of amendments thereafter), while amendments under Art. 34 remain confidential until either inspection of the file of the elected Office under national law becomes possible or inspection of the file of the International Bureau becomes possible after 30 months (see annotations to Art. 30). 7

Most designated Offices allow filing of amendments on entry into the national phase (see, for example, AG-NP(EP.18)). After the international application has entered the national phase, the applicant has an opportunity to amend the international application under Art. 28 and 41 before each designated Office. This opportunity is implemented before the EPO in R. 161 EPC (see annotations to Art. 22). 8

Article 19
Amendment of the Claims before the International Bureau

(1)

The applicant shall, after having received the international search report, be entitled to one opportunity to amend the claims of the international application by filing amendments with the International Bureau within the prescribed time limit. He may, at the same time, file a brief statement, as provided in the Regulations, explaining the amendments and indicating any impact that such amendments might have on the description and the drawings.

R. 11.12	Formal requirements for amendments of the PCTa
R. 12.2	Language of changes in the PCTa
R. 46.1	Time limit: two months from transmittal of ISR to the International Bureau and applicant or 16 months from priority date, whichever time limit expires later
R. 46.3	Language of amendments under Art. 19
R. 48.2(a)(vi)	Publication of the amendments under Art. 19
Art. 28	See the annotations for an overview of amendments in different phases
R. 53.9(a), R. 66.1(c), R. 66.1(d); R. 66.4*bis*	Effect of amendments under Art. 19 in the IPE

PCT Newsletter 11/2023 p. 11	Pract. Adv. referring to submission of amendments in ePCT

9 After receipt of the ISR, the applicant has the possibility to amend the claims of the international application under Art. 19. The applicant may only amend the claims, not the description or drawings. This is notwithstanding the correction of obvious errors according to R. 91.

10 The demand for IPE (Art. 34) must indicate whether an amendment under Art. 19 is to be taken into account for the IPE or considered reversed by an amendment under Art. 34 (R. 53.9(a), R. 66.1(c)). An amendment under Art. 19 filed after the demand will only be taken into account if received before the IPEA begins to draw up the IPER (R. 66.1(d); R. 66.4*bis*).

(2)
The amendments shall not go beyond the disclosure in the international application as filed.

11 While this requirement is not enforceable in the international phase (AG-IP 9.009, 11.047), designated Offices may disregard amendments going beyond the disclosure of the international application as filed (Art. 19(3)).

AG-IP 9.009, 11.047	The filed amendments will not be checked for added matter during Chapter I
Art. 46	Added matter in translation of the PCTa
Art. 28(2)	Added matter before designated Office
Art. 34(2)(b)2	Added matter in amendments during the IPE
Art. 41(2)	Added matter before elected Office

(3)
If the national law of any designated State permits amendments to go beyond the said disclosure, failure to comply with paragraph (2) shall have no consequence in that State.

12 See AG-NP for each State.

Article 20
Communication to Designated Offices

(1)

(a) The international application, together with the international search report (including any indication referred to in Article 17(2)(b)) or the declaration referred to in Article 17(2)(a), shall be communicated to each designated Office, as provided in the Regulations, unless the designated Office waives such requirement in its entirety or in part.

Art. 17(2)(a), (b)	Non-searchable matter, search not possible
R. 47	Transmission to the designated Offices:
R. 45*bis*.8(b)	Transmittal of the SISR as ISR under Art. 20(1), R. 47 by SISA to designated Office
R. 45*bis*.6(e)	Transmittal of request for review and decision concerning lack of unity of invention is transmitted together with the SISR (R. 45*bis*.7)
R. 93bis	Further restriction on transmittal: Transmittal only on request, at a specific time and, where applicable, in electronic form
	The applicant may validly transmit documents under Art. 20(1), (2) to the designated Office even without a representative. Explanations on effective acts of a foreign applicant before the EPO (R. 159 EPC) can be found under Euro-PCT Guide 5.3.006.

A 'First Notice' (Form PCT/IB/308) is issued at the end of 19 months after the priority date, informing the applicant about the designated Office adhering to the 20-month time limit for entry into the national phase to which the PCTa has been transmitted. With the 'Second and Supplementary Notice', the applicant is informed about the designated Office observing the 30-month time limit for national phase entry, to which the PCTa has been sent electronically and for which transmission of the PCTa is not required. In both cases, the applicant does not have to send a copy of the PCTa to these Offices (PCT Newsletter 11/2013, p. 10). Most countries have waived this requirement for transmission (this can be seen, among other things, from Form PCT/IB/308, Second and Supplementary Notice, which is sent from the International Bureau to the applicant in a PCTa 28 months after the priority date). 1

Approximately 17 countries, including CN and EP, have not waived the transmission of the PCTa. These countries are: AZ, BY, CN, EP, KG, KP, KR, MD, MK, MZ, NA, NG, PG, RU, TM. The International Bureau sends them the application electronically in accordance with R. 47 and R. 93*bis*.

(b) The communication shall include the translation (as prescribed) of the said report or declaration.

(2)

If the claims have been amended by virtue of Article 19(1), the communication shall either contain the full text of the claims both as filed and as amended or shall contain the full text of the claims as filed and specify the amendments, and shall include the statement, if any, referred to in Article 19(1).

(3)

At the request of the designated Office or the applicant, the International Searching Authority shall send to the said Office or the applicant, respectively, copies of the documents cited in the international search report, as provided in the Regulations.

R. 44.3	Copies of the documents cited may be requested within seven years of the filing date of the PCTa; copies of the documents cited are of particular interest in the case of non-patent literature
R. 45*bis*.7	Application of R. 45*bis*.7 for SISR

Article 21
International Publication

INTRODUCTION

The International Bureau publishes the application (Art. 21(1)) in a form governed by the AIs, Part 4 (R. 48.1). The publication is only in electronic form (AG-IP 9.015; AIs 406(b)). The international publication contains: 1

- a front page with bibliographic data;
- the abstract and the accompanying figure (R. 48.2(a)(i), (b), (d));
- the description, claims, and drawings, if any (R. 48.2(a)(ii)–(iv));
- if available, the ISR or the declaration under Art. 17(2)(a) that no meaningful search could be made (Art. 21(3); R. 48.2(a)(v); R. 48.2(c));
- any amended claims filed in response to Art. 19(1) (R. 48.2(f));
- any statement explaining amendments to the claims under Art. 19(1) (R. 48.2(a)(vi));
- any not-granted request for the correction of an obvious mistake referred to in R. 91.3(d) (R. 48.2(a)(vii));
- data relating to any deposited biological material furnished under R. 13*bis* separately from the description (R. 48.2(a)(viii));
- any information concerning a priority claim considered defective under R. 26*bis*.2(b)–(d) (R. 48.2(a)(ix));
- any declaration under R. 4.17 relating to the identity of an inventor, inventorship, applicant's entitlement, or non-prejudicial disclosures (R. 48.2(a)(x));
- any information concerning a request under R. 26*bis*.3 for restoration of the right of priority, including the decision of the receiving Office on such a request and information as to the criterion for restoration upon which the decision was based (R. 48.2(a)(xi)).

The applicant may request the International Bureau to omit from the publication matter irrelevant for the invention or which should be kept secret (R. 48.2(l) and (n)). This matter will not be accessible in the files of the International Authorities (R. 94.1(d)). 2

(1)

The International Bureau shall publish international applications.

Art. 153(3) EPC	International publication replaces publication of the European patent application

(2)

(a) Subject to the exceptions provided for in subparagraph (b) and in Article 64(3), the international publication of the international application shall be effected promptly after the expiration of 18 months from the priority date of that application.

3 Publication of the international application and official communications normally takes place on Thursdays when the International Bureau is not closed. In this case, it is recommended to check with the International Bureau (www.wipo.int/export/sites/www/pct/de/seminar/basic_1/document.pdf), p. 154, 155. Early completion of the technical preparation will be announced in due time in the PCT Newsletter.

Art. 64(3)	Waiver of publication	
R. 48	International publication	
	R. 48.1	Form and means of international publication
	R. 48.2	Contents
	R. 48.5	Notification of national publication

4 The technical preparations for publication are completed by the 15th calendar day prior to the date of publication. The date of publication is normally a Thursday; any exception will always be published in advance in the Newsletter. If the date is critical, the applicant is recommended to contact the International Bureau for the exact day of publication or check the publication schedule in ePCT with strong authentication.

5 Any change an applicant wants to be taken into consideration for publication should reach the International Bureau at least one day before the 15-day time limit to allow the International Bureau to process the change, i.e. 16 days before the publication date. If, for example, the application is to be published on Thursday April 16, 2020, then the technical preparations are to be completed on Wednesday April 1, 2020, and any withdrawal or amendment should be received by the International Bureau at the latest at midnight at the end of Tuesday March 31, 2020 (CET). Where an application is exceptionally published on a Friday because the International Bureau is closed on Thursday, the withdrawal or amendment should be received at the latest at midnight at the end of Tuesday, 17 days before the publication date (AG-IP 9.014). Note that the PCT RO Guidelines §337 states in contrast that in such a case the publication may take place on the preceding Wednesday. The exceptions will always be published in the Newsletter beforehand.

The PCTa will not be published if only States have been designated which do not require the publication of the application (Art. 64(3)). As only the US has given a declaration to this effect, this possibility is of minor importance (AG-IP 9.012(iv)). 6

R. 48.6	Announcing of certain facts about withdrawals
R. 17.2(b)	Copy of the priority document may not be published before publication
R. 34.1(b)(ii)	PCTa is prior art from the date of international publication
AIs 801 et seq.	TPOs are possible from the date of international publication until the expiry of 28 months from the priority date via ePCT. After examination of the TPO by the International Bureau, the TPO are published without the cited documents but including a statement by the applicant. See also introduction to Art. 33, AG-IP 11.109 et seq. and PCT EPO Guidelines E-II.

(b) The applicant may ask the International Bureau to publish his international application any time before the expiration of the time limit referred to in subparagraph (a). The International Bureau shall proceed accordingly, as provided in the Regulations.

R. 48.4	Early publication at the applicant's request only after payment of a special publication fee
PCT Newsletter 10/2022, p. 12–14	See practical advice for factors to consider before requesting early publication: the publication can be used as prior art if there are competitors who file an application on a related subject matter. Some national laws calculate royalties for infringements from the earlier publication date. In some States publication is a pre-condition to start national examination. A published PCTa can be cited more readily in advertisements, negotiations, or for attracting investors. The time in which the content is kept secret will be shorter in case of early publication. This may be useful for a competitor. After the decision to request early publication and before the request, procedural issues need to be considered, e.g. whether bibliographical changes under R. 92 should be made, whether physical defects need to be corrected, whether a correction or addition of priority claims under R. 26*bis* is required, or whether references to deposited biological material under R. 13*bis*.4(c) shall be included.

(3)

The international search report or the declaration referred to in Article 17(2)(a) shall be published as prescribed in the Regulations.

Art. 17(2)(a)	Non-searchable subject matter
R. 45	Translation of the ISR

R. 48.2(a)(v)	Publication of the ISR
R. 48.2(g)	If the ISR is not yet available at the time of publication, a separate supplementary publication is made
AIs 404	International publication number of the international application; entered in the European Patent Register under R. 143 EPC (OJ 2014, A86)

7 The ISA establishes the ISR within the prescribed period in the form as set out in R. 43 (Art. 18(1)). Rectifications of obvious mistakes will be taken into account by the ISA (R. 91.1; R. 43.6*bis*). The report relates to the invention first mentioned in the claims and to those inventions for which additional fees have been paid (Art. 17(3)(a)). The report may not contain opinions or explanations (R. 43.9). The ISR is published (Art. 21(3)) in the language in which the application is to be published (Art. 21(4); R. 48.3; see R. 43.4 for exceptions). If the application is not published in English, the ISR, or the declaration that no meaningful search could be made, is translated into English (Art. 18(3); R. 45.1).

8 If the ISR is not yet available at the time of completion of the technical preparations for the publication, for example, due to a request for early publication under Art. 21(2)(b), the publication will so state, and also that the ISR will be published separately (R. 48.2(g); AG-IP 9.015). Where amended claims have been filed, these are included in the publication (R. 48.2(f)), and may therefore be useful for a better definition of the scope of the claims in view of provisional protection in the designated States (Art. 29). The publication also allows the applicant to effect the amendments with a single notification for all designated Offices.

9 If, at the time of completion of the technical preparations, the period for amending the claims under Art. 19 has not yet expired, the publication will so state, and also that any later-filed amendments under Art. 19 will be published (R. 48.2(h)).

(4)

The language and form of the international publication and other details are governed by the Regulations.

R. 48.1	Form and means of international publication
R. 48.3	Language of publication

10 The application is published in the language as filed if that language is a language of publication, i.e. Arabic, Chinese, English, French, German, Japanese, Korean, Portuguese, Russian or Spanish (R. 48.3(a)). English is the most frequently used language of publication; in 2023 42 % of the international applications were published in English (PCT Yearly Review 2024, https://www.wipo.int/edocs/pubdocs/en/wipo-pub-901-2024-en-patent-cooperation-treaty-yearly-review-2024.pdf, p. 75).

(5)

There shall be no international publication if the international application is withdrawn or is considered withdrawn before the technical preparations for publication have been completed.

R. 90*bis*.1(c)	Prevention of publication by withdrawal of the international application
R. 90*bis*.3(d), (e)	Deferment of publication by withdrawal of the earliest priority claim with the consequence of recalculation of time limits (www.wipo.int/export/sites/www/pct/de/seminar/basic_1/document.pdf, p. 158)
R. 48.6(c)	Withdrawal of a designation or priority claim after completion of the technical preparation

An applicant desiring to avoid publication of the international application should not rely on a deemed withdrawal by not paying fees. Some receiving Offices are known not to have followed up on lack of payment with declaring the application to be considered withdrawn, causing the application still to be published. It is best practice to avoid publication by active withdrawal as set out in the introduction to R. 90*bis* (see also Pract. Adv. NL 10/2014 https://www.wipo.int/pct/en/newslett/practical_advice/pa_102014.html). 11

The withdrawal may be made conditional on the international application not being published (PCT RO Guidelines 318 https://www.wipo.int/pct/en/texts/ro/ro314_321.html). 12

According to official practice, the technical preparations for publication are generally completed 15 days in advance (AG-IP 9.014). Earlier completion if the publication date falls on a Thursday on which the International Bureau is not open for official business or if official holidays fall within the 15-day period. In case of doubt, it is recommended to ask the International Bureau for information (www.wipo.int/export/sites/www/pct/de/seminar/basic_1/document.pdf, p. 155). An earlier conclusion of the technical preparation will be announced in good time in the PCT Newsletter. 13

(6)

If the international application contains expressions or drawings which, in the opinion of the International Bureau, are contrary to morality or public order, or if, in its opinion, the international application contains disparaging statements as defined in the Regulations, it may omit such expressions, drawings, and statements, from its publications, indicating the place and number of words or drawings omitted, and furnishing, upon request, individual copies of the passages omitted.

R. 9	Expressions not to be used

14 Expressions or drawings in the international application which, in the opinion of the International Bureau, are contrary to morality or public order or disparaging may be omitted from the publication.

Article 22
Copy, Translation, and Fee, to Designated Offices

INTRODUCTION

1. General Aspects of Entry into National Phase

The international phase of the application is followed by a national phase before each designated Office where the applicant wishes to obtain a national patent for the invention. The procedure in the national phase is governed mainly by national law. The expressions 'international phase' and 'national phase' are not used in the PCT but are convenient expressions for the processing of the international application before International Authorities and before national Offices (AG-IP 3.001 and 3.004). 1

A national Office is called a 'designated Office' if the applicant has designated the Office under Chapter I (Art. 2(xiii)) and enters the national phase with an international preliminary report on patentability under Chapter I (IPRP I), i.e. a written opinion of the ISA. The national Office is called an 'elected Office' if the applicant has elected the Office under Chapter II (Art. 2(xiv)) and enters the national phase with an IPRP II, i.e. an IPER of the IPEA, which is to be taken into account by the national Office. A reference to a designated Office in this book must be construed as a reference also to an elected Office, unless the context indicates differently; for example, a designated Office in the context of Chapter I does not refer to an elected Office. 2

If the designated Office processes the international application under a regional law, such as the EPC, instead of a national law, the national phase is called a regional phase. A reference to national law, national phase, and national Office in this book must be construed as a reference also to regional law, regional phase, and regional Office (Art. 2(x) and 2(xii); AG-IP 3.001). 3

The entry into the national phase requires the applicant to carry out certain acts before each designated Office. These acts are governed by provisions of both the PCT and national law. The following paragraphs outline the PCT provisions for entry into the national phase and indicate where provisions of national law may supplement them. The procedure for entry into the regional phase before the EPO as a designated or elected Office is set out in No. 1.4 below. 4

5 Most requirements for entering the national phase before a designated Office and an elected Office are similar (R. 76.5). Where in the following the same requirements are applicable before both Offices, a reference to the PCT first mentions the provision applicable to a designated Office, followed by the equivalent provision applicable to an elected Office between square brackets, for example, Art. 22 [Art. 39].

6 See also No. 6 'Overview of Procedure' in the Introduction.

1.1 Start of National Phase

1.1.1 Time Limit

7 The start of the national phase, i.e. when a designated Office may start the processing of the international application, is defined in the PCT in a negative manner by stating when processing by the designated Office is not allowed. A designated Office may not process the international application prior to expiry of 30 months from the priority date (Art. 22(1); Art. 23(1) [Art. 39(1)(a); Art. 40(1)]). This is called the 'processing prohibition' for the designated Offices. A designated Office usually starts processing promptly after expiry of the time limit. The applicant need not request the Office to start processing.

8 National law of a designated State may fix a time limit expiring later than 30 months (Art. 22(3); R. 50 [Art. 39(1)(b); R. 77]). Several States, including the EPO, have extended the time limit to 31 months from the priority date. The time limits applicable for entering the national phase under Chapters I and II of the PCT are given in AG-NP for each designated Office; a complete list of time limits is available at the WIPO website (https://www.wipo.int/pct/en/texts/time_limits.html) and in Annex 2 below.

9 The time limit is the same for starting the national phase under Chapter I (i.e. without a demand; Art. 22(1)) and under Chapter II (i.e. with a demand for IPE; Art. 39(1)(a)).

10 For most designated Offices the time limit for entry into the national phase is the same for Chapter I and Chapter II. However, a few national Offices still have, by way of a reservation, different time limits for entering the national phase under Chapter I and under Chapter II. These are: LU, using 20 months, and TZ, using 21 months under Chapter I. Note, however, that an applicant can use the EPO for LU and the ARIPO for TZ, which regional Offices both apply a time limit of 31 months under Chapter I. The time limit under Chapter II is 30 months for LU and 31 months for TZ. (See Introduction to the PCT in this book, No. 6.2.2.)

11 A designated Office may, exceptionally, start processing the international application earlier than expiry of the time limit if the applicant lifts the processing prohibition by filing an express request under Art. 23(2) [Art. 40(2)] with the designated Office. He may do so either voluntarily, for example, to speed up processing of the international application, or involuntarily. The latter case arises where the processing of the international application has been interrupted prematurely, for example, because the application is considered withdrawn, in which case the applicant must enter the national phase early before each designated Office and use the special review and excuse procedure as described in No. 1.6 below in order to safeguard rights.

1.1.2 *Entry into National Phase*

Before expiry of the time limit when national processing may start, the applicant must carry out several acts before each designated Office. These acts are similar to the acts to be carried out for a national application filed with the national Office and which have not yet been carried out in the international phase; they may include the payment of fees and the filing of a translation of the international application. The acts are prescribed by both PCT (see, for example, Art. 22 [Art. 39]) and national law, and are described in more detail in No. 1.2 below. 12

The carrying out of the acts by the applicant before the designated Office is often called 'entry into the national phase', although this phrase does not occur in the PCT. The PCT only mentions acts to be carried out before expiry of a time limit (Art. 22) and start of the processing of the international application before the designated Office after expiry of the time limit (Art. 23; Art. 27(2)). The notion of 'entry into the national phase' could be confusing in suggesting that the international application becomes a national application only on entry. Instead, the international application has the effect of a regular national application in each designated State already from the international filing date according to Art. 11(3), but burdened with a temporal processing prohibition under Art. 23(1). 13

The transition from the international to the national phase can be envisaged as follows. A designated Office is notified of its designation by the International Bureau under R. 47.1(a) after international publication and prepares its own file for the international application. Before expiry of the time limit, the applicant must complete the file by submitting the required documents and paying the necessary fees. The expiry of the time limit lifts the processing prohibition of the designated Office and soon after the expiry the designated Office starts processing the international application by opening the file and checking whether all acts have been completed in due time. 14

If no or not all acts have been completed before expiry of the time limit for national phase entry and entry is still desired, the international phase may be extended by withdrawing a priority claim (www.wipo.int/pct/en/newslett/practical_advice/pa_012003.html). If the only priority claim is withdrawn, the time limit will typically be extended by 12 months. A disadvantage of the withdrawal is the possibility of additional detrimental prior art coming up. Another solution is to enter the national phase late and apply remedies available under national law (see No. 1.5 below). 15

Where the applicant wants to enter the national phase early by filing the express request, the applicant must also complete all acts necessary to start national processing (AG-NP 3.004). If an applicant completes all necessary acts but does not file an express request, the designated Office will only start processing the application after expiry of the time limit (Art. 23(1)). A request for early entry may be filed in respect of a particular national Office while the international phase of the international application continues for the other Offices until expiry of the time limit (PCT News Letter 08/2006, www.wipo.int/pct/en/newslett/practical_advice/pa_082006.html). 16

1.1.3 Acceleration of Prosecution

17 The prosecution of the international application may be accelerated by an early entry into the national phase. Further possibilities to accelerate the prosecution are:

- by requesting the designated Office to accelerate the prosecution according to national rules; or
- by filing a PPH request with the designated Office, provided the prerequisites for a PPH request are fulfilled (see annotation to Art. 16).

18 Acceleration before the EPO as designated Office can be achieved by filing a request for accelerated search and/or a separate request for accelerated examination under the 'PACE program', especially if this is combined with a waiver to receive a communication pursuant to R. 161 and 162 EPC (Euro-PCT 5.1.037–5.1.038). For PCT applications entering the European phase where the EPO did not act as (S)ISA, the EPO strives to issue the supplementary European search report within six months from expiry of the time limit under R. 161(2) (https://www.epo.org/law-practice/legal-texts/html/guidelines/e/e_viii_4_1.htm).

1.2 Acts for Entry into National Phase

19 The entry into the national phase before an Office of a State or acting for a State requires the applicant to carry out the acts set out in Art. 22 [Art. 39(1)] if not already completed and any other acts required by national law.

20 Shortly before the end of the international phase, the International Bureau sends the international application to those designated Offices that so requested (Art. 20(1)(a) [Art. 36(3)(a)]) and informs the applicant accordingly using Form PCT/IB/308 (R. 47.1(c) [R 61.3]; R. 93*bis*.1). Although it is the purpose of the form to notify the applicant that no copy of the international application is required to be furnished to the designated Offices, this communication contains in fact a reminder of the upcoming 30-month time limit (PCT News 11/2013, Practical Advice). The applicant has to monitor the time limit because normally the designated Offices do not warn the applicant. Only some designated Offices, for example, the EPO, send the applicant a reminder before expiry of the time limit for entering the national phase (see AG-NP 3.003). The acts to be carried out by the applicant are described in the following sections. (See AG-IP 5.099-5.104 for the furnishing of sequence listings.)

21 Failure to comply with the requirements of Art. 22 [Art. 39(1)] for any designated State in due time will result in the international application losing the effect of a regular national application in that State; failure to meet the time limit has the same consequences as the withdrawal of a national application in that State (Art. 24(1)(iii) [Art. 39(2)]). The designated Office may invite the applicant to remedy the failure using any available national provisions (Art. 24(2) [Art. 39(3)]; see, for example, R. 160 EPC; No. 1.5 below).

1.2.1 *Start of Processing in National Phase*

Some designated Offices require an explicit request from the applicant to start processing the international application after expiry of the time limit. 22

Other Offices, for example, the EPO, regard the notification of its designation or election by the International Bureau under R. 47.1 [R 61.2] and the receipt of a copy of the international application sent by the International Bureau under Art. 20(1) as a sufficient basis to start the national phase immediately after expiry of the time limit of Art. 22 [Art. 39(1)] without a request by the applicant. 23

The EPO has specific requirements for the entry into the European phase of a PCT application (see EPO Entry into the European phase (https://www.epo.org/en/applying/international/entry-european-phase)). These requirements include the submission of a translation of the international application (if not already in one of the EPO's official languages), specification of the application documents on which the European grant procedure is to be based, payment of the filing fee and any additional fees, and payment of the designation fee, search fee (if applicable), examination fee, and the third year renewal fee if it has fallen due before the expiry of the 31-month period. These steps must be completed within 31 months from the priority date of the application. It is important to note that the EPO does not start processing the application in the European phase before the expiry of the 31-month period. If an applicant wishes for the EPO to start processing their application earlier, an explicit request for early processing must be made. This request can be filed by selecting the relevant checkbox in EPO Form 1200, provided that the relevant steps have been completed (GL Exam E-IX, 2.1). Therefore, even though the EPO considers the notification of its designation or election by the International Bureau under R. 47.1 and the receipt of a copy of the international application as a basis for the national phase, the processing of the application only starts after the expiry of the 31-month period or upon an explicit early processing request by the applicant, assuming all necessary steps and payments have been made. 24

Comparing the practice at the EPO and at the German Patent and Trade Mark Office (DPMA), which might not require a fee for entering the national phase if the DPMA was the receiving Office (AG-NP Annex DE.I Fees), it is evident that the EPO's procedures are distinct in requiring both the completion of procedural steps and payment of fees for the national phase to commence. This distinction underlines the importance of understanding specific Office requirements for the national phase entry of a PCT application. 25

1.2.2 *Form for National Phase Entry*

Most national Offices provide a special form for entry into the national phase before that Office. Offices that do not start the national phase automatically may include in the form a possibility to request the start of the processing. The form typically includes a check list for the acts to be performed and its use is recommended but never compulsory (R. 49.4 [R 76.5]). The EPO provides Form 1200. 26

1.2.3 *Kind of Protection*

27 On filing an international application, the PCT request form indicates by default that the applicant desires protection for all kinds of protection available (patent, utility model, etc.) (R. 4.9(a)(ii)).

28 Upon entry into the national phase, the applicant must indicate for each designated State which kind(s) of protection he desires if this is different from a patent (R. 49*bis*.1(a), (b) [R 76.5]). This indication is also required for protection in the form of a continuation or continuation-in-part of an earlier application; the relevant earlier application must also be indicated (R. 49*bis*.1(d) [R 76.5]). Some designated Offices allow filing the indications at a later time (AP-NP 4.029).

29 If upon filing an international application, an applicant intends to make such an indication under R. 49*bis*.1, the request must so indicate (R. 4.11). Information on the kind of protection available in each State via the PCT can be found in AG-IP Annex B (https://www.wipo.int/pct/en/guide/index.html) and in the overview on the WIPO site (www.wipo.int/export/sites/www/pct/en/texts/pdf/typesprotection.pdf).

1.2.4 *Transmission of Copy of International Application*

30 The International Bureau communicates a copy of the international application to each designated Office (Art. 20(1)(a); R. 47.1(a)) promptly after expiry of 28 months from the priority date (AG-IP 9.028).

31 The International Bureau includes the search report with any prescribed translations in the communication (Art. 20(1)(b)). For international applications in respect of which no demand has been filed, the International Bureau will additionally include the IPRP I, which has the same content as the written opinion established by the ISA (R. 44*bis*.1(a)).

32 Any amendments of the claims under Art. 19 and the brief statement (Art. 19(1); R. 46.4) explaining the amendments are regarded as part of the international application for the purpose of Art. 22 (R. 49.3) and are also included in the communication under Art. 20(2).

33 Where an IPE has been carried out, the International Bureau communicates the IPRP II, together with any translation as prescribed, with its annexes in the original language, to each elected Office (Art. 36(3)(a)). The annexes include replacement sheets showing corrections and amendments under Art. 19 and/or Art. 34 and any letters (R. 46.5(b); R. 66.8(a), (b)) explaining such (R. 70.16). Amendments under Art. 19 considered reversed by amendments under Art. 34 are not annexed unless the IPEA considers that the relevant amendment goes beyond the disclosure of the international application as filed (R. 70.16).

34 According to Art. 22(1) [Art. 39(1)(a)], the applicant must furnish a copy of the international application, unless already provided by the International Bureau (Art. 20; R. 47.1(a)), within the time limit for entering the national phase. Under normal circumstances, no designated Office requires a copy of the international application

to be submitted by the applicant (AG-NP 4.027). Most States require the International Bureau to communicate the international application under Art. 20; R. 47.1(a).

Where this communication has not or could not yet have taken place, the designated Office has two options. The first option, applied by the Offices of a few States, is to request the applicant to provide a copy of the international application under R. 47.1(c). This often happens when entering the national phase early. The second option, applied by most Offices (including the EPO), is to use the exception to Art. 22(1) [Art. 39(1)(a)] as provided in R. 49.1(a-*bis*) [R 76.5] and never request the applicant to furnish a copy of the international application; instead, the International Bureau will later provide the copy (R. 93*bis*.1(a)). The Offices of some States request the applicant to provide a copy of the international application only where it was filed in the official language of that State. The option chosen by each designated Office is indicated in AG-NP Annex (search for 'copy of the international application' in the Annex for a specific designated Office). 35

1.2.5 Translation of International Application

A designated Office may require a translation of the international application if the language in which it was filed or published is not a language accepted by the Office (Art. 22(1); AG-NP 4.008 (https://www.wipo.int/pct/en/guide/np04.html#_4.008); R. 49.2 [R 76.5]). AG-NP Annex indicates the accepted languages for each designated Office. Where more than one language is accepted, the applicant may choose the language of the translation (R. 49.2 [R 76.5]). The translation must be furnished within the time limit for entering the national phase (Art. 22(1) [Art. 39(1)(a)]). Some States allow furnishing the translation at a later time (see Art. 22(3) and AG-NP Annex for each State). 36

The translation must contain the description, the claims, any text matter in the drawings, and the abstract (R. 49.5(a) [R 76.5]; AG-NP 4.010). If the claims are amended under Art. 19, a designated or elected Office may also require a translation of both the claims as filed and as amended (for the complete set of claims) and the request (R. 49.5(a), (b) [R 76.5]). The statement explaining amendments under Art. 19 should also be translated; any Office may disregard the statement if not translated (R. 49.3; R. 49.5(c) [R 76.5]). The EPO as designated or elected Office disregards claim amendments under Art. 19 for which a translation is not furnished in due time (PCT Gazette 2019, p. 27). Where an IPRP II has been established, a translation of an amendment under Art. 19 will only be required if that amendment is annexed to the IPRP II (R. 76.5(iv)). 37

An elected Office may require the applicant to translate any replacement sheet annexed to the report and transmit it to the elected Office (R. 74.1). 38

The content of the translation as required by each designated Office is indicated in the AG-NP Annex. The physical requirements for the translation are stated in R. 49.5 [R 76.5]. National law may determine the number of copies to be furnished of any translation (R. 51*bis*.1(c), [R 76.5]) and the certification or verification of the translations (R. 51*bis*.1(d), 2(b) [R 76.5]). Information for special requirements under national law is available in AG-NP. 39

40 All designated Offices allow the correction of translation errors (AG-NP 6.002). Where a translation error has caused the scope of a granted patent to exceed the scope of the international application in its original language, the Office concerned may retroactively limit the scope of the patent (Art. 46).

1.2.6 Payment of Fees

41 The applicant must pay the national fee (if any) to each designated Office within the time limit for entering the national phase (Art. 22(1); R. 49.1(a)(ii) [Art. 39(1)(a); R. 76.5]). The national fee comprises in general several fees. The currency, the amount of the national fee, and any reductions are indicated in AG-NP Annex for each designated Office.

42 Designated Offices may require that an annual fee be paid to maintain the international application; the fee is usually called (patent) annuity or renewal fee. The national rules governing patent annuities differ from one designated Office to another designated Office. If an annuity falls due before expiry of the time limit of Art. 22 [Art. 39(1)], a designated Office may not require payment on the due date because of the processing prohibition of Art. 23(1). Such an annuity must normally be paid before expiry of the time limit for national entry. The national rules governing patent annuities of each designated Office, stating the amounts, when they fall due, and the provision on entry are given in AG-NP Annex.

43 Many designated Offices charge a claims fee if the number of claims exceeds a certain number on entry into the national phase. Some Offices determine the amount of the fee only after the applicant has had an opportunity to amend the application in the national phase. The conditions are given in AG-NP Annex for each designated Office.

1.2.7 Naming of Inventor

44 Where national law requires the indication of the name and address of the inventor(s) but allows this data to be furnished after the filing of the PCTa, the applicant must furnish the data upon entry into the national phase (Art. 22(1) [Art. 39(1)(a)]). Designated Offices may require more information in the national phase about items that are mentioned in the PCT, such as identity, entitlement or evidence (Art. 27(1), (2); R. 51*bis*; AG-NP 5.001, 4.001(iv), 4.030–4.031 and AG-NP Annex for each Office).

1.2.8 Priority Documents

45 A certified copy of the priority document must be filed in the international phase with the receiving Office or the International Bureau for each valid priority claim (see annotations to Art. 8) (unless made accessible electronically to the receiving Office or International Bureau via the DAS program). The International Bureau will forward copies of the priority document to each designated Office at its request; a designated Office may not require an applicant who has duly filed a certified copy of the priority document in the international phase to furnish such a copy in the national

phase (R. 17.2(a)). A designated Office may only request a simple photocopy of the original priority document and its certificate of filing (AP-NP 5.009).

A designated Office may request the applicant to furnish a translation of the priority document after expiration of the time limit of Art. 22 (R. 17.2(a)) [Art. 39(1) (R. 76.4)]. See AG-NP Annex when each designated Office requires a translation of the priority document. A designated Office may only request such a translation where the validity of the priority claim is relevant for the patentability of the invention (R. 51*bis*.1(e)(i)), or where the international filing data has been accorded on the basis of an incorporation by reference (R. 51*bis*.1(e)(ii)). 46

1.2.9 Amendment and Correction before Designated Office

The PCT requires that any designated Office give the applicant at least one opportunity to amend the description, claims, and drawings in accordance with national law and within a time limit set by the national Office (Art. 28(1), (3) [Art. 41(1), (3)]). The PCT prescribes a time limit of at least one month after entry into the national phase (R. 52). National law may extend the time limit for filing amendments (R. 52.1(b) [R 78.1(b)]). The time limit may be extended if the International Bureau was late in transmitting the international application and search report under Art. 20 (R. 52) or the IPRP II under Art. 36 (R. 78) to the designated Office. 47

The applicant may file different amendments for different designated Offices; the amendments may not go beyond the disclosure in the international application as filed, unless the national law of the designated State permits them to go beyond the original disclosure (Art. 28(2) [Art. 41(2)]). The requirements of each designated Office for amendments are set out in AG-NP Annex. 48

The correction of an obvious mistake under R. 91 may be presented as an amendment under Art. 28 [Art. 41], even if the authorization of the rectification has been refused during the international phase and the applicant has made a request for publication of the request for correction under R. 91.3(d) (AG-NP 6.014–6.017). A designated Office need not take a correction into account if it has already started the processing or examination of the international application when it receives the authorization (R. 91.3(e)). 49

1.2.10 Unity of Invention

Unity of invention is a requirement for the international application, which is checked in the international phase (Art. 17(3) [Art. 34(3)]) and normally checked again in the national phase. Designated Offices may require the applicant to restrict the claims, to divide the application or to pay extra fees in order to maintain parts of the international application according to national law. Information on the procedure and the restriction requirements can be found in the AG-NP Annex. The procedure before the EPO is set out in No. 1.4.3 below. 50

1.2.11 Representation

51 Once processing of an international application has started in a designated Office, the Office may apply national law for any requirement that the applicant be represented by an agent having the right to represent applicants before the Office and/or that the applicant have an address in the designated State for receiving notifications (Art. 27(7); R. 51*bis*.1(b) [R 76.5]). Most Offices require representation for applicants that have neither their residence nor place of business in the territory of the State (AG-NP 5.006). Since a national Office cannot start processing before expiry of the time limit for national phase entry (Art. 23(1)), acts carried out before any designated Office before the expiry do not require an agent (see, for example, Euro-PCT Guide 5.3.008). Hence, entry into the national phase can be carried out without a local representative, while processing and prosecution does require a local representative.

1.3 Procedure before Designated or Elected Office

52 Each designated Office, not being a registration Office, will start the processing of the application with a search. If the quality of the ISR is deemed sufficient, there will be no additional or supplementary search in the national phase. A designated Office will usually regard the ISR only as sufficient if it has drafted the report itself as ISA in the international phase. The supplementary search usually focusses on prior art in the local language of the designated Office.

53 Subsequently, the designated Office will carry out a substantive examination of the application, which may result in the grant of a patent. A designated Office will also use the IPRP I as prepared by the ISA. An elected Office will examine the application using the IPRP II as prepared by the IPEA as a basis, thereby reducing the cost and duration of the examination – in theory. In practice, this will be true for some Offices but certainly not for the USPTO. The USPTO basically ignores the IPRP (Chapter I or II) and carries out its own search and examination, unless the USPTO acted as ISA or IPEA.

54 An elected Office may not require that the applicant furnish papers connected with the examination of the same international application in any other elected Office (Art. 42). In other words, if an international application has been preliminarily examined under Chapter II, the elected Offices may not ask the applicant to provide a so-called 'information disclosure statement' informing them about search results from other elected Offices. The rationale is that the Offices should exchange this information among themselves, alleviating the applicant from this burden (see Records of the Washington Diplomatic Conference on the Patent Cooperation Treaty, Notes on Article 42, sole paragraph, p. 52 (https://www.wipo.int/export/sites/www/pct/en/texts/pdf/washington.pdf). This basic idea, signed in Washington back in 1970, is implemented by the Common Citation Document (CCD), set up in November 2011. The CCD is a publicly accessible database listing all prior art documents found by any of the participating Offices for a particular member of a patent family. (https://www.trilateral.net/citation).

Despite the existence of the CCD, some Offices still contravene Art. 42 (namely GB, IL, IN, and US) and instead of asking other Offices to furnish documents or to retrieve them from the CCD, they oblige the applicant to furnish these documents. 55

1.4 EPO as Designated or Elected Office

The EPO will act as a designated Office within the meaning of Art. 2(xiii) PCT for those States for which both the EPC and the PCT is in force and which have been validly designated in the international application for a European patent (Art. 153(1)(a) EPC; Preamble to the EPC). The EPO will act as an elected Office within the meaning of Art. 2(xiv) PCT if the applicant has elected any of the said States which are bound by Chapter II (Art. 153(1)(b) EPC). All EPC Contracting States are PCT Contracting States (www.epo.org/about-us/foundation/member-states.html and www.wipo.int/pct/en/texts/reg_des.html) and all PCT Contracting States are bound by PCT Chapter II (www.wipo.int/pct/en/pct_contracting_states.html, Footnote 1 in the list of PCT Contracting States). 56

An international application for which the EPO is a designated or elected Office and which has been accorded an international filing date is equivalent to a regular European application and is called a Euro-PCT application (Art. 11(3) and (4) PCT; Art. 153(2) EPC). A Euro-PCT application will be treated as prior art according to Art. 54(3) EPC, i.e. as a European prior right, if the requirements for publication in Art. 153(3) and (4) EPC have been complied with and the filing fee has been paid (Art. 153(5) EPC and R. 165 EPC). 57

The procedure and requirements to which the EPO as designated or elected Office subjects the international application are governed by the EPC, except where the PCT provides otherwise (Art. 150(2) EPC; Art. 27 PCT). 58

1.4.1 Entry into Regional Phase before EPO

An overview of important procedural steps before the EPO as designated Office and as elected Office is given on the EPO website (https://www.epo.org/en/applying/international/entry-european-phase). 59

The EPC has made use of the facility of Art. 22(3) [Art. 39(1)(b)] and has fixed in R. 159(1) EPC the time limit for entering the regional phase before the EPO to 31 months from priority, both where the EPO acts as designated Office and where the EPO acts as elected Office. The 31-month time limit is an EPC time limit and should therefore be calculated according to R. 131(4) EPC. 60

The applicant must perform the following acts to enter the regional phase before the EPO (R. 159 EPC), preferably using Form 1200 – or its electronic equivalent: 61

1. supply, where applicable, a translation of the international application (R. 159(1)(a) EPC);
2. indicate the documents to be used as basis for the grant procedure (R. 159(1)(b) EPC);

3. pay the filing fee including, where applicable, the additional fee if the international application comprises more than 35 pages (R. 159(1)(c); Rfees2(1)1a);
4. pay the designation fee if the time limit of R. 39 EPC has already expired (R. 159(1)(d) EPC), pay where applicable the fee for extension or validation in non-EPC Contracting States;
5. pay the search fee in respect of the supplementary European search, if required (R. 159(1)(e) EPC);
6. pay, where applicable, the claims fees (R. 162(1) EPC);
7. file the request for examination if the time limit of R. 70(1) EPC has already expired (R. 159(1)(f) EPC);
8. pay any renewal fee already fallen due (R. 159(1)(g) EPC);
9. file, where applicable, the certificate of exhibition (R. 159(1)(h) EPC);
10. provide the data concerning the inventor, if not yet submitted (R. 163(1) EPC);
11. where priority is claimed, furnish the number and a copy of the priority application, if not yet submitted (R. 163(2) EPC);
12. where applicable, file a sequence listing conforming to the prescribed standard, if not yet submitted (R. 163(3) EPC);
13. provide indications of address, nationality, or residence or principal place of business of the applicant, if not already provided (R. 163(4) EPC);
14. appoint a professional representative if required under Art. 133(2) (R. 163(5) EPC).

62 If the requirements of items 1, 3, 4, 5 or 7 in the above list are not performed within 31 months, the Euro-PCT application is deemed to be withdrawn (R. 160(1) EPC). Item 4 requires that on the international filing date the desired State is a member of EPC or the extension/validation agreement applies, otherwise entry in the national phase of that State is necessary (Euro-PCT Guide 5.1.009, 5.8.004, 5.8.015; see also Introduction to the PCT in this book, No. 4.2).

63 If the requirements of items 10, 13 or 14 in the above list are not corrected in due time, the European patent application will be refused.

64 If the deficiency of item 11 in the above list is not corrected in due time, the right of priority will be lost for the European patent application.

65 Failure to comply with the Rules mentioned in items 2, 6, 8, 9 and 12 does not directly result in a loss of rights because R. 160(1) EPC does not refer to these items. Either the Office does not require the information, the payments are not applicable, or the applicant will be invited to comply at a later stage (Euro-PCT Guide 5). There is a grace period for the renewal fee (R. 51(2) EPC).

66 The EPO is prohibited from starting the processing of an international application before expiry of the 31-month time limit, unless the applicant expressly requested to start earlier (Art. 23(1) and (2); Art. 40(1) and (2) PCT). A request for early processing may be filed with the EPO at any time before expiry of the 31-month time limit. The EPO will start processing if the applicant both files an express request and complies with the requirements stipulated in R. 159(1) EPC as if the 31-month time limit in that Rule expired on the date early processing is requested (Euro-PCT Guide 5.1.023).

This means that the applicant must comply at least with items 1, 2, 3, and 5 of the above list. Which further requirements of R. 159(1) EPC must be complied with depends on the date on which early processing is requested, since the (regular) time limits for paying the designation fee (R. 39(1) EPC), the renewal fee (R. 51(1) EPC), and for filing the request for examination and paying the examination fee (R. 70(1) EPC) may not yet have expired on the date the request for early processing is filed (see OJ EPO 2013 p.156; Euro-PCT Guide 5.1.024; GL Exam EPO E-IX, 2.8 and R. 159(1) EPC). 67

Entry into the European phase may be carried out by filing on paper using Form 1200 or by using EPO Online Filing (OLF), EPO Filing 2.0 or the EPO Web-Form Filing service (Euro-PCT Guide 5.1.016, 5.1.017 https://www.epo.org/applying/international/guide-for-applicants/html/e/ga_c5_1_6.html; online filing web page https://www.epo.org/applying/online-services/online-filing.html). 68

1.4.2 Procedure before EPO

The EPO has not waived the communication of the international application from the International Bureau to the EPO under Art. 20(1)(a), R. 47.1. Therefore, the International Bureau will communicate a copy of the international application to the EPO as designated Office. The applicant, thus, does not need to furnish a copy of the international application mentioned in Art. 22(1) (R. 49.1(a-*bis*) [R 76.5]; GL Exam EPO E-IX, 2.7). 69

The EPO has made use of the facility of Art. 27(7), R. 51*bis*.1(b) PCT. Hence, if not already complied with upon entry into the regional phase before the EPO, the EPO will invite an applicant having residence and principal place of business outside the territory of an EPC Contracting State to appoint a representative having the right to practice before the EPO (Art. 133(2) EPC via Art. 150(2) EPC; R. 163(5) EPC). Acts performed without representation where representation is mandatory are deemed not to have taken place and may normally be remedied by requesting further processing (Art. 163; Art. 121 EPC). A non-resident applicant may also carry out any act himself before expiry of the time limit for entry into the regional phase to comply with the requirements of R. 159 EPC. The only act a non-resident applicant may carry out without representation during the regional phase is to pay fees (Euro-PCT Guide 5.3.010). It should be noted that an agent appointed in the international phase is not automatically appointed for the national/regional phase of an international application (Euro-PCT Guide 2.11.020). 70

Where the EPO has acted as ISA, the search examiner will also be the primary examiner of the examining division in the regional phase before the EPO. Hence, a positive IPRP often causes the European patent to be granted rapidly (AG-IP 10.083). However, as the search examiner in the PCT phase is a single person, while grant of a European patent requires the consent of an examining division consisting of three people, an examiner may change his opinion during the regional phase before the EPO. 71

The EPO withdrew all but one (R. 66.1*bis*(b), recognition of written opinions by other ISAs) of its reservations under the PCT when the EPC 2000 entered into force (December 13, 2007), including the reservation under PCT R. 49.6 (reinstatement 72 after expiry of the time limit for entry into the regional phase). The latter withdrawal results in the somewhat strange situation in that reinstatement (or re-establishment) of rights may be requested for payment of the filing fee and filing of a translation of the international application (RFees 2(1)13, fee for reinstatement, referring to PCT R. 49.6(d)(i)). This does not concord with R. 136(3) EPC, where re-establishment for these acts is ruled out because further processing is available. This is an example where the provisions of the PCT (R. 49.6) prevail over those of the EPC (R. 136(3)), laid down in Art. 150(2) EPC, last sentence, (Euro-PCT 5.7.013–5.7.016).

1.4.3 Unity of Invention on Entry into European Phase

73 Unity of invention is a requirement that will be examined both in the international and in the national phase. The EPO as designated Office examines the unity of the claims pending after the applicant has had the opportunity to amend them under R. 161 EPC. If the EPO considers the claims non-unitary, it will invite the applicant to pay further search fees for claimed inventions the EPO has not searched in the international phase. If the applicant does not pay further search fees, the examining division will request him to delete the unsearched claims. If several non-unitary inventions have been searched, the EPO will invite the applicant to restrict the application to a single invention searched by the EPO for prosecution. Inventions thus excised may be pursued in a divisional application (R. 164 EPC; Euro-PCT Guide 5.15.006).

1.5 Loss of Effect in Designated States

74 If an applicant does not perform the acts stated in Art. 22 for entry into the national phase before a designated Office in due time, i.e. furnish where required a copy of the international application and a translation, pay any national fee, and furnish any prescribed data, the international application will lose the effect of a national application in respect of that Office (Art. 24(1)(iii) [Art. 39(2)]). Non-performance of the required acts will terminate the procedure before that Office automatically (AG-NP 4.003). The termination will not affect the procedure before other Offices (AG-NP 4.003).

75 A designated Office may not reject an international application on the ground of non-compliance with the requirements of the PCT without first giving the applicant an opportunity to correct the application to the extent and according to the procedure provided by national law (Art. 26). The correction possibilities for the different acts upon entering the national phase are set out in AG-NP Annex for each designated Office. For the EPO see also Euro-PCT Guide 5.4–5.13.

76 Where entry into the national phase before a designated Office has failed because the international application or the designation is deemed withdrawn in the international phase (Art. 24(1)(ii)), the applicant may ask that Office to excuse the delay and maintain the effect of the international application (Art. 24(1)(iii) and Art. 24(2)). The review and excuse procedure is set out below.

1.6 *Review and Excuse Procedure*

The international phase will be terminated prematurely if the international application is regarded as withdrawn or is refused. The International Authorities lose their competence to continue processing the application, and the procedures in Art. 22 and Art. 39 for entry into the national phase of a pending international application are no longer applicable. There are no means of redress or appeal in the international phase, on the one hand because there is no time for it in the tight PCT schedule, and on the other hand because the different States could not agree on this issue (EPO Board of Appeal decisions J20/89 and J15/91). 77

However, the PCT contains provisions that a loss of rights incurred by the applicant in the international phase may be remedied in the national phase before each of the designated Offices in which the applicant wishes his rights to be maintained. The remedy is available for both an erroneous determination of a loss of rights, i.e. where the loss of rights was not justified under the provisions of the PCT, and a correct determination, for example, a loss of rights due to a missed time limit. To make use of the remedy, the applicant must terminate the international phase early by entering the national phase before the desired Offices immediately after the loss of rights has occurred. The designated Offices will review whether the decision causing the loss of rights was justified and/or apply an excuse under national law. The early national entry deprives the applicant of his right to postpone payment of the national fees and filing of the translation until 30 months from the priority date. 78

1.6.1 *Erroneous Determinations*

The first type of negative determinations of an International Authority are erroneous determinations of the receiving Office or the International Bureau, refusing the international application or regarding the international application as withdrawn. The applicant may remedy the loss of rights by entering the national phase before each designated Office where he desires to continue prosecution (Art. 25(1) and (2)) and request a review of the negative determination. Details of the procedure are given in No. 1.6.3 below. Each designated Office reviews the negative determination and, if it decides that the determination is due to an error or omission of the receiving Office or the International Bureau, the designated Office must treat the international application as if the error or omission had not occurred (AG-NP 6.018–6.021). 79

The following cases are liable to a review: 80

- The receiving Office does not accord an international filing date because the international application does not meet the requirements of Art. 11(1) and the applicant has not duly corrected the deficiencies after an invitation to do so (Art. 11(2)(a), R. 20.4). The negative decision with reasons is sent to the applicant and the International Bureau (R. 20.4(i)–(ii)).
- The receiving Office considers the international application withdrawn because certain defects have been found in the application (Art. 14(1)(a)) and the applicant has not duly corrected them after an invitation (Art. 14(1)(b)), or because certain fees (Art. 3(4)(iv) and Art. 4(2)) have not been paid

in time (Art. 14(3)), or because the receiving Office has discovered that an international filing date has been accorded in spite of non-compliance with one of the requirements of Art. 11(1) (Art. 14(4); R. 27.1; R. 29.1).

- The International Bureau may consider the application withdrawn because it has not received the record copy of the application in time (Art. 12(3); R. 22.3; R. 24.2(c)). R. 22.1(d) and (e) give the applicant the opportunity to send a copy of the application to the receiving Office, to be certified and passed on to the International Bureau in case the receiving Office is slow in transmitting such.

1.6.2 Correct Determinations

81 The second type of negative determinations are correct determinations of an International Authority, refusing the international application or regarding the international application as withdrawn. These determinations are often caused by an error of the applicant, such as failure to meet a PCT time limit. The applicant may remedy the loss of rights by entering the national phase before each designated Office where he desires to continue prosecution (Art. 25(1) and (2)) and request an excuse of the error. A designated Office may remedy such losses of rights under Art. 24(2). Where the loss of rights relates to non-observance of a time limit caused by an interruption in the mail service or an unavoidable loss or delay in the mail, a designated Office must excuse any delay in meeting the time limit if it would excuse such a delay under its national law. A designated Office may also excuse any such delay for other reasons (Art. 48(2)).

82 R 82*bis*.1 states that time limits fixed in the PCT and fixed by an Office are liable to excuse. In particular, R. 82*bis*.2 mentions 'further processing' and '*restitutio in integrum*' (or re-establishment of rights) as means of excuse under national law. Details about available remedies for each designated Office are given in the AG-NP Annex.

83 R 49.6 obliges all States to apply on request reinstatement of rights for failure to meet the time limit for entry into the national phase (also see Art. 3(1)(b)(i) PLT). This is not binding for those States that declared incompatibility with their national law (see list of states under R. 49.6(f) or www.wipo.int/pct/en/texts/reservations/res_incomp.html).

1.6.3 Procedure before National Office

84 An applicant may remedy in the national phase a loss of rights that occurred in the international phase by entering the national phase early for each designated Office before which he wishes to continue prosecution of the application. Art. 25 provides the legal basis for the early national entry in the case of a review by a designated Office. However, Art. 24(2) on excuse does not contain provisions on how to effect the excuse. A generally accepted solution is to regard the procedure for obligatory early national entry in Art. 25 as applying both to review of an erroneous determination (Art. 25) and to excuse in case of a correct determination (Art. 24(2)). Both cases require entry into the national phase under Art. 25(1) and (2).

Thereto, the applicant must request the International Bureau to send copies of the documents in the file which are necessary for reviewing the determination to any of the designated Offices named by the applicant (Art. 25(1)(a)). The request must be filed within two months from the date of the notification of the negative determination (Art. 25(1)(c) and R. 51.1), i.e. not the date the notification was received but was dispatched (see R. 80.6). Within the same two months (R. 51.3) the applicant must enter the national phase early before each designated Office by filing an express request to start processing (Art. 23(2)), paying the national fee and providing any translation as prescribed (Art. 25(2)(a)), and complying with any further national requirements for entry. The applicant must file with the designated Office, where appropriate, a request to review the negative determination and a request to excuse an error of the applicant (AG-NP 6.026). 85

Where only a request for excuse is filed, the time limit for national entry is not the two months of R. 51.1 and 51.3 but is fixed in national law for the excuse applied. 86

The review of a correct determination of a failure to meet a PCT time limit will often result in a decision confirming the loss of rights. Nevertheless, where the applicant has also filed a request to excuse, the designated Office must under Art. 48(2)(a) excuse the delay in meeting a time limit for reasons admitted under its national law. A designated Office may also excuse the delay for other reasons (Art. 48(2)(b)). Therefore, a request for review of an erroneous determination is preferably accompanied by a request for an excuse in case the designated Office decides that the determination was correct. 87

1.6.4 Review of Erroneous Determinations by EPO as Designated Office

The time limit for entry into the regional phase before the EPO for a review under Art. 25 PCT is two months from the date of the communication of loss of rights, as fixed in R. 51.1 and 51.3. The time limit for entry into the regional phase before the EPO for an excuse under Art. 24(2) PCT is, however, determined by the remedy applied under national law, i.e. further processing or re-establishment (Euro-PCT Guide 5.14.004). Where both review and excuse are requested, the shortest time limit must be used for national entry. 88

If the examining division of the EPO decides (see R. 159(2) EPC) that the loss of rights was not justified under the PCT and was due to an error or omission of the receiving Office or the International Bureau, it will treat the application as if the error or omission had not occurred (Art. 25(2)(a) PCT). The application will be regarded as a valid European application for the States for which the EPO acts as designated Office. If the examining division decides that the contested determination was correct, the loss of rights will not be reversed. Such a decision can be appealed according to Art. 106(1) EPC. However, it is usually preferable to request not only a review but also an excuse. The requested excuse may allow the EPO to revive the application as set out in No. 1.6.5 (Euro-PCT Guide 5.14.004). 89

1.6.5 *Excuse Following Correct Determination by EPO as Designated Office*

90 The EPO is bound by Art. 48(2)(a) to excuse failures under the PCT in a way similar to failures under the EPC. The EPO will therefore excuse a delay in meeting a time limit in the international phase if a corresponding delay in respect of a European patent application can be remedied, for example, using further processing or re-establishment under Art. 24(2). If the EPO excuses the delay, it will deal with the international application as a valid Euro-PCT application. If the EPO does not accept the remedy, the applicant may appeal the decision (Euro-PCT Guide 5.14.004).

91 Further processing under Art. 121 EPC should be available to remedy a failure to meet the two-month time limit of R. 51.1 PCT (and other non-excluded time limits set in the PCT), instead of the less-reliable re-establishment of rights provisions (Art. 122 EPC). Therefore, if a failed time limit has been fixed in the PCT or by an International Authority (R. 82*bis*.1(i), (ii)), the applicant should request further processing before the EPO (Art. 121 EPC) to retract the legal consequences of the failure. He must file with the EPO the request to uphold the application (Art. 24(2)), pay the fee for further processing, complete the omitted act, and enter the regional phase within two months from the date of the communication informing the applicant of the withdrawal of the international application. The start of the two-month time limit is determined by R. 80.6 PCT, and the time limit is extended on, for example, weekends, according to R. 134 EPC.

92 A failure to meet the two-month time limit for filing the request for further processing under Art. 121, R. 135(1) EPC and R. 51.1 PCT may be excused under Art. 48(2)(a) PCT using re-establishment of rights. If an applicant only becomes aware of the withdrawal of the international application after expiry of the two-month time limit, he must request within the time limit set by R. 136 EPC re-establishment into the right for further processing and also request further processing. Art. 48(2)(a) PCT excludes re-establishment in cases similar to the ones excluded for re-establishment in Art. 122(4) and R. 136(3) EPC.

93 For a review of the decision on the restoration of the right of priority taken in the international phase see R. 49*ter*.

Article 22
Copy, Translation, and Fee, to Designated Offices

(1)

The applicant shall furnish a copy of the international application (unless the communication provided for in Article 20 has already taken place) and a translation thereof (as prescribed), and pay the national fee (if any), to each designated Office not later than at the expiration or 30 months from the priority date. Where the national law of the designated State requires the indication of the name of and other prescribed data concerning the inventor but allows that these indications be furnished at a time later than that of the filing of a national application, the applicant shall, unless they were contained in the request, furnish

the said indications to the national Office of or acting for the State not later than at the expiration of 30 months from the priority date.

Editor's Note (WIPO): 'The 30-month time limit, as in force from April 1, 2002, does not apply in respect of any designated Office which has notified the International Bureau of incompatibility with the national law applied by that Office. The 20-month time limit, as in force until March 31, 2002, continues to apply after that date in respect of any such designated Office for as long as Article 22(1), as modified, continues not to be compatible with the applicable national law. Information received by the International Bureau concerning any such incompatibility is published in the Gazette and on the WIPO website at: www.wipo.int/pct/en/texts/reservations/res_incomp.html.' Currently, these are the LU and TZ Offices. 94

Time Limit

Art. 24(1)(iii)	In the event of *failure to observe the time limit*, the fiction of withdrawal shall apply
R. 49*bis*.1	When the applicant performs the acts referred to in Art. 22, he must provide further information if he wishes to obtain a specific type of protection. This information can be obtained by interpreting the payment of a corresponding fee.
R. 49*bis*.2	Time of furnishing indications
R. 49.6	Reinstatement of rights after failure to perform the acts referred to in Art. 22
R. 82*quater*.1(c) and 2(b)	Excuse of delay in meeting time limits
R. 82*quater*.3(c)	Extension of time limits due to general disruption
Art. 76(1), R. 36 EPC	Legal fiction of Art. 11(3) PCT is not sufficient for pendency within the meaning of R. 36 EPC, requirements of Art. 22 PCT must be fulfilled, EPO J 18/09 (OJ EPO 2011 p. 480 supplemented by OJ EPO 2013 p. 156).
Art. 153, R. 159 EPC	If the international application is deemed to be withdrawn by declaration of the receiving Office (Art. 14(1) (b) PCT), the *review procedure* under Art. 25 and 24(2) in conjunction with Art. 48(2) PCT may be invoked. If the applicant makes use of a comparable European remedy (i.e. the request for further processing of the application under Art. 121 EPC), the conditions for the use of this remedy before the EPO as designated Office must also be met. Therefore, in addition to the action to be taken within the two-month period under R. 51.1 PCT vis-à-vis the International Bureau (Art. 25(1)(a) PCT), the actions under Art. 25(2)(a) PCT vis-à-vis the EPO as designated Office must also be taken within the two-month period under R. 51.3 PCT (see Examining Division 125

	decision of June 5, 1984, OJ EPO 1984 p. 565). The time limit under Art. 22 PCT does not apply in the case of early termination of the international phase.
Art. 153, R. 159 EPC	In the event of a *delay or loss in mail*, the applicant may invoke R. 82 PCT, subject to the conditions provided for therein (in particular, he must prove that he sent the document by registered airmail five days before the expiry of the time limit). Please note R. 82*quater*.1 for the case of *force majeure* and R. 82*quater*.2 for the case of unavailability of electronic means of communication. The relevant provisions of the EPC (in particular R. 83 and 85) apply to the other time limits not arising directly from the PCT.

Translation

R. 49.5	Contents of and physical requirements for the translation
R. 95	Information and translation from designated and elected Offices
Art. 153, R. 159 EPC	Elements of the translation
R. 40.2(c) 4	The translation of the objection to the finding of non-uniformity and the decision thereon must be filed with the designated Offices within the time limit under Art. 22. However, only a few Offices insist on this.
R. 45*bis*.6(e)	Submission of a translation of the SISR together with the translation of the international application
GL Exam E-IX, 2.7.	The EPO does not require the applicant to transmit a copy of the application under Art. 22(1) PCT even if it was not transmitted from the International Bureau to the EPO (R. 49.1(a-*bis*) PCT, GL Exam E-IX, 2.1.2. PCT Gazette 1986 p. 2367; R. 159(1), 160 EPC). There is no communication from WIPO to the applicant under R. 47.1(c) PCT.
R. 3, R. 4 EPC, GL Exam E-IX, 2.1.3	If the PCTa has been filed in an official language of the EPO, i.e. DE, FR or GB, this language remains the language of the procedure after the regional phase before the EPO has been initiated. The language of procedure cannot be changed by filing a translation when the regional phase is initiated before the EPO (G 4/08).
Art. 14(3) EPC	Language of the procedure

Transmission

R. 49	Furnishing of a copy and a translation of the application and payment of fee under Art. 22	
	R. 49.1	Notification
	R. 49.2	Languages

R. 49.3	Statements under Art. 19; indications under R. 13*bis*.4
R. 49.4	Use of a national form

Art. 153, R. 159(1) EPC	Fees payable to the EPO. Notification of deemed withdrawal under R. 160(3) EPC to applicant in case of non-payment and if he has not waived notification by declaring in Form 1200. For requirements for entering the European phase before the EPO, see the general notes above.
R. 160 EPC	Invitation to pay fees. If necessary, further processing under R. 135 EPC.

(2)

Where the International Searching Authority makes a declaration, under Article 17(2)(a), that no international search report will be established, the time limit for performing the acts referred to in paragraph (1) of this Article shall be the same as that provided for in paragraph (1).

(3)

Any national law may, for performing the acts referred to in paragraphs (1) or (2), fix time limits which expire later than the time limit provided for in those paragraphs.

R. 50	Faculty under Art. 22(3)
R. 50.1	Exercise of faculty
Art. 39(1)	Time limit for entry in case of filing a demand for IPE

An overview of the time limits, including grace periods, arranged by country can be found in this book under 'List of Member States of the PCT' and at www.wipo.int/pct/en/texts/time_limits.html. **95**

Art. 24(1)(iii)	Missing the time limit under Art. 22 may result in loss of effect of international application
R. 49.6	Reinstatement of rights after failure to perform the acts referred to in Art. 22 is possible in general

Article 23
Delaying of National Procedure

(1)

No designated Office shall process or examine the international application prior to the expiration of the applicable time limit under Article 22.

(2)

Notwithstanding the provisions of paragraph (1), any designated Office may, on the express request of the applicant, process or examine the international application at any time.

EPO	The requirements for an effective request for early processing also depend on the date on which early processing is requested. For the requirements and consequences, see EPO OJ EPO 2015 A94, p. 3, OJ EPO 2013 p. 156, OJ EPO 2011 p. 48 and Euro-PCT Guide 5.1.023 et seq., 5.14.
Art. 25	Early entry into national regional phase. According to Art. 40(2) early entry may also be initiated during the preliminary international examination.
Art. 40(1)	Corresponding regulation for the elected Office
R. 159 EPC	Requirements for an effective request for early processing

Article 24
Possible Loss of Effect in Designated States

INTRODUCTION

Consequences of Withdrawal of the International Application

If the receiving Office declares that an international application is considered withdrawn (Art. 14(1)(b), (3), (4)) for reasons mentioned in annotations to Art. 14, it will notify the applicant and the International Bureau of the declaration (R. 29.1(ii)). An applicant may also voluntarily withdraw the international application by sending a notice to the receiving Office or the International Bureau (R. 90*bis*.1). The effect of being withdrawn or being considered withdrawn is that the international application ceases to have the effect of a regular national application as provided in Art. 11(3) in any designated State, with the same consequences as the withdrawal of a national application in that State (Art. 24(1)). This effect applies to the following cases (Art. 24(1)(i)–(iii)): 1

(i) voluntary withdrawal of the international application or a designation of a State (R. 90*bis*.1, 2; see annotations to Art. 14);
(ii) the international application is considered withdrawn if:
  - the record copy is not received by the International Bureau in time (Art. 12(3)); it seems that the International Bureau does not apply Art. 12(3) in practice;
  - defects in the international application are not corrected (Art. 14(1)(b); R. 26.5);
  - the transmittal fee, the international filing fee, the search fee or, where required, the late payment fee is not paid (Art. 14(3)(a); R. 27.1);
  - after accordance of the filing date, the receiving Office notices defects under Art. 11(1)(i)–(iii) (Art. 14(4));
(iii) the applicant fails to perform the acts necessary to enter the national phase in time (Art. 22 and 39).

The decision of the receiving Office to consider the application withdrawn cannot, in principle, be appealed in the international phase because the PCT does not provide for any appeal during the international phase. However, some receiving Offices do reconsider their decisions on petition, and some national courts or appeal boards have accepted appeals against decisions taken by national Offices acting as 2 receiving Office. The reconsideration mitigates the consequences a single error in the international phase might have, i.e. the loss of the application for all designated States, in particular those States whose national law does not provide remedies as mentioned in Art. 48(2) for an excuse of a delay in meeting a time limit. A favorable decision will be accepted by the national Office acting as designated Office if it also acted as the receiving Office, but other national Offices need not accept the favorable decision (AG-IP 6.054).

3 The PCT provides for a review of the decision relating to the accordance of an international filing date and to a declaration of considered withdrawn only in the national phase (Art. 25). The PCT, therefore, allows an applicant to enter the national phase before each designated Office with a (considered) withdrawn international application and apply national law to remedy the loss of rights. Thereto, Art. 24(2) and 25 provide the necessary connection between the loss of rights in the international phase and the remedy available under national law. The so-called review and excuse procedure to be carried out before each designated Office is set out in the annotations to Art. 22.

(1)

Subject, in case (ii) below, to the provisions of Article 25, the effect of the international application provided for in Article 11(3) shall cease in any designated State with the same consequences as the withdrawal of any national application in that State:

- **(i) if the applicant withdraws his international application or the designation of that State;**
- **(ii) if the international application is considered withdrawn by virtue of Articles 12(3), 14(1)(b), 14(3)(a), or 14(4), or if the designation of that State is considered withdrawn by virtue of Article 14(3)(b);**

Art. 11(3)	Effect of the international application	
R. 90*bis*	Withdrawals	
	R. 90*bis*.1	Withdrawal of the international application
	R. 90*bis*.2	Withdrawal of designations
	R. 90*bis*.5	Signature requirements for withdrawals
	R. 90*bis*.6	Effect of withdrawal

The PCTa is deemed withdrawn:

Art. 12(3)	... if the record copy is not received by the International Bureau within 17 months from the priority date (R. 22.3)
Art. 14(1)(b), R. 26.5	... if the defect has not been remedied within the time limit and, for physical requirements, if it affects reasonable uniform international publication
Art. 14(3)(a)	... if the prescribed fees have not been paid

Art. 14(4)	... if the minimum requirements for the accordance of a filing date are not complied with
Art. 14(3)(b)	... if the prescribed designation fee has not been paid. Since the designation fee has been abolished, this Article no longer has any effect.

(iii) if the applicant fails to perform the acts referred to in Article 22 within the applicable time limit.

Art. 22	These acts include the communication (if not already done by the International Bureau under Art. 20) of a copy and a translation of the application and the payment of fees to the designated Offices within 30 months, unless the Offices provide deviating provisions (Art. 22(3)).
AIs 112	Ceasing of effect under Art. 24(1)(iii) and Art. 39(2), review under Art. 25(2) and maintaining of effect under Art. 24(2) and Art. 39(3).

(2)

Notwithstanding the provisions of paragraph (1), any designated Office may maintain the effect provided for in Article 11(3) even where such effect is not required to be maintained by virtue of Article 25(2).

Art. 11(3)	Effect of a regular national application
Art. 48(2)(a), R. 82*bis*(2)	Allows for national/regional review, with the procedure following Art. 25. Essentially, there is a review of the facts by the designated or elected Offices.
AIs 112	Ceasing of effect under Art. 24(1)(iii) and Art. 39(2), review under Art. 25(2) and maintaining of effect under Art. 24(2) and Art. 39(3)

Article 25
Review by Designated Offices

(1)

(a) Where the receiving Office has refused to accord an international filing date or has declared that the international application is considered withdrawn, or where the International Bureau has made a finding under Article 12(3), the International Bureau shall promptly send, at the request of the applicant, copies of any document in the file to any of the designated Offices named by the applicant.

(b) Where the receiving Office has declared that the designation of any given State is considered withdrawn, the International Bureau shall promptly send, at the request of the applicant, copies of any document in the file to the national Office of such State.

Art. 26	Opportunity to correct before designated Offices	
Art. 48	Delay in meeting certain time limits	
R. 82*bis*	Excuse by designated or elected Office of delays in meeting certain time limits	
	R. 82*bis*.1	Meaning of 'time limit' in Art. 48(2)
	R. 82*bis*.2	Reinstatement of rights and other provisions to which Art. 48(2) applies
R. 82*quater*	Excuse of delay in meeting time limits and extension of time limits	

(c) The request under subparagraphs (a) or (b) shall be presented within the prescribed time limit.

R. 51.1	The time limit for filing the request for copies under Art. 25(1) is two months from notification of the negative determination. Reinstatement under the EPC is possible. R. 80.6 is to be taken into account for the calculation of the time limit.

R. 51.3 The time limit for paying the national fee and providing a translation is two months from the date of notification of the negative determination. For the calculation of the time limit, R. 80.6 is to be taken into account. Decision of the EPO Examining Division 25, OJ EPO 1984 p. 565, decision ground No. 9: The expiry of the time limit terminates the international phase.

(2)

(a) Subject to the provisions of subparagraph (b), each designated Office shall, provided that the national fee (if any) has been paid and the appropriate translation (as prescribed) has been furnished within the prescribed time limit, decide whether the refusal, declaration, or finding, referred to in paragraph (1) was justified under the provisions of this Treaty and the Regulations, and, if it finds that the refusal or declaration was the result of an error or omission on the part of the receiving Office or that the finding was the result of an error or omission on the part of the International Bureau, it shall, as far as effects in the State of the designated Office are concerned, treat the international application as if such error or omission had not occurred.

R. 51.3 Refers to time limit under R. 51.1: two months from notification to applicant

R. 80.6 Date of documents

The designated Office has to take a decision. 1

1. If the receiving Office has made a mistake, the application must be maintained (Art. 25(2)(a)).
2. If the receiving Office acted lawfully, i.e. there is a default by the applicant, and
   - 2.1 the error is not a failure to observe the time limit, the application may be maintained (Art. 24(2)).
   - 2.2 a time limit has not been met, so
     - 2.2.1 the application must be maintained in accordance with national law (Art. 48(2)(b), Art. 24(2)), provided that the respective provisions apply, e.g. reinstatement is to be granted or further processing applies.
     - 2.2.2 the application may also be maintained for other reasons not arising under national law (Art. 48(2)(b), Art. 24(2)).

Art. 20(3) Transmission of copies of the documents cited in the ISR

R. 51.2 Furthermore, a copy of the negative determination that it is not an application (R. 20.4) must be sent. Alternative possibilities are:
1. a new application claiming priority if the time limit has not yet expired;
2. a request for reinstatement or further processing.

Art. 121 and R. 135 EPC 2000	Further processing
	Decision of the EPO Examining Division 25 (OJ EPO 1984 p. 565). The EPO, as designated Office, may excuse failure to observe time limits in the procedure under the PCT because of formal defects under Art. 14(1)(b) and R. 26.2 (R. 159(2) EPC). The applicant must perform the following acts within two months: a) request WIPO to send the documents according to Art. 25(1)(a) or (b), R. 51.1; b) pay the national fees (filing fee, examination fee, designation fee, search fee) (R. 159(1) EPC) to the EPO (no reinstatement of payment periods G 5/93) and, if applicable, file a translation (reinstatement possible) of the application (Art. 25(2), R. 51.3 PCT, R. 159(1)(a) EPC); c) file a request for further processing/reinstatement including payment of the further processing/reinstatement fee; continue to perform the omitted acts (reinstatement for missing provision G 3/91 is not given) according to Art. 24(2) and Art. 48(2), R. 82*bis*(2), Art. 121, 122 EPC.
AIs 112	Ceasing of effect under Art. 24(1)(iii) and Art. 39(2), review under Art. 25(2) and maintaining of effect under Art. 24(2) and Art. 39(3).

(b) Where the record copy has reached the International Bureau after the expiration of the time limit prescribed under Article 12(3) on account of any error or omission on the part of the applicant, the provisions of subparagraph (a) shall apply only under the circumstances referred to in Article 48(2).

Art. 12(3)	The record copy must be received by the International Bureau within 17 months from the priority date (R. 22.3)
Art. 48(2)	Excuse of delay by national Office under national law (reinstatement/further processing)

Article 26
Opportunity to Correct before Designated Offices

No designated Office shall reject an international application on the grounds of non-compliance with the requirements of this Treaty and the Regulations without first giving the applicant the opportunity to correct the said application to the extent and according to the procedure provided by the national law for the same or comparable situations in respect of national applications.

The Office must apply national/regional law, e.g. EPC in addition (Singer/Stauder 6th ed. Art. 150 EPC marginal no. 29). 1

Article 27
National Requirements

(1)

No national law shall require compliance with requirements relating to the form or contents of the international application different from or additional to those which are provided for in this Treaty and the Regulations.

Art. 150 EPC	General primacy of the PCT Articles and Rules in case of lack of conformity with the EPC; complementary application of the EPC

(2)

The provisions of paragraph (1) neither affect the application of the provisions of Article 7(2) nor preclude any national law from requiring, once the processing of the international application has started in the designated Office, the furnishing:

(i) when the applicant is a legal entity, of the name of an officer entitled to represent such legal entity,

(ii) of documents not part of the international application but which constitute proof of allegations or statements made in that application, including the confirmation of the international application by the signature of the applicant when that application, as filed, was signed by his representative or agent.

R. 51*bis*	Certain national requirements allowed under Art. 27(1), (2), (6), (7)	
	R. 51*bis*.1	Certain national requirements allowed
	R. 51*bis*.1(a)(i) in conjunction with R. 163 EPC	Indication of the inventor (R. 4.6)
	R. 51*bis*.1(a)(ii)	Transfer of rights, entitlement of the applicant

	R. 51*bis*.1(a)(iv)	Declaration of inventorship
	R. 51*bis*.2(i)	Requesting evidence relating to the identity of the inventor is generally not allowed

(3)

Where the applicant, for the purposes of any designated State, is not qualified according to the national law of that State to file a national application because he is not the inventor, the international application may be rejected by the designated Office.

R. 18.4	Information on requirements under national law as to the applicant

(4)

Where the national law provides, in respect of the form or contents of national applications, for requirements which, from the viewpoint of applicants, are more favorable than the requirements provided for by this Treaty and the Regulations in respect of international applications, the national Office, the courts and any other competent organs of or acting for the designated State may apply the former requirements, instead of the latter requirements, to international applications, except where the applicant insists that the requirements provided for by this Treaty and the Regulations be applied to his international application.

(5)

Nothing in this Treaty and the Regulations is intended to be construed as prescribing anything that would limit the freedom of each Contracting State to prescribe such substantive conditions of patentability as it desires. In particular, any provision in this Treaty and the Regulations concerning the definition of prior art is exclusively for the purposes of the international procedure and, consequently, any Contracting State is free to apply, when determining the patentability of an invention claimed in an international application, the criteria of its national law in respect of prior art and other conditions of patentability not constituting requirements as to the form and contents of applications.

(6)

The national law may require that the applicant furnish evidence in respect of any substantive condition of patentability prescribed by such law.

(7)

Any receiving Office or, once the processing of the international application has started in the designated Office, that Office may apply the national law as far as it relates to any requirement that the applicant be represented by an agent having

the right to represent applicants before the said Office and/or that the applicant have an address in the designated State for the purpose of receiving notifications.

1. General

1 Whether an applicant himself may carry out the necessary acts for his international application before an Office or whether he must act through an agent is determined by national law, not by the PCT. In view of the complexity of the PCT and of drafting patent applications, applicants are strongly advised to use professional assistance from patent attorneys or patent agents and act through them before the Offices, unless they are specialist in patent law themselves (AG-IP 1.004). The provisions for appointment, right to practice, renunciation and the acts an agent may perform are partly laid down in national law and partly in the PCT. See definitions of 'representation' and 'common representative' in Art. 49 and R. 90.

2 A receiving Office or, once the national phase has started, a designated Office may apply national law for requirements that the applicant be represented by an agent (Art. 27(7); R. 51*bis*.1(b)). Most Offices have done so and AG-IP Annex C indicates for each receiving Office whether the applicant must be represented. If so, the appointment of an agent is necessary; such an agent must have the right to practice before the Office.

3 Some receiving Offices do not require representation by an agent (for example, International Bureau, US); others require representation only for applicants not having a residence within the territory of the Contracting State (for example, DE, EP, JP) (AG-IP Annex C). Similar rules apply to compulsory representation before the designated Offices (see AG-NP).

4 An applicant need not be represented by an agent before the ISA nor before the IPEA because Art. 27(7) allows the application of national law as far as it relates to any requirement that the applicant be represented only before receiving Offices and designated Offices but not before ISAs or IPEAs. However, an applicant may be represented before the ISA by an agent. In most cases, it is highly advisable for the applicant to be represented.

5 The applicant may also appoint an agent specifically for the procedure before the IPEA; that agent must have the right to practice before the national Office which acts as IPEA (R. 90.1(c)).

6 An agent having the right to practice before the national Office or intergovernmental organization with which the international application was filed, also has the right to practice before the ISA in respect of that application (Art. 49; R. 90.1(a)). The ISA may require proof of the right to practice (R. 83.1), which it may request from the national Office before which the agent allegedly has the right to practice (R. 83.2).

7 An agent may appoint a sub-agent to represent the applicant specifically before the ISA, provided the person appointed as sub-agent has the right to practice before the national Office which acts as ISA (R. 90.1(d)(ii)). The applicant himself may appoint an agent to represent him specifically before the ISA, provided the person

appointed as agent has the right to practice before the national Office which acts as ISA (R. 90.1(b)).

The rules concerning the legal position, revocation, and renunciation of appointments apply to the international phase during all stages (AG-IP 10.023). 8

2. Representation before EPO as Designated or Elected Office

In general, no person will be compelled to be represented by a professional representative; however, applicants not having their residence or principal place of business in an EPC Contracting State must be represented by a professional representative before the EPO as designated or elected Office (Art. 133(2); R. 163(5) EPC). However, until expiry of the 31-month period for entry into the European phase, applicants not having their residence or principal place of business in an EPC Contracting State may carry out themselves the steps required to initiate the procedure before the EPO as a designated or elected Office. Payment of official fees to the EPO may be made by anybody. An appointment of an agent in the international phase does not automatically have effect in the national phase before the EPO; an explicit appointment for the regional phase before the EPO is required (Euro-PCT Guide 2.11.020; Art. 27(7) PCT; Art. 133(2) EPC; Art. 150(2) EPC; R. 159(1) EPC; GL Exam EPO E-IX,2.3.1; Euro-PCT Guide 5.3.007, 5.3.0011). 9

Art. 49	Right to practice before international authorities
R. 4.4(d)	Address to which notifications shall be sent
R. 51*bis*.1(b)(i)	National law may require indication of an agent and address in the designated State
R. 90	Appointment of agents and common representatives. See also annotations related to the entitlement of the agent in Art. 49 and R. 83.1*bis*.
Art. 133(2) EPC	The filing of an application is effective even without a representative, but a representative must be appointed in the subsequent procedure

(8)

Nothing in this Treaty and the Regulations is intended to be construed as limiting the freedom of any Contracting State to apply measures deemed necessary for the preservation of its national security or to limit, for the protection of the general economic interests of that State, the right of its own residents or nationals to file international applications.

R. 22.1	Transmittal of the record copy unless prescriptions concerning national security prevent the international application from being treated
AIs 330	Transmittal of record copy prevented or delayed by national security prescriptions

R. 15.4(iii), R. 16.2(iii)	Refund of fees if prescriptions concerning national security prevent the international application from being treated

10 A list of national security regulations: https://www.wipo.int/pct/en/texts/nat_sec.html with a link to state secrets concerning DE according to Patent Law § 52 and Act on International Patent Conventions (IntPatÜbkG) Art. III § 2. https://www.dpma.de/english/our_office/law/index.html.

Article 28
Amendment of the Claims, the Description, and the Drawings, before Designated Offices

(1)

The applicant shall be given the opportunity to amend the claims, the description, and the drawings, before each designated Office within the prescribed time limit. No designated Office shall grant a patent, or refuse the grant of a patent, before such time limit has expired except with the express consent of the applicant.

(2)

The amendments shall not go beyond the disclosure in the international application as filed unless the national law of the designated State permits them to go beyond the said disclosure.

AG-IP 11.047	Consequences of added subject matter in the national phase
Art. 19(2)	Added subject matter in amendments according to Art. 19
Art. 46	Added subject matter in translation of the PCTa
Art. 34(2)(b)2	Added subject during IPE
Art. 41(2)	Added subject matter before elected Office

(3)

The amendments shall be in accordance with the national law of the designated State in all respects not provided for in this Treaty and the Regulations.

(4)

Where the designated Office requires a translation of the international application, the amendments shall be in the language of the translation.

Art. 19	Amendments before the International Bureau during Chapter I

Art. 34	Amendments before the IPEA during Chapter II
R. 11.12	Physical requirements for amendments, etc., of the international application
R. 12.2	Language of amendments of the international application

Amendments During Chapter I:

Art. 19	Amendment of the claims before the International Bureau. Publication of amendments (R. 48(a)(vi), (f)).	
R. 46	Amendment of the claims before the International Bureau	
	R. 46.1	The *time limit* is normally *two months* from the date of transmittal of the ISR.
	R. 46.2	Amendments shall be filed with the International Bureau
	R. 46.3	Amendments shall be filed in the language of publication under R. 48.3
	R. 46.4	Statement accompanying amendments
	R. 46.5	Form of amendments
R. 62	Transmission of copy of amendments under Art. 19 by the International Bureau to the IPEA with copy of written opinion by ISA	
	R. 62.1	Amendments submitted before the demand for IPE
	R. 62.2	Amendments submitted after the demand for IPE
AIs 205	Numbering and identification of claims upon amendment	
AIs 417	Processing of amendments under Art. 19	

Amendments During the National Procedure Following Chapter I:

Art. 28	Amendments of claims, description, and drawings before designated Offices	
R. 52	Amendments of claims, description, and drawings before designated Offices	
	R. 52.1	Time limit for amendments. This is e.g. one month from entry into the national phase.
R. 159(1)(b) EPC	Submission of new amendments or indication of maintenance of amendments made on entry into the regional phase (Euro-PCT Guide 5.1.020)	
R. 161 EPC	Possibility to amend again during Euro-PCT phase within six months from notification (GL Exam E-IX, 3)	
R. 137(5) EPC	Amendments after receipt of the supplementary European search report (GL Exam E-IX, 4.2)	

Amendments During Chapter II:

Art. 34(2)(b)	Amendments of claims, description and drawings before the IPEA

R. 53	The demand for IPE	
	R. 53.9	Statement concerning amendments under Art. 19
	R. 55.3	Language of translation of amendments and letters
R. 62	Copy of amendments under Art. 19 for the IPEA with a copy of the written opinion of the ISA	
	R. 62.2	Amendments made after the demand is filed
R. 66	Procedure before the IPEA	
	R. 66.4	Additional opportunity for submitting amendments or arguments
	R. 66.4*bis*	Consideration of amendments, arguments and rctifications of obvious mistakes
	R. 66.5	Definition of 'amendment'
	R. 66.8	Form of the amendments
R. 70.11	Mention of the amendments in the preliminary report on patentability Chapter II	

Amendment During the National Procedure Following Chapter II:

Art. 41	Amendment of claims, description, drawings before elected Offices	
R. 78	Amendment of claims, description, drawings before elected Offices	
	R. 78.1	Time limit for amendment of claims is in general one month from entry into national phase.
	R. 78.3	Applies accordingly for utility models
R. 159(1)(b) EPC	Submission of new amendments or indication of maintenance of amendments made on entry into the regional phase	
R. 161 EPC	Possibility to amend again during Euro-PCT phase within six months from notification (GL Exam E-IX, 3)	
R. 137(5) EPC	Amendments after receipt of the supplementary European search report (GL Exam E-IX, 4.2)	

Article 29
Effects of the International Publication

INTRODUCTION

1 The effects of the publication of the international application on protection of any rights of the applicant in a designated State are the same as those which the national law of that State provides for the compulsory national publication of unexamined national applications as such (Art. 29(1)). The rights may relate to provisional protection in a designated State or to a prior right effect of the international application. A designated State may make the protection of the applicant's rights effective only after the publication, or making available in a different form of a translation in a language of the State if the international application is published in a different language (Art. 29(2)). The protection may also be made dependent on the expiration of 18 months from the priority date (Art. 29(3)) and on receipt of a copy of the published application by the designated Office (Art. 29(4)). AG-IP Annex B gives the requirements for provisional protection of each designated Office.

2 The publication of an international application for which the EPO is a designated Office will take the place of the publication of a European patent application under Art. 93 EPC (Art. 29(1) PCT; Art. 153(3) EPC). However, where the international application is published in a language other than English, French or German, the EPO will publish a translation in English, French or German supplied by the applicant (Art. 29(2)(i) PCT; Art. 153(4) EPC).

3 An international application will only have the prior right effect of Art. 54(3) EPC if the application is supplied to the EPO in English, French or German, the filing fee of R. 159(1)(c) EPC is paid to the EPO as designated Office, and the EPO has published the application (Art. 153(5) EPC; R. 165 EPC). If, for example, an international application is in Japanese and the applicant only requires a prior right effect in Europe, the applicant must furnish a translation in English, French or German to the EPO and pay the filing fee (R. 159(1)(c) EPC; R. 165 EPC; GL Exam EPO G-IV, 5.2). Since the EPO typically takes a few months for such publications and the EPO has not guaranteed it will publish a withdrawn application, if the applicant decides to withdraw the European application after having paid the filing fee to avoid payment of further fees, there may be no publication after the withdrawal, and the applicant would not obtain the prior right effect.

The provisional protection of Art. 67(1), (2) EPC in the designated EPC Contracting States will be effective from the date of the international publication for those international applications published in English, French or German and for which the EPO is a designated Office (indirect consequence of Art. 153(4) EPC). The provisional protection will be effective from the date of the above-mentioned publication of the translation by the EPO if the international publication was not in English, French or German (Art. 153(4) EPC; Euro-PCT Guide 5.16.003). The provisional protection is subject to any national requirements of the designated States regarding translations of claims in a national language (Art. 153(4) EPC, referring to Art. 67(3) EPC; see NatLaw table III for the national requirements, https://www.epo.org/law-practice/legal-texts/national-law.html). 4

(1)

As far as the protection of any rights of the applicant in a designated State is concerned, the effects, in that State, of the international publication of an international application shall, subject to the provisions of paragraphs (2) to (4), be the same as those which the national law of the designated State provides for the compulsory national publication of unexamined national applications as such.

Art. 11(3), (4)	Effect of international application

(2)

If the language in which the international publication has been effected is different from the language in which publications under the national law are effected in the designated State, the said national law may provide that the effects provided for in paragraph (1) shall be applicable only from such time as:

(i) a translation into the latter language has been published as provided by the national law, or

(ii) a translation into the latter language has been made available to the public, by laying open for public inspection as provided by the national law, or

(iii) a translation into the latter language has been transmitted by the applicant to the actual or prospective unauthorized user of the invention claimed in the international application, or

(iv) both the acts described in (i) and (iii), or both the acts described in (ii) and (iii), have taken place.

1. Language

R. 48.3	Language of publication is Arabic, Chinese, English, French, German, Japanese, Portuguese, Russian, Spanish
Art. 46	In case of incorrect translation of the international application, the original language version is binding
R. 17	The priority document

R. 17.2	Availability of copies
R. 48	International publication
Art. 67 EPC	Rights conferred by a European patent application after publication

2. Effect at the EPO

Art. 67, 153(3)–(5) EPC	Rights conferred by a European patent application after publication; publication of the international application and its transmission to the EPO

(3)

The national law of any designated State may provide that, where the international publication has been effected, on the request of the applicant, before the expiration of 18 months from the priority date, the effects provided for in paragraph (1) shall be applicable only from the expiration of 18 months from the priority date.

(4)

The national law of any designated State may provide that the effects provided for in paragraph (1) shall be applicable only from the date on which a copy of the international application as published under Article 21 has been received in the national Office of or acting for such State. The said Office shall publish the date of receipt in its gazette as soon as possible.

Article 30 Confidential Nature of the International Application

INTRODUCTION

1. Access to Files

1 The accessibility of documents in the file of an international application depends on the international filing date, the procedural stage the international application is at, and the Office that holds the file (Art. 38; International Bureau: R. 94.1; receiving Office: R. 94.1*bis*; ISA: R. 94.1*ter*; IPEA: R. 94.2; designated Office: R. 94.2*bis*; elected Office: R. 94.3). Sensitive personal data can be omitted from access (annotation to R. 48.2). National rules of a designated Office relating to accessibility prevail only if they are more favorable to the applicant than the PCT Rules (Art. 27(4)).

1.1 Access Prior to International Publication

2 Prior to the international publication of an application, the international application is confidential for third parties (Art. 30(1)(a)). The International Bureau and other International Authorities may only furnish copies of documents in their files to the applicant or a person authorized by the applicant (Art. 30(2)(a); R. 94.1(a); R. 94.1*bis*(a); R. 94.1*ter*(a); R. 94.2), subject to payment of the cost of the service (R. 94.1(a)). Copies of documents may also be furnished to judicial authorities (Art. 30(2)(c); AG-IP 11.072). A national Office may inform third parties that it has been designated; such information should contain only an identification of the receiving Office, name of the applicant, international filing date, international application number, and title of the invention (Art. 30(2)(b)).

3 ePCT with strong authentication provides full access to the file for the applicant.

1.2 Access after International Publication

4 Once the International Bureau has published the international application under Art. 21, the content of the international application and parts of the content of its file become public. See introduction to Art. 21 for the contents of the international

publication (Art. 21; R. 48). Copies of the international application as published and held in the file of the International Bureau may be obtained by downloading them from the WIPO website via PATENTSCOPE (AG-IP 9.021; Art. 50) and in paper form by ordering from the International Bureau or other International Authorities against payment of a fee. The entire publicly accessible file content of international applications filed on or after January 1, 2009 is available on PATENTSCOPE. Only some documents of the file of international applications filed on or after July 1, 1998 and prior to January 1, 2009 are available via PATENTSCOPE; others are available in paper form and subject to reimbursement of costs (R. 94.1(b))). Prior to July 1, 1998 there was no file inspection at the International Bureau (https://www.wipo.int/export/sites/www/pct/en/docs/document.pdf, p. 155). PATENTSCOPE is one of the electronic services offered on the WIPO IP Portal (https://ipportal.wipo.int/about) and provides access to published patent applications and patent collections of participating national and regional Offices (https://patentscope.wipo.int/search/en/search.jsf and https://www.wipo.int/patentscope/en/faqs_patentscope.html).

5 After the publication of an international application, the International Bureau will furnish copies of priority documents to any person upon request, provided the international application was not withdrawn prior to publication or the relevant priority claim was not withdrawn or considered not to have been made prior to publication (R. 17.2(c)).

6 The written opinion of international applications filed on or after July 1, 2014 will be publicly available from the date of international publication, including any translation and observations on the translation (R. 94.1(b); R. 43*bis*.1; R. 44*bis*.3; R. 44*bis*.4) and observations on the written opinion (AG-IP 7.030).

7 The ISR or declaration that no search has been carried out is published together with the international application or later separately (R. 48.2(a)(v), (g); R. 43; R. 17(2)(a)). Further documents, such as information sheets are accessible on PATENTSCOPE (OJ EPO 2017 A106). Any SISR is neither published with the international application nor separately but will be available on PATENTSCOPE as soon as it has been established (R. 45*bis*.7; AG-IP 8.053).

8 At this stage of the procedure any documents established during the IPE are not accessible to the public (R. 94.1(b); Art. 38).

9 The table 'Access to Files' in the Annex of this book gives an overview of how and when third parties can obtain access to information in the files of the Offices depending on the nature of the information and presented in the order of the stage of the procedure.

(1)

(a) Subject to the provisions of subparagraph (b), the International Bureau and the International Searching Authorities shall not allow access by any person or authority to the international application before the international publication of that application, unless requested or authorized by the applicant.

Art. 38	Confidential nature of the IPE
R. 48.2(l)	Omission from access
R. 94.3	Access to files held by the elected Office after publication, including documents referring to Chapter II, if the IPER has been established (GL Exam E-IX, 2.10) (see the overview 'Access to Files' in the Annex of this book)
Art. 153(3)-(5), R. 159(1)(a) EPC; GL Exam E-IX, 2.10	The EPO as designated Office allows file inspection after international publication. If the Euro-PCT application was published by the International Bureau in a language other than an official language of the EPO, the EPO will publish the translation filed at the entry into the European phase Euro-PCT Guide No. 5.16.003.

(b) The provisions of subparagraph (a) shall not apply to any transmittal to the competent International Searching Authority, to transmittals provided for under Article 13, and to communications provided for under Article 20.

(2)

(a) No national Office shall allow access to the international application by third parties, unless requested or authorized by the applicant, before the earliest of the following dates:

(i) date of the international publication of the international application,

(ii) date of the receipt of the communication of the international application under Article 20,

(iii) date of the receipt of a copy of the international application under Article 22.

(b) The provisions of subparagraph (a) shall not prevent any national Office from informing third parties that it has been designated, or from publishing that fact. Such information or publication may, however, contain only the following data: identification of the receiving Office, name of the applicant, international filing date, international application number, and title of the invention.

(c) The provisions of subparagraph (a) shall not prevent any designated Office from allowing access to the international application for the purposes of the judicial authorities.

(3)

The provisions of paragraph (2)(a) shall apply to any receiving Office except as far as transmittals provided for under Article 12(1) are concerned.

(4)

For the purposes of this Article, the term "access" covers any means by which third parties may acquire cognizance, including individual communication and general publication, provided, however, that no national Office shall generally publish an international application or its translation before the international publication or, if international publication has not taken place by the expiration of 20 months from the priority date, before the expiration of 20 months from the said priority date.

Chapter II: International Preliminary Examination

For general information regarding Chapter II see the 'Introduction to the PCT', No. 6.2.2 in this book.

Article 31
Demand for International Preliminary Examination

(1)

On the demand of the applicant, his international application shall be the subject of an international preliminary examination as provided in the following provisions and the Regulations.

INTRODUCTION

The PCT offers the possibility to subject the international application to an IPE (Art. 31(1)) to formulate a non-binding opinion on whether the claimed invention appears to be novel, to involve an inventive step, and to be industrially applicable (Art. 33(1)–(4)). Since the examination is optional, an applicant must request it by filing a demand (Art. 31(1)). The examination is carried out by an IPEA (Art. 32(1); R. 59). 1

The examination is preliminary in that it does not lead to the grant of a patent but has to be followed by an examination carried out by a designated Office or has to be endorsed by a designated Office; no designated Office is bound by the opinion. The IPE is governed by the provisions of Chapter II of the PCT, i.e. Art. 31–42, giving this part of the international phase its name 'Chapter II stage'. The Chapter II stage is preceded by the Chapter I stage, i.e. Art. 3–30, in which the international application is received, the international search is carried out and the international application is published. 2

The examination's results assist in the national phase in elected Offices, as chosen by the applicant through a demand that automatically elects all designated States. 3

A PCT Contracting State may opt out of Chapter II (Art. 64(1)), not accepting the examination results. Currently, all Contracting States adhere to Chapter II. 4

The IPEA issues the 'international preliminary examination report' (Art. 35), also known as 'international preliminary report on patentability (Chapter II of the PCT)' or IPRP II, after WIPO aligned the terminology with the introduction of the ISA's written opinion, termed 'international preliminary report on patentability (Chapter 5

I of the PCT)'. While WIPO avoids 'IPER', the EPO uses it. This text refers to IPRP I and IPRP II interchangeably.

6 During the Chapter I stage, an ISA establishes an ISR for each international application, including a preliminary non-binding written opinion on the patentability of the claimed invention. The optional IPE provides the applicant with a second opinion on patentability. Applicants should balance the cost of the IPE against the usefulness of a second opinion, considering the application's content, the initial written opinion, and their strategy for the national phase.

7 Initially, applicants cannot amend their application or exchange arguments with the ISA. Only after receiving the ISR can they amend the application's claims. The IPE, governed by the provisions of Chapter II, allows applicants to amend all parts of the application and exchange arguments with the IPEA.

8 This facility for amendment and dialogue during the patent application's prosecution could be pivotal, given the limited exchange opportunities during the national phase examination. The outcomes of the international examination might expedite the review and patent issuance in the elected Office.

9 The IPE becomes particularly beneficial if the ISA's written opinion is negative, allowing the applicant to file amendments and/or arguments addressing the ISA's concerns. Engaging with the IPEA is necessary for a more favorable opinion than the ISA's. Without significant submissions from the applicant, the IPEA is likely to concur with the ISA. However, if the ISA's opinion is positive, pursuing an IPE may be worthwhile for applicants seeking to refine or broaden their claims.

10 An IPEA generally will not examine claims not searched by the ISA or if an Art. 17(2) declaration has been made, thus the IPE cannot remedy a restricted search by the ISA. The PCT Chapter II process offers a chance to address ISA objections in one go, avoiding multiple responses across different languages and patent systems in the designated Offices' national phases.

11 Another advantage of requesting an IPE is the IPEA's 'top-up' search (R. 66.1*ter*), aimed at uncovering any new prior art that became available after the ISR was established.

12 The Office acting as IPEA and establishing the IPER may offer further benefits upon national entry. For instance, the EPO as an elected Office grants a 75 % reduction in the examination fee if it has prepared the IPER for the application.

13 The applicant must indicate the wish to subject the international application to an IPE by filing a request, called a 'demand' (Art. 31(1); R. 53). The following sections set out the requirements for the demand, which applicant may file it, where to file it, and which fees to pay. The demand must indicate the States ('elected States') that will use the results of the IPE in the national phase in the assessment of the patentability. The demand must also indicate whether the IPE should take into account amendments of the claims made earlier under Art. 19. The demand may contain amendments of the claims, description, and drawings under Art. 34 (R. 53.9).

The demand shall be filed: 14

Where: Art. 31(6)	The demand shall be filed with the IPEA designated by the receiving Office under R. 59.1(a)
When: R. 54*bis*	The time limit for making a demand is 22 months from the priority date or three months from the date of notification of the search report – whichever is later (until December 31, 2003: Art. 39(1) (a) the demand had to be filed within 19 months from the priority date)
How: Art. 31(3)	Art. 39(1) and (3) A demand must be filed separately from the PCTa. The demand must be made using the prescribed Form PCT/IPEA/401 (R. 53.1(a); AG-IP 10.012–10.034). The form contains a demand that the international application be the subject of the IPE. The demand must identify the international application and the applicant. Copies of printed demand forms are available free of charge from the receiving Office, the IPEA (R. 53.1(b)), and the WIPO website. Many receiving Offices provide a copy of the form on their own websites. The demand may be filed by fax (R. 92.1(4)). The demand must be signed by the applicant or his attorney (R. 53.2 (b), R. 90.3). If there is more than one applicant, all must sign (R. 53.8) or the duly appointed common attorney or representative (R. 90.3).
Fee: Art. 31(5)	See below
R. 57	Determines the processing fee, for WIPO
R. 58	Examination fee, for the IPEA
R. 57.3	The time limit for payment of the processing fee and the examination fee is one month from the filing of the demand or 22 months from the priority date – whichever is later. The grace period for late payment is one month from the date of the invitation (R. 58*bis*).
Art. 31(2)(a), R. 54.2	Entitlement to file the demand
R. 55.1	Language of the demand: As a rule, the language of publication
R. 60.1	Correction of deficiencies in the demand
R. 61.4	Publication of the demand in the Gazette
R. 90*bis*.4	Withdrawal of the demand
Art. 34	Amendments of the specification in Chapter II
Art. 31(4)(a)	Election of States ('elected States')
Art. 31(6)(b)	Later election of States.

(2)

(a) Any applicant who is a resident or national, as defined in the Regulations, of a Contracting State bound by Chapter II, and whose international application

has been filed with the receiving Office of or acting for such State, may make a demand for international preliminary examination.

15 An applicant must be a resident or national of a Contracting State bound by Chapter II to have the right to make a demand (Art. 31(2)(a); see also R. 54). The Assembly has not made any exceptions to the residence/nationality requirement as allowed by Art. 31(2)(b). The demand must give the applicant's name, address, nationality and residence (R. 53.4; R. 4.4 and 4.5). The applicant must sign the demand (R. 53.8; AG-IP 10.031).

16 Where a demand is filed by several applicants, at least one of them must be entitled to make a demand (R. 54.2). It is sufficient if the demand states the name, address, nationality and residence of at least one of the applicants that has the right to file the demand (R. 60.1(a-*bis*), overruling R. 53.4, R. 4.5(a)(ii) and (iii)). At least one of the applicants must sign the demand (R. 60.1(a-*ter*), overruling R. 53.8).

17 Where two or more applicants have designated different States (R. 4.5(d)), the demand should also indicate each applicant for the corresponding elected State (R. 53.4; R. 4.5(d)).

R. 54, R. 53.4	Applicant who is entitled to make a demand. At least one applicant shall fulfill the requirements.	
	R. 54.1	Residence and nationality
	R. 54.2	Right to make a demand
	R. 54.3	International applications filed with the International Bureau as receiving Office
	R. 54.4	Applicant not entitled to make a demand

(b) The Assembly may decide to allow persons entitled to file international applications to make a demand for international preliminary examination even if they are residents or nationals of a State not party to this Treaty or not bound by Chapter II.

(3)

The demand for international preliminary examination shall be made separately from the international application. The demand shall contain the prescribed particulars and shall be in the prescribed language and form.

R. 55.1	Language of demand	
R. 53	The demand	
	R. 53.1	Form
	R. 53.2	Contents
	R. 53.3	The petition

	R. 53.4	The applicant
	R. 53.5	Agent or common representative
	R. 53.6	Identification of the PCTa
	R. 53.7	Election of States
	R. 53.8	Signature
	R. 53.9	Statement concerning amendments
R. 60.1	Correction of defects in the demand	
R. 62	Copy of the written opinion by the ISA and of amendments under Art. 19 for the IPEA	
	R. 62.1	Amendments filed before the demand was filed
	R. 62.2	Amendments filed after filing the demand
R. 92*bis*	Recording of changes in certain indications in the request or the demand	
	R. 92*bis*.1	Recording of changes by the International Bureau

(4)

(a) The demand shall indicate the Contracting State or States in which the applicant intends to use the results of the international preliminary examination ("elected States"). Additional Contracting States may be elected later. Election may relate only to Contracting States already designated under Article 4.

(b) Applicants referred to in paragraph (2)(a) may elect any Contracting State bound by Chapter II. Applicants referred to in paragraph (2)(b) may elect only such Contracting States bound by Chapter II as have declared that they are prepared to be elected by such applicants.

The demand must indicate the Contracting States in which the applicant intends 18
to use the results of the IPE. These States are called 'elected States'. (Art. 31(4)(a)) A demand constitutes the election of all Contracting States designated in the international application (R. 53.7). Since the request designates all Contracting States automatically (R. 4.9(a)(i)), the demand elects all Contracting States automatically. Exclusions are not possible, but withdrawal of an election is possible. Where there are two or more applicants, they may elect different Contracting States.

Art. 1	Contracting States
R. 53.7	The filing of a demand shall constitute the election of all Contracting States which are designated and are bound by Chapter II of the Treaty
Art. 64(1)(a)	Expiry of reservations in respect of Chapter II: – Spain (ES) can be elected since September 6, 1997, irrespective of the international filing date – Greece (GR) can be elected, irrespective of the international filing date

- Liechtenstein (LI) can be elected since September 1, 1995, regardless of the international filing date
- Switzerland (CH) can be elected since September 1, 1995, regardless of the international filing date

For CH/LI, however, Art. 153(1) EPC (deadweight effect) takes precedence, i.e. the election of one of the two States CH or LI is deemed to be a election of both States on the basis of the Patent Protection Treaty of December 22, 1978, OJ 1980, 407 as a regional treaty within the meaning of Art. 45.

(5)

The demand shall be subject to the payment of the prescribed fees within the prescribed time limit.

19 The demand is subject to payment of fees, i.e. a handling fee and a preliminary examination fee. The amount of the fees and any reductions are listed in AG-IP Annex E for each IPEA.

20 The handling fee is collected by the IPEA to which the demand is submitted and is for the benefit of the International Bureau (R. 57.1) to carry out various administrative tasks, such as translating the IPRP II into English where required. The amount of the handling fee is fixed in item 3 of the Schedule of Fees (R. 57.2(a); R. 96.1). The 'handling fee' should not be confused with the 'supplementary search handling fee' payable if the applicant files a supplementary international search request (R. 45*bis*.2).

21 The preliminary examination fee is collected by the IPEA for its own benefit for carrying out the examination (R. 58.1(c), (a)). The amount of the fee is fixed by each IPEA and stated in AG-IP Annex E.

22 The handling fee may be reduced by 90% for applicants from developing countries (see Schedule of Fees 5; AG-IP Annex E). The EPO as IPEA provides a 75% reduction of the preliminary examination fee for nationals/residents of a State listed by the World Bank as a low-income or lower-middle-income economy (OJ EPO 2024 A69). See also AG-IP 10.040 and 10.041 for the available fee reductions.

23 The handling fee and the preliminary examination fee must be paid within one month from the date on which the demand was submitted or 22 months from the priority date, whichever expires later (R. 57.3(a); R. 58.1(b)). Where the demand was not filed with a competent IPEA and transmitted to it under R. 59.3, the fees must be paid within one month from the date of receipt of the demand by the competent IPEA or 22 months from the priority date, whichever expires later (R. 57.3(b)). The amounts payable are the amounts applicable on the date of payment (R. 57.3(d)).

24 If the handling fee or preliminary examination fee is not duly paid within the time limit of R. 57.3, the IPEA invites the applicant to pay within one month from the date of the invitation (R. 58*bis*.1(a)). An IPEA may charge a late payment fee to be paid within the same time limit (R. 58*bis*.1(a)). The EPO as IPEA levies such a late payment fee (OJ EPO 1998 p.282; Euro-PCT Guide 4.1.062). A payment received

before the IPEA sends the invitation is regarded as received within the period of R. 57.3 (R. 58*bis*.1(c)).

The amount of the late payment fee is 50% of the amount of the unpaid fees, but it will be at least equal to the amount of the handling fee and not more than twice the amount of the handling fee (R. 58*bis*.2). **25**

Where the applicant has not paid in full the amount due, including any late payment fee, in due time in response to the invitation, the IPEA will consider the demand as not having been submitted (R. 58*bis*.1(b)). A payment received by the IPEA before it considers the demand as not having been submitted will be regarded as having been received within the one-month period from the invitation (R. 58*bis*.1(d)). **26**

Where the demand is regarded as not having been submitted, there will be no valid elections and no IPRP II will be drawn up. **27**

The handling fee will be refunded if the demand is withdrawn before the IPEA has forwarded the demand to the International Bureau (see introduction to Art. 33) or if the demand is regarded as not having been submitted (R. 57.4). An IPEA may refund the preliminary examination fee if the demand is considered not to have been submitted (R. 58.3; see AG-IP Annex E for the conditions and the amount of the refund for each IPEA). **28**

R. 57	The handling fee	
	R. 57.1	Requirement to pay
	R. 57.2	Amount; transfer
	R. 57.3	The time limit for payment is one month from filing the demand or 22 months from the priority date (R. 57.3); however, a grace period of one month from the demand is granted with a surcharge (R. 58*bis*)
	R. 57.4	Refund
R. 58	The preliminary examination fee	
	R. 58.1	Right to ask for a fee
	R. 58.1(b), 57.3	The time limit for payment is one month from filing the demand or 22 months from the priority date; a period of grace of one month from the invitation is granted, but with a surcharge (R. 58*bis*). The EPO waives the surcharge if the fee is paid within one month of notification of the ISR.
	R. 58.3	Refund
R. 58*bis*	Extension of time limits for payment of fees	
	R. 58*bis*.1	Invitation by the IPEA
	R. 58*bis*.1(b)	In the event of non-payment, the demand is deemed not to have been filed
	R. 58*bis*.2	Late payment of fee

(6)

(a) The demand shall be submitted to the competent International Preliminary Examining Authority referred to in Article 32.

29 The demand must be filed with the competent IPEA (Art. 31(6)(a)). If the demand is filed instead with the receiving Office, International Bureau, ISA, or an incompetent IPEA, the demand will be forwarded to the competent IPEA, retaining the date of receipt of the Office to which the applicant sent the demand (R. 59.3; AG-IP 10.007–10.008).

30 The demand must be submitted using a filing method permitted by the IPEA. AG-IP Annex B indicates the filing methods by post and fax and AG-IP Annex E the electronic filing method permitted by each IPEA. While the demand may be filed by post or fax, IPEAs generally prefer that it is filed electronically. Applicants may use the ePCT method of filing of the International Bureau (Pract. Adv. NL 01/2014) or a permitted proprietary online filing system of a national Office.

31 The EPO offers the following online filing methods: EPO's Online Filing Software, the Online Filing 2.0 (OJ EPO 2021, A20), Web-form filing (OJ EPO 2018 A45) and ePCT (OJ EPO 2016 A78). The USPTO also offers electronic filing.

Art. 16(2)	Competent ISA	
R. 59	Competent IPEA	
	R. 59.1	Demands under Art. 31(2)(a)
	R. 59.2	Demands under Art. 31(2)(b)
	R. 59.3	Transmittal of the demand to the competent IPEA

(b) Any later election shall be submitted to the International Bureau.

32 This requirement has become superfluous since all States are elected automatically in accordance with R. 53.7.

(7)

Each elected Office shall be notified of its election.

R. 61	Notification of the demand and elections	
	R. 61.1	Notification to the International Bureau and the applicant
	R. 61.2	Notification to the elected Offices
	R. 61.3	Information for the applicant
	R. 61.4	Publication in the Gazette
AIs 418	Notifications to elected Offices where the demand is considered not to have been submitted or made	
AIs 431	Publication of notice of submission of demand	

Article 32 The International Preliminary Examining Authority

INTRODUCTION

The preliminary examination is carried out by the IPEA (Art. 32(1)). Any national Office or intergovernmental organization satisfying the requirements relating to manpower and documentation can be appointed as IPEA by the Assembly upon conclusion of an Agreement between such Office or organization and the International Bureau (Art. 32(3); R. 63). All IPEAs are listed in https://www.wipo.int/pct/en/access/isa_ipea_agreements.html and AG-IP Annex E. 1

Each receiving Office, except the International Bureau, has specified one or more IPEAs that are competent to carry out the preliminary examination of an international application filed with it (Art. 32(2); R. 59.1(a)). AG-IP Annex C gives the competent IPEA(s) for each receiving Office. The choice of IPEA by the receiving Office is often based on the presumed quality of the examinations of the IPEA and its language capabilities. Some IPEAs are competent only if that Office as ISA has carried out the international search. If the receiving Office specifies several IPEAs, the applicant of an international application filed with this receiving Office may choose the IPEA to carry out the IPE (R. 59.1(a)) (AG-IP 10.006). 2

Where the International Bureau is receiving Office, the competent IPEA is the one which would have been competent had the application been filed with the receiving Office that is the national Office of, or acting for, a Contracting State of which the applicant is a national or resident (R. 59.1(b)). Where two or more IPEAs are competent, the choice is left to the applicant (R. 59.1(b)) (AG-IP 10.006). 3

(1)

International preliminary examination shall be carried out by the International Preliminary Examining Authority.

The Offices acting as IPEA are AT, AU, BR, CA, CL, CN, EA EG, EP, ES, FI, IL, IN, JP, KR, PH, RU, SE, SG, TR, UA, and US. DK, IS, SE and NO have a common patent authority, Nordic Patent Institute (NPI, abbreviation: XN). The joint patent Office 4

Visegrad Patent Institute (VPI) of the Offices of CZ, HU, PL and SK acts as IPEA under the country code XV. See https://www.wipo.int/pct/en/access/isa_ipea_agreements.html.

Art. 152 EPC R. 158(2) EPC	EPO as IPEA

(2)

In the case of demands referred to in Article 31(2)(a), the receiving Office, and, in the case of demands referred to in Article 31(2)(b), the Assembly, shall, in accordance with the applicable agreement between the interested International Preliminary Examining Authority or Authorities and the International Bureau, specify the International Preliminary Examining Authority or Authorities competent for the preliminary examination.

Art. 16	Choice of ISA may affect competence of the IPEA
Art. 34(4)	Proceedings before the IPEA, excluded subject matter
R. 59	Competent authority entrusted with IPE, see Art. 16(2) for EPC States
	The EPO is competent as ISA for applications for which the competent receiving Office has designated the EPO as ISA. This is not limited to receiving Offices from EPC Member States. The latest status in this respect can be found in Annex C of the PCT Applicant's Guide.
	However, it will only act as IPEA if the ISA was the EPO, the Office in AT, FI, ES, XN, XV, TR or SE (AG-IP Annex E (EP)).

(3)

The provisions of Article 16(3) shall apply, *mutatis mutandis*, in respect of International Preliminary Examining Authorities.

Art. 16(3)	Appointment of an IPEA	
R. 63	Minimum requirements for the authorities in charge of IPE	
	R. 63.1	List of minimum requirements

Article 33
The International Preliminary Examination

INTRODUCTION

1. International Preliminary Examination

The objective of the preliminary examination is to formulate a preliminary, non-binding opinion on whether the claimed invention is novel, involves an inventive step, and is industrially applicable (Art. 33(1)). The definitions used for prior art, novelty, inventive step, and industrial applicability (Art. 33(2)–(4); R. 64; R. 65) are almost identical to those of the EPC. These definitions are acceptable to all PCT Contracting States. A Contracting State may in its national examination apply additional or different conditions for patentability (Art. 33(5)). The major differences between the PCT and the EPC are that the PCT does not recognize oral disclosures as prior art (R. 64.2) and does not consider prior rights to form part of the prior art (R. 64.3). 1

The IPE is based on the international application as filed (R. 66.1(a)). The applicant may indicate in the demand whether or not any amendments of the claims under Art. 19 or any amendments of the claims, description, or drawings under Art. 34 filed together with the demand must be taken into account in the examination, and whether an Art. 34 amendment of the claims reverses an earlier Art. 19 amendment. (R. 53.9; R. 66.1; AG-IP 10.026). 2

If the claims, description, or drawings have been amended under Art. 19 but the filed replacement sheets were not accompanied by a letter indicating the basis for the amendments (R. 46.5(b)(iii)), the IPE may proceed as if the amendments had not been made (R. 70.2(c-*bis*)). Timely rectification of obvious mistakes in the international application will be taken into account by the IPEA (R. 91.1; R. 66.1(d-*bis*); R. 66.4*bis*)). 3

The IPEA will normally carry out a top-up search to discover prior art which has been published or has become available to the IPEA for search after the date on which the ISR was established (R. 66.1*ter*). An IPEA will not carry out a top-up search if it serves no useful purpose, for example, where the entire application relates to subject matter which it is not required to be examined (AG-IP 10.062A). The IPRP II will indicate the date on which the top-up search was made or state that no top-up search was made (R. 70.2(f)). 4

5 The examiner may exclude the following subject matter from the examination:

- subject matter not searched by the ISA (Art. 17(2)(a); R. 39.1; R. 66.1(e); see introduction to Art. 17);
- subject matter in fields excluded from patentability (Art. 34(4)(a)(i); R. 67.1, similar to R. 39.1);
- subject matter for which no meaningful examination can be carried out because it is not supported by the description or because it is unclear (Art. 34(4)(a)(ii)).

6 Any exclusion will be mentioned in the opinion (Art. 34(2)(c); R. 66.2(a)(i) and (vi)) and, if the applicant does not amend the subject matter, also in the report (Art. 35(3); R. 70.2(d); R. 70.12(iii)).

7 The IPEA checks whether the international application complies with the requirement of unity of invention (Art. 34(3)(a); R. 68). The IPEA applies the same requirements for unity of invention as the ISA (AG-IP 10.072).

8 The examination need not extend to claims relating to an invention that does not form unity with the main invention and for which no examination fee or additional fee has been paid (Art. 34(3)).

9 The IPEA will inform the applicant of its preliminary opinion in one or more written opinions and will conclude the examination by issuing the IPER.

2. Third Party Observations

10 Many Offices allow third parties to file observations under the PCT referring to prior art which they believe to be relevant to the question of whether the invention claimed in an international application is new and/or involves an inventive step. TPOs have their legal basis in the Administrative Instructions, Part 8, sections 801–805, not in the PCT. See the WIPO overview (https://www.wipo.int/scp/en/revocation_mechanisms/third_party/index.html) for a summary of the service. The Offices that accept TPOs are listed on the WIPO third party website.

11 A TPO can be made at any time from the date of publication of the international application until the expiration of 28 months from the priority date, provided that the application is not withdrawn or considered withdrawn. No fee is payable for the use of this service (AG-IP 11.109–11.110).

12 There is no express provision in the PCT for filing TPOs. More information on the service can be found in AIs Part 8.

13 A third party may only submit a single observation for any application, and once submitted, it cannot be retracted or modified. A maximum of ten observations may be submitted on any particular international application (Pract. Adv.NL 05/2024).

14 An observation must be filed using ePCT, either directly or through a link on the bibliographical data tab of the published international application in PATENTSCOPE. The use of ePCT requires a standard WIPO user account, which can be created by anyone. Each observation must include at least one citation that refers to a document

published before the international filing date or a patent document having a priority date before the international filing date, together with a brief explanation of how each document is considered to be relevant to the questions of novelty and/or inventive step of the claimed invention. Observations should be submitted in a language of publication (AIs 802); copies of prior art documents may be in any language (AG-IP 11.111, 11.113).

Although the third party must identify himself to the International Bureau when logging into the WIPO user account, the third party can indicate when submitting an observation that he would like the observation to be published anonymously (AIs 801(b)(i)), in which case the International Bureau will not reveal any details about the third party to the public, the applicant, any International Authority, or any designated Office (AG-IP 11.112). 15

The International Bureau will review each observation to determine whether it is an observation on the questions of novelty and/or inventive step. If approved, the International Bureau will promptly notify the observation to the applicant and any International Authorities that have not yet issued their report, and make it available to the public via PATENTSCOPE. The International Bureau will also transmit the observations to the designated Offices after the expiration of 30 months from the priority date. However, the designated Offices are not obliged to take them into account during national processing (AG-IP 11.116–11.117). 16

The applicant may respond to observations by a third party (although this is not required) until 30 months from the priority date (AIs 804(b)), either through the ePCT system, using the private services option, or by sending a letter to the International Bureau. The applicant's response will also be promptly made available to International Authorities and for public inspection in PATENTSCOPE (AG-IP 11.114). 17

The applicant will be notified directly about the first TPO, and all subsequent observations will be notified to the applicant promptly after the expiration of 28 months from the priority date. The applicant may comment on TPOs until the expiration of 30 months from the priority date. 18

Observations will be transmitted to any competent (S)ISA, and/or IPEA involved in the processing of the application during the international phase, if the International Bureau has not yet received the ISR, SISR or IPRP, respectively. To the extent that the observations are received by those Authorities in time to be taken into account in drawing up their respective reports, any prior art referred to in the observations should be considered, provided that either the third party has included a copy of the prior art with the observation or the prior art is otherwise immediately available to the examiner (WIPO Third Party Observations FAQ). The observations will also be transmitted to the designated Offices promptly after the expiration of 30 months from the priority date (AIs 805). The designated Offices are, however, not obliged to take them into account during national processing (WIPO third party website). 19

The PCT system for TPOs is different from the EPC system. Under PCT, TPOs must refer to at least one prior art document relevant to the novelty and/or inventive step of the invention claimed in the international application. Additionally, under PCT, only novelty and inventive step may be discussed (AG-IP 11.111). In contrast, 20 under Art. 115 EPC, TPOs may be filed without citing any prior art. Moreover, under the EPC, issues such as clarity, sufficiency of disclosure, patentability in the broad sense, and unallowable amendments/added matter may also be mentioned (see GL/EPO E-VI 3).

3. Proceedings after Receipt of the Demand

21 On receipt of the demand, the IPEA sends a copy of the demand to the International Bureau (R. 61.1(a)) and notifies the applicant of the date of receipt (R. 61.1(b)). Subsequently, the International Bureau notifies the elected Offices and the applicant of the elections (Art. 31(7); R. 61.2, 3) and publishes information about the demand and elections in the Gazette, in particular in PATENTSCOPE (R. 61.4). The International Bureau forwards a copy of any Art. 19 amendments and any accompanying letter explaining the differences and basis for the amendments (R. 46.5(b)) to the IPEA, unless the IPEA indicates that it has already received such a copy (R. 62.1(ii)). The International Bureau will also forward a copy of the written opinion of the ISA to the IPEA and, if required, an English translation (R. 62*bis*.1), except where the IPEA and the ISA are the same Authority (R. 62.1(i)).

22 The IPEA may request the International Bureau to send a copy of the priority application (R. 66.7(a)). Where the priority application is not in a language accepted by the IPEA and the IPEA needs a translation, it may request the applicant to furnish a translation (R. 66.7(b)). Where the applicant does not submit a copy of the priority application under R. 17.1 or does not furnish its translation, the IPER may be drawn up as if no priority had been claimed (R. 66.7).

Article 33
The International Preliminary Examination

(1)

The objective of the international preliminary examination is to formulate a preliminary and non-binding opinion on the questions whether the claimed invention appears to be novel, to involve an inventive step (to be non-obvious), and to be industrially applicable.

R. 55	Languages of the IPE	
	R. 55.2	Translation of PCTa
	R. 55.3	Language and translation of amendments and letters
R. 70.1, 70.15	Title and form of the IPRP/IPER	
	R. 70.1	Various terms are synonymous: 'report', 'international preliminary examination report (IPER)' and 'international preliminary report on patentability (IPRP)' (see heading of R. 70)
	R. 70.15	IPRP II

	R. 70.14	Under this provision, only one examiner is responsible for the IPE (Art. 35).
GL Exam EPO E-IX, 4.3.3	IPER forms the basis for the EPO's decision on examination in the regional phase; deviations from this are only made in exceptional cases.	

(2)

For the purposes of the international preliminary examination, a claimed invention shall be considered novel if it is not anticipated by the prior art as defined in the Regulations.

R. 64	Prior art for IPE	
	R. 64.1	Prior art
	R. 64.2	Non-written disclosures
	R. 64.3	Certain published documents only become prior art in the national/regional phase.
AIs 801 et seq.	TPOs concerning the prior art, see Introduction above	

(3)

For the purposes of the international preliminary examination, a claimed invention shall be considered to involve an inventive step if, having regard to the prior art as defined in the Regulations, it is not, at the prescribed relevant date, obvious to a person skilled in the art.

R. 64	Prior art for IPE	
R. 65	Inventive step or non-obviousness	
	R. 65.1	Approach to prior art
	R. 65.2	Relevant date

(4)

For the purposes of the international preliminary examination, a claimed invention shall be considered industrially applicable if, according to its nature, it can be made or used (in the technological sense) in any kind of industry. "Industry" shall be understood in its broadest sense, as in the Paris Convention for the Protection of Industrial Property.

R. 67	Subject matter of the application under Art. 34(4)(a)(i)	
	R. 67.1	Definition
R. 67.1(i)–(iv)	Non-technical, not industrially applicable inventions	

(5)

The criteria described above merely serve the purposes of international preliminary examination. Any Contracting State may apply additional or different criteria for the purpose of deciding whether, in that State, the claimed invention is patentable or not.

(6)

The international preliminary examination shall take into consideration all the documents cited in the international search report. It may take into consideration any additional documents considered to be relevant in the particular case.

Article 34
Procedure before the International Preliminary Examining Authority

INTRODUCTION

In the PCT system, applicants are provided with distinct opportunities to amend their international applications to potentially overcome objections related to novelty, inventive step, or industrial applicability before entering the national phase of patent prosecution. These opportunities are crucial for applicants aiming to strengthen their patent applications based on the ISR or the written opinion of the ISA. 1

Before the opportunity to amend under Art. 34, applicants can amend only the claims of the international application under Art. 19 PCT after receiving the ISR. These amendments need to be indicated whether they should be taken into account for the IPE or considered reversed by an amendment under Art. 34. An amendment under Art. 19 filed after the demand will only be considered if received before the IPEA begins drafting the IPER. 2

The applicant has under Art. 34 a second opportunity to amend the claims and a first opportunity to amend the description and any drawings. The filing of amendments is free of charge (AG-IP 10.071). 3

The first opportunity to file amendments under Art. 34 is together with the demand; they may also be filed during the examination if time permits until the IPRP II is established (Art. 34(2)(b); R. 66.1(b); AG-IP 10.024). Amendments under Art. 34 will only be taken into account if they are filed in the period from the filing of the demand until the IPRP II is established (Art. 34(2)(b); R. 66.1(b) (d)); amendments received later need not be taken into account (R. 66.4*bis*). 4

If the applicant intends to file amendments but is not in a position to submit them together with the demand, that intention should preferably be mentioned in a letter filed with the demand (AG-IP 10.028). In such a situation, under current practice, the EPO acting as IPEA will, shortly after the demand is filed, invite the applicant to file the amendments within a period of one month. 5

The amendment, i.e., any change other than the rectification of obvious mistakes (R. 66.5), may not go beyond the disclosure in the international application as filed (Art. 34(2)(b); R. 70.2(c)). Non-compliance will be reported (AG-IP 11.047). The 6 applicant may indicate that an Art. 34 amendment supersedes an amendment made earlier under Art. 19 (R. 66.1(c)).

7 Amendments concerning the description or drawings should be presented in the form of individual replacement pages for any pages containing amendments and an accompanying letter indicating the differences between the replaced and replacement sheets, the basis for the amendments in the application as filed, and preferably the reasons for the amendments (R. 66.8(a); AG-IP 10.071). Where the only amendment is the deletion of an entire sheet, a letter explaining the reasons for the amendment suffices (R. 66.8(b)). Any amendments made to the claims must be presented as for an Art. 19 amendment (R. 66.8(c)). If the claims, description, or drawings are amended but the basis for the amendments is not furnished, the IPRP II may be established as if the amendments had not been made (R. 70.2(c-*bis*)).

8 The applicant has the right to respond to the written opinion by communicating in writing and orally with the IPEA (Art. 34(2)(a), (d)). Both the applicant or the agent and the IPEA may request an interview. The interview may be in person, by telephone, or in informal writing. Where the applicant or the agent requests an interview, the IPEA will grant at least one such interview (R. 66.3; R. 66.6; ISPE 19.41–19.46; AG-IP 10.067, 10.068).

Article 34
Procedure before the International Preliminary Examining Authority

(1)

Procedure before the International Preliminary Examining Authority shall be governed by the provisions of this Treaty, the Regulations, and the agreement which the International Bureau shall conclude, subject to this Treaty and the Regulations, with the said Authority.

R. 66	Procedure before the IPEA
R. 66.1*ter*	Top-up searches
R. 69	Start of and time limit for IPE
R. 69.1	Start of IPE

(2)

(a) The applicant shall have a right to communicate orally and in writing with the International Preliminary Examining Authority.

Art. 14(2)(c) and (d)	Written opinion

W 4/93 EPO	The right of the applicants to communicate orally with the IPEA (Art. 34(2)(a) PCT) does not include the right to formal oral proceedings (Reasons, 9).
AG-IP 10.067	Communication of applicant with IPEA

(b) The applicant shall have a right to amend the claims, the description, and the drawings, in the prescribed manner and within the prescribed time limit, before the international preliminary examination report is established. The amendment shall not go beyond the disclosure in the international application as filed ***(added subject matter).***

Art. 19 Introduction	General annotations referring to amendments under Chapter I
Art. 19(2)	Added subject matter in amendments according to Art. 19
Art. 46	Added subject matter in translation of the PCTa
Art. 28(2)	Added subject matter before designated Office
Art. 41(2)	Added subject matter before elected Office
R. 70(2)(c)	Added matter will be ignored during IPE
R. 66.1(b)	Time limit for filing amendments
R. 70.11	Mention of amendments in IPRP II
R. 91	Rectification of obvious mistakes in amendments under Art. 34
AG-IP 10.070	In case of non-compliance with sentence 2 (added matter), IPEA will comment in written opinion and IPRP II and report will be established as if amendment had not been made.

Amendments under Chapter II:

Art. 34(2)(b)	Amendment of the *claims*, the *description*, and the *drawings* before the IPEA
R. 53	The demand for IPE
R. 53.9	Statement concerning amendments under Art. 19

The options to make amendments in accordance with Art. 19 or Art. 34 exist independently of each other. There are differences with regard to the requirements and effects. Amendments under Art. 19 can be made once, after receipt of the search report by the applicant and before expiry of the time limit under R. 46.1. Amendments under Art. 34 require a request for IPE and can be made several times until the IPER is drawn up in accordance with R. 66.1(b). Further differences exist with regard to the addressee (Art. 19: International Bureau; Art. 34: IPEA), the subject matter of the amendment (Art. 19: only claims; Art. 34: also descriptions and drawings), the language (Art. 19, R. 12: language of publication; Art. 34, R. 55.3 language of publication or translation of the PCTa). Relevant differences with regard to the effects are that amendments under Art. 19 are published with the application in accordance with Art. 21; R. 48.2(f) and (h). This is not provided for in Art. 34. As a result, Art. 9

19 can achieve a different protective effect under Art. 29 with regard to an amended scope of the claims compared to the application. Confidentiality is given for Art. 19 until publication of the PCTa, for Art. 34 until third parties have access to the files of the IPE according to R. 94.

R. 13*ter*.1(e)	Amending the description or a sequence listing filed after the filing date
R. 55.3	Language and Translation of Amendments and accompanying Letters
R. 62	Copy of the written opinion by the ISA and of amendments under Art. 19 for the IPEA
R. 62.2	Amendments made after the demand is filed
R. 66	Procedure before the IPEA
R. 66.1(d-*bis*)	Taking into account of rectifications of obvious mistakes
R. 66.4	Additional opportunity for submitting amendments or arguments
R. 66.4*bis*	Consideration of amendments, arguments and rectifications of obvious mistakes
R. 66.5	Amendment
R. 66.8	Form of amendments
R. 70.11	Mention of amendments in the IPRP II
R. 91	Rectification of obvious mistakes in amendments under Art. 34

Amendment in the National Procedure Following Chapter II:

Art. 41, R. 78	Amendments to the *claims*, the *description*, and the *drawings* before the elected Offices
R. 78.1	Time limit for filing amendments. This is generally one month from the start of the national phase.
R. 78.3	Correspondingly for utility models
R. 159(1)(b) EPC	Submission of new amendments or indication of maintenance of amendments made on entry into the regional phase, use of Form 1200 is recommended (Information sheet on Form EPO 1200, Euro-PCT Guide 5.1.020)
R. 161 EPC	Renewed possibility of amendment during the Euro-PCT phase within a period of six months from notification in compliance with R. 137(4) EPC (Information Sheet on Form 1200, OJ 2011, 354, OJ 2010, 406 with further details, GL Exam E-IX 3)
R. 137(5) EPC	Amendments after receipt of the supplementary European search report, GL Exam E-IX 4.2

(c) The applicant shall receive at least one written opinion from the International Preliminary Examining Authority unless such Authority considers that all of the following conditions are fulfilled:

(i) the invention satisfies the criteria set forth in Article 33(1),

(ii) the international application complies with the requirements of this Treaty and the Regulations in so far as checked by that Authority,

(iii) no observations are intended to be made under Article 35(2), last sentence.

Art. 34(2)(b)	Filing of amendments and arguments, preferably with the demand
R. 66.1*bis*	The written opinion established by the ISA under R. 43*bis*.1 shall be considered to be a written opinion of the IPEA for the purposes of R. 66.2(a). Subject to exceptions under R. 66.1*bis*(b).
R. 66.1	Documents forming the basis of the IPE
R. 66.1*ter*	Top-up search conducted by IPEA
AG-IP 10.066	No new written opinion will be issued if there are no objections against the claims. The IPEA will then proceed directly to issuing of the IPRP II.
R. 66.2	Written opinion of the IPEA in case of non-compliance with certain requirements
R. 66.3 and 4	Opportunities for submitting amendments or arguments
R. 66.4*bis*	Consideration of amendments, arguments and rectifications of obvious mistakes

(d) The applicant may respond to the written opinion.

R. 66.3	Formal response of the applicant
R. 66.6	Informal communications between IPEA and applicant

(3)

(a) If the International Preliminary Examining Authority considers that the international application does not comply with the requirement of unity of invention as set forth in the Regulations, it may invite the applicant, at his option, to restrict the claims so as to comply with the requirement or to pay additional fees.

R. 13	Requirement of unity of invention, see details in the Introduction to R. 13.
R. 68	Lack of unity of invention during IPE
R. 66.1*ter*	Impact on the scope of the Top-up search
R. 68.2	Invitation to restrict or to pay additional fees in case of non-unity
R. 68.3	Additional fees
R. 158(1) EPC	Additional fee for IPE

(b) The national law of any elected State may provide that, where the applicant chooses to restrict the claims under subparagraph (a), those parts of the international application which, as a consequence of the restriction, are not to be the subject of international preliminary examination shall, as far as effects in that State are concerned, be considered withdrawn unless a special fee is paid by the applicant to the national Office of that State.

Art. 17, R. 40	Lack of unity of invention (international search)
Art. 34(3)(a), R. 68	Lack of unity of invention (IPE)
Art. 3(4)(iii)	Unity of invention

10 A PCTa cannot be divided. Only additional fees for search or examination can be paid. The possibility of division is only available in the national/regional phases.

R. 13	Unity of invention
R. 13.1	Requirement (of unity)
R. 13.2	Cases in which the requirement of unity of invention is deemed to be fulfilled. In short: where the characterizing features are identical. Very detailed examples can be found in the AIs Annex B.
R. 13.3	Determination of unity of invention not affected by manner of claiming
R. 13.4	Dependent claims are unitary
R. 13.5	Unity of invention for utility models
W 52/92 EPO	For the determination of non-unity *a priori* (before the search), the problem is to be determined on the basis of the description and the prior art considered therein from the applicant's point of view
W 8/87 EPO	According to R. 13.1 PCT, lack of unity can be established *a posteriori* (after the search), i.e. after examination of the common distinguishing features
G 2/89 EPO	Lack of unity may be determined *a priori* or *a posteriori* – with a request for payment of an additional fee
R. 68	Lack of unity of invention (IPE)
R. 68.1	No invitation to restrict or pay, despite lack of unity
R. 68.2	Invitation to restrict or pay. Contents: – The applicant may choose between restriction or paying additional fees; – Information on the restriction option; – Amount of the additional fees; – Reasons for lack of unity;

- Time limit for compliance: one month from the invitation;
- There is the possibility of protest under R. 68.3(c) (see below);
- Time limit for payment of the protest fee: one month from the invitation;
- The amount of the protest fee is determined by IPEA.

Established Case Law (e.g. W 8/87 EPO)	The invitation under Art. 34(3)(a) PCT to pay additional fees is only legally effective if the lack of unity is sufficiently substantiated. According to R. 68.2(ii), the reasons for lack of unity must be stated in the invitation.
W 6/99 EPO	Before issuing an invitation under R. 68.2, a written communication raising the objection of lack of unity *a posteriori* must be sent and the applicant's response awaited
G 1/89 EPO	The EPO, as ISA, may request an additional search fee under Art. 17(3)(a) PCT if it considers the application *a posteriori* to be non-unitary. The relevant communication under R. 40.1 PCT must contain, in addition to the list of inventions defined in the new independent claims (resulting from the combination of the dropped main or secondary claim) and the invitation to pay further search fees under Art. 17(3)(a) PCT, the reasoning for objections of lack of unity. An invitation to pay which does not contain these reasons is not legally binding with regard to the lack of unity established *a posteriori*.
W 21/03 EPO	The fee may only be charged in 'clear cases'
W 6/96 EPO	Doubts on the question of unity of invention work in favor of the applicant.
W 3/03 EPO	The objection should be raised at the latest with the first written opinion and not in a possible second one.
R. 68.3(a)	The amount of the additional fee is determined by the IPEA. At the EPO it corresponds to the amount of the fee for IPE (R. 158(2) EPC, Art. 2(1) item 19 RFees).
R. 68.3(b)	The additional fee is due to the IPEA. The time limit for payment of the additional fee is one month from the invitation.

If the additional fee was not paid, the EPO previously selected the first group of 11
inventions in the regional phase or requested the submission of suitable claims (R. 164 EPC 2000). No further search or examination fees could be requested. Only the filing of a divisional application remained.

Since November 1, 2014, it has been possible to pay further search fees in the regional 12
phase in the event of non-unity being objected to in the international phase. This possibility exists irrespective of which authority previously searched as ISA. If the time limit is missed, further processing is possible in accordance with R. 135(2) EPC applicable from November 1, 2014. If the EPO has searched as ISA, this applies if no Office action has been issued by November 1, 2014. In other cases, this applies if the supplementary European search report was drawn up on or after November 1, 2014. (OJ 2013, 503; OJ 2014, A70).

R. 68.2(iii)	The time limit for payment of the additional fees is one month from the invitation under Art. 34(3)(a)
R. 68.3(c)	The applicant may protest against the invitation (with reasons), subject to simultaneous payment of the additional fee – under protest – and payment of the protest fee
W 16/92 EPO	The applicant's statement of grounds for protest must contain comprehensible reasons. The mere assertion that the application is unitary is not sufficient to avoid the protest being rejected as inadmissible.
G 2/89 EPO	The ISA's decision on unity is not binding for the IPEA
W 9/94 EPO	If the IPEA objects to unity, a statement of grounds of protest based solely on non-objection by the ISA is generally not sufficient within the meaning of R. 68.3(c)
R. 68.2(v)	A protest fee must be paid together with the protest
R. 68.3(e)	If the protest fee is not paid on time, the protest is deemed not to have been filed. There is no grace period. The additional fee will not be refunded. Instead, the additional examination will be carried out.

13 The time limit for filing a protest and paying the protest fee is one month from the invitation under Art. 34(3)(a). However, the EPO deviated from this until the EPC 2000 came into force. The previous two-stage procedure applied to applications which were pending at the time the EPC 2000 entered into force. For international applications filed since the date of entry into force of the EPC 2000 (December 13, 2007), the one-step procedure applies and the Communication of March 1, 2005 (OJ 2005, 225) cited below, replaced by Communication of June 24, 2007 (Special edition no. 3 OJ 2007, 142 et seq.) and replaced on July 1, 2010 by decision of June 24, 2010 (OJ 5/2010, 320), which does not affect the procedure before the EPO as ISA and IPEA, but only regulates the applicability to the EPO as SISA (Communication of June 24, 2010, OJ 5/2010, 322). This was in turn replaced by the decision of June 9, 2015 (OJ 2015, A59), which redefines the composition of the review body.

14 See also practical advice in PCT Newsletter 6/2021, p.11.

Single-Stage Procedure

15 The review body (see also the term 'review panel' below) is the sole instance for examining a protest. If additional fees are paid under protest and the protest fee is duly paid, the protest is submitted to the review body for a decision.

1. If the review body finds that the protest was fully justified, the additional fees and the protest fee shall be refunded.
2. If the review body finds that the protest was only partially justified, the corresponding additional fees, but not the protest fee, shall be refunded.

W 20/01 EPO	If an applicant has paid the additional fees late under protest, the protest must still be taken into account if the ISA has carried out

	the supplementary search as if the additional fees had been paid on time
W 3/93 EPO	For the time limit under R. 40.1(ii) (Payment of additional fees in international search), re-establishment is allowed, although Art. 48(2) does not refer to the ISA, i.e. re-establishment in the PCT without initiation of the national phase under Art. 25(2). Analogously applicable to R. 68.3 (additional fees in IPE).
R. 68.3(c) 2nd sentence	The protest is examined by a review panel
R. 68.3(c) 2 2nd half-sentence	The additional fee may be refunded
W 4/93 EPO	Submission of new reasons and evidence on the occasion of the communication of the review result is inadmissible in principle. A deficiency in the statement of grounds in the invitation to pay additional fees shall not be remedied by the subsequent submission of grounds in the communication of the result of the review of the protest.
W 11/93 EPO e.g. Art. 155(3) EPC previous practice	The 'review panels' according to R. 68.3(c), second sentence, are the Boards of Appeal for all applications filed before the entry into force of the EPC 2000 (December 13, 2007). The Board of Appeal cannot examine *ex officio* whether lack of unity exists for reasons other than those mentioned in the invitation. For all applications filed after the date of entry into force of the EPC 2000 (December 13, 2007), the 'review panel' is a review body consisting of three members, one of whom is the chair and another the examiner who issued the invitation to pay additional fees under Art. 17(3)(a) or 34(3)(a) or established the SISR or the communication under R. 45*bis*.6(a)(ii) (decision of June 9, 2015, OJ 2015, A59).
W 4/93 EPO	The right of the applicants to communicate orally with the IPEA (Art. 34(2)(a) PCT) does not include the right to formal oral proceedings. An informal interview under R. 66.6 PCT is usually not expedient in protest proceedings under R. 68.3(c) PCT (Reasons, 9).
W 4/94 EPO	If no new arguments have been put forward in the statement of grounds of protest, a statement of grounds by the authority referring back to the results of the review under R. 68.3(c) is not objectionable
W 3/02 EPO	The suspension of grant proceedings under R. 14 EPC (vindication) after entry into the regional phase before the EPO does not extend to protest proceedings pending before the Board of Appeal
R. 68.3(c) 2 2nd half-sentence	Possible refund of the additional fee if the protest was justified

R. 68.3(e) 3rd sentence	Likewise refund of the protest fee if the protest was fully justified
R. 68.3(c) 3, AIs 403 and 603	The protest and the decision thereon are transmitted to the elected Offices at the request of the applicant. Transmission of a translation of the protest and the decision thereon to the elected Offices, applying R. 40.2(c)(4) *mutatis mutandis*, with the start of the national/regional phases.

(c) If the applicant does not comply with the invitation referred to in subparagraph (a) within the prescribed time limit, the International Preliminary Examining Authority shall establish an international preliminary examination report on those parts of the international application which relate to what appears to be the main invention and shall indicate the relevant facts in the said report. The national law of any elected State may provide that, where its national Office finds the invitation of the International Preliminary Examining Authority justified, those parts of the international application which do not relate to the main invention shall, as far as effects in that State are concerned, be considered withdrawn unless a special fee is paid by the applicant to that Office.

R. 68.4	Procedure in the case of insufficient restriction of the claims
R. 68.5	Main invention
R. 70.13	75% reduction of the examination fee at the EPO under Art. 14(2) RFees if examination is to be carried out for the subject matter dealt with in the IPRP, OJ EPO 2023 A28 p.6

(4)

(a) If the International Preliminary Examining Authority considers

(i) that the international application relates to a subject matter on which the International Preliminary Examining Authority is not required, under the Regulations, to carry out an international preliminary examination, and in the particular case decides not to carry out such examination, or

R. 67	Subject matter for which no IPE is required by IPEA
R. 67.1	Non-technical and non-industrially applicable inventions are not examined. An exception to this is made if the EPO would carry out an examination under the European procedure (Annex C of the WIPO-EPO Agreement, https://www.wipo.int/pct/en/access/isa_ipea_agreements.html, Art. 16(3)(b)).
R. 39	Subject matter for which no international search is required by ISA
R. 66.1(e)	Impact of non-establishment of ISR with respect to some subject matter on IPE
Art. 152 EPC	See first the earlier agreement between the EPO and WIPO under the PCT as amended on November 1, 2001 (OJ 2001, 601 et seq.,

OJ 2007, 617 et seq.) and the Notice from the President of the EPO of Novermber 26, 2001 concerning the limitation of the EPO's competence as PCT authority for US applicants with respect to biotechnology, business methods, and telecommunications and the applicability of the limitation to parallel European direct filing and regional phase applications (OJ 2002, 52 et seq.). Repeal with regard to biotechnology and telecommunications from January 1, 2004 (Communication of October 31, 2003, OJ 2003, 633). Extended with regard to business methods until March 1, 2009 (Communication of December 1, 2004, OJ 2005, 149 and of July 27, 2006, OJ 10/2006, 555). Amendment by IPC since January 1, 2006: G 06F17/60 corresponds to G06Q, G06Q 10/00, 30/00, 40/00, 50/00, 90/00, 99/00 (OJ 2006, 149). Amendment by IPC since January 1, 2006: G 06F17/60 corresponds to G06Q, G06Q 10/00, 30/00, 40/00, 50/00, 90/00, 99/00 (OJ 2006, 149). Amendments as of March 1, 2009 in Annex A of the WIPO-EPO Agreement, PCT Gazette February 26, 2009, OJ 2010, 304, 2014, A40, Supplementary Publication 4/2016, p. 402. Business methods corresponding to the IPCs mentioned are still not searched. Although the restriction for business methods has been deleted from the WIPO-EPO Agreement since January 1, 2015 (PCT Gazette November 20, 2014, p. 175), the Notice on Business Methods in OJ 2007, 592 is still applicable according to the Notice of the EPO (OJ 2014, A117), see also annotation to Art. 16(2).

R. 66.1*ter* Effect on the scope of the supplementary international search

(ii) that the description, the claims, or the drawings, are so unclear, or the claims are so inadequately supported by the description, that no meaningful opinion can be formed on the novelty, inventive step (non-obviousness), or industrial applicability, of the claimed invention,

the said Authority shall not go into the questions referred to in Article 33(1) and shall inform the applicant of this opinion and the reasons therefor.

Art. 35(3) If the IPEA is of the opinion that any situations mentioned in Art. 34(4)(a) exist at the time of establishing the IPRP/IPER, this opinion and its reasons must be stated in the report: the application to involve subject matter not required for examination under the Regulations, or when the application's descriptions, claims, or drawings are so unclear, or the claims are inadequately supported by the description, that no meaningful opinion on novelty, inventive step, or industrial applicability can be formed

(b) If any of the situations referred to in subparagraph (a) is found to exist in, or in connection with, certain claims only, the provisions of that subparagraph shall apply only to the said claims.

Article 35
The International Preliminary Examination Report

INTRODUCTION

1 The IPEA will prepare an international preliminary report on patentability, the IPRP II. It states whether the claims appear to satisfy the criteria of novelty, inventive step, and industrial applicability, but does not contain any statements whether or not the claimed invention is or seems patentable according to any national law (Art. 35(2)). The report cites the documents believed to support the conclusions, possibly with explanations (Art. 35(2)). The report will also indicate any unexamined subject matter (Art. 35(3)).

2 Replacement sheets containing amendments and corrections of obvious mistakes which have been taken into account and also those that have not been taken into account in the IPE will be annexed to the report (Art. 36(1); R. 70.2(e); R. 70.16). The report is drawn up in the language in which the international application is published, or, where the examination is carried out on a translation furnished under R. 55.2, in the language of the translation (R. 70.17). Form requirements for the report are given in R. 70.

3 The IPRP II remains confidential in the international phase (Art. 38). An elected Office may allow access to it.

(1)

The international preliminary examination report shall be established within the prescribed time limit and in the prescribed form.

R. 69.2	The time limit for drawing up the international examination report is generally 28 months from the priority date if the request was filed before the expiry of 19 months; or six months after the start of international examination or receipt of the translation if this time limit expires later.
R. 70	IPRP by the IPEA (International Preliminary Examination Report)
	R. 70.1 Definition

	R. 70.2	The report is based on the amended claims
	R. 70.3	Identifications
	R. 70.4	Dates
	R. 70.5	Classification
	R. 70.9	Non-written disclosures
	R. 70.10	Certain published documents
	R. 70.11	Mention of amendments
	R. 70.12	Mention of certain defects and other matters
	R. 70.13	Remarks concerning unity of invention
	R. 70.14	Authorized officer
	R. 70.15	Form; Title: international preliminary report on patentability (Chapter II of the PCT)
	R. 70.16	Annexes to the Report
	R. 70.17	Languages of the Report and the Annexes
AIs 604	Guidelines for Explanations Contained in the International Preliminary Examination Report	
AIs 612	Authorized officer	

(2)

The international preliminary examination report shall not contain any statement on the question whether the claimed invention is or seems to be patentable or unpatentable according to any national law. It shall state, subject to the provisions of paragraph (3), in relation to each claim, whether the claim appears to satisfy the criteria of novelty, inventive step (non-obviousness), and industrial applicability, as defined for the purposes of the international preliminary examination in Article 33(1) to (4). The statement shall be accompanied by the citation of the documents believed to support the stated conclusion with such explanations as the circumstances of the case may require. The statement shall also be accompanied by such other observations as the Regulations provide for.

R. 70.6	Statement under Art. 35(2) in the IPER/IPRP
R. 70.7	Citations under Art. 35(2) in the IPER/IPRP
R. 70.8	Explanations under Art. 35(2) in the IPER/IPRP

(3)

(a) If, at the time of establishing the international preliminary examination report, the International Preliminary Examining Authority considers that any of the situations referred to in Article 34(4)(a) *(non-searchable matter)* exists, that report shall state this opinion and the reasons therefor. It shall not contain any statement as provided in paragraph (2).

(b) If a situation under Article 34(4)(b) *(non-searchable matter only for some claims)* is found to exist, the international preliminary examination report shall, in relation to the claims in question, contain the statement as provided in subparagraph (a), whereas, in relation to the other claims, it shall contain the statement as provided in paragraph (2).

Art. 34(6) Unclear claims or no obligation to examine

Article 36
Transmittal, Translation, and Communication, of the International Preliminary Examination Report

(1)

The international preliminary examination report, together with the prescribed annexes, shall be transmitted to the applicant and to the International Bureau.

R. 71	Transmission
R. 73.1	International Bureau prepares copies
R. 73.2	Communication to elected Offices

(2)

(a) The international preliminary examination report and its annexes shall be translated into the prescribed languages.

(b) Any translation of the said report shall be prepared by or under the responsibility of the International Bureau, whereas any translation of the said annexes shall be prepared by the applicant.

R. 70.2	Amended claims as basis of the report
R. 70.16	Annexes to the report
R. 70.17	Language of the report and the annexes
R. 72	Translation of IPRP II and of the written opinion of the ISA
R. 74	Content of translation of annexes

(3)

(a) The international preliminary examination report, together with its translation (as prescribed) and its annexes (in the original language), shall be communicated by the International Bureau to each elected Office.

(b) The prescribed translation of the annexes shall be transmitted within the prescribed time limit by the applicant to the elected Offices.

R. 74	Time limit for transmission under Art. 39 is 30/31 months.

(4)

The provisions of Article 20(3) shall apply, *mutatis mutandis*, to copies of any document which is cited in the international preliminary examination report and which was not cited in the international search report.

Art. 20(3)	The International Bureau shall send copies of citations
R. 71.2(a)	Copies of cited documents
R. 71.2(b)	Costs of preparing and mailing copies

Article 37
Withdrawal of Demand or Election

INTRODUCTION

During the international phase the applicant may withdraw the application, designations, priority claims, the supplementary search request, the demand, or elections before the expiration of 30 months from the priority date (Art. 37; R. 90*bis*.1(a), 2(a), 3(a), 3*bis*(a), 4(a); see also annotations to Art. 22). Note that the extended period of 31 months for entering the national phase under Art. 22(3) and Art. 39(1)(b) is not applicable here because R. 90*bis*.2(a), 3(a), 4(a) specifically mention only 30 months. Withdrawals after expiry of the 30 months must be made before the designated or elected Offices, the effect of which being governed by national law. 1

The withdrawal of the election of a Contracting State will result in the State reverting from an elected State to a designated State, where the results of the IPE will not be used in the national phase. If all elections are withdrawn, the demand is considered withdrawn (Art. 37(2)) and the processing of the application by the IPEA is discontinued (R. 90*bis*.6(c)). 2

An applicant might wish to prevent publication of an international application, for example, for strategic considerations relating to business needs or objectives. Another reason could be a reduced prospect of grant because of prior art revealed in the international search. Not publishing an application will keep it confidential and avoids giving an insight to competitors. An unpublished application will not belong to the prior art and, consequently, it cannot be used to refuse grant of another application. This can be relevant if an applicant filed other closely related applications in the same technical area. 3

There will be no international publication if the international application is withdrawn or is considered withdrawn at least one day before the technical preparations for publication have been completed (Art. 21(5); R. 90*bis*.1(c)). Even if a receiving Office declares that an international application has been withdrawn, the publication of the international application will only be prevented if the notification of withdrawal transmitted by the receiving Office reaches the International Bureau before technical preparations are complete (R. 29.1(v)). It is strongly recommended to send the notice of withdrawal directly to the International Bureau through ePCT https://pct.wipo.int/ePCT. Only if ePCT cannot be used, the notice can be filed using an internet backup 4 document upload system provided by the International Bureau (https://pct.wipo.int/ePCTExternal/pages/UploadDocument.xhtml). (AG-IP 9.023A)

5 The notice of withdrawal must be filed with the International Bureau (Art. 37(3)(a); R. 90*bis*.4(b)), which will notify the IPEA and the elected Offices concerned (Art. 37(3)(b)). If the withdrawal is filed instead with the IPEA, the IPEA will date-mark the withdrawal and forward it to the International Bureau, which will consider the date marked as the date of receipt (R. 90*bis*.4(c)). The withdrawal must be signed (R. 90*bis*.5, R. 2.1) and is free of charge (AG-IP 11.060).

6 A special situation may arise when the election of LU or TZ is withdrawn because of their use of 20/21 months instead of 30/31 months for national entry as designated Office; see Art. 37(4); AG-IP 11.061 and PCT Reservations, Declarations, Notification and Incompatibilities (https://www.wipo.int/pct/en/texts/reservations/res_incomp.html).

(1)

The applicant may withdraw any or all elections.

R. 90*bis*.4 Withdrawal of demand or elections

(2)

If the election of all elected States is withdrawn, the demand shall be considered withdrawn.

R. 90*bis*.6 Effect of withdrawal

(3)

(a) Any withdrawal shall be notified to the International Bureau.

(b) The elected Offices concerned and the International Preliminary Examining Authority concerned shall be notified accordingly by the International Bureau.

(4)

(a) Subject to the provisions of subparagraph (b), withdrawal of the demand or of the election of a Contracting State shall, unless the national law of that State provides otherwise, be considered to be withdrawal of the international application as far as that State is concerned.

(b) Withdrawal of the demand or of the election shall not be considered to be withdrawal of the international application if such withdrawal is effected prior to the expiration of the applicable time limit under Article 22; however, any Contracting State may provide in its national law that the aforesaid shall apply only if its national Office has received, within the said time limit, a copy of the international application, together with a translation (as prescribed), and the national fee.

R. 90*bis*.6 Effect of withdrawal

The time limit under Art. 22 is generally 30 months. This means that, as a rule, the withdrawal of the demand does not constitute a withdrawal of the PCTa. The applicant should exercise care in respect of designated Offices which do not apply the 30-month time limit (AG-IP 11.062). 7

If the withdrawal takes place before substantive examination has begun, the IPE fee may be refunded. In this case, the EPO refunds 100% of the examination fee (Euro-PCT Guide 5.9.014). 8

Article 38
Confidential Nature of the International Preliminary Examination

INTRODUCTION

1. Access to Documents of International Preliminary Examination

1 Promptly after the filing of a demand for preliminary examination, the International Bureau will publish information on the demand (R. 61.4, AIs 431).

2 The file of the IPE kept by the IPEA is, in principle, confidential, unless access is requested or authorized by the applicant (Art. 38(1)). However, once an IPRP has been established, the IPEA will allow an elected Office to access it (Art. 38(1); R. 94.2).

3 If no examination has been demanded or no IPRP II (see Introduction to the PCT, No. 1.6.2) will be established by the IPEA, an examination report (IPRP I) is issued by the International Bureau on behalf of the ISA at expiry of 30 months from the priority date and is available on PATENTSCOPE, including any translation and observations (R. 44*bis*.1; R. 43*bis*.1; AG-IP 7.031). An IPRP I has the same content as the written opinion of the ISA, which is available earlier.

4 After the IPEA has established the international preliminary report on patentability (IPRP II, R. 70), the International Bureau communicates the report and any annexes to the elected Offices (Art. 36(3)(a); R. 73.2). The report may be available for public inspection in the files of an elected Office, depending on national law (R. 94.3; AG-IP 11.074). An elected Office may also request the International Bureau to make the report and related documents received from IPEA under R. 71.1 since January 1, 2020 available to third parties via PATENTSCOPE on behalf of the elected Office at the expiration of 30 months from the priority date (R. 94.1(c); AG-IP 9.027, 10.080). The Offices that have made such a request are listed on the WIPO website. (https://www.wipo.int/pct/en/texts/access_iper.html)

5 The wording of R. 94.1(c) about access to the file held by the International Bureau obscures its actual effect. The true effect can be unveiled as follows.

1. The copies are made available to third parties. This means that file inspection is possible for everyone.

2. Access provided by the International Bureau concerns both IPRP I and IPRP II.
3. A request for access to the file is made by an elected Office, for example, the EPO, for all international applications and not for individual ones. These requests are published in the PCT Gazette, for example, see 2004, p.1742.
4. It is irrelevant whether the requesting Office has actually started the national or regional phase (see R. 94.3 and OJ EPO 2003 p. 382).
5. The documents are made available on the WIPO website (https://patentscope.wipo.int/search/de/structuredSearch.jsf).

As a result, the IPRP I and II will be available on the WIPO website for everyone, 6 but only after 30 months from the priority date (AG-IP 10.080; AG-IP No. 7.031). After this period, these reports are no longer confidential, as was required by Art. 38. Access to documents established under Chapter I before the expiry of 30 months is in accordance with Art. 38, even if the documents subsequently become part of the Chapter II procedure (www.wipo.int/edocs/mdocs/pct/en/pct_wg_6/pct_wg_6_24.pdf, p. 57, No. 292).

Additionally, any person may inspect *any* documents relating to an international ap- 7 plication contained in the file of the elected Office (R. 94.3), including *any* documents relating to the IPE, for example, the correspondence between the applicant and the IPEA. The inspection may be allowed to the same extent as provided by the national law applicable to the elected Office for access to the file of a national application and only after publication of the international application (R. 94.3).

The EPO makes documents relating to PCT applications held by it in its capacity 8 of receiving Office or (S)ISA available for inspection free of charge through the European Patent Register, i.e. through online file inspection. Access is provided to third parties after the publication of the international application. Documents omitted from file inspection under R. 48.2(l) or R. 94.1(d) or (e) or under R. 144 EPC are not accessible. File inspection on paper copies is possible in exceptional cases (OJ EPO 2019 A17; A16).

In its capacity as a designated Office, the EPO allows access to its files and may 9 communicate information from its files relating to international applications once international publication has taken place. In its capacity as an elected Office, the EPO allows access to its files (including the entire PCT Chapter II file) and may communicate information from its files relating to international applications once international publication has taken place and, as far as the PCT Chapter II file is concerned, the IPRP has been completed (GL Exam EPO E-IX, 2.10).

The receiving Office, ISA (including the SISA) and IPEA keep the records of interna- 10 tional applications for at least ten years from the international filing date (R. 93.1, 93.3). The International Bureau keeps the file, including the record copy, for at least 30 years from the date of receipt of the record copy under Art. 12(1) (R. 93.2) and the basic records, theoretically, indefinitely.

The table in Annex 3 below gives an overview of how and when third parties can 11 obtain access to information in the files of the Offices depending on the nature of the information and presented in the order of the stage of the procedure.

(1)

Neither the International Bureau nor the International Preliminary Examining Authority shall, unless requested or authorized by the applicant, allow access within the meaning, and with the proviso, of Article 30(4) to the file of the international preliminary examination by any person or authority at any time, except by the elected Offices once the international preliminary examination report has been established.

(2)

Subject to the provisions of paragraph (1) and Articles 36(1) and (3) *(transmittal of IPRP II to applicant, International Bureau, elected Office)* **and 37(3)(b)** *(notification of withdrawal of demand or election)*, **neither the International Bureau nor the International Preliminary Examining Authority shall, unless requested or authorized by the applicant, give information on the issuance or nonissuance of an international preliminary examination report and on the withdrawal or nonwithdrawal of the demand or of any election.**

12 See table 'Access to Files' in the Annex of this book.

Art. 30	Confidential nature of the international application
Art. 36	Transmittal of IPER to applicant, International Bureau, and elected Office
Art. 37	Notification of the elected Office and IPEA by International Bureau regarding withdrawal of election
R. 94	Access to files
R. 61.4	Publication of the demand for IPE
R. 48.2(l)	Omission from access

Article 39
Copy, Translation, and Fee, to Elected Offices

INTRODUCTION

1 The significance of Art. 39 lies in the extension of the suspensive effect under Art. 22, 23 for those countries which have declared the incompatibility of Art. 22 with national law and for which the 20 or 21-month time limit applies (see annotations to Art. 22). In order to obtain the suspensive effect for entry into the national phase for these countries, the request for IPE must be filed before the expiry of 19 months, despite the provision of R. 54*bis* (AG-IP 5.006, 10.010). However, the suspensive effect can also be achieved by selecting these countries not for the national phase but through the regional phase (see note on Art. 22 at the end and PCT Newsletter 02/2005 p. 6).

(1)

(a) If the election of any Contracting State has been effected prior to the expiration of the 19th month from the priority date, the provisions of Article 22 shall not apply to such State and the applicant shall furnish a copy of the international application (unless the communication under Article 20 has already taken place) and a translation thereof (as prescribed), and pay the national fee (if any), to each elected Office not later than at the expiration of 30 months from the priority date.

Art. 22	Time limit for actions before designated Offices	
Art. 31	Indication of elected Offices in the demand for IPE	
R. 57	Handling fee	
R. 58	Preliminary examination fee. There is no remedy in the international phase if all time limits for payment of fees are missed, but only in the national phase.	
R. 49	Requirements for translations	
R. 76	Translation of priority document; application of certain rules to procedures before elected Offices	
	R. 76.4	Time limit for the translation of the priority document shall be determined in accordance with Art. 39

	R. 76.5	Application of R. 13*ter*.3 (standardized sequence listing), R. 20.8 (incorporation of elements, filing date), R. 22.1(g) (record copy), R. 47.1 (transmittal of international application and search report by International Bureau), R. 49 (transmittal, translation and payment of fees), R. 49*bis* (indications as to protection sought for purposes of national processing), R. 49*ter*.2 (effect of restoration of right of priority) and R. 51*bis* (national requirements)

R. 82*quater*	Excuse of delay in meeting time limits and extension of time limits
Art. 45, Art. 153(1) EPC	The election of one EPC State leads to the election of all States.
Art. 158(3), (4)	Transmittal of the application in the required language and payment of fees
Art. 64(1)(a)	Expiry of reservations regarding Chapter II
R. 95	Details of entry into the national phase and submission of translations to the International Bureau
R. 70.16	Amendments under Art. 19 (after service of the search report) and R. 66.8 (during the IPE procedure) are annexed to the preliminary examination report and are thus subject to translation under R. 49.5.
G 4/08	If the international application has been filed in an official language of the EPO, i.e. DE, FR or GB, this language remains the language of the procedure after the regional phase before the EPO has started. The language of procedure cannot be changed by filing a translation when the regional phase has started before the EPO (GL Exam E-IX, 2.1.3).

(b) Any national law may, for performing the acts referred to in subparagraph (a), fix time limits which expire later than the time limit provided for in that subparagraph.

2 The extended time limits allowed by national law under Art. 39(1)(b) do not in some cases coincide with the extended time limits under Art. 22(3), e.g. in AZ.

Art. 22	Time limits and extension of time limits before designated Offices An overview of the time limits, including extension of time limits, arranged by country can be found under 'Member States of the PCT' in the Annexes to this book and at www.wipo.int/pct/en/texts/time_limits.html.
Art. 48(2), R. 82*bis*.2	Reinstatement after failure to perform the acts under Art. 39
R. 77.1	Exercise of faculty under Art. 39(1)(b)

(2)

The effect provided for in Article 11(3) shall cease in the elected State with the same consequences as the withdrawal of any national application in that State if the applicant fails to perform the acts referred to in paragraph (1)(a) within the time limit applicable under paragraph (1)(a) or (b).

R. 160 EPC	Legal consequence is the fiction of withdrawal
AIs 112	Ceasing of effect under Art. 24(1)(iii) and Art. 39(2), review under Art. 25(2) and maintaining of effect under Art. 24(2) and Art. 39(3)

(3)

Any elected Office may maintain the effect provided for in Article 11(3) even where the applicant does not comply with the requirements provided for in paragraph (1)(a) or (b).

Art. 24(2)	Contains a corresponding provision
Art. 25(2)	Contains a corresponding provision
Art. 48	Reinstatement, further processing
AIs 112	Ceasing of effect under Art. 24(1)(iii) and Art. 39(2), review under Art. 25(2) and maintaining of effect under Art. 24(2) and Art. 39(3)

Article 40
Delaying of National Examination and Other Processing

(1)

If the election of any Contracting State has been effected prior to the expiration of the 19th month from the priority date, the provisions of Article 23 shall not apply to such State and the national Office of or acting for that State shall not proceed, subject to the provisions of paragraph (2), to the examination and other processing of the international application prior to the expiration of the applicable time limit under Article 39.

(2)

Notwithstanding the provisions of paragraph (1), any elected Office may, on the express request of the applicant, proceed to the examination and other processing of the international application at any time.

EPO	The requirements for an effective request for early processing also depend on the date on which early processing is requested. For the requirements and consequences, see OJ EPO 2015 A94 p. 3, OJ EPO 2013 p. 156, that supplements OJ EPO 2011 p. 48; Euro-PCT Guide 5.1.023 et seq., 5.14.003.
Art. 23(2)	Contains a corresponding provision
Art. 39	Time limit of 30/31 months
R. 49*ter.*2(b)	Time limit for the request for restoration of the right of priority
R. 159 EPC	Requirements for an effective request for early processing

Article 41
Amendment of the Claims, the Description, and the Drawings, before Elected Offices

(1)

The applicant shall be given the opportunity to amend the claims, the description, and the drawings, before each elected Office within the prescribed time limit. No elected Office shall grant a patent, or refuse the grant of a patent, before such time limit has expired, except with the express consent of the applicant.

(2)

The amendments shall not go beyond the disclosure in the international application as filed, unless the national law of the elected State permits them to go beyond the said disclosure.

AG-IP 11.047	Consequences of added subject matter in the national phase
Art. 19(2)	Added subject matter in amendments according to Art. 19
Art. 46	Added subject matter in translation of the PCTa
Art. 28(2)	Added subject matter before designated Office
Art. 34(2)(b)(2)	Added subject during IPE

(3)

The amendments shall be in accordance with the national law of the elected State in all respects not provided for in this Treaty and the Regulations.

(4)

Where an elected Office requires a translation of the international application, the amendments shall be in the language of the translation.

R. 11.12	Amendments etc.
R. 12.2	Language of amendments in the international applications

R. 92*bis*	Recording of changes in certain indications in the request of the international application or in the demand for IPE

1 For the possibilities of amendments in the various phases (during Chapter I or II, or after Chapter I or II in the national or regional phase) see annotations to Art. 28.

Article 42
Results of National Examination in Elected Offices

No elected Office receiving the international preliminary examination report may require that the applicant furnish copies, or information on the contents, of any papers connected with the examination relating to the same international application in any other elected Office.

The Records of the Washington Diplomatic Conference on the Patent Cooperation Treaty, drafted during the 1970 Washington Conference (available at https://www.wipo.int/export/sites/www/pct/en/docs/texts/washington_p1_to_162.pdf, p. 52) state with regard to Art. 42: 1

> 'NOTES ON ARTICLE 42
>
> SOLE PARAGRAPH: There is a growing tendency in examining Offices to obligate the applicant to produce copies, or information on the contents, of any papers connected with the examination of the same invention in other examining Offices. Sometimes it is even required that the applicant furnish translations of such papers. Such requirements may become extremely costly and vexatious for the applicant. Article 42 would exclude such requirements, provided the other Offices were also elected under Chapter II. Such other Offices would hardly lose anything because, instead of the said papers, they would receive the international preliminary examination report, which generally will be more valuable to them as it is prepared according to agreed international criteria.

On the other hand, nothing in this Article prevents any elected Office from asking any other elected Office to exchange with it – direct, that is, without the intervention of the applicant and without placing any burden on him – information on the examination results in the national phase, provided such exchange is permitted by the applicable laws.' 2

This makes it clear that applicants are to be relieved of the burden of the so-called '*information disclosure statement*' (IDS). The Offices are to exchange information directly among themselves, if necessary. 3

4 As of December 2023, the following countries are in breach of Art. 42, as they (may) require an IDS even for applications that have gone through the IPE: BR, CA, CO, GB, IE, IL, IN, MX, MY, NO and US. However, in some of these countries, requiring an IDS is only an option for the examiner, so a violation of Art. 42 does not always occur. Art. 42 is regularly violated by GB, IL, IN, US. The US is of considerable practical relevance.

Chapter III: Common Provisions

Article 43
Seeking Certain Kinds of Protection

In respect of any designated or elected State whose law provides for the grant of inventors' certificates, utility certificates, utility models, patents or certificates of addition, inventors' certificates of addition, or utility certificates of addition, the applicant may indicate, as prescribed in the Regulations, that his international application is for the grant, as far as that State is concerned, of an inventor's certificate, a utility certificate, or a utility model, rather than a patent, or that it is for the grant of a patent or certificate of addition, an inventor's certificate of addition, or a utility certificate of addition, and the ensuing effect shall be governed by the applicant's choice. For the purposes of this Article and any Rule thereunder, Article 2(ii) shall not apply.

R. 49*bis*.1(a)	Indications as to protection sought for purposes of national processing
R. 4.9(a)(ii)	All kinds of protection are automatically requested

Article 44
Seeking Two Kinds of Protection

In respect of any designated or elected State whose law permits an application, while being for the grant of a patent or one of the other kinds of protection referred to in Article 43, to be also for the grant of another of the said kinds of protection, the applicant may indicate, as prescribed in the Regulations, the two kinds of protection he is seeking, and the ensuing effect shall be governed by the applicant's indications. For the purposes of this Article, Article 2(ii) shall not apply.

1 The WIPO list of types of protection can be found under: https://www.wipo.int/pct/en/texts/typesprotection.html.

Art. 43	Seeking certain kinds of protection
R. 4.9(a)(ii)	Request covers automatically all kind of protections
R. 49*bis*.1(b)	Indications as to protection sought for purposes of national processing

Article 45
Regional Patent Treaties

(1)

Any treaty providing for the grant of regional patents ("regional patent treaty"), and giving to all persons who, according to Article 9, are entitled to file international applications the right to file applications for such patents, may provide that international applications designating or electing a State party to both the regional patent treaty and the present Treaty may be filed as applications for such patents.

(2)

The national law of the said designated or elected State may provide that any designation or election of such State in the international application shall have the effect of an indication of the wish to obtain a regional patent under the regional patent treaty.

For PCT Contracting States for which regional patents can be applied for, see: www.wipo.int/pct/en/texts/reg_des.html, www.wipo.int/pct/en/texts/typesprotection.html. 1

In No. 4 of the 'Introduction to the PCT' in this book, regional patents are explained. 2
See the 'List of Territories' in this book to find which patent treaties are applicable in a certain territory.

There are regional treaties under which applicants from Member States can obtain a 3
regional patent via the PCT. It may also be stipulated that only a regional patent and not a national patent can be granted via the PCT in the State concerned (national route closed). In this case, the designation of the State in question has the effect that a corresponding regional patent is deemed to be designated.

If the national route via PCT is closed, no other type of protection (e.g. utility model, 4
see Art. 43) can be obtained via PCT; if an application for another IP right is desired, a direct national application is required (PCT Newsletter 4/2022, p. 10 footnote 3).

In addition to closing the national route, the following situation may exist: for an au- 5
tonomous territory of a State, the application of the regional patent may be excluded, so that the autonomous territory cannot be reached via PCT or directly regionally,

such as in NL (see annotations to Art. 1). Furthermore, for autonomous territories of a State, the respective national legislation may exclude that the national law of the State extends to this autonomous territory. In this case, a national application in the autonomous territory may be possible for that autonomous territory (e.g. Aruba). These situations may be alternative or cumulative.

6 Regional organizations that are PCT members (status on March 18, 2024):

7 *AP ARIPO Patent*

- regional phase only, not national phase for: SZ
- regional in addition or instead of national phase for: BW, CV (for international applications since October 14, 2022), GH, GM, KE, LR, LS, MW, MZ, NA, RW, SC (for international applications since January 1, 2022), SD, SL, ST, TZ, UG, ZM, ZW

8 *EA Eurasian Patent*

- regional or national phase for: AM, AZ, BY, KG, KZ, RU, TJ, TM

9 *EP European Patent*

- regional phase only, no national phase for: BE, CY, FR, GR, IE, (IT until June 30, 2020), LV, ME (since October 1, 2022, OJ EPO 2022 A82), MT, MC, NL, SI, SM; (Art. 4(1)(ii) PCT, Art. 153(1) EPC)
- regional and national phase for: AL, AT, BG, CH, CZ, DE, DK, EE, ES, FI, GB, HR, HU, IS, IT (for international applications since July 1, 2020) LI, LT, LU, LV, MT, MK, NO, PL, PT, RO, RS, SE, SK, SM, TR
- Extension States are States which are Contracting States to the PCT but not to the EPC (i.e. not covered by the EP designation) but are potential candidates for accession to the EPC and for which an extension agreement with the EPO is in force on the international filing date: currently Bosnia-Herzegovina (BA) and ME from March 1, 2010 to September 31, 2022 (OJ EPO 2022 A82). See GL Exam A-III, 12.1 and https://new.epo.org/en/legal/extension-validation-system
- Validation agreements, i.e. agreements with States for which no EPC accession is currently envisaged. For European or international patent applications filed as from the date of validity of the validation agreement, a request for validation is deemed to have been filed in the respective State. Currently applicable for Morocco (MA), for the Republic of Moldova (MD), for Tunisia (TN), for Cambodia (KH), for Georgia (GE, OJ EPO 2023 A104, A105).

10 *OA OAPI Patent*

- regional phase only, no national phase for: BF, BJ, CF, CG, CI, CM, GA, GN, GQ, GW, KM, ML, MR, NE, SN, TD, TG

Organizations that are not PCT members: 11

- Bilateral treaty
- CH – LI unitary jurisdiction based on the Patent Protection Treaty of December 22, 1978, OJ EPO 1980 p. 407. CH and LI are members of the PCT, but the association forming a unitary jurisdiction is not a member.

Multilateral treaty 12

- unitary patent of the Gulf Cooperation Council (GCC) is not a member of the PCT and has not accepted applications since January 6, 2021 (https://gccpo.org/AboutUsEn/ShowNews?id=66). Members are: Bahrain (BH), Qatar (QA), Kuwait (KW), Oman (OM), Saudi Arabia (SA), United Arab Emirates (AE) (see J. Wrede: 'Das GCC-Patent', Mitteilungen der deutschen Patentanwälte 2014 p. 385).

Article 46
Incorrect Translation of the International Application

If, because of an incorrect translation of the international application, the scope of any patent granted on that application exceeds the scope of the international application in its original language, the competent authorities of the Contracting State concerned may accordingly and retroactively limit the scope of the patent, and declare it null and void to the extent that its scope has exceeded the scope of the international application in its original language.

1 The word 'scope' must be interpreted as 'scope of protection'.

Art. 19(2)	Prohibition to introduce added matter when amending the claims after receipt of the ISR
Art. 34(2)(b)2	Prohibition to introduce added matter when amending the claims, description, or drawings during the IPE
Art. 28(2)	Added subject matter before designated Office
Art. 41(2)	Added subject matter before elected Office
R. 70(2)(c)	Added matter will be ignored during IPE

Article 47
Time Limits

(1)

The details for computing time limits referred to in this Treaty are governed by the Regulations.

R. 79	Calendar	
	R. 79.1	Expressing dates
R. 80	Computation of time limits	
	R. 80.1	Periods expressed in years
	R. 80.2	Periods expressed in months
	R. 80.3	Periods expressed in days
	R. 80.4	Local dates
	R. 80.5	Expiration on a non-working day or official holiday
	R. 80.6	Date of documents in case of service
	R. 80.7	End of a working day
Art. 48	Delay in meeting certain time limits	
R. 82	Irregularities in mail services	
R. 82*quater*	Excuse of delay in meeting time limits and extension of time limits	

(2)

(a) All time limits fixed in Chapters I and II of this Treaty may, outside any revision under Article 60, be modified by a decision of the Contracting States.

(b) Such decisions shall be made in the Assembly or through voting by correspondence and must be unanimous.

(c) The details of the procedure are governed by the Regulations.

R. 81	Modification of time limits fixed in the Treaty	
	R. 81.1	Proposal

R. 81.2	Decision by the Assembly
R. 81.3	Voting by correspondence

1 The PCT frequently uses the term 'time limit' and sometimes 'period' for the same notion, i.e. a period of time with a well-defined start, duration and expiration in which an applicant has to perform a certain act before an Office. The computation of time limits is governed by Art. 47, R. 79 and R. 80.

2 For an overview of historical modifications of the time limits under this paragraph, refer to annotations under Art. 60.

Article 48
Delay in Meeting Certain Time Limits

INTRODUCTION

1. Mail Irregularities During the International Phase

If a time limit fixed in the PCT is not met because of a delay or loss in the mail delivery service, for example, because of an interruption due to a strike, any loss of rights can be reversed if the following requirements of R. 82 are complied with (Art. 48(1)). The party must provide evidence that the letter was sent by registered airmail at least five days prior to the expiration of the period (R. 82.1(a)). If no airmail is available or where surface mail normally reaches its destination within two days, surface mail may be used (R. 82.1(a)). Where the evidence of the mailing is satisfactory, the delay in arrival will be excused, or, if the letter was lost in the mail, substitution by a new copy will be permitted, provided the party proves that the substitute is identical with the original (R. 82.1(b)). The evidence and, where applicable, the substitute letter, must be submitted within one month after the discovery of the delay or loss, but at least within six months after the expiration of the missed time limit (R. 82.1(c)). (AG-IP 11.063). 1

2. Excuse in National Phase of Time Limits Not Met in International Phase

The PCT has a few remedies in the international phase for a failure to meet a time limit. Most of them relate to time limits for payment of a fee. If not paid in time, the Office will invite the applicant to pay the fee together with a late payment fee (see, for example, R. 16*bis*). If still not paid, a loss of rights sets in, usually that the international application is considered withdrawn. Such a loss of rights can, in principle, not be remedied in the international phase (AG-IP 6.054). 2

However, the PCT allows Offices to apply remedies permitted under the national law of a Contracting State, but only with effect for that State (Art. 48(2)). Possible national remedies are reinstatement of rights, restoration, further processing, *restitutio in integrum* (or re-establishment), other provisions for excuse of delay, and other provisions providing for the extension of time limits or for excusing delays in meeting time limits (R. 82*bis*.2). Such remedies can only be obtained by entering the national 3 phase before the designated Office and carrying out the review and excuse procedure as set out in annotations to Art. 22.

4 Some Offices acting as receiving Office, ISA or IPEA may allow the application of national remedies in the international phase to excuse failure to meet a time limit, thereby extending the effect of the national remedy to all designated or elected States (see also AG-IP 6.054). Although this practice goes against Art. 48(2), it is used to mitigate the effect of the failure before Offices that do not have suitable national remedies, such as JP (AG-IP 6.054; for EPO practice, see EPO Board of Appeal decisions W4/87 r. 7, https://www.epo.org/law-practice/case-law-appeals/recent/w870004ep1.html and W3/93, https://www.epo.org/law-practice/case-law-appeals/recent/w930003ep1.html).

(1)

Where any time limit fixed in this Treaty or the Regulations is not met because of interruption in the mail service or unavoidable loss or delay in the mail, the time limit shall be deemed to be met in the cases and subject to the proof and other conditions prescribed in the Regulations.

R. 82	Irregularities in the mail service	
	R. 82.1	Delay or loss in mail
R. 82*quater*	Excuse of delay in meeting time limits and extension of time limits	

(2)

(a) Any Contracting State shall, as far as that State is concerned, excuse, for reasons admitted under its national law, any delay in meeting any time limit.

(b) Any Contracting State may, as far as that State is concerned, excuse, for reasons other than those referred to in subparagraph (a), any delay in meeting any time limit.

R. 82*bis*	Excuse by the designated or elected State of delays in meeting certain time limits	
	R. 82*bis*.1	Meaning of 'time limit' in Art. 48(2) (delay under national law)
	R. 82*bis*.2	Reinstatement of rights and other provisions to which Art. 48(2) applies
R. 82*quater*	Excuse of delay in meeting time limits and extension of time limits due to *force majeure*	
Art. 25, 24	Termination of the international phase, remedy before national Office	

J 5/80	Art. 48(2)(a) is to be interpreted broadly. Art. 121 EPC 1973, Art. 122 EPC 1973 and R. 85(a) EPC 1973 apply on transition to the national phase. The time limit is treated as having expired before the EPO under the EPC.
T 227/97	Reinstatement is always given if it is given under the EPC. R. 31(2)(a) EPC and R. 13*bis*.4 PCT are equivalent.
R. 26*bis*	Correction or addition of priority claim
R. 49*ter*	Effect of restoration of right of priority

Article 49
Right to Practice before International Authorities

INTRODUCTION

1 An agent appointed on filing of an international application must have the right to practice before the national Office with which the international application was filed (AG-IP 5.042). The requirements for the right to practice are laid down in national law and are summarized in AG-IP Annex C for each receiving Office.

2 The applicant may appoint the agent for the receiving Office also as agent for all other Offices acting in the international phase, i.e. the International Bureau, ISA and IPEA (Art. 49; R. 90.1(a)). Such an agent need not have the right to practice before these other Offices. For example, an applicant may appoint an agent having the right to practice before the USPTO and file his international application with the USPTO and appoint the same agent for the EPO as ISA and IPEA, even though the agent does not have the right to practice before the EPO as national Office. Note that this automatic right to practice before the ISA and IPEA does not extend to designated Offices. The applicant may, instead of the agent for the receiving Office, appoint another agent specifically to practice before the (S)ISA or IPEA, provided the agent has the right to practice before the national Office which acts as (S)ISA or IPEA (R. 90.1(b), (b-*bis*), (c)). Such an agent may be more familiar with the practice of the ISA and in particular of the IPEA.

Any attorney, patent agent, or other person, having the right to practice before the national Office with which the international application was filed, shall be entitled to practice before the International Bureau and the competent International Searching Authority and competent International Preliminary Examining Authority in respect of that application.

3 The power under national regulations is mentioned in the Summary of Annex C AG-NP.

Art. 10 Receiving Office

Art. 27(7)	Representation (warning): where an applicant is not a resident or national of an EPC Member State, a representative must be appointed before the EPO as receiving Office	
R. 18.1	Applicant: residence or nationality	
R. 18.1(c)	International Bureau as receiving Office	
R. 83	Right to practice before international authorities	
	R. 83.1	Proof of right
	R. 83.1*bis* (a)(b)	Right to practice before the International Bureau acting as receiving Office: the right to practice before the ISA and IPEA is derived from this right (R. 83.1*bis*(b))
	R. 83.2	Information on right to practice
R. 90	Agents and common representatives	
	R. 90.1	Appointment as agent
	R. 90.2	Common representative
	R. 90.3	Effect of acts by or in relation to agents and common representatives
	R. 90.4	Manner of appointment of agent or common representative (power of attorney)
	R. 90.5	General power of attorney
	R. 90.6	Revocation and renunciation of agent

Chapter IV: Technical Services

Article 50
Patent Information Services

INTRODUCTION

1 According to the post-Conference documents (Records of the Washington Conference, 1970, p. 752), the 'Treaty has two principal aims, one in the field of procedures for obtaining legal protection for inventions, the other in the field of the dissemination of technical information and the organization of technical assistance, particularly for developing countries'. It facilitates public access to new inventions through international publication, abstracts, and ISRs at 18 months from priority. Already then it was envisaged that the International Bureau provides information services, and a weekly Gazette publishes essential details. Developing countries should receive these services at reduced costs, potentially covered by profits or grants-in-aid (Records of the Washington Conference, 1970, p. 752, no. 64).

(1)

The International Bureau may furnish services by providing technical and any other pertinent information available to it on the basis of published documents, primarily patents and published applications (referred to in this Article as "the information services").

2 As to the form of providing such information services, refer to Art. 55(4), which states that the International Bureau shall provide a Gazette and other publications as provided for in the Regulations. In 2024, most of the information services are online, providing free access, for example to PATENTSCOPE, with 4.9 million PCT applications and in total 117 million (June 2024), national, regional, or international patent documents.

3 The Gazette has to be in English and French (R. 86.2). Since April 1, 2006 the paper based PCT Gazette subscription model is no longer available and the information in Section II are included in PATENTSCOPE and the information in Section IV ('Official Notices') as PDF files. Further, most of the information is also included in the various information resources, such as the PCT Applicant's Guide and the various website tables on the specificities of each territory or Office. Thus, in practice, if the Treaty or the Regulations today refer to publication in the Gazette, it means either PATENTSCOPE, the Official Notices or, to a certain extent, also anywhere else on WIPO's PCT website.

PATENTSCOPE (https://patentscope.wipo.int/search/en/structuredSearch.jsf) is a searchable database with data and documents relating to specific international applications (previously Section I-III Gazette); the original aim of providing information services is to facilitate the acquisition by developing countries of technical knowledge and technology, including published know-how. Currently, PATENTSCOPE contains many more documents and data from national and regional patent collections and various free of charge search tools in more than the ten publication languages (refer to annotations to para. (3). 4

The Official Notices (PCT Gazette) Collection (https://www.wipo.int/pct/en/official_notices/index.html), is a collection of all previous Section IV Gazette notifications in electronic form, going back to 1978 as yearly PDF documents. Combined PDFs for the first two and the second two decades are available to enable PCT users to do an efficient full text search through all years. Refer also to annotations to R. 86. 5

(2)

The International Bureau may provide these information services either directly or through one or more International Searching Authorities or other national or international specialized institutions, with which the International Bureau may reach agreement.

Some ISAs have their own databases on patents and published applications (in particular the IP5 Offices, e.g. Espacenet for the EPO). To a certain extent such databases are also provided to other countries. 6

(3)

The information services shall be operated in a way particularly facilitating the acquisition by Contracting States which are developing countries of technical knowledge and technology, including available published know-how.

PATENTSCOPE (http://patentscope.wipo.int/search/en/search.jsf;jsessionid=98389B05A9639FD400881E9627C8EEC5.wapp1) offers free access to over 4.9 million PCT applications as part of its collection of 117 million patent documents. PATENTSCOPE additionally contains the national patent data collections of 80 national or regional patent Offices (http://patentscope.wipo.int/search/en/help/data_coverage.jsf). The interface features a number of powerful tools, including cross-lingual (https://patentscope.wipo.int/search/en/clir/clir.jsf?new=true) and chemical compound (https://www.wipo.int/patentscope/en/news/pctdb/2016/news_0008.html) (including substructures and Markush (https://www.wipo.int/patentscope/en/news/pctdb/2021/news_0006.html)) searches, XML data and hyperlinks to citations in ISRs (https://www.wipo.int/patentscope/en/news/pctdb/2019/news_0002.html), as well as machine translation (https://patentscope.wipo.int/translate/translate.jsf?interfaceLanguage=en). Information on patent families (https://www.wipo.int/patentscope/en/news/pctdb/2021/news_0002.html) and non-patent literature (https://www.wipo.int/patentscope/en/news/pctdb/2021/news_0001.html) was added. Following a WIPO Development Agenda recommendation, information on 7 national phase processing of PCT applications, and thus legal status data, is available for 84 Offices (https://patentscope.wipo.int/search/en/help/national_phase_entry.jsf) (refer to R. 86 and R. 95 amended in 2016). Global Dossier public information is available for ten Offices (https://patentscope.wipo.int/search/en/help/global_dossier_coverage.jsf). The redesigned version of the Patent Register Portal (https://inspire.wipo.int/patent-register-portal/) contains legal status information for over 200 national and regional collections, including a search functionality by PCT application number. The new tool WIPO Inspire (https://inspire.wipo.int) provides a collection of reports on different functionalities of patent databases.

(4)

The information services shall be available to Governments of Contracting States and their nationals and residents. The Assembly may decide to make these services available also to others.

8 The WIPO website and Portal are freely accessible to the public, including governments and nationals and residents via the Internet. Previously information was sent by paper copies, including copies of the Gazette to Contracting States and also applicants. While certain paper services as the paper Gazette, including the Official Notices, were already discontinued in 2006 (refer to annotations to para. (1)), after the Covid-19 pandemic paper notifications are no longer sent by the International Bureau, not even for individual applications. Documents and data are provided to Offices and applicants by the International Bureau via PATENTSCOPE, ePCT (www.wipo.int/pct-eservices/en/ and https://pct.wipo.int/ePCTExternal/pages/landing_offices.xhtml), eDI (www.wipo.int/patentscope/en/data/index.html#ipos) and exceptionally on DVD-R.

(5)

(a) Any service to Governments of Contracting States shall be furnished at cost, provided that, when the Government is that of a Contracting State which is a developing country, the service shall be furnished below cost if the difference can be covered from profit made on services furnished to others than Governments of Contracting States or from the sources referred to in Article 51(4).

(b) The cost referred to in subparagraph (a) is to be understood as cost over and above costs normally incident to the performance of the services of a national Office or the obligations of an International Searching Authority.

9 Currently, most services are provided to Offices and Authorities of Contracting States without cost since the budget is provided by the filing fees. Some data services on PATENTSCOPE are provide to commercial users at cost (https://www.wipo.int/patentscope/en/data/).

(6)

The details concerning the implementation of the provisions of this Article shall be governed by decisions of the Assembly and, within the limits to be fixed by the Assembly, such working groups as the Assembly may set up for that purpose.

Refer to annotations to Art. 53. 10

(7)

The Assembly shall, when it considers it necessary, recommend methods of providing financing supplementary to those referred to in paragraph (5).

Article 51
Technical Assistance

(1)

The Assembly shall establish a Committee for Technical Assistance (referred to in this Article as "the Committee").

1 The Committee for Technical Assistance (PCT/CTA) established by the first PCT Assembly (refer to document PCT/A/I/14 (https://www.wipo.int/meetings/en/doc_details.jsp?doc_id=19549)) never met. However, other WIPO Committees dealt with PCT technical assistance. The PCT Interim Committee met from 1970 to 1978 (refer to meeting documents (https://www.wipo.int/meetings/en/topic.jsp?group_id=277)). Membership of the PCT/CTA comprises all PCT Contracting States. The WIPO Permanent Committee for the Acquisition by Developing Countries of Technology Related to Industrial Property (AT/PC), established in 1973, and the WIPO Permanent Committee for Development Cooperation related to Industrial Property (PC/IP), established 1976, were discussing technical assistance and merged in 1988 into the WIPO Permanent Committee for Cooperation for Development Related to Intellectual Property (PCIPD). Since 2007 technical assistance activities are now discussed in the WIPO Committee on Development and Intellectual Property (CDIP); refer also to WIPO activities for technical assistance (https://www.wipo.int/cooperation/en/technical_assistance/). Since none of the meeting expressly called on the PCT/CTA for its guidance on the PCT there was no need to convene the Committee (refer to PCT/WG/5/5 (https://www.wipo.int/meetings/en/doc_details.jsp?doc_id=201684) for a detailed overview on WIPO's PCT Technical Assistance work from 1970 to 2012); for activities refer to WIPO activities for technical assistance and the CDIP (https://www.wipo.int/policy/en/cdip/).

(2)

(a) The members of the Committee shall be elected among the Contracting States, with due regard to the representation of developing countries.

(b) The Director General shall, on his own initiative or at the request of the Committee, invite representatives of intergovernmental organizations concerned with technical assistance to developing countries to participate in the work of the Committee.

(3)

(a) The task of the Committee shall be to organize and supervise technical assistance for Contracting States which are developing countries in developing their patent systems individually or on a regional basis.

(b) The technical assistance shall comprise, among other things, the training of specialists, the loaning of experts, and the supply of equipment both for demonstration and for operational purposes.

(4)

The International Bureau shall seek to enter into agreements, on the one hand, with international financing organizations and intergovernmental organizations, particularly the United Nations, the agencies of the United Nations, and the Specialized Agencies connected with the United Nations concerned with technical assistance, and, on the other hand, with the Governments of the States receiving the technical assistance, for the financing of projects pursuant to this Article.

During the existence of the PCT Interim Committee for Technical Assistance between 1970 and 1978, the International Bureau obtained assistance under Art. 51(4) from the United Nations Development Programme (UNDP) for the financing of technical assistance projects within the scope of Art. 51, resulting in the funding and supervision of various technical assistance projects by UNDP. Funding declined in 1990 but several follow up activities were done, including contacts with the World Bank and the Inter-American Development Bank (refer to an overview in PCT/WG/5/5) and also special Fund-in-Trust (FIT) arrangements with Member States. Work intensified with a Conference on Building Partnerships for Mobilizing Resources for Development (https://www.wipo.int/meetings/en/details.jsp?meeting_id = 19405) that took place in November 2009. For current activities refer to WIPO FIT webpage (https://www.wipo.int/cooperation/en/funds_in_trust/japan_fitip_global/index.html). 2

(5)

The details concerning the implementation of the provisions of this Article shall be governed by decisions of the Assembly and, within the limits to be fixed by the Assembly, such working groups as the Assembly may set up for that purpose.

Refer to annotations to para. (1). 3

Article 52
Relations with Other Provisions of the Treaty

Nothing in this Chapter shall affect the financial provisions contained in any other Chapter of this Treaty. Such provisions are not applicable to the present Chapter or to its implementation.

1 This Article clarifies that the provisions in Chapter IV Patent Information Services (Art. 50 to Art. 52) are separate from the financial provisions of the Treaty (refer to Art. 57 Finances in Chapter V, Administrative Provisions).

Chapter V: Administrative Provisions

Article 53
Assembly

(1)

(a) The Assembly shall, subject to Article 57(8), consist of the Contracting States.

A definition of Contracting State, i.e. States party to the Treaty, is given in Art. 1. 1

(b) The Government of each Contracting State shall be represented by one delegate, who may be assisted by alternate delegates, advisors, and experts.

(2)

(a) The Assembly shall:

(i) deal with all matters concerning the maintenance and development of the Union and the implementation of this Treaty;

The PCT Assembly meets regularly every year as part of the meeting of the WIPO Assemblies. It adopts recommendations for amendments to the PCT Regulations as prepared by the PCT Working Group. It also appoints new ISAs/IPEAs upon recommendation by the Committee on Technical Cooperation. The WIPO Assemblies meet annually, every two years in an Ordinary Session with budgetary decision and every other two years in an extraordinary session (refer to Art. 53(11)). The PCT Union Assembly documents have a continuous numbering from 1978 (PCT/A/...). 2

(ii) perform such tasks as are specifically assigned to it under other provisions of this Treaty;

Art. 9(2)	The applicant: residents and nationals of non-Contracting States PCT Art. 9(2) allows the Assembly to authorize the filing of PCTa by residents or nationals of non-Contracting States (not the case currently, as the PCT is a closed system).
Art. 16(3)	Assembly appoints ISAs
Art. 32(2)(3)	Assembly appoints IPEAs

Art. 47(2)(b)	Revision of time limits
Art. 50(7)	Assembly recommends methods of supplementary financing
Art. 51(1), (5)	Assembly establishes a Committee for Technical Assistance
Art. 53(9), 54(5)(c)	Assembly establishes Executive Committee
Art. 53(12)	Adoptions of Rules of Procedure for the Assembly
Art. 55(4), (7)	Assembly requires new publications and provides direction for Revision Conferences
Art. 56	Assembly establishes Committee for Technical Cooperation
Art. 57	Assembly decides on budget (finance)
Art. 58	Assembly adopts the amendments of the Regulations
Art. 60(2)	Convocation of Revision Conference
Art. 61	Assembly proposes revision of certain Articles
Art. 65(2)	Assembly determines gradual application possibility to file a PCTa or a demand in case of new Contracting States or new IPEAs

(iii) give directions to the International Bureau concerning the preparation for revision conferences;

Art. 55(7)	Assembly provides direction for Revision Conferences
Art. 60	Revision of the Treaty

(iv) review and approve the reports and activities of the Director General concerning the Union, and give him all necessary instructions concerning matters within the competence of the Union;

(v) review and approve the reports and activities of the Executive Committee established under paragraph (9), and give instructions to such Committee;

Art. 53(9), 54(5)(c)	Assembly establishes Executive Committee

(vi) determine the program and adopt the triennial budget of the Union, and approve its final accounts;

3 Editor's Note (WIPO): 'Since 1980, the program and budget of the Union have been biennial.'

(vii) adopt the financial regulations of the Union;

(viii) establish such committees and working groups as it deems appropriate to achieve the objectives of the Union;

Currently, the following PCT member States bodies meet: 4

- International Patent Cooperation Union (PCT Union): Assembly (https://www.wipo.int/meetings/en/topic.jsp?group_id=135) (PCT/A)
- PCT Committee for Technical Cooperation (https://www.wipo.int/meetings/en/topic.jsp?group_id=130) (PCT/CTC)
- PCT Working Group (https://www.wipo.int/meetings/en/topic.jsp?group_id=238) (PCT/WG)
- Meeting of International Authorities under the PCT (https://www.wipo.int/meetings/en/topic.jsp?group_id=128) (PCT/MIA)
- PCT Text Processing Task Force (https://www.wipo.int/meetings/en/details.jsp?meeting_id=81130)

The following Committees and Working Groups have been established in the past: 5

Reform of the PCT 6

- Working Group on Reform of the PCT (November 2001 to April 2007) (https://www.wipo.int/meetings/en/topic.jsp?group_id=133) (PCT/R/WG)
- Committee on Reform of the PCT (May 21 to May 25, 2001 and July 1 to July 5, 2002) (https://www.wipo.int/meetings/en/topic.jsp?group_id=127) (PCT/R)

PCT Informal Consultation Meeting on Electronic Filing 7

- First and only Session, July 11 to July 14, 2000 (https://www.wipo.int/meetings/en/topic.jsp?group_id=131) (PCT/AI/1)

PCT Committees and Working Group Meetings held between the adoption, June 19, 1970 and the entry into force January 24, 1978 of the PCT 8

- PCT Committee for Administrative and Legal Matters (https://www.wipo.int/meetings/en/topic.jsp?group_id=129) (PCT/CAL)
- PCT Interim Committee for Technical Assistance (https://www.wipo.int/meetings/en/topic.jsp?group_id=277) (PCT/TAS)
- PCT Interim Committee for Technical Cooperation (https://www.wipo.int/pct/en/meetings/tco/) (PCT/TCO)
- PCT Interim Advisory Committee for Administrative Questions (https://www.wipo.int/pct/en/meetings/aaq/) (PCT/AAQ)
- PCT Working Group on Budgetary Question (https://www.wipo.int/meetings/en/details.jsp?meeting_id=376) (PCT/WG/BUD)
- PCT Preparatory Committee (https://www.wipo.int/meetings/en/details.jsp?meeting_id=437) (PCT/PREP/I)

(ix) determine which States other than Contracting States and, subject to the provisions of paragraph (8), which intergovernmental and international non-governmental organizations shall be admitted to its meetings as observers;

(x) take any other appropriate action designed to further the objectives of the Union and perform such other functions as are appropriate under this Treaty.

(b) With respect to matters which are of interest also to other Unions administered by the Organization, the Assembly shall make its decisions after having heard the advice of the Coordination Committee of the Organization.

(3)

A delegate may represent, and vote in the name of, one State only.

(4)

Each Contracting State shall have one vote.

9 Normally the Assemblies will make decisions by consensus, even if legally two-thirds of the votes cast is required (quorum Art. 53(5) and (6)). In the absence of a quorum, R. 85.1 enables a decision to be sought by including in writing the absent Contracting States.

(5)

(a) One-half of the Contracting States shall constitute a quorum.

10 A quorum is a minimum number for a valid meeting.

(b) In the absence of the quorum, the Assembly may make decisions but, with the exception of decisions concerning its own procedure, all such decisions shall take effect only if the quorum and the required majority are attained through voting by correspondence as provided in the Regulations.

11 In practice all decisions are by consensus.

R. 85	Absence of a quorum in the Assembly
R. 85.1	Voting by correspondence
Art. 58(2)(b)	Amendment of Regulations under the PCT requires three-fourths of votes
Art. 47(2)(b)	Amendment of time limits in the Treaty requires unanimity

12 Some decisions are legally by unanimity or three-fourths of votes (e.g., R. 61(2)(b)).

(6)

(a) Subject to the provisions of Articles 47(2)(b), 58(2)(b), 58(3) and 61(2)(b), the decisions of the Assembly shall require two-thirds of the votes cast.

(b) Abstentions shall not be considered as votes.

Refer to annotations to para. (4). In practice, most decisions are made by consensus. 13

(7)

In connection with matters of exclusive interest to States bound by Chapter II, any reference to Contracting States in paragraphs (4), (5), and (6), shall be considered as applying only to States bound by Chapter II.

Currently, all Contracting States are bound by Chapter II (the last Contracting State that became bound by Chapter II was ES in 1997: PCT Notification No. 120 (https://www.wipo.int/wipolex/en/treaties/notifications/details/treaty_pct_120)). 14

(8)

Any intergovernmental organization appointed as International Searching or Preliminary Examining Authority shall be admitted as observer to the Assembly.

Examples of this are EPO, EAPO, ARIPO, Visegrad Patent Institute, Nordic Patent Institute, and OAPI. 15

(9)

When the number of Contracting States exceeds forty, the Assembly shall establish an Executive Committee. Any reference to the Executive Committee in this Treaty and the Regulations shall be construed as references to such Committee once it has been established.

Art. 54 Executive Committee

Despite the number of 158 Contracting States (as of January 7, 2025), an Executive Committee has not yet been established. 16

(10)

Until the Executive Committee has been established, the Assembly shall approve, within the limits of the program and triennial budget, the annual programs and budgets prepared by the Director General.

The budget of WIPO is currently biennial (since 1980). Discussion about the program is annual in the WIPO Program and Budget Committee (PBC) (https://www.wipo.int/policy/en/pbc/). 17

(11)

(a) The Assembly shall meet in every second calendar year in ordinary session upon convocation by the Director General and, in the absence of exceptional circumstances, during the same period and at the same place as the General Assembly of the Organization.

(b) The Assembly shall meet in extraordinary session upon convocation by the Director General, at the request of the Executive Committee *(after its formation)*, or at the request of one-fourth of the Contracting States.

18 Currently the Assembly meets every year, one year in an ordinary and the following year in an extraordinary session.

(12)

The Assembly shall adopt its own rules of procedure.

19 WIPO has general rules of procedure (https://www.wipo.int/policy/en/rules_of_procedure.html) and certain bodies have special rules of procedure such as the PCT Union, refer to compilation of special rules of procedure: (https://www.wipo.int/export/sites/www/treaties/en/docs/pdf/special_rules.pdf).

Article 54
Executive Committee

INTRODUCTION

Art. 54 regulates the activities of the Executive Committee. No Executive Committee has yet been established (refer to WIPO Governance Structure in document WO/PBC/17/2 REV (https://www.wipo.int/meetings/en/doc_details.jsp?doc_id = 168239) and WO/PBC/18/20 (https://www.wipo.int/meetings/en/doc_details.jsp?doc_id = 284119)). In 1985, the Assembly agreed to postpone the decision concerning the establishment of the Executive Committee, until any Contracting State or the Director General proposed to reconsider the matter (refer to document PCT/A/XIII/3 (https://www.wipo.int/edocs/mdocs/govbody/en/pct_a_xiii/pct_a_xiii_3.pdf), para. 11 (v)). 1

With regard to the current governance structure as far as the PCT is concerned, please note that the WIPO Program and Budget Committee (PBC) (https://www.wipo.int/policy/en/pbc/) has regular meetings, including matters concerning the PCT and the Members of the Executive Committee of the Paris Convention are part of the WIPO Coordination Committee (A/64/4 (https://www.wipo.int/edocs/mdocs/govbody/en/a_64/a_64_4-main1.pdf), refer to Art. 54(7) as far as the relationship to the Coordination Committee is concerned). 2

(1)

When the Assembly has established an Executive Committee, that Committee shall be subject to the provisions set forth hereinafter.

(2)

(a) The Executive Committee shall, subject to Article 57(8), consist of States elected by the Assembly from among States members of the Assembly.

(b) The Government of each State member of the Executive Committee shall be represented by one delegate, who may be assisted by alternate delegates, advisors, and experts.

(3)

The number of States members of the Executive Committee shall correspond to one-fourth of the number of States members of the Assembly. In establishing the number of seats to be filled, remainders after division by four shall be disregarded.

(4)

In electing the members of the Executive Committee, the Assembly shall have due regard to an equitable geographical distribution.

(5)

(a) Each member of the Executive Committee shall serve from the close of the session of the Assembly which elected it to the close of the next ordinary session of the Assembly.

(b) Members of the Executive Committee may be re-elected but only up to a maximum of two-thirds of such members.

(c) The Assembly shall establish the details of the rules governing the election and possible re-election of the members of the Executive Committee.

(6)

(a) The Executive Committee shall:

(i) prepare the draft agenda of the Assembly;

(ii) submit proposals to the Assembly in respect of the draft program and biennial budget of the Union prepared by the Director General;

(iii) [deleted]

(iv) submit, with appropriate comments, to the Assembly the periodical reports of the Director General and the yearly audit reports on the accounts;

(v) take all necessary measures to ensure the execution of the program of the Union by the Director General, in accordance with the decisions of the Assembly and having regard to circumstances arising between two ordinary sessions of the Assembly;

(vi) perform such other functions as are allocated to it under this Treaty.

(b) With respect to matters which are of interest also to other Unions administered by the Organization, the Executive Committee shall make its decisions after having heard the advice of the Coordination Committee of the Organization.

(7)

(a) The Executive Committee shall meet once a year in ordinary session upon convocation by the Director General, preferably during the same period and at the same place as the Coordination Committee of the Organization.

(b) The Executive Committee shall meet in extraordinary session upon convocation by the Director General, either on his own initiative or at the request of its Chairman or one-fourth of its members.

(8)

(a) Each State member of the Executive Committee shall have one vote.

(b) One-half of the members of the Executive Committee shall constitute a quorum.

(c) Decisions shall be made by a simple majority of the votes cast.

(d) Abstentions shall not be considered as votes.

(e) A delegate may represent, and vote in the name of, one State only.

(9)

Contracting States not members of the Executive Committee shall be admitted to its meetings as observers, as well as any intergovernmental organization appointed as International Searching or Preliminary Examining Authority.

(10)

The Executive Committee shall adopt its own rules of procedure.

Article 55
International Bureau

(1)

Administrative tasks concerning the Union shall be performed by the International Bureau.

1 The International Bureau acts through WIPO colleagues in the Patent and Technology Sector. The Sector organized as follows:

- PCT Legal and International Affairs Department (https://www.wipo.int/about-wipo/en/activities_by_unit/index.jsp?id = 1036), responsible for:
  - PCT Legal and User Relations Division (https://www.wipo.int/about-wipo/en/activities_by_unit/index.jsp?id = 102)
  - PCT International Cooperation Division (https://www.wipo.int/about-wipo/en/activities_by_unit/index.jsp?id = 98)
- PCT Translation Division (https://www.wipo.int/about-wipo/en/activities_by_unit/index.jsp?id = 108)
- PCT Services Department (https://www.wipo.int/about-wipo/en/activities_by_unit/index.jsp?id = 106), responsible for:
  - PCT Operations Division (https://www.wipo.int/about-wipo/en/activities_by_unit/index.jsp?id = 104)
  - PCT Business Development Division (https://www.wipo.int/about-wipo/en/activities_by_unit/index.jsp?id = 94)
  - PCT Information Systems Division (https://www.wipo.int/about-wipo/en/activities_by_unit/index.jsp?id = 96)

(2)

The International Bureau shall provide the secretariat of the various organs of the Union.

2 The International Bureau is the Secretariat for the PCT Assembly, the PCT Working Group, Meeting of International Authorities, the Committee for Technical Cooperation.

(3)

The Director General shall be the chief executive of the Union and shall represent the Union.

The Director General's responsibilities are – in practice – often delegated to the Patent and Technology Sector. 3

(4)

The International Bureau shall publish a Gazette and other publications provided for by the Regulations or required by the Assembly.

R. 86	Gazette
R. 48	International publication

(5)

The Regulations shall specify the services that national Offices shall perform in order to assist the International Bureau and the International Searching and Preliminary Examining Authorities in carrying out their tasks under this Treaty.

R. 95	E.g. furnishing of translations

(6)

The Director General and any staff member designated by him shall participate, without the right to vote, in all meetings of the Assembly, the Executive Committee and any other committee or working group established under this Treaty or the Regulations. The Director General, or a staff member designated by him, shall be *ex officio* secretary of these bodies.

Currently, in practice this is often either the Deputy Director General of the Patents and Technology Sector or the Director or any other Staff in the PCT Business Development Division. For specific expertise other staff members will be invited, such as the Office of the Legal Counsel, Finance or the Director of the PCT Legal and User Relations Division. 4

(7)

(a) The International Bureau shall, in accordance with the directions of the Assembly and in cooperation with the Executive Committee, make the preparations for the revision conferences.

Art. 60	Revisions of the Treaty

5 There have been amendments and modifications to the Treaty so far in 1979, 1984 and 2001, but no revisions *per se* (for the content of the revisions refer to annotations to Art. 60). Further amendments, modifications and revisions are unlikely and usually only the Regulations will be revised.

(b) The International Bureau may consult with intergovernmental and international non-governmental organizations concerning preparations for revision conferences.

(c) The Director General and persons designated by him shall take part, without the right to vote, in the discussions at revision conferences.

(8)

The International Bureau shall carry out any other tasks assigned to it.

Art. 12	Receipt of record copy
Art. 13	Transmittal of copies
Art. 16(2)(b), Art. 34	Receives ISA/IPEA agreements
Art. 19	Amendments of claims
Art. 20, R. 47	Communication to designated Offices
R. 19(iii)	Receiving Office of the International Bureau
Art. 21, R. 48	International publication
Art. 25	Copy for review by designated Offices
Art. 36	Translation of IPRP II/IPER
Art. 37	Receives withdrawal of demand
Art. 50	Patent information services
Art. 57	Receives fees
Art. 63	Publishes statistics

6 The International Bureau has various functions in the PCT system and provides several electronic systems:

- A search platform for published international applications, previously Section I to III PCT Gazette, in form of PATENTSCOPE (https://patentscope.wipo.int/search/en/structuredSearch.jsf) (refer to Art. 50); the platform includes many national and regional patent documents, legal status information (national phase entry data) and non-patent literature.
- A platform for filing and managing international applications, as well as for handling international application as a receiving Office, electronic search copies and payment information for ISAs and IPEAs, in the form of ePCT (https://pct.wipo.int/ePCT/about-epct.xhtml?lang=en).

- PCT Operations is responsible for the processing of international applications, in particular, the international publication and translation, the work is organized in Processing Teams.
- PCT Translations provides translation into English and French, as applicable, in particular, for PCT work products (ISR, IPRP I or II) and abstracts.
- The receiving Office of the International Bureau (RO/IB) (https://www.wipo.int/pct/en/filing/filing.html) acts as the currently sixth largest receiving Office (behind IP5 Offices), either at the choice of applicants, in cases no other Office is competent (R. 19.4) and on behalf of some developing countries.
- The International Bureau provides PCT Training, training on IT (in particular ePCT) but also on other aspects of the PCT system. It provides technical assistance on the PCT to developing countries (refer to Art. 53) and technical assistance with regard to ePCT for Offices. It provides legal advice to applicants within the framework of the PCT (PCT Infoline, PCT eservices, PCT Legal and User Relations Division). It maintains the PCT part of the WIPO website (https://www.wipo.int/pct/en/), in up to ten languages. It provides the legal texts (https://www.wipo.int/pct/en/texts/index.html), in ten languages. It publishes weekly the Official Notices (PCT Gazette) (https://www.wipo.int/pct/en/official_notices/index.html) and updates to the PCT Applicant's Guide (https://www.wipo.int/pct/en/guide). It provides a monthly PCT Newsletter (https://www.wipo.int/pct/en/newslett/) and publishes PCT Highlights (https://www.wipo.int/pct/en/highlights/).

Article 56
Committee for Technical Cooperation

(1)

The Assembly shall establish a Committee for Technical Cooperation (referred to in this Article as "the Committee").

1 The PCT Committee for Technical Cooperation (https://www.wipo.int/meetings/en/topic.jsp?group_id = 130) has met 32 times (from September 1978 to, most recently, October 2022). It currently meets to discuss and recommend appointing new ISAs/IPEAs to the PCT Assembly. Previously it met also on technical matters such as the minimum documentation. Currently, such issues are discussed in the PCT Meeting of International Authorities or the PCT Working Group, or in task forces set up by the PCT Working Group. For minimum requirements for ISAs, refer to R. 36.

(2)

(a) The Assembly shall determine the composition of the Committee and appoint its members, with due regard to an equitable representation of developing countries.

2 Currently all Contracting States are members of the Committee for Technical Cooperation.

(b) The International Searching and Preliminary Examining Authorities shall be *ex officio* members of the Committee. In the case where such an Authority is the national Office of a Contracting State, that State shall not be additionally represented on the Committee.

(c) If the number of Contracting States so allows, the total number of members of the Committee shall be more than double the number of *ex officio* members.

(d) The Director General shall, on his own initiative or at the request of the Committee, invite representatives of interested organizations to participate in discussions of interest to them.

(3)

The aim of the Committee shall be to contribute, by advice and recommendations:

(i) to the constant improvement of the services provided for under this Treaty,

(ii) to the securing, so long as there are several International Searching Authorities and several International Preliminary Examining Authorities, of the maximum degree of uniformity in their documentation and working methods and the maximum degree of uniformly high quality in their reports, and

(iii) on the initiative of the Assembly or the Executive Committee, to the solution of the technical problems specifically involved in the establishment of a single International Searching Authority.

Art. 16 The ISA

With the growing number of ISAs, it has become quite unlikely that the initial objective of establishing a single ISA (refer to Art. 16(1) and (2)) will be achieved. Art. 16(1) refers to the International Patent Institute, the predecessor of the EPO. 3

(4)

Any Contracting State and any interested international organization may approach the Committee in writing on questions which fall within the competence of the Committee.

(5)

The Committee may address its advice and recommendations to the Director General or, through him, to the Assembly, the Executive Committee, all or some of the International Searching and Preliminary Examining Authorities, and all or some of the receiving Offices.

(6)

(a) In any case, the Director General shall transmit to the Executive Committee the texts of all the advice and recommendations of the Committee. He may comment on such texts.

(b) The Executive Committee may express its views on any advice, recommendation, or other activity of the Committee, and may invite the Committee to study and report on questions falling within its competence. The Executive Committee may submit to the Assembly, with appropriate comments, the advice, recommendations and report of the Committee.

(7)

Until the Executive Committee has been established, references in paragraph (6) to the Executive Committee shall be construed as references to the Assembly.

(8)

The details of the procedure of the Committee shall be governed by the decisions of the Assembly.

Article 57
Finances

(1)

(a) The Union shall have a budget.

(b) The budget of the Union shall Include the income and expenses proper to the Union and its contribution to the budget of expenses common to the Unions administered by the Organization.

(c) Expenses not attributable exclusively to the Union but also to one or more other Unions administered by the Organization shall be considered as expenses common to the Unions. The share of the Union in such common expenses shall be in proportion to the interest the Union has in them.

Art. 52	Relations with other provisions
R. 84	Expenses of delegations

Currently, there is a common WIPO budget to all Unions. The PCT contribution finances the expenses of the other Unions. The origin of the unitary contribution system and the unitary presentation in the WIPO budget goes back to 1993, refer to Art. 11 of the WIPO Convention. 1

(2)

The budget of the Union shall be established with due regard to the requirements of coordination with the budgets of the other Unions administered by the Organization.

(3)

Subject to the provisions of paragraph (5), the budget of the Union shall be financed from the following sources:

(i) fees and charges due for services rendered by the International Bureau in relation to the Union;

Fees are the main PCT income. Most services are now provided electronically and free of charge. 2

(ii) sale of, or royalties on, the publications of the International Bureau concerning the Union;

(iii) gifts, bequests, and subventions;

(iv) rents, interests, and other miscellaneous income.

(4)

The amounts of fees and charges due to the International Bureau and the prices of its publications shall be so fixed that they should, under normal circumstances, be sufficient to cover all the expenses of the International Bureau connected with the administration of this Treaty.

R. 96	Schedule of fees
Sect. 113 AIs	Special fees payable to the International Bureau

3 Currently, most of the information exchange is free of charge, electronically via ePCT, PATENTSCOPE, PDF publications on WIPO's website and via e-mail. (Paper) publications have only a very minor and subsidiary role.

(5)

(a) Should any financial year close with a deficit, the Contracting States shall, subject to the provisions of subparagraphs (b) and (c), pay contributions to cover such deficit.

(b) The amount of the contribution of each Contracting State shall be decided by the Assembly with due regard to the number of international applications which has emanated from each of them in the relevant year.

(c) If other means of provisionally covering any deficit or any part thereof are secured, the Assembly may decide that such deficit be carried forward and that the Contracting States should not be asked to pay contributions.

(d) If the financial situation of the Union so permits, the Assembly may decide that any contributions paid under subparagraph (a) be reimbursed to the Contracting States which have paid them.

(e) A Contracting State which has not paid, within two years of the due date as established by the Assembly, its contribution under subparagraph (b) may not exercise its right to vote in any of the organs of the Union. However, any organ of the Union may allow such a State to continue to exercise its right to vote in that organ so long as it is satisfied that the delay in payment is due to exceptional and unavoidable circumstances.

4 Currently there is a surplus in income in fees and this paragraph is practically not relevant.

(6)

If the budget is not adopted before the beginning of a new financial period, it shall be at the same level as the budget of the previous year, as provided in the financial regulations.

(7)

(a) The Union shall have a working capital fund which shall be constituted by a single payment made by each Contracting State. If the fund becomes insufficient, the Assembly shall arrange to increase it. If part of the fund is no longer needed, it shall be reimbursed.

(b) The amount of the initial payment of each Contracting State to the said fund or of its participation in the increase thereof shall be decided by the Assembly on the basis of principles similar to those provided for under paragraph (5)(b).

(c) The terms of payment shall be fixed by the Assembly on the proposal of the Director General and after it has heard the advice of the Coordination Committee of the Organization.

(d) Any reimbursement shall be proportionate to the amounts paid by each Contracting State, taking into account the dates at which they were paid.

(8)

(a) In the headquarters agreement concluded with the State on the territory of which the Organization has its headquarters, it shall be provided that, whenever the working capital fund is insufficient, such State shall grant advances. The amount of these advances and the conditions on which they are granted shall be the subject of separate agreements, in each case, between such State and the Organization. As long as it remains under the obligation to grant advances, such State shall have an *ex officio* seat in the Assembly and on the Executive Committee.

(b) The State referred to in subparagraph (a) and the Organization shall each have the right to denounce the obligation to grant advances, by written notification. Denunciation shall take effect three years after the end of the year in which it has been notified.

The headquarters of WIPO is located in Switzerland (CH). The relevant details are **5**
regulated by the Host Country Agreement (Art. 12 WIPO Convention). This is an exception to the principle that the Assembly decides (Art. 53).

(9)

The auditing of the accounts shall be effected by one or more of the Contracting States or by external auditors, as provided in the financial regulations. They shall be designated, with their agreement, by the Assembly.

Article 58
Regulations

INTRODUCTION

1 In practice, the Regulations are regularly amended, usually every year in order to make specific improvements or update to the PCT legal framework. While most existing Rules deal with the implementation of specific Treaty provisions, sometimes entirely new provisions are added that have no corresponding Article in the Treaty, such as Supplementary International Searches (R. 45*bis*).

(1)

The Regulations annexed to this Treaty provide Rules:

(i) concerning matters in respect of which this Treaty expressly refers to the Regulations or expressly provides that they are or shall be prescribed,

(ii) concerning any administrative requirements, matters, or procedures,

(iii) concerning any details useful in the implementation of the provisions of this Treaty.

(2)

(a) The Assembly may amend the Regulations.

(b) Subject to the provisions of paragraph (3), amendments shall require three-fourths of the votes cast.

2 In practice, amendments to the Regulations are decided by consensus by the PCT Assemblies based upon previous recommendations made by the PCT Working Group (also by consensus in practice).

(3)

(a) The Regulations specify the Rules which may be amended

(i) only by unanimous consent, or

R. 88	Amendment of the Regulations
R. 88.1	Requirement of unanimity
Art. 53	The Assembly
	Documents of the preparatory PCT Working Group and the deciding PCT Assembly can be found at www.wipo.int/pct/en/meetings/index.html.

(ii) only if none of the Contracting States whose national Office acts as an International Searching or Preliminary Examining Authority dissents, and, where such Authority is an intergovernmental organization, if the Contracting State member of that organization authorized for that purpose by the other member States within the competent body of such organization does not dissent.

R. 88	Amendment of the Regulations
R. 88.3	Requirement of absence of opposition of certain States
R. 88.4	Procedure

(b) Exclusion, for the future, of any such Rules from the applicable requirement shall require the fulfillment of the conditions referred to in subparagraph (a)(i) or (a)(ii), respectively.

(c) Inclusion, for the future, of any Rule in one or the other of the requirements referred to in subparagraph (a) shall require unanimous consent.

(4)

The Regulations provide for the establishment, under the control of the Assembly, of Administrative Instructions by the Director General.

R. 89	Administrative Instructions
R. 89.1	Scope
R. 89.2	Source
R. 89.3	Publication and entry into force

(5)

In the case of conflict between the provisions of the Treaty and those of the Regulations, the provisions of the Treaty shall prevail.

Occasionally, together with amendments to Rules, the Assembly adopts an interpre- 3
tation for the application of a Rule in specific cases. This Understanding of the PCT Assembly is published in the PCT Gazette (PCT Gazette, for example, November 30, 2023, March 5, 2020, February 8, 2018, January 18, 2007, February 23, 2006) and is given priority by the EPO as the authentic interpretation of the legislature when

interpreting the Rule (J 14/21 para. 12). The content of the Understandings of the PCT Assembly are mentioned in the respective Rules.

Chapter VI: Disputes

Article 59
Disputes

Subject to Article 64(5), any dispute between two or more Contracting States concerning the interpretation or application of this Treaty or the Regulations, not settled by negotiation, may, by any one of the States concerned, be brought before the International Court of Justice by application in conformity with the Statute of the Court, unless the States concerned agree on some other method of settlement. The Contracting State bringing the dispute before the Court shall inform the International Bureau; the International Bureau shall bring the matter to the attention of the other Contracting States.

Art. 64(5) states: 'Each State may declare that it does not consider itself bound by Article 59. With regard to any dispute between any Contracting State having made such a declaration and any other Contracting State, the provisions of Article 59 shall not apply.' 1

Currently, AM, BH, BY, CL, CU, DZ, FR, GE, HU, IN, ID, KG, KZ, LA, LC, MA, MY, MZ, OM, QA, MD, RO, RU, SA, TJ, TH, TM, TN, UA, UZ and VC have made such a reservation. 2

Both Art. 28 of the Paris Convention and Art. 59 PCT only provide for a dispute settlement procedure between Contracting Parties or States of the respective international treaties. The procedures foreseen in those provisions are, however, not open to individual companies. 3

Thus, determination and resolution of matters, such as entitlement, are exclusively within the competence of the national authorities under the national laws of the countries concerned, which include the designated/elected States and in certain cases the receiving Offices with which the international application was filed. A person wishing to take steps against another person claiming rights to an international application or to the claimed invention contained therein may be able to seek an order from a court having competent jurisdiction in the matter. 4

In the PCT's history, no disputes between PCT Contracting States have ever been taken to the International Court of Justice. 5

Chapter VII: Revision and Amendment

Article 60
Revision of the Treaty

INTRODUCTION

1. Revision

1 The Treaty may be *revised* by a special conference of Contracting States (Art. 60(1)). Such conferences are rare because of the large number of Contracting States and the fact that WIPO must pay the expenses of some delegates.

2. Amendment

2.1 Amendment of the Treaty (Articles)

2 The Assembly of delegates of the Contracting States (see Art. 53) itself may *amend* certain Articles (Art. 61(2)(a)). The provisions that can be changed by a simple amendment are enumerated in Art. 60(4) and 61(1).

2.2 Amendment of the Regulations (Rules)

3 The Assembly may also *amend the Regulations* of the Treaty (Art. 58(2)(a)). The amendment of some Rules requires unanimous consent (Art. 58(3)(a)(i); R. 88.1).

3. Modification

4 Furthermore, Art. 47(2) provides for the possibility to *modify* the time limits fixed in Chapters I and II of the Treaty. This can be achieved by a unanimous decision (Art. 47(2)(b)) of the Assembly (Art. 53) of the Contracting States (Art. 47(2), R. 81).

(1)

This Treaty may be revised from time to time by a special conference of the Contracting States.

Art. 58(2)(a) The Assembly may amend the Regulations.

R. 88	Amendment of the Regulations
R. 88.1	Requirement of unanimity

Most Articles of the Treaty have not been amended or modified for the than 50 years. Amendments are usually done through changes to the Regulations (refer to document History of the Regulations (https://www.wipo.int/export/sites/www/pct/en/docs/texts/pct-regulations-history.pdf)) and Administrative Instructions (and its Annexes, e.g. Annex F on Electronic Filing). **5**

With regard to options for a possible revision and also the above-mentioned implications of revisions, refer to document PCT/R/WG/3/3 (https://www.wipo.int/edocs/mdocs/pct/en/pct_r_wg_3/pct_r_wg_3_3.pdf). Accordingly, on the basis of Art. 60 and established practice for the revisions of treaties, a revised PCT could only be the result of a two-stage process, involving: (i) the adoption of a revised text by the Contracting States at a special conference; and (ii) the ratification of, or accession to, the revised Treaty by States on an individual basis. Where a Treaty has been amended through a revision, the general rule is that the 'amending agreement does not bind any State already a party to the treaty which does not become a party to the amending agreement' (refer to Art. 40(4) of the Vienna Convention on the Law of Treaties). **6**

(2)

The convocation of any revision conference shall be decided by the Assembly.

(3)

Any intergovernmental organization appointed as International Searching or Preliminary Examining Authority shall be admitted as observer to any revision conference.

(4)

Articles 53(5) *(quorum)*, (9) *(Executive Committee)* and (11) *(frequency of meetings)*, 54 *(Executive Committee)*, 55(4) to (8) *(Gazette and task of International Bureau)*, 56 *(Committee for Technical Cooperation)*, and 57 *(Finances)*, may be amended either by a revision conference or according to the provisions of Article 61.

Art. 58(2)(a)	The Assembly may amend the Regulations.
Art. 47(2)	Time limits may be modified by a decision of the Contracting States independently of a revision under Art. 60
Art. 53	The Assembly

The above-mentioned Articles can be changed by a revision according to Art. 60 only. **7**

4. History of Changes

4.1 Revision

8 So far, there have been no revisions of the Treaty.

4.2 Amendments

4.2.1 Amendment of Articles

9 An Amendment (Art. 61) of the Treaty with regard to Art. 53 and 54 took place in 1979 and entered into force in 1984. The amendment of September 28, 1979 changed the budgetary period in PCT Art. 54(6)(a)(ii). All WIPO Unions, including the PCT, moved from a triennial or annual to a uniformly biennial financial period. Further, the meeting cycle of the PCT Assembly in Art. 53(11) was amended (refer to PCT Notification 43).

4.2.2 Amendment of the Regulations (Rules)

10 Amendments to the Rules according to Art. 58(2)(a)) are agreed upon almost every year. Decisions on Rule changes by the Assembly are often taken in the year preceding the year of entry into force and published in the PCT Gazette and in the PCT Newsletter. For details see the documents of the meetings of the PCT Assembly and of the PCT Working Group (www.wipo.int/pct/en/meetings/index.html). Amended Rules usually enter into force in July and sometimes in January. Since 2022, Assemblies are held in July, however the entry into force date seems to still tend towards July of the following year in order to provide adequate time for implementation. All Rule changes are compiled and made available by the International Bureau in a document called History of the Regulations (https://www.wipo.int/export/sites/www/pct/en/docs/texts/pct-regulations-history.pdf). More recent changes by year are available in the archive to the amendments (https://www.wipo.int/pct/en/texts/rule_changes_archive.html).

4.3 Modifications

11 The 1984 modification (refer to Art. 47(2)) entered into force on January 1, 1985 and gave more time for national phase entry under Chapter II in Art. 39 from 25 to 30 months, and increased the time limit for cases of no search report to the regular time limit (Art. 17(2)) (refer to document PCT/A/XI/9 Annex VII and https://www.wipo.int/export/sites/www/pct/en/docs/official-notices/section-iv/sectioniv1984.pdf, p. 132).

12 The 2001 modification (refer to Art. 47(2)) that entered into force on April 1, 2002 increased the time limit for national phase entry under Chapter I in Art. 22 from 20 to 30 months (refer to PCT Notification 153 (https://www.wipo.int/wipolex/en/treaties/notifications/details/treaty_pct_153) and Certified Copy (https://www.wipo.int/wipolex/en/treaties/notifications/details/treaty_pct_153-annex); refer also to document PCT/A/30/7 (https://www.wipo.int/edocs/mdocs/govbody/en/pct_a_30/

pct_a_30_7.pdf), p. 7). The fact that LU and TZ are still applying the 20-month time limit, due to the possibility to make a notification of incompatibility with national law on those changes in 2001, shows that the gradual and individual entry into force of such modifications of time limits in the Treaty has some inconveniences and limitations in a complex system such as the PCT.

Article 61
Amendment of Certain Provisions of the Treaty

(1)

(a) Proposals for the amendment of Articles 53(5) *(quorum)*, **(9)** *(Executive Committee)* **and (11)** *(frequency of meetings)*, **54** *(Executive Committee)*, **55(4) to (8)** *(Gazette and task of International Bureau)*, **56** *(Committee for Technical Cooperation)*, **and 57** *(Finances)*, **may be initiated by any State member of the Assembly, by the Executive Committee, or by the Director General.**

(b) Such proposals shall be communicated by the Director General to the Contracting States at least six months in advance of their consideration by the Assembly.

1 These provisions on amendments of administrative provisions have been used in 1979 for the biennial budgetary cycle (refer to annotations to Art. 60(4)).

(2)

(a) Amendments to the Articles referred to in paragraph (1) shall be adopted by the Assembly.

(b) Adoption shall require three-fourths of the votes cast.

(3)

(a) Any amendment to the Articles referred to in paragraph (1) shall enter into force one month after written notifications of acceptance, effected in accordance with their respective constitutional processes, have been received by the Director General from three-fourths of the States members of the Assembly at the time it adopted the amendment.

(b) Any amendment to the said Articles thus accepted shall bind all the States which are members of the Assembly at the time the amendment enters into force, provided that any amendment increasing the financial obligations of the Contracting States shall bind only those States which have notified their acceptance of such amendment.

(c) Any amendment accepted in accordance with the provisions of subparagraph (a) shall bind all States which become members of the Assembly after the date on which the amendment entered into force in accordance with the provisions of subparagraph (a).

Chapter VIII: Final Provisions

Article 62
Becoming Party to the Treaty

(1)

Any State member of the International Union for the Protection of Industrial Property may become party to this Treaty by:

(i) signature followed by the deposit of an instrument of ratification, or

(ii) deposit of an instrument of accession.

1 The Paris Union has to be joined first or at the same time. The Treaty enters into force in the ratifying or acceding State three months after the deposit of the instrument of ratification or of the instrument of accession (refer to Art. 63(2)).

2 The Treaty was open for signature until December 31, 1970, refer to Art. 67(2).

3 For States part of the Paris Union but not the PCT, refer to: States bound by the Paris Convention but not the PCT (https://www.wipo.int/pct/en/paris_non_pct.html).

(2)

Instruments of ratification or accession shall be deposited with the Director General.

(3)

The provisions of Article 24 of the Stockholm Act of the Paris Convention for the Protection of Industrial Property shall apply to this Treaty.

4 Article 24 – Territories of the Paris Convention reads as follows:

> '(1) Any country may declare in its instrument of ratification or accession, or may inform the Director General by written notification any time thereafter, that this Convention shall be applicable to all or part of those territories, designated in the declaration or notification, for the external relations of which it is responsible.
>
> (2) Any country which has made such a declaration or given such a notification may, at any time, notify the Director General that this Convention shall cease to be applicable to all or part of such territories.'

(3)

(a) Any declaration made under para. (1) shall take effect on the same date as the ratification or accession in the instrument of which it was included, and any notification given under such paragraph shall take effect three months after its notification by the Director General.

(b) Any notification given under para. (2) shall take effect twelve months after its receipt by the Director General.'

The list of PCT Contracting States (https://www.wipo.int/pct/en/pct_contracting_states.html) (formerly Annex A of the PCT Applicant's Guide) contains notifications to which territories the PCT is extended as far as they have been received. An Overview can be found in the Annexes to this book in the 'List of Territories'. For a complete list of territories contact the national Office of the State concerned. This is particularly relevant for GB, (refer to https://www.gov.uk/government/publications/extension-of-uk-intellectual-property-rights-abroad/extension-of-uk-ip-right-abroad-countries-a-to-b), FR, NL and US. 5

(4)

Paragraph (3) shall in no way be understood as implying the recognition or tacit acceptance by a Contracting State of the factual situation concerning a territory to which this Treaty is made applicable by another Contracting State by virtue of the said paragraph.

The application of the PCT to a dependent territory by a Contracting State does not imply that the other Contracting States recognizes the factual situation of such dependent territory, for example if such dependent territory is politically disputed. 6

Refer also to R. 32 PCT. 7

Article 63
Entry into Force of the Treaty

(1)

(a) Subject to the provisions of paragraph (3), this Treaty shall enter into force three months after eight States have deposited their instruments of ratification or accession, provided that at least four of those States each fulfill any of the following conditions:

(i) the number of applications filed in the State has exceeded 40,000 according to the most recent annual statistics published by the International Bureau,

(ii) the nationals or residents of the State have filed at least 1,000 applications in one foreign country according to the most recent annual statistics published by the International Bureau,

(iii) the national Office of the State has received at least 10,000 applications from nationals or residents of foreign countries according to the most recent annual statistics published by the International Bureau.

(b) For the purposes of this paragraph, the term "applications" does not include applications for utility models.

1 The Treaty entered into force on January 24, 1978 (refer to PCT Notification 14 (https://www.wipo.int/wipolex/en/treaties/notifications/details/treaty_pct_14)). Thus, this legal provision has only historical value. Statistics can be found in the PCT Yearly Review (https://www.wipo.int/pct/en/activity/index.html) and the WIPO IP Statistics Data Center (https://www3.wipo.int/ipstats/pmh-search/pct).

(2)

Subject to the provisions of paragraph (3), any State which does not become party to this Treaty upon entry into force under paragraph (1) shall become bound by this Treaty three months after the date on which such State has deposited its instrument of ratification or accession.

2 States that joined the Treaty after January 24, 1978 either by accession (without previously having signed the Treaty) or by ratification (having signed but not yet ratified the Treaty) become bound three months after the deposit of instrument. WIPO publishes a PCT Notification (https://www.wipo.int/wipolex/en/

treaties/ShowResults?start_year = ANY&end_year = ANY&search_what = N&country_id = ALL&treaty_id = 6) and a list of all Contracting States (https://www.wipo.int/pct/en/pct_contracting_states.html), the respective date of entry into force and recent accessions and ratifications are available.

(3)

The provisions of Chapter II and the corresponding provisions of the Regulations annexed to this Treaty shall become applicable, however, only on the date on which three States each of which fulfill at least one of the three requirements specified in paragraph (1) have become party to this Treaty without declaring, as provided in Article 64(1), that they do not intend to be bound by the provisions of Chapter II. That date shall not, however, be prior to that of the initial entry into force under paragraph (1).

The declaration in this is paragraph is obsolete since Chapter II entered into force on **3**
March 29, 1978 (PCT Notifications 17 (https://www.wipo.int/wipolex/en/treaties/notifications/details/treaty_pct_17)). All States are bound by Chapter II, except Uruguay, which will be bound by the PCT as from January 7, 2025. States wishing not to be bound by Chapter II have to make an Art. 64(1) reservation.

Article 64
Reservations

INTRODUCTION

1 The PCT allows a Contracting State to make reservations about the application of certain provisions of the PCT for that State because of incompatibility of the provisions with national law. The reservations modify the international procedure to encompass national peculiarities. Several of the more important reservations are given below. An up-to-date list of all 'PCT Reservations, Declarations, Notifications and Incompatibilities' can be found on the WIPO website (www.wipo.int/pct/en/texts/reservations/res_incomp.html)

2 Only two Contracting States still uphold the declaration that Art. 22(1) as in force from April 1, 2002 does not apply to its designated Office. The 20-month time limit for national entry after the Chapter I phase continues to apply. See annotations to Art. 22.

3 Many declarations have been made about incompatibility of several Rules and of Section 703 of the Administrative Instructions AIs 703 (https://www.wipo.int/pct/en/texts/ai/s703.html).

(1)

(a) Any State may declare that it shall not be bound by the provisions of Chapter II.

4 There are currently now no more reservations under Art. 64(1)(a) and all PCT Contracting States are bound by Chapter II. ES was the last Contracting State withdrawing its declaration concerning Chapter II on September 6, 1997 (PCT Notification 120 (https://www.wipo.int/treaties/en/notifications/pct/treaty_pct_120.html)).

(b) States making a declaration under subparagraph (a) shall not be bound by the provisions of Chapter II and the corresponding provisions of the Regulations.

(2)

(a) Any State not having made a declaration under paragraph (1)(a) may declare that:

(i) it shall not be bound by the provisions of Article 39(1) with respect to the furnishing of a copy of the international application and a translation thereof (as prescribed),

There are no reservations under Art. 64(2)(a)(i). 5

(ii) the obligation to delay national processing, as provided for under Article 40, shall not prevent publication, by or through its national Office, of the international application or a translation thereof, it being understood, however, that it is not exempted from the limitations provided for in Articles 30 and 38.

A declaration in respect of Art. 64(2)(a)(ii) has been made by FI, NO, PL, SE. 6

(b) States making such a declaration shall be bound accordingly.

(3)

(a) Any State may declare that, as far as it is concerned, international publication of international applications is not required.

The US has made such a declaration which would only be effective if the US were the only designated State and the appropriate declaration is made by the applicant (Art. 64(3)(b)). However, according to R. 4.9(a)(i) all Contracting States are automatically designated. The applicant would have to withdraw the designation of all other States except the US according to R. 90bis.2(a) to achieve this goal. 7

(b) Where, at the expiration of 18 months from the priority date, the international application contains the designation only of such States as have made declarations under subparagraph (a), the international application shall not be published by virtue of Article 21(2).

If all designations except the US designation are withdrawn before technical preparations for international publication (that is, not just before international publication), then the PCT application will not be published at 18 months, in accordance with Art. 64(3) except that the applicant may specifically request that publication take place anyway (see Art. 64(3)(c)(i)). Publication of such PCT applications will take place much later than the usual 18 months upon notification by the US designated Office that the US patent has been granted; the text published under the PCT will be the text of the application as it was at 18 months, it will not be the text of the granted US patent. 8

(c) Where the provisions of subparagraph (b) apply, the international application shall nevertheless be published by the International Bureau:

(i) at the request of the applicant, as provided in the Regulations,

9 Publication under Articles 21(2)(b) and 64(3)(c)(i) shall be effected by the International Bureau promptly after the applicant has asked for it (request for early publication).

(ii) when a national application or a patent based on the international application is published by or on behalf of the national Office of any designated State having made a declaration under subparagraph (a), promptly after such publication but not before the expiration of 18 months from the priority date.

10 This would only be the case for US patent applications or patents.

(4)

(a) Any State whose national law provides for prior art effect of its patents as from a date before publication, but does not equate for prior art purposes the priority date claimed under the Paris Convention for the Protection of Industrial Property to the actual filing date in that State, may declare that the filing outside that State of an international application designating that State is not equated to an actual filing in that State for prior art purposes.

11 The US has made such a declaration (see also AG-IP Annex B(US) (https://pctlegal.wipo.int/eGuide/view-doc.xhtml?doc-code=US&doc-lang=en)).

Art. 11(3)	Limited effect as national application: E.g. in the US: The foreign PCT application remains new in relation to later other applications (according to Art. 4). However, it was not an earlier application as of the international filing date with respect to later other applications in the US (Hilmer doctrine), unless the international application was published in English. The Hilmer doctrine was abolished by the America Invents Act. 'The new prior art as well as grace period law applies to all US applications as of the filing date of March 16, 2013. The new law also applies to US applications that at any time have at least one claim whose subject matter has an effective filing date after March 16, 2013. 35 U.S.C. 102 and 103 in effect on March 16, 2013, will apply to any application that ever contains a claim that has an effective filing date on or after 16, 2013.' (VPP-Rundbrief No. 3/2012, p. 140)

12 AG-IP Annex B (US) states the following: 'However, this declaration only applies to applications that are not subject to the First Inventor to File provisions of the America Invents Act, that is, applications that contain or ever contained a claim having an effective filing date prior to 16 March 2013.'

13 Despite these developments, the declaration has not yet been withdrawn.

(b) Any State making a declaration under subparagraph (a) shall to that extent not be bound by the provisions of Article 11(3).

(c) Any State making a declaration under subparagraph (a) shall, at the same time, state in writing the date from which, and the conditions under which, the prior art effect of any international application designating that State becomes effective in that State. This statement may be modified at any time by notification addressed to the Director General.

(5)

Each State may declare that it does not consider itself bound by Article 59. With regard to any dispute between any Contracting State having made such a declaration and any other Contracting State, the provisions of Article 59 shall not apply.

Such a declaration has been made by: AM, BH, BY, CL, CU, DZ, FR, GE, HU, IN, ID, 14
KZ, KG, LA, LC, MD, MT, MY, MZ, OM, QA, RO, RU, ZA, TH, TJ, TM, TN, UA, UZ, VC.

(6)

(a) Any declaration made under this Article shall be made in writing. It may be made at the time of signing this Treaty, at the time of depositing the instrument of ratification or accession, or, except in the case referred to in paragraph (5), at any later time by notification addressed to the Director General. In the case of the said notification, the declaration shall take effect six months after the day on which the Director General has received the notification, and shall not affect international applications filed prior to the expiration of the said six-month period.

(b) Any declaration made under this Article may be withdrawn at any time by notification addressed to the Director General. Such withdrawal shall take effect three months after the day on which the Director General has received the notification and, in the case of the withdrawal of a declaration made under paragraph (3), shall not affect international applications filed prior to the expiration of the said three-month period.

(7)

No reservations to this Treaty other than the reservations under paragraphs (1) to (5) are permitted.

The Treaty foresees only a limited number of reservations. Thus, a Contracting State 15
cannot claim that it is not bound by any other provision of the Treaty.

Article 65
Gradual Application

(1)

If the agreement with any International Searching or Preliminary Examining Authority provides, transitionally, for limits on the number or kind of international applications that such Authority undertakes to process, the Assembly shall adopt the measures necessary for the gradual application of this Treaty and the Regulations in respect of given categories of international applications. This provision shall also apply to requests for an international type search under Article 15(5).

1 There has not been such gradual application of the Treaty with regard to ISAs and IPEAs. Nevertheless, some ISAs/IPEAs have limitations as to the number of international applications they search for applications from certain receiving Offices (refer to ISA and IPEA Agreements (https://www.wipo.int/pct/en/access/isa_ipea_agreements.html); e.g. Annex A of Agreements for Israeli Office: the number of international applications searched with regard to RO/US applications is limited to 100). Further, past declarations concerning Chapter II (refer to annotations to Art. 64(1)) were mainly linked to the fact that the corresponding ISA/IPEA was not yet (fully) ready to do IPEs (refer for example to document PCT/A/V/9 (https://www.wipo.int/meetings/en/doc_details.jsp?doc_id=134154) para. 22).

(2)

The Assembly shall fix the dates from which, subject to the provision of paragraph (1), international applications may be filed and demands for international preliminary examination may be submitted. Such dates shall not be later than six months after this Treaty has entered into force according to the provisions of Article 63(1), or after Chapter II has become applicable under Article 63(3), respectively.

Article 66
Denunciation

(1)

Any Contracting State may denounce this Treaty by notification addressed to the Director General.

This provision has not been applied so far. 1

(2)

Denunciation shall take effect six months after receipt of the said notification by the Director General. It shall not affect the effects of the international application in the denouncing State if the international application was filed, and, where the denouncing State has been elected, the election was made, prior to the expiration of the said six-month period.

Article 67
Signature and Languages

(1)

(a) This Treaty shall be signed in a single original in the English and French languages, both texts being equally authentic.

(b) Official texts shall be established by the Director General, after consultation with the interested Governments, in the German, Japanese, Portuguese, Russian and Spanish languages, and such other languages as the Assembly may designate.

1 In September 1978, upon a proposal by the International Bureau, the Assembly designated Arabic and Italian as languages in which the Director General shall establish, under Art. 67(1)(b), official texts of the PCT (PCT/A/II/5, p. 7, para. 47 and 50). In September 1993, the Assembly designated Chinese(PCT/A/XXI/5, p. 6, para. 42). There is not yet an official text of the Treaty for the publication language Korean.

(2)

This Treaty shall remain open for signature at Washington until December 31, 1970.

Article 68
Depositary Functions

(1)

The original of this Treaty, when no longer open for signature, shall be deposited with the Director General.

The Treaty was open for signature until December 31, 1970 (refer to Art. 67(2)). 1

(2)

The Director General shall transmit two copies, certified by him, of this Treaty and the Regulations annexed hereto to the Governments of all States party to the Paris Convention for the Protection of Industrial Property and, on request, to the Government of any other State.

(3)

The Director General shall register this Treaty with the Secretariat of the United Nations.

(4)

The Director General shall transmit two copies, certified by him, of any amendment to this Treaty and the Regulations to the Governments of all Contracting States and, on request, to the Government of any other State.

Article 69
Notifications

The Director General shall notify the Governments of all States party to the Paris Convention for the Protection of Industrial Property of:

(i) signatures under Article 62,

1 That means as a State becoming party to the Treaty.

(ii) deposits of instruments of ratification or accession under Article 62,

2 Refer to list of PCT Notifications below.

(iii) the date of entry into force of this Treaty and the date from which Chapter II is applicable in accordance with Article 63(3),

3 Refer to PCT Notification No. 14: the PCT entered into force on 24 January 1978 (https://www.wipo.int/wipolex/en/treaties/notifications/details/treaty_pct_14); and PCT Notification No. 17: Chapter II became applicable on 29 March 1978 (https://www.wipo.int/wipolex/en/treaties/notifications/details/treaty_pct_17).

(iv) any declarations made under Article 64(1) to (5),

4 Refer to PCT Notifications and table of PCT Reservations, Declarations, Notifications and Incompatibilities (https://www.wipo.int/pct/en/texts/reservations/res_incomp.html)

(v) withdrawals of any declarations made under Article 64(6)(b),

5 Refer to PCT Notifications above.

(vi) denunciations received under Article 66, and

There are no such denunciations so far; however, the United Kingdom ceded its responsibility for Hong Kong (PCT Notifications 122). 6

(vii) any declarations made under Article 31(4).

Notifications are done in the Official Notices (PCT Gazette) Collection at: https:// 7
www.wipo.int/pct/en/official_notices/index.html and the PCT Notifications at: https://www.wipo.int/wipolex/en/treaties/ShowResults?start_year = ANY&end_year = ANY&search_what = N&country_id = ALL&treaty_id = 6.

Regulations under the Patent Cooperation Treaty

(as in force from July 1, 2024)

Table of Contents of Regulations

PART C: RULES CONCERNING CHAPTER II OF THE TREATY

Part A: Introductory Rules

Rule 1
Abbreviated Expressions

1.1 Meaning of Abbreviated Expressions

(a) In these Regulations, the word "Treaty" means the Patent Cooperation Treaty.

(b) In these Regulations, the words "Chapter" and "Article" refer to the specified Chapter or Article of the Treaty.

See also Terms and Abbreviations concerning Intellectual Property Information and Documentation (https://www.wipo.int/standards/en/part_08.html). 1

Rule 2
Interpretation of Certain Words

2.1 "Applicant"

Whenever the word "applicant" is used, it shall be construed as meaning also the agent or other representative of the applicant, except where the contrary clearly follows from the wording or the nature of the provision, or the context in which the word is used, such as, in particular, where the provision refers to the residence or nationality of the applicant.

2.2 "Agent"

Whenever the word "agent" is used, it shall be construed as meaning an agent appointed under Rule 90.1, unless the contrary clearly follows from the wording or the nature of the provision, or the context in which the word is used.

R. 90	Appointment as agent or common representative

2.2*bis* "Common Representative"

Whenever the expression "common representative" is used, it shall be construed as meaning an applicant appointed as, or considered to be, the common representative under Rule 90.2.

R. 90	Appointment as agent or common representative
R. 151 EPC	The EPC definition does not correspond to the PCT definition for the common representative.

2.3 "Signature"

Whenever the word "signature" is used, it shall be understood that, if the national law applied by the receiving Office or the competent International Searching or Preliminary Examining Authority requires the use of a seal instead of a signature, the word, for the purposes of that Office or Authority, shall mean seal.

1 There is no definition of a signature for paper submissions in the PCT Rules and Articles. So far it has been assumed that it is a handwritten signature in ink. A

clarification that signature means also 'handwritten, printed, typed or stamped' – similar to the PLT – has been proposed but not adopted (PCT Circular C.PCT 1625). The use of seals is mandatory in JP and KR, it is also possible in CN. For the use of official seals at the EPO see OJ EPO 2020 A37. For a PCTa the options are electronic signature as facsimile signature (pictorial reproduction, AIs Annex F 3.3.1), text string signature (characters selected by the signatory, AIs Annex F 3.3.2), click wrap signature (AIs Annex F 3.3.3), or enhanced electronic signature (confirmed with certificates, AIs Annex F 3.3.4).

R. 9(3) PLT	Enables the approval of other signature types such as stamped signature, seal, bar code
AIs Annex F 3.3	Definition of signature for electronic submissions

2.4 "Priority Period"

(a) Whenever the term "priority period" is used in relation to a priority claim, it shall be construed as meaning the period of 12 months from the filing date of the earlier application whose priority is so claimed. The day of filing of the earlier application shall not be included in that period.

(b) Rule 80.5 shall apply *mutatis mutandis* to the priority period.

Art. 8	Claiming priority and requirements for claiming priority
R. 26*bis*	Correction or addition of a priority claim, GL Exam A-VI, 1.4
R. 80.5	Expiration on a non-working day or official holiday
R. 82	Irregularities in the mail service, not applicable
R. 82*quater*	*Force majeure* not applicable

Part B: Rules Concerning Chapter I of the Treaty

See detailed overview in the Introduction to Art. 3.

Rule 3
The Request (Form)

3.1 Form of Request

The request shall be made on a printed form or be presented as a computer print-out.

3.2 Availability of Forms

Copies of the printed form shall be furnished free of charge to the applicants by the receiving Office, or, if the receiving Office so desires, by the International Bureau.

Art. 4	Detailed overview referring to the request in the Introduction to Art. 4
AIs 102	Use of the forms

3.3 Check List

(a) The request shall contain a list indicating:

(i) the total number of sheets constituting the international application and the number of the sheets of each element of the international application: request, description (separately indicating the number of sheets of any sequence listing part of the description), claims, drawings, abstract;

R. 13*ter*	Sequence listings

(ii) where applicable, that the international application as filed is accompanied by a power of attorney (i.e., a document appointing an agent or a common representative), a copy of a general power of attorney, a priority document, a sequence listing in electronic form, a document relating to the payment of fees, or any other document (to be specified in the check list);

(iii) the number of that figure of the drawings which the applicant suggests should accompany the abstract when the abstract is published; in exceptional cases, the applicant may suggest more than one figure.

(b) The list shall be completed by the applicant, failing which the receiving Office shall make the necessary indications, except that the number referred to in paragraph (a)(iii) shall not be indicated by the receiving Office.

3.4 Particulars

Subject to Rule 3.3, particulars of the printed request form and of a request presented as a computer print-out shall be prescribed by the Administrative Instructions.

Rule 4
The Request (Contents)

1 See detailed overview in the Introduction to Art. 4.

4.1 Mandatory and Optional Contents; Signature *(R. 4.15)*

Art. 3	The international application
Art. 4	The request
Art. 14	Certain defects in the international application

(a) The request shall contain:

(i) a petition,

(ii) the title of the invention,

(iii) indications concerning the applicant and the agent, if there is an agent,

(iv) indications concerning the inventor where the national law of at least one of the designated States requires that the name of the inventor be furnished at the time of filing a national application.

R. 4.1(a)(iv), 4.6(a)	It is possible to avoid publication of indications concerning the inventor like postal addresses and email addresses under R. 48.2(b)(l). It is not possible to keep the name of the inventor confidential (PCT Newsletter 06/2024).
Art. 4(4)	Failure to indicate the name of the inventor
R. 4.1(c)(i)	Request may omit name of inventor where law of designated State does not require
Art. 4(1)(v)	Name of the inventor
R. 6.4	Inventor

(b) The request shall, where applicable, contain:

(i) a priority claim *(R. 4.10)*,

(ii) indications relating to an earlier search as provided in Rules 4.12(i) and 12*bis*.1(b) and (d),

R. 41	Taking into account results of earlier search: where earlier search was carried out by the same ISA it may be taken into account (with the consequence that search fees may be refunded).
R. 12*bis*.1	Furnishing by the applicant of documents related to earlier search in case of request under R. 4.12

(iii) a reference to a parent application or parent patent,

(iv) an indication of the applicant's choice of competent International Searching Authority.

(c) The request may contain:

(i) indications concerning the inventor where the national law of none of the designated States requires that the name of the inventor be furnished at the time of filing a national application,

Art. 4(1)(v)	Name of the inventor
Art. 4(4)	Failure to indicate in the request the name of the inventor
R. 4.1(a)(iv)	Mandatory indications concerning the inventor (name)
R. 4.6	Inventor

(ii) a request to the receiving Office to prepare and transmit the priority document to the International Bureau where the application whose priority is claimed was filed with the national Office or intergovernmental authority which is the receiving Office,

(iii) declarations as provided in Rule 4.17,

R. 4.17	Additional declarations that might be required by national law, such as 'declaration of inventorship', assignment, etc.

(iv) a statement as provided in Rule 4.18,

R. 4.18	Statement of incorporation by reference of the priority of an earlier application. Such a statement is included as a precaution in the application Form PCT/RO/101.

(v) a request for restoration of the right of priority,

R. 26*bis*.3	Restoration of right of priority by receiving Office

(vi) a statement as provided in Rule 4.12(ii) *(same as earlier application)*.

R. 4.12	Indications relating to an earlier search

(d) The request shall be signed.

Art. 14(1)(a)(i)	Missing signature
Art. 14(1)(b)	Correction of defects, R. 26
R. 2.3	Signature
R. 4.15	The request shall be signed by all of the applicants
R. 90.3, Art. 49	The request shall be signed by the common agent or representative
R. 53.8 Art. 14(1)(b)	Missing signature of the request can be corrected
R. 92.1(b), Art. 14(1)(a)(i)	Missing signature of any letter submitted by the applicant can be corrected
AIs 316	Procedure in case of missing signature of the international application

Licensing Indications

2 An applicant desiring to attract licensees for the invention contained in his international application can request the International Bureau to put a licensing indication on the public part of the PATENTSCOPE website. The applicant can file the request using a special form (Form PCT/IB/382 available in all publication languages: https://www.wipo.int/pct/en/forms/) or send a letter to the International Bureau indicating that the claimed invention is available for licensing. The applicant may include licensing terms. The service is free of charge (AG-IP 11.102–11.108).

3 Licensing indications may be submitted at any time from the filing of the international application until the expiration of the 30-month time period. The indications will be visible in the bibliographic data relating to the particular application but will not be part of the published international application itself (AG-IP 11.103, 11.106; Art. 21; R. 4.1, 48.2).

4 The PCT has no express provision for indicating licensing information.

4.2 The Petition

The petition shall be to the following effect and shall preferably be worded as follows: "The undersigned requests that the present international application be processed according to the Patent Cooperation Treaty."

4.3 Title of the Invention

The title of the invention shall be short (preferably from two to seven words when in English or translated into English) and precise.

4.4 Names and Addresses

(a) Names of natural persons shall be indicated by the person's family name and given name(s), the family name being indicated before the given name(s).

(b) Names of legal entities shall be indicated by their full, official designations.

(c) Addresses shall be indicated in such a way as to satisfy the customary requirements for prompt postal delivery at the indicated address and, in any case, shall consist of all the relevant administrative units up to, and including, the house number, if any. Where the national law of the designated State does not require the indication of the house number, failure to indicate such number shall have no effect in that State. In order to allow rapid communication with the applicant, it is recommended to indicate any teleprinter address, telephone and facsimile machine numbers, or corresponding data for other like means of communication, of the applicant or, where applicable, the agent or the common representative.

R. 4.4(c) refers to communication from the Office to the applicant and prescribes details for the address. An example for another 'like means' is e-mail communication. Since July 1, 2008, there have been more extensive possibilities for e-mail communication by adapting the forms and AIs 706, 710. The e-mail address can be added and changed in accordance with R. 92*bis*.The e-mail address may be used by the International Bureau in case of failure of electronic systems (AIs 710(a)(v), Gazette November 16, 2023). See Introduction to R. 92 No. 2.2 for further information of correspondence of Office to applicant by e-mail. For communication of Offices to the applicant that trigger a time limit see R. 92.3. For different means of communication emanating from Office to applicant see Introduction to Part F of the Regulations. 5

(d) For each applicant, inventor, or agent, only one address may be indicated, except that, if no agent has been appointed to represent the applicant, or all of them if more than one, the applicant or, if there is more than one applicant, the common representative, may indicate, in addition to any other address given in the request, an address to which notifications shall be sent.

Letters are always sent to an appointed agent/representative. If none has been appointed, the correspondence will be sent to the applicant's address. If the applicant wishes a different address to be used, he must indicate this in a separate field (AG-IP 5.051). 6

Art. 27(7)	National requirements may apply for the requirements to indicate an address for the purpose of receiving notifications. The use of addresses for service is subject to the rules applicable to representation.
R. 90.1	Appointment as agent
R. 92*bis*.1	Recording of changes (address of the applicant or address for service) by the International Bureau

Art. 134 EPC	Appointment of an authorised agent/representative is necessary where the applicant is not resident in a EPC Contracting State (this refers to PCTa in the European phase, direct European applications or international phase before the EPO, OJ EPO 2014 A99 II.6, Art. 150(2) EPC). The EPO only sends correspondence to an address if no authorized agent/representative has been or has to be appointed. Since November 1, 2014, an address for correspondence may also be used by natural persons and not only by legal persons. For the international phase, the address of any person in any country may be given. For the European phase, the own address of the acting person must be indicated, i.e. not work place address. The address of a subdivision of a company is permitted if it is not another legal entity (OJ EPO 2014 A99).
R. 151 EPC	Several applicants

7 For statements of WIPO concerning R. 4.4(d) see PCT/A/VII/15, p.3, para. 17 (https://www.wipo.int/edocs/mdocs/govbody/en/pct_a_vii/pct_a_vii_15.pdf).

4.5 The Applicant

(a) The request shall indicate:

(i) the name,

(ii) the address, and

(iii) the nationality and residence

of the applicant or, if there are several applicants, of each of them.

(b) The applicant's nationality shall be indicated by the name of the State of which he is a national.

R. 18.1	Residence and nationality
AIs 105	Indication of the PCTa with two or more applicants
R. 26.2*bis*(b)	For the purpose of Art. 14(1)(a)(ii) the requirements of R. 4.4 and R. 4.5 in case of several applicants are fulfilled if the indications under R. 4.5(a)(ii) and (iii) are provided with reference to one of the applicants who is entitled under R. 19.2 to file the application (information No. 2 in Annex A Form PCT/RO/106)
R. 51*bis*.1(a)(vii)	Designated Office may require missing indications under R. 4.5(a)(ii) and (iii) (Information in No. 2 in Annex A Form PCT/RO/106)

(c) The applicant's residence shall be indicated by the name of the State of which he is a resident *(R. 18.1)*.

(d) The request may, for different designated States, indicate different applicants. In such a case, the request shall indicate the applicant or applicants for each designated State or group of designated States.

R. 18.4	National requirements relating to the applicant. Although the US removed the requirement that inventors be named as applicants, US law will still oblige the inventors to be involved in the national stage process (Newsletter 7–8/2012).
AIs 203	Different applicants for different designated States

For statements of WIPO concerning R. 4.5(d) see PCT/A/XVIII/9 p.3, para.17 (https://www.wipo.int/meetings/en/doc_details.jsp?doc_id=2337). 8

(e) Where the applicant is registered with the national Office that is acting as receiving Office, the request may indicate the number or other indication under which the applicant is so registered.

4.6 The Inventor

(a) Where Rule 4.1(a)(iv) *(Compulsory naming of inventors on the filing date)* or (c)(i) *(voluntary)* applies, the request shall indicate the name and address of the inventor or, if there are several inventors, of each of them.

R. 4.1(a)(iv), 4.1(c)(i)	It is possible to avoid the publication of indications concerning the inventor like postal addresses and email addresses under R. 48.2(b)(l). It is not possible to keep the name of the inventor confidential (PCT Newsletter 06/2024).
Art. 4(1)(v)	Indications concerning the inventor in the request. For late furnishing of indications concerning inventors see Art. 4(4).
Art. 4(4)	Failure to indicate the name of the inventor
Art. 4*ter* Paris Convention, Art. 62 EPC	Right of the inventor to be mentioned
Art. 81 EPC	Designation of the inventor/statement indicating the origin of the right
§ 37 PatG	Designation of the inventor/indication how right to the patent has been acquired

(b) If the applicant is the inventor, the request, in lieu of the indication under paragraph (a), shall contain a statement to that effect.

(c) The request may, for different designated States, indicate different persons as inventors *(R. 4.5(d))* where, in this respect, the requirements of the national laws of the designated States are not the same. In such a case, the request shall contain a separate statement for each designated State or group of States in which a particular person, or the same person, is to be considered the inventor, or in which particular persons, or the same persons, are to be considered the inventors.

Para. (c) mentions persons as inventors. On the question of whether artificial 9
intelligence can be named as inventor and on the rejection by various patent Offices,

see the essays by several authors in *Mitteilungen der deutschen Patentanwälte*, e.g. Köllner in Mitt. 2020 p. 193 and 386. Publication WO 2020/079499 A1 names an artificial intelligence called DABUS as inventor on the title page.

4.7 The Agent

(a) If an agent is appointed, the request shall so indicate, and shall state the agent's name and address.

R. 90	Agents and common representatives
R. 90.4	The power of attorney can be granted by signing the request form by the applicants
R. 90.4(a)	The power of attorney must be signed by all applicants

(b) Where the agent is registered with the national Office that is acting as receiving Office, the request may indicate the number or other indication under which the agent is so registered.

4.8 Common Representative

If a common representative is appointed, the request shall so indicate.

R. 90	Agents and common representatives

4.9 Designation of States; Kinds of Protection; National and Regional Patents

(a) The filing of a request shall constitute:

(i) the designation of all Contracting States that are bound by the Treaty on the international filing date;

(ii) an indication that the international application is, in respect of each designated State to which Article 43 or 44 applies, for the grant of every kind of protection which is available by way of the designation of that State;

(iii) an indication that the international application is, in respect of each designated State to which Article 45(1) applies, for the grant of a regional patent and also, unless Article 45(2) applies, a national patent.

Art. 44	Kinds of protection
Art. 45	Regional patent treaties
R. 4.5(d)	Different applicants for different designated States
R. 4.11	Indication referring to patent of addition or continuation-in-part and similar

R. 49*bis*.1	The indication of certain kinds of protections is only possible at the time of entry into the national phase before the designated Office. Without further specification, it is assumed that granting of a patent is requested, PCT Newsletter 4/2022, p. 11.
Art. 9(3), R. 18.4(c)	In case where there are several applicants and one of the applicants, who is not a resident or national of a PCT Contracting State, is designated as the only applicant for a certain designated State, this designation is nevertheless valid

(b) Notwithstanding paragraph (a)(i), if, on October 5, 2005, the national law of a Contracting State provides that the filing of an international application which contains the designation of that State and claims the priority of an earlier national application having effect in that State *(internal priority)* shall have the result that the earlier national application ceases to have effect with the same consequences as the withdrawal of the earlier national application, any request in which the priority of an earlier national application filed in that State is claimed may contain an indication that the designation of that State is not made, provided that the designated Office notifies the International Bureau by January 5, 2006, that this paragraph shall apply in respect of designations of that State and that the notification is still in force on the international filing date. The information received shall be promptly published by the International Bureau in the Gazette.

Art. 8	Claiming priority
Art. 4 Paris Convention	Priority of an earlier foreign application (foreign priority)

The following countries currently have a provision on the fiction of withdrawal when claiming internal priority: DE, JP and KR (www.wipo.int/pct/de/texts/reservations/res_incomp.html). 10

For DE:

§ 40 PatG stipulates that claiming the priority of an earlier domestic patent application (internal priority) has the effect of deemed withdrawal of the priority application (https://www.dpma.de/english/patents/application/index.html, https://www.gesetze-im-internet.de/englisch_patg/englisch_patg.html). 11

However, the internal priority is only validly claimed for an international patent application according to Art. III § 4(4) of the Act on International Patent Conventions (DE-IntPatÜbkG) if all formal requirements according to Art. III § 4(2), § 6(2) DE-IntPatÜbkG are fulfilled, in particular the national (filing) fee is paid upon entry into the international phase (BlPMZ 2001 p. 220). Pursuant to Art. III, § 4(2) DE-IntPatÜbkG, the international application enters into the national phase without further action by the applicant, provided the DPMA is both receiving Office and designated Office and the international application has been filed in the German language. According to Art. III § 4(2) 2 DE-IntPatÜbkG, the filing fee is deemed to have been paid upon 12 payment of the transmittal fee if the DPMA was the receiving Office for the PCTa. Under these conditions, the priority application would be considered withdrawn. Namely, the case of unintentional withdrawal due to the fiction of withdrawal when claiming priority of a German application can only occur if the application is filed at the DPMA, but not at the EPO as receiving Office.

13 Consequently, if the applicant wants to avoid the automatic withdrawal of the earlier national application, he may exclude Germany from the automatic designation, pursuant to R. 4.9(b), or may consider withdrawing the designation of Germany, pursuant to R. 90*bis*.2, subsequent to the filing of the international application but before entry into the national phase (https://pctlegal.wipo.int/eGuide/view-doc.xhtml?doc-code=DE&doc-lang=en#NATIONAL%20CHAPTER).

For JP:

14 In JP the deemed withdrawal takes effect after the expiry of 16 months calculated from the filing date of the earlier application. Within this period, the withdrawal of the JP designation can take place (PCT Newsletter, 4/2015, p. 5 and AG-IP Annex B (JP)).

For KR:

15 In KR a time limit of 15 months from the priority date applies (AG-IPAnnex B (KR)).

R. 90*bis*.2	For all States other than DE, JP and KR, the designation can only be withdrawn under this Rule
AIs 319	Procedure in accordance with R. 4.9(b)

4.10 Priority Claim

Art. 8	Claiming priority
R. 2.4	Priority period
R. 17	Priority document

(a) Any declaration referred to in Article 8(1) ("priority claim") may claim the priority of one or more earlier applications filed either in or for any country party to the Paris Convention for the Protection of Industrial Property or in or for any Member of the World Trade Organization that is not party to that Convention. Any priority claim shall be made in the request; it shall consist of a statement to the effect that the priority of an earlier application is claimed and shall indicate:

16 For a list of the Member States of the Paris Convention and the WTO, see the List of Territories in the Annex and the references therein. The earlier application may be a patent, utility model or inventor's certificate, PCT EPO Guidelines A-VI 1.1.

R. 26*bis*	Correction or addition of priority claim

R. 90*bis*.3	Withdrawals of priority claims
R. 91	Rectification of obvious mistakes
R. 17	Priority document
AIs 302, 409	Priority claim considered not to have been made
AIs 314, 402	Correction or addition of a priority claim under R. 26*bis*

(i) the date on which the earlier application was filed;
(ii) the number of the earlier application;

R. 26*bis*.2(c)(i)	A priority claim shall not be considered void due to a missing indication of the official number of the earlier application
AIs 408	Priority application number

(iii) where the earlier application is a national application, the country party to the Paris Convention for the Protection of Industrial Property or the Member of the World Trade Organization that is not party to that Convention in which it was filed;
(iv) where the earlier application is a regional application, the authority entrusted with the granting of regional patents under the applicable regional patent treaty;
(v) where the earlier application is an international application, the receiving Office with which it was filed.

(b) In addition to any indication required under paragraph (a)(iv) or (v):
(i) where the earlier application is a regional application or an international application, the priority claim may indicate one or more countries party to the Paris Convention for the Protection of Industrial Property for which that earlier application was filed;
(ii) where the earlier application is a regional application and at least one of the countries party to the regional patent treaty is neither party to the Paris Convention for the Protection of Industrial Property nor a Member of the World Trade Organization, the priority claim shall indicate at least one country party to that Convention or one Member of that Organization for which that earlier application was filed.

(c) For the purposes of paragraphs (a) *(national patents)* and (b) *(regional patents)*, Article 2(vi) *(national means national or regional)* shall not apply.

Priority of an application filed in or in respect of a WTO member which is not a party to the Paris Convention may be claimed before the EPO as a receiving Office for applications filed on or after December 13, 2007, Euro-PCT Guide 2.15.001. 17

4.11 Reference to Continuation or Continuation-in-Part, or Parent Application or Grant

(a) If:

(i) the applicant intends to make an indication under Rule 49*bis*.1(a) or (b) of the wish that the international application be treated, in any designated State, as an application for a patent of addition, certificate of addition, inventor's certificate of addition or utility certificate of addition; or

(ii) the applicant intends to make an indication under Rule 49*bis*.1(d) of the wish that the international application be treated, in any designated State, as an application for a continuation or a continuation-in-part of an earlier application;

the request shall so indicate and shall indicate the relevant parent application or parent patent or other parent grant.

(b) The inclusion in the request of an indication under paragraph (a) shall have no effect on the operation of Rule 4.9.

R. 26*quater*	Correction or addition of indications under R. 4.11

4.12 Taking into Account Results of Earlier Search

If the applicant wishes the International Searching Authority to take into account, in carrying out the international search, the results of an earlier international, international-type or national search carried out by the same or another International Searching Authority or by a national Office ("earlier search"):

(i) the request shall so indicate and shall specify the Authority or Office concerned and the application in respect of which the earlier search was carried out;

(ii) the request may, where applicable, contain a statement to the effect that the international application is the same, or substantially the same, as the application in respect of which the earlier search was carried out, or that the international application is the same, or substantially the same, as that earlier application except that it is filed in a different language.

R. 4.12	'Earlier search' includes both the search carried out by the Authority or the Office itself and a commissioned search (PCT Assembly report PCT/A/36/13, also on the interpretation of the term 'substantially the same' in para. (ii))
R. 12*bis*.1	Filing of documents pertaining to an earlier search with a request under R. 4.12: (a) copies of the results, (b) exceptionally, request that receiving Office to transmit, (c) and (d) exceptions to the filing requirement
R. 12*bis*.2	Furnishing of documents relating to earlier searches: (a) upon request by ISA, possible also in respect of additional documents, (b) and (c) unless documents are available there

R. 23*bis*	Transmittal of documents from receiving Office to ISA
R. 41	Taking into account results of earlier search in case of request under R. 4.12: must be taken into account if carried out by the same ISA and may be taken into account if carried out by another ISA or another Office. In other cases, the ISA may take the results into account under R. 41.2(b).

For statements of WIPO concerning R. 4.12 see PCT/A/36/13, p.29, para. 137(iii) and (iv) (https://www.wipo.int/edocs/mdocs/govbody/en/pct_a_36/pct_a_36_13.pdf). 18

4.13 and 4.14 [Deleted]

4.14*bis* Choice of International Searching Authority

If two or more International Searching Authorities are competent for the searching of the international application, the applicant shall indicate his choice of International Searching Authority in the request.

Art. 16(2)	Choice of ISA by receiving Office

4.15 Signature

The request shall be signed by the applicant or, if there is more than one applicant, by all of them.

R. 2.3	Signature
R. 4.17(iv)	Declaration of inventorship
R. 4.15	Each applicant must sign the application.
R. 51*bis*.1(a) (vi)	Designated Offices may require missing signatures (No. 2 Annex A PCT/RO/106)
R. 60.1(a-*ter*)	Corresponding formal requirements under Chapter II
R. 53.8	Signature of the demand for IPE
R. 90.3, Art. 49	Effect of acts by agents or common representatives
Art. 14(1)(a)(i)	Missing signature leads to missing representation
R. 92.1(b), Art. 14(1)(a)(i)	Missing signature of a letter may be corrected
AIs 316	Procedure where international application lacks prescribed signature

4.16 Transliteration or Translation of Certain Words

(a) Where any name or address is written in characters other than those of the Latin alphabet, the same shall also be indicated in characters of the Latin alphabet either as a mere transliteration or through translation into English.

The applicant shall decide which words will be merely transliterated and which words will be so translated.

(b) The name of any country written in characters other than those of the Latin alphabet shall also be indicated in English.

4.17 Declarations Relating to National Requirements Referred to in Rule 51*bis*.1(a)(i) to (v)

The request may, for the purposes of the national law applicable in one or more designated States, contain one or more of the following declarations, worded as prescribed by the Administrative Instructions:

R. 26*ter*	Correction or addition of declarations under R. 4.17
R. 26*ter*.1	In the case of corrections or additions concerning statements under R. 4.17, a time limit of 16 months from the priority date or before completion of the technical preparations for publication (AG-IP 6.045) applies. The technical preparations are usually completed 15 days before the publication date, see annotations to Art. 21(5). The declaration shall be sent to the International Bureau. If received after the time limit, the International Bureau informs the applicant. It does not publish the declaration and does not send it to the designated Office. It informs the applicant that such declarations must be filed directly with the designated Office. The International Bureau returns an inventor's declaration signed by at least one inventor. (AIs 419(d), AG-.IP 6.050).
R. 26*ter*.2(a)	Receiving Office or International Bureau invites the applicant to correct the defects within the time limit mentioned
AIs 327	No correction *ex officio* of indications under R. 4.17
R. 51*bis*.2	No further evidence for declarations under R. 4.17
AIs 303	No deletion *ex officio* of indications under R. 4.17
R. 48.2(a)(x)	Declarations submitted in time will be published with the A1 document (time limit R. 26*ter*.1: 16 months).
R. 48.2(b)(iv)	The publication is independent of the question of whether the declaration according to R. 4.17 was made correctly.
AIs 406	All international applications and declarations are published in electronic form. Since April 1, 2006, each declaration of the applicant under R. 4.17 is available for each designated Office via the Internet (available at http://patentscope.wipo.int/search/en/search.jsf). Therefore, the applicant does not need to indicate to which designated Office the declaration refers. Furthermore, the International Bureau does not need to send the declarations to the designated Offices either (PCT Newsletter 11/2006, 7). The applicant is informed of the publication by receiving the Form (PCT/IB/311). It states that sending the publication in paper form can be requested by e-mail and is available on PATENTSCOPE.

AIs 419	Processing in the event of expiry of the time limit under R. 26*ter*

(i) a declaration as to the identity of the inventor, as referred to in Rule 51*bis*.1(a)(i) (declaration of inventorship);

(ii) a declaration as to the applicant's entitlement, as at the international filing date, to apply for and be granted a patent, as referred to in Rule 51*bis*.1(a)(ii) *("assignment" for the US)*;

If the inventor is designated in the international phase, but the applicant's entitlement to file the application is not indicated in the international phase, the EPO does not request indications as to the entitlement in the regional phase (GL Exam E-IX, 2.3.4). The situation is different for an EP direct application. Here, the applicant's entitlement must be indicated in the inventor's designation (GL Exam E-IX, 2.3.4). **19**

(iii) a declaration as to the applicant's entitlement, as at the international filing date, to claim priority of the earlier application, as referred to in Rule 51*bis*.1(a)(iii);

This declaration is not checked for correctness by the receiving Office. For the entitlement to claim priority, it is important that applicants ensure that on the international filing date all applicants who filed the priority of an earlier application are indicated in the PCTa as applicants or have validly transferred their rights to the applicants as successors in title before the filing date (Euro-PCT Guide 2.15.003). For more details, see PCT EPO Guidelines A-VI 1.6 and Art. 8 Introduction. **20**

(iv) a declaration of inventorship, as referred to in Rule 51*bis*.1(a)(iv), which shall be signed as prescribed by the Administrative Instructions *("declaration of inventorship" for the US)*;

	The private or professional address of the inventor is visible in PATENTSCOPE. A change of address under R. 92*bis* is also visible, but in a non-searchable image format. (PCT Newsletter 10/2020, p. 14).
	Via ePCT, signatures of inventors can be obtained electronically and made available (PCT Newsletter 10/2019, p. 7). For managing external signatures in ePCT see Pract. Adv. NL 7–8/2023.
R. 4.6	Indication of the name and address of the inventor
R. 4.17(iv)	A declaration of inventorship for the US requires the signature of the inventor. Even if the inventor has personally signed the PCT request (Form PCT/RO/101, last sheet) and the inventor's declaration is filed as part of the application together with the PCT request, this separate signature is required on the declaration (Form PCT/RO101, declaration sheet (iv)

AIs 211–215	Wording of the declarations on the identity of the inventor or on the entitlement

(v) a declaration as to non-prejudicial disclosures or exceptions to lack of novelty, as referred to in Rule 51*bis*.1(a)(v).

4.18 Statement of Incorporation by Reference

Where the international application, on the date on which one or more elements referred to in Article 11(1)(iii) were first received by the receiving Office, claims the priority of an earlier application, the request may contain a statement that, where an element of the international application referred to in Article 11(1)(iii) (d) or (e) *(description or claims in their entirety)*, or a part of the description, claims or drawings referred to in Rule 20.5(a), or an element or part of the description, claims or drawings referred to in Rule 20.5*bis*(a) is not otherwise contained in the international application but is completely contained in the earlier application, that element or part is, subject to confirmation under Rule 20.6 *(ensuring international filing date)*, incorporated by reference in the international application for the purposes of Rule 20.6. Such a statement, if not contained in the request on that date, may be added to the request if, and only if, it was otherwise contained in, or submitted with, the international application on that date.

21 The regulation is applicable to PCTa for which reference is made to one or more elements mentioned in Art. 11(1)(iii) for the first time on or after July 1, 2020. The reference to R. 20.5*bis*(a) was added.

Art. 11(1)(iii)	Elements: (a) treatment as PCTa, (b) designation of Contracting State, (c) applicant's name, (d) description, (e) claims
R. 20.3	Completely missing parts
R. 20.5	Partially missing parts
R. 20.5(a)	Request for rectification of defects in case of missing parts
R. 20.5*bis*(a)	Erroneously filed elements or parts
R. 4.18	Statement of incorporation by reference. It is included in the application Form PCT/RO/101 as a precaution and cannot be filed subsequently.
R. 20.6, R. 20.7	Confirmation within two months and subsequent submission of documents
AIs 309	Procedure in case of later submitted sheets furnished for the purposes of incorporation by reference

4.19 Additional Matter

(a) The request shall contain no matter other than that specified in Rules 4.1 to 4.18, provided that the Administrative Instructions may permit, but cannot

make mandatory, the inclusion in the request of any additional matter specified in the Administrative Instructions.

(b) If the request contains matter other than that specified in Rules 4.1 to 4.18 or permitted under paragraph (a) by the Administrative Instructions, the receiving Office shall *ex officio* delete the additional matter.

AIs 303 Deletion of additional matter in the request

Rule 5
The Description

Art. 3	The international application
Art. 5	The description
R. 12	Language

5.1 Manner of the Description

(a) The description shall first state the title of the invention *(R. 4.3)* as appearing in the request and shall:

(i) specify the technical field to which the invention relates;

(ii) indicate the background art which, as far as known to the applicant, can be regarded as useful for the understanding, searching and examination of the invention, and, preferably, cite the documents reflecting such art;

(iii) disclose the invention, as claimed, in such terms that the technical problem (even if not expressly stated as such) and its solution can be understood, and state the advantageous effects, if any, of the invention with reference to the background art;

(iv) briefly describe the figures in the drawings, if any;

(v) set forth at least the best mode contemplated by the applicant for carrying out the invention claimed; this shall be done in terms of examples, where appropriate, and with reference to the drawings, if any; where the national law of the designated State does not require the description of the best mode but is satisfied with the description of any mode (whether it is the best contemplated or not), failure to describe the best mode contemplated shall have no effect in that State;

(vi) indicate explicitly, when it is not obvious from the description or nature of the invention, the way in which the invention is capable of exploitation in industry and the way in which it can be made and used, or, if it can only be used, the way in which it can be used; the term "industry" is to be understood in its broadest sense as in the Paris Convention for the Protection of Industrial Property.

(b) The manner and order specified in paragraph (a) shall be followed except when, because of the nature of the invention, a different manner or a different order would result in a better understanding and a more economic presentation.

(c) Subject to the provisions of paragraph (b), each of the parts referred to in paragraph (a) shall preferably be preceded by an appropriate heading as suggested in the Administrative Instructions.

AIs 204	Headings of the parts of the description

5.2 Nucleotide and/or Amino Acid Sequence Disclosure

(a) Where the international application contains disclosure of nucleotide and/or amino acid sequences that, pursuant to the Administrative Instructions, are required to be included in a sequence listing, the description shall include a sequence listing part of the description complying with the standard provided for in the Administrative Instructions.

The formal requirements for a sequence listing and further details are regulated in the AIs. Sequence listings may no longer be submitted in paper form or in a format other than XML. Nevertheless, the possibility of filing in paper form under R. 89*bis*.1(a) is maintained for emergency purposes to ensure the accordance of a filing date if filing under WIPO Standard ST.26 is not possible (PCT/WG/13/8 No. 6). The receiving Office will only examine whether it is *prima facie* a sequence listing. It is assumed that only in exceptional cases a receiving Office finds deficiencies and only the ISA invites the applicant to correct the deficiency under R. 13*ter*.1. If the applicant himself identifies a deficiency, the usual possibilities of correction, amendment, or rectification exist. In case of problems with a receiving Office, the International Bureau offers assistance to the applicant (PCT Circular C.PCT 1627, p. 6. PCT/WG/13/8 No. 11). 1

See also https://www.wipo.int/standards/de/sequence/faq.html. 2

Art. 34	Procedure of amendments (IPEA)
R. 13*ter*	Furnishing sequence listings with or without invitation by ISA or IPEA
R. 20	Correction of defects before the receiving Office
R. 26.1	Invitation from the receiving Office to correct a sequence listing
R. 91	Rectification of obvious mistakes in the international application and other documents
AIs 208	Reference to Annex C of the AIs regarding requirements for the sequence listings
AIs 707 (a-*bis*)	If the prescribed format is used, the sequence listing is not taken into account in the calculation of the international filing fee
AIs 710	As long as the International Bureau does not receive any information from the receiving Office concerning the accepted format, it is assumed that the respective receiving Office accepts the format ST.26 but not ST.25 (PCT Circular C.PCT 1622).

AIs Annex C	Information on sequences to be included in the sequence listing and information on furnishing. For details, reference is made there to WIPO Standard ST.26, which applies to all PCTa filed since July 1, 2022 (PCT Circular C.PCT 1627 p. 5). For a PCTa filed before July 1, 2022, sequence listings in WIPO ST.25 format can be uploaded in ePCT as subsequently filed documents, e.g. under R. 13*ter* or as a rectification or amendment. The document types currently available in ePCT will continue to be used – without distinction between WIPO ST.25 and ST.26 standards (https://www.wipo.int/standards/de/sequence/faq.html).
ST.26	https://www.wipo.int/export/sites/www/standards/en/pdf/03-26-01.pdf https://www.wipo.int/standards/en/sequence/faq.html
Annex C	For requirements before the receiving Offices, see AG-IP
EPO	OJ EPO 2021 A96 and OJ EPO 2021 A97 No. 27 et seq. No. 19 et seq. regulate the procedure before the EPO as ISA, SISA or IPEA: if there is no sequence listing that complies with the regulations, an invitation to file a suitable sequence listing according to R. 13*ter*.1 is issued. It is recommended to use the latest version of the software (OJ EPO 2023 A47). If the sequence listing file seems to be in a format other than XML at the EPO as receiving Office, the sequence listing file will not be considered part of the PCTa. The EPO converts the file into the format of the main part of the description and invites the applicant, within a time limit, to confirm that this content is to be part of the description. If the applicant fails to comply with the time limit or makes an explicit declaration to that effect, the file does not form part of the PCTa and does not form part of the priority document under R. 17.1(b) (OJ EPO 2022 A60). For the EPO as designated or elected Office OJ EPO 2021 A96 and OJ EPO 2021 A97 No. 27 et seq. apply (see also AG-NP EP.03 and C (EP) Info on ST.26 in Gazette June 30, 2022). To avoid the risk of adding and/or losing subject matter when converting sequence listings from ST.25 to ST.26 format, see the notice concerning the handling of ST.25 sequence listings filed as a safeguard as part of divisional applications to which ST.26 applies (OJ EPO 2024 A54).
DPMA	Implementation of the international standard in the German Patent Ordinance as of July 1, 2022, DPMA Notice of September 24, 2022 (https://www.dpma.de/english/our_office/publications/important_notices/notice_24062022/index.html)

(b) Language-dependent free text included in the sequence listing part of the description shall not be required to be included in the main body of the description.

R. 12.1(d)	Language of the free text

Free text included in the sequence listing is dispensable in the body of the description because it is more difficult to understand at that point than in the context of the sequence listing. The receiving Office does not examine the contents of sequence listings for lack of knowledge (PCT Circular C.PCT, Circular 1627 p. 2). If the receiving Office finds a language not admitted, it may, in the absence of language competence, forward the PCTa to the International Bureau under R. 19.4 (see No. 28 under https://www.wipo.int/standards/en/sequence/faq.html). 3

Rule 6
The Claims

6.1 Number and Numbering of Claims

(a) The number of the claims shall be reasonable in consideration of the nature of the invention claimed.

(b) If there are several claims, they shall be numbered consecutively in Arabic numerals.

(c) The method of numbering in the case of the amendment of claims shall be governed by the Administrative Instructions.

Art. 3	The international application
Art. 6	The claims
AIs 205	Numbering and identification of claims upon amendment: no renumbering required

6.2 References to Other Parts of the International Application

(a) Claims shall not, except where absolutely necessary, rely, in respect of the technical features of the invention, on references to the description or drawings. In particular, they shall not rely on such references as: "as described in part ... of the description," or "as illustrated in figure ... of the drawings."

(b) Where the international application contains drawings, the technical features mentioned in the claims shall preferably be followed by the reference signs relating to such features. When used, the reference signs shall preferably be placed between parentheses. If inclusion of reference signs does not particularly facilitate quicker understanding of a claim, it should not be made. Reference signs may be removed by a designated Office for the purposes of publication by such Office.

6.3 Manner of Claiming

(a) The definition of the matter for which protection is sought shall be in terms of the technical features of the invention.

(b) Whenever appropriate, claims shall contain:

(i) a statement indicating those technical features of the invention which are necessary for the definition of the claimed subject matter but which, in combination, are part of the prior art,

(ii) a characterizing portion – preceded by the words "characterized in that," "characterized by," "wherein the improvement comprises," or any other words to the same effect – stating concisely the technical features which, in combination with the features stated under (i), it is desired to protect.

Single-part claims are also admissible. 1

(c) Where the national law of the designated State does not require the manner of claiming provided for in paragraph (b), failure to use that manner of claiming shall have no effect in that State provided the manner of claiming actually used satisfies the national law of that State.

6.4 Dependent Claims

(a) Any claim which includes all the features of one or more other claims (claim in dependent form, hereinafter referred to as "dependent claim") shall do so by a reference, if possible at the beginning, to the other claim or claims and shall then state the additional features claimed. Any dependent claim which refers to more than one other claim ("multiple dependent claim") shall refer to such claims in the alternative only. Multiple dependent claims shall not serve as a basis for any other multiple dependent claim. Where the national law of the national Office acting as International Searching Authority does not allow multiple dependent claims to be drafted in a manner different from that provided for in the preceding two sentences, failure to use that manner of claiming may result in an indication under Article 17(2)(b) in the international search report. Failure to use the said manner of claiming shall have no effect in a designated State if the manner of claiming actually used satisfies the national law of that State.

(b) Any dependent claim shall be construed as including all the limitations contained in the claim to which it refers or, if the dependent claim is a multiple dependent claim, all the limitations contained in the particular claim in relation to which it is considered.

(c) All dependent claims referring back to a single previous claim, and all dependent claims referring back to several previous claims, shall be grouped together to the extent and in the most practical way possible.

6.5 Utility Models

Any designated State in which the grant of a utility model is sought on the basis of an international application may, instead of Rules 6.1 to 6.4, apply in respect of the matters regulated in those Rules the provisions of its national law concerning utility models once the processing of the international application has started in that State, provided that the applicant shall be allowed at least two

months from the expiration of the time limit applicable under Article 22 to adapt his application to the requirements of the said provisions of the national law.

Art. 2(ii)	'Patent' also means 'utility model'
Art. 3	The international application
Art. 44	Seeking two kinds of protection

Rule 7
The Drawings

7.1 Flow Sheets and Diagrams

Flow sheets and diagrams are considered drawings.

Art. 3	The international application
Art. 7(1)	The drawings necessary for the understanding of the invention

7.2 Time Limit

The time limit referred to in Article 7(2)(ii) *(drawings requested by the designated Office)* shall be reasonable under the circumstances of the case and shall, in no case, be shorter than two months from the date of the written invitation requiring the filing of drawings or additional drawings under the said provision.

Art. 7(2)	The drawings not necessary for the understanding of the invention
R. 11.13	Special requirements for drawings
Art. 14(2)	Missing drawings have a different consequence than other defects mentioned in Art. 14. It is recommended to file a PCTa with informal drawings rather than not meeting the priority time limit. Pract. Adv. NL 04/2019 and 05/2019.

Rule 8
The Abstract

INTRODUCTION

1 An international application must contain an abstract (Art. 3(2)). The abstract merely serves the purpose of technical information and cannot be taken into account for any other purpose, particularly not for the interpretation of the scope of protection (Art. 3(3)). The requirements the abstract must comply with are set out in R. 8 and R. 11; amongst other things, it must be concise, preferably 50 to 150 words when in English or translated into English (R. 8.1(b)). See annotations to Art. 14 for the correction of non-compliance with the physical requirements as set out in R. 8 and R. 11.

2 The request must indicate the figure of the drawings to accompany the abstract on the front page of the international publication (R. 3.3(a)(iii)). If the applicant does not specify the number of the figure or the ISA considers the figure suggested by the applicant inappropriate, the ISA determines the figure to accompany the abstract (R. 8.2(a)). If the ISA finds that no figure is useful, the abstract will be published without a figure (R. 8.2(b)).

3 A missing abstract is regarded as a defect (Art. 14(1)(a)(iv)), which does not affect the international filing date. The receiving Office will invite the applicant to furnish the abstract, failure of which can result in the international application being considered withdrawn (Art. 14(1)(b); see annotations to Art. 14 for the procedure). The receiving Office notifies the ISA of a missing abstract; the ISA will proceed with the international search, but stops if it is notified that the application is considered withdrawn (R. 38.1). However, if the ISA has not received a notification that the receiving Office has invited the applicant to correct the defect and the abstract is missing or the abstract does not comply with R. 8, the ISA will establish the abstract itself (R. 38.2).

4 The applicant may comment on the abstract established by the ISA; the ISA decides whether to modify the abstract accordingly (R. 38.3). An obvious mistake in the abstract may not be corrected using R. 91, but the applicant may, within one month from the date of mailing of the ISR, submit comments on and/or propose modifications of the abstract established by the ISA (R. 91.1(g)(ii); R. 38.3). The ISR either states that the ISA approves the abstract submitted by the applicant or that the report is accompanied by the abstract as established by the ISA (R. 44.2).

It is important to draft an abstract carefully, in the first place because a high-quality abstract is important for an effective prior art search, in the second place to avoid delays caused by the ISA in rewriting the abstract and in subsequently reworking the translation, and in the third place to avoid republication of the international application (Pract. Adv. NL 04/2017 www.wipo.int/pct/en/newslett/practical_advice/pa_042017.html). 5

8.1 Contents and Form of the Abstract

(a) The abstract shall consist of the following:

(i) a summary of the disclosure as contained in the description, the claims, and any drawings; the summary shall indicate the technical field to which the invention pertains and shall be drafted in a way which allows the clear understanding of the technical problem, the gist of the solution of that problem through the invention, and the principal use or uses of the invention;

(ii) where applicable, the chemical formula which, among all the formulae contained in the international application, best characterizes the invention.

(b) The abstract shall be as concise as the disclosure permits (preferably 50 to 150 words if it is in English or when translated into English).

(c) The abstract shall not contain statements on the alleged merits or value of the claimed invention or on its speculative application.

(d) Each main technical feature mentioned in the abstract and illustrated by a drawing in the international application shall be followed by a reference sign, placed between parentheses.

R. 38	Missing or defective abstract
R. 48.2	Publication of the abstract
Art. 3(2) and (3)	Abstract as content of the international application: for technical information only and not for the purpose of interpreting the scope of protection
AIs 207	Arrangement of elements and numbering of sheets of the international application

8.2 Figure

(a) If the applicant fails to make the indication referred to in Rule 3.3(a)(iii), or if the International Searching Authority finds that a figure or figures other than that figure or those figures suggested by the applicant would, among all the figures of all the drawings, better characterize the invention, it shall, subject to paragraph (b), indicate the figure or figures which should accompany the abstract when the latter is published by the International Bureau. In such case, the abstract shall be accompanied by the figure or figures so indicated by the International Searching Authority. Otherwise, the abstract shall, subject to paragraph (b), be accompanied by the figure or figures suggested by the applicant.

(b) If the International Searching Authority finds that none of the figures of the drawings is useful for the understanding of the abstract, it shall notify the International Bureau accordingly. In such case, the abstract, when published by the International Bureau, shall not be accompanied by any figure of the drawings even where the applicant has made a suggestion under Rule 3.3(a)(iii).

6 For statements of WIPO concerning R. 8.2 see PCT/A/XI/9, p.3, para.21 (https://www.wipo.int/about-wipo/ru/assemblies/2022/a-63/doc_details.jsp?doc_id=2333).

8.3 Guiding Principles in Drafting

The abstract shall be so drafted that it can efficiently serve as a scanning tool for purposes of searching in the particular art, especially by assisting the scientist, engineer or researcher in formulating an opinion on whether there is a need for consulting the international application itself.

Rule 9
Expressions, Etc., Not to Be Used

9.1 Definition

The international application shall not contain:

(i) expressions or drawings contrary to morality;

(ii) expressions or drawings contrary to public order;

(iii) statements disparaging the products or processes of any particular person other than the applicant, or the merits or validity of applications or patents of any such person (mere comparisons with the prior art shall not be considered disparaging *per se*);

(iv) any statement or other matter obviously irrelevant or unnecessary under the circumstances.

AIs 217(c)	Correction concerning expressions under R. 9.1
Art. 53(a) EPC	'Subject matter' contrary to public order or morality (as opposed to merely 'expressions') is not expressly excluded in the PCT, unlike in the EPC (Art. 53(a) EPC). The EPO may exclude such subject matter, PCT EPO Guidelines G-II.4.

9.2 Noting of Lack of Compliance

The receiving Office, the International Searching Authority, the Authority specified for supplementary search and the International Bureau may note lack of compliance with the prescriptions of Rule 9.1 and may suggest to the applicant that he voluntarily correct his international application accordingly, in which case the receiving Office, the competent International Searching Authority, the competent Authority specified for supplementary search and the International Bureau, as applicable, shall be informed of the suggestion.

Art. 21(6)	International Bureau may omit expressions contrary to morality or public order from publication.
R. 48.2(l) – (n)	Procedure of omission of certain content from international publication

R. 94	Access to files
AIs 217	Correction concerning expressions under R. 9.2

9.3 Reference to Article 21(6)

"Disparaging statements," referred to in Article 21(6), shall have the meaning as defined in Rule 9.1(iii).

Rule 10
Terminology and Signs

10.1 Terminology and Signs

(a) Units of weights and measures shall be expressed in terms of the metric system, or also expressed in such terms if first expressed in terms of a different system.

(b) Temperatures shall be expressed in degrees Celsius, or also expressed in degrees Celsius, if first expressed in a different manner.

(c) [Deleted]

(d) For indications of heat, energy, light, sound, and magnetism, as well as for mathematical formulae and electrical units, the rules of international practice shall be observed; for chemical formulae, the symbols, atomic weights, and molecular formulae, in general use, shall be employed.

(e) In general, only such technical terms, signs and symbols should be used as are generally accepted in the art.

Signs and symbols that are not generally accepted may be used if they are not likely to be confused with existing symbols, and if they are simple and clearly explained in the text of the description (AG-IP 5.157). 1

(f) When the international application or its translation is in Chinese, English or Japanese, the beginning of any decimal fraction shall be marked by a period, whereas, when the international application or its translation is in a language other than Chinese, English or Japanese, it shall be marked by a comma.

10.2 Consistency

The terminology and the signs shall be consistent throughout the international application.

All designated Offices will accept prescribed terminology (AG-IP 5.156). 2

Rule 11
Physical Requirements of the International Application

R. 26.5 Whether a failure to comply with the formal requirements under R. 11 has consequences – for example, that the PCTa is deemed withdrawn – is at the discretion of the receiving Office (Pract. Adv. NL 03/2016)

11.1 Number of Copies

(a) Subject to the provisions of paragraph (b), the international application and each of the documents referred to in the check list (Rule 3.3(a)(ii)) shall be filed in one copy.

(b) Any receiving Office may require that the international application and any of the documents referred to in the check list (Rule 3.3(a)(ii)), except the receipt for the fees paid or the check for the payment of the fees, be filed in two or three copies. In that case, the receiving Office shall be responsible for verifying the identity of the second and the third copies with the record copy.

R. 157(2) EPC One copy must be filed with the EPO; filing by fax is possible until June 30, 2024 (OJ EPO 2024 A41). If filing by fax, a letter of confirmation must also be filed (Euro-PCT Guide 2.2.019, 2.2.025 and OJ EPO 2019 A19).

11.2 Fitness for Reproduction

(a) All elements of the international application (i.e., the request, the description, the claims, the drawings, and the abstract) shall be so presented as to admit of direct reproduction by photography, electrostatic processes, photo offset, and microfilming, in any number of copies.

(b) All sheets shall be free from creases and cracks; they shall not be folded.

(c) Only one side of each sheet shall be used.

(d) Subject to Rule 11.10(d) and Rule 11.13(j), each sheet shall be used in an upright position (i.e., the short sides at the top and bottom).

11.3 Material to Be Used

All elements of the international application shall be on paper which shall be flexible, strong, white, smooth, non-shiny, and durable.

11.4 Separate Sheets, Etc.

(a) Each element (request, description, claims, drawings, abstract) of the international application shall commence on a new sheet.

(b) All sheets of the international application shall be so connected that they can be easily turned when consulted, and easily separated and joined again if they have been separated for reproduction purposes.

11.5 Size of Sheets

The size of the sheets shall be A4 (29.7 cm x 21 cm). However, any receiving Office may accept international applications on sheets of other sizes provided that the record copy, as transmitted to the International Bureau, and, if the competent International Searching Authority so desires, the search copy, shall be of A4 size.

11.6 Margins

(a) The minimum margins of the sheets containing the description, the claims, and the abstract, shall be as follows:

- top: 2 cm
- left side: 2.5 cm
- right side: 2 cm
- bottom: 2 cm.

(b) The recommended maximum, for the margins provided for in paragraph (a), is as follows:

- top: 4 cm
- left side: 4 cm
- right side: 3 cm
- bottom: 3 cm.

(c) On sheets containing drawings, the surface usable shall not exceed 26.2 cm x 17.0 cm. The sheets shall not contain frames around the usable or used surface. The minimum margins shall be as follows:

- top: 2.5 cm
- left side: 2.5 cm
- right side: 1.5 cm
- bottom: 1 cm.

(d) The margins referred to in paragraphs (a) to (c) apply to A4-size sheets, so that, even if the receiving Office accepts other sizes, the A4-size record copy and, when so required, the A4-size search copy shall leave the aforesaid margins.

(e) Subject to paragraph (f) and to Rule 11.8(b), the margins of the international application, when submitted, must be completely blank.

(f) The top margin may contain in the left-hand corner an indication of the applicant's file reference, provided that the reference appears within 1.5 cm from the top of the sheet. The number of characters in the applicant's file reference shall not exceed the maximum fixed by the Administrative Instructions.

AIs 109 The file number may consist of a maximum of 25 Latin letters and/or Arabic numerals in total

11.7 Numbering of Sheets

(a) All the sheets contained in the international application shall be numbered in consecutive Arabic numerals.

(b) The numbers shall be centered at the top or bottom of the sheet, but shall not be placed in the margin.

AIs 207 Arrangement of elements and numbering of sheets of the international application

11.8 Numbering of Lines

(a) It is strongly recommended to number every fifth line of each sheet of the description, and of each sheet of claims.

(b) The numbers should appear in the right half of the left margin.

11.9 Writing of Text Matter

(a) The request, the description, the claims and the abstract shall be typed or printed.

(b) Only graphic symbols and characters, chemical or mathematical formulae, and certain characters in the Chinese or Japanese language may, when necessary, be written by hand or drawn.

(c) The typing shall be 1½-spaced.

(d) All text matter shall be in characters the capital letters of which are not less than 0.28 cm high, and shall be in a dark, indelible color, satisfying the requirements specified in Rule 11.2 *(fitness for reproduction)*, provided that any text matter in the request may be in characters the capital letters of which are not less than 0.21 cm high.

AIs 707 Effect of font size on calculation of fees: the international filing fee should be calculated on the basis of the number of sheets that the application would contain if presented as a print-out complying with the minimum margin and character size requirements. The receiving Office should rely on the number of pages of the international application as calculated by the electronic filing software.

(e) As far as the spacing of the typing and the size of the characters are concerned, paragraphs (c) and (d) shall not apply to texts in the Chinese or Japanese language.

11.10 Drawings, Formulae, and Tables, in Text Matter

(a) The request, the description, the claims and the abstract shall not contain drawings.

(b) The description, the claims and the abstract may contain chemical or mathematical formulae.

(c) The description and the abstract may contain tables; any claim may contain tables only if the subject matter of the claim makes the use of tables desirable.

(d) Tables and chemical or mathematical formulae may be placed sideways on the sheet if they cannot be presented satisfactorily in an upright position thereon; sheets on which tables or chemical or mathematical formulae are presented sideways shall be so presented that the tops of the tables or formulae are at the left side of the sheet.

11.11 Words in Drawings

(a) The drawings shall not contain text matter, except a single word or words, when absolutely indispensable, such as "water," "steam," "open," "closed," "section on AB," and, in the case of electric circuits and block schematic or flow sheet diagrams, a few short catchwords indispensable for understanding.

(b) Any words used shall be so placed that, if translated, they may be pasted over without interfering with any lines of the drawings.

11.12 Alterations, Etc.

Each sheet shall be reasonably free from erasures and shall be free from alterations, overwritings, and interlineations. Non-compliance with this Rule may be authorized if the authenticity of the content is not in question and the requirements for good reproduction are not in jeopardy.

11.13 Special Requirements for Drawings

(a) Drawings shall be executed in durable, black, sufficiently dense and dark, uniformly thick and well-defined, lines and strokes without colorings.

Photographs are undesired, but are permissible if the representation as a drawing is 1
not sufficient. They must meet certain requirements (AG-IP 5.159, 5.133).

(b) Cross-sections shall be indicated by oblique hatching which should not impede the clear reading of the reference signs and leading lines.

(c) The scale of the drawings and the distinctness of their graphical execution shall be such that a photographic reproduction with a linear reduction in size to two-thirds would enable all details to be distinguished without difficulty.

(d) When, in exceptional cases, the scale is given on a drawing, it shall be represented graphically.

(e) All numbers, letters and reference lines, appearing on the drawings, shall be simple and clear. Brackets, circles or inverted commas shall not be used in association with numbers and letters.

(f) All lines in the drawings shall, ordinarily, be drawn with the aid of drafting instruments.

(g) Each element of each figure shall be in proper proportion to each of the other elements in the figure, except where the use of a different proportion is indispensable for the clarity of the figure.

(h) The height of the numbers and letters shall not be less than 0.32 cm. For the lettering of drawings, the Latin and, where customary, the Greek alphabets shall be used.

R. 11.9(d)	The minimum size of letters refers to numbers and capital letters
R. 26.3	Review of the PCTa under R. 11 only as far as relevant for publication for technical reasons (PCT Newsletter 3/2007, p. 6)

(i) The same sheet of drawings may contain several figures. Where figures on two or more sheets form in effect a single complete figure, the figures on the several sheets shall be so arranged that the complete figure can be assembled without concealing any part of any of the figures appearing on the various sheets.

(j) The different figures shall be arranged on a sheet or sheets without wasting space, preferably in an upright position, clearly separated from one another. Where the figures are not arranged in an upright position, they shall be presented sideways with the top of the figures at the left side of the sheet.

(k) The different figures shall be numbered in Arabic numerals consecutively and independently of the numbering of the sheets.

(l) Reference signs not mentioned in the description shall not appear in the drawings, and vice versa.

(m) The same features, when denoted by reference signs, shall, throughout the international application, be denoted by the same signs.

(n) If the drawings contain a large number of reference signs, it is strongly recommended to attach a separate sheet listing all reference signs and the features denoted by them.

11.14 Later Documents

Rules 10, and 11.1 to 11.13, also apply to any document – for example, replacement sheets, amended claims, translations – submitted after the filing of the international application.

Rule 12 Language of the International Application and Translations for the Purposes of International Search and International Publication

12.1 Languages Accepted for the Filing of International Applications

(a) An international application shall be filed in any language which the receiving Office accepts for that purpose.

(b) Each receiving Office shall, for the filing of international applications, accept at least one language which is both:

(i) a language accepted by the International Searching Authority, or, if applicable, by at least one of the International Searching Authorities, competent for the international searching of international applications filed with that receiving Office, and

R. 12.3	Translation for the purposes of international search
R. 55	Language for IPE

(ii) a language of publication.

R. 48.3	Languages of publication: Arabic, Chinese, English, French, German, Japanese, Korean, Portuguese, Russian, Spanish
R. 12.4	Translation for the purposes of international publication

(c) Notwithstanding paragraph (a), the request shall be filed in any language of publication which the receiving Office accepts for the purposes of this paragraph.

Annex C (IB)	Any language is permitted before the International Bureau
AIs 103	Languages of the forms used by international authorities

R. 92.2	Language for written correspondence
Art. 11(1)(ii), R. 20.1(c) and (d), R. 26.3*ter*	Mixed languages used in abstract, drawings, description, claims
R. 26.3*ter*(c)	Request in language not accepted by receiving Office
R. 19.4(a)(ii)	Transmittal to the International Bureau as receiving Office
Art. 14 EPC, R. 3, 157 EPC	The languages before the EPO are the official languages English, French, German. Amendments must be filed in the language of the procedure. Dutch is accepted as a language for the search, provided the application was filed in NL (Annex A of the WIPO-EPO Agreement, see https://www.wipo.int/pct/en/access/isa_ipea_agreements.html Art. 16(3)(b)).

(d) Notwithstanding paragraph (a), any language-dependent free text contained in the sequence listing part of the description shall be filed in a language which the receiving Office accepts for that purpose. Any language accepted under this paragraph but not accepted under paragraph (a) shall meet the requirements of paragraph (b). The receiving Office may permit but shall not require the language-dependent free text to be filed in more than one language in accordance with the Administrative Instructions.

R. 13*ter*	Sequence listings

1 The receiving Office does not have to check the language of the language-dependent free text in the sequence listing. If it finds on its own initiative that an inadmissible language is used, it sends the PCTa to the International Bureau as receiving Office under R. 19.4(a)(ii) (PCT Circular C.PCT 1642, p. 2). For text elements in the sequence listing part of the description, the receiving Office may now allow languages different from those allowed for the main part of the PCTa. According to PCT/WG/13/8 No. 8, this is intended to facilitate filing for the applicant and to provide flexibility for the receiving Office. No translation shall be required merely because of a deviation from the language of the main part, provided that it is a language accepted for searching or publication (PCT/WG/13/8 No. 8).

AIs 332(a-*bis*)	Each receiving Office notifies the International Bureau of the accepted language.
Annex C	PCT Applicant's Guide informs about admitted language according to para. (d), for example DE: German or German and English, for EP: English or the language of the PCTa (German, French), for International Bureau: any language or English and any other language.

12.1*bis* Language of Elements and Parts Furnished under Rule 20.3, 20.5, 20.5*bis* or 20.6 *(missing and erroneously filed elements)*

An element referred to in Article 11(1)(iii)(d) or (e) furnished by the applicant under Rule 20.3(b), 20.5*bis*(b), 20.5*bis*(c) or 20.6(a) and a part of the description, claims or drawings furnished by the applicant under Rule 20.5(b), 20.5(c), 20.5*bis*(b), 20.5*bis*(c) or 20.6(a) shall be in the language of the international application as filed or, where a translation of the application is required under Rule 12.3(a) or 12.4(a), in both the language of the application as filed and the language of that translation.

The regulation is applicable to PCTa for which reference is made to one or more elements mentioned in Art. 11(1)(iii) for the first time on or after July 1, 2020. The reference to R. 20.5*bis*(a) was added because of the insertion of R. 20.5*bis*. The reference to R. 20.5(c) was added because it had been forgotten when R. 12.1*bis* was introduced (PCT/WG/12/9 Annex p. 3). 2

12.1*ter* Language of Indications Furnished under Rule 13*bis*.4

Any indication in relation to deposited biological material furnished under Rule 13*bis*.4 shall be in the language in which the international application is filed, provided that, where a translation of the international application is required under Rule 12.3(a) or 12.4(a), any such indication shall be furnished in both the language in which the application is filed and the language of that translation.

12.2 Language of Changes in the International Application

(a) Any amendment of the international application shall, subject to Rules 46.3 and 55.3, be in the language in which the application is filed.

R. 92.2(b)	Correspondence may also be submitted in other languages. Amendments, however, are to be filed only in the language of the procedure.

(b) Any rectification under Rule 91.1 of an obvious mistake in the international application shall be in the language in which the application is filed, provided that:

(i) where a translation of the international application is required under Rule 12.3(a), 12.4(a) or 55.2(a), rectifications referred to in Rule 91.1(b)(ii) and (iii) *(Corrections addressed to the IPEA and ISA)* shall be filed in both the language of the application and the language of that translation;

(ii) where a translation of the request is required under Rule 26.3ter(c), rectifications referred to in Rule 91.1(b)(i) *(correction of the request)* need only be filed in the language of that translation.

(c) Any correction under Rule 26 of a defect in the international application shall be in the language in which the international application is filed. Any correction under Rule 26 of a defect in a translation of the international application

furnished under Rule 12.3 or 12.4, any correction under Rule 55.2(c) of a defect in a translation furnished under Rule 55.2(a), or any correction of a defect in a translation of the request furnished under Rule 26.3*ter*(c), shall be in the language of the translation.

12.3 Translation for the Purposes of International Search

(a) Where the language in which the international application is filed is not accepted by the International Searching Authority that is to carry out the international search, the applicant shall, within one month from the date of receipt of the international application by the receiving Office, furnish to that Office *(receiving Office)* a translation of the international application into a language which is all of the following:

R. 12.3(c)	Time limit: one month
R. 12.3(c)(ii)	Grace period one or two months, in each case plus surcharge if applicable
R. 12.3(e)	Late furnishing fee is 25 % of the international filing fee
R. 12.3(d) S. 2	Time limit is considered to be met if the necessary acts are performed before the expiry of 15 months from the priority date
AIs 305*bis*	Preparation, identification and transmittal of the copies of the translation of the international application under R. 12.3, 12.4 and 26.3ter(e)
AIs 308	Marking of the sheets of the international application and of the translation thereof under R. 12.3, 12.4, 20.4 and 26.3ter(e)
AIs 311	Renumbering in the case of deletion, substitution or addition of sheets of the international application and of the translation thereof
AIs 335	Procedure relating to sequence listings

(i) a language accepted by that Authority *(ISA)*, and

(ii) a language of publication, and

(iii) a language accepted by the receiving Office under Rule 12.1(a), unless the international application is filed in a language of publication.

R. 48.3	Languages of publication: Arabic, Chinese, English, French, German, Japanese, Korean, Portuguese, Russian or Spanish
AG-IP 6.014	Providing a translation of a language-dependent free text in a sequence listing

(a-*bis*) For any sequence listing part of the description, paragraph (a) shall only apply to the language-dependent free text; any translation of the language-dependent free text shall be provided in accordance with the Administrative Instructions.

In principle, no translation was required for the sequence listing part of the description if the standard according to Annex C to AIs 707 was complied with (AG-IP 6.013). Since July 1, 2022 a translation of the free text is required. If possible, the applicant should file translations of this free text at the same time as further translations of the main part of the description (PCT/WG/13/8 Nos. 11, 13 and commentary on R. 12.3 in the Annex to the document). 3

(b) Paragraph (a) shall not apply to the request.

(c) Where, by the time the receiving Office sends to the applicant the notification under Rule 20.2(c) *(notification of the filing date and file number)*, the applicant has not furnished a translation required under paragraph (a), the receiving Office shall, preferably together with that notification, invite the applicant:

(i) to furnish the required translation within the time limit under paragraph (a) *(one month)*;

(ii) in the event that the required translation is not furnished within the time limit under paragraph (a), to furnish it and to pay, where applicable, the late furnishing fee referred to in paragraph (e), within one month from the date of the invitation or two months from the date of receipt of the international application by the receiving Office, whichever expires later.

Para. (b) was amended with effect from July 1, 2022 because the subject matter was then regulated in para. (a-*bis*). 4

R. 12.3(d) S. 2 Time limit may be considered to be met

(d) Where the receiving Office has sent to the applicant an invitation under paragraph (c) and the applicant has not, within the applicable time limit under paragraph (c)(ii), furnished the required translation and paid any required late furnishing fee, the international application shall be considered withdrawn and the receiving Office shall so declare. Any translation and any payment received by the receiving Office before that Office makes the declaration under the previous sentence and before the expiration of 15 months from the priority date shall be considered to have been received before the expiration of that time limit.

(e) The furnishing of a translation after the expiration of the time limit under paragraph (a) may be subjected by the receiving Office to the payment to it, for its own benefit, of a late furnishing fee equal to 25% of the international filing fee referred to in item 1 of the Schedule of Fees, not taking into account any fee for each sheet of the international application in excess of 30 sheets.

For statements of the Assembly concerning R. 12.3, see PCT/A/XXIV/10, p.5, para. 19 (https://www.wipo.int/edocs/mdocs/govbody/en/pct_a_xxiv/pct_a_xxiv_10-main1.pdf). 5

12.4 Translation for the Purposes of International Publication

(a) Where the language in which the international application is filed is not a language of publication and no translation is required under Rule 12.3(a), the applicant shall, within 14 months from the priority date, furnish to the receiving Office a translation of the international application into any language of publication which the receiving Office accepts for the purposes of this paragraph.

R. 12.4(a)	Time limit: 14 months
R. 12.4(c)	Grace period of two months, plus surcharge if necessary
R. 12.4(e)	Late furnishing fee is 25% of the international filing fee
R. 12.4(d)	Time limit is considered to be met if the necessary acts are performed before the expiry of 17 months from the priority date.
R. 28	Defects noted by the International Bureau
AIs 305*bis*	Preparation, identification and transmittal of the copies of the translation of the international application under R. 12.3, 12.4 and 26.3ter(e)
AIs 308	Marking of the sheets of the international application and of the translation thereof under R. 12.3, 12.4, 20.4 and 26.3ter(e)
AIs 311	Renumbering in case of deletion, substitution or addition of sheets of the international application and of the translation thereof
AIs 335	Procedure relating to sequence listings

(a-*bis*) For any sequence listing part of the description, paragraph (a) shall only apply to the language-dependent free text; any translation of the language-dependent free text shall be provided in accordance with the Administrative Instructions.

6 The system is the same as in R. 12.3. However, R. 12.4 concerns a situation in which the ISA has no reason to require a translation and the International Bureau can therefore proceed according to R. 28. As the Working Group considers this situation unlikely, there are no further procedural instructions for this (PCT/WG/13/8 No. 13 and commentary on R. 12.4 in the Annex to the document).

(b) Paragraph (a) shall not apply to the request.

7 Para. (b) has been amended because the subject matter is partly regulated in para. (a-*bis*) since July 1, 2022. See the annotations on this above.

(c) Where the applicant has not, within the time limit referred to in paragraph (a), furnished a translation required under that paragraph, the receiving Office shall invite the applicant to furnish the required translation, and to pay, where applicable, the late furnishing fee required under paragraph (e), within 16 months from the priority date. Any translation received by the receiving Office before that

Office sends the invitation under the previous sentence shall be considered to have been received before the expiration of the time limit under paragraph (a).

(d) Where the applicant has not, within the time limit under paragraph (c), furnished the required translation and paid any required late furnishing fee, the international application shall be considered withdrawn and the receiving Office shall so declare. Any translation and any payment received by the receiving Office before that Office makes the declaration under the previous sentence and before the expiration of 17 months from the priority date shall be considered to have been received before the expiration of that time limit.

(e) The furnishing of a translation after the expiration of the time limit under paragraph (a) may be subjected by the receiving Office to the payment to it, for its own benefit, of a late furnishing fee equal to 25% of the international filing fee referred to in item 1 of the Schedule of Fees, not taking into account any fee for each sheet of the international application in excess of 30 sheets.

Rule 12*bis*
Submission by the Applicant of Documents Relating to Earlier Search

12*bis*.1 Furnishing by the Applicant of Documents Related to Earlier Search in Case of Request under Rule 4.12

(a) Where the applicant has, under Rule 4.12, requested the International Searching Authority to take into account the results of an earlier search carried out by the same or another International Searching Authority or by a national Office, the applicant shall, subject to paragraphs (b) to (d), submit to the receiving Office, together with the international application, a copy of the results of the earlier search, in whatever form (for example, in the form of a search report, a listing of cited prior art or an examination report) they are presented by the Authority or Office concerned.

R. 4.12	Taking into account results of earlier search
R. 23*bis*	Transmittal of documents from receiving Office to ISA
AG-IP 5.073	Taking into account of results of earlier search

(b) Where the earlier search was carried out by the same Office as that which is acting as the receiving Office, the applicant may, instead of submitting the copy referred to in paragraph (a), indicate the wish that the receiving Office prepare and transmit it to the International Searching Authority. Such request shall be made in the request and may be subjected by the receiving Office to the payment to it, for its own benefit, of a fee.

1 The EPO does not charge a fee for this.

(c) Where the earlier search was carried out by the same International Searching Authority, or by the same Office as that which is acting as the International Searching Authority, no copy referred to in paragraph (a) shall be required to be submitted under that paragraph.

(d) Where a copy referred to in paragraph (a) is available to the receiving Office or the International Searching Authority in a form and manner acceptable to it, for example, from a digital library, and the applicant so indicates in the request, no copy shall be required to be submitted under that paragraph.

R. 41	Taking into account results of an earlier search in the case of the request under R. 4.12: if carried out by the same ISA, the results must be taken into account, if carried out by other ISA or another Office, the results may be taken into account. In addition, the search results shall be taken into account in the case of claimed priority of an earlier application from the same Office and where a earlier search was undertaken by this Office. In other cases, the ISA may take into account the results under R. 41.2(b).

12*bis*.2 Invitation by the International Searching Authority to Furnish Documents Related to Earlier Search in Case of Request under Rule 4.12

(a) The International Searching Authority may, subject to paragraphs (b) and (c), invite the applicant to furnish to it, within a time limit which shall be reasonable under the circumstances:

(i) a copy of the earlier application concerned;

(ii) where the earlier application is in a language which is not accepted by the International Searching Authority, a translation of the earlier application into a language which is accepted by that Authority;

(iii) where the results of the earlier search are in a language which is not accepted by the International Searching Authority, a translation of those results into a language which is accepted by that Authority;

(iv) a copy of any document cited in the results of the earlier search.

(b) Where the earlier search was carried out by the same International Searching Authority, or by the same Office as that which is acting as the International Searching Authority, or where a copy or translation referred to in paragraph (a) is available to the International Searching Authority in a form and manner acceptable to it, for example, from a digital library, or in the form of the priority document, no copy or translation referred to in paragraph (a) shall be required to be submitted under that paragraph.

(c) Where the request contains a statement under Rule 4.12(ii) to the effect that the international application is the same, or substantially the same, as the application in respect of which the earlier search was carried out, or that the international application is the same, or substantially the same, as that earlier application except that it is filed in a different language, no copy or translation referred to in paragraphs (a)(i) and (ii) shall be required to be submitted under those paragraphs.

R. 4.12	Indications and statements concerning earlier search in PCTa to be taken into account by Authorities or Offices
R. 4.12(ii)	For the interpretation of the term 'substantially the same', see PCT Assembly Report PCT/A/36/13.

Rule 13
Unity of Invention

INTRODUCTION

1 The search fee is intended to cover the expenses of the search of a single invention. Hence, an application must comply with the requirement of unity of invention (Art. 3(4)(iii); R. 13).

2 The PCT has no provisions for filing divisional applications (see AG-IP 10.073), which can only be filed in the national phase where national law permits so. For example, under the EPC, only a pending European patent application may be divided (R. 36(1) EPC; GL Exam EPO A-IV, 1.1.1). An international application is deemed to be a pending European application when the EPO actually acts as designated Office (Art. 153(2) EPC), i.e. when the requirements of R. 159(1)(a) and (c) have been complied with on expiry of the 31-month period (J18/09; GL Exam EPO E-IX, 2.4.1) or, if a request for early processing has been filed, the acts under R. 159(1) EPC set out in GL Exam EPO E-IX, 2.8 have been completed (GL Exam EPO E-IX, 2.4.1).

3 The need for filing a divisional application with the EPO has been reduced strongly by R. 164 EPC, allowing an applicant to continue prosecution in the regional phase before the EPO with claims not searched in the international phase.

4 An international application must comply with the requirement of unity of invention (Art. 3(4)(iii)). There is unity of invention if the claims relate to a single invention or to a group of inventions so linked as to form a single general inventive concept. A group of inventions forms a single general inventive concept only if there is a technical relationship among the inventions involving one or more of the same or corresponding special technical features. Special technical features define a contribution which an invention makes over the prior art (R. 13.1; R. 13.2).

5 The formulation for the requirement of unity of invention for a group of inventions in R. 13.2 PCT is verbally identical to the one in R. 44(1) EPC. The requirement for unity of a utility model may be determined by national law (R. 13.5). AG-IP 5.115–5.123 contain requirements for different categories of claims, the Markush formulation and intermediate and final products.

6 Any designated Office must accept an international application which complies with the PCT requirement of unity of invention (Art. 27(1); AG-IP 5.123). As a

consequence, the USPTO as designated Office may not apply its deviating rules for unity of invention in the national phase of an international application. However, a divisional application, continuation or continuation-in-part based on the international application is subject to national rules for unity of invention.

If the ISA finds that the application does not comply with the requirement of unity of invention, it will usually issue an invitation to pay additional fees and specify the reasons for its finding (Art. 17(3)(a); R. 40). An ISA may annex to the invitation the results of the search of the first invention (AG-IP 7.017); some ISAs, such as the EPO, even include a written opinion. 7

The invitation indicates the amount to be paid (R. 40.1(ii)) and includes a reasoned statement as to why the international application is considered not to comply with the requirement of unity of invention (R. 40.1(i)). The number of additional fees to be paid depends on the number of additional inventions. The amount of the additional fee is determined by the ISA (R. 40.2(a)) and is payable directly to the ISA (R. 40.2(b)); see AG-IP Annex D. The period for payment is one month from the date of mailing of the invitation (R. 40.1(ii)). 8

In response to the invitation, the applicant may pay an additional fee for each additional invention to be searched or not pay any additional fee at all (AG-IP 7.021). The payment of additional fees will be indicated in the final ISR covering all inventions paid for (R. 43.7). 9

If the applicant does not agree with the finding of lack of unity by the ISA, he can pay one or more additional fees under protest, also within the period of one month. This will result in a review of the protest by a review body of the ISA (R. 40.2(c)). A review requires that at least one additional fee is paid. 10

The applicant must support the protest by a reasoned statement as to why the requirement of unity is complied with or why the amount of additional fees is excessive (R. 40.2(c)). The ISA may require that the applicant pay a protest fee for the review of the protest (R. 40.2(e)). The protest fee must be paid within the same period as the additional fee(s) (R. 40.1(iii)). If the protest fee is not paid, the protest is considered not to have been made (R. 40.2(e)). The amount of the protest fee levied by each ISA is stated in AG-IP Annex D. 11

Depending on the outcome of the review, the review body may order a total or partial reimbursement of the additional fees to the extent that it finds the protest justified (R. 40.2(c)). Where it finds that the protest was entirely justified, the protest fee will also be refunded (R. 40.2(e)). Upon request of the applicant, the text of the protest and the corresponding decision will be notified to the designated Offices together with the ISR (R. 40.2(c)). The protest procedure is one of the two instances of a procedure resembling an appeal in the international phase. 12

The invitation to pay one or more additional international search fees, even if it comprises the results of the partial international search for the first invention, must not be confused with the ISR. Most importantly, claims cannot be amended at this point in the procedure, even if the amendments would overcome the objection of lack of unity of invention. 13

14 See Art. 22 Introduction No. 1.4.3 for an overview where unity of inventions is examined.

15 Definition and formal criteria concerning the assessment of and reasoning for unity of invention are the same in the PCT and in the EPC (PCT EPO Guidelines F-V 1 with links to GL Exam sources). For lack of unity during international search and examination, see PCT EPO Guidelines F-V 2 and 3 that refer mainly to ISPE Guidelines 10.60, 10.83, 10.71 et seq.

Rule 13
Unity of Invention

13.1 Requirement

The international application shall relate to one invention only or to a group of inventions so linked as to form a single general inventive concept ("requirement of unity of invention").

Art. 64, 27, R. 51*bis*	There are no reservations to R 13, i.e. the question of unity is guided by R. 13 in all regional and national phases
R. 13.2	Same or corresponding special technical features
Art. 17, R. 40	Lack of unity in international search, consequences R. 45*bis*.5(e)
R. 45*bis*.6	Lack of unity in supplementary international search
R. 66.1*ter*	Lack of unity in top-up search
Art. 34(3), R. 68	Lack of unity in IPE
AIs 206	AIs Annex B gives detailed examples of unity of invention. Among other things, the Markush practice is explained in AIs Annex B Part 2 III.
R. 164 EPC	Lack of unity on entry into the European phase, Euro-PCT Guide 5.15.001 et seq.

13.2 Circumstances in Which the Requirement of Unity of Invention Is to Be Considered Fulfilled

Where a group of inventions is claimed in one and the same international application, the requirement of unity of invention referred to in Rule 13.1 shall be fulfilled only when there is a technical relationship among those inventions involving one or more of the same or corresponding special technical features. The expression "special technical features" shall mean those technical features that define a contribution which each of the claimed inventions, considered as a whole, makes over the prior art.

13.3 Determination of Unity of Invention Not Affected by Manner of Claiming

The determination whether a group of inventions is so linked as to form a single general inventive concept shall be made without regard to whether the inventions are claimed in separate claims or as alternatives within a single claim.

13.4 Dependent Claims

Subject to Rule 13.1, it shall be permitted to include in the same international application a reasonable number of dependent claims, claiming specific forms of the invention claimed in an independent claim, even where the features of any dependent claim could be considered as constituting in themselves an invention.

W 54/91	Dependent claims generally fulfill the requirement of unity of invention in conjunction with the independent claim on which they depend (established case law)

13.5 Utility Models

Any designated State in which the grant of a utility model is sought on the basis of an international application may, instead of Rules 13.1 to 13.4, apply in respect of the matters regulated in those Rules the provisions of its national law concerning utility models once the processing of the international application has started in that State, provided that the applicant shall be allowed at least two months from the expiration of the time limit applicable under Article 22 to adapt his application to the requirements of the said provisions of the national law.

For statements of WIPO concerning R. 13, see PCT/A/XVIII/9, p.4, para. 25 (https://www.wipo.int/edocs/mdocs/govbody/en/pct_a_xviii/pct_a_xviii_9.pdf). 16

Rule 13*bis*
Inventions Relating to Biological Material

INTRODUCTION

1 Normally, an invention is disclosed by means of a written description (Art. 5). Where this is not possible (if microorganisms are involved) disclosure is effected by a deposit. The term 'biological material' is covered by the term 'microorganism' under the Budapest Treaty which allows depositing independently from the territory of the State in which protection is sought (https://www.wipo.int/treaties/en/registration/budapest/).

2 An international application may refer to biological material and/or to its deposit with a depositary institution (R. 13*bis*; AG-IP 11.075–11.088). AG-IP Annex L gives the requirements of each designated Office for when to furnish what information on the deposit and provides a list of the institutions with which deposits may be made. An applicant may in general send indications of the reference to a deposit of biological material, such as the name of the institute, date of deposition, and accession number, to the International Bureau within 16 months from the priority date or after the 16 months but before completion of the technical preparations for international publication (R. 13*bis*.4(a)). However, some designated Offices require that the indications are filed with the International Bureau earlier than 16 months (R. 13*bis*.4(b); see AG-IP Annex L).

3 See Introduction to Art. 3 for the filing of the description.

13*bis*.1 Definition

For the purposes of this Rule, "reference to deposited biological material" means particulars given in an international application with respect to the deposit of biological material with a depositary institution or to the biological material so deposited.

13*bis*.2 References (General)

Any reference to deposited biological material shall be made in accordance with this Rule and, if so made, shall be considered as satisfying the requirements of the national law of each designated State.

R. 31 EPC — Requirements to be complied with according to EPO communication of July 7, 2010 (OJ EPO 2010 p. 498), PCT Gazette of October 28, 2010, for international applications where EPO is designated or elected Office

13*bis*.3 References: Contents; Failure to Include Reference or Indication

(a) A reference to deposited biological material shall indicate:

(i) the name and the address of the depositary institution with which the deposit was made;

(ii) the date of deposit of the biological material with that institution;

(iii) the accession number given to the deposit by that institution; and

(iv) any additional matter of which the International Bureau has been notified pursuant to Rule 13*bis*.7(a)(i), provided that the requirement to indicate that matter was published in the Gazette in accordance with Rule 13*bis*.7(c) at least two months before the filing of the international application.

See details in Annex L of the AG-IP. 4

(b) Failure to include a reference to deposited biological material or failure to include, in a reference to deposited biological material, an indication in accordance with paragraph (a), shall have no consequence in any designated State whose national law does not require such reference or such indication in a national application.

13*bis*.4 References: Time Limit for Furnishing Indications

(a) Subject to paragraphs (b) and (c), if any of the indications referred to in Rule 13*bis*.3(a) is not included in a reference to deposited biological material in the international application as filed but is furnished to the International Bureau:

(i) within 16 months from the priority date, the indication shall be considered by any designated Office to have been furnished in time;

(ii) after the expiration of 16 months from the priority date, the indication shall be considered by any designated Office to have been furnished on the last day of that time limit if it reaches the International Bureau before the technical preparations for international publication have been completed.

(b) If the national law applicable by a designated Office so requires in respect of national applications, that Office may require that any of the indications referred to in Rule 13*bis*.3(a) be furnished earlier than 16 months from the priority date, provided that the International Bureau has been notified of such requirement pursuant to Rule 13*bis*.7(a)(ii) and has published such requirement in the Gazette in accordance with Rule 13*bis*.7(c) at least two months before the filing of the international application.

(c) Where the applicant makes a request for early publication under Article 21(2)(b), any designated Office may consider any indication not furnished before the technical preparations for international publication have been completed as not having been furnished in time.

(d) The International Bureau shall notify the applicant of the date on which it received any indication furnished under paragraph (a), and:

(i) if the indication was received before the technical preparations for international publication have been completed, publish the indication furnished under paragraph (a), and an indication of the date of receipt, together with the international application;

(ii) if the indication was received after the technical preparations for international publication have been completed, notify that date and the relevant data from the indication to the designated Offices.

R. 12.1*ter*	Language of indications furnished under R. 13*bis*.4
Art. 21(5)	Completion of the technical preparations for publication

13*bis*.5 References and Indications for the Purposes of One or More Designated States; Different Deposits for Different Designated States; Deposits with Depositary Institutions Other than Those Notified

(a) A reference to deposited biological material shall be considered to be made for the purposes of all designated States, unless it is expressly made for the purposes of certain of the designated States only; the same applies to the indications included in the reference.

(b) References to different deposits of the biological material may be made for different designated States.

(c) Any designated Office may disregard a deposit made with a depositary institution other than one notified by it under Rule 13*bis*.7(b).

13*bis*.6 Furnishing of Samples

Pursuant to Articles 23 and 40, no furnishing of samples of the deposited biological material to which a reference is made in an international application shall, except with the authorization of the applicant, take place before the expiration of the applicable time limits after which national processing may start under the said Articles. However, where the applicant performs the acts referred to in Articles 22 or 39 after international publication but before the expiration of the said time limits, the furnishing of samples of the deposited biological material may take place, once the said acts have been performed. Notwithstanding the previous provision, the furnishing of samples of the deposited biological material may take place under the national law applicable by any designated Office as soon as, under that law, the international publication has the effects of the compulsory national publication of an unexamined national application.

AIs 209	Indications as to deposited biological material on a separate sheet

Art. 153(4) EPC R. 32(1), R. 33(1) EPC	Reference to procedures at the EPO in PCT Gazette of January 12, 2012

13*bis*.7 National Requirements: Notification and Publication

(a) Any national Office may notify the International Bureau of any requirement of the national law:

(i) that any matter specified in the notification, in addition to those referred to in Rule 13*bis*.3(a)(i), (ii) and (iii), is required to be included in a reference to deposited biological material in a national application;

(ii) that one or more of the indications referred to in Rule 13*bis*.3(a) are required to be included in a national application as filed or are required to be furnished at a time specified in the notification which is earlier than 16 months from the priority date.

EPO Notice on amended requirements in PCT Gazette October 28, 2010, Newsletter 11/2010, p. 2 5

(b) Each national Office shall notify the International Bureau of the depositary institutions with which the national law permits deposits of biological materials to be made for the purposes of patent procedure before that Office or, if the national law does not provide for or permit such deposits, of that fact.

See details in Annex L of the AG-IP. 6

(c) The International Bureau shall promptly publish in the Gazette requirements notified to it under paragraph (a) and information notified to it under paragraph (b).

Rule 13*ter*
Nucleotide and/or Amino Acid Sequence Listings

INTRODUCTION

1 The sequence listings are part of the description (R. 3.3(a)(i), R. 5.2(a)). Details referring to the filing, translation, and the procedure related to sequence listings at the receiving Office are mentioned in the Introduction to Art. 3, annotations to Art. 5, AG-IP 5.099, AG-IP 11.088. R. 13*ter* refers to the procedure before the ISA and IPEA.

R. 3.3(a)(i)	Sequence listing as part of the description
R. 5.2(a)	Nucleotide and/or amino acid sequence disclosure – as part of the description

13*ter*.1 Procedure before the International Searching Authority

(a) Where the international application contains disclosure of nucleotide and/or amino acid sequences that, pursuant to the Administrative Instructions, are required to be included in a sequence listing, the International Searching Authority may invite the applicant to furnish to it, for the purposes of the international search, a sequence listing complying with the standard provided for in the Administrative Instructions, unless such listing is already available to it in a form, language and manner acceptable to it, and to pay to it, where applicable, the late furnishing fee referred to in paragraph (c), within a time limit fixed in the invitation.

2 If the application documents do not comply with the Rules and AIs, the ISA may invite the applicant to provide the correct form (R. 13*ter*.1(a)), subject to payment of a late furnishing fee (R. 13*ter*.1(c)). No designated Office may request a sequence listing other than the one complying with the standard (R. 13*ter*.3).

3 Noting that the receiving Office will not be obliged to make detailed checks on sequence listings and may therefore not invite the applicant to provide a translation required under R. 12.3, the ISA should have the power to request such a translation without going back to the receiving Office, in the same way that it can for formal defects (PCT/WG/13/8 Commentary on R. 13*ter* in the Annex to the document, p. 7).

R. 89*bis* In the case of electronic filing with the EPO, the provisions for R. 13*ter*, R. 30 EPC and the publications mentioned below must be observed

EPO: For the EPO acting as ISA, SISA or IPEA, the invitation is based on R. 13*ter*.1, the decision OJ EPO 2021 A96 (replaced OJ EPO 2011 p. 372, 376 as of July 1, 2022) and the notice OJ EPO 2021 p. A97 (replaced OJ EPO 2013 p. 542 as of July 1, 2022). The non-extendable time limit is one month and receipt before the beginning of the international search is deemed to be within the time limit (OJ EPO 2021 A97 No. 22). The said notice also sets out the procedure to be followed in the event of deficiencies. For the EPO as designated or elected Office, Art. 5 of the decision and No. 27 of the notice apply. Details of the requirements for transmission in electronic form can also be found in the AG Annex C(EP).

(b) [Deleted]

Para. (b) was deleted on July 1, 2022 because it refers to filing in paper form, but the standard ST.26 only provides for electronic form (comment in Annex to PCT/WG/13/8). 4

(c) The furnishing of a sequence listing in response to an invitation under paragraph (a) may be subjected by the International Searching Authority to the payment to it, for its own benefit, of a late furnishing fee whose amount shall be determined by the International Searching Authority but shall not exceed 25% of the international filing fee referred to in item 1 of the Schedule of Fees, not taking into account any fee for each sheet of the international application in excess of 30 sheets.

AG-IP Annex D, Annex SISA Late furnishing fee

EPO: Specification of a late filing fee on the basis of Art. 4 of decision OJ EPO 2021 A96. A refund of the fee is only possible if the fee amounts were paid inadvertently, without reason or in excess (continuation of the WIPO EPO Agreement, Annex D, Part II, para. 1). For the current amount, see AG-IP Annex D (EP).

(d) If the applicant does not, within the time limit fixed in the invitation under paragraph (a), furnish the required sequence listing and pay any required late furnishing fee, the International Searching Authority shall only be required to search the international application to the extent that a meaningful search can be carried out without the sequence listing.

EPO: Notice OJ EPO 2021 A97 replaces OJ EP 2011 p., 376: in the case of para. (d), the ISR is replaced in whole or in part by the statement under Art. 17(2) without further request. No performance of IPE by EPO as IPEA as far as meaningful examination according to R. 66.1(e) is not possible. Notification to applicant and note according to R. 66.2(a)(vii) and R. 70.12(iv). No request under R. 13*ter*.2. by EPO as IPEA The EPO advises against filing a sequence listing at this late stage because, at least in the case of extensive sequences, it is not in a position, with reasonable effort, to compare the original application documents with the subsequently filed sequence listing. A declaration by the applicant that the subsequently filed sequence listing does not go beyond the disclosure content does not exempt the EPO from the examination under Art. 34(2), R. 66.2. The IPER is drawn up only on the basis of the sequences available in the description on the filing date, which is noted in the report. The EPO as SISA starts the supplementary international search only if the sequence listing is available according to the regulations.

(e) Any sequence listing not contained in the international application as filed, whether furnished in response to an invitation under paragraph (a) or otherwise, shall not form part of the international application, but this paragraph shall not prevent the applicant from amending the description in relation to a sequence listing pursuant to Article 34(2)(b).

5 A separately filed sequence listing can be viewed via PATENTSCOPE after publication of the PCTa, AG-IP 7.011.

(f) [Deleted]

13*ter*.2 Procedure before the International Preliminary Examining Authority

Rule 13*ter*.1 shall apply *mutatis mutandis* to the procedure before the International Preliminary Examining Authority.

AG-IP Annex E Late furnishing fee

13*ter*.3 Sequence Listing for Designated Office

No designated Office shall require the applicant to furnish to it a sequence listing other than a sequence listing complying with the standard provided for in the Administrative Instructions.

R. 76.5 Application before elected Office

Rule 14
The Transmittal Fee

14.1 The Transmittal Fee

(a) Any receiving Office may require that the applicant pay a fee to it, for its own benefit, for receiving the international application, transmitting copies to the International Bureau and the competent International Searching Authority, and performing all the other tasks which it must perform in connection with the international application in its capacity of receiving Office ("transmittal fee").

AG-IP Annex C	Transmittal fee
Art. 152, R. 157(4) EPC, Art. 2(1) No. 18Rfees	Transmittal fee for filing and forwarding the international application
DE:	Art. III Sec 1(2) Act on International Patent Conventions (DE-IntPatÜbkG) in conjunction with No. 313 900 Patent Costs Act (https://www.dpma.de/docs/english/formulare/allg_eng/a9510_1.pdf)
AG-IP Annex C	Consult Offices by ST.3 Code; for some developing country Offices this is included in Annex C of the International Bureau, which acts as receiving Office for those Offices. Applicants who qualify for the 90% reduction of the international filing fee do not have to pay the transmittal fee to RO/IB.

Refer to annotations to Art. 3 for an overview of fees that are paid to the receiving Office, including the transmittal fee. 1

(b) The amount of the transmittal fee, if any, shall be fixed by the receiving Office.

(c) The transmittal fee shall be paid within one month from the date of receipt of the international application. The amount payable shall be the amount applicable on that date of receipt.

R. 16*bis*.1(a)	Extension of time limit

R. 16*bis*.1(c), R. 29, Art. 14(3)	Legal consequence of non-payment is the fiction of withdrawal
AP-IP 5.192, Euro-PCT Guide 2.27.010	The amount payable shall be the amount applicable on that date of receipt of the PCTa – and not the date of receipt of the fee.
R. 19.4(c)	Date of actual receipt of PCTa by the International Bureau if forwarded to International Bureau

Rule 15
The International Filing Fee

15.1 The International Filing Fee

Each international application shall be subject to the payment of a fee for the benefit of the International Bureau ("international filing fee") to be collected by the receiving Office.

R. 4.9	Designation of States; kinds of protection, national and regional patents
R. 15.2	Amount, transfer
R. 15.3	Time limit for payment; amount payable
R. 16*bis*.1(a)	Extension of time limit
AIs 304	Invitation to pay fees before date on which they are due
R. 16*bis*.2	Late payment fee
Art. 14(3)	PCTa considered withdrawn in case of non-payment.
R. 15.4	Refund

For further information on fee payment and the currently applicable fees, please consult the PCT webpage at: www.wipo.int/pct/en/fees/ 1

15.2 Amount; Transfer

(a) The amount of the international filing fee is as set out in the Schedule of Fees.

(b) The international filing fee shall be payable in the currency or one of the currencies prescribed by the receiving Office ("prescribed currency").

(c) Where the prescribed currency is the Swiss franc, the receiving Office shall transfer the said fee to the International Bureau in Swiss francs in accordance with Rule 96.2.

(d) Where the prescribed currency is a currency other than the Swiss franc and that currency:

(i) is freely convertible into Swiss francs, the Director General shall establish, for each receiving Office which prescribes such a currency for the payment of the international filing fee, an equivalent amount of that fee in the prescribed currency according to directives given by the Assembly, and the amount in that currency shall be transferred by the receiving Office to the International Bureau in accordance with Rule 96.2;

(ii) is not freely convertible into Swiss francs, the receiving Office shall be responsible for the conversion of the international filing fee from the prescribed currency into Swiss francs and shall transfer that fee in Swiss francs, in the amount set out in the Schedule of Fees, to the International Bureau in accordance with Rule 96.2. Alternatively, if the receiving Office so wishes, it may convert the international filing fee from the prescribed currency into euros or US dollars and transfer the equivalent amount of that fee in euros or US dollars, as established by the Director General according to directives given by the Assembly as referred to in item (i), to the International Bureau in accordance with Rule 96.2.

R. 96.2	Regulation for simplification and cost reduction in the transfer and clearing of fee payments between different Offices
AIs 114	Notification and Transfer of fees in accordance with Annex G of the AIs
Art. 16(3), Art. 11(2), (4)	See the respective agreements between ISA/IPEA and WIPO

2 The Directives of the PCT Assembly Relating to the Establishment of Equivalent Amounts of Certain Fees as in force from July 1, 2010 are available at: www.wipo.int/pct/en/fees/equivalent_amounts.html

15.3 Time Limit for Payment; Amount Payable

The international filing fee shall be paid to the receiving Office within one month from the date of receipt of the international application. The amount payable shall be the amount applicable on that date of receipt.

AIs 304	Invitation to pay fees before the date on which they are due
R. 16*bis*.1(a)	Extension of time limit
R. 16*bis*.2	Late payment fee
AP-IP 5.192, Euro-PCT Guide 2.27.010	The amount payable shall be the amount applicable on that date of receipt of the PCTa – and not the date of receipt of the fee
R. 19.4(c)	Date of actual receipt of PCTa by the International Bureau if forwarded to International Bureau
R. 15.4	Refund

15.4 Refund

The receiving Office shall refund the international filing fee to the applicant:

(i) if the determination under Article 11(1) is negative ,

(ii) if, before the transmittal of the record copy to the International Bureau, the international application is withdrawn or considered withdrawn, or

(iii) if, due to prescriptions concerning national security, the international application is not treated as such.

Art. 27(8)	Annotations on the expressions 'national security' and 'state secret'
Art. 11(1)	Negative determination means no filing date has been accorded
R. 20.4	Negative determination

Rule 16
The Search Fee

16.1 Right to Ask for a Fee

(a) Each International Searching Authority may require that the applicant pay a fee ("search fee") for its own benefit for carrying out the international search and for performing all other tasks entrusted to International Searching Authorities by the Treaty and these Regulations.

OJ EPO 2024 A5, Art. 4(1):	Time of payment is decisive for the application of amended amounts

(b) The search fee shall be collected by the receiving Office. The said fee shall be payable in the currency prescribed by that Office ("prescribed currency").

(c) Where the prescribed currency is the currency in which the International Searching Authority has fixed the said fee ("fixed currency"), the receiving Office shall transfer the said fee to that Authority in that currency in accordance with Rule 96.2.

(d) Where the prescribed currency is not the fixed currency and that currency:

(i) is freely convertible into the fixed currency, the Director General shall establish, for each receiving Office which prescribes such a currency for the payment of the search fee, an equivalent amount of that fee in the prescribed currency according to directives given by the Assembly, and the amount in that currency shall be transferred by the receiving Office to the International Searching Authority in accordance with Rule 96.2;

(ii) is not freely convertible into the fixed currency, the receiving Office shall be responsible for the conversion of the search fee from the prescribed currency into the fixed currency and shall transfer that fee in the fixed currency, in the amount fixed by the International Searching Authority, to the International Searching Authority in accordance with Rule 96.2.

(e) Where, in respect of the payment of the search fee in a prescribed currency, other than the fixed currency, the amount actually received under paragraph (d)(i) of this Rule by the International Searching Authority in the prescribed currency is, when converted by it into the fixed currency, less than that fixed

by it, the difference will be paid to the International Searching Authority by the International Bureau, whereas, if the amount actually received is more, the difference will belong to the International Bureau.

For further information on fee payment and the currently applicable fees, please consult the PCT webpage at: www.wipo.int/pct/en/fees/. 1

As a comment on para. (e) according to PCT/WG/12/20 Annex I, p. 5: 'Under the new arrangements for transfer of fees via the International Bureau, the International Bureau would always transfer the search fee to the ISA in the fixed currency. Differences between the fee in the fixed currency and the amount in the prescribed currency when converted to the fixed currency would be dealt with directly by the International Bureau. Consequently, this provision would only apply with regard to those fees that continued to be transferred directly from the receiving Office to the International Searching Authority.' 2

(f) As to the time limit for payment of the search fee and the amount payable, the provisions of Rule 15.3 relating to the international filing fee shall apply *mutatis mutandis*.

AIs 114	Notification and transfer of fees according to Annex G of AIs
R. 15.3	Time limit: one month from receipt of the international application
R. 16*bis*.1(a)	Extension of time limit
AG-IP Annex D	Amount and reduction of the fee
AP-IP 5.192, Euro-PCT Guide 2.27.010	The amount payable shall be the amount applicable on the date of receipt of the PCTa – and not the date of receipt of the fee
R. 19.4(c)	Date of actual receipt of PCTa by the International Bureau if forwarded to International Bureau
R. 45*bis*.3(b)	Corresponding application for supplementary search fee
R. 96.2	Simplification and cost reduction in the transfer and clearing of fee payments between different Offices. For the specification of equivalent amounts of certain PCT fees see the annotation to R. 96.2.

16.2 Refund

The receiving Office shall refund the search fee to the applicant:

- **(i) if the determination under Article 11(1)** *(accordance of filing date)* **is negative,**
- **(ii) if, before the transmittal of the search copy to the International Searching Authority, the international application is withdrawn or considered withdrawn, or**
- **(iii) if, due to prescriptions concerning national security, the international application is not treated as such.**

Art. 27(8)	National security
R. 23.1	Time of transmittal of search copy to the ISA
AIs 322	Invitation to submit a request for refund of the search fee
AIs 510	Refund of search fee in case of withdrawal of PCTa
EPO	If the EPO as ISA has issued a standardized non-search declaration under Art. 17(2), R. 39 and has not carried out a subsequent search in the European phase, there will be no refund of the search fee. There is no legal basis for a refund in this case, neither in the PCT nor in the WIPO-EPO Agreement or in a decision of the EPO (T 0506/08). There is also no possibility of appeal (T 0506/08).

3 For statements of WIPO concerning R. 16.2, see PCT/A/XVIII/9, p.4, para. 29 (https://www.wipo.int/edocs/mdocs/govbody/en/pct_a_xviii/pct_a_xviii_9.pdf).

16.3 Partial Refund

Where the International Searching Authority takes into account, under Rule 41.1, the results of an earlier search in carrying out the international search, that Authority shall refund the search fee paid in connection with the international application to the extent and under the conditions provided for in the agreement under Article 16(3)(b).

Art. 16(3)(b)	Agreement between WIPO and ISA
EPO	Annex D. II. (3) and Art. 5 (2) of the WIPO-EPO Agreement (https://www.wipo.int/pct/en/access/isa_ipea_agreements.html)) allows a (partial) refund of the fee for the international preliminary search

Rule 16*bis* Extension of Time Limits for Payment of Fees

16*bis*.1 Invitation by the Receiving Office

(a) Where, by the time they are due under Rules 14.1(c), 15.3 and 16.1(f), the receiving Office finds that no fees were paid to it, or that the amount paid to it is insufficient to cover the transmittal fee, the international filing fee and the search fee, the receiving Office shall, subject to paragraph (d), invite the applicant to pay to it the amount required to cover those fees, together with, where applicable, the late payment fee under Rule 16*bis*.2, within a time limit of one month from the date of the invitation.

(b) [Deleted]

(c) Where the receiving Office has sent to the applicant an invitation under paragraph (a) and the applicant has not, within the time limit referred to in that paragraph, paid in full the amount due, including, where applicable, the late payment fee under Rule 16*bis*.2, the receiving Office shall, subject to paragraph (e):

(i) make the applicable declaration under Article 14(3), and

(ii) proceed as provided in Rule 29.

(d) Any payment received by the receiving Office before that Office sends the invitation under paragraph (a) shall be considered to have been received before the expiration of the time limit under Rule 14.1(c), 15.3 or 16.1(f), as the case may be.

(e) Any payment received by the receiving Office before that Office makes the applicable declaration under Article 14(3) *(deemed withdrawn)* shall be considered to have been received before the expiration of the time limit referred to in paragraph (a).

Art. 7(3) RFees — In the absence of payment provisions in the PCT, the national provisions before the EPO thus have to take into account the EPC provisions on the effective date of payment before applying the PCT provisions on late payment of fees

1 Besides the very limited safeguard in R. 16*bis*.1(3), there is no legal provision for reviving an application considered withdrawn. Thus, any invitation for late payment, Form PCT/RO/133, should be taken seriously.

16*bis*.2 Late Payment Fee

(a) The payment of fees in response to an invitation under Rule 16*bis*.1(a) may be subjected by the receiving Office to the payment to it, for its own benefit, of a late payment fee. The amount of that fee shall be:

(i) 50% of the amount of unpaid fees which is specified in the invitation, or,

(ii) if the amount calculated under item (i) is less than the transmittal fee, an amount equal to the transmittal fee.

(b) The amount of the late payment fee shall not, however, exceed the amount of 50% of the international filing fee referred to in item 1 of the Schedule of Fees, not taking into account any fee for each sheet of the international application in excess of 30 sheets.

2 R 16*bis*.2 leaves no discretion as to the amount. The Offices can only decide whether or not to apply a surcharge.

3 In connection with the Covid-19 pandemic, the International Bureau waived the payment of that fee until futher notice (https://www.wipo.int/pct/en/news/2020/news_0017.html) and recommended that the receiving Offices refrain from charging this fee (https://www.wipo.int/pct/en/news/2020/news_0017.html).

4 The EPO specifies a late payment fee (OJ EPO 1992 p. 383, AG-IP Annex C(EP)).

5 The DPMA does not mention that fee (https://www.dpma.de/english/services/fees/patents/index.html).

Rule 17
The Priority Document

17.1 Obligation to Submit Copy of Earlier National or International Application

(a) Where the priority of an earlier national or international application is claimed under Article 8, a copy of that earlier application, certified by the authority with which it was filed ("the priority document"), shall, unless that priority document has already been filed with the receiving Office together with the international application in which the priority claim is made, and subject to paragraphs (b) and (b-*bis*), be submitted by the applicant to the International Bureau or to the receiving Office not later than 16 months after the priority date, provided that any copy of the said earlier application which is received by the International Bureau after the expiration of that time limit shall be considered to have been received by that Bureau on the last day of that time limit if it reaches it before the date of international publication of the international application.

Art. 21	International publication: 18 months
R. 4.10	Priority claim
R. 17.1(c), R. 163(2) EPC	A priority document that was produced in paper must be filed in paper with the EPO as receiving Office, i.e. not by fax or web filing. A priority document drawn up in electronic form may be filed electronically if it has been digitally signed by the issuing authority and the signature is recognized by the EPO (Euro-PCT Guide 5.13.005, 2.16.004). If this has not been observed, the filing of the priority document must be undertaken on entry into the European phase. If the priority document is not available at the time of entry, the EPO will invite filing within two months from the date of the communication under R. 163(2) EPC.
R. 89*bis*	Filing, processing and communication of PCTa and other documents in electronic form or by electronic means in accordance with AIs Part 7 and Annex F
R. 17.1(b-*bis*), AIs 715, 716	Providing and retrieving the priority document from a digital library

AIs 421	Invitation to furnish a copy of the priority document
EPO	Electronic filing of priority documents (OJ EPO 2018 A94)

1 For detailed information on how to furnish priority documents please see annotations to Art. 8, No. 3.

(b) Where the priority document is issued by the receiving Office, the applicant may, instead of submitting the priority document, request the receiving Office to prepare and transmit the priority document to the International Bureau. Such request shall be made not later than 16 months after the priority date and may be subjected by the receiving Office to the payment of a fee.

2 If a first application and a subsequent PCT application have been filed with the same Office, as a national or regional Office and as a receiving Office, for example the EPO, a corresponding request must be filed.

AG-IP Annex C	Fees for issue of a copy of priority document. For filing of priority documents via the digital library (DAS), see para. (b-*bis*).
Art. 3(1) RFees	There is a fee at the EPO (https://www.epo.org/en/applying/fees/international-fees/important-fees, code no. 029), if not requested using MyEPO Portfolio OJ EPO 2024 A5
AIs 323	Transmittal of priority documents to International Bureau
DPMA	For the fee see Annex C (DE) AG-IP
International Bureau	In general there is a fee, but the fee is waived in case of R 17.1(b) or if available via DAS, (Annex C (IB), AG-IP No. 5.070). The International Bureau will inform the applicant of the date of receipt of the priority document (AG-IP 5.070D).
Form PCT/RO/101	Check box no. VI

(b-*bis*) Where the priority document is, in accordance with the Administrative Instructions, made available to the International Bureau from a digital library prior to the date of international publication of the international application, the applicant may, instead of submitting the priority document, request the International Bureau, prior to the date of international publication, to obtain the priority document from such digital library.

Art. 21(2)	International publication 18 months from the priority date
AIs 715	Availability of priority documents from digital libraries
AIs 716	Request that priority document be obtained from a digital library under R. 17.1(b-*bis*)
Form PCT/RO/101	Check box no. VI

Information on whether certain authorities grant the applicant the possibility under R. 17.1(b-*bis*) and whether they participate in DAS can be found in Annex B AG-IP and at www.wipo.int/das/en/participating_offices. It should be observed that the Office where the earlier application was filed is a DAS depositing Office (PCT Newsletter 11/2019, p. 3). 3

The digital library is WIPO's DAS, which also includes documents from participating national and regional Offices and participating receiving Offices other than the RO/IB (AG-IP 5.070A). The EPO and CH participate. DE participates as depositing Office as from November 25, 2024 and prepares to participate as accessing Office as well (DPMA Notice No. 5/2024). The applicant must first request availability and then retrieval. For entry in the file at the EPO as designated or elected Office before January 1, 2022, see Euro-PCT Guide 5.13.007. For explanations on how DAS works in the context of ePCT, see Pract. Adv. NL 3/2022. 4

The USPTO provides digital copies of priority documents for patent applications filed with the USPTO as first filing Office for retrieval via DAS. However, the applicant may not request the USPTO as receiving Office (RO/US) to obtain a priority document from a digital library and transmit it to the International Bureau (AG-IP Annex B (US)). 5

(c) If the requirements of none of the three preceding paragraphs are complied with, any designated Office may, subject to paragraph (d), disregard the priority claim, provided that no designated Office shall disregard the priority claim before giving the applicant an opportunity to furnish the priority document within a time limit which shall be reasonable under the circumstances.

(d) No designated Office shall disregard the priority claim under paragraph (c) *(furnishing in national phase)* **if the earlier application referred to in paragraph (a) was filed with it in its capacity as national Office or if the priority document is, in accordance with the Administrative Instructions, available to it from a digital library.**

AIs 715	Availability of priority documents from digital libraries
AIs 716	Request that priority document be obtained from a digital library
R. 163(2) EPC	After the regional phase has been initiated, an official time limit is set for providing the official number of the priority application and the priority document. The time limit cannot be extended and in case of non-compliance the priority claim is lost, but further processing may be requested (Euro-PCT Guide 5.13.010). With regard to the priority document, the applicant may request that the EPO obtain the documents via DAS if the applicant provides the access code and if the countries participate in this system, e.g. also US, KR, CN, JP. If the earlier application was a European application or a PCTa filed with the EPO as receiving Office, a copy is automatically included in the file. If retrieval is not possible or has not been

requested, the applicant is invited to file a copy subsequently under R. 53 EPC. OJ EPO 2021 A83 and OJ EPO 2021 A84 apply to PCTa entering the European phase at the EPO on or after January 1, 2022. OJ EPO 2020 A57 applies to the previous procedure. See AG-IP Annex B and Euro-PCT Guide 5.13.012 for the case where the International Bureau has not transmitted the priority document although the applicant filed a corresponding requested.

17.2 Availability of Copies

(a) Where the applicant has complied with Rule 17.1(a), (b) or (b-*bis*), the International Bureau shall, at the specific request of the designated Office, promptly but not prior to the international publication of the international application, furnish a copy of the priority document to that Office. No such Office shall ask the applicant himself to furnish it with a copy. The applicant shall not be required to furnish a translation to the designated Office before the expiration of the applicable time limit under Article 22. Where the applicant makes an express request to the designated Office under Article 23(2) prior to the international publication of the international application, the International Bureau shall, at the specific request of the designated Office, furnish a copy of the priority document to that Office promptly after receiving it.

R. 51*bis*.1(e)	Furnishing a translation of the priority document under national law
R. 76.4	Time limit for the translation of a priority document
Art. 88(1), R. 53 EPC	As a rule, the EPO receives the priority document from the International Bureau, so that it does not have to be filed by the applicant on entry into the regional phase. If the priority document needs to be translated, the EPO will invite the applicant to file a translation (Euro-PCT Guide 5.13.013).

(b) The International Bureau shall not make copies of the priority document available to the public prior to the international publication of the international application.

6 Copies are usually provided to the public via PATENTSCOPE.

(c) Where the international application has been published under Article 21, the International Bureau shall furnish a copy of the priority document to any person upon request and subject to reimbursement of the cost unless, prior to that publication:

(i) the international application was withdrawn *(R. 90bis.3)*,

(ii) the relevant priority claim was withdrawn or considered, under Rule 26*bis*.2(b) *(formal deficiencies)*, **not to have been made.**

For statements of WIPO concerning R. 17.2, see PCT/A/XXIV/10, p. 7, para. 30 (https://www.wipo.int/edocs/mdocs/govbody/en/pct_a_xxiv/pct_a_xxiv_10-main1.pdf). 7

Rule 18
The Applicant

18.1 Residence and Nationality

(a) Subject to the provisions of paragraphs (b) and (c), the question whether an applicant is a resident or national of the Contracting State of which he claims to be a resident or national shall depend on the national law of that State and shall be decided by the receiving Office.

(b) In any case,

(i) possession of a real and effective industrial or commercial establishment in a Contracting State shall be considered residence in that State, and

(ii) a legal entity constituted according to the national law of a Contracting State shall be considered a national of that State.

(c) Where the international application is filed with the International Bureau as receiving Office, the International Bureau shall, in the circumstances specified in the Administrative Instructions, request the national Office of, or acting for, the Contracting State concerned to decide the question referred to in paragraph (a). The International Bureau shall inform the applicant of any such request. The applicant shall have an opportunity to submit arguments directly to the national Office. The national Office shall decide the said question promptly.

1 For statements of WIPO concerning R. 18.1, see PCT/CAL/V/6, p. 3, para. 22 (https://www.wipo.int/edocs/mdocs/pct/en/pct_cal_v/pct_cal_v_6.pdf).

2 For detailed information refer to annotations to Art. 11.

18.2 [Deleted]

18.3 Two or More Applicants

If there are two or more applicants, the right to file an international application shall exist if at least one of them is entitled to file an international application according to Article 9.

Art. 9	Entitlement of the applicant

R. 4.5(d)	Different applicants may be indicated for different designated States

18.4 Information on Requirements under National Law as to Applicants

(a) and (b) [Deleted]

(c) The International Bureau shall, from time to time, publish information on the various national laws in respect of the question who is qualified (inventor, successor in title of the inventor, owner of the invention, or other) to file a national application and shall accompany such information by a warning that the effect of the international application in any designated State may depend on whether the person designated in the international application as applicant for the purposes of that State is a person who, under the national law of that State, is qualified to file a national application.

R. 4.5(d)	When designating the US in a PCTa, the inventors had to be named as applicants prior to September 16, 2012. This was possible as different applicants can be indicated for different States.

Rule 19
The Competent Receiving Office

19.1 Where to File

(a) Subject to the provisions of paragraph (b), the international application shall be filed, at the option of the applicant,

Art. 10	The receiving Office
R. 19.4	Remedy for lack of competence
R. 35	Competent ISA

(i) with the national Office of or acting for the Contracting State of which the applicant is a resident,

(ii) with the national Office of or acting for the Contracting State of which the applicant is a national, or

(iii) irrespective of the Contracting State of which the applicant is a resident or national, with the International Bureau.

R. 18.1	Residence
R. 35.3	Competence where the International Bureau is the receiving Office under R. 19.1(a)(iii)
Art. 27(8)	The national Offices have the possibility to review the PCTa from a national security perspective
Art. 151 S. 2, Art. 75(2), R. 157(1) EPC	PCTa must be filed with the EPO, the International Bureau or the national Office if the EPC Contracting State has provided for this in its national law (Euro-PCT Guide 2.1.001, OJ EPO 2014 A9)

(b) Any Contracting State may agree with another Contracting State or any intergovernmental organization that the national Office of the latter State or the intergovernmental organization shall, for all or some purposes, act instead of the national Office of the former State as receiving Office for applicants who are residents or nationals of that former State. Notwithstanding such agreement, the

national Office of the former State shall be considered the competent receiving Office for the purposes of Article 15(5).

Annex B of the PCT Applicant's Guide contains information on which Office of another Contracting State (e.g. CH for LI) or of an intergovernmental organization such as the International Bureau or ARIPO, EAPO, EPO, OAPI (e.g. EPO for BE) is competent as receiving Office. For a few Contracting States, the International Bureau is the only competent receiving Office (AG-IP Annex C (IB)). 1

Art. 1	The term 'Contracting State' with annotation concerning overseas territories of a State
Art. 9	Entitlement to file the application
Art. 15(5)	Request for a search similar to an international search for a national application
Art. 45	Regional patent treaties
Art. 151(1), R. 157 EPC	PCT applicant shall be resident/national to Contracting State of EPC and PCT

(c) In connection with any decision made under Article 9(2) *(non-Paris Convention States whose nationals may file PCTa)*, **the Assembly shall appoint the national Office or the intergovernmental organization which will act as receiving Office for applications of residents or nationals of States specified by the Assembly. Such appointment shall require the previous consent of the said national Office or intergovernmental organization.**

Art. 9(2)	The assembly has not yet made a decision

For statements of WIPO concerning R. 19.1, see PCT/CAL/V/6, p. 4, paras 24 and 25 (https://www.wipo.int/edocs/mdocs/pct/en/pct_cal_v/pct_cal_v_6.pdf). 2

19.2 Two or More Applicants

If there are two or more applicants:

(i) the requirements of Rule 19.1 shall be considered to be met if the national Office with which the international application is filed is the national Office of or acting for a Contracting State of which at least one of the applicants is a resident or national;

Art. 31(2)(a)	The 'binding nature of Chapter II' for this State leads to the entitlement of at least one applicant to file a request for IPE

(ii) the international application may be filed with the International Bureau under Rule 19.1(a)(iii) if at least one of the applicants is a resident or national of a Contracting State.

19.3 Publication of Fact of Delegation of Duties of Receiving Office

(a) Any agreement referred to in Rule 19.1(b) shall be promptly notified to the International Bureau by the Contracting State which delegates the duties of the receiving Office to the national Office of or acting for another Contracting State or an intergovernmental organization.

(b) The International Bureau shall, promptly upon receipt, publish the notification in the Gazette.

19.4 Transmittal to the International Bureau as Receiving Office

(a) Where an international application is filed with a national Office which acts as a receiving Office under the Treaty but

(i) that national Office is not competent under Rule 19.1 or 19.2 to receive that international application, or

(ii) that international application is not in a language accepted under Rule 12.1(a) or the language-dependent free text contained within the sequence listing part of the description is not in a language accepted under Rule 12.1(d) by that national Office but is in a language accepted under that Rule by the International Bureau as receiving Office, or

3 The International Bureau accepts applications in any language (AG-IP 6.034).

(ii-*bis*) all or part of the international application is filed in electronic form in a format not accepted by that national Office, or

4 The intention of para. (ii-*bis*) is to facilitate filing when a receiving Office cannot process the PCTa filed. This may be the case, for example, if an applicant has to file the PCTa with a particular receiving Office for reasons of national security, but the receiving Office does not accept electronic filing, or if the uploading of a sequence listing fails on the receiving Office's online system (comment in Annex to PCT/WG/13/8). Para. (ii-*bis*) applies if the receiving Office does not accept the filing of sequence listings in XML format (AG-IP 5.100 et seq.).

(iii) that national Office and the International Bureau agree, for any reason other than those specified under items (i), (ii) and (ii-*bis*), and with the authorization of the applicant, that the procedure under this Rule should apply,

that international application shall, subject to paragraph (b), be considered to have been received by that Office on behalf of the International Bureau as receiving Office under Rule 19.1(a)(iii).

5 Upon request from the applicant, the International Bureau is competent in any case where the International Bureau and the receiving Office agree. In practice, the International Bureau had so far agreed to all such requests.

[In September and October 2019] 'The Assembly of the PCT Union: [...] (ii) adopted the Understanding set out in para. 7 of document PCT/A/51/2' (PCT/A/51/4, p. 5, para. 17). Para. 7(a) of document PCT/A/51/2 reads: 'In adopting new Rule 20.8(a-*bis*), the Assembly agreed that, where a correct element or part cannot be incorporated by reference under Rules 20.5*bis*(a)(ii) and (d) because of the operation of Rule 20.8(a-*bis*), the receiving Office concerned and the International Bureau shall agree, under Rule 19.4(a)(iii), with the authorization of the applicant, that the procedures under Rule 19.4 shall apply, in which case the international application shall, subject to Rule 19.4(b), be considered to have been received by that Office on behalf of the International Bureau as receiving Office under Rule 19.1(a)(iii).' 6

(https:/www.wipo.int/edocs/mdocs/govbody/en/pct_a_51/pct_a_51_2.pdf, Publication in Gazette March 5, 2020) 7

(b) Where, pursuant to paragraph (a), an international application is received by a national Office on behalf of the International Bureau as receiving Office under Rule 19.1(a)(iii), that national Office shall, unless prescriptions concerning national security prevent the international application from being so transmitted, promptly transmit it to the International Bureau. Such transmittal may be subjected by the national Office to the payment of a fee, for its own benefit, equal to the transmittal fee charged by that Office under Rule 14. The international application so transmitted shall be considered to have been received by the International Bureau as receiving Office under Rule 19.1(a)(iii) on the date of receipt of the international application by that national Office.

(c) For the purposes of Rules 14.1(c), 15.3 and 16.1(f) *(amount payable for transmittal fee, international filing fee and search fee)*, **where the international application was transmitted to the International Bureau under paragraph (b), the date of receipt of the international application shall be considered to be the date on which the international application was actually received by the International Bureau. For the purposes of this paragraph, the last sentence of paragraph (b) shall not apply.**

Art. 3(4)(i)	PCTa in prescribed language
R. 5.2	Sequence listings
R. 12.1(a)	Possible publication language and language accepted by the competent ISA
R. 12.1(d)	Language-dependent free text in sequence protocol, accepted by ISA
R. 89*bis*	Electronic filing

For refund of fees paid to the non-competent Office, see AG-IP No. 6.034. 8

For statements of WIPO concerning R. 19.4, see PCT/CAL/V/6, p. 4, paras 29 and 30 (https://www.wipo.int/edocs/mdocs/pct/en/pct_cal_v/pct_cal_v_6.pdf) and PCT/A/XXI/5, p.4, paras 25 and 26 (https://www.wipo.int/edocs/mdocs/govbody/en/pct_a_xxi/pct_a_xxi_5.pdf). 9

Rule 20
International Filing Date

INTRODUCTION

1. Missing Elements or Parts of the International Application

1 An element or part missing from the international application as filed may be added after the day on which the first documents were filed. The addition may be achieved, where possible, by referring to an earlier application that contains the entire element or part. Alternatively, the missing part can be filed later. Such a reference results in the missing element or part being incorporated by reference in the international application. Depending on the circumstances, the international application with the missing element or part supplemented may retain its original international filing date or may be re-dated. For the check of requirements and the accordance of an international filing date by the receiving Office, see annotations to Art. 11.

2 An 'element' for the purpose of supplementing the application as filed is the entire description or all of the claims (R. 4.18 referring to Art. 11(1)(iii)(d) and (e)). A 'part' is a part of the description, a part of the claims, or a part or all of the drawings (R. 4.18 and R. 20.5(a)). Note that a missing element will affect the accordance of the international filing date; a missing part will not. The PCT distinguishes the following two cases:

1. Filing an international application by reference

3 The case relates to an international application that claims the priority of an earlier application and where on filing one or more elements or parts are not included in the international application and are incorporated by a reference to the earlier application. The receiving Office will treat the element or part as if it had actually been contained in the international application as originally filed if the following two requirements are both complied with.

(i) The applicant must add a statement under R. 4.18 to the international application as filed that the element or part is completely contained in the earlier application and are incorporated by reference in the international application (R. 4.18).

(ii) The applicant must confirm the incorporation by providing the information stated in R. 20.6 within the two-month time limit mentioned in the annotations to Art. 11 No. 3 (R. 20.3(a)(ii); AG-IP 6.027–6.031).

The PCT has no remedy where an element is missing from the international application and no statement under R. 4.18 is included in the application as filed. The only option for the applicant is to file the international application again. 4

The possibility of filing an international application by reference was included in the PCT to make filing an application by fax easier in that the pages of the description, claims and/or drawings did not need to be fed through a fax machine but could be replaced by a brief reference to an earlier application. It has become outdated with the advent of electronic filing. 5

2. Filing missing parts

The second case relates to an international application where a part of the description, claims or drawings is missing, including the case where all of the drawings are missing, but excluding the case where an entire element is missing. The receiving Office will invite the applicant either to submit the missing part or to confirm that the missing part was incorporated by reference, both within the two-month time limit of R. 20.7 (R. 20.5(a); AG-IP 6.027–6.031, Art. 11 Introduction). 6

If the applicant submits the missing part, the date of receipt of the missing part will become the international filing date (R. 20.5(b), (c)). If, on second thoughts, the applicant does not want a change in the international filing date, he may request the receiving Office to disregard the submitted missing part and maintain the original international filing date (R. 20.5(e)). 7

However, if the applicant confirms that the missing part was completely contained in an earlier application of which the international application claims priority and that the missing part was incorporated by reference in the international application and submits the information required under R. 4.18 and 20.6, the application will retain the original international filing date (R. 20.5(d)). 8

An ISA may charge the applicant additional fees under R. 40*bis*.1 if it is notified of a correction of a missing part only after it has begun to draw up the ISR. 9

The following table summarizes the provisions of R. 20 concerning missing parts. 10

missing	completely	in part
description	R. 20.3(a)(ii)	R. 20.5(a)
claims	R. 20.3(a)(ii)	R. 20.5(a)
drawings	R. 20.5(a)	R. 20.5(a)

(Table originally published in Köllner, PCT-Handbuch, 15th edition, 2020, Wolters Kluwer Germany) 11

A receiving Office or a designated Office may declare that several of the provisions on incorporation by reference are incompatible with its national law (R. 20.8). If an Office has informed the International Bureau accordingly, then the provisions do not apply with respect to that Office. Details of the declarations can be found on the 'PCT Reservations, Declarations, Notifications and Incompatibilities' webpage 12 of the PCT website (www.wipo.int/pct/en/texts/reservations/res_incomp.html). If a receiving Office cannot incorporate by reference because of an incompatibility, the applicant may request the receiving Office to transmit the international application to the International Bureau (R. 19.4(a)(iii)), so the International Bureau as receiving Office can make an incorporation by reference under R. 4.18 (AG-IP 6.027).

13 Designated and elected Offices have a limited power to review a decision made by a receiving Office concerning the incorporation by reference (R. 82*ter.*1(b)–(d); AG-NP 6.012). Note that receiving Offices have diverging interpretations of incorporation by reference; see Pract. Adv. NL 07–08/2015 (https://www.wipo.int/pct/en/newslett/practical_advice/pa_072015.html).

2. Erroneously Filed Description, Claims or Drawings or Parts Thereof

14 R 20.5*bis* deals with erroneously filed elements and parts, whereas R. 20.5 deals with missing parts. R. 20.5*bis* entered into force on July 1, 2020 with the purpose of harmonizing diverging practice between Offices (PCT/WG/11/21 para. 6 and 19 (https://www.wipo.int/edocs/mdocs/pct/en/pct_wg_11/pct_wg_11_21.pdf).

15 R 20.5*bis* permits correction of an erroneously filed element or part of the international application by a correct element or part (Pract. Adv. NL 07–08/2020, https://www.wipo.int/pct/en/newslett/practical_advice/pa_072020.html). Since it is one of the principles of incorporation by reference that it can only add subject matter to an application, not remove, incorporation by reference cannot replace any erroneously filed elements or parts of an application. Hence, the word 'correct' instead of 'replace' is used in R. 20.5*bis* and the different treatment of a filed and incorporated element and part. The correction must be made within the two-month time limit of R. 20.7.

16 The correct element or part may be filed with the receiving Office or incorporated by reference:

- If the correct element or part is filed, the international application is re-dated to the date of receipt of the correct element or part. The correct element or part will be included in the application and the erroneously filed element or part removed from it (R. 20.5*bis*(b), (c)).
- If the correct element or part is incorporated by reference, the international application is not re-dated (R. 20.5*bis*(d)). The erroneously filed element or part will remain in the application (R. 20.5*bis*(d)). It is the understanding of the PCT Assembly that the ISA need not take the erroneously filed element or part remaining in the application into account (see presentation 'PCT – July 2020 Rule changes', slide 8, https://www.wipo.int/edocs/mdocs/pct/en/wipo_webinar_pct_2020_1/wipo_webinar_pct_2020_1_presentation.pdf).

17 The procedure in R. 20.5*bis* to correct an erroneously filed element or part by the corresponding correct element or part of the priority application corresponds to the procedure under R. 20.5 for missing parts. An ISA may charge the applicant additional fees under R. 40*bis*.1 if it is notified of a correction of an erroneously filed element or part only after it has begun to draw up the ISR. ISA/EP does charge the fee.

3. Comparison of Incorporation by Reference in PCT and EPC

Since November 1, 2022 the procedure under the EPC is in alignment with the PCT procedure. Under R. 56(3) EPC the relevant priority must be claimed on the date of filing if it is to serve as a basis for adding missing parts without changing the date of filing. If a declaration of priority is added thereafter under R. 52(3) EPC it cannot serve as a basis for such a correction. Furthermore, new R. 56a EPC aligns the EPC with R. 20.5*bis* PCT (OJ EPO 2022 A71, OJ EPO 2022 A3, https://www.epo.org/en/legal/epc/2020/r56a.html). 18

Rule 20
International Filing Date

20.1 Determination under Article 11(1)

(a) Promptly after receipt of the papers purporting to be an international application, the receiving Office shall determine whether the papers fulfill the requirements of Article 11(1).

(b) For the purposes of Article 11(1)(iii)(c), it shall be sufficient to indicate the name of the applicant in a way which allows the identity of the applicant to be established even if the name is misspelled, the given names are not fully indicated, or, in the case of legal entities, the indication of the name is abbreviated or incomplete.

(c) For the purposes of Article 11(1)(ii) *(application in prescribed language)*, it shall be sufficient that the part which appears to be a description (other than any sequence listing part thereof) and the part which appears to be a claim or claims be in a language accepted by the receiving Office under Rule 12.1(a).

R. 26.3*ter*, R. 26.5	For drawings a different language is allowed
R. 26.3*ter*	Invitation to correct defects under Art. 3(4)(i)
R. 26.5	Decision of the receiving Office
R. 89*bis*	Electronic filing

(d) If, on October 1, 1997, paragraph (c) is not compatible with the national law applied by the receiving Office, paragraph (c) shall not apply to that receiving Office for as long as it continues not to be compatible with that law, provided that the said Office informs the International Bureau accordingly by December 31, 1997. The information received shall be promptly published by the International Bureau in the Gazette.

Publication at https://www.wipo.int/pct/en/texts/reservations/res_incomp.html. A notice from the US was published. 19

AIs 105	Identification of international application with two or more applicants
AIs 307	System of numbering international applications

20.2 Positive Determination under Article 11 (1)

(a) If the receiving Office determines that, at the time of receipt of the papers purporting to be an international application, the requirements of Article 11 (1) were fulfilled, the receiving Office shall accord as the international filing date the date of receipt of the international application.

(b) The receiving Office shall stamp the request of the international application which it has accorded an international filing date as prescribed by the Administrative Instructions. The copy whose request has been so stamped shall be the record copy of the international application.

(c) The receiving Office shall promptly notify the applicant of the international application number and the international filing date. At the same time, it shall send to the International Bureau a copy of the notification sent to the applicant, except where it has already sent, or is sending at the same time, the record copy to the International Bureau under Rule 22.1 (a).

AIs 110	Dates
AIs 301	Notification of receipt of purported international application
AIs 308	Marking of sheets of the international application and translation thereof under R. 12.3, 12.4, 20.4 and 26.3ter(e)
AIs 324	Copy of notification of the international application number and the international filing date under R. 20.2(c)

20.3 Defects under Article 11 (1)

(a) Where, in determining whether the papers purporting to be an international application fulfill the requirements of Article 11 (1) *(for accordance of filing date)*, the receiving Office finds that any of the requirements of Article 11 (1) are not, or appear not to be fulfilled, it shall promptly invite the applicant, at the applicant's option:

(i) to furnish the required correction under Article 11 (2); or

(ii) where the requirements concerned are those relating to an element referred to in Article 11 (1) (iii) (d) *(whole description)* or (e) *(whole claims)*, to confirm in accordance with Rule 20.6(a) that the element is incorporated by reference under Rule 4.18;

and to make observations, if any, within the applicable time limit under Rule 20.7. If that time limit expires after the expiration of 12 months from the filing date of any application whose priority is claimed, the receiving Office shall call that circumstance to the attention of the applicant.

R. 20.7(a)(i)	Time limit is two months for response with correction
R. 29.4(b)	For R. 20.7(a)(i), a request under R. 29.4(b) shall be deemed to be a request under R. 20.3(a)(ii).
R. 4.18	Remedy by incorporation by reference

(b) Where, following an invitation under paragraph (a) or otherwise:

(i) the applicant furnishes to the receiving Office the required correction under Article 11(2) after the date of receipt of the purported international application but on a later date falling within the applicable time limit under Rule 20.7, the receiving Office shall accord that later date as the international filing date and proceed as provided in Rule 20.2(b) and (c);

(ii) an element referred to in Article 11(1)(iii)(d) or (e) *(description, claim)* is, under Rule 20.6(b) *(incorporation by reference)*, considered to have been contained in the international application on the date on which one or more elements referred to in Article 11(1)(iii) were first received by the receiving Office, the receiving Office shall accord as the international filing date the date on which all of the requirements of Article 11(1) are fulfilled and proceed as provided in Rule 20.2(b) and (c).

R. 20.7(a)(i)	Time limit is two months for response with correction
R. 20.6(b)	Since the missing documents are deemed to be included in the initial incomplete submission, the application date is the date of initial receipt of parts. There is no postponement of the application date.
R. 12.1*bis*	Language of submitted elements and parts

(c) If the receiving Office later discovers, or on the basis of the applicant's reply realizes, that it has erred in issuing an invitation under paragraph (a) since the requirements of Article 11(1) were fulfilled when the papers were received, it shall proceed as provided in Rule 20.2.

AIs 309	Procedure in the case of later submitted sheets furnished for the purposes of incorporation by reference
AIs 310	Procedure in the case of later submitted sheets not furnished for the purposes of incorporation by reference

20.4 Negative Determination under Article 11(1)

If the receiving Office does not receive, within the applicable time limit under Rule 20.7, a correction or confirmation referred to in Rule 20.3(a), or if a correction or confirmation has been received but the application still does not fulfill the requirements of Article 11(1), the receiving Office shall:

(i) promptly notify the applicant that the application is not and will not be treated as an international application and shall indicate the reasons therefor;

(ii) notify the International Bureau that the number it has marked on the papers will not be used as an international application number;

(iii) keep the papers constituting the purported international application and any correspondence relating thereto as provided in Rule 93.1; and

(iv) send a copy of the said papers to the International Bureau where, pursuant to a request by the applicant under Article 25(1), the International Bureau needs such a copy and specially asks for it.

R. 20.7(a)(i)	Time limit is two months for response with correction
R. 12.3(c)	Invitation to furnish a translation
AIs 308	Marking of the sheets of the international application and of the translation thereof under R. 12.3, 12.4, 20.4 and 26.3ter(e)
AIs 309	Marking of later submitted sheets, furnished for the purposes of incorporation by reference
AIs 310	Procedure in the case of later submitted sheets not furnished for the purposes of incorporation by reference

20.5 Missing Parts

(a) Where, in determining whether the papers purporting to be an international application fulfill the requirements of Article 11(1), the receiving Office finds that a part of the description, claims or drawings is or appears to be missing, including the case where all of the drawings are or appear to be missing ("missing part") but not including the case where an entire element referred to in Article 11(1)(iii)(d) *(whole description)* or (e) *(whole claims)* is or appears to be missing and not including the case referred to in Rule 20.5*bis*(a), it shall promptly invite the applicant, at the applicant's option:

(i) to complete the purported international application by furnishing the missing part; or

(ii) to confirm, in accordance with Rule 20.6(a), that the part was incorporated by reference under Rule 4.18;

and to make observations, if any, within the applicable time limit under Rule 20.7. If that time limit expires after the expiration of 12 months from the filing date of any application whose priority is claimed, the receiving Office shall call that circumstance to the attention of the applicant.

R. 20.7(a)(i)	Time limit is two months for response with correction
R. 20.5	aims at harmonizing the different practices in different Offices (PCT/WG/11/21 No. 6).

Art. 11(1)(iii)	lists what 'elements' are, namely: request, designation of at least one Contracting State, name of the applicant, description, claims, but not the drawings. If only individual pages are missing, it is a missing 'part'.
R. 20.3(a)(ii), R. 20.6	Procedure in the case of missing elements, e.g. complete description

R 20.5 governs the case where parts of the PCTa are missing. In contrast, R. 20.5*bis* governs the case where wrong parts have been filed by mistake, i.e. documents filed are not correct and should therefore be exchanged. The further procedure is basically similar, see AG-IP 6.025(ii). 20

For illustration see the table in annotation to R. 20 No. 1.2 above. 21

(b) Where, following an invitation under paragraph (a) or otherwise, the applicant furnishes to the receiving Office, on or before the date on which all of the requirements of Article 11(1) are fulfilled but within the applicable time limit under Rule 20.7, a missing part referred to in paragraph (a) so as to complete the purported international application, that part shall be included in the application, and the receiving Office shall accord as the international filing date the date on which all of the requirements of Article 11(1) are fulfilled and proceed as provided in Rule 20.2(b) and (c).

R. 20.7(a)(i)	Time limit is two months for response with correction

Since the requirements of Art. 11(1) are usually fulfilled by the subsequent filing, the international filing date is postponed to the date of the subsequent filing. 22

(c) Where, following an invitation under paragraph (a) or otherwise, the applicant furnishes to the receiving Office, after the date on which all of the requirements of Article 11(1) were fulfilled but within the applicable time limit under Rule 20.7, a missing part referred to in paragraph (a) so as to complete the international application, that part shall be included in the application, and the receiving Office shall correct the international filing date to the date on which the receiving Office received that part, notify the applicant accordingly and proceed as provided for in the Administrative Instructions.

R. 20.7(a)(i)	Time limit is two months for response with correction
R. 12.1*bis*	Language of elements and parts

This results in a postponement of the international filing date, which may already have been recognized. However, it is possible to change this correction according to para. (e). 23

The PCT RO Guidelines contain further details on paras (b) and (c), in particular in No. 200 et seq. (https://www.wipo.int/pct/en/texts/gdlines.html). 24

(d) Where, following an invitation under paragraph (a) or otherwise, a part referred to in paragraph (a) is, under Rule 20.6(b), considered to have been contained in the purported international application on the date on which one or more elements referred to in Article 11(1)(iii) were first received by the receiving Office, the receiving Office shall accord as the international filing date the date on which all of the requirements of Article 11(1) are fulfilled and proceed as provided in Rule 20.2(b) and (c).

25 In contrast to paras (b) and (c), the correction by the applicant is not made by way of filing but by way of incorporation by reference.

R. 20.6(b)	Since the missing documents are deemed to be included in the initial incomplete submission, the international filing date is the date of initial receipt of parts. There is no postponement of the international filing date.
R. 40*bis*	Additional fees in case of correction of parts/elements of the PCTa
R. 82*ter*.1	Review in the national/regional phase.

(e) Where the international filing date has been corrected under paragraph (c), the applicant may, in a notice submitted to the receiving Office within one month from the date of the notification under paragraph (c), request that the missing part concerned be disregarded, in which case the missing part shall be considered not to have been furnished and the correction of the international filing date under that paragraph shall be considered not to have been made, and the receiving Office shall proceed as provided for in the Administrative Instructions.

R. 82*ter*.1(d)	Request to disregard a part or element before designated or elected Office
AIs 308*bis*	Marking of later submitted sheets
AIs 309	Procedure in the case of later submitted sheets furnished for the purposes of incorporation by reference
AIs 310	Procedure in the case of later submitted sheets not furnished for the purposes of incorporation by reference
AIs 310*bis*	Procedure in the case of later submitted sheets resulting in the correction of the international filing date under R. 20.5(c) or 20.5*bis*(c)

26 The request according to para. (e) can be useful if, for example, the priority can no longer be claimed due to the postponement of the filing date, which could be avoided if necessary.

20.5*bis* Erroneously Filed Elements and Parts

(a) Where, in determining whether the papers purporting to be an international application fulfill the requirements of Article 11(1), the receiving Office finds that an entire element referred to in Article 11(1)(iii)(d) *(whole description)* or (e) *(whole claims)* has or appears to have been erroneously filed, or that a part of the description, claims or drawings has or appears to have been erroneously filed, including the case where all drawings have or appear to have been erroneously filed ("erroneously filed element or part"), it shall promptly invite the applicant, at the applicant's option:

(i) to correct the purported international application by furnishing the correct element or part; or

(ii) to confirm, in accordance with Rule 20.6(a), that the correct element or part was incorporated by reference under Rule 4.18;

and to make observations, if any, within the applicable time limit under Rule 20.7. If that time limit expires after the expiration of 12 months from the filing date of any application whose priority is claimed, the receiving Office shall call that circumstance to the attention of the applicant.

Art. 11(1)(iii)	lists what 'elements' are, namely: request, designation of at least one Contracting State, name of the applicant, description, claims but not the drawings. If only individual pages are missing, it is a missing 'part'.
R. 20.7	Time limit for exchange: two months
R. 20.8(a-*bis*)	Incompatibility with national law (receiving Office)
R. 20.8(b-*bis*)	Incompatibility with national law (designated Office)

While R. 20.5 regulates the case that missing parts can be submitted subsequently, R. 20.5*bis* deals with the case that components or parts have been submitted, but they are the wrong parts or components. The procedure is similar to that in R. 20.5. See also PCT/WG/12/9, comments in Annex p. 9–12. 27

Para. (a) refers to the erroneously filed whole description and whole claims. In contrast, the parallel provision R. 20.5 does not refer to the whole description and the whole claims missing because these are the subject of the separate R. 20.3. 28

The receiving Office does not check whether something has been filed erroneously (it only checks for missing elements), but draws the applicant's attention to it if it has the impression (No. 194A PCT/GL/RO/20). 29

(b) Where, following an invitation under paragraph (a) or otherwise, the applicant furnishes to the receiving Office, on or before the date on which all of the requirements of Article 11(1) are fulfilled but within the applicable time limit under Rule 20.7, a correct element or part so as to correct the purported international application, that correct element or part shall be included in the application, the erroneously filed element or part concerned shall be removed from the application and the receiving Office shall accord as the international filing date the date on which all of the requirements of Article 11(1) are fulfilled

and proceed as provided in Rule 20.2(b) and (c) and as provided for in the Administrative Instructions.

(c) Where, following an invitation under paragraph (a) or otherwise, the applicant furnishes to the receiving Office, after the date on which all of the requirements of Article 11(1) were fulfilled but within the applicable time limit under Rule 20.7, a correct element or part so as to correct the international application, that correct element or part shall be included in the application, the erroneously filed element or part concerned shall be removed from the application, and the receiving Office shall correct the international filing date to the date on which the receiving Office received that correct element or part, notify the applicant accordingly and proceed as provided for in the Administrative Instructions.

30 Paras (b) and (c) regulate how to proceed after the request for correction, if the applicant opts for filing documents under paras (b) and (c) instead of incorporation by reference under para. (d). The paragraphs correspond to the rules for the subsequent filing of missing parts under R. 20.5, but the erroneously filed parts will be removed. Removed parts are not published as part of the PCTa (PCT Newsletter 7–8/2020, p. 16).

31 The legal consequence with regard to the international filing date is the same in terms of the wording. Whether para. (b) or (c) is applicable depends on whether the correction is received before or after all the elements for granting the filing date are present. If it is received before according to para. (b), the filing date is accorded for the first time according to Art. 11.

32 If the correction under para. (c) is received after accordance of an international filing date but within the time limit under R. 20.7, the conditions for according a filing date already existed before the correction. Thereafter, the filing date is corrected and shifts to the later date of receipt of the correction. To preserve the original filing date, the applicant may – as in the case of missing parts – request disregard under para. (e).

(d) Where, following an invitation under paragraph (a) or otherwise, a correct element or part is, under Rule 20.6(b) *(incorporation by reference)*, considered to have been contained in the purported international application on the date on which one or more elements referred to in Article 11(1)(iii) were first received by the receiving Office, the erroneously filed element or part concerned shall remain in the application, and the receiving Office shall accord as the international filing date the date on which all of the requirements of Article 11(1) are fulfilled and proceed as provided in Rule 20.2(b) and (c) and as provided for in the Administrative Instructions.

R. 20.8 a-*bis*) Incompatibility with national law (receiving Office)

R. 20.8 b-*bis*) Incompatibility with national law (designated Office)

33 With the adaptation of R. 20.5*bis*, the PCT Assembly also adopted the following understanding (Publication in Gazette March 5, 2020, p. 33): 'In adopting new Rule 20.5*bis*, the Assembly agreed that Article 15 should be interpreted such that,

in the case of incorporation by reference of a correct element or part under Rule 20.5*bis*(d), the International Searching Authority would only be required to carry out the international search on the basis of the international application ("the claims, with due regard to the description and the drawings, if any") including the correct element or part incorporated by reference, and would not need to take into account any erroneously filed element or part which, pursuant to Rule 20.5*bis*(d), remained in the application. The Assembly further agreed that Article 15 should be interpreted such that, in the case referred to in Rule 40*bis*.1, where no additional fees were paid within the prescribed time limit, the International Searching Authority would only be required to carry out the international search on the basis of the international application ("the claims, with due regard to the description and the drawings, if any") including the erroneously filed element or part, and would not need to take into account any correct element or part included in the application under Rule 20.5*bis*(c) or incorporated by reference under Rule 20.5*bis*(d).'

Para. (d) regulates the special form of correction by way of incorporation by reference in accordance with the Rules for missing parts. The 'correct' element incorporated by reference is deemed to be contained in the original version of the PCTa (OJ EPO 2020 A81 p. 11). The filing date is retained (OJ EPO 2020 A81 p. 11 with diagrams for overview). In contrast to the Rule on missing parts, however, it is clarified what happens to the documents that were filed erroneously. In the case of incorporation by reference, and thus in contrast to paras (b) and (c), these elements/parts are not removed but remain part of the application. They will be published together with the correct elements with the PCTa, but with the indication 'ERRONEOUSLY FILED' (PCT Newsletter 7–8/2020, p. 16). The applicant should therefore consider whether publication is a problem. In principle, withdrawal and refiling of the PCTa is an alternative. The applicant should check whether a later filing date is within the priority period or whether a request for restoration of the priority right under R. 26*bis*, R. 49*ter* has a chance of success. **34**

EPO	Since November 1, 2022 R. 20.5*bis*(a)(ii) and R. 20.5*bis*(d) are no longer incompatible as R. 56a EPC entered into force (Gazette July 7, 2022, p. 173). For applications filed since November 1, 2022, OJ EPO 2022 A71 applies (before that date see OJ EPO 2020 A81).

Procedure before the ISA: the basis of the international search is formed by the corrected documents. This also applies if the erroneously filed documents remain in the PCTa according to R. 20.5*bis*(d). The ISA does not have to take into account documents filed in error which remain in the PCTa. However, it need not take the correction into account if the additional fee under R. 40*bis*.1 is not paid and the preparation of the ISR has been started (PCT/A/51/4 No. 17 in conjunction with PCT/A/51/2 No. 7, AG-IP 7.004A, 7.004B). **35**

EPO as ISA	The EPO's declaration of incompatibility had no influence on the functions as ISA and the procedure remains unchanged (OJ EPO 2022 A71 p. 8) after the incompatibility ceased. ISA searches on the basis of the PCTa as decided by the receiving Office, i.e. with the 'correct' documents, if applicable, including the decision on

the international filing date. However, the EPO as ISA checks whether the decision of the receiving Office was correct with regard to the criterion 'completely contained' (PCT EPO Guidelines B-III 2.3.3). If the EPO as ISA is informed of the correction by the receiving Office after the search has begun but before it is completed and the applicant pays an additional fee (R. 40*bis*.1, Art. 2(1) No. 2 RFees, OJ EPO 2020 A36), the EPO as ISA also completes the search already begun on the basis of the 'incorrect' documents originally filed and issues a non-official ISR/WO-ISA relating thereto. This is not an ISR/WO-ISA within the meaning of R. 43 and R. 43*bis* and only applies to the applicant and the designated Offices which have notified an incompatibility under R. 20.8(b-*bis*) (OJ EPO 2020 A81 pp. 2, 3, 12 with diagrams for overview).

EPO as IPEA — The procedure before the IPEA remains unchanged, too, after the declaration of incompatibility ceased: The EPO's declaration of incompatibility had no influence on the functions as IPEA. The IPE is based on the official ISR/WO-ISA as defined in R. 43 and R. 43*bis*. As far as can be seen, no IPE is established on the basis of an additional non-official ISR/WO-ISA.

EPO as designated Office or elected Office — Corrections allowed by the receiving Office in the international phase under para. (b) or (c) (subsequent filing of correct documents) are effective. This also applies to PCTa filed since November 1, 2022, irrespective of the date of entry into the European phase, in the case of incorporation by reference, so that the filing date is not changed (OJ EPO 2022 A71). Until October 31, 2022, this did not apply in the case of incorporation by reference according to para. (d) (R. 20.8(c), erroneously filed parts) – due to the applicable reservation (OJ EPO 2020 A81 p. 5 et seq. with overview diagrams).

Art. 11(1)	Accordance of international filing date if requirements are fulfilled at the time of receipt
R. 4.18	Statement of incorporation by reference
R. 12.1*bis*	Language of elements and parts furnished
R. 20.2(b), (c)	Accordance of international filing date, further procedure in accordance with AIs
R. 20.6(b)	Effect of incorporation by reference on international filing date
R. 40*bis*	Additional fees in case of correction of elements/parts of the PCTa
R. 49*ter*.2	Request for restoration of right of priority
AIs 308*bis*	Marking of later submitted sheets
AIs 309	Marking of later submitted sheets, furnished for the purposes of incorporation by reference
AIs 310	Procedure in the case of later submitted sheets not furnished for the purposes of incorporation by reference

AIs 310*bis*	Procedure in the case of later submitted sheets resulting in the correction of the international filing date under R. 20.5(c) or 20.5*bis*(c)
AIs 311	Renumbering in the case of deletion, substitution, or addition of sheets of the PCTa and of the translation thereof

(e) Where the international filing date has been corrected under paragraph (c), the applicant may, in a notice submitted to the receiving Office within one month from the date of the notification under paragraph (c), request that the correct element or part be disregarded, in which case the correct element or part shall be considered not to have been furnished, the erroneously filed element or part concerned shall be considered not to have been removed from the application and the correction of the international filing date under paragraph (c) shall be considered not to have been made, and the receiving Office shall proceed as provided for in the Administrative Instructions.

For statements of WIPO concerning R. 20.5*bis*, see PCTA/51/2 p.3, para. 7(b) (https://www.wipo.int/edocs/mdocs/govbody/en/pct_a_51/pct_a_51_2.pdf). 36

20.6 Confirmation of Incorporation by Reference of Elements and Parts

(a) The applicant may submit to the receiving Office, within the applicable time limit under Rule 20.7, a written notice confirming that an element or part is incorporated by reference in the international application under Rule 4.18, accompanied by:

(i) a sheet or sheets embodying the entire element as contained in the earlier application or embodying the part concerned;

(ii) where the applicant has not already complied with Rule 17.1(a), (b) or (b-*bis*) in relation to the priority document, a copy of the earlier application as filed;

(iii) where the earlier application is not in the language in which the international application is filed, a translation of the earlier application into that language or, where a translation of the international application is required under Rule 12.3(a) or 12.4(a), a translation of the earlier application into both the language in which the international application is filed and the language of that translation; and

(iv) in the case of a part of the description, claims or drawings, an indication as to where that part is contained in the earlier application and, where applicable, in any translation referred to in item (iii).

R. 20.7(a)(i)	Time limit is two months for response with correction

The PCT RO Guidelines contain further details on para. (a), in particular in No. 204 et seq. (www.wipo.int/pct/en/texts/gdlines.html). 37

(b) Where the receiving Office finds that the requirements of Rule 4.18 and paragraph (a) have been complied with and that the element or part referred to in paragraph (a) is completely contained in the earlier application concerned, that element or part shall be considered to have been contained in the purported international application on the date on which one or more elements referred to in Article 11(1)(iii) were first received by the receiving Office.

(c) Where the receiving Office finds that a requirement under Rule 4.18 or paragraph (a) has not been complied with or that the element or part referred to in paragraph (a) is not completely contained in the earlier application concerned, the receiving Office shall proceed as provided for in Rule 20.3(b)(i), 20.5(b), 20.5(c), 20.5*bis*(b) or 20.5*bis*(c) *(date of receipt as later filing date)*, as the case may be.

R. 4.18	Statement of incorporation by reference
R. 12.1*bis*	Language of elements and parts
R. 20.5(e)	Possibility in the case of R. 20.6(c) to request disregard of the missing part, this leads to the original filing date being retained.
R. 20.5*bis*	Erroneously filed elements or parts
R. 20.8	Transitional Rule for the validity of reservations in EPO Notice of November 7, 2007 on the withdrawal of reservations under the PCT (OJ EPO 2007 p. 692 et seq.)
AIs 305*ter*	Identification and transmittal of the translation of an earlier application furnished under R. 20.6(a)(ii)
AIs 309	Procedure in the case of later submitted sheets furnished for the purposes of incorporation by reference
AIs 310	Procedure in the case of later submitted sheets not furnished for the purposes of incorporation by reference
AIs 310*ter*	Procedure in the case of later submitted sheets furnished after expiration of the applicable time limit referred to in R. 20.7
AIs 335	Procedure relating to sequence listings
AIs 411*bis*	Receipt of translation of earlier application under R. 20.6(a)(iii)
AIs 413	Incorporation by reference under R. 20.6, correction of defects under R. 26.4 and rectification of obvious mistakes under R. 91

20.7 Time Limit

(a) The applicable time limit referred to in Rules 20.3(a) *(no accordance of filing date)* and (b) *(subsequent correction)*, 20.4 *(no accordance of filing date)*, 20.5(a) *(missing parts)*, (b) *(subsequent correction)* and (c) *(correction of filing date)*, 20.5*bis*(a) *(erroneously filed elements and parts)*, (b) *(subsequent correction)* and (c) *(correction of filing date)*, and 20.6(a) *(incorporation by reference)* shall be:

(i) where an invitation under Rule 20.3(a), 20.5(a) or 20.5*bis*(a), as applicable, was sent to the applicant, two months from the date of the invitation;

(ii) where no such invitation was sent to the applicant, two months from the date on which one or more elements referred to in Article 11(1)(iii) were first received by the receiving Office.

(b) Where neither a correction under Article 11(2) nor a notice under Rule 20.6(a) confirming the incorporation by reference of an element referred to in Article 11(1)(iii)(d) or (e) *(description, claims)* is received by the receiving Office prior to the expiration of the applicable time limit under paragraph (a), any such correction or notice received by that Office after the expiration of that time limit but before it sends a notification to the applicant under Rule 20.4(i) shall be considered to have been received within that time limit.

In the case of correction of an erroneous filed document, the same time limit is applicable as in the case of subsequent filing of missing parts. The time limit is not extendable (PCT/GL/RO/20 No. 46). 38

20.5*bis*	Erroneously filed elements and parts
R. 29.4(b)	For R. 20.7(a)(i), an invitation under R. 29.4(b) shall be deemed to be an invitation under R. 20.3(a)(ii).
R. 82*ter*.1(b)	Effects of incorporation by reference at the national phase. The designated Offices may, under certain conditions, review the incorporation allowed by the receiving Office.
AIs 309	Procedure in the case of later submitted sheets furnished for the purposes of incorporation by reference
AIs 310	Procedure in the case of later submitted sheets not furnished for the purposes of incorporation by reference
AIs 310*bis*	Procedure in the case of later submitted sheets resulting in the correction of the international filing date under R. 20.5(c) or 20.5*bis(c)*
AIs 310*ter*	Procedure in the case of later submitted sheets furnished after expiration of the applicable time limit referred to in R. 20.7
AIs 335	Procedure relating to sequence listings

20.8 Incompatibility with National Laws

(a) If, on October 5, 2005, any of Rules 20.3(a)(ii) and (b)(ii), 20.5(a)(ii) and (d), and 20.6 *(incorporation by reference)* are not compatible with the national law applied by the receiving Office, the Rules concerned shall not apply to an international application filed with that receiving Office for as long as they continue not to be compatible with that law, provided that the said Office informs the International Bureau accordingly by April 5, 2006. The information received shall be promptly published by the International Bureau in the Gazette.

Notifications concerning R. 20.8(a) have been received from CU, CZ, DE, ID, KR, MX (status January 20, 2021). 39

(a-*bis*) If, on October 9, 2019, any of Rules 20.5*bis*(a)(ii) and (d) are not compatible with the national law applied by the receiving Office, the Rules concerned shall not apply to an international application filed with that receiving Office for as long as they continue not to be compatible with that law, provided that the said Office informs the International Bureau accordingly by April 9, 2020. The information received shall be promptly published by the International Bureau in the Gazette.

40 Member States which have declared reservations in respect of R. 20.8(a-*bis*) are invited to apply, at the request of the applicant, the procedure under R. 19.4(a)(iii) (PCT/A/51/4, No. 17 in conjunction with PCT/A/51/2, No. 7, p. 3. PCT/A/51/2, No. 7 p. 3). The applicant may request the receiving Office which has declared a reservation to transmit the PCTa to the International Bureau which has not declared a reservation (AG-IP 6.027).

41 Reservations concerning R. 20.8(a-*bis*) have been received from CL, CU, CZ, DE, ES, FR, ID, KR, MX (status on January 20, 2024). Announcement of compatibility at the EPO as of November 1, 2022 (Gazette July 7, 2022, p. 173; annotations under R. 20.5*bis*(e)).

42 [In September and October 2019] 'The Assembly of the PCT Union: […] (ii) adopted the Understanding set out in para. 7 of document PCT/A/51/2' (PCT/A/51/4, p. 5, para. 17). (Paragraph 7 (a) of document PCT/A/51/2) (a) 'In adopting new Rule 20.8(a-*bis*), the Assembly agreed that, where a correct element or part cannot be incorporated by reference under Rules 20.5*bis*(a)(ii) and (d) because of the operation of Rule 20.8(a-*bis*), the receiving Office concerned and the International Bureau shall agree, under Rule 19.4(a)(iii), with the authorization of the applicant, that the procedures under Rule 19.4 shall apply, in which case the international application shall, subject to Rule 19.4(b), be considered to have been received by that Office on behalf of the International Bureau as receiving Office under Rule 19.1(a)(iii).' The understanding of the PCT Assembly has been published in Gazette March 5, 2020.

(a-*ter*) Where an element or a part cannot be incorporated by reference in the international application under Rules 4.18 and 20.6 because of the operation of paragraph (a) or paragraph (a-*bis*) of this Rule, the receiving Office shall proceed as provided for in Rule 20.3(b)(i), 20.5(b), 20.5(c), 20.5*bis*(b) or 20.5*bis*(c), as the case may be. Where the receiving Office proceeds as provided for in Rule 20.5(c) or 20.5*bis*(c), the applicant may proceed as provided for in Rule 20.5(e) or 20.5*bis*(e), as the case may be.

(b) If, on October 5, 2005, any of Rules 20.3(a)(ii) and (b)(ii), 20.5(a)(ii) and (d), and 20.6 *(incorporation by reference)* are not compatible with the national law applied by the designated Office, the Rules concerned shall not apply in respect of that Office in relation to an international application in respect of which the acts referred to in Article 22 have been performed before that Office for as long as they continue not to be compatible with that law, provided that the said Office

informs the International Bureau accordingly by April 5, 2006. The information received shall be promptly published by the International Bureau in the Gazette.

Notifications concerning R. 20.8(b) have been received from CU, CZ, DE, ID, KR, MX, TR (status January 20, 2024). CN has withdrawn its notification of incompatibility as from January 20, 2024 (Gazette January 18, 2024, p. 17) 43

(b-*bis*) If, on October 9, 2019, any of Rules 20.5*bis*(a)(ii) and (d) are not compatible with the national law applied by the designated Office, the Rules concerned shall not apply in respect of that Office in relation to an international application in respect of which the acts referred to in Article 22 have been performed before that Office for as long as they continue not to be compatible with that law, provided that the said Office informs the International Bureau accordingly by April 9, 2020. The information received shall be promptly published by the International Bureau in the Gazette.

Notifications concerning R. 20.8(b-*bis*) have been received from CL, CU, CZ, DE, ES, ID, KR, MX, TR (status January 20, 2024). Announcement of compatibility at the EPO as from November 1, 2022 (Gazette July 7, 2022, p. 173). CN has withdrawn its notification of incompatibility as from January 20, 2024 (Gazette January 18, 2024, p. 17) 44

(c) Where an element or part is considered to have been incorporated by reference in the international application by virtue of a finding of the receiving Office under Rule 20.6(b), but that incorporation by reference does not apply to the international application for the purposes of the procedure before a designated Office because of the operation of paragraph (b) or paragraph (b-*bis*) of this Rule, the designated Office may treat the application as if the international filing date had been accorded under Rule 20.3(b)(i), 20.5(b) or 20.5*bis*(b), or corrected under Rule 20.5(c) or 20.5*bis*(c), as the case may be, provided that Rule 82*ter*.1(c) and (d) shall apply *mutatis mutandis*.

An 'Understanding of the PCT Assembly' has been published in Gazette January 18, 2007: 'In connection with the adoption of amended Rules 20.8(c) and 76.5, the Assembly noted that: (a) where an element or part is considered to have been incorporated by reference in the international application by virtue of a finding of the receiving Office under Rule 20.6(b), but that incorporation by reference does not apply to the international application for the purposes of the procedure before a designated or elected Office because of the operation of Rule 20.8(b), the time limit for performing the acts referred to in Articles 22 and 39 before such designated or elected Office would be calculated on the basis of the priority date referred to in Article 2(xi) having due regard to the international filing date as accorded by the receiving Office; and (b) the same should apply where that incorporation by reference does not apply to the international application for the purposes of the procedure before a designated or elected Office because of the operation of Rule 82*ter*.1(b) as adopted by 45 the Assembly in October 2005 with effect from April 1, 2007.' (PCT/A35/7 p.3, Annex IV, https://www.wipo.int/edocs/mdocs/govbody/en/pct_a_35/pct_a_35_7.pdf).

R. 76.5 Application before the elected Office

Rule 21
Preparation of Copies

21.1 Responsibility of the Receiving Office

(a) Where the international application is required to be filed in one copy, the receiving Office shall be responsible for preparing the home copy and the search copy required under Article 12(1).

(b) Where the international application is required to be filed in two copies, the receiving Office shall be responsible for preparing the home copy.

(c) If the international application is filed in less than the number of copies required under Rule 11.1(b), the receiving Office shall be responsible for the prompt preparation of the number of copies required, and shall have the right to fix a fee for performing that task and to collect such fee from the applicant.

21.2 Certified Copy for the Applicant

Against payment of a fee, the receiving Office shall furnish to the applicant, on request, certified copies of the international application as filed and of any corrections thereto.

Art. 3(1) RFees For the fee at the EPO see code 029 https://www.epo.org/en/applying/fees/international-fees/important-fees.

Rule 22
Transmittal of the Record Copy and Translation

22.1 Procedure

(a) If the determination under Article 11(1) *(accordance of a filing date)* is positive, and unless prescriptions concerning national security prevent the international application from being treated as such, the receiving Office shall transmit the record copy to the International Bureau. Such transmittal shall be effected promptly after receipt of the international application or, if a check to preserve national security must be performed, as soon as the necessary clearance has been obtained. In any case, the receiving Office shall transmit the record copy in time for it to reach the International Bureau by the expiration of the 13th month from the priority date. If the transmittal is effected by mail, the receiving Office shall mail the record copy not later than five days prior to the expiration of the 13th month from the priority date.

Art. 12(1)	Transmittal of record copy
Art. 27(8)	National security prescriptions, notes referring to state secret
AIs 305	Identifying the copies of the PCTa
AIs 330	Transmittal of record copy prevented or delayed by national security prescriptions
EPO	Transmission of the PCT Direct letter with the PCTa to the International Bureau, see annotations to R. 43*bis*.1(c) and OJ EPO 2017 A21

(b) If the International Bureau has received a copy of the notification under Rule 20.2(c) *(notification of file number and application date)* but is not, by the expiration of 13 months from the priority date, in possession of the record copy, it shall remind the receiving Office that it should transmit the record copy to the International Bureau promptly.

(c) If the International Bureau has received a copy of the notification under Rule 20.2(c) *(notification of file number and application date)* but is not, by the expiration of 14 months from the priority date, in possession of the record copy, it shall notify the applicant and the receiving Office accordingly.

(d) After the expiration of 14 months from the priority date, the applicant may request the receiving Office to certify a copy of his international application as being identical with the international application as filed and may transmit such certified copy to the International Bureau.

(e) Any certification under paragraph (d) shall be free of charge and may be refused only on any of the following grounds:

- (i) the copy which the receiving Office has been requested to certify is not identical with the international application as filed;
- (ii) prescriptions concerning national security prevent the international application from being treated as such;
- (iii) the receiving Office has already transmitted the record copy to the International Bureau and that Bureau has informed the receiving Office that it has received the record copy.

(f) Unless the International Bureau has received the record copy, or until it receives the record copy, the copy certified under paragraph (e) and received by the International Bureau shall be considered to be the record copy.

(g) If, by the expiration of the time limit applicable under Article 22 *(20/21 months)*, the applicant has performed the acts referred to in that Article but the designated Office has not been informed by the International Bureau of the receipt of the record copy, the designated Office shall inform the International Bureau. If the International Bureau is not in possession of the record copy, it shall promptly notify the applicant and the receiving Office unless it has already notified them under paragraph (c).

R. 76.5 Application before the elected Office

(h) Where the international application is to be published in the language of a translation furnished under Rule 12.3 or 12.4, that translation shall be transmitted by the receiving Office to the International Bureau together with the record copy under paragraph (a) or, if the receiving Office has already transmitted the record copy to the International Bureau under that paragraph, promptly after receipt of the translation.

22.2 [Deleted]

22.3 Time Limit under Article 12(3)

The time limit referred to in Article 12(3) *(delayed transmittal to International Bureau)* shall be three months from the date of the notification sent by the International Bureau to the applicant under Rule 22.1(c) *(reminder to send copy)* or (g).

1 For statements of WIPO concerning R. 22.3, see PCT/CAL/II/9, p.4 para. 21 (https://www.wipo.int/edocs/mdocs/pct/en/pct_cal_ii/pct_cal_ii_9.pdf) and PCT/A/XI/9, p.5, para. 28 (https://www.wipo.int/edocs/mdocs/govbody/en/pct_a_xi/pct_a_xi_9.pdf).

Rule 23
Transmittal of the Search Copy, Translation and Sequence Listing

23.1 Procedure

(a) Where no translation of the international application is required under Rule 12.3(a) *(translation for the international search)*, the search copy shall be transmitted by the receiving Office to the International Searching Authority at the latest on the same day *(R. 22, 13 months from priority date)* as the record copy is transmitted to the International *(R. 22.1(a))* Bureau unless no search fee has been paid. In the latter case, it shall be transmitted promptly after payment of the search fee.

(b) Where a translation of the international application is furnished under Rule 12.3, a copy of that translation and of the request, which together shall be considered to be the search copy under Article 12(1), shall be transmitted by the receiving Office to the International Searching Authority, unless no search fee has been paid. In the latter case, a copy of the said translation and of the request shall be transmitted promptly after payment of the search fee.

Art. 12(1)	Definition of search copy and record copy
R. 22.1(a)	Transmittal of record copy and translation to International Bureau
EPO	For transmission of the PCT Direct letter with the PCTa to the EPO, see annotation to R. 43*bis*.1(c) and OJ EOP 2017 A21.

(c) Any sequence listing in electronic form which is furnished for the purposes of Rule 13ter but submitted to the receiving Office instead of the International Searching Authority shall be promptly transmitted by that Office to that Authority.

R. 5.2	Sequence listings disclosure
R. 13*ter*	Procedure for sequence listings
EPO	Filing sequence listings in the EPO OJ EPO 2021 A96, A97

Rule 23*bis*
Transmittal of Documents Relating to Earlier Search or Classification

23*bis*.1 Transmittal of Documents Relating to Earlier Search in Case of Request under Rule 4.12

(a) The receiving Office shall transmit to the International Searching Authority, together with the search copy, any copy referred to in Rule 12*bis*.1(a) related to an earlier search in respect of which the applicant has made a request under Rule 4.12, provided that any such copy:

(i) has been submitted by the applicant to the receiving Office together with the international application;

(ii) has been requested by the applicant to be prepared and transmitted by the receiving Office to that Authority; or

(iii) is available to the receiving Office in a form and manner acceptable to it, for example, from a digital library, in accordance with Rule 12*bis*.1(d).

(b) If it is not included in the copy of the results of the earlier search referred to in Rule 12*bis*.1(a), the receiving Office shall also transmit to the International Searching Authority, together with the search copy, a copy of the results of any earlier classification effected by that Office, if already available.

R. 4.12	Taking into account of results of earlier search
R. 12*bis*.1	Furnishing by the applicant of documents relating to earlier search in case of request under R. 4.12

23*bis*.2 Transmittal of Documents Relating to Earlier Search or Classification for the Purposes of Rule 41.2

(a) For the purposes of Rule 41.2, where the international application claims the priority of one or more earlier applications filed with the same Office as that which is acting as the receiving Office and that Office has carried out an earlier search in respect of such an earlier application or has classified such earlier application, the receiving Office shall, subject to Article 30(2)(a) as applicable by virtue of Article 30(3) and paragraphs (b), (d) and (e), transmit to the

International Searching Authority, together with the search copy, a copy of the results of any such earlier search, in whatever form (for example, in the form of a search report, a listing of cited prior art or an examination report) they are available to the Office, and a copy of the results of any such earlier classification effected by the Office, if already available. The receiving Office may, subject to Article 30(2)(a) as applicable by virtue of Article 30(3), also transmit to the International Searching Authority any further documents relating to such an earlier search which it considers useful to that Authority for the purposes of carrying out the international search.

Art. 30(2)(a)	No file access before the national Office before international publication
Art. 30(3)	Validity before receiving Offices
R. 94.1*bis*	File access before the receiving Office after international publication
R. 41	Taking into account the results of an earlier search in the case of the request under R. 4.12: if carried out by the same ISA, results must be taken into account (R. 41.1(i)), if carried out by another ISA or another Office, results may be taken into account (R. 41.1(ii)). In addition, the search results shall be taken into account in the case of claimed priority of an earlier application from the same Office and earlier search by the same Office (R. 41.2(a)). In other cases, the ISA may take into account the results under R. 41.2(b).

(b) Notwithstanding paragraph (a), a receiving Office may notify the International Bureau by April 14, 2016 that it may, on request of the applicant submitted together with the international application, decide not to transmit the results of an earlier search to the International Searching Authority. The International Bureau shall publish any notification under this provision in the Gazette.

Notifications regarding R. 23*bis*.2(b) have been received from DE, FI, SE (PCT Gazette of October 20, 2016, p. 204). It is possible for the applicant to request these Offices not to forward the relevant documents (AG-IP 5.073C; see continuation sheet No. VII 2.2, PCT/RO/101/). 1

(c) At the option of the receiving Office, paragraph (a) shall apply *mutatis mutandis* where the international application claims the priority of one or more earlier applications filed with an Office different from the one which is acting as the receiving Office and that Office has carried out an earlier search in respect of such an earlier application or has classified such earlier application, and the results of any such earlier search or classification are available to the receiving Office in a form and manner acceptable to it, for example, from a digital library.

(d) Paragraphs (a) and (c) shall not apply where the earlier search was carried out by the same International Searching Authority or by the same Office as that which is acting as the International Searching Authority, or where the receiving Office is aware that a copy of the earlier search or classification results is available to the International Searching Authority in a form and manner acceptable to it, for example, from a digital library.

(e) To the extent that, on October 14, 2015, the transmission of the copies referred to in paragraph (a), or the transmission of such copies in a particular form, such as those referred to in paragraph (a), without the authorization by the applicant is not compatible with the national law applied by the receiving Office, that paragraph shall not apply to the transmission of such copies, or to the transmission of such copies in the particular form concerned, in respect of any international application filed with that receiving Office for as long as such transmission without the authorization by the applicant continues not to be compatible with that law, provided that the said Office informs the International Bureau accordingly by April 14, 2016. The information received shall be promptly published by the International Bureau in the Gazette.

R. 41.2 Taking into account results of an earlier search and classification in other cases. Declarations concerning R. 23*bis*.2(c) have been received from AU, CZ, FI, HU, IL, JP, NO, SE, SG, US (PCT Gazette of October 20, 2016, p. 210 ff.). Nevertheless, it is possible for these Offices that the applicant agrees to transmission by marking the continuation sheet for No. VII 2.3, Form PCT/RO/101 (AG-IP 5.073A).

Rule 24
Receipt of the Record Copy by the International Bureau

24.1 [Deleted]

24.2 Notification of Receipt of the Record Copy

(a) The International Bureau shall promptly notify:

(i) the applicant,

(ii) the receiving Office, and

(iii) the International Searching Authority (unless it has informed the International Bureau that it wishes not to be so notified),

of the fact and the date of receipt of the record copy. The notification shall identify the international application by its number, the international filing date and the name of the applicant, and shall indicate the filing date of any earlier application whose priority is claimed. The notification sent to the applicant shall also contain a list of the designated Offices and, in the case of a designated Office which is responsible for granting regional patents, of the Contracting States designated for such regional patent.

R. 90*bis*.2 Withdrawal of designations

The applicant can check the correct designations especially in case of withdrawal or exclusion of certain designations (DE/JP/KR) (AG-IP 9.003 https://www.wipo.int/export/sites/www/pct/guide/en/gdvol1/pdf/gdvol1.pdf). 1

(b) [Deleted]

(c) If the record copy is received after the expiration of the time limit fixed in Rule 22.3, the International Bureau shall promptly notify the applicant, the receiving Office, and the International Searching Authority, accordingly.

Rule 25
Receipt of the Search Copy by the International Searching Authority

25.1 Notification of Receipt of the Search Copy

The International Searching Authority shall promptly notify the International Bureau, the applicant, and – unless the International Searching Authority is the same as the receiving Office – the receiving Office, of the fact and the date of receipt of the search copy.

Art. 12	Transmittal of the international application to the International Bureau and the ISA
R. 12.1	Transmission to ISA is effected by receiving Office provided that certain conditions are fulfilled. Omission of payment of fees or of translation may cause delay in the establishment of the ISR (AG-IP 6.059 https://www.wipo.int/export/sites/www/pct/guide/en/gdvol1/pdf/gdvol1.pdf).
R. 23.1	Procedure of transmittal of search copy, translation and sequence listing
R. 25.1	Notification of receipt of search copy
AIs 412	Notification of lack of transmittal of search copy

Rule 26
Checking by, and Correcting before, the Receiving Office of Certain Elements of the International Application

This Rule refers to the checking of elements of the PCTa after the accordance of an international filing date by the receiving Office. See the overview in the Introduction to Art. 14. 1

26.1 Invitation under Article 14(1)(b) to Correct

The receiving Office shall issue the invitation to correct provided for in Article 14(1)(b) as soon as possible, preferably within one month from the receipt of the international application. In the invitation, the receiving Office shall invite the applicant to furnish the required correction, and give the applicant the opportunity to make observations, within the time limit under Rule 26.2.

A correction is also possible on the applicant's own initiative without a request (Pract. Adv. NL 06/2007). 2

26.2 Time Limit for Correction

The time limit referred to in Rule 26.1 shall be two months from the date of the invitation to correct. It may be extended by the receiving Office at any time before a decision is taken.

The wording allows an extension of the time limit even after the expiry of the time limit. 3

26.2*bis* Checking of Requirements under Article 14(1)(a)(i) and (ii)

(a) For the purposes of Article 14(1)(a)(i), if there is more than one applicant, it shall be sufficient that the request be signed by one of them.

It is irrelevant which applicant signs and whether that applicant is entitled by virtue of his nationality or residence to file an application at the receiving Office or whether he is entitled at all. Although the Rule expressly refers only to the application form, 4 it is generally assumed that it is sufficient for an agent to sign the application form, provided he submits a power of attorney from at least one applicant (Reischle, *Mitteilungen der deutschen Patentanwälte* 2004, 533).

R. 4.15	Signature by all applicants
R. 51*bis*.1(a)(vi)	Designated Office may require missing signatures
R. 60.1(a-*ter*)	Corresponding requirements for the purposes of R. 53.8 (demand under Chapter II)
R. 90.4, 90.5	Waiver of submission of powers of attorney
R. 90*bis*	No waiver in case of declaration of withdrawal

(b) For the purposes of Article 14(1)(a)(ii), if there is more than one applicant, it shall be sufficient that the indications required under Rule 4.5(a)(ii) and (iii) be provided in respect of one of them who is entitled according to Rule 19.1 to file the international application with the receiving Office.

R. 60.1(a-*bis*)	Formal requirements for the demand under Chapter II

26.3 Checking of Physical Requirements under Article 14(1)(a)(v)

(a) Where the international application is filed in a language of publication, the receiving Office shall check:

(i) the international application for compliance with the physical requirements referred to in Rule 11 only to the extent that compliance therewith is necessary for the purpose of reasonably uniform international publication;

(ii) *(in force until June 30, 2024)* any translation furnished under Rule 12.3 for compliance with the physical requirements referred to in Rule 11 to the extent that compliance therewith is necessary for the purpose of satisfactory reproduction.

(ii) *(in force as from July 1, 2024)* any translation furnished under Rule 12.3 or 26.3*ter* for compliance with the physical requirements referred to in Rule 11 to the extent that compliance therewith is necessary for the purpose of satisfactory reproduction.

5 A reference to R. 26.3*ter* has been added on July 1, 2024. Amendments apply to PCTa with an international filing date that is on or after that date (PCT/A/55/2). See annotations to R. 26.3*ter*.

(b) Where the international application is filed in a language which is not a language of publication, the receiving Office shall check:

(i) the international application for compliance with the physical requirements referred to in Rule 11 only to the extent that compliance therewith is necessary for the purpose of satisfactory reproduction;

(ii) *(in force until June 30, 2024)* any translation furnished under Rule 12.3 or 12.4 and the drawings for compliance with the physical requirements referred to in Rule 11 to the extent that compliance therewith is necessary for the purpose of reasonably uniform international publication.

(ii) *(in force as from July 1, 2024)* any translation furnished under Rule 12.3, 12.4 or 26.3*ter* and the drawings for compliance with the physical requirements referred to in Rule 11 to the extent that compliance therewith is necessary for the purpose of reasonably uniform international publication.

A reference to R. 26.3*ter* has been added on July 1, 2024. Amendments apply to PCTa with an international filing date that is on or after that date (PCT/A/55/2). See annotations to R. 26.3*ter*. 6

26.3*bis* Invitation under Article 14(1)(b) to Correct Defects under Rule 11

The receiving Office shall not be required to issue the invitation under Article 14(1)(b) to correct a defect under Rule 11 where the physical requirements referred to in that Rule are complied with to the extent required under Rule 26.3.

AIs 108	Correspondence intended for the applicant
AIs Part 7	Electronic transmission of communications
AIs 704(d)	Consequences of missing signature

26.3*ter* Invitation to Correct Defects under Article 3(4)(i)

(a) *(in force until June 30, 2024)* Where the abstract or any text matter of the drawings is filed in a language which is different from the language of the description and the claims, the receiving Office shall, unless

(a) *(in force as from July 1, 2024)* Where the abstract or any text matter of the drawings is filed in a language which is different from the language, subject to Rules 12.1*bis* and 26.3*ter*(e), of the description and the claims, the receiving Office shall, unless

(i) a translation of the international application is required under Rule 12.3(a) *(for international search)*, or

(ii) the abstract or the text matter of the drawings is in the language in which the international application is to be published,

invite the applicant to furnish a translation of the abstract or the text matter of the drawings into the language in which the international application is to be published. Rules 26.1 *(invitation to correct defects)*, 26.2 *(time limit for correction of defects)*, 26.3, 26.3*bis*, 26.5 *(legal consequences)* and 29.1 *(finding by receiving Office)* shall apply *mutatis mutandis*.

A reference to new R. 26.3*ter*(e) has been added on July 1, 2024. Amendments apply to PCTa with an international filing date that is on or after that date (PCT/A/55/2). Para. (a) applies in the rare cases where an applicant furnishes the translation of 7 the mixed-language claims and description into a single language that is not the same language as the abstract and/or text matter of the drawings. Accordingly, the receiving Office invites the applicant to file a translation of the abstract and/or text matter of the drawings into this single language. This will ensure that the entire PCTa is available to the receiving Office in a single language, also for the purpose of search and publication. The aim of the amendments is to provide a clear legal basis for the receiving Office to request a translation and harmonize the procedure (PCT/WG/16/8).

8 Further amendments have been proposed to enter into force on July 1, 2025 in order to limit the scope of exceptions from the requirement of the receiving Office to invite to furnish a translation of abstract and text matter of drawings into the language in which the PCTa is to be published ensuring that the PCTa is published in a single language (PCT/A/56/2). For earlier statements of WIPO concerning R. 26.3*ter*(a) see PCT/A/XVIII/9, p.4 para. 23 (https://www.wipo.int/edocs/mdocs/govbody/en/pct_a_xviii/pct_a_xviii_9.pdf).

Art. 3(4)(i)	Requires using the prescribed language in the PCTa (annotations in Introduction)
R. 12	Language of the PCTa and translations for international search and publication
AIs 308	Marking of sheets of the PCTa and the translation thereof under R. 12.3, 12.4, 20.4 and 26.3*ter*(e)

(b) If, on October 1, 1997, paragraph (a) is not compatible with the national law applied by the receiving Office, paragraph (a) shall not apply to that receiving Office for as long as it continues not to be compatible with that law, provided that the said Office informs the International Bureau accordingly by December 31, 1997. The information received shall be promptly published by the International Bureau in the Gazette.

9 A reservation by the US has been published.

(c) Where the request does not comply with Rule 12.1(c) *(language)*, the receiving Office shall invite the applicant to file a translation so as to comply with that Rule. Rules 3 *(request)*, 26.1 *(invitation to correct defects)*, 26.2 *(time limit for correction of defects)*, 26.5*(legal consequences)* and 29.1 *(finding by receiving Office)* shall apply *mutatis mutandis*.

(d) If, on October 1, 1997, paragraph (c) is not compatible with the national law applied by the receiving Office, paragraph (c) shall not apply to that receiving Office for as long as it continues not to be compatible with that law, provided that the said Office informs the International Bureau accordingly by December 31, 1997. The information received shall be promptly published by the International Bureau in the Gazette.

(e) *(in force from July 1, 2024)* Where the description of an international application is filed in a language which is different from the language of the claims,

or parts of the description or parts of the claims are filed in a language which is different from the language of the remainder of this element, and where all such languages are accepted by the receiving Office under Rule 12.1(a), the receiving Office shall, as appropriate, invite the applicant to furnish, within one month of the date of receipt of the international application by the receiving Office, a translation of the description or the claims, or any part thereof, such that the description and claims are in a single language which is all of the following:

(i) one of the languages contained in the description or claims as filed;

(ii) a language accepted by the International Searching Authority that is to carry out the international search; and

(iii) the language in which the international application is to be published.

Rule 12.3(c) to (e) shall apply *mutatis mutandis.*

New para. (e) has been added on July 1, 2024. Amendments apply to PCTa with an international filing date that is on or after that date (PCT/A/55/2). The Rule ensures that the receiving Office can invite the applicant to furnish a translation of the description or claims. With the wording 'as appropriate' the scope of the Rule does not extend to cases where more than one language is required for the proper understanding of the claimed invention. This applies where the International Bureau acts as receiving Office and no text in a language of publication is included in the PCTa. The International Bureau invites the applicant to specify a language of publication into which the applicant will supply a translation of the entire claims and description (PCT/WG/16/8 p.3 and Annexes). 10

A reservation by the US has been published. 11

R. 12.3(c)	Invitation to furnish within one month, further time limit and fee
R. 12.3(d)	In case of non-compliance PCTa is declared withdrawn
R. 12.3(e)	Late furnishing fee
AIs 305*bis*	Preparation, identification, transmittal of copies of the translation of the PCTa. under R. 12.3, 12.4 and 26.3*ter*(e). Amendments in force from July 1, 2024 (Circular C. PCT 1668, 1664).
AIs 308	Marking of sheets of the PCTa and the translation thereof under R. 12.3, 12.4, 20.4 and 26.3*ter*(e)
RO Guidelines	Promulgation of new 65A to 65D and further amendments in PCT Circular C.PCT 1674 referring to C.PCT 1671 with effect from July1, 2024. If not all three criteria under para. (e) can be satisfied the applicant is invited to furnish a translation of the PCTa under R. 12.3 or 12.4.
Pract. Adv. NL 7–8/2024	If the applicant believes that certain words cannot or should not be translated but is invited to furnish a translation the applicant should contact the receiving Office.

26.4 Procedure

A correction of the request offered to the receiving Office may be stated in a letter addressed to that Office if the correction is of such a nature that it can be transferred from the letter to the request without adversely affecting the clarity and the direct reproducibility of the sheet on to which the correction is to be transferred; otherwise, and in the case of a correction of any element of the international application other than the request, the applicant shall be required to submit a replacement sheet embodying the correction and the letter accompanying the replacement sheet shall draw attention to the differences between the replaced sheet and the replacement sheet.

AIs 325, 413, 217	Correction of defects and obvious mistakes
AIs 335	Procedure for sequence listings
R. 91	Rectification of obvious mistakes
R. 9.2	Correction of expressions or drawings
R. 26.4	Procedure for correction of request to the receiving Office

26.5 Decision of the Receiving Office

The receiving Office shall decide whether the applicant has submitted the correction within the applicable time limit under Rule 26.2, and, if the correction has been submitted within that time limit, whether the international application so corrected is or is not to be considered withdrawn, provided that no international application shall be considered withdrawn for lack of compliance with the physical requirements referred to in Rule 11 if it complies with those requirements to the extent necessary for the purpose of reasonably uniform international publication.

R. 48	International publication

Rule 26*bis*
Correction or Addition of Priority Claim

26*bis*.1 Correction or Addition of Priority Claim

(a) The applicant may correct a priority claim or add a priority claim to the request by a notice submitted to the receiving Office or the International Bureau within a time limit of 16 months from the priority date or, where the correction or addition would cause a change in the priority date, 16 months from the priority date as so changed, whichever 16-month period expires first, provided that such a notice may be submitted until the expiration of four months from the international filing date. The correction of a priority claim may include the addition of any indication referred to in Rule 4.10 *(priority claim)*.

PCT Newsletter 9/98 legal advice: the later of four months from filing date or 16 months from priority date is relevant. 1

AIs 314, 402	Correction or addition of a priority claim
R. 52(3) EPC	Allows a correction of the priority claim
R. 26*bis*.2(e)	Correction or addition of priority claim after the time limit of R. 26*bis*.1(a)

(b) Any notice referred to in paragraph (a) received by the receiving Office or the International Bureau after the applicant has made a request for early publication under Article 21(2)(b) shall be considered not to have been submitted, unless that request is withdrawn before the technical preparations for international publication have been completed.

(c) Where the correction or addition of a priority claim causes a change in the priority date, any time limit which is computed from the previously applicable priority date and which has not already expired shall be computed from the priority date as so changed.

Art. 21(5)	Completion of the technical preparations
R. 90*bis*.3(e)	Withdrawal of priority claims

R. 91.1(g)(iv)	Correction of priority claim due to obvious mistake can only be performed under R. 91 as long as the priority date does not change

26*bis*.2 Defects in Priority Claims

(a) Where the receiving Office or, if the receiving Office fails to do so, the International Bureau, finds in relation to a priority claim:

(i) that the international application has an international filing date which is later than the date on which the priority period expired and that a request for restoration of the right of priority under Rule 26*bis*.3 has not been submitted;

(ii) that the priority claim does not comply with the requirements of Rule 4.10 *(claiming a priority)*; or

(iii) that any indication in the priority claim is inconsistent with the corresponding indication appearing in the priority document;

the receiving Office or the International Bureau, as the case may be, shall invite the applicant to correct the priority claim. In the case referred to in item (i), where the international filing date is within two months from the date on which the priority period expired, the receiving Office or the International Bureau, as the case may be, shall also notify the applicant of the possibility of submitting a request for the restoration of the right of priority in accordance with Rule 26*bis*.3, unless the receiving Office has notified the International Bureau under Rule 26*bis*.3(j) of the incompatibility of Rule 26*bis*.3(a) to (i) with the national law applied by that Office.

(b) If the applicant does not, before the expiration of the time limit under Rule 26*bis*.1(a), submit a notice correcting the priority claim, that priority claim shall, subject to paragraph (c), for the purposes of the procedure under the Treaty, be considered not to have been made ("considered void") and the receiving Office or the International Bureau, as the case may be, shall so declare and shall inform the applicant accordingly. Any notice correcting the priority claim which is received before the receiving Office or the International Bureau, as the case may be, so declares and not later than one month after the expiration of that time limit shall be considered to have been received before the expiration of that time limit.

R. 26*bis*.1(a), R. 26*bis*.2(b)2	Time limit 16 months from priority or four months from filing date plus one month
AIs 302, 409	Priority claim considered not to have been made

(c) A priority claim shall not be considered void only because:

(i) the indication of the number of the earlier application referred to in Rule 4.10(a)(ii) is missing;

(ii) an indication in the priority claim is inconsistent with the corresponding indication appearing in the priority document; or

(iii) the international application has an international filing date which is later than the date on which the priority period expired, provided that the international filing date is within the period of two months from that date.

R. 26*bis*.3	Relation to the restoration of right of priority by receiving Office
R. 26*bis*.2(c)(iii)	governs, according to para. (a)(i), the case where no request for restoration of priority has been filed. R. 26*bis*.3 governs the case where the applicant has filed a request for restoration.
R 26*bis*.1(c)	The claimed priority date is relevant for the calculation of time limits in the international phase, as the cut-off date for prior art at the time of the written opinion of ISA (R. 43*bis*.1(b), R. 64(b)) and IPEA (R. 64.1(b)(iii)) and for the time limit for entry into the national or regional phases according to Art. 22 and 39. Effectiveness is irrelevant.

(d) Where the receiving Office or the International Bureau has made a declaration under paragraph (b) or where the priority claim has not been considered void only because paragraph (c) applies, the International Bureau shall publish, together with the international application, information concerning the priority claim as prescribed by the Administrative Instructions, as well as any information submitted by the applicant concerning such priority claim which is received by the International Bureau prior to the completion of the technical preparations for international publication. Such information shall be included in the communication under Article 20 where the international application is not published by virtue of Article 64(3).

(e) Where the applicant wishes to correct or add a priority claim but the time limit under Rule 26*bis*.1 has expired, the applicant may, prior to the expiration of 30 months from the priority date and subject to the payment of a special fee whose amount shall be fixed in the Administrative Instructions, request the International Bureau to publish information concerning the matter, and the International Bureau shall promptly publish such information.

Art. 21(5)	Completion of technical preparations
AIs 113	Special fees: Annex B (IB) AG-IP. The fee is payable to the International Bureau.

26*bis*.3 Restoration of Right of Priority by Receiving Office

(a) Where the international application has an international filing date which is later than the date on which the priority period expired but within the period of two months from that date, the receiving Office shall, on the request of the applicant, and subject to paragraphs (b) to (g) of this Rule, restore the right of priority if the Office finds that a criterion applied by it ("criterion for restoration")

is satisfied, namely, that the failure to file the international application within the priority period:

(i) occurred in spite of due care required by the circumstances having been taken; or

(ii) was unintentional.

Each receiving Office shall apply at least one of those criteria and may apply both of them.

R. 26*bis*.1	Filing date within priority period, addition of a priority claim
R. 26*bis*.3	Filing date after priority period
R. 49*ter*	Review of the observance of due care before the designated Office
EP: Art. 122(1) EPC	Comparable requirements for excusing missed time limits, J13/16 point 4.6 et seq. The wording 'all due care required under the circumstances' calls for a stricter standard under the EPC as compared to the PCT in R. 26*bis*.3 and R. 49*ter* (Teschemacher, Mitteilungen der deutschen Patentanwälte 2019, 311 (316), compare AG-NP EP.28, status April 1, 2022). receiving Office and designated Office accept requests.
DE	does not accept this requests, R. 26*bis*.3(j)
CN	applies 'unintentional' as designated Office and as receiving Office 'due care' and 'unintentional'
JP	applies as receiving Office and designated Office 'unintentional'
KR	does not accept this requests, R. 26*bis*.3(j)
US	applies as receiving Office and designated Office 'unintentional'
List of Offices:	https://www.wipo.int/pct/en/texts/restoration.html#D

2 See also annotations on the effect in the national phase in the Introductuon to R. 49*ter*. For statements of WIPO concerning R. 26*bis*.3(a) see PCT/A/34/6, p.57 Annex IV, p.1, para. 3 (https://www.wipo.int/edocs/mdocs/govbody/en/pct_a_34/pct_a_34_6.pdf).

(b) A request under paragraph (a) shall:

(i) be filed with the receiving Office within the time limit applicable under paragraph (e);

(ii) state the reasons for the failure to file the international application within the priority period; and

(iii) preferably be accompanied by any declaration or other evidence required under paragraph (f).

(c) Where a priority claim in respect of the earlier application is not contained in the international application, the applicant shall submit, within the time limit applicable under paragraph (e), a notice under Rule 26*bis*.1(a) adding the priority claim.

(d) The submission of a request under paragraph (a) may be subjected by the receiving Office to the payment to it, for its own benefit, of a fee for requesting restoration, payable within the time limit applicable under paragraph (e). The amount of that fee, if any, shall be fixed by the receiving Office. The time limit for payment of the fee may be extended, at the option of the receiving Office, for a period of up to two months from the expiration of the time limit applicable under paragraph (e).

AG-IP Annex C	Fee for requesting restoration of right of priority
Art. 2(1) RFees No. 13 (Code 013):	For the fee at the EPO see https://www.epo.org/en/applying/fees/international-fees/important-fees. No fee is payable at the International Bureau (R. 26*bis*.3(d)) Annex C (IB).

(e) The time limit referred to in paragraphs (b)(i), (c) and (d) shall be two months from the date on which the priority period expired, provided that, where the applicant makes a request for early publication under Article 21(2)(b), any request under paragraph (a) or any notice referred to in paragraph (c) submitted, or any fee referred to in paragraph (d) paid, after the technical preparations for international publication have been completed shall be considered as not having been submitted or paid in time.

Art. 21(5)	Completion of the technical preparations

(f) The receiving Office may require that a declaration or other evidence in support of the statement of reasons referred to in paragraph (b)(ii) be filed with it within a time limit which shall be reasonable under the circumstances.

For statements of WIPO concerning R. 26*bis*.3(f), see PCT/A/34/6, p.57 Annex IV, p.1, 3
para. 4 (https://www.wipo.int/edocs/mdocs/govbody/en/pct_a_34/pct_a_34_6.pdf).

(g) The receiving Office shall not refuse, totally or in part, a request under paragraph (a) without giving the applicant the opportunity to make observations on the intended refusal within a time limit which shall be reasonable under the circumstances. Such notice of intended refusal by the receiving Office may be sent to the applicant together with any invitation to file a declaration or other evidence under paragraph (f).

(h) The receiving Office shall promptly:

(i) notify the International Bureau of the receipt of a request under paragraph (a);

(ii) make a decision upon the request;

(iii) notify the applicant and the International Bureau of its decision and the criterion for restoration upon which the decision was based;

(iv) subject to paragraph (h-*bis*), transmit to the International Bureau all documents received from the applicant relating to the request under paragraph (a) (including a copy of the request itself, any statement of reasons referred to in paragraph (b)(ii) and any declaration or other evidence referred to in paragraph (f)).

(h-*bis*) The receiving Office shall, upon a reasoned request by the applicant or on its own decision, not transmit documents or parts thereof received in relation to the request under paragraph (a), if it finds that:

(i) this document or part thereof does not obviously serve the purpose of informing the public about the international application;

(ii) publication or public access to any such document or part thereof would clearly prejudice the personal or economic interests of any person; and

(iii) there is no prevailing public interest to have access to that document or part thereof.

Where the receiving Office decides not to transmit documents or parts thereof to the International Bureau, it shall notify the International Bureau accordingly.

Para. (h-*bis)*	provides for an exception to the duty of the receiving Office to forward documents in para. (h)
AIs 315	Procedure before the receiving Office

(i) Each receiving Office shall inform the International Bureau of which of the criteria for restoration it applies and of any subsequent changes in that respect. The International Bureau shall promptly publish such information in the Gazette.

(j) If, on October 5, 2005, paragraphs (a) to (i) are not compatible with the national law applied by the receiving Office, those paragraphs shall not apply in respect of that Office for as long as they continue not to be compatible with that law, provided that the said Office informs the International Bureau accordingly by April 5, 2006. The information received shall be promptly published by the International Bureau in the Gazette.

R. 26*bis*.3(j)	Notifications of incompatibility with national law of: BR, CO, CU, CZ, DE, DZ, GR, ID, IN, KR, PH.

4 At www.wipo.int/pct/en/texts/restoration.html there is a list, arranged by country, with information on whether the Office will accept a request for restoration of priority, what criteria apply and what the fee is, if any.

5 At the EPO, the criterion of 'due care' applies (PCT EPO Guidelines A-VI 1.5 with further references and examples). The request should be addressed to a receiving Office which has not declared incompatibility. In the event that the desired receiving Office has declared incompatibility, attention is drawn to the following possibilities: the International Bureau may be chosen as receiving Office. The receiving Office that has declared incompatibility may transmit the application to the International Bureau in accordance with R. 19.4(a)(iii).

R. 26*bis*.2(c)(iii)	A time limit of two months for taking into account the priority right also applies to receiving Offices which have declared incompatibility
R. 26*bis*.3(a)	The competent authority for the decision concerning the restoration of the right of priority during the international phase is the receiving Office
R. 49*ter*	Effects of restoration of the right of priority by the receiving Office. In case of declared incompatibility, the designated Office is not bound by a restoration decision. Otherwise, a decision by the receiving Office is in principle binding, but subject to limited review. Therefore, there is no guarantee for the national phase. If restoration is refused, there is the possibility of restoration in the national phase. No State is bound by the refusal.
	R. 49*ter*.2(a) The designated Office may consider the rejected request of the receiving Office as a request for restoration
	R. 49*ter*.2 The competent authority during the national phase is the designated Office. The request for restoration during the national phase is useful in the following cases: – the receiving Office has declared incompatibility and there has been no transmission to the International Bureau under R. 19.4, – the receiving Office has refused the request for restoration, or – the request in the international phase was not submitted. Restoration in the national phase is not possible if the designated Office has declared incompatibility.
R. 26*bis*.2(d)	Free publication of certain information on a priority claim
R. 26*bis*.2(e)	Publication against fee in case of correction/addition after expiration of time limit R. 26*bis*.1

Details can be found in the PCT RO Guidelines at www.wipo.int/export/sites/www/pct/en/texts/pdf/ro.pdf. For further remedies in connection with the Covid-19 pandemic, see PCT Newsletter 3/2020, p. 6 and https://www.wipo.int/pct/en/covid_19/covid_update.html. 6

Rule 26*ter*
Correction or Addition of Declarations under Rule 4.17

26*ter*.1 Correction or Addition of Declarations

The applicant may correct or add to the request any declaration referred to in Rule 4.17 *(naming of inventor, declaration, etc.)* by a notice submitted to the International Bureau within a time limit of 16 months from the priority date, provided that any notice which is received by the International Bureau after the expiration of that time limit shall be considered to have been received on the last day of that time limit if it reaches it before the technical preparations for international publication have been completed.

1 If received after the expiration of the time limit, the International Bureau informs the applicant. It does not publish the declaration and does not transmit it to the designated Office. It informs the applicant that such declarations must be filed directly with the designated Office. Under these conditions, the International Bureau returns any declaration of inventorship signed by at least one inventor to the applicant (AIs 419(d), AG-IP 6.050).

Art. 21(5)	Completion of the technical preparations
AIs 214	Declaration of inventorship
AIs 216	Notice of correction or addition of a declaration
AIs 419	Processing of a declaration

26*ter*.2 Processing of Declarations

(a) Where the receiving Office or the International Bureau finds that any declaration referred to in Rule 4.17 is not worded as required or, in the case of the declaration of inventorship referred to in Rule 4.17(iv), is not signed as required, the receiving Office or the International Bureau, as the case may be, may invite the applicant to correct the declaration within a time limit of 16 months from the priority date.

(b) Where the International Bureau receives any declaration or correction under Rule 26*ter*.1 after the expiration of the time limit under Rule 26*ter*.1, the

International Bureau shall notify the applicant accordingly and shall proceed as provided for in the Administrative Instructions.

Rule 26*quater* Correction or Addition of Indications under Rule 4.11

26*quater*.1 Correction or Addition of Indications

The applicant may correct or add to the request any indication referred to in Rule 4.11 by a notice submitted to the International Bureau within a time limit of 16 months from the priority date, provided that any notice which is received by the International Bureau after the expiration of that time limit shall be considered to have been received on the last day of that time limit if the notice reaches the International Bureau before the technical preparations for international publication have been completed.

26*quater*.2 Late Correction or Addition of Indications

Where any correction or addition of an indication referred to in Rule 4.11 is not timely received under Rule 26*quater*.1, the International Bureau shall notify the applicant accordingly and shall proceed as provided for in the Administrative Instructions.

1 The possibility of correcting or adding indications under R. 4.11 was at the discretion of the respective receiving Office before the introduction of R. 26*quater*. R. 26*quater* is similar to R. 26*ter*. (PCT/WG/12/8)

R. 4.11	Indication that the PCTa be treated as continuation or continuation-in-part in a national phase
AIs 317*bis*	The receiving Office informs the International Bureau of the date of receipt
AIs 419*bis*	The International Bureau shall inform the applicant of any correction or addition made. In case of delay, the International Bureau shall inform the applicant of the possibility of sending the correction or addition to the designated Office.

Rule 27
Lack of Payment of Fees

27.1 Fees

(a) For the purposes of Article 14(3)(a), "fees prescribed under Article 3(4)(iv)" means: the transmittal fee (Rule 14), the international filing fee (Rule 15.1), the search fee (Rule 16), and, where required, the late payment fee (Rule 16*bis*.2).

(b) For the purposes of Article 14(3)(a) and (b), "the fee prescribed under Article 4(2)" means the international filing fee (Rule 15.1) and, where required, the late payment fee (Rule 16*bis*.2).

Art. 11	Filing date and effects of the international application
Art. 14	Certain defects in the international application
R. 29	International application considered withdrawn

Defects in payment do not influence the international filing date. The international application may be considered withdrawn and excluded from further processing but may be invoked as a priority application under the Paris Convention (AG-IP 6.009). 1

Rule 28
Defects Noted by the International Bureau

28.1 Note on Certain Defects

(a) If, in the opinion of the International Bureau, the international application contains any of the defects referred to in Article 14(1)(a)(i), (ii) or (v), the International Bureau shall bring such defects to the attention of the receiving Office.

(b) The receiving Office shall, unless it disagrees with the said opinion, proceed as provided in Article 14(1)(b) and Rule 26.

Art. 14	Checking of signature, indications concerning applicant, physical requirements
R. 26	Checking and correcting of certain elements of the international application

1 For statements of WIPO concerning R. 28.1, see PCT/A/XI/9 p. 5 para. 30 (https://www.wipo.int/edocs/mdocs/govbody/en/pct_a_xi/pct_a_xi_9.pdf).

Rule 29
International Applications Considered Withdrawn

29.1 Finding by Receiving Office

(in force until June 30, 2024) If the receiving Office declares, under Article 14(1)(b) and Rule 26.5 (failure to correct certain defects), or under Article 14(3)(a) (failure to pay the prescribed fees under Rule 27.1(a)), or under Article 14(4) (later finding of non-compliance with the requirements listed in items (i) to (iii) of Article 11(1)), or under Rule 12.3(d) or 12.4(d) (failure to furnish a required translation or, where applicable, to pay a late furnishing fee), or under Rule 92.4(g)(i) (failure to furnish the original of a document), that the international application is considered withdrawn:

(in force as from July 1, 2024) If the receiving Office declares, under Article 14(1)(b) and Rule 26.5 (failure to correct certain defects), or under Article 14(3)(a) (failure to pay the prescribed fees under Rule 27.1(a)), or under Article 14(4) (later finding of non-compliance with the requirements listed in items (i) to (iii) of Article 11(1)), or under Rule 12.3(d), 12.4(d) or 26.3*ter* (failure to furnish a required translation or, where applicable, to pay a late furnishing fee), or under Rule 92.4(g)(i) (failure to furnish the original of a document), that the international application is considered withdrawn:

(i) the receiving Office shall transmit the record copy (unless already transmitted), and any correction offered by the applicant, to the International Bureau;

(ii) the receiving Office shall promptly notify both the applicant and the International Bureau of the said declaration, and the International Bureau shall in turn notify each designated Office which has already been notified of its designation;

(iii) the receiving Office shall not transmit the search copy as provided in Rule 23, or, if such copy has already been transmitted, it shall notify the International Searching Authority of the said declaration;

(iv) the International Bureau shall not be required to notify the applicant of the receipt of the record copy;

(v) no international publication of the international application shall be effected if the notification of the said declaration transmitted by the receiving Office reaches the International Bureau before the technical preparations for international publication have been completed.

1 A reference to new R. 26.3*ter*(e) has been added on July 1, 2024. Amendments apply to PCTa with an international filing date that is on or after that date (PCT/A/55/2).

Art. 21(5)	Completion of the technical preparations
R. 48.6	Announcing of certain facts
R. 90*bis*.1	Withdrawal of the international application
R. 90*bis*.2	Withdrawal of designations

29.2 [Deleted]

29.3 Calling Certain Facts to the Attention of the Receiving Office

If the International Bureau or the International Searching Authority considers that the receiving Office should make a finding under Article 14(4), it shall call the relevant facts to the attention of the receiving Office.

29.4 Notification of Intent to Make Declaration under Article 14(4)

(a) Before the receiving Office issues any declaration under Article 14(4), it shall notify the applicant of its intent to issue such declaration and the reasons therefor. The applicant may, if he disagrees with the tentative finding of the receiving Office, submit arguments to that effect within two months from the date of the notification.

(b) Where the receiving Office intends to issue a declaration under Article 14(4) in respect of an element mentioned in Article 11(1)(iii)(d) *(description)* or (e) *(claims)*, the receiving Office shall, in the notification referred to in paragraph (a) of this Rule, invite the applicant to confirm in accordance with Rule 20.6(a) that the element is incorporated by reference under Rule 4.18. For the purposes of Rule 20.7(a)(i), the invitation sent to the applicant under this paragraph shall be considered to be an invitation under Rule 20.3(a)(ii).

R. 20.3(a)(ii)	Confirmation of incorporation by reference by the applicant
R. 20.7(a)(i)	Two-month period from response to invitation according to R. 20.3(a) to correct missing or erroneously filed parts or elements

(c) Paragraph (b) shall not apply where the receiving Office has informed the International Bureau in accordance with Rule 20.8(a) of the incompatibility of Rules 20.3(a)(ii) and (b)(ii) and 20.6 with the national law applied by that Office.

R. 20.8(a)	Incompatibility with national laws of incorporation by reference
R. 20.6	Confirmation of incorporation by reference of elements and parts
AIs 312	Notification of decision not to issue a declaration that the international application is considered withdrawn

Rule 30
Time Limit under Article 14(4)

30.1 Time Limit

The time limit referred to in Article 14(4) shall be four months from the international filing date.

Art. 14(4)	Withdrawal due to finding of defects after accordance of international filing date within time limit
R. 29.3	International Bureau and ISA shall inform the receiving Office about defects
R. 29.4	Notification to the applicant
R. 82*ter*	Rectification of errors before designated Office

Rule 31
Copies Required under Article 13

31.1 Request for Copies

(a) Requests under Article 13(1) may relate to all, some kinds of, or individual international applications in which the national Office making the request is designated. Requests for all or some kinds of such international applications must be renewed for each year by means of a notification addressed by that Office before November 30 of the preceding year to the International Bureau.

(b) Requests under Article 13(2)(b) shall be subject to the payment of a fee covering the cost of preparing and mailing the copy.

For the amount of the fees see AG-IP Annex B (IB) 1

31.2 Preparation of Copies

The preparation of copies required under Article 13 shall be the responsibility of the International Bureau.

R. 93*bis*	Note: restricted transmission, electronic download if necessary. Transmission only on request, at a specific time and, if applicable, in electronic form.

Rule 32
Extension of Effects of International Application to Certain Successor States

32.1 Extension of International Application to Successor State

(a) The effects of any international application whose international filing date falls in the period defined in paragraph (b) are extended to a State ("the successor State") whose territory was, before the independence of that State, part of the territory of a Contracting State designated in the international application which subsequently ceased to exist ("the predecessor State"), provided that the successor State has become a Contracting State through the deposit, with the Director General, of a declaration of continuation the effect of which is that the Treaty is applied by the successor State.

AIs 430 Notification of designations

(b) The period referred to in paragraph (a) starts on the day following the last day of the existence of the predecessor State and ends two months after the date on which the declaration referred to in paragraph (a) was notified by the Director General to the Governments of the States party to the Paris Convention for the Protection of Industrial Property. However, where the date of independence of the successor State is earlier than the date of the day following the last day of the existence of the predecessor State, the successor State may declare that the said period starts on the date of its independence; such a declaration shall be made together with the declaration referred to in paragraph (a) and shall specify the date of independence.

(c) Information on any international application whose filing date falls within the applicable period under paragraph (b) and whose effect is extended to the successor State shall be published by the International Bureau in the Gazette.

32.2 Effects of Extension to Successor State

(a) Where the effects of the international application are extended to the successor State in accordance with Rule 32.1,

(i) the successor State shall be considered as having been designated in the international application, and

(ii) the applicable time limit under Article 22 or 39(1) in relation to that State shall be extended until the expiration of at least six months from the date of the publication of the information under Rule 32.1(c).

(b) The successor State may fix a time limit which expires later than that provided in paragraph (a)(ii). The International Bureau shall publish information on such time limits in the Gazette.

Rule 33 Relevant Prior Art for the International Search

33.1 Relevant Prior Art for the International Search

(a) For the purposes of Article 15(2), relevant prior art shall consist of everything which has been made available to the public anywhere in the world by means of written disclosure (including drawings and other illustrations) and which is capable of being of assistance in determining that the claimed invention is or is not new and that it does or does not involve an inventive step (i.e., that it is or is not obvious), provided that the making available to the public occurred prior to the international filing date.

(b) When any written disclosure refers to an oral disclosure, use, exhibition, or other means whereby the contents of the written disclosure were made available to the public, and such making available to the public occurred on a date prior to the international filing date, the international search report shall separately mention that fact and the date on which it occurred if the making available to the public of the written disclosure occurred on a date which is the same as, or later than, the international filing date.

(c) Any published application *(subsequently published applications)* or any patent whose publication date is the same as, or later than, but whose filing date, or, where applicable, claimed priority date, is earlier than the international filing date of the international application searched, and which would constitute relevant prior art for the purposes of Article 15(2) had it been published prior to the international filing date, shall be specially mentioned in the international search report.

1 An amendment of R. 33.1(a) has been proposed to broaden the definition of relevant prior art to include non-written disclosures as of January 1, 2026 (PCT/A/56/2).

33.2 Fields to Be Covered by the International Search

(a) The international search shall cover all those technical fields, and shall be carried out on the basis of all those search files, which may contain material pertinent to the invention.

(b) Consequently, not only shall the art in which the invention is classifiable be searched but also analogous arts regardless of where classified.

(c) The question what arts are, in any given case, to be regarded as analogous shall be considered in the light of what appears to be the necessary essential function or use of the invention and not only the specific functions expressly indicated in the international application.

(d) The international search shall embrace all subject matter that is generally recognized as equivalent to the subject matter of the claimed invention for all or certain of its features, even though, in its specifics, the invention as described in the international application is different.

33.3 Orientation of the International Search

(a) International search shall be made on the basis of the claims, with due regard to the description and the drawings (if any) and with particular emphasis on the inventive concept towards which the claims are directed.

(b) In so far as possible and reasonable, the international search shall cover the entire subject matter to which the claims are directed or to which they might reasonably be expected to be directed after they have been amended.

AIs 801–805 Third Party Observation System. See also Euro-PCT Guide E-II.

Rule 34
Minimum Documentation

34.1 Definition

(a) The definitions contained in Article 2(i) and (ii) shall not apply for the purposes of this Rule.

(b) The documentation referred to in Article 15(4) ("minimum documentation") shall consist of:

(i) the "national patent documents" as specified in paragraph (c),

(ii) the published international (PCT) applications, the published regional applications for patents and inventors' certificates, and the published regional patents and inventors' certificates,

(iii) such other published items of non-patent literature as the International Searching Authorities shall agree upon and which shall be published in a list by the International Bureau when agreed upon for the first time and whenever changed.

(c) Subject to paragraphs (d) and (e), the "national patent documents" shall be the following:

(i) the patents issued in and after 1920 by France, the former Reichspatentamt of Germany, Japan, the former Soviet Union, Switzerland (in the French and German languages only), the United Kingdom, and the United States of America,

(ii) the patents issued by the Federal Republic of Germany, the People's Republic of China, the Republic of Korea and the Russian Federation,

(iii) the patent applications, if any, published in and after 1920 in the countries referred to in items (i) and (ii),

(iv) the inventors' certificates issued by the former Soviet Union,

(v) the utility certificates issued by, and the published applications for utility certificates of, France,

(vi) such patents issued by, and such patent applications published in, any other country after 1920 as are in the English, French, German or Spanish language and in which no priority is claimed, provided that the national Office of the interested country sorts out these documents and places them at the disposal of each International Searching Authority.

AG-IP 7.004 It is emphasized, however, that, where the ISA has more than the 'minimum documentation' at its disposal, it is obliged also to consult that additional documentation to the extent permitted by its facilities.

(d) Where an application is republished once (for example, an *Offenlegungsschrift* as an *Auslegeschrift*) or more than once, no International Searching Authority shall be obliged to keep all versions in its documentation; consequently, each such Authority shall be entitled not to keep more than one version. Furthermore, where an application is granted and is issued in the form of a patent or a utility certificate (France), no International Searching Authority shall be obliged to keep both the application and the patent or utility certificate (France) in its documentation; consequently, each such Authority shall be entitled to keep either the application only or the patent or utility certificate (France) only.

(e) Any International Searching Authority whose official language, or one of whose official languages, is not Chinese, Japanese, Korean, Russian or Spanish is entitled not to include in its documentation those patent documents of the People's Republic of China, Japan, the Republic of Korea, the Russian Federation and the former Soviet Union as well as those patent documents in the Spanish language, respectively, for which no abstracts in the English language are generally available. English abstracts becoming generally available after the date of entry into force of these Regulations shall require the inclusion of the patent documents to which the abstracts refer no later than six months after such abstracts become generally available. In case of the interruption of abstracting services in English in technical fields in which English abstracts were formerly generally available, the Assembly shall take appropriate measures to provide for the prompt restoration of such services in the said fields.

(f) For the purposes of this Rule, applications which have only been laid open for public inspection are not considered published applications.

Amendments to R. 34 shall enter into force on January 1, 2026 (PCT/A/55/2). 1

Rule 35
The Competent International Searching Authority

1 See also Art. 16 with annotations to acceleration of prosecution using PPH.

35.1 When Only One International Searching Authority Is Competent

Each receiving Office shall, in accordance with the terms of the applicable agreement referred to in Article 16(3)(b), inform the International Bureau which International Searching Authority is competent for the searching of the international applications filed with it, and the International Bureau shall promptly publish such information.

35.2 When Several International Searching Authorities Are Competent

(a) Any receiving Office may, in accordance with the terms of the applicable agreement referred to in Article 16(3)(b), specify several International Searching Authorities:

(i) by declaring all of them competent for any international application filed with it, and leaving the choice to the applicant, or

(ii) by declaring one or more competent for certain kinds of international applications filed with it, and declaring one or more others competent for other kinds of international applications filed with it, provided that, for those kinds of international applications for which several International Searching Authorities are declared to be competent, the choice shall be left to the applicant.

(b) Any receiving Office availing itself of the faculty provided in paragraph (a) shall promptly inform the International Bureau, and the International Bureau shall promptly publish such information.

2 Since July 1, 2018, the EPO had been engaged in a collaborative pilot project with patent Offices in KR, US, JP, and CN as part of the IP5 Collaborative Search and Examination (CS&E) initiative. This pilot aimed to enhance the preparation of ISRs and written opinions at the applicant's request, as referenced in OJ 2018, A47, and OJ 2019, A65. Under this cooperation, the ISR was not solely prepared by one ISA; instead, examiners from the other four ISAs also contributed to searching the subject

matter of the claims. Consequently, applicants received comprehensive search results from the world's leading patent Offices before progressing to the national/regional phase. Limited to 500 searches, participation in the project was voluntary and free of charge. Initially, only applications in English were eligible, with German and French applications admitted from January 1, 2019, as noted in OJ 2018, A95. Additional language allowances were to be announced by the ISAs as needed. The pilot was initially set to conclude on June 1, 2021, and the EPO stopped accepting new participation requests as of OJ 2020, A46, with a planned extension to June 2022 (PCT/WG/13/13).

However, at their annual meeting in June 2023 in Honolulu, USA, the IP5 Heads of Office reviewed the outcomes of this pilot. Based on the final report of the IP5 Collaborative Search and Examination Pilot under the PCT, it was decided not to implement the CS&E in its piloted form. The report recognized the project's contributions but concluded that, for the time being, the initiative would not proceed as originally piloted. This decision marks the end of this particular phase of collaborative patent examination efforts among the world's leading patent Offices. 3

35.3 When the International Bureau Is Receiving Office under Rule 19.1(a)(iii)

(a) Where the international application is filed with the International Bureau as receiving Office under Rule 19.1(a)(iii), an International Searching Authority shall be competent for the searching of that international application if it would have been competent had that international application been filed with a receiving Office competent under Rule 19.1(a)(i) or (ii), (b) or (c) or Rule 19.2(i).

(b) Where two or more International Searching Authorities are competent under paragraph (a), the choice shall be left to the applicant.

(c) Rules 35.1 and 35.2 shall not apply to the International Bureau as receiving Office under Rule 19.1(a)(iii).

ISAs are the Offices of AT, AU, BR, CA, CL, CN, EA (since July 1, 2022), EG, EP, ES, FI, IL, IN, JP, KR, PH, RU, SE, SG, TR, UA, US, XN (Nordic Patent Institute NPI of the Offices of DK, IS, SE, NO) and the XV (Visegrad Patent Institute (VPI) of the offices of CZ, HU, PL, SK). EPO only acts as IPEA if ISA was the EPO, the Office in AT, FI, ES, XN, XV, TR or SE (AG-IP Annex E (EP)). See WIPO agreements at www.wipo.int/pct/en/access/isa_ipea_agreements.html and PCT Applicant's Guide Annex D, updated by PCT Gazette. 4

Rule 36
Minimum Requirements for International Searching Authorities

36.1 Definition of Minimum Requirements

The minimum requirements referred to in Article 16(3)(c) shall be the following:

(i) the national Office or intergovernmental organization must have at least 100 full-time employees with sufficient technical qualifications to carry out searches;

(ii) that Office or organization must have in its possession, or have access to, at least the minimum documentation referred to in Rule 34, properly arranged for search purposes, on paper, in microform or stored on electronic media;

(iii) that Office or organization must have a staff which is capable of searching the required technical fields and which has the language facilities to understand at least those languages in which the minimum documentation referred to in Rule 34 is written or is translated;

(iv) that Office or organization must have in place a quality management system and internal review arrangements in accordance with the common rules of international search;

1 ISPE Guidelines, Chapter 21 Common Quality Framework for International Search and Preliminary Examination, https://www.wipo.int/pct/en/texts/ispe/21_01_03.html.

(v) that Office or organization must hold an appointment as an International Preliminary Examining Authority.

2 Amendments to R. 36 shall enter into force on January 1, 2026 (PCT/A/55/2). An Understanding of the PCT Assembly has been published in Gazette November 30, 2023.

Rule 37
Missing or Defective Title

37.1 Lack of Title

If the international application does not contain a title and the receiving Office has notified the International Searching Authority that it has invited the applicant to correct such defect, the International Searching Authority shall proceed with the international search unless and until it receives notification that the said application is considered withdrawn.

37.2 Establishment of Title

If the international application does not contain a title and the International Searching Authority has not received a notification from the receiving Office to the effect that the applicant has been invited to furnish a title, or if the said Authority finds that the title does not comply with Rule 4.3, it shall itself establish a title. Such title shall be established in the language in which the international application is to be published or, if a translation into another language was transmitted under Rule 23.1(b) and the International Searching Authority so wishes, in the language of that translation.

Rule 38
Missing or Defective Abstract

38.1 Lack of Abstract

If the international application does not contain an abstract and the receiving Office has notified the International Searching Authority that it has invited the applicant to correct such defect, the International Searching Authority shall proceed with the international search unless and until it receives notification that the said application is considered withdrawn.

R. 8	Abstract
R. 48.2	Content of the international publication

38.2 Establishment of Abstract

If the international application does not contain an abstract and the International Searching Authority has not received a notification from the receiving Office to the effect that the applicant has been invited to furnish an abstract, or if the said Authority finds that the abstract does not comply with Rule 8, it shall itself establish an abstract. Such abstract shall be established in the language in which the international application is to be published or, if a translation into another language was transmitted under Rule 23.1(b) and the International Searching Authority so wishes, in the language of that translation.

AIs 515	Modification of abstract in response to applicant's comments

38.3 Modification of Abstract

The applicant may, until the expiration of one month from the date of mailing of the international search report, submit to the International Searching Authority:

(i) proposed modifications of the abstract; or

(ii) where the abstract has been established by the Authority, proposed modifications of, or comments on, that abstract, or both modifications and comments;

and the Authority shall decide whether to modify the abstract accordingly. Where the Authority modifies the abstract, it shall notify the modification to the International Bureau.

Rule 39
Subject Matter under Article 17(2)(a)(i)

39.1 Definition

No International Searching Authority shall be required to search an international application if, and to the extent to which, its subject matter is any of the following:

(i) scientific and mathematical theories,

(ii) plant or animal varieties or essentially biological processes for the production of plants and animals, other than microbiological processes and the products of such processes,

(iii) schemes, rules or methods of doing business, performing purely mental acts or playing games,

1 The EPO, as an ISA for PCT applications, does not search business method applications lacking technical character (Euro-PCT Guide, 3.3.006). In such cases, a declaration is issued under PCT Art. 17(2). R. 39.1 allows discretion, which the EPO exercises according to EPC standards (Annex C, WIPO-EPO Agreement; OJ EPO 2007 p. 592; Euro-PCT Guide, 3.3.005). This is also reflected in amendments to the WIPO-EPO Agreement (https://www.wipo.int/pct/en/access/isa_ipea_agreements.html, Art. 16(3) and Art. 17(2)(a)(i)).

(iv) methods for treatment of the human or animal body by surgery or therapy, as well as diagnostic methods,

(v) mere presentations of information,

(vi) computer programs to the extent that the International Searching Authority is not equipped to search prior art concerning such programs.

R. 66.1(e)	In IPE, the IPEA is not required to examine applications for business methods
R. 66.1*ter*	In the case of claim in respect of which no ISR has been established and which are not the subject of IPE (R. 66.1(e)), no top-up search is carried out
Art. 17(2)	If the EPO as ISA has issued a standardized non-search declaration under Art. 17(2), R. 39, and has not carried out a subsequent

search in the European phase, the Board of Appeal of the EPO is not competent to request a (partial) refund of search fees in the event of an appeal against the decision. There is no legal basis for a refund either in the PCT or in the WIPO-EPO Agreement or in a decision of the EPO (T 0506/08).

Rule 40
Lack of Unity of Invention (International Search)

40.1 Invitation to Pay Additional Fees; Time Limit

The invitation to pay additional fees provided for in Article 17(3)(a) shall:

(i) specify the reasons for which the international application is not considered as complying with the requirement of unity of invention;

(ii) invite the applicant to pay the additional fees within one month from the date of the invitation, and indicate the amount of those fees to be paid; and

(iii) invite the applicant to pay, where applicable, the protest fee referred to in Rule 40.2(e) within one month from the date of the invitation, and indicate the amount to be paid.

Art. 64, 27, R. 51*bis*	There are no reservations to R. 13, i.e. the requirement of unity of invention is governed by R. 13 in all regional and national phases be it as designated or elected Office
R. 13.2	The common characterizing features
Art. 17, R. 40	Lack of unity of invention in international searches
R. 45*bis*.5(e)	Lack of unity of invention in supplementary searches in case the lack was objected to by the ISR
R. 45*bis*.6	Lack of unity of invention first objected to in supplementary search
R. 66.1*ter*	Lack of unity of invention in top-up searches before the IPEA
Art. 34(3), R. 68	Lack of unity of invention in IPE
AIs 206	Unity of invention. AIs Annex B (https://www.wipo.int/pct/en/texts/ai/annex_b.html) comprises detailed examples of unity of invention. Further examples can be found in AIs 206, including an explanation of the Markush practice in AIs Annex B Part 2 III.
W 0013/05–3.3.01	A precise statement of reasons with reference to the relevant passage in the ISPE Guidelines for Searches, Chapter 10 Unity of

	invention, is required if lack of unity is not clearly recognizable, https://www.wipo.int/pct/en/texts/ispe/index.html
EPO	For the procedure at the EPO see annotation to Art. 17(3)(a).

40.2 Additional Fees

(a) The amount of the additional fees due for searching under Article 17(3)(a) shall be determined by the competent International Searching Authority.

AG-IP Annex D	Additional search fee
Art. 2(1) no. 2 RFees, R. 158(1) EPC:	In principle, the amount of the international search fee applicable on the date of filing is charged. Subsequent fee increases are not taken into account.
R. 16	International search fee

(b) The additional fees due for searching under Article 17(3)(a) shall be payable direct to the International Searching Authority.

(c) Any applicant may pay the additional fees under protest, that is, accompanied by a reasoned statement to the effect that the international application complies with the requirement of unity of invention or that the amount of the required additional fees is excessive. Such protest shall be examined by a review body constituted in the framework of the International Searching Authority, which, to the extent that it finds the protest justified, shall order the total or partial reimbursement to the applicant of the additional fees. On the request of the applicant, the text of both the protest and the decision thereon shall be notified to the designated Offices together with the international search report. The applicant shall submit any translation thereof with the furnishing of the translation of the international application required under Article 22.

(d) The membership of the review body referred to in paragraph (c) may include, but shall not be limited to, the person who made the decision which is the subject of the protest.

(e) The examination of a protest referred to in paragraph (c) may be subjected by the International Searching Authority to the payment to it, for its own benefit, of a protest fee. Where the applicant has not, within the time limit under Rule 40.1(iii), paid any required protest fee, the protest shall be considered not to have been made and the International Searching Authority shall so declare. The protest fee shall be refunded to the applicant where the review body referred to in paragraph (c) finds that the protest was entirely justified.

Apart from protest, there is the possibility to submit informal comments on the 1
Written Opinion of the International Searching Authority (WO-ISA). For the informal comments, see also annotations to R. 43*bis*.1(c).

For the amount of the protest fee, see the AG-IP Annex D. 2

3 If additional fees are not paid, it may be possible to file a divisional application or make an additional fee payment in the national phase (PCT Newsletter 6/2021 p. 11).

4 For the procedure at the EPO, see annotations to Art. 17(3)(a).

Rule 40*bis*
Additional Fees in Case of Missing Parts or Correct Elements and Parts Included in the International Application or Considered to Have Been Contained in the International Application

40*bis*.1 Invitation to Pay Additional Fees

The International Searching Authority may invite the applicant to pay additional fees where the fact that a missing part or a correct element or part:

(i) is included in the international application under Rule 20.5(c) or Rule 20.5*bis*(c), respectively; or

(ii) is considered, under Rule 20.5(d) or Rule 20.5*bis*(d), respectively, to have been contained in the international application on the date on which one or more elements referred to in Article 11(1)(iii) were first received by the receiving Office;

is notified to that Authority only after it has begun to draw up the international search report. The invitation shall invite the applicant to pay the additional fees within one month from the date of the invitation and indicate the amount of those fees to be paid. The amount of the additional fees shall be determined by the International Searching Authority but shall not exceed the search fee; the additional fees shall be payable directly to that Authority. Provided any such additional fees have been paid within the prescribed time limit, the International Searching Authority shall establish the international search report on the international application including any such missing part or any such correct element or part.

For statements of WIPO concerning R. 40*bis*.1 see PCTA/51/2 p.3, para. 7(b) (https://www.wipo.int/edocs/mdocs/govbody/en/pct_a_51/pct_a_51_2.pdf). 1

The provision is applicable to PCT application in which reference is made for the first time on or after July 1, 2020 to one or more elements mentioned in Art. 11(1)(iii). The provision allows the ISA to charge fees in the case of subsequent filing of missing 2 parts or corrections if the preparation of the ISR has already begun. This applies not only to the newly regulated case of correction of erroneously filed documents under R. 20.5*bis*, but also to the case of filing missing documents under R. 20.5. It is at the discretion of the examiner to decide whether the effort involved in taking into account the documents received later justifies an invitation to pay a fee (PCT/GL/ISPE/12, No. 15.11A). If the fee is not paid in due time, the ISA will issue the ISR and the written opinion without taking into account these superseded documents (PCT/GL/ISPE/12, point 15.11C). At the EPO, an additional fee equal to the search fee must be paid only in the case of R. 20.5*bis*, but not in the case of missing parts under R. 20.5 (OJ 2020 A36, PCT EPO Guidelines A-III 5.1).

R. 20.5*bis*	Erroneously filed elements and parts
Art. 11(1)	Minimum elements of the PCT application for the accordance of the international filing date
Art. 15(3)	Basis of the international search
Art. 17(1)	Procedure before the ISA
R. 43	The ISR
R. 43*bis*	Written opinion of the ISA
AG-IP Annex D	Additional search fee
Art. 2(2) No. 2 RFees	Fees payable to the EPO (OJ 2020 A36, OJ EPO 2020 A81). See also: https://www.epo.org/en/applying/fees/international-fees/important-fees.

Rule 41 Taking into Account Results of Earlier Search and Classification

41.1 Taking into Account Results of Earlier Search in Case of a Request under Rule 4.12

Where the applicant has, under Rule 4.12, requested the International Searching Authority to take into account the results of an earlier search and has complied with Rule 12*bis*.1 and:

(i) the earlier search was carried out by the same International Searching Authority, or by the same Office as that which is acting as the International Searching Authority, the International Searching Authority shall, to the extent possible, take those results into account in carrying out the international search;

(ii) the earlier search was carried out by another International Searching Authority, or by an Office other than that which is acting as the International Searching Authority, the International Searching Authority may take those results into account in carrying out the international search.

R. 4.12	Taking into account results of earlier search
R. 12*bis*.1	Furnishing by the applicant of documents related to earlier search in case of request under R. 4.12
R. 16.3	Partial refund of the search fee
EP:	R. 41.1 allows in conjunction with Annex D. II.(3) and Art. 5(2) of the WIPO-EPO Agreement (https://www.wipo.int/pct/en/access/isa_ipea_agreements.html, Art. 16(3)(b)) a (partial) refund of the fee for the international preliminary search

41.2 Taking into Account Results of Earlier Search and Classification in Other Cases

(a) Where the international application claims the priority of one or more earlier applications in respect of which an earlier search has been carried out by the same International Searching Authority, or by the same Office as that which is acting as the International Searching Authority, the International Searching Authority shall, to the extent possible, take the results of any such earlier search into account in carrying out the international search.

(b) Where the receiving Office has transmitted to the International Searching Authority a copy of the results of any earlier search or of any earlier classification under Rule 23*bis*.2(a) or (c), or where such a copy is available to the International Searching Authority in a form and manner acceptable to it, for example, from a digital library, the International Searching Authority may take those results into account in carrying out the international search.

R. 23*bis*.2 Transmission of documents pertaining to a earlier search or classification for the purposes of R. 41.2.

Rule 42
Time Limit for International Search

42.1 Time Limit for International Search

The time limit for establishing the international search report or the declaration referred to in Article 17(2)(a) *(declaration that no ISR will be established)* shall be three months from the receipt of the search copy by the International Searching Authority, or nine months from the priority date, whichever time limit expires later.

R. 23.1	Transmittal of search copy on the same day as transmittal of record copy
R. 22.1(b)	Transmittal of record copy at the latest 13 months from priority date

Rule 43
The International Search Report

43.1 Identifications

The international search report shall identify the International Searching Authority which established it by indicating the name of such Authority, and the international application by indicating the international application number, the name of the applicant, and the international filing date.

43.2 Dates

The international search report shall be dated and shall indicate the date on which the international search was actually completed. It shall also indicate the filing date of any earlier application whose priority is claimed or, if the priority of more than one earlier application is claimed, the filing date of the earliest among them.

43.3 Classification

(a) The international search report shall contain the classification of the subject matter at least according to the International Patent Classification.

(b) Such classification shall be effected by the International Searching Authority.

43.4 Language

Every international search report and any declaration made under Article 17(2)(a) shall be in the language in which the international application to which it relates is to be published, provided that:

(i) if a translation of the international application into another language was transmitted under Rule 23.1(b) and the International Searching Authority so wishes, the international search report and any declaration made under Article 17(2)(a) may be in the language of that translation;

(ii) if the international application is to be published in the language of a translation furnished under Rule 12.4 which is not accepted by the International Searching Authority and that Authority so wishes, the international search report and any declaration made under Article 17(2)(a) may be in a language which is both a language accepted by that Authority and a language of publication referred to in Rule 48.3(a).

43.5 Citations

(a) The international search report shall contain the citations of the documents considered to be relevant.

(b) The method of identifying any cited document shall be regulated by the Administrative Instructions.

(c) Citations of particular relevance shall be specially indicated.

(d) Citations which are not relevant to all the claims shall be cited in relation to the claim or claims to which they are relevant.

(e) If only certain passages of the cited document are relevant or particularly relevant, they shall be identified, for example, by indicating the page, the column, or the lines, where the passage appears. If the entire document is relevant but some passages are of particular relevance, such passages shall be identified unless such identification is not practicable.

Art. 15(3)	Basis of the international search
Art. 17(1)	Procedure before the ISA
AIs 505	Identification of documents of particular importance in the ISR

43.6 Fields Searched

(a) The international search report shall list the classification identification of the fields searched. If that identification is effected on the basis of a classification other than the International Patent Classification, the International Searching Authority shall publish the classification used.

(b) If the international search extended to patents, inventors' certificates, utility certificates, utility models, patents or certificates of addition, inventors' certificates of addition, utility certificates of addition, or published applications for any of those kinds of protection, of States, periods, or languages, not included in the minimum documentation as defined in Rule 34, the international search report shall, when practicable, identify the kinds of documents, the States, the periods, and the languages to which it extended. For the purposes of this paragraph, Article 2(ii) shall not apply.

(c) If the international search was based on, or was extended to, any electronic data base, the international search report may indicate the name of the data base and, where considered useful to others and practicable, the search terms used.

43.6*bis* Consideration of Rectifications of Obvious Mistakes

(a) A rectification of an obvious mistake that is authorized under Rule 91.1 shall, subject to paragraph (b), be taken into account by the International Searching Authority for the purposes of the international search and the international search report shall so indicate.

(b) A rectification of an obvious mistake need not be taken into account by the International Searching Authority for the purposes of the international search if it is authorized by or notified to that Authority, as applicable, after it has begun to draw up the international search report, in which case the report shall, if possible, so indicate, failing which the International Searching Authority shall notify the International Bureau accordingly and the International Bureau shall proceed as provided for in the Administrative Instructions.

R. 40*bis*	Additional fees in case of missing parts or correct elements and parts included in the PCTa or considered to have been contained in the PCTa
R. 66.1(d-*bis*)	Taking into account of the correction of obvious mistakes by the IPEA
R. 70.2(e)	Mention of the correction of obvious mistakes in the IPRP/IPER
AIs 413	Incorporation by reference and corrections

43.7 Remarks Concerning Unity of Invention

If the applicant paid additional fees for the international search, the international search report shall so indicate. Furthermore, where the international search was made on the main invention only or on less than all the inventions (Article 17(3)(a)), the international search report shall indicate what parts of the international application were and what parts were not searched.

43.8 Authorized Officer

The international search report shall indicate the name of the officer of the International Searching Authority responsible for that report.

AIs 514	Authorized officer

43.9 Additional Matter

The international search report shall contain no matter other than that specified in Rules 33.1(b) and (c), 43.1 to 43.3, 43.5 to 43.8, and 44.2, and the indication referred to in Article 17(2)(b), provided that the Administrative Instructions may permit the inclusion in the international search report of any additional matter specified in the Administrative Instructions. The international search report shall not contain, and the Administrative Instructions shall not permit the inclusion of, any expressions of opinion, reasoning, arguments, or explanations.

43.10 Form

The physical requirements as to the form of the international search report shall be prescribed by the Administrative Instructions.

Rule 43*bis* Written Opinion of the International Searching Authority

43*bis*.1 Written Opinion

(a) Subject to Rule 69.1(b-*bis*), the International Searching Authority shall, at the same time as it establishes the international search report or the declaration referred to in Article 17(2)(a), establish a written opinion as to:

R. 42.1 Time limit for the preparation of the ISR

(i) whether the claimed invention appears to be novel, to involve an inventive step (to be non-obvious), and to be industrially applicable;

(ii) whether the international application complies with the requirements of the Treaty and these Regulations in so far as checked by the International Searching Authority.

The written opinion shall also be accompanied by such other observations as these Regulations provide for.

1 The written opinion according to R. 43*bis* is named WO-ISA by the EPO in its function as ISA (Euro-PCT Guide 3.2.005). Examination of requirements by the EPO are regulated in PCT EPO Guidelines Part F of the Regulations.

(b) For the purposes of establishing the written opinion, Articles 33(2) to (6) *(novelty, inventive step)* and 35(2) and (3) *(IPRP II)* and Rules 43.4 *(language of the ISR)*, 43.6*bis* *(obvious mistakes)*, 64 *(prior art)*, 65 *(inventive step)*, 66.1(e) *(non-searchable subject matter)*, 66.7 *(priority document)*, 67 *(exclusion from patentability)*, 70.2(b) and (d) *(basis of the IPRP II)*, 70.3 *(identification of the authority)*, 70.4(ii) *(date)*, 70.5(a) *(patent classification)*, 70.6 to 70.10 *(indications in the IPRP II)*, 70.12 *(defects)*, 70.14 *(authorized officer)* and 70.15(a) *(title of the report)* shall apply *mutatis mutandis*.

AIs 421 Request for a copy of the priority document

AIs 514	Authorized officer

(c) The written opinion shall contain a notification informing the applicant that, if a demand for international preliminary examination is made, the written opinion shall, under Rule 66.1*bis*(a) but subject to Rule 66.1*bis*(b), be considered to be a written opinion of the International Preliminary Examining Authority for the purposes of Rule 66.2(a), in which case the applicant is invited to submit to that Authority, before the expiration of the time limit under Rule 54bis.1(a), a written reply together, where appropriate, with amendments.

Art. 17	Procedure before the ISA
Art. 18	ISR
R. 89*bis*	Electronic file management
EPO	Applicants' informal comments must be considered in the *PCT Direct procedure* at the EPO, which is distinct from filing with the International Bureau. A 'PCT Direct letter' can be used to address objections in the EPO's search opinion on an earlier priority application. This letter is filed with the EPO as the receiving Office alongside the PCTa but does not form part of the application. A crucial condition is that the PCTa claims priority from a prior European or national application searched by the EPO. For more information, see OJ 2017 A21 and PCT EPO Guidelines A-IV.1. The EPO conducts national searches for AL, AT, BE, CY, FR, GB, GR, HR, IT, LT, LU, LV, MC, MT, NL, SI, SM, and TR (AG Annex D (EP)). The procedure is available at the EPO as an ISA for PCTa, irrespective of the receiving Office chosen.
Art. 17(3)(a)	Since April 1, 2017, the EPO sends a preliminary opinion on patentability to the applicant in cases of inconsistencies
R. 161 EPC	Invitation to applicants to comment after entry into the European phase; reaction of the applicant is mandatory in case of a negative decision to avoid disadvantages (fiction of withdrawal) since April 1, 2010, amendments to IPRP I by EPO as ISA (not EPO as IPEA) can be considered as a reply, but can also be filed independently. R. 137 EPC must be observed (Euro-PCT Guide 5.4.027 et seq.).

2 Unlike the IPRP II procedure, influencing the examination through amendments under Art. 34, written arguments, or oral discussions with the examiner is not possible. Amendments under Art. 19 are only allowed after the search report is prepared, which means they are not considered in the written opinion. However, following a PCT Assembly decision (Report dated September 29 – October 1, 2002, para. 47, Doc. No. PCT/A31/10, FN 1), informal comments on the written opinion can be submitted. These comments should be sent only to the International Bureau and must be clearly identified as such. To ensure they are available to the designated Office during the national phase entry, it's advisable to file these comments before the 28-month time limit from the priority date. These comments are included with the IPRP I for submission to the designated Offices, unless an IPRP II is prepared.

An informal comment is not forwarded automatically, but the applicant may submit it to the IPEA (AG-IP 7.030). It is important to note that commenting on the search report is not an option (AG-IP 7.025A).

Rule 44
Transmittal of the International Search Report, Written Opinion, Etc.

44.1 Copies of Report or Declaration and Written Opinion

The International Searching Authority shall, on the same day, transmit one copy of the international search report or of the declaration referred to in Article 17(2)(a), and one copy of the written opinion established under Rule 43*bis*.1 to the International Bureau and one copy to the applicant.

44.2 Title or Abstract

The international search report shall either state that the International Searching Authority approves the title and the abstract as submitted by the applicant or be accompanied by the text of the title and/or abstract as established by the International Searching Authority under Rules 37 and 38.

44.3 Copies of Cited Documents

(a) The request referred to in Article 20(3) *(transmittal of copies of document cited in the ISR)* may be presented any time during seven years from the international filing date of the international application to which the international search report relates.

Art. 20(3)	Copies of the identified documents are of particular interest, especially in case of non-patent literature

(b) The International Searching Authority may require that the party (applicant or designated Office) presenting the request pay to it the cost of preparing and mailing the copies. The level of the cost of preparing copies shall be provided for in the agreements referred to in Article 16(3)(b) between the International Searching Authorities and the International Bureau.

Art. 3(1) RFees	OJ EPO 2019 A15, abolition of the administrative fee for copies as they are available online, except for certified copies. EPO only provides copies free of charge in exceptional cases upon reasoned

	request. Certified copies are also only available on reasoned request.
R. 45*bis*.7	Charging of copying costs by SISA for SISR

(c) [Deleted]

(d) Any International Searching Authority may perform the obligations referred to in paragraphs (a) and (b) through another agency responsible to it.

Art. 17	Procedure before the ISA
Art. 18	The ISR
R. 89*bis*	Electronic file management

Rule 44*bis*
International Preliminary Report on Patentability by the International Searching Authority

44*bis*.1 Issuance of Report; Transmittal to the Applicant

(a) Unless an international preliminary examination report has been or is to be established, the International Bureau shall issue a report on behalf of the International Searching Authority (in this Rule referred to as "the report") as to the matters referred to in Rule 43*bis*.1(a). The report shall have the same contents as the written opinion established under Rule 43*bis*.1.

(b) The report shall bear the title "international preliminary report on patentability (Chapter I of the Patent Cooperation Treaty)" together with an indication that it is issued under this Rule by the International Bureau on behalf of the International Searching Authority.

(c) The International Bureau shall promptly transmit one copy of the report issued under paragraph (a) to the applicant.

Time limit	The IPRP I is created by the International Bureau 30 months after the priority date (R. 44*bis*.2(a)). At this time, the IPRP I must be sent to the designated Offices. In practice, only a cover sheet is added to the ISR. The IPRP I can therefore be viewed on PATENTSCOPE after 30 months (see the recommendations of Working Group PCT/WG/6/13, www.wipo.int/edocs/mdocs/pct/en/pct_wg_6/pct_wg_6_13.pdf, adopted by the PCT Assembly on October 2, 2013).
R. 69.1	Time limit for drawing up the IPRP II: 28 months

44*bis*.2 Communication to Designated Offices

(a) Where a report has been issued under Rule 44*bis*.1, the International Bureau shall communicate it to each designated Office in accordance with Rule 93*bis*.1 but not before the expiration of 30 months from the priority date.

(b) Where the applicant makes an express request to a designated Office under Article 23(2), the International Bureau shall communicate a copy of the written opinion established by the International Searching Authority under Rule 43*bis*.1 to that Office promptly upon the request of that Office or of the applicant.

Art. 23(2)	Request for early processing

44*bis*.3 Translation for Designated Offices

(a) Any designated State may, where a report has been issued under Rule 44*bis*.1 in a language other than the official language, or one of the official languages, of its national Office, require a translation of the report into English. Any such requirement shall be notified to the International Bureau, which shall promptly publish it in the Gazette.

(b) If a translation is required under paragraph (a), it shall be prepared by or under the responsibility of the International Bureau.

(c) The International Bureau shall transmit a copy of the translation to any interested designated Office and to the applicant at the same time as it communicates the report to that Office.

(d) In the case referred to in Rule 44*bis*.2(b), the written opinion established under Rule 43*bis*.1 shall, upon request of the designated Office concerned, be translated into English by or under the responsibility of the International Bureau. The International Bureau shall transmit a copy of the translation to the designated Office concerned within two months from the date of receipt of the request for translation, and shall at the same time transmit a copy to the applicant.

44*bis*.4 Observations on the Translation

The applicant may make written observations as to the correctness of the translation referred to in Rule 44*bis*.3(b) or (d) and shall send a copy of the observations to each of the interested designated Offices and to the International Bureau.

Art. 17	Procedure before the ISA
Art. 18	ISR
R. 89*bis*	Electronic file management

Rule 45
Translation of the International Search Report

45.1 Languages

International search reports and declarations referred to in Article 17(2)(a) shall, when not in English, be translated into English.

Art. 17(2)(a)	Declaration of non-establishment of ISR
Art. 21(3)	Publication of ISR or of non-establishment

Rule 45*bis*
Supplementary International Searches

INTRODUCTION

1 The procedure aims to reduce the likelihood that new documents relevant to the state of the art will be found in the national phase at considerable cost and should take into account the growing linguistic diversity of the state of the art. This approach is intended to enhance the prospects of the national procedure, bolster the designated Office's confidence in the outcomes of the international phase, and ultimately reduce the need for additional national searches.

2 Details on the implementation of the supplementary international search at the EPO can be found in the Euro-PCT Guide. 3.4.001 et seq.

45*bis*.1 Supplementary Search Request

(a) The applicant may, at any time prior to the expiration of 22 months from the priority date, request that a supplementary international search be carried out in respect of the international application by an International Searching Authority that is competent to do so under Rule 45*bis*.9. Such requests may be made in respect of more than one such Authority.

AIs 102(f), (g)	Form PCT/IB/375 must be used. For the method of sending communications from the Office to the applicant, see annotations to R. 4.4(c).
R. 90	An agent may be appointed
	Appointment specifically for representation before the EPO as SISA possible (Euro-PCT Guide 3.4.017)
R. 90*bis*.3*bis*	Withdrawal of the request for a supplementary search
R. 90*bis*.6(b)	Discontinuation of processing after withdrawal of the international application

(b) A request under paragraph (a) ("supplementary search request") shall be submitted to the International Bureau and shall indicate:

(i) the name and address of the applicant and of the agent (if any), the title of the invention, the international filing date and the international application number;

AIs 108	Correspondence address
AIs 109, 110	File reference, dates

(ii) the International Searching Authority that is requested to carry out the supplementary international search ("Authority specified for supplementary search"); and

(iii) where the international application was filed in a language which is not accepted by that Authority, whether any translation furnished to the receiving Office under Rule 12.3 or 12.4 is to form the basis of the supplementary international search.

R. 92.2(d)	Correspondence language with International Bureau in English or French and in other languages permitted under the Administrative Instructions. Applies to request for supplementary search (AG-IP 8.009).

3 For authorized languages, see Annex SISA PCT Applicant's Guide, for EP as SISA: German, English, French; Agreement WIPO-EPO Annex B, see https://www.wipo.int/pct/en/access/isa_ipea_agreements.html and Art. 16(3)(b).

(c) The supplementary search request shall, where applicable, be accompanied by:

(i) where neither the language in which the international application was filed nor that in which a translation (if any) has been furnished under Rule 12.3 or 12.4 is accepted by the Authority specified for supplementary search, a translation of the international application into a language which is accepted by that Authority;

4 See annotation to R. 45*bis*.1(b)(iii).

(ii) preferably, a copy of a sequence listing in electronic form complying with the standard provided for in the Administrative Instructions, if required by the Authority specified for supplementary search.

R. 5.2	Sequence listing
R. 13*ter*	Is applicable via R. 45*bis*.5. Annex SISA for the authorized form of transmission of the sequence listing

(d) Where the International Searching Authority has found that the international application does not comply with the requirement of unity of invention, the supplementary search request may contain an indication of the wish of the applicant to restrict the supplementary international search to one of the inventions as identified by the International Searching Authority other than the main invention referred to in Article 17(3)(a).

R. 13	Unity of invention
R. 45*bis*.5(d)	Limitation of the supplementary search to the subject matter of the international search. However, there is no obligation for SISA to search other claims not searched by ISA (Euro-PCT Guide 3.4.011).

(e) The supplementary search request shall be considered not to have been submitted, and the International Bureau shall so declare:

(i) if it is received after the expiration of the time limit referred to in paragraph (a); or

(ii) if the Authority specified for supplementary search has not stated, in the applicable agreement under Article 16(3)(b), its preparedness to carry out such searches or is not competent to do so under Rule 45*bis*.9(b).

45*bis*.2 Supplementary Search Handling Fee

(a) The supplementary search request shall be subject to the payment of a fee for the benefit of the International Bureau ("supplementary search handling fee") as set out in the Schedule of Fees.

(b) The supplementary search handling fee shall be paid in the currency in which the fee is set out in the Schedule of Fees or in any other currency prescribed by the International Bureau. The amount in such other currency shall be the equivalent, in round figures, as established by the International Bureau, of the amount as set out in the Schedule of Fees, and shall be published in the Gazette.

For the fee, see AG-IP Annex SISA, Schedule of Fees item 2 and 5. International Bureau only accepts Swiss francs (AG-IP 8.031). 5

(c) The supplementary search handling fee shall be paid to the International Bureau within one month from the date of receipt of the supplementary search request. The amount payable shall be the amount applicable on the date of payment.

(d) The International Bureau shall refund the supplementary search handling fee to the applicant if, before the documents referred to in Rule 45*bis*.4(e)(i) to (iv) are transmitted to the Authority specified for supplementary search, the international application is withdrawn or considered withdrawn, or the supplementary search request is withdrawn or is considered not to have been submitted under Rule 45*bis*.1(e).

R. 45*bis*.4(d) No refund, but different for R. 45*bis*.3(d) (PCT Working Group comment p. 2, 3 PCT/WG/2/10)

45*bis*.3 Supplementary Search Fee

(a) Each International Searching Authority carrying out supplementary international searches may require that the applicant pay a fee ("supplementary search fee") for its own benefit for carrying out such a search.

6 See AG-IP Annex SISA for each Office. Introduction of the EPO fee since July 1, 2010 (OJ 2009, 593). Further details in WIPO-SISA Agreement Annex D I. and www.wipo.int/pct/en/access/isa_ipea_agreements.html.

(b) The supplementary search fee shall be collected by the International Bureau. Rules 16.1(b) to (e) *(currency)* shall apply *mutatis mutandis.*

(c) As to the time limit for payment of the supplementary search fee and the amount payable, the provisions of Rule 45*bis*.2(c) *(1 month)* shall apply *mutatis mutandis.*

(d) The International Bureau shall refund the supplementary search fee to the applicant if, before the documents referred to in Rule 45*bis*.4(e)(i) to (iv) are transmitted to the Authority specified for supplementary search, the international application is withdrawn or considered withdrawn, or the supplementary search request is withdrawn or is considered not to have been submitted under Rules 45*bis*.1(e) or 45*bis*.4(d).

R. 45*bis*.2(d) Other reasons for refund

7 Refund and reduction of fees in all newer agreements in Annex D instead of C of the WIPO-SISA Agreement, www.wipo.int/pct/en/access/isa_ipea_agreements.html and AG-IP Annex SISA.

R. 90*bis*.6(b) Effect of withdrawal, discontinuation of processing

(e) The Authority specified for supplementary search shall, to the extent and under the conditions provided for in the applicable agreement under Article 16(3)(b) *(e.g. WIPO-EPO agreement)*, refund the supplementary search fee if, before it has started the supplementary international search in accordance with Rule 45*bis*.5(a), the supplementary search request is considered not to have been submitted under Rule 45*bis*.5(g).

8 The conditions and amount of the refund are regulated in the respective WIPO-SISA agreement, now mostly under Annex D instead of C (www.wipo.int/pct/en/access/isa_ipea_agreements.html), see also AG-IP Annex SISA.

45*bis*.4 Checking of Supplementary Search Request; Correction of Defects; Late Payment of Fees; Transmittal to Authority Specified for Supplementary Search

(a) Promptly after receipt of a supplementary search request, the International Bureau shall check whether it complies with the requirements of Rule 45*bis*.1(b) and (c)(i) and shall invite the applicant to correct any defects within a time limit of one month from the date of the invitation.

(b) Where, by the time they are due under Rules 45*bis*.2(c) and 45*bis*.3(c), the International Bureau finds that the supplementary search handling fee and the supplementary search fee have not been paid in full, it shall invite the applicant to pay to it the amount required to cover those fees, together with the late payment fee under paragraph (c), within a time limit of one month from the date of the invitation.

Before expiry of the one-month period, only an invitation regarding outstanding fees will be issued, thereafter an invitation is ony issued in conjunction with an invitation regarding the late fee using Form PCT/IB/377 (PCT Applicant's Guide 8.035). 9

(c) The payment of fees in response to an invitation under paragraph (b) shall be subject to the payment to the International Bureau, for its own benefit, of a late payment fee whose amount shall be 50% of the supplementary search handling fee.

For the fee, see AG-IP Annex SISA. International Bureau only accepts Swiss francs (AG-IP 8.031). 10

(d) If the applicant does not furnish the required correction or does not pay the amount in full of the fees due, including the late payment fee, before the expiration of the time limit applicable under paragraph (a) or (b), respectively, the supplementary search request shall be considered not to have been submitted and the International Bureau shall so declare and shall inform the applicant accordingly.

(e) On finding that the requirements of Rule 45*bis*.1(b) and (c)(i), 45*bis*.2(c) and 45*bis*.3(c) have been complied with, the International Bureau shall promptly, but not before the date of receipt by it of the international search report or the expiration of 17 months from the priority date, whichever occurs first, transmit to the Authority specified for supplementary search a copy of each of the following:

(i) the supplementary search request;

(ii) the international application;

(iii) any sequence listing furnished under Rule 45*bis*.1(c)(ii); and

(iv) any translation furnished under Rule 12.3, 12.4 or 45*bis*.1(c)(i) which is to be used as the basis of the supplementary international search;

and, at the same time, or promptly after their later receipt by the International Bureau:

R. 45*bis*.5(a)	Refund of fees at the EPO under WIPO Agreement Annex D.II. (8) (see annotations to Art. 16(3)(b)) if the international application is withdrawn before the start of the supplementary international search but the documents under (i) to (iv) are available

(v) the international search report and the written opinion established under Rule 43*bis*.1;

(vi) any invitation by the International Searching Authority to pay additional fees referred to in Article 17(3)(a); and

(vii) any protest by the applicant under Rule 40.2(c) and the decision thereon by the review body constituted in the framework of the International Searching Authority.

(f) Upon request of the Authority specified for supplementary search, the written opinion referred to in paragraph (e)(v) shall, when not in English or in a language accepted by that Authority, be translated into English by or under the responsibility of the International Bureau. The International Bureau shall transmit a copy of the translation to that Authority within two months from the date of receipt of the request for translation, and shall at the same time transmit a copy to the applicant.

45*bis*.5 Start, Basis and Scope of Supplementary International Search

(a) The Authority specified for supplementary search shall start the supplementary international search promptly after receipt of the documents specified in Rule 45*bis*.4(e)(i) to (iv), provided that the Authority may, at its option, delay the start of the search until it has also received the documents specified in Rule 45*bis*.4(e)(v) or until the expiration of 22 months from the priority date, whichever occurs first.

R. 45*bis*.4(e)	Refund of fees at the EPO under WIPO Agreement Annex D.II.(8) (see annotations to Art. 16(3)(b)) if the international application is withdrawn before the start of the supplementary international search but the documents under (i) to (iv) are available
Art. 16(3)(b)	EPO as SISA will only start the supplementary international search if the sequence listing is available in accordance with the provisions (OJ 2021 A97 and WIPO Agreement Annex B(3), see annotations to Art. 16(3)(b)). If no copy is received, the applicant will be invited to file it subsequently and pay a late filing fee (Euro-PCT Guide 3.4.015).

(b) The supplementary international search shall be carried out on the basis of the international application as filed or of a translation referred to in Rule

45*bis*.1(b)(iii) or 45*bis*.1(c)(i), taking due account of the international search report and the written opinion established under Rule 43*bis*.1 where they are available to the Authority specified for supplementary search before it starts the search. Where the supplementary search request contains an indication under Rule 45*bis*.1(d), the supplementary international search may be restricted to the invention specified by the applicant under Rule 45*bis*.1(d) *(lack of unity of invention)* and those parts of the international application which relate to that invention.

Amendments under Art. 19 or Art. 34 are not taken into account, as they are not expressly mentioned in R. 45*bis*. (Seminar presentation dated December 23, 2020 p. 117 at https://www.wipo.int/export/sites/www/pct/en/docs/pct-seminar.pdf). 11

(c) For the purposes of the supplementary international search, Article 17(2) *(non-establishment of a report)* and Rules 13*ter*.1 *(Procedure regarding nucleotide and amino acid sequences)*, 33 *(prior art)* and 39 *(no search for certain subject matters)* shall apply *mutatis mutandis*.

R. 13*ter*.1(c)	Fee
Annex	AG-IP Annex SISA provides information on whether the authority requires a sequence listing in electronic form.

(d) Where the international search report is available to the Authority specified for supplementary search before it starts the search under paragraph (a), that Authority may exclude from the supplementary search any claims which were not the subject of the international search.

R. 45*bis*.1(d)	Limitation of the search due to lack of unity of invention
EPO	Will search claims as SISA if EPO would have searched claims as ISA (Euro-PCT Guide 3.4.011)

(e) Where the International Searching Authority has made the declaration referred to in Article 17(2)(a) and that declaration is available to the Authority specified for supplementary search before it starts the search under paragraph (a), that Authority may decide not to establish a supplementary international search report, in which case it shall so declare and promptly notify the applicant and the International Bureau accordingly.

Art. 17(2)(a)	No search by ISA due to unsuitable subject matter or insufficient disclosure
R. 13	No search by ISA due to lack of unity of invention and lack of payment of fees. The SISA does not have to carry out a search on claims which have not been searched by the ISA (AG-IP 8.044).

For the partial search and procedure at the EPO see annotations under Art. 17(3)(a).

(f) The supplementary international search shall cover at least the documentation indicated for that purpose in the applicable agreement under Article 16(3)(b).

Art. 16(3)(b)	See Annex SISA in AG-IP and Annex B of the ISA/IPEA Agreement www.wipo.int/pct/en/access/isa_ipea_agreements.html.
EP	EP as for international search: content of the official documentation collection in addition to, but not limited to, the PCT minimum test material according to R. 34 (Annex B(2) WIPO-EPO Agreement)

(g) If the Authority specified for supplementary search finds that carrying out the search is entirely excluded by a limitation or condition referred to in Rule 45*bis*.9(a), other than a limitation under Article 17(2) as applicable by virtue of Rule 45*bis*.5(c), the supplementary search request shall be considered not to have been submitted, and the Authority shall so declare and shall promptly notify the applicant and the International Bureau accordingly.

R. 45*bis*.5(a)	Refund of fees at the EPO under WIPO Agreement Annex D.II. (7) (see annotations to Art. 16(3)(b))
R. 45*bis*.9	Limitations and conditions under the WIPO-SISA agreement

(h) The Authority specified for supplementary search may, in accordance with a limitation or condition referred to in Rule 45*bis*.9(a), decide to restrict the search to certain claims only, in which case the supplementary international search report shall so indicate.

45*bis*.6 Unity of Invention

(a) If the Authority specified for supplementary search finds that the international application does not comply with the requirement of unity of invention, it shall:

Art. 64, 27, R. 51*bis*	There are no reservations to R. 13, i.e. the question of unity of invention is thus governed by R. 13 in all regional and national phases.
R. 13	Common characterizing features
Art. 17, R. 40	Lack of unity in international search, effect of R. 45*bis*.5(e)
R. 66.1*ter*	Lack of unity in top-up search
Art. 34(3), R. 68	Lack of unity in IPE

AIs 206	Unity of invention. AIs Annex B shows detailed examples of unity of invention. Further examples can be found in AIs 206, e.g. the Markush practice is explained in AIs Annex B Part 2 III.

(i) establish the supplementary international search report on those parts of the international application which relate to the invention first mentioned in the claims ("main invention");

(ii) notify the applicant of its opinion that the international application does not comply with the requirement of unity of invention and specify the reasons for that opinion; and

(iii) inform the applicant of the possibility of requesting, within the time limit referred to in paragraph (c), a review of the opinion.

In contrast to the main search, there is no possibility to extend the search by paying additional fees, but there is the possibility of a review procedure (R. 45*bis*.6(c)). An extension by payment of additional fees exists under R. 164 EPC since November 1, 2014 upon entry into the European phase (Euro-PCT Guide 3.4.020 et seq.). 12

R. 45*bis*.1(d)	allows the applicant to indicate the invention for which the supplementary international search is to be carried out. However, there is no obligation for SISA to search other claims not searched by ISA. (Euro-PCT Guide 3.4.011)

(b) In considering whether the international application complies with the requirement of unity of invention, the Authority shall take due account of any documents received by it under Rule 45*bis*.4(e)(vi) and (vii) before it starts the supplementary international search.

The Authority specified for supplementary search is not bound by the decision of the main ISA regarding unity of invention (AG-IP 8.044). 13

(c) The applicant may, within one month from the date of the notification under paragraph (a)(ii), request the Authority to review the opinion referred to in paragraph (a). The request for review may be subjected by the Authority to the payment to it, for its own benefit, of a review fee whose amount shall be fixed by it.

Determination of the fee and amount by WIPO-SISA agreement (Annex SISA PCT Applicant's Guide, www.wipo.int/pct/en/access/isa_ipea_agreements.html). 14

AG-IP Annex SISA	Review fee
Art. 2(1) No. 22 RFees	Introduction of the EPO's review fee since July 1, 2010 (OJ 2009, 593)

(d) If the applicant, within the time limit under paragraph (c), requests a review of the opinion by the Authority and pays any required review fee, the opinion shall be reviewed by the Authority. The review shall not be carried out only by the person who made the decision which is the subject of the review. Where the Authority:

(i) finds that the opinion was entirely justified, it shall notify the applicant accordingly;

(ii) finds that the opinion was partially unjustified but still considers that the international application does not comply with the requirement of unity of invention, it shall notify the applicant accordingly and, where necessary, proceed as provided for in paragraph (a)(i);

(iii) finds that the opinion was entirely unjustified, it shall notify the applicant accordingly, establish the supplementary international search report on all parts of the international application and refund the review fee to the applicant.

(e) On the request of the applicant, the text of both the request for review and the decision thereon shall be communicated to the designated Offices together with the supplementary international search report. The applicant shall submit any translation thereof with the furnishing of the translation of the international application required under Article 22.

R. 45*bis*.8(b)	Transmission of the SISR like the ISR under Art. 20(1), R. 47 by SISA to the designated Office
R. 40.2, 68.3	Rules for protest and review procedures for EPO as SISA correspond to the Rules for EPO as ISA and IPEA (OJ 2015 A59)

(f) Paragraphs (a) to (e) shall apply *mutatis mutandis* where the Authority specified for supplementary search decides to restrict the supplementary international search in accordance with the second sentence of Rule 45*bis*.5(b) or with Rule 45*bis*.5(h), provided that any reference in the said paragraphs to the "international application" shall be construed as a reference to those parts of the international application which relate to the invention specified by the applicant under Rule 45*bis*.1(d) or which relate to the claims and those parts of the international application for which the Authority will carry out a supplementary international search, respectively.

45*bis*.7 Supplementary International Search Report

(a) The Authority specified for supplementary search shall, within 28 months from the priority date, establish the supplementary international search report, or make the declaration referred to in Article 17(2)(a) as applicable by virtue of Rule 45*bis*.5(c) that no supplementary international search report will be established.

15 Form PCT/SISA/501 (communication of the results of the Supplementary International Search, including any relevant documents identified during the search) or PCT/

SISA/502 (declaration of Non-Establishment of Supplementary International Search Report) is used.

(b) Every supplementary international search report, any declaration referred to in Article 17(2)(a) as applicable by virtue of Rule 45*bis*.5(c) and any declaration under Rule 45*bis*.5(e) shall be in a language of publication.

R. 48.3	Publication languages

(c) For the purposes of establishing the supplementary international search report, Rules 43.1 *(indications)*, 43.2 *(dates)*, 43.5 *(considered documents)*, 43.6 *(fields searched)*, 43.6*bis* *(obvious mistakes)*, 43.8 *(authorized officer)* and 43.10 *(form)* shall, subject to paragraphs (d) and (e), apply *mutatis mutandis*. Rule 43.9 *(expressions of opinion)* shall apply *mutatis mutandis*, except that the references therein to Rules 43.3, 43.7 and 44.2 shall be considered non-existent. Article 20(3) *(copies)* and Rule 44.3 *(request of copies, costs)* shall apply *mutatis mutandis*.

Art. 20(3)	Transmission of copies to designated Office or applicant
R. 44.3	Charging of copying costs by SISA. Amount results from Annex SISA PCT Applicant's Guide based on agreement with WIPO at www.wipo.int/pct/en/access/isa_ipea_agreements.html, updated by PCT Gazette.

The Supplementary International Search Report (SISR) is not published separately; 16
however, after the international application is published, the SISR becomes available on PATENTSCOPE at http://patentscope.wipo.int/search/de/structuredSearch.jsf (AG-IP 8.053.)

(d) The supplementary international search report need not contain the citation of any document cited in the international search report, except where the document needs to be cited in conjunction with other documents that were not cited in the international search report.

(e) The supplementary international search report may contain explanations:

(i) with regard to the citations of the documents considered to be relevant;

This means that the supplementary international search report may include more 17
detailed explanations of cited documents when such detail is essential for fully understanding the prior art (AG-IP 8.049).(AG-IP 8.049)

(ii) with regard to the scope of the supplementary international search.

The EPO does not issue a separate written opinion, but only gives explanations which 18
are equivalent to a written opinion as ISA (OJ 5/2010, 318).

R. 161 EPC	Invitation to comment on negative objections under R. 45*bis*.7(e) after entry into the European phase at the EPO (in force since April 1, 2010: OJ 2009, p. 582; OJ 2010 pp. 316, 319, 406; amended on May 1, 2011, OJ 2011 p. 354)
R. 164 EPC	Invitation after entry into the European phase to pay further search fees or to limit the application in case of lack of unity. The new procedure described under Art. 17(3)(a) also applies to supplementary European searches. Here, too, a written opinion on the invention first mentioned in the patent claims will be drawn up and sent with the invitation to pay further search fees (OJ 2017 A20)).

45*bis*.8 Transmittal and Effect of the Supplementary International Search Report

(a) The Authority specified for supplementary search shall, on the same day, transmit one copy of the supplementary international search report or the declaration that no supplementary international search report shall be established, as applicable, to the International Bureau and one copy to the applicant.

R. 90*bis*.3*bis*	Relevant for time limit for withdrawal of the request for supplementary search

(b) Subject to paragraph (c), Article 20(1) *(transmittal to designated Office)* and Rules 45.1 *(translation into English)*, 47.1(d) *(translation to designated Office)* and 70.7(a) *(indications in the IPRP II)* shall apply as if the supplementary international search report were part of the international search report.

Art. 20(1)	Transmittal of the SISR or declaration of non-establishment by SISA to the designated Office as for the ISR by ISA to the designated Office under R. 47, together with translation

(c) A supplementary international search report need not be taken into account by the International Preliminary Examining Authority for the purposes of a written opinion or the international preliminary examination report if it is received by that Authority after it has begun to draw up that opinion or report.

AIs 420(b)	If IPEA is not the same authority as SISA, International Bureau will send SISR or declaration of non-establishment to IPEA without delay

45*bis*.9 International Searching Authorities Competent to Carry Out Supplementary International Search

(a) An International Searching Authority shall be competent to carry out supplementary international searches if its preparedness to do so is stated in the

applicable agreement under Article 16(3)(b) *(WIPO-SISA agreements)*, subject to any limitations and conditions set out in that agreement.

Art. 16	Authorities competent to carry out the supplementary international search: AT, EA since July 1, 2022 (PCT Gazette May 12, 2022), EP, FI, PH, RU, SE, SG, TR, UA, XN, XV (i.e. CZ, HU, PL, SK)

Current agreements with WIPO can be accessed at www.wipo.int/pct/en/access/isa_ipea_agreements.html, where Art. 3(4) is referenced in each agreement. 19

Applicants have free choice among the competent authorities, except for the authority that conducted the international search, as highlighted in a seminar presentation dated December 23, 2020 (see p. 113 at https://www.wipo.int/export/sites/www/pct/en/docs/pct-seminar.pdf). In contrast to ISA and IPEA, the competence of SISA does not depend on the receiving Office (PCT Newsletter 12/2008, p. 2) 20

Details on fees and procedures before the above-mentioned authorities can be found in Annex SISA, PCT Applicant's Guide and www.wipo.int/pct/en/guide/index.html. 21

(b) The International Searching Authority carrying out the international search under Article 16(1) in respect of an international application shall not be competent to carry out a supplementary international search in respect of that application.

(c) The limitations referred to in paragraph (a) may, for example, include limitations as to the subject matter for which supplementary international searches will be carried out, other than limitations under Article 17(2) as applicable by virtue of Rule 45*bis*.5(c), limitations as to the total number of supplementary international searches which will be carried out in a given period, and limitations to the effect that the supplementary international searches will not extend to any claim beyond a certain number of claims.

The agreements between the ISAs and WIPO generally contain a provision in Art. 4 that no search will be carried out under R. 39.1 unless the subject matter is authorized under national law. 22

EP	The restrictions relating to the subject matter listed in Annex C to the EPO-WIPO Agreement apply both when the EPO acts as ISA and when it acts as SISA (see annotations to R. 39.1). The same applies to all other reasons for not performing a (full) search, i.e. complex applications, lack of sequence listings and lack of unity (Euro-PCT Guide 3.4.010).

See respective WIPO Agreements, in annotations to Art. 16(3) and AG-IP Annex (SISA). 23

Rule 46
Amendment of Claims before the International Bureau

46.1 Time Limit

The time limit referred to in Article 19 shall be two months from the date of transmittal of the international search report to the International Bureau and to the applicant by the International Searching Authority or 16 months from the priority date, whichever time limit expires later, provided that any amendment made under Article 19 which is received by the International Bureau after the expiration of the applicable time limit shall be considered to have been received by that Bureau on the last day of that time limit if it reaches it before the technical preparations for international publication have been completed.

Art. 21(5)	Completion of technical preparations generally 15 days before publication
R. 48.2(h)	If the two months since the transmission of the ISR are after the completion of the technical preparations for publication of the PCTa (Art. 21(5)), the amended claims will be published subsequently in the form of an A4 document.
R. 90*bis*.3(e)	International publication after completion of technical preparations (AG-IP 9.004)

1 The date of dispatch on the last page of the ISR 'date of mailing' is decisive for the start of the time limit, not the date of completion of the international search. To take account of the postal route, the letter is dated two days earlier.

46.2 Where to File

Amendments made under Article 19 shall be filed directly with the International Bureau.

46.3 Language of Amendments

If the international application has been filed in a language other than the language in which it is published, any amendment made under Article 19 shall be in the language of publication.

R. 12.2	If Art. 19 is not applicable, R. 12.2 applies.

46.4 Statement

(a) The statement referred to in Article 19(1) shall be in the language in which the international application is published and shall not exceed 500 words if in the English language or if translated into that language. The statement shall be identified as such by a heading, preferably by using the words "Statement under Article 19(1)" or their equivalent in the language of the statement.

(b) The statement shall contain no disparaging comments on the international search report or the relevance of citations contained in that report. Reference to citations, relevant to a given claim, contained in the international search report may be made only in connection with an amendment of that claim.

46.5 Form of Amendments

(a) The applicant, when making amendments under Article 19, shall be required to submit a replacement sheet or sheets containing a complete set of claims in replacement of all the claims originally filed.

(b) The replacement sheet or sheets shall be accompanied by a letter which:

(i) shall identify the claims which, on account of the amendments, differ from the claims originally filed, and shall draw attention to the differences between the claims originally filed and the claims as amended;

(ii) shall identify the claims originally filed which, on account of the amendments, are cancelled;

(iii) shall indicate the basis for the amendments in the application as filed.

R. 70.2(c-*bis*)	Non-recognition of amendments in IPRP II
R. 66.1*ter*	Non-recognition of amendments in the supplementary search and limitation to the scope of the IPER at the EPO
AIs 205	Numbering and identification of claims upon amendment

Rule 47
Communication to Designated Offices

47.1 Procedure

(a) The communication provided for in Article 20 shall be effected by the International Bureau to each designated Office in accordance with Rule 93*bis*.1 but, subject to Rule 47.4, not prior to the international publication of the international application.

R. 93*bis*	Restricted transmission, electronic download if necessary. Transmission only on request, at a specific time and, if applicable, in electronic form.
R. 76.5	Application of procedure before elected Office

(a-*bis*) The International Bureau shall notify each designated Office, in accordance with Rule 93*bis*.1, of the fact and date of receipt of the record copy and of the fact and date of receipt of any priority document.

(b) Any amendment received by the International Bureau within the time limit under Rule 46.1 which was not included in the communication provided for in Article 20 shall be communicated promptly to the designated Offices by the International Bureau, and the latter shall notify the applicant accordingly.

(c) The International Bureau shall, promptly after the expiration of 28 months from the priority date, send a notice to the applicant indicating:

(i) the designated Offices which have requested that the communication provided for in Article 20 be effected under Rule 93*bis*.1 and the date of such communication to those Offices; and

(ii) the designated Offices which have not requested that the communication provided for in Article 20 be effected under Rule 93*bis*.1.

1 Editor's note (WIPO) (https://www.wipo.int/export/sites/www/pct/en/docs/texts/pct-regs.pdf p.103 FN 8): 'Rule 47.1(c) and (e) shall apply to any international application whose international filing date is on or after January 1, 2004 and in respect of a designated Office which has made a notification under paragraph (2) of the decisions of the Assembly set out in Annex IV of document PCT/A/30/7 (to the effect that the modification of the time limit fixed in Article 22(1) was not compatible

with the national law applied by that Office on October 3, 2001), and which has not withdrawn that notification under paragraph (3) of those decisions, as though the reference in each of Rule 47.1(c) and (e) to "28 months" was a reference to "19 months," with the consequence that two notifications under Rule 47.1(c) shall, if applicable, be sent in respect of such an application.'

Currently, this is applicable to LU and TZ as detailed on www.wipo.int/pct/en/ texts/time_limits.html. 2

As a result, the International Bureau will issue two notifications under R. 47.1(c): a 'First Notice' after 19 months from the priority date (Form PCT/IB/308 (First Notice)) for the aforementioned States, and a 'Second and Supplementary Notice' after 28 months from the priority date (Form PCT/IB/308 (Second and Supplementary Notice)) for all other Member States. Refer to the annotations to Art. 20 for further details. 3

(c-*bis*) The notice referred to in paragraph (c) shall be accepted by designated Offices:

(i) in the case of a designated Office referred to in paragraph (c)(i), as conclusive evidence that the communication provided for in Article 20 was effected on the date specified in the notice;

(ii) in the case of a designated Office referred to in paragraph (c)(ii), as conclusive evidence that the Contracting State for which that Office acts as designated Office does not require the furnishing, under Article 22, by the applicant of a copy of the international application.

(d) Each designated Office shall, when it so requires, receive the international search reports and the declarations referred to in Article 17(2)(a) also in the translation referred to in Rule 45.1.

(e) Where any designated Office has not, before the expiration of 28 months from the priority date, requested the International Bureau to effect the communication provided for in Article 20 in accordance with Rule 93*bis*.1, the Contracting State for which that Office acts as designated Office shall be considered to have notified the International Bureau, under Rule 49.1(a-*bis*), that it does not require the furnishing, under Article 22, by the applicant of a copy of the international application.

See annotation to para. (c). 4

47.2 Copies

The copies required for communication shall be prepared by the International Bureau. Further details concerning the copies required for communication may be provided for in the Administrative Instructions.

47.3 Languages

(a) The international application communicated under Article 20 shall be in the language in which it is published.

(b) Where the language in which the international application is published is different from the language in which it was filed, the International Bureau shall furnish to any designated Office, upon the request of that Office, a copy of that application in the language in which it was filed.

47.4 Express Request under Article 23(2) prior to International Publication

Where the applicant makes an express request to a designated Office under Article 23(2) *(early start of national phase)* prior to the international publication of the international application, the International Bureau shall, upon request of the applicant or the designated Office, promptly effect the communication provided for in Article 20 to that Office.

Rule 48
International Publication

48.1 Form and Means

The form in which and the means by which international applications are published shall be governed by the Administrative Instructions.

48.2 Contents

(a) The publication of the international application shall contain:

(i) a standardized front page;

(ii) the description;

(iii) the claims;

(iv) the drawings, if any;

(v) subject to paragraph (g), the international search report or the declaration under Article 17(2)(a) *(non-establishment of ISR)*;

(vi) any statement filed under Article 19(1) *(amendment of claims)*, unless the International Bureau finds that the statement does not comply with the provisions of Rule 46.4;

(vii) where the request for publication under Rule 91.3(d) *(rejected request for correction)* was received by the International Bureau before the completion of the technical preparations for international publication, any request for rectification of an obvious mistake, any reasons and any comments referred to in Rule 91.3(d);

R. 91.3(d) — If the request for publication of the rejection of a request for rectification under R. 91.3(d) is filed before completion of the technical preparations, it will be published with the international publication, provided that the corresponding fee has also been paid (R. 91.3(d) and AIs 113)

R. 48.2(k), R. 48.2(i) — If the request is filed after the technical preparations have been completed, the rejected request for rectification shall be published in accordance with R. 48.2(k) and the approved request for rectification shall be published in accordance with R. 48.2(i)

Art. 21(5) — Completion of the technical preparations

(viii) the indications in relation to deposited biological material furnished under Rule 13*bis* separately from the description, together with an indication of the date on which the International Bureau received such indications;

(ix) any information concerning a priority claim referred to in Rule 26*bis*.2(d) *(existing or void claim)*;

(x) any declaration referred to in Rule 4.17, and any correction thereof under Rule 26*ter*.1, which was received by the International Bureau before the expiration of the time limit under Rule 26*ter*.1;

(xi) any information concerning a request under Rule 26*bis*.3 for restoration of the right of priority and the decision of the receiving Office upon such request, including information as to the criterion for restoration upon which the decision was based.

(b) Subject to paragraph (c), the front page shall include:

(i) data taken from the request sheet and such other data as are prescribed by the Administrative Instructions;

(ii) a figure or figures where the international application contains drawings, unless Rule 8.2(b) *(drawings not useful)* applies;

(iii) the abstract; if the abstract is both in English and in another language, the English text shall appear first;

(iv) where applicable, an indication that the request contains a declaration referred to in Rule 4.17 which was received by the International Bureau before the expiration of the time limit under Rule 26*ter*.1;

(v) where the international filing date has been accorded by the receiving Office under Rule 20.3(b)(ii), 20.5(d) or 20.5*bis*(d) on the basis of the incorporation by reference under Rules 4.18 and 20.6 of an element or part, an indication to that effect, together with an indication as to whether the applicant, for the purposes of Rule 20.6(a)(ii), relied on compliance with Rule 17.1(a), (b) or (b-*bis*) in relation to the priority document or on a separately submitted copy of the earlier application concerned;

(vi) where applicable, an indication that the published international application contains information under Rule 26*bis*.2(d) *(existing or void claim)*;

(vii) where applicable, an indication that the published international application contains information concerning a request under Rule 26*bis*.3 for restoration of the right of priority and the decision of the receiving Office upon such request;

(viii) where applicable, an indication that an erroneously filed element or part has been removed from the international application in accordance with Rule 20.5*bis*(b) or (c).

R. 20.5*bis*	Erroneously filed elements and parts
R. 26*bis*.3(f)	Receiving Office may require evidence in support of request for restoration of the right of priority

R. 26*bis*.3(h)(iv)	Transmission of documents to the International Bureau
R. 26*bis*.3(h-*bis*)	Exceptions to the duty to forward

(c) Where a declaration under Article 17(2)(a) has issued, the front page shall conspicuously refer to that fact and need include neither a drawing nor an abstract.

(d) The figure or figures referred to in paragraph (b)(ii) shall be selected as provided in Rule 8.2. Reproduction of such figure or figures on the front page may be in a reduced form.

(e) If there is not enough room on the front page for the totality of the abstract referred to in paragraph (b)(iii), the said abstract shall appear on the back of the front page. The same shall apply to the translation of the abstract when such translation is required to be published under Rule 48.3(c).

(f) If the claims have been amended under Article 19, the publication of the international application shall contain the full text of the claims both as filed and as amended. Any statement referred to in Article 19(1) shall be included as well, unless the International Bureau finds that the statement does not comply with the provisions of Rule 46.4. The date of receipt of the amended claims by the International Bureau shall be indicated.

R. 48(h)	Subsequent publication is possible

(g) If, at the time of the completion of the technical preparations for international publication, the international search report is not yet available, the front page shall contain an indication to the effect that that report was not available and that the international search report (when it becomes available) will be separately published together with a revised front page.

(h) If, at the time of the completion of the technical preparations for international publication, the time limit for amending the claims under Article 19 has not expired, the front page shall refer to that fact and indicate that, should the claims be amended under Article 19, then, promptly after receipt by the International Bureau of such amendments within the time limit under Rule 46.1, the full text of the claims as amended will be published together with a revised front page. If a statement under Article 19(1) has been filed, that statement shall be published as well, unless the International Bureau finds that the statement does not comply with the provisions of Rule 46.4.

This is done in the form of an A4 document (see https://www.wipo.int/patentscope/ 1
en/data/kind_codes.html).

Art. 19(1), R. 46.1	The time limit is two months from transmittal of ISR to International Bureau and applicant or 16 months from priority date
R. 46.4	Requirements for the statement under Art. 19(1)

(i) If the authorization by the receiving Office, the International Searching Authority or the International Bureau of a rectification of an obvious mistake in the international application under Rule 91.1 *(refused rectification)* is received by or, where applicable, given by the International Bureau after completion of the technical preparations for international publication, a statement reflecting all the rectifications shall be published, together with the sheets containing the rectifications, or the replacement sheets and the letter furnished under Rule 91.2, as the case may be, and the front page shall be republished.

Para. (i)	only refers to authorization by the receiving Office, ISA, or International Bureau
R. 91.1(b)(iii)	According to the Working Group's commentary on the amendment of R. 48.2, document PCT/WG/3/8 pp. 3, Annex, p. 4, it is clear that para. (i) does not apply where the rectification of an obvious mistake is authorized by the IPEA under R. 91.1(b)(iii) for compliance with Art. 38
R. 70	Corrections can be provided to the elected Offices as an annex to the report according to R. 70.16 or, if not possible, via the International Bureau according to R. 70.2(e) and AIs 413 (PCT WG/3/8 p. 3, Annex p. 4)

(j) If, at the time of completion of the technical preparations for international publication, a request under Rule 26*bis*.3 for restoration of the right of priority is still pending, the published international application shall contain, in place of the decision by the receiving Office upon that request, an indication to the effect that such decision was not available and that the decision, when it becomes available, will be separately published.

(k) If a request for publication under Rule 91.3(d) was received by the International Bureau after the completion of the technical preparations for international publication, the request for rectification, any reasons and any comments referred to in that Rule shall be promptly published after the receipt of such request for publication, and the front page shall be republished.

(l) The International Bureau shall, upon a reasoned request by the applicant received by the International Bureau prior to the completion of the technical preparations for international publication, omit from publication any information, if it finds that:

(i) this information does not obviously serve the purpose of informing the public about the international application;

(ii) publication of such information would clearly prejudice the personal or economic interests of any person; and

(iii) there is no prevailing public interest to have access to that information.

Rule 26.4 shall apply *mutatis mutandis* as to the manner in which the applicant shall present the information which is the subject of a request made under this paragraph.

Para. (l)	grants the applicant a right of request to exclude personal information from publication of the application for lack of prevailing public interest.
Para. (m)	allows the authorities to inform the applicant of the possibility
Para. (n)	allows the International Bureau to inform the other authorities involved (PCT/WG/7/30 No. 410 et seq.)

In contrast to the request for limitation of access to files under R. 94, the time limit under para. (l) must be observed here. 2

Sensitive personal data may be omitted from publication (R. 94.1(d); R. 94.1*bis*(c); R. 94.1*ter*(c); R. 94.2(c); R. 48.2(l)(ii))) upon reasoned request (Form PCT/IB/384). Many Offices omit documents for internal use from file inspection (for example, R. 94.1(g)). 3

According to information from the WIPO helpdesk, the omission by the International Bureau will be effective against everyone; therefore, data protection in the international phase is binding for the designated and elected Offices. PCT takes precedence over national law unless national law is more favorable to the applicant (Art. 27(4)). 4

Art. 21(5)	Completion of the technical preparations
R. 9.2	Possibility for the authorities to point out excludable contents of the PCTa
R. 26.4	Examination and correction of certain elements of the PCTa before the receiving Office. Corresponding applicability means: filing of explanatory letters and replacement sheets. The replacement sheets are published, the replaced sheets and explanatory letters are part of the file of the International Bureau, but no public access is granted to them (PCT/WG/8/12, Nos. 14, 15).
R. 94.1	Access to files held by the International Bureau
AIs 218	Processing of a request for omission of information before the International Bureau

(m) Where the receiving Office, the International Searching Authority, the Authority specified for supplementary search or the International Bureau notes any information meeting the criteria set out under paragraph (l), that Office, Authority or Bureau may suggest to the applicant to request the omission from international publication in accordance with paragraph (l).

(n) Where the International Bureau has omitted information from international publication in accordance with paragraph (l) and that information is also contained in the file of the international application held by the receiving Office, the International Searching Authority, the Authority specified for supplementary search or the International Preliminary Examining Authority, the International Bureau shall promptly notify that Office and Authority accordingly.

For the relation between paras (l), (m), (n) see annotations to para. (l) 5

6 The applicant is also informed by the International Bureau if it has decided that the information is not excluded from publication (AG-IP 9.016A).

7 The documents are available from the International Bureau at https://patentscope.wipo.int/search/en/structuredSearch.jsf.

R. 4.1	See general annotations for licensing indications at the end of R. 4.1
AIs 801 et seq.	Third party prior art observations after the international publication and before the expiry of 28 months from the priority date via ePCT: after examination by the International Bureau, the observation is published without the relevant documents together with a statement by the applicant (AG-IP 11.109 et seq.)

48.3 Languages of Publication

(a) If the international application is filed in Arabic, Chinese, English, French, German, Japanese, Korean, Portuguese, Russian or Spanish ("languages of publication"), that application shall be published in the language in which it was filed.

8 For statements of WIPO concerning R. 48.3, criteria for future addition of further languages, see PCT/A/38, Annex III (https://www.wipo.int/edocs/mdocs/govbody/en/pct_a_38/pct_a_38_6.pdf).

(b) If the international application is not filed in a language of publication and a translation into a language of publication has been furnished under Rule 12.3 or 12.4, that application shall be published in the language of that translation.

(c) If the international application is published in a language other than English, the international search report to the extent that it is published under Rule 48.2(a)(v), or the declaration referred to in Article 17(2)(a), the title of the invention, the abstract and any text matter pertaining to the figure or figures accompanying the abstract shall be published both in that language and in English. The translations, if not furnished by the applicant under Rule 12.3, shall be prepared under the responsibility of the International Bureau.

R. 87.1	Service of publications

48.4 Earlier Publication on the Applicant's Request

(a) Where the applicant asks for publication under Articles 21(2)(b) and 64(3)(c)(i) and the international search report, or the declaration referred to in Article 17(2)(a), is not yet available for publication together with the international application, the International Bureau shall collect a special publication fee whose amount shall be fixed in the Administrative Instructions.

Art. 21(2)(b) For factors to be considered before requesting early publication, see annotations to Art. 21(2)(b)

AIs 113 Special fee payable to the International Bureau: Annex B (IB) AG-IP

(b) Publication under Articles 21(2)(b) and 64(3)(c)(i) shall be effected by the International Bureau promptly after the applicant has asked for it and, where a special fee is due under paragraph (a), after receipt of such fee.

48.5 Notification of National Publication

Where the publication of the international application by the International Bureau is governed by Article 64(3)(c)(ii), the national Office concerned shall, promptly after effecting the national publication referred to in the said provision, notify the International Bureau of the fact of such national publication.

48.6 Announcing of Certain Facts

(a) If any notification under Rule 29.1(ii) reaches the International Bureau at a time later than that at which it was able to prevent the international publication of the international application, the International Bureau shall promptly publish a notice in the Gazette reproducing the essence of such notification.

(b) [Deleted]

(c) If the international application, the designation of any designated State or the priority claim is withdrawn under Rule 90*bis* after the technical preparations for international publication have been completed, notice of the withdrawal shall be published in the Gazette.

Art. 21(5) Completion of the technical preparations

Rule 49
Copy, Translation and Fee under Article 22

Art. 22 Introduction	Detailed overview of start and entry into national phase
R. 76.5	Application before the elected Office

49.1 Notification

(a) Any Contracting State requiring the furnishing of a translation or the payment of a national fee, or both, under Article 22, shall notify the International Bureau of:

(i) the languages from which and the language into which it requires translation,

(ii) the amount of the national fee.

(a-*bis*) Any Contracting State not requiring the furnishing, under Article 22, by the applicant of a copy of the international application (even though the communication of the copy of the international application by the International Bureau under Rule 47 has not taken place by the expiration of the time limit applicable under Article 22) shall notify the International Bureau accordingly.

Art. 22	Copy, translation of PCTa and fee to designated Offices
GL Exam E-IX, 2.1.2	EPO does not require the applicant to transmit a copy of the application under Art. 22(1) even if the transmission from the International Bureau to the EPO has not taken place (R. 49.1(a-*bis*), PCT Gazette 14/1986, 2367; R. 159(1), 160, Art. 153(3)-(5) EPC 2000). The International Bureau does not send a notice to the applicant under R. 47.1(c).

(a-*ter*) Any Contracting State which, pursuant to Article 24(2), maintains, if it is a designated State, the effect provided for in Article 11(3) even though a copy of the international application is not furnished by the applicant by the expiration of the time limit applicable under Article 22 shall notify the International Bureau accordingly.

(b) Any notification received by the International Bureau under paragraphs (a), (a-*bis*) or (a-*ter*) shall be promptly published by the International Bureau in the Gazette.

The EPO notified the International Bureau (see PCT Gazette 14/1986, 2367) under this Rule. 1

(c) If the requirements under paragraph (a) change later, such changes shall be notified by the Contracting State to the International Bureau and that Bureau shall promptly publish the notification in the Gazette. If the change means that translation is required into a language which, before the change, was not required, such change shall be effective only with respect to international applications filed later than two months after the publication of the notification in the Gazette. Otherwise, the effective date of any change shall be determined by the Contracting State.

49.2 Languages

The language into which translation may be required must be an official language of the designated Office. If there are several of such languages, no translation may be required if the international application is in one of them. If there are several official languages and a translation must be furnished, the applicant may choose any of those languages. Notwithstanding the foregoing provisions of this paragraph, if there are several official languages but the national law prescribes the use of one such language for foreigners, a translation into that language may be required.

49.3 Statements under Article 19; Indications under Rule 13*bis*.4

For the purposes of Article 22 and the present Rule, any statement made under Article 19(1) and any indication furnished under Rule 13*bis*.4 shall, subject to Rule 49.5(c) and (h), be considered part of the international application.

49.4 Use of National Form

No applicant shall be required to use a national form when performing the acts referred to in Article 22.

At the EPO, Form 1200 is recommended for this (AG-NP EP.01), or its electronic equivalent. 2

49.5 Contents of and Physical Requirements for the Translation

(a) For the purposes of Article 22, the translation of the international application shall contain the description (subject to paragraph (a-*bis*)), the claims, any text matter of the drawings and the abstract. If required by the designated Office, the translation shall also, subject to paragraphs (b), (c-*bis*) and (e),

(i) contain the request,

(ii) if the claims have been amended under Article 19, contain both the claims as filed and the claims as amended (the claims as amended shall be furnished in the form of a translation of the complete set of claims furnished under Rule 46.5(a) in replacement of all the claims originally filed), and

R. 49.5(c-*bis*) Legal consequences

(iii) be accompanied by a copy of the drawings.

3 R 45.5 deals with a condition for entering the national phase. That has to be distinguished from the fact that after an amendment of the PCTa during the national phase it might be necessary to furnish new drawings (statement of WIPO concerning R. 49.5(a)(iii) see PCT/A/XI/9, p.10, para. 60 (https://www.wipo.int/edocs/mdocs/govbody/en/pct_a_xi/pct_a_xi_9.pdf).

(a-*bis*) No designated Office shall require the applicant to furnish to it a translation of any text matter contained in the sequence listing part of the description if such sequence listing part complies with Rule 12.1(d) and includes the language-dependent free text in a language which the designated Office accepts for the purpose, save that a designated Office which supplies published sequence listings to database providers may require a translation of the sequence listing part of the description into English, in accordance with the Administrative Instructions, where the language-dependent free text is not included in English.

R. 5.2(b) Language-dependent free text in the sequence listing part of the description

(b) Any designated Office requiring the furnishing of a translation of the request shall furnish copies of the request form in the language of the translation free of charge to the applicants. The form and contents of the request form in the language of the translation shall not be different from those of the request under Rules 3 and 4; in particular, the request form in the language of the translation shall not ask for any information that is not in the request as filed. The use of the request form in the language of the translation shall be optional.

(c) Where the applicant did not furnish a translation of any statement made under Article 19(1), the designated Office may disregard such statement.

PCT/A/XI/9, p.10, para. 61 The designated Office 'could take it into account, for instance, if it was drafted in a language which was understood by its examiners. On the other hand, disregarding the statement would be the only possible sanction in case of failure to furnish a translation thereof.'

(https://www.wipo.int/edocs/mdocs/govbody/en/pct_a_xi/pct_a_xi_9.pdf).

(c-*bis*) Where the applicant furnishes, to a designated Office which requires under paragraph (a)(ii) a translation of both the claims as filed and the claims as amended, only one of the required two translations, the designated Office may disregard the claims of which a translation has not been furnished or invite the applicant to furnish the missing translation within a time limit which shall be reasonable under the circumstances and shall be fixed in the invitation. Where the designated Office chooses to invite the applicant to furnish the missing translation and the latter is not furnished within the time limit fixed in the invitation, the designated Office may disregard those claims of which a translation has not been furnished or consider the international application withdrawn.

Art. 153(2) EPC, R. 159 EPC	EPO procedure: the EPO disregards untranslated claims amended under Art. 19 (Euro-PCT Guide 5.5.006 et seq.). As a rule, there is no invitation to subsequent filing of a translation. Clarification by the EPO that the PCTa is not considered withdrawn (PCT Gazette February 7, 2019).
R. 49.5(l).	Reservations to para. (c-*bis*) by BR and US
PCT/CAL/IV/6, p. 11, para. 79	'The International Bureau stressed that the proposed provision did not deny the right of the designated Offices to require a translation of the claims both as filed and as amended. Rather, the proposal provided a safeguard for applicants who overlook the requirement of furnishing both translations by giving them the opportunity, upon invitation by the designated Office, to comply with it.' (https://www.wipo.int/edocs/mdocs/pct/en/pct_cal_iv_part_i/pct_cal_iv_part_i_6.pdf).
PCT/A/XVIII/9, p. 6, para. 41	The effect of withdrawal is only referring 'to the loss of effect of the international application in the designated State referred to in Article 24' (https://www.wipo.int/edocs/mdocs/govbody/en/pct_a_xviii/pct_a_xviii_9.pdf).

(d) If any drawing contains text matter, the translation of that text matter shall be furnished either in the form of a copy of the original drawing with the translation pasted on the original text matter or in the form of a drawing executed anew.

(e) Any designated Office requiring under paragraph (a) the furnishing of a copy of the drawings shall, where the applicant failed to furnish such copy within the time limit applicable under Article 22, invite the applicant to furnish such copy within a time limit which shall be reasonable under the circumstances and shall be fixed in the invitation.

(f) The expression "Fig." does not require translation into any language.

(g) Where any copy of the drawings or any drawing executed anew which has been furnished under paragraph (d) or (e) does not comply with the physical requirements referred to in Rule 11, the designated Office may invite the applicant

to correct the defect within a time limit which shall be reasonable under the circumstances and shall be fixed in the invitation.

PCT/A/XI/9, p. 11, para. 59	'since this was merely a defect concerning a physical requirement under Rule 11, it should not consider the international application withdrawn and it should not disregard the drawing.' (https://www.wipo.int/edocs/mdocs/govbody/en/pct_a_xi/pct_a_xi_9.pdf).

(h) Where the applicant did not furnish a translation of the abstract or of any indication furnished under Rule 13*bis*.4, the designated Office shall invite the applicant to furnish such translation, if it deems it to be necessary, within a time limit which shall be reasonable under the circumstances and shall be fixed in the invitation.

(i) Information on any requirement and practice of designated Offices under the second sentence of paragraph (a) shall be published by the International Bureau in the Gazette.

(j) No designated Office shall require that the translation of the international application comply with physical requirements other than those prescribed for the international application as filed.

(k) Where a title has been established by the International Searching Authority pursuant to Rule 37.2 *(title of the invention)*, the translation shall contain the title as established by that Authority.

R. 49.5(l).	Reservations to para. (k) by the US

(l) If, on July 12, 1991, paragraph (c-*bis*) or paragraph (k) is not compatible with the national law applied by the designated Office, the paragraph concerned shall not apply to that designated Office for as long as it continues not to be compatible with that law, provided that the said Office informs the International Bureau accordingly by December 31, 1991. The information received shall be promptly published by the International Bureau in the Gazette.

4 A notice was published from BR regarding para. (c-*bis*) and from the US regarding paras (c-*bis*) and (k).

49.6 Reinstatement of Rights after Failure to Perform the Acts Referred to in Article 22

Art. 22	Entry into the national phase after Chapter I

(a) Where the effect of the international application provided for in Article 11(3) has ceased because the applicant failed to perform the acts referred to in Article

22 within the applicable time limit, the designated Office shall, upon request of the applicant, and subject to paragraphs (b) to (e) of this Rule, reinstate the rights of the applicant with respect to that international application if it finds that any delay in meeting that time limit was unintentional or, at the option of the designated Office, that the failure to meet that time limit occurred in spite of due care required by the circumstances having been taken.

A comparison with the wording of R. 26*bis*.3 shows that in principle the criterion 'unintentional' is to be applied here for all designated Offices, unless the designated Office has expressly chosen the criterion 'due care'. 5

(b) The request under paragraph (a) shall be submitted to the designated Office, and the acts referred to in Article 22 shall be performed, within whichever of the following periods expires first:

(i) two months from the date of removal of the cause of the failure to meet the applicable time limit under Article 22; or

(ii) 12 months from the date of the expiration of the applicable time limit under Article 22;

provided that the applicant may submit the request at any later time if so permitted by the national law applicable by the designated Office.

(c) The request under paragraph (a) shall state the reasons for the failure to comply with the applicable time limit under Article 22.

(d) The national law applicable by the designated Office may require:

(i) that a fee be paid in respect of a request under paragraph (a);

Art. 2(1) No. 13 RFees	For the fee at the EPO, see https://www.epo.org/en/applying/fees/international-fees/important-fees Code 013

(ii) that a declaration or other evidence in support of the reasons referred to in paragraph (c) be filed.

(e) The designated Office shall not refuse a request under paragraph (a) without giving the applicant the opportunity to make observations on the intended refusal within a time limit which shall be reasonable under the circumstances.

(f) If, on October 1, 2002, paragraphs (a) to (e) are not compatible with the national law applied by the designated Office, those paragraphs shall not apply in respect of that designated Office for as long as they continue not to be compatible with that law, provided that the said Office informs the International Bureau accordingly by January 1, 2003. The information received shall be promptly published by the International Bureau in the Gazette.

R. 49.6(f)	This information is also published on the WIPO website at https://www.wipo.int/pct/en/texts/reservations/res_incomp.html.

	A communication has been published by: CA, CN, DE, IN, KR, LV, MX, NZ, PH, PL.
R. 135 EPC	Request for further processing as alternative to request under R. 49.6 in case of failure to observe time limit R. 160 EPC

6 For further remedies in connection with the Covid-19 pandemic, see PCT Newsletter 3/2020, p. 6 and https://www.wipo.int/pct/en/covid_19/covid_update.html.

Rule 49*bis* Indications as to Protection Sought for Purposes of National Processing

Art. 22 Introduction	No. 1.2.3 referring to kind of protection in the overview of entry into national phase
R. 76.5	Application before the elected Office

49*bis*.1 Choice of Certain Kinds of Protection

(a) If the applicant wishes the international application to be treated, in a designated State in respect of which Article 43 applies, as an application not for the grant of a patent but for the grant of another kind of protection referred to in that Article, the applicant, when performing the acts referred to in Article 22, shall so indicate to the designated Office.

(b) If the applicant wishes the international application to be treated, in a designated State in respect of which Article 44 applies, as an application for the grant of more than one kind of protection referred to in Article 43, the applicant, when performing the acts referred to in Article 22, shall so indicate to the designated Office and shall indicate, if applicable, which kind of protection is sought primarily and which kind is sought subsidiarily.

(c) In the cases referred to in paragraphs (a) and (b), if the applicant wishes the international application to be treated, in a designated State, as an application for a patent of addition, certificate of addition, inventor's certificate of addition or utility certificate of addition, the applicant, when performing the acts referred to in Article 22, shall indicate the relevant parent application, parent patent or other parent grant.

(d) If the applicant wishes the international application to be treated, in a designated State, as an application for a continuation or a continuation-in-part of an earlier application, the applicant, when performing the acts referred to in Article 22, shall so indicate to the designated Office and shall indicate the relevant parent application.

(e) Where no express indication under paragraph (a) is made by the applicant when performing the acts referred to in Article 22 but the national fee referred to in Article 22 paid by the applicant corresponds to the national fee for a particular kind of protection, the payment of that fee shall be considered to be an indication of the wish of the applicant that the international application is to be treated as an application for that kind of protection and the designated Office shall inform the applicant accordingly.

R. 4.9	As a result of the amendment of para. (a) in 2004, information on certain kinds of protection is not possible until the national phase is entered
R. 90*bis*	Withdrawal of designations

49*bis*.2 Time of Furnishing Indications

(a) No designated Office shall require the applicant to furnish, before performing the acts referred to in Article 22, any indication referred to in Rule 49*bis*.1 or, where applicable, any indication as to whether the applicant seeks the grant of a national patent or a regional patent.

(b) The applicant may, if so permitted by the national law applicable by the designated Office concerned, furnish such indication or, if applicable, convert from one kind of protection to another, at any later time.

Rule 49*ter*
Effect of Restoration of Right of Priority by Receiving Office; Restoration of Right of Priority by Designated Office

INTRODUCTION

A decision taken by a receiving Office in the international phase on the restoration of the right of priority (R. 26*bis*.3) is not automatically valid in a national phase. A decision taken in the international phase refusing the restoration can be reviewed in the national phase. If the receiving Office does not accept a request for restoration because of incompatibility with its national law (R. 26*bis*.3(j)), a decision can be taken in the national phase. A designated Office will not review or take a decision on restoration if it has declared that restoration of the right of priority is incompatibility with its national law (R. 49*ter*.1(g) and R. 49*ter*.2(h); AG-NP 6.004–6.0011). 1

WIPO website gives an overview of incompatibilities (www.wipo.int/pct/en/texts/reservations/res_incomp.html) and of the different criteria applied for restoration (www.wipo.int/pct/en/texts/restoration.html). The possibilities for restoration before each receiving Office are given in AG-IP Annex C and the possibilities and procedure for restoration before each designated Office are given in AG-NP Annex. 2

National Offices apply different criteria for restoration and may use stricter criteria than those applied by the receiving Office ('due care' and 'unintentional') that took the decision. Hence, a decision in the international phase restoring the right of priority may be overturned in the national phase. If the designated Office has not declared incompatibility, a request for review of the decision can be filed directly with this designated Office within one month from expiry of the time limit for entry into the national phase or from the request for early entry. A request is recommended if the restoration in the international phase was not possible, or if the receiving Office refused the request. The request must contain arguments supporting that the failure to file the international application within the priority period occurred in spite of due care or unintentionally, depending on the criterion applied by the designated Office. If required, a fee must be paid. Offices may apply requirements that are less strict. The applicant will have the opportunity to make observations before an Office refuses his request (R. 49*ter*.2). 3

4 The following table shows the possible outcomes and the relevant provisions governing these cases:

RO \ DO	incompatible	restored	refused
incompatible	–	R. 49*ter*.2(a)	R. 49*ter*.2(a)
restored	–	R. 49*ter*.1(a), (b)	R. 49*ter*.1(c), (d)
refused	–	R. 49*ter*.2(a), R. 49*ter*.1(e), (f)	R. 49*ter*.2(a), R. 49*ter*.1(a), (b)

(Table originally published in Köllner, PCT-Handbuch, 17th edition, 2023, Wolters Kluwer Germany)

5 For further remedies in connection with the Covid-19 pandemic, see PCT Newsletter 3/2020, p. 6 and www.wipo.int/pct/de/covid_19/covid_update.html.

Art. 48(2)	Delay in meeting certain time limits, notes on reinstatement
R. 76.5	Application before the elected Office

Rule 49*ter*
Effect of Restoration of Right of Priority by Receiving Office; Restoration of Right of Priority by Designated Office

49*ter*.1 Effect of Restoration of Right of Priority by Receiving Office

(a) Where the receiving Office has restored a right of priority under Rule 26*bis*.3 based on a finding by it that the failure to file the international application within the priority period occurred in spite of due care required by the circumstances having been taken, that restoration shall, subject to paragraph (c), be effective in each designated State.

(b) Where the receiving Office has restored a right of priority under Rule 26*bis*.3 based on a finding by it that the failure to file the international application within the priority period was unintentional, that restoration shall, subject to paragraph (c), be effective in any designated State whose applicable national law provides for restoration of the right of priority based on that criterion or on a criterion which, from the viewpoint of applicants, is more favorable than that criterion.

(c) A decision by the receiving Office to restore a right of priority under Rule 26*bis*.3 shall not be effective in a designated State where the designated Office, a court or any other competent organ of or acting for that designated State finds that a requirement under Rule 26*bis*.3(a), (b)(i) or (c) was not complied with, taking into account the reasons stated in the request submitted to the receiving Office under Rule 26*bis*.3(a) and any declaration or other evidence filed with the receiving Office under Rule 26*bis*.3(b)(iii).

(d) A designated Office shall not review the decision of the receiving Office unless it may reasonably doubt that a requirement referred to in paragraph (c) was complied with, in which case the designated Office shall notify the applicant accordingly, indicating the reasons for that doubt and giving the applicant an opportunity to make observations within a reasonable time limit.

(e) No designated State shall be bound by a decision of the receiving Office refusing a request under Rule 26*bis*.3 for restoration of the right of priority.

(f) Where the receiving Office has refused a request for the restoration of the right of priority, any designated Office may consider that request to be a request for restoration submitted to that designated Office under Rule 49*ter*.2(a) within the time limit under that Rule.

(g) If, on October 5, 2005, paragraphs (a) to (d) are not compatible with the national law applied by the designated Office, those paragraphs shall not apply in respect of that Office for as long as they continue not to be compatible with that law, provided that the said Office informs the International Bureau accordingly by April 5, 2006. The information received shall be promptly published by the International Bureau in the Gazette.

R. 49*ter*.1(g)	Notifications of incompatibility with national law have been received from: BR, CO, CU, CZ, DE, DZ, ID, IN, KR, LT, MX, PH. CN has withdrawn its notification of incompatibility as from January 20, 2024 (Gazette January 18, 2024, p. 17)
PCT/A/34/6 Annex IV para. 6	'the giving of a notification of incompatibility under Rule 49*ter*.1(g) will have both procedural and substantive effects; for example, there will be consequences both in terms of calculating the time limit for national phase entry before the designated Office concerned and in terms of the assessment of novelty and inventive step during the national search and examination.' (https://www.wipo.int/edocs/mdocs/govbody/en/pct_a_34/pct_a_34_6.pdf).

The EPO applies the criterion of 'due care' (AG-IP Annex C(EP), AG-NP (EP)). 6

49*ter*.2 Restoration of Right of Priority by Designated Office

(a) Where the international application claims the priority of an earlier application and has an international filing date which is later than the date on which the priority period expired but within the period of two months from that date, the designated Office shall, on the request of the applicant in accordance with paragraph (b), restore the right of priority if the Office finds that a criterion applied by it ("criterion for restoration") is satisfied, namely, that the failure to file the international application within the priority period:

(i) occurred in spite of due care required by the circumstances having been taken; or

(ii) was unintentional.

Each designated Office shall apply at least one of those criteria and may apply both of them.

PCT/A/34/6 Annex IV para. 7	'[A] designated Office may, if it wishes, apply both criteria for restoration and leave the choice to the applicant as to which criterion is sought to be applied in a specific case. Furthermore, a designated Office will be free to apply, upon request of the applicant, first the "due care" criterion and then, if the designated Office finds that that criterion is not complied with, the "unintentionality" criterion.' (https://www.wipo.int/edocs/mdocs/govbody/en/pct_a_34/pct_a_34_6.pdf).
EP: Art. 122(1) EPC	The standards at the different receiving Offices are different. In terms of wording, the standard in the EPC 'all due care required by the circumstances' is stricter when compared to the PCT in R. 26*bis*.3 and R. 49*ter* (Teschemacher, Mitteilungen der deutschen Patentanwälte 2019, 311 (316), AG-NP EP.28)
EP: R. 112(1) EPC	The criterion of 'due care' is stricter than that of 'unintentional omission'. If the EPO as designated Office applies a stricter criterion (due care) than the receiving Office (e.g. restoration of the right of priority due to unintentional omission at the USPTO), the receiving section no longer informs the applicant by means of Form 1201 that a request under R. 49*ter* must be filed with the EPO as designated Office upon entry into the European phase (OJ EPO 2023 A66). Instead the website can be consulted (https://www.epo.org/en/applying/international/entry-european-phase). The previously filed request for restoration of the priority right at the USPTO has no effect in this respect. Reinstatement under Art. 122 EPC within the time limit for filing the request for restoration of the right of priority is excluded under Art. 48(2)(a) PCT in conjunction with R. 136(3) EPC. See also Decision of the Board of Appeal J 13/16 (https://new.epo.org/en/boards-of-appeal/decisions/j160013eu1). See also Teschemacher, Mitteilungen der deutschen Patentanwälte 2019, 311 (316).

DE	does not accept this request, see annotations to R. 49*ter*.2(h) below.
CN	applies 'unintentional' as designated Office and as receiving Office 'due care' and 'unintentional'.
JP	applies as receiving Office and designated Office 'unintentional'.
KR	does not accept this requests, R. 49*ter*.2(h).
US	applies as receiving Office and designated Office 'unintentional
List of Offices:	https://www.wipo.int/pct/en/texts/restoration.html#D

(b) A request under paragraph (a) shall:

(i) be filed with the designated Office within a time limit of one month from the applicable time limit under Article 22 *(furnishing of PCTa within 30 months from priority date)* **or, where the applicant makes an express request to the designated Office under Article 23(2)** *(early processing of the PCTa)*, within a time limit of one month from the date of receipt of that request by the designated Office;

R. 76.5	Application before the elected Office
PCT/A/34/6 Annex IV para. 8	'[W]here the effect of the international application provided for in Article 11(3) ceases because the applicant fails to perform the acts referred to in Article 22 or 39(1) within the applicable time limit but the designated Office reinstates the rights of the applicant with respect to that international application in accordance with Rule 49.6 or 76.5(ii), respectively, such reinstatement will extend to all time limits calculated on the basis of the applicable time limit under Article 22 or 39(1), respectively, including the time limit under Rule 49*ter*.2(b)(i)' (https://www.wipo.int/edocs/mdocs/govbody/en/pct_a_34/pct_a_34_6.pdf).

(ii) state the reasons for the failure to file the international application within the priority period and preferably be accompanied by any declaration or other evidence required under paragraph (c); and

(iii) be accompanied by any fee for requesting restoration required under paragraph (d).

(c) The designated Office may require that a declaration or other evidence in support of the statement of reasons referred to in paragraph (b)(ii) be filed with it within a time limit which shall be reasonable under the circumstances.

(d) The submission of a request under paragraph (a) may be subjected by the designated Office to the payment to it, for its own benefit, of a fee for requesting restoration.

Art. 2(1) No. 13 RFees	For the fee at the EPO, see https://www.epo.org/en/applying/fees/international-fees/important fees Code 013

(e) The designated Office shall not refuse, totally or in part, a request under paragraph (a) without giving the applicant the opportunity to make observations on the intended refusal within a time limit which shall be reasonable under the circumstances. Such notice of intended refusal may be sent by the designated Office to the applicant together with any invitation to file a declaration or other evidence under paragraph (c).

(f) Where the national law applicable by the designated Office provides, in respect of the restoration of the right of priority, for requirements which, from the viewpoint of applicants, are more favorable than the requirements provided for under paragraphs (a) and (b), the designated Office may, when determining the right of priority, apply the requirements under the applicable national law instead of the requirements under those paragraphs.

(g) Each designated Office shall inform the International Bureau of which of the criteria for restoration it applies, of the requirements, where applicable, of the

national law applicable in accordance with paragraph (f), and of any subsequent changes in that respect. The International Bureau shall promptly publish such information in the Gazette.

(h) If, on October 5, 2005, paragraphs (a) to (g) are not compatible with the national law applied by the designated Office, those paragraphs shall not apply in respect of that Office for as long as they continue not to be compatible with that law, provided that the said Office informs the International Bureau accordingly by April 5, 2006. The information received shall be promptly published by the International Bureau in the Gazette.

R. 49*ter*.2(h)	Notifications of incompatibility with national law have been received from: BR, CA, CO, CU, CZ, DE, DZ, ID, IN, KR, MX, NO, PH. CN has withdrawn its notification of incompatibility as from January 20, 2024 (Gazette January 18, 2024, p. 18)
R. 26*bis*.3(a)	The competent authority for the decision concerning the restoration of the right of priority during the international phase is the receiving Office
R. 49*ter*.2	The competent authority during the national phase is the designated Office
PCT/A/34/6, Annex IV, para. 9	'[A]ny designated Office whose national law provides for a criterion more stringent than the "due care" criterion or does not provide for restoration of the right of priority at all may make use of the reservation provision in Rule 49*ter*.2(h). Designated Offices whose applicable national law provides for the restoration of the right of priority based on requirements similar but not identical to the requirements under Rule 49*ter*.2(a) and (b) will not need to make use of the reservation provision if the requirements under the applicable national law are, from the viewpoint of applicants, at least as favorable as the requirements under Rule 49*ter*.2(a) and (b).' (https://www.wipo.int/edocs/mdocs/govbody/en/pct_a_34/pct_a_34_6.pdf).

Rule 50
Faculty under Article 22(3)

50.1 Exercise of Faculty

(a) Any Contracting State allowing a time limit expiring later than the time limits provided for in Article 22(1) or (2) shall notify the International Bureau of the time limits so fixed.

R. 159(1) EPC	The EPO has set the time limit at 31 months
Art. 22(3)	A complete list of the individual time limits set by the individual Contracting States can be found in the Annex to this book and at www.wipo.int/pct/en/texts/pdf/time_limits.html

(b) Any notification received by the International Bureau under paragraph (a) shall be promptly published by the International Bureau in the Gazette.

(c) Notifications concerning the shortening of the previously fixed time limit shall be effective in relation to international applications filed after the expiration of three months computed from the date on which the notification was published by the International Bureau.

(d) Notifications concerning the lengthening of the previously fixed time limit shall become effective upon publication by the International Bureau in the Gazette in respect of international applications pending at the time or filed after the date of such publication, or, if the Contracting State effecting the notification fixes some later date, as from the latter date.

Rule 51
Review by Designated Offices

51.1 Time Limit for Presenting the Request to Send Copies

The time limit referred to in Article 25(1)(c) shall be two months computed from the date of the notification sent to the applicant under Rule 20.4(i) *(negative determination under Art. 11(1))*, 24.2(c) *(delayed receipt of record copy)* or 29.1(ii) *(application considered withdrawn)*.

Art. 25(1)	Request to review non-accordance of international filing date or declaration of withdrawal
R. 80.6	Date of documents

51.2 Copy of the Notification

Where the applicant, after having received a negative determination under Article 11(1), requests the International Bureau, under Article 25(1), to send copies of the file of the purported international application to any of the named Offices he has attempted to designate, he shall attach to his request a copy of the notification referred to in Rule 20.4(i).

51.3 Time Limit for Paying National Fee and Furnishing Translation

The time limit referred to in Article 25(2)(a) shall expire at the same time as the time limit prescribed in Rule 51.1 *(two months)*.

Rule 51*bis* Certain National Requirements Allowed under Article 27

R. 76.5	Application before the elected Office

51*bis*.1 Certain National Requirements Allowed

(a) Subject to Rule 51*bis*.2, the national law applicable by the designated Office may, in accordance with Article 27, require the applicant to furnish, in particular:

(i) any document relating to the identity of the inventor,

R. 4.17(i)	Declaration relating to identity of inventor
Art. 27(2)(ii)	National requirements, e.g. at EPO R. 163 EPC

(ii) any document relating to the applicant's entitlement to apply for or be granted a patent,

R. 4.17(ii)	Declaration relating to entitlement, 'assignment' for US

(iii) any document containing any proof of the applicant's entitlement to claim priority of an earlier application where the applicant is not the applicant who filed the earlier application or where the applicant's name has changed since the date on which the earlier application was filed,

Although certain indications must only be provided upon entry into the national phase, in order to simplify the procedure, indications can already be made with the PCTa or thereafter before the International Bureau effective for all designated Offices – preferably via ePCT. Submitting any declarations after filing has the advantage that the number of pages and thus possibly the fees are not increased at the time of filing. The procedure is to be distinguished from the information on subsequent amendments according to R. 92*bis*. On the other hand, it should be noted that certain acts must be performed before the international filing date, such as a transfer of rights in connection with the priority right. The use of standardized templates can avoid errors, but there is no guarantee that it will be accepted. Therefore, the applicant 1 should consult the AG-NP for information relating to the individual national Office (PCT Newsletter 1/2022, p. 9).

R. 4.17(iii)	Declaration as to the applicant's entitlement prior to the expiration of 16 months under R. 26*ter*.1
R. 4.17(iv)	Declaration of inventorship as part of the PCTa. Even if the US has accepted since September 16, 2012 for the PCTa that the applicant is a person other than the inventor, the obligation to send a declaration – with amended requirements – remains, however, for the national procedure (PCT Newsletter 7–8/2012, p. 1).

(iv) where the international application designates a State whose national law requires, on October 9, 2012, the furnishing of an oath or declaration of inventorship, any document containing an oath or declaration of inventorship,

R. 4.17(iv)	Declaration of inventorship, for US
R. 26*ter*.1	In the case of corrections or additions concerning declarations under R. 4.17, a time limit of 16 months from the priority date or before completion of the technical preparations for publication (AG-IP 6.045) applies
R. 26*ter*.2(b)	If received after the expiration of the time limit, the International Bureau informs the applicant accordingly and neither publishes the declaration nor transmits it to the designated Office. It informs the applicant that such statements must be filed directly with the designated Office. The International Bureau returns any declaration of inventorship signed by at least one inventor to the applicant (AIs 419(d), AG-IP 6.050).
Art. 21(5)	Completion of the technical preparations

(v) any evidence concerning non-prejudicial disclosures or exceptions to lack of novelty, such as disclosures resulting from abuse, disclosures at certain exhibitions and disclosures by the applicant during a certain period of time *(R. 4.17(v))*;

PCT/A/XI/9 p. 12, para. 63	The Rule refers to the evidence of the statement but not the statement itself. The evidence falls under Art. 27(2)(ii) and may be required only once the processing of the PCTa had started in the designated Office (https://www.wipo.int/edocs/mdocs/govbody/en/pct_a_xi/pct_a_xi_9.pdf).

(vi) the confirmation of the international application by the signature of any applicant for the designated State who has not signed the request;

R. 26.2*bis*(a)	Consequently, the application is not deemed to be withdrawn pursuant to Art. 14(1)(b).

(vii) any missing indication required under Rule 4.5(a)(ii) and (iii) in respect of any applicant for the designated State;

(viii) in the cases referred to in Rule 82*ter*.1, a translation of any erroneously filed element or part removed from the international application in accordance with Rule 20.5*bis*(b) or (c).

With effect from July 1, 2020, the reference to R. 20.5*bis* was added. 2

20.5*bis*	Erroneously filed elements and parts
R. 4.5(a), 26.2*bis*(b)	Indications under R. 4.5(a)(ii) (address) and (iii) (nationality and residence) sufficient in respect of one of the applicants
R. 82*ter*.1	Error by receiving Office regarding the international filing date or priority claim

(b) The national law applicable by the designated Office may, in accordance with Article 27(7), require that

(i) the applicant be represented by an agent having the right to represent applicants before that Office and/or have an address in the designated State for the purpose of receiving notifications,

(ii) the agent, if any, representing the applicant be duly appointed by the applicant.

(c) The national law applicable by the designated Office may, in accordance with Article 27(1), require that the international application, the translation thereof or any document relating thereto be furnished in more than one copy.

(d) The national law applicable by the designated Office may, in accordance with Article 27(2)(ii), require that the translation of the international application furnished by the applicant under Article 22 be:

(i) verified by the applicant or the person having translated the international application in a statement to the effect that, to the best of his knowledge, the translation is complete and faithful;

(ii) certified by a public authority or sworn translator, but only where the designated Office may reasonably doubt the accuracy of the translation.

(e) The national law applicable by the designated Office may, in accordance with Article 27, require the applicant to furnish a translation of the priority document, provided that such a translation may only be required:

(i) where the validity of the priority claim is relevant to the determination of whether the invention concerned is patentable; or

(ii) where the international filing date has been accorded by the receiving Office under Rule 20.3(b)(ii), 20.5(d) or 20.5*bis*(d) on the basis of the incorporation by reference under Rules 4.18 and 20.6 of an element or part, for the purposes of determining under Rule 82*ter*.1(b) whether that element or part is completely contained in the priority document concerned, in which case the national law applicable by the designated Office may also require the applicant to furnish, in the case of a part of the description, claims or drawings, an indication as to where that part is contained in the translation of the priority document.

3 With effect from July 1, 2020, the reference to R. 20.5*bis* was added.

R. 20.5*bis* Erroneously filed elements and parts

4 There are no remaining reservations concerning R. 20.5 (missing parts) and R. 20.5*bis* (erroneously filed parts).

51*bis*.2 Certain Circumstances in Which Documents or Evidence May Not Be Required

The designated Office shall not, unless it may reasonably doubt the veracity of the indications or declaration concerned, require any document or evidence:

(i) relating to the identity of the inventor (Rule 51*bis*.1(a)(i)) (other than a document containing an oath or declaration of inventorship (Rule 51*bis*.1(a)(iv)), if indications concerning the inventor, in accordance with Rule 4.6, are contained in the request or if a declaration as to the identity of the inventor, in accordance with Rule 4.17(i), is contained in the request or is submitted directly to the designated Office;

(ii) relating to the applicant's entitlement, as at the international filing date, to apply for and be granted a patent (Rule 51*bis*.1(a)(ii)), if a declaration as to that matter, in accordance with Rule 4.17(ii), is contained in the request or is submitted directly to the designated Office;

(iii) relating to the applicant's entitlement, as at the international filing date, to claim priority of an earlier application (Rule 51*bis*.1(a)(iii)), if a declaration as to that matter, in accordance with Rule 4.17(iii), is contained in the request or is submitted directly to the designated Office;

(iv) containing an oath or declaration of inventorship (Rule 51*bis*.1(a)(iv)), if a declaration of inventorship, in accordance with Rule 4.17(iv), is contained in the request or is submitted directly to the designated Office.

51*bis*.3 Opportunity to Comply with National Requirements

(a) Where any of the requirements referred to in Rule 51*bis*.1(a)(i) to (iv) and (c) to (e), or any other requirement of the national law applicable by the designated Office which that Office may apply in accordance with Article 27(1) or (2), is not already fulfilled during the same period within which the requirements under Article 22 must be complied with, the designated Office shall invite the applicant to comply with the requirement within a time limit which shall not be less than two months from the date of the invitation. Each designated Office may require that the applicant pay a fee for complying with national requirements in response to the invitation.

(b) Where any requirement of the national law applicable by the designated Office which that Office may apply in accordance with Article 27(6) or (7) is not already fulfilled during the same period within which the requirements under Article 22 must be complied with, the applicant shall have an opportunity to comply with the requirement after the expiration of that period.

(c) If, on March 17, 2000, paragraph (a) is not compatible with the national law applied by the designated Office in relation to the time limit referred to in that paragraph, the said paragraph shall not apply in respect of that Office in relation to that time limit for as long as the said paragraph continues not to be compatible with that law, provided that the said Office informs the International Bureau accordingly by November 30, 2000. The information received shall be promptly published by the International Bureau in the Gazette.

A notification has been received from SG against R. 51*bis*.3(c) (https://www.wipo.int/pct/en/texts/reservations/res_incomp.html). 5

Rule 52
Amendment of the Claims, the Description, and the Drawings, before Designated Offices

52.1 Time Limit

(a) In any designated State in which processing or examination starts without special request, the applicant shall, if he so wishes, exercise the right under Article 28 within one month from the fulfillment of the requirements under Article 22, provided that, if the communication under Rule 47.1 has not been effected by the expiration of the time limit applicable under Article 22, he shall exercise the said right not later than four months after such expiration date. In either case, the applicant may exercise the said right at any later time if so permitted by the national law of the said State.

EPO	A request is necessary

(b) In any designated State in which the national law provides that examination starts only on special request, the time limit within or the time at which the applicant may exercise the right under Article 28 shall be the same as that provided by the national law for the filing of amendments in the case of the examination, on special request, of national applications, provided that such time limit shall not expire prior to, or such time shall not come before, the expiration of the time limit applicable under paragraph (a).

Art. 28	Amendment of claims, description, drawings before designated Office
Art. 22	Copy, translation, fee to designated Office
Art. 41, R. 78	Amendments before elected Office

1 For the start of the national phase, see annotation No. 1.2.1 and 1.2.9 to Art. 22.

2 For amendments in the international phase see Art. 19, 34, R. 46, 66, 70.

Part C: Rules Concerning Chapter II of the Treaty

Rule 53
The Demand

53.1 Form

(a) The demand shall be made on a printed form or be presented as a computer print-out. The particulars of the printed form and of a demand presented as a computer print-out shall be prescribed by the Administrative Instructions.

(b) Copies of printed demand forms shall be furnished free of charge by the receiving Office or by the International Preliminary Examining Authority.

For communication from the Office to the applicant, see annotations to R. 4.4(c). 1

Art. 31	Demand for IPE
R. 60.1	Deficiencies in the demand
R. 89*bis*	Electronic form of filing

53.2 Contents

(a) The demand shall contain:

(i) a petition,

(ii) indications concerning the applicant and the agent if there is an agent,

(iii) indications concerning the international application to which it relates,

(iv) where applicable, a statement concerning amendments.

(b) The demand shall be signed.

R. 60.1	Deficiencies in the demand

53.3 The Petition

The petition shall be to the following effect and shall preferably be worded as follows: "Demand under Article 31 of the Patent Cooperation Treaty: The undersigned requests that the international application specified below be the subject of international preliminary examination according to the Patent Cooperation Treaty."

R. 60.1 Deficiencies in the demand

53.4 The Applicant

As to the indications concerning the applicant, Rules 4.4 *(name, address)* and 4.16 *(transcription of words)* shall apply, and Rule 4.5 *(name, address, State)* shall apply *mutatis mutandis*.

R. 60.1 Deficiencies in the demand

53.5 Agent or Common Representative

If an agent or common representative is appointed, the demand shall so indicate. Rules 4.4 and 4.16 shall apply, and Rule 4.7 shall apply *mutatis mutandis*.

R. 60.1 Deficiencies in the demand

R. 90 Appointment of an agent or common representative

53.6 Identification of the International Application

The international application shall be identified by the name and address of the applicant, the title of the invention, the international filing date (if known to the applicant) and the international application number or, where such number is not known to the applicant, the name of the receiving Office with which the international application was filed.

R. 60.1 Deficiencies in the demand

53.7 Election of States

The filing of a demand shall constitute the election of all Contracting States which are designated and are bound by Chapter II of the Treaty.

Art. 31(4) Declaration of election in the application

R. 60.1 Deficiencies in the demand

R. 61 Notification of the demand and elections

53.8 Signature

The demand shall be signed by the applicant or, if there is more than one applicant, by all applicants making the demand.

Art. 31(3) Request for IPE

R. 60.1 Deficiencies in the demand

R. 60.1(a-*ter*) Provided that at least one applicant has signed the request, the IPEA does not request missing signatures. If a representative has signed, a power of attorney must be filed if the requirement under Annex E (EP) of the PCT Applicant's Guide has not been waived (EPO has waived power of attorney, as at June 3, 2021). (Notes to VII to Form PCT/IPEA/401 and in AG-IPs Guide 10.031).

R. 90.3(a) Agent and common representative

R. 90.4(a), (d) Appointment of an agent; waiver of requirements

R. 90*bis*.5 Signature by all applicants in case of declaration of withdrawal during the international phase

R. 90.4(a) Authorization of an agent or common representative to sign a declaration of withdrawal

53.9 Statement Concerning Amendments

(a) If amendments under Article 19 have been made, the statement concerning amendments shall indicate whether, for the purposes of the international preliminary examination, the applicant wishes those amendments:

(i) to be taken into account, in which case a copy of the amendments and of the letter required under Rule 46.5(b) shall preferably be submitted with the demand; or

R. 46.5(b) Explanatory accompanying letter to the replacement sheet for changes before the International Bureau

(ii) to be considered as reversed by an amendment under Article 34.

(b) If no amendments under Article 19 have been made and the time limit for filing such amendments has not expired, the statement may indicate that, should the International Preliminary Examining Authority wish to start the international preliminary examination at the same time as the international search in accordance with Rule 69.1(b), the applicant wishes the start of the international preliminary examination to be postponed in accordance with Rule 69.1(d).

Form PCT/IPEA/401 2

(c) If any amendments under Article 34 are submitted with the demand, the statement shall so indicate.

R. 55.3 Language and translation of amendments and cover letters

R. 60.1(g) Invitation to submit missing amendments

R. 62 Forwarding of letters by International Bureau to IPEA. PCT Applicant's Guide 9.010: Recommendation to send directly to IPEA to avoid delays and uncertainties.

3 The options to make amendments in accordance with Art. 19 or Art. 34 exist independently of each other, each with its own requirements and effects. Amendments under Art. 19 can be made once after the applicant receives the search report and before the expiry of the time limit under R. 46.1. Amendments under Art. 34 require a demand for IPE and can be made several times until the IPER is drawn up in accordance with R. 66.1(b). Further differences include the addressee (Art. 19: International Bureau; Art. 34: IPEA), the subject matter of the amendment (Art. 19: only claims; Art. 34: descriptions and drawings as well), and the language (Art. 19, R. 12: language of publication; Art. 34, R. 55.3: language of publication or translation of the PCT application). Significant differences also exist in the effects of these amendments. Art. 19 amendments are published with the application in accordance with Art. 21, R. 48.2(f) and (h), which is not the case for Art. 34. As a result, Art. 19 can achieve a different protective effect under Art. 29 with regard to an amended scope of the claims compared to the application. Confidentiality is maintained for Art. 19 amendments until the publication of the PCT application, and for Art. 34 amendments until third parties have access to the files of the IPE according to R. 94.

Rule 54
The Applicant Entitled to Make a Demand

54.1 Residence and Nationality

(a) Subject to the provisions of paragraph (b), the residence or nationality of the applicant shall, for the purposes of Article 31(2), be determined according to Rule 18.1(a) and (b).

(b) The International Preliminary Examining Authority shall, in the circumstances specified in the Administrative Instructions, request the receiving Office or, where the international application was filed with the International Bureau as receiving Office, the national Office of, or acting for, the Contracting State concerned to decide the question whether the applicant is a resident or national of the Contracting State of which he claims to be a resident or national. The International Preliminary Examining Authority shall inform the applicant of any such request. The applicant shall have an opportunity to submit arguments directly to the Office concerned. The Office concerned shall decide the said question promptly.

54.2 Right to Make a Demand

The right to make a demand under Article 31(2) shall exist if the applicant making the demand or, if there are two or more applicants, at least one of them is a resident or national of a Contracting State bound by Chapter II and the international application has been filed with a receiving Office of or acting for a Contracting State bound by Chapter II.

Art. 31(2)(a)	See annotations there on the binding nature of Chapter II. The wording of the Article still requires that nationality and filing with the receiving Office must relate to the same State. R. 54.2 does not require this. This is a softening of Art. 31(2)(a). In any case, care must be taken to ensure that the nationality or domicile is present at the time of filing the demand for the IPE.
R. 18.1	Domicile, residence, and nationality
R. 54.4	Legal consequences of lack of entitlement

54.3 International Applications Filed with the International Bureau as Receiving Office

Where the international application is filed with the International Bureau as receiving Office under Rule 19.1(a)(iii), the International Bureau shall, for the purposes of Article 31(2)(a), be considered to be acting for the Contracting State of which the applicant is a resident or national.

R. 59.3	Transmittal of the demand to the competent IPEA in case it was sent to a non-competent Office

54.4 Applicant Not Entitled to Make a Demand

If the applicant does not have the right to make a demand or, in the case of two or more applicants, if none of them has the right to make a demand under Rule 54.2, the demand shall be considered not to have been submitted.

R. 57.4(ii)	The fiction that the demand was not submitted leads to a refund of the processing fee

Rule 54*bis*
Time Limit for Making a Demand

54*bis*.1 Time Limit for Making a Demand

(a) A demand may be made at any time prior to the expiration of whichever of the following periods expires later:

(i) three months from the date of transmittal to the applicant of the international search report or the declaration referred to in Article 17(2)(a), and of the written opinion established under Rule 43*bis*.1; or

(ii) 22 months from the priority date.

(b) Any demand made after the expiration of the time limit applicable under paragraph (a) shall be considered as if it had not been submitted and the International Preliminary Examining Authority shall so declare.

R 54*bis* regulates the time limit for filing the demand while R. 69 governs the start of 1
the examination. The expiry of the R. 54*bis*.1 time limit, according to R. 69.1(a), is exceptionally only a prerequisite for the start of the IPE if the applicant requests so. However, additional prerequisites for the start of the examination may apply, such as the filing of the demand, payment of fees, and the submission of certain documents. Filing the demand is a prerequisite for the effectiveness of amendments under Art. 34. Independently, there is the possibility to file amendments under Art. 19, but only between the receipt of the search report by the applicant and before the expiry of the time limit under R. 46.1. Therefore, Art. 19 can also be relevant at the time of filing the demand, provided its conditions are met. The possibilities for amendments under Art. 34 remain unaffected. Filing amendments under Art. 19 can be advantageous if a different protective effect is desired through subsequent publication due to a changed scope of claims compared to the application.

The function of R. 54*bis*.1(a) is to set a time limit during which the applicant can 2
influence the procedure by submitting amendments under Art. 34 or objections.

R. 57.4(ii)	Refund of the handling fee in case of fiction of non-submission
R. 66.1*bis*	Because of the fiction, it is advisable to file amendments under Art. 34 and counter-arguments with the demand under Chapter II or at the latest before expiry of the time limit under R. 54*bis*.1(a).

3 There is no grace period for filing the demand for examination, only for the payment of fees.

R. 58*bis*.1(a) (i), (ii)	Grace period for fees: one month from the invitation, identical for processing and examination fees.
R. 58*bis*.1(c), (d)	In due time if paid before the communication under R. 58*bis*.1(a) was sent
R. 58*bis*.2	Late payment fee

Rule 55
Languages (International Preliminary Examination)

INTRODUCTION

1 The demand must be filed in a language that is accepted by the IPEA. It may be the language in which the international application has been filed or, if the international application has been translated for the international publication, the language of publication (R. 55.1). Where the competent IPEA does not accept either of these languages, the applicant must file both the demand and a translation of the international application, including any elements or parts incorporated by reference under R. 20.6(b), in a language which is both a language accepted by the IPEA and a language of publication (R. 55.2(a); R. 55.2(a-*bis*)). The languages accepted by each IPEA are given in AG-IP Annex E.

2 If a translation of the international application in a publication language acceptable to the IPEA was transmitted to the ISA as search copy and the IPEA and ISA are part of the same Office, the applicant need not furnish a copy of the translation; the IPEA will use the search copy (R. 55.2(b)). If the IPEA does not have a copy of the international application in an accepted language either from the applicant or the ISA, it will invite the applicant to furnish a translation within an extendable period of at least one month from the invitation (R. 55.2(c)). Failure to supply the translation will result in the demand being considered not to have been submitted and the IPEA will so declare (R. 55.2(d)).

55.1 Language of Demand

The demand shall be in the language of the international application or, if the international application has been filed in a language other than the language in which it is published, in the language of publication. However, if a translation of the international application is required under Rule 55.2, the demand shall be in the language of that translation.

R. 60.1	Invitation to correct defects in case of non-compliance with R. 55.1

55.2 Translation of International Application

(a) Where neither the language in which the international application is filed nor the language in which the international application is published is accepted by the International Preliminary Examining Authority that is to carry out the international preliminary examination, the applicant shall, subject to paragraph (b), furnish with the demand a translation of the international application into a language which is both:

(i) a language accepted by that Authority, and

(ii) a language of publication.

R. 48.3	Publication languages

(a-*bis*) A translation of the international application into a language referred to in paragraph (a) shall include any element referred to in Article 11(1)(iii)(d) or (e) furnished by the applicant under Rule 20.3(b) *(missing parts submitted after filing)*, 20.5*bis*(b), 20.5*bis*(c) or 20.6(a) and any part of the description, claims or drawings furnished by the applicant under Rule 20.5(b) *(missing parts)*, 20.5(c), 20.5*bis*(b), 20.5*bis*(c) or 20.6(a) *(confirmation of incorporation by reference)* which is considered to have been contained in the international application under Rule 20.6(b).

3 The amendment applies to PCT applications in which reference is made for the first time on or after July 1, 2020, to one or more elements mentioned in Art. 11(1)(iii). Newly introduced was the reference to R. 20.5*bis*. Additionally, a reference to R. 20.5(c) has been added. Although R. 20.5(c) itself was not amended, its reference had been inadvertently omitted when R. 55.2(a-*bis*) was introduced, as noted in PCT/WG/12/9 Annex, p. 20.

Art. 11(1)(iii)(d)	Description
Art. 11(1)(iii)(e)	Claims
R. 20.3(b)	Subsequent filing/incorporation within the time limit
R. 20.5(b)	Missing parts
R. 20.5(c)	Subsequent submission of parts
R. 20.5*bis*	Erroneously filed parts or components
R. 20.5*bis*(b)	Subsequent filing before a date of filing is accorded
R. 20.5*bis*(c)	Subsequent filing after a date of filing has been accorded
R. 20.6(a)	Confirmation of incorporation by reference

(a-*ter*) The International Preliminary Examining Authority shall check any translation furnished under paragraph (a) for compliance with the physical requirements referred to in Rule 11 to the extent that compliance therewith is necessary for the purposes of the international preliminary examination.

(b) Where a translation of the international application into a language referred to in paragraph (a) was transmitted to the International Searching Authority under Rule 23.1(b) and the International Preliminary Examining Authority is part of the same national Office or intergovernmental organization as the International Searching Authority, the applicant need not furnish a translation under paragraph (a). In such a case, unless the applicant furnishes a translation under paragraph (a), the international preliminary examination shall be carried out on the basis of the translation transmitted under Rule 23.1(b).

(c) If a requirement referred to in paragraphs (a), (a-*bis*) and (a-*ter*) is not complied with and paragraph (b) does not apply, the International Preliminary Examining Authority shall invite the applicant to furnish the required translation or the required correction, as the case may be, within a time limit which shall be reasonable under the circumstances. That time limit shall not be less than one month from the date of the invitation. It may be extended by the International Preliminary Examining Authority at any time before a decision is taken.

(d) If the applicant complies with the invitation within the time limit under paragraph (c), the said requirement shall be considered to have been complied with. If the applicant fails to do so, the demand shall be considered not to have been submitted and the International Preliminary Examining Authority shall so declare.

For statements of WIPO concerning R. 55.2, see PCT/A/XXIV/10, p.5, para. 19 (https://www.wipo.int/edocs/mdocs/govbody/en/pct_a_xxiv/pct_a_xxiv_10-main1.pdf). 4

55.3 Language and Translation of Amendments and Letters

(a) Subject to paragraph (b), if the international application has been filed in a language other than the language in which it is published, any amendment under Article 34, as well as any letter referred to in Rule 66.8(a), Rule 66.8(b) and Rule 46.5(b) as applicable by virtue of Rule 66.8(c), shall be submitted in the language of publication.

(b) Where a translation of the international application is required under Rule 55.2:

(i) any amendment and any letter referred to in paragraph (a); and

Art. 34	Amendment of claims, description and drawings
R. 66.8(a)	Amendment of the description or drawings (Art. 34)
R. 66.8(b)	Deletion, minor amendment
R. 66.8(c)	Amendment of claims under Art. 19 or Art. 34

(ii) any amendment under Article 19 which is to be taken into account under Rule 66.1(c) or (d) and any letter referred to in Rule 46.5(b);

shall be in the language of that translation. Where such amendments or letters have been or are submitted in another language, a translation shall also be submitted.

Art. 19	Amendments to claims
R. 66.1(c)	Relation between amendments under Art. 19 and amendments under Art. 34
R. 66.1(d)	Timely amendments under Art. 19 or Art. 34 after demand for IPE
R. 46.5(b)	Content of cover letters for amendments under Art. 19

(c) If an amendment or letter is not submitted in a language as required under paragraph (a) or (b), the International Preliminary Examining Authority shall invite the applicant to submit the amendment or letter in the required language within a time limit which shall be reasonable under the circumstances. That time limit shall not be less than one month from the date of the invitation. It may be extended by the International Preliminary Examining Authority at any time before a decision is taken.

(d) If the applicant fails to comply, within the time limit under paragraph (c), with the invitation to furnish an amendment in the required language, the amendment shall not be taken into account for the purposes of the international preliminary examination. If the applicant fails to comply, within the time limit under paragraph (c), with the invitation to furnish a letter referred to in paragraph (a) in the required language, the amendment concerned need not be taken into account for the purposes of the international preliminary examination.

Rule 56
[Deleted]

Rule 57
The Handling Fee

57.1 Requirement to Pay

Each demand for international preliminary examination shall be subject to the payment of a fee for the benefit of the International Bureau ("handling fee") to be collected by the International Preliminary Examining Authority to which the demand is submitted.

1 The fee is payable to the IPEA.

57.2 Amount; Transfer

(a) The amount of the handling fee is as set out in the Schedule of Fees.

2 See AG-IP Annex E for each Office.

(b) The handling fee shall be payable in the currency or one of the currencies prescribed by the International Preliminary Examining Authority ("prescribed currency").

(c) Where the prescribed currency is the Swiss franc, the Authority shall transfer the said fee to the International Bureau in Swiss francs in accordance with Rule 96.2.

(d) Where the prescribed currency is a currency other than the Swiss franc and that currency:

(i) is freely convertible into Swiss francs, the Director General shall establish, for each Authority which prescribes such a currency for the payment of the handling fee, an equivalent amount of that fee in the prescribed currency according to directives given by the Assembly, and the amount in that currency shall be transferred by the Authority to the International Bureau in accordance with Rule 96.2;

(ii) is not freely convertible into Swiss francs, the Authority shall be responsible for the conversion of the handling fee from the prescribed currency into Swiss francs and shall transfer that fee in Swiss francs, in the amount set out in the Schedule of Fees, to the International Bureau in accordance with Rule 96.2. Alternatively, if the Authority so wishes, it may convert the handling fee from the prescribed currency into euros or US dollars and transfer the equivalent amount of that fee in euros or US dollars, as established by the Director General according to directives given by the Assembly as referred to in item (i), to the International Bureau in accordance with Rule 96.2.

The changes apply to the transfer of fees for PCT applications made by an Office on or after July 1, 2020, including the fees according to R. 16 in conjunction with R. 45*bis*.3(b). A reference to R. 96.2 has been inserted, a regulation aimed at simplifying and reducing costs in the transfer and reconciliation of fee payments between different Offices. 3

AI114	Fee Transfer according to Annex G

For the determination of an equivalent value of certain PCT fees, see the annotations to R. 96.2. 4

Art. 16(3) PCT and Art. 11(2), (4)	Respective agreements between the ISAs/IPEAs and WIPO

57.3 Time Limit for Payment; Amount Payable

(a) Subject to paragraphs (b) and (c), the handling fee shall be paid within one month from the date on which the demand was submitted or 22 months from the priority date, whichever expires later.

(b) Subject to paragraph (c), where the demand was transmitted to the International Preliminary Examining Authority under Rule 59.3, the handling fee shall be paid within one month from the date of receipt by that Authority or 22 months from the priority date, whichever expires later.

(c) Where, in accordance with Rule 69.1(b), the International Preliminary Examining Authority wishes to start the international preliminary examination at the same time as the international search, that Authority shall invite the applicant to pay the handling fee within one month from the date of the invitation.

(d) The amount of the handling fee payable shall be the amount applicable on the date of payment.

R. 58	Preliminary examination fee
R. 58*bis*	Extension of time limit for payment of fees: one month from invitation, additional fee

57.4 Refund

The International Preliminary Examining Authority shall refund the handling fee to the applicant:

(i) if the demand is withdrawn before the demand has been sent by that Authority to the International Bureau, or

(ii) if the demand is considered, under Rule 54.4 or 54*bis*.1(b), not to have been submitted.

AIs 613	Invitation to submit a request for refund of fees under R. 57.4 or 58.3
EPO	Refund according to EPO-WIPO Agreement, see annotation to R. 58.3

Rule 58
The Preliminary Examination Fee

58.1 Right to Ask for a Fee

(a) Each International Preliminary Examining Authority may require that the applicant pay a fee ("preliminary examination fee") for its own benefit for carrying out the international preliminary examination and for performing all other tasks entrusted to International Preliminary Examining Authorities under the Treaty and these Regulations.

(b) The amount of the preliminary examination fee, if any, shall be fixed by the International Preliminary Examining Authority. As to the time limit for payment of the preliminary examination fee and the amount payable, the provisions of Rule 57.3 *(time limit one month from making demand or 22 month from priority date)* relating to the handling fee shall apply *mutatis mutandis.*

For the amount of the fee and applicable reductions, see the AG-IP Annex E. 1

(c) The preliminary examination fee shall be payable directly to the International Preliminary Examining Authority. Where that Authority is a national Office, it shall be payable in the currency prescribed by that Office, and where the Authority is an intergovernmental organization, it shall be payable in the currency of the State in which the intergovernmental organization is located or in any other currency which is freely convertible into the currency of the said State.

58.2 [Deleted]

58.3 Refund

The International Preliminary Examining Authorities shall inform the International Bureau of the extent, if any, to which, and the conditions, if any, under which, they will refund any amount paid as a preliminary examination fee where the demand is considered as if it had not been submitted, and the International Bureau shall promptly publish such information.

R. 57.4(ii) Demand deemed not to have been filed under R. 54.4, 54*bis*.1(b)

R. 57.4(i)	Refund in the event of withdrawal of the demand
R. 90*bis*.4 and 6	Withdrawal of the demand and the effect of withdrawal
AIs 613	Invitation to file a request for reimbursement of fees under R. 57.4 or R. 58.3

2 The EPO as IPEA refunds the full fee amount under the WIPO-EPO Agreement Art. 5(3), Annex D. Part II. (5) in the case of the above fiction, and in case of withdrawal of the international application or the demand before the start of the examination according to Annex D. Part II. (6).

3 A technically generated verifiable date establishes the start of search and examination at the EPO (OJ EPO 2013 p. 153). This clearly determines whether a withdrawal occurred before the start of the search or examination.

Rule 58*bis*
Extension of Time Limits for Payment of Fees

58*bis*.1 Invitation by the International Preliminary Examining Authority

(a) Where the International Preliminary Examining Authority finds:

(i) that the amount paid to it is insufficient to cover the handling fee and the preliminary examination fee; or

(ii) by the time they are due under Rules 57.3 and 58.1(b), that no fees were paid to it;

the Authority shall invite the applicant to pay to it the amount required to cover those fees, together with, where applicable, the late payment fee under Rule 58*bis*.2, within a time limit of one month from the date of the invitation.

R. 57.3	The time limit for paying the handling fee is one month after receipt of the demand
R. 58.1(b)	The time limit for paying the preliminary examination fee is also one month after receipt of the demand (R. 57(3))
R. 58*bis*.1(c), (d)	A payment after expiry of the grace period can still be considered to have been received on time

(b) Where the International Preliminary Examining Authority has sent an invitation under paragraph (a) and the applicant has not, within the time limit referred to in that paragraph, paid in full the amount due, including, where applicable, the late payment fee under Rule 58*bis*.2, the demand shall, subject to paragraph (c), be considered as if it had not been submitted and the International Preliminary Examining Authority shall so declare.

(c) Any payment received by the International Preliminary Examining Authority before that Authority sends the invitation under paragraph (a) shall be considered to have been received before the expiration of the time limit under Rule 57.3 or 58.1(b), as the case may be.

(d) Any payment received by the International Preliminary Examining Authority before that Authority proceeds under paragraph (b) shall be considered to have been received before the expiration of the time limit under paragraph (a).

58*bis*.2 Late Payment Fee

(a) The payment of fees in response to an invitation under Rule 58*bis*.1(a) may be subjected by the International Preliminary Examining Authority to the payment to it, for its own benefit, of a late payment fee. The amount of that fee shall be:

(i) 50% of the amount of unpaid fees which is specified in the invitation, or,

(ii) if the amount calculated under item (i) is less than the handling fee, an amount equal to the handling fee.

(b) The amount of the late payment fee shall not, however, exceed double the amount of the handling fee.

1 According to the decision of the President of the EPO (dated February 26, 1998, OJ 1998, 282), a surcharge is due: 'The fee for late payment is 50% of the amount of unpaid fees indicated in the invitation. It shall be at least equal to, but not more than double, the handling fee under Rule 57.2(a) PCT.'

2 WIPO does not charge a fee because it passes on the demand.

Rule 59
The Competent International Preliminary Examining Authority

59.1 Demands under Article 31 (2) (a)

(a) For demands made under Article 31(2)(a) *(residents/nationals of States bound by PCT Chapter II)*, each receiving Office of or acting for a Contracting State bound by the provisions of Chapter II shall, in accordance with the terms of the applicable agreement referred to in Article 32(2) and (3), inform the International Bureau which International Preliminary Examining Authority is or which International Preliminary Examining Authorities are competent for the international preliminary examination of international applications filed with it. The International Bureau shall promptly publish such information. Where several International Preliminary Examining Authorities are competent, the provisions of Rule 35.2 shall apply *mutatis mutandis.*

The information published by WIPO can also be found in Annex C of the PCT Applicant's Guide. 1

(b) Where the international application was filed with the International Bureau as receiving Office under Rule 19.1(a)(iii), Rule 35.3(a) and (b) *(competent authority)* shall apply *mutatis mutandis.* Paragraph (a) of this Rule shall not apply to the International Bureau as receiving Office under Rule 19.1(a)(iii).

IPEA are the Offices of AT, AU, BR, CA, CL, CN, EA (since July 1, 2022), EG, EP, ES, FI, IL, IN, JP, KR, PH, RU, SE, SG, TR, UA, US, XN (Nordic Patent Institute NPI of the Offices DK, IS, NO), XV (Visegrad Patent Institute VPI of the Offices of CZ, HU, PL, SK). EPO only acts as IPEA if ISA was the EPO, the Office in AT, FI, ES, XN, XV, TR or SE (FN 1 PCT Applicant's Guide int. P. Annex E (EP), as at July 1, 2022). See WIPO agreements at www.wipo.int/pct/en/access/isa_ipea_agreements.html and PCT Applicant's Guide Annex E, updated by PCT Gazette. 2

Art. 152, R. 158(2) EPC	EPO as IPEA

59.2 Demands under Article 31 (2) (b)

As to demands made under Article 31 (2) (b), *(applicants not residents/nationals of States bound by PCT Chapter II)* the Assembly, in specifying the International Preliminary Examining Authority competent for international applications filed with a national Office which is an International Preliminary Examining Authority, shall give preference to that Authority; if the national Office is not an International Preliminary Examining Authority, the Assembly shall give preference to the International Preliminary Examining Authority recommended by that Office.

59.3 Transmittal of the Demand to the Competent International Preliminary Examining Authority

(a) If the demand is submitted to a receiving Office, an International Searching Authority, or an International Preliminary Examining Authority which is not competent for the international preliminary examination of the international application, that Office or Authority shall mark the date of receipt on the demand and, unless it decides to proceed under paragraph (f), transmit the demand promptly to the International Bureau.

(b) If the demand is submitted to the International Bureau, the International Bureau shall mark the date of receipt on the demand.

(c) Where the demand is transmitted to the International Bureau under paragraph (a) or submitted to it under paragraph (b), the International Bureau shall promptly:

(i) if there is only one competent International Preliminary Examining Authority, transmit the demand to that Authority and inform the applicant accordingly, or

(ii) if two or more International Preliminary Examining Authorities are competent, invite the applicant to indicate, within the time limit applicable under Rule 54*bis*.1 (a) or 15 days from the date of the invitation, whichever is later, the competent International Preliminary Examining Authority to which the demand should be transmitted.

(d) Where an indication is furnished as required under paragraph (c)(ii), the International Bureau shall promptly transmit the demand to the competent International Preliminary Examining Authority indicated by the applicant. Where no indication is so furnished, the demand shall be considered not to have been submitted and the International Bureau shall so declare.

(e) Where the demand is transmitted to a competent International Preliminary Examining Authority under paragraph (c), it shall be considered to have been received on behalf of that Authority on the date marked on it under paragraph (a) or (b), as applicable, and the demand so transmitted shall be considered to have been received by that Authority on that date.

3 This date does not apply to the time limit for the payment of the fee under R. 57.3.

(f) Where an Office or Authority to which the demand is submitted under paragraph (a) decides to transmit that demand directly to the competent International Preliminary Examining Authority, paragraphs (c) to (e) shall apply *mutatis mutandis.*

Rule 60
Certain Defects in the Demand

INTRODUCTION

1 If the demand does not contain the prescribed particulars or is not in the prescribed language or form (Art. 31(3); R. 53; R. 55.1), the IPEA will invite the applicant to correct the defects within a period of at least one month from the date of the invitation (R. 60.1(a)). The period may be extended upon request filed before expiry of the period. A common defect is that the demand does not indicate all applicants for the elected States as required by R. 53.4 and R. 4.5(d). Note that R. 60.1(a-*bis*) overrules R. 4.5(a)(ii) and 4.5(a)(iii) but not R. 4.5(a)(i) about indication of the name.

2 When the defects are duly corrected, the date of the demand remains the date it was first received. However, if the defect does not permit identifying the international application, the date of the demand will become the date of receipt of the correction (R. 60.1(b); AG-IP 10.048).

3 If the defects are not duly corrected, the demand will be considered as not having been submitted, and the IPEA will so declare (R. 60.1(c)).

60.1 Defects in the Demand

(a) Subject to paragraphs (a-*bis*) and (a-*ter*), if the demand does not comply with the requirements specified in Rules 53.1 *(form)*, 53.2(a)(i) to (iii), 53.2(b) *(content)*, 53.3 to 53.8 *(title, applicant, representative, State, signature)* and 55.1 *(other language)*, the International Preliminary Examining Authority shall invite the applicant to correct the defects within a time limit which shall be reasonable under the circumstances. That time limit shall not be less than one month from the date of the invitation. It may be extended by the International Preliminary Examining Authority at any time before a decision is taken.

(a-*bis*) For the purposes of Rule 53.4 *(indications concerning applicant)*, if there are two or more applicants, it shall be sufficient that the indications referred to in Rule 4.5(a)(ii) and (iii) be provided in respect of one of them who has the right according to Rule 54.2 to make a demand.

R. 26.2*bis*(b) Corresponding formal requirements for international applications (a-*ter*) For the purposes of Rule 53.8 *(signature)*, if there are two or more applicants, it shall be sufficient that the demand be signed by one of them.

R. 26.2*bis*(a)	Corresponding formal requirements for international applications
R. 90.4, 90.5	Waiver of submission of a power of attorney
R. 90*bis*	No waiver in the case of a declaration of withdrawal

(b) If the applicant complies with the invitation within the time limit under paragraph (a), the demand shall be considered as if it had been received on the actual filing date, provided that the demand as submitted permitted the international application to be identified; otherwise, the demand shall be considered as if it had been received on the date on which the International Preliminary Examining Authority receives the correction.

(c) If the applicant does not comply with the invitation within the time limit under paragraph (a), the demand shall be considered as if it had not been submitted and the International Preliminary Examining Authority shall so declare.

(d) [Deleted]

(e) If the defect is noticed by the International Bureau, it shall bring the defect to the attention of the International Preliminary Examining Authority, which shall then proceed as provided in paragraphs (a) to (c).

(f) If the demand does not contain a statement concerning amendments, the International Preliminary Examining Authority shall proceed as provided for in Rules 66.1 and 69.1(a) or (b).

(g) Where the statement concerning amendments contains an indication that amendments under Article 34 are submitted with the demand (Rule 53.9(c)) but no such amendments are, in fact, submitted, the International Preliminary Examining Authority shall invite the applicant to submit the amendments within a time limit fixed in the invitation and shall proceed as provided for in Rule 69.1(e).

R. 69.1	The Authority waits with the examination until the changes have been received

Rule 61
Notification of the Demand and Elections

61.1 Notification to the International Bureau and the Applicant

(a) The International Preliminary Examining Authority shall indicate on the demand the date of receipt or, where applicable, the date referred to in Rule 60.1(b). The International Preliminary Examining Authority shall promptly either send the demand to the International Bureau and keep a copy in its files or send a copy to the International Bureau and keep the demand in its files.

(b) The International Preliminary Examining Authority shall promptly notify the applicant of the date of receipt of the demand. Where the demand has been considered under Rules 54.4, 55.2(d), 58*bis*.1(b) or 60.1(c) as if it had not been submitted, the International Preliminary Examining Authority shall notify the applicant and the International Bureau accordingly.

R. 54.2	Entitlement to file the demand for IPE
Art. 31(2)	Conditions for filing the demand for IPE
AIs 614	Proof of entitlement to make a demand

61.2 Notification to the Elected Offices

(a) The notification provided for in Article 31(7) *(notification of elected Offices)* shall be effected by the International Bureau.

(b) The notification shall indicate the number and filing date of the international application, the name of the applicant, the filing date of the application whose priority is claimed (where priority is claimed) and the date of receipt by the International Preliminary Examining Authority of the demand.

(c) The notification shall be sent to the elected Office together with the communication provided for in Article 20. Elections effected after such communication shall be notified promptly after they have been made.

(d) Where the applicant makes an express request to an elected Office under Article 40(2) *(early processing)* prior to the international publication of the international application, the International Bureau shall, upon request of the applicant or the elected Office, promptly effect the communication provided for in Article 20 *(transmittal of PCTa)* to that Office.

61.3 Information for the Applicant

The International Bureau shall inform the applicant in writing of the notification referred to in Rule 61.2 *(notification of elected Offices)* and of the elected Offices notified under Article 31(7).

Notifications under R. 61.2 and 61.3 are issued using Form PCT/IB/331, which is sent simultaneously to the applicant and the elected Offices listed therein. It also includes information on whether the election of the Offices mentioned was made within 19 months of the priority date. This was relevant as long as Art. 22 stipulated a 20-month time limit for entering the national phase under Chapter I. Currently, only LU and TZ have a 20 or 21-month time limit. The notification is sent only to those elected Offices that have requested this notification under R. 93*bis*.1. The ePCT profile of the Offices in 'Current Distribution' shows which Offices receive which forms, see https://pct.wipo.int/ePCTExternal/pages/OfficeProfile.xhtml. In this case, for example, the EPO receives Form PCT/IB/331. 1

According to AIs 102, the use of the form is mandatory and it is sent to all applicants who make use of Chapter II. The applicant cannot waive this notification but can only choose delivery methods. See the annotation to R. 4.4(c) for more details. 2

Art. 22	30-month time limit for transmitting PCT applications to designated Offices
Art. 39(1)(a)	30-month time limit for transmitting PCT applications to elected Offices, non-application of Art. 22 if the Office is chosen within a 19-month period
R. 93*bis*.1	Transmission upon request; transmission via a digital library

61.4 Publication in the Gazette

The International Bureau shall, promptly after the filing of the demand but not before the international publication of the international application, publish in the Gazette information on the demand and the elected States concerned, as provided in the Administrative Instructions.

Art. 38	Confidential nature of the IPE
AIs 431	Publication of the application

Rule 62
Copy of the Written Opinion by the International Searching Authority and of Amendments under Article 19 for the International Preliminary Examining Authority

62.1 Copy of Written Opinion by International Searching Authority and of Amendments Made before the Demand Is Filed

Upon receipt of a demand, or a copy thereof, from the International Preliminary Examining Authority, the International Bureau shall promptly transmit to that Authority:

(i) a copy of the written opinion established under Rule 43*bis*.1, unless the national Office or intergovernmental organization that acted as International Searching Authority is also acting as International Preliminary Examining Authority; and

(ii) a copy of any amendment under Article 19, any statement referred to in that Article, and the letter required under Rule 46.5(b), unless that Authority has indicated that it has already received such a copy.

62.2 Amendments Made after the Demand Is Filed

If, at the time of filing any amendments under Article 19, a demand has already been submitted, the applicant shall preferably, at the same time as he files the amendments with the International Bureau, also file with the International Preliminary Examining Authority a copy of such amendments, any statement referred to in that Article and the letter required under Rule 46.5(b). In any case, the International Bureau shall promptly transmit a copy of such amendments, statement and letter to that Authority.

AG-IP 10.053	Consideration of amendments under Art. 19 by the IPEA
AG-IP 9.010	Filing amendments under Art. 19 with the IPEA

Rule 62*bis*
Translation for the International Preliminary Examining Authority of the Written Opinion of the International Searching Authority

62*bis*.1 Translation and Observations

(a) Upon request of the International Preliminary Examining Authority, the written opinion established under Rule 43*bis*.1 shall, when not in English or in a language accepted by that Authority, be translated into English by or under the responsibility of the International Bureau.

(b) The International Bureau shall transmit a copy of the translation to the International Preliminary Examining Authority within two months from the date of receipt of the request for translation, and shall at the same time transmit a copy to the applicant.

(c) The applicant may make written observations as to the correctness of the translation and shall send a copy of the observations to the International Preliminary Examining Authority and to the International Bureau.

Rule 63
Minimum Requirements for International Preliminary Examining Authorities

63.1 Definition of Minimum Requirements

The minimum requirements referred to in Article 32(3) shall be the following:

(i) the national Office or intergovernmental organization must have at least 100 full-time employees with sufficient technical qualifications to carry out examinations;

(ii) that Office or organization must have at its ready disposal at least the minimum documentation referred to in Rule 34, properly arranged for examination purposes;

1 An understanding of the PCT Assembly referring to the amendments in 2026 has been published in Gazette November 30, 2023, p. 224:

2 'Furthermore, the PCT Assembly adopted the following Understanding with regard to the interpretation of Rules 36.1(ii) and 63.1(ii): "In adopting the amendments to Rules 36.1 and 63.1 setting out the minimum requirements referred to in Articles 16(3)(c) and 32(3), respectively, the Assembly agreed that, in the case of an intergovernmental organization that has been established for the collaboration between national Offices of the States that are members of that intergovernmental organization and does not itself issue patents or publish patent applications, the requirements in Rules 36.1(ii) and 63.1(ii) for the organization are that the national Offices of those States make available for consultation, as part of the minimum documentation, any patent issued, and any patent application published, by them and, where applicable, by their legal predecessor(s)."'

(iii) that Office or organization must have a staff which is capable of examining in the required technical fields and which has the language facilities to understand at least those languages in which the minimum documentation referred to in Rule 34 is written or is translated;

(iv) that Office or organization must have in place a quality management system and internal review arrangements in accordance with the common rules of international preliminary examination;

ISPE Guidelines, Chapter 21 Common Quality Framework for International Search and Preliminary Examination, available at www.wipo.int/pct/en/texts/pdf/ispe.pdf. 3

(v) that Office or organization must hold an appointment as an International Searching Authority.

Amendments to R. 63 shall enter into force on January 1, 2026 (PCT/A/55/2). 4

Rule 64
Prior Art for International Preliminary Examination

64.1 Prior Art

(a) For the purposes of Article 33(2) and (3), everything made available to the public anywhere in the world by means of written disclosure (including drawings and other illustrations) shall be considered prior art provided that such making available occurred prior to the relevant date.

(b) For the purposes of paragraph (a), the relevant date shall be:

(i) subject to items (ii) and (iii), the international filing date of the international application under international preliminary examination;

(ii) where the international application under international preliminary examination claims the priority of an earlier application and has an international filing date which is within the priority period, the filing date of such earlier application, unless the International Preliminary Examining Authority considers that the priority claim is not valid;

(iii) where the international application under international preliminary examination claims the priority of an earlier application and has an international filing date which is later than the date on which the priority period expired but within the period of two months from that date, the filing date of such earlier application, unless the International Preliminary Examining Authority considers that the priority claim is not valid for reasons other than the fact that the international application has an international filing date which is later than the date on which the priority period expired.

R. 33	Relevant prior art for the international search
R. 64(b)(iii)	Reference to R. 26*bis*.3 restoration of the priority right
AIs 801 et seq.	Third Party Observation System. See also Euro-PCT Guide E-II.

1 An amendment of R. 64.1(a) has been proposed to broaden the definition of relevant prior art to include non-written disclosures as of January 1, 2026 (PCT/A/56/2).

64.2 Non-Written Disclosures

In cases where the making available to the public occurred by means of an oral disclosure, use, exhibition or other non-written means ("non-written disclosure") before the relevant date as defined in Rule 64.1 (b) and the date of such non-written disclosure is indicated in a written disclosure which has been made available to the public on a date which is the same as, or later than, the relevant date, the non-written disclosure shall not be considered part of the prior art for the purposes of Article 33(2) and (3). Nevertheless, the international preliminary examination report shall call attention to such non-written disclosure in the manner provided for in Rule 70.9.

An amendment of R. 64.2 has been proposed to broaden the definition of relevant prior art to include non-written disclosures as of January 1, 2026 (PCT/A/56/2). Prior to this date non-written disclosures can only be considered in the national/ regional phase of the procedure (e.g. oral disclosure at trade fairs). 2

64.3 Certain Published Documents

In cases where any application or any patent which would constitute prior art for the purposes of Article 33(2) and (3) had it been published prior to the relevant date referred to in Rule 64.1 was published on a date which is the same as, or later than, the relevant date but was filed earlier than the relevant date or claimed the priority of an earlier application which had been filed prior to the relevant date, such published application or patent shall not be considered part of the prior art for the purposes of Article 33(2) and (3). Nevertheless, the international preliminary examination report shall call attention to such application or patent in the manner provided for in Rule 70.10.

Older, unpublished applications are not prior art in the procedure before the IPEA. Rather, they must be taken into account in the national procedure. 3

Rule 65
Inventive Step or Non-Obviousness

65.1 Approach to Prior Art

For the purposes of Article 33(3), the international preliminary examination shall take into consideration the relation of any particular claim to the prior art as a whole. It shall take into consideration the claim's relation not only to individual documents or parts thereof taken separately but also its relation to combinations of such documents or parts of documents, where such combinations are obvious to a person skilled in the art.

13.03–13.13 ISPE Guidelines	Considerations in determining inventive step

1 The concept of the 'person skilled in the art' is central to the evaluation of inventive step or non-obviousness, a key criterion for patentability. This hypothetical individual or team represents someone with average knowledge and skills in the technical field related to the patent application. They are presumed to have access to all relevant prior art and the common general knowledge at the time the invention was made.

2 The determination of whether an invention is obvious involves assessing whether it would have been straightforward for this skilled person to achieve the invention, considering the state of technology and information available at the relevant time. This assessment is not just about the individual elements of the invention but requires considering the invention as a whole. It's crucial to avoid applying hindsight from the invention itself when evaluating the prior art and the steps a skilled person would have taken.

3 The process involves several steps: first, understanding the invention as claimed and identifying all relevant prior art. Then, determining the differences between the prior art and the claimed invention and assessing whether these differences would have been obvious to the skilled person. This assessment takes into account not only the explicit teachings of the prior art but also the implicit knowledge a skilled person would infer from it.

4 Moreover, the PCT ISPE Guidelines (Chapter 13) highlight that inventive step evaluation must consider the possibility of combining various teachings from different pieces of prior art. However, such combinations are considered obvious only if a

skilled person, motivated by the common technical challenges known at the time, would reasonably have been expected to combine such teachings to arrive at the invention.

In essence, the 'person skilled in the art' serves as a benchmark against which the 5
inventive step is measured. This concept ensures that patents are granted only for advancements that contribute meaningfully beyond the existing state of the art, reflecting a genuine leap in innovation rather than a mere aggregation of known techniques or knowledge.

65.2 Relevant Date

For the purposes of Article 33(3), the relevant date for the consideration of inventive step (non-obviousness) is the date prescribed in Rule 64.1 *(filing or priority date).*

Rule 66
Procedure before the International Preliminary Examining Authority

66.1 Basis of the International Preliminary Examination

(a) Subject to paragraphs (b) to (d), the international preliminary examination shall be based on the international application as filed.

(b) The applicant may submit amendments under Article 34 at the time of filing the demand or, subject to Rule 66.4*bis*, until the international preliminary examination report is established.

(c) Any amendments under Article 19 made before the demand was filed shall be taken into account for the purposes of the international preliminary examination unless superseded, or considered as reversed, by an amendment under Article 34 *(Article 34(2)(b))*.

(d) Any amendments under Article 19 made after the demand was filed and any amendments under Article 34 submitted to the International Preliminary Examining Authority shall, subject to Rule 66.4*bis*, be taken into account for the purposes of the international preliminary examination.

(d-*bis*) A rectification of an obvious mistake that is authorized under Rule 91.1 shall, subject to Rule 66.4*bis*, be taken into account by the International Preliminary Examining Authority for the purposes of the international preliminary examination.

(e) Claims relating to inventions in respect of which no international search report has been established need not be the subject of international preliminary examination.

Art. 34(3)	Proceedings before the IPEA: lack of unity
Art. 34(4)(a)(i)	Unsearchable/searched subject matter
Art. 34(4)(a)(ii)	Unclear application affects the scope of the IPE and the IPRP II
Art. 17(2), (3)	Proceedings before the ISA: lack of unity, unsearchable/searched subject matter, unclear application has an impact on the preparation of the ISR. It does not matter whether the applicant files

	amendments or counter-arguments which allegedly overcome the reasons for non-searchability (Euro-PCT Guide 4.2.027).
R. 39	Unsearchable subject matter
R. 67	Unexaminable subject matter
R. 66.1*ter*	Effect on the scope of the supplementary international search

66.1*bis* Written Opinion of the International Searching Authority

(a) Subject to paragraph (b), the written opinion established by the International Searching Authority under Rule 43*bis*.1 shall be considered to be a written opinion of the International Preliminary Examining Authority for the purposes of Rule 66.2(a).

The fiction means that the IPEA does not normally have to (but may) issue a new written decision. This always applies if IPEA has already acted as ISA (Reischle, *Mitteilungen der deutschen Patentanwälte* 2004, 530). 1

The written opinion under R. 43*bis* is referred to by the EPO in its function as ISA as WO-ISA (Euro-PCT Guide, para. 3.2.005). 2

(b) An International Preliminary Examining Authority may notify the International Bureau that paragraph (a) shall not apply to the procedure before it in respect of written opinions established under Rule 43*bis*.1 by the International Searching Authority or Authorities specified in the notification, provided that such a notification shall not apply to cases where the national Office or intergovernmental organization that acted as International Searching Authority is also acting as International Preliminary Examining Authority. The International Bureau shall promptly publish any such notification in the Gazette.

A notice from the EPO was published (PCT Newsletter 1/2004, p. 4). The EPO will only refrain from issuing a new decision if it has acted as the ISA in this PCT application. 3

(c) Where the written opinion established by the International Searching Authority under Rule 43*bis*.1 is not, by virtue of a notification under paragraph (b), considered to be a written opinion of the International Preliminary Examining Authority for the purposes of Rule 66.2(a), the International Preliminary Examining Authority shall notify the applicant accordingly in writing.

(d) A written opinion established by the International Searching Authority under Rule 43*bis*.1 which is not, by virtue of a notification under paragraph (b), considered to be a written opinion of the International Preliminary Examining Authority for the purposes of Rule 66.2(a) shall nevertheless be taken into account by the International Preliminary Examining Authority in proceeding under Rule 66.2(a).

66.1*ter* Top-up Searches

The International Preliminary Examining Authority shall conduct a search ("top-up search") to discover documents referred to in Rule 64 *(prior art)* which have been published or have become available to the said Authority for search subsequent to the date on which the international search report was established, unless it considers that such a search would serve no useful purpose. If the Authority finds that any of the situations referred to in Article 34(3) *(lack of unity of invention)* or (4) *(irrelevant subject matter, unclear application)* or Rule 66.1(e) *(no ISR established)* exists, the top-up search shall cover only those parts of the international application that are the subject of international preliminary examination.

4 The purpose of the top-up search is to find further relevant documents related to the prior art, especially intermediate literature that became accessible later. The top-up search is normally conducted by the EPO at the beginning of the examination under Chapter II (Euro-PCT Guide, para. 4.2.012 et seq.).

5 The EPO will in particular refrain from conducting a top-up search if it would not cite written evidence of the relevant prior art (e.g., in the case of 'notorious knowledge of a person skilled in the art' in the field of computer-implemented inventions), because a search in this case would not be meaningful, OJ EPO 2014 A57.

R. 46.5(b)	Form of amendments according to Art. 19 before the International Bureau. If the amendments are insufficient, the EPO limits the top-up search to the scope of the claims on which the IPER is based (OJ EPO 2014 A57).
R. 64.1	Prior art for IPE. If new documents are found in the top-up search that lead to objections against patentability, the EPO as IPEA issues a second written opinion or conducts a telephone consultation. Without substantive response from the applicant, a second written opinion is only issued if the top-up search reveals new relevant prior art; otherwise, the IPER is issued directly. Relevant documents identified in the top-up search are mentioned in the IPER, unless they have become irrelevant due to the response to the written opinion. If the top-up search only finds intermediate literature (P) or potentially conflicting applications (E) and there are no other objections, a second written opinion is only issued if the documents would lead to objections under Art. 54(3) in the regional phase before the EPO; otherwise, an IPER is issued (OJ EPO 2014 A57 and OJ EPO 2011p. 532).
R. 66.8	Form of amendments according to Art. 34 in the procedure before the IPEA. If the amendments are insufficient, the EPO limits the top-up search to the scope of the claims on which the IPER is based. OJ EPO 2014 A57.
R. 70.2(c), (c-*bis*)	The basis for the top-up search are the application documents as they were at the beginning of the examination under Chapter II (Euro-PCT Guide 4.2.013).

R. 70.2(f)	Indication of the date of the top-up search in the IPRP II or information about the non-conduct of the top-up search.
R. 70.7	Indication of identified documents in the IPRP II

66.2 Written Opinion of the International Preliminary Examining Authority

(a) If the International Preliminary Examining Authority

(i) considers that any of the situations referred to in Article 34(4) exists,

Art. 34(4)	Irrelevant subject matter, unclear application, non-obviousness
R. 67	Lack of technicity

(ii) considers that the international preliminary examination report should be negative in respect of any of the claims because the invention claimed therein does not appear to be novel, does not appear to involve an inventive step (does not appear to be non-obvious), or does not appear to be industrially applicable,

(iii) notices that there is some defect in the form or contents of the international application under the Treaty or these Regulations,

(iv) considers that any amendment goes beyond the disclosure in the international application as filed,

(v) wishes to accompany the international preliminary examination report by observations on the clarity of the claims, the description, and the drawings, or the question whether the claims are fully supported by the description,

(vi) considers that a claim relates to an invention in respect of which no international search report has been established and has decided not to carry out the international preliminary examination in respect of that claim, or

(vii) considers that a nucleotide and/or amino acid sequence listing is not available to it in such a form that a meaningful international preliminary examination can be carried out,

the said Authority shall notify the applicant accordingly in writing. Where the national law of the national Office acting as International Preliminary Examining Authority does not allow multiple dependent claims to be drafted in a manner different from that provided for in the second and third sentences of Rule 6.4(a), the International Preliminary Examining Authority may, in case of failure to use that manner of claiming, apply Article 34(4)(b). In such case, it shall notify the applicant accordingly in writing.

(b) The notification shall fully state the reasons for the opinion of the International Preliminary Examining Authority.

(c) The notification shall invite the applicant to submit a written reply together, where appropriate, with amendments.

(d) The notification shall fix a time limit for the reply. The time limit shall be reasonable under the circumstances. It shall normally be two months after the date of notification. In no case shall it be shorter than one month after the said date. It shall be at least two months after the said date where the international search report is transmitted at the same time as the notification. It shall, subject to paragraph (e), not be more than three months after the said date.

(e) The time limit for replying to the notification may be extended if the applicant so requests before its expiration.

66.3 Formal Response to the International Preliminary Examining Authority

(a) The applicant may respond to the invitation referred to in Rule 66.2(c) of the International Preliminary Examining Authority by making amendments or – if he disagrees with the opinion of that Authority – by submitting arguments, as the case may be, or do both.

(b) Any response shall be submitted directly to the International Preliminary Examining Authority.

66.4 Additional Opportunity for Submitting Amendments or Arguments

(a) If the International Preliminary Examining Authority wishes to issue one or more additional written opinions, it may do so, and Rules 66.2 and 66.3 shall apply.

6 EPO as IPEA:

7 If the written opinion on the ISR in the sense of R. 43*bis* was prepared by the EPO, the EPO usually does not issue any further opinion before the preparation of the IPRP, in accordance with para. 19.14 of the ISPE Guidelines during the IPE (www.wipo.int/export/sites/www/pct/en/texts/pdf/ispe.pdf). Before the issuance of the IPRP, preferably along with the request for IPE, an applicant or their representative may submit a request for a telephone consultation with the EPO examiner responsible for drafting the report, which should include the specific points the applicant wishes to discuss. Such consultation is usually granted if requested in a timely manner; the granting of further consultations is at the sole discretion of the examiner according to para. 19.12 of the ISPE Guidelines (OJ EPO 2005 p. 493).

8 In case of an objection by the EPO that suggests a negative IPRP, i.e., a deficiency that the applicant would have to address under R. 161(1) EPC if they decide to enter the European phase, the EPO generally issues an additional written opinion unless a telephone consultation has been requested. This opinion is called a 'second written opinion' because the first opinion of the EPO is either the WO-ISA of the EPO as ISA according to R. 43*bis*.1, which is considered the first written opinion for Chapter II under R. 66.1*bis*(a), or because the first opinion was issued by the EPO as IPEA if the WO-ISA was not prepared by the EPO R. 66.1*bis*(c), 66.3.

The issuance of the second opinion presupposes that the applicant has submitted amendments and/or counterarguments under R. 66.1(a)–(d), 66.4*bis* or that the applicant has timely submitted a response to the opinion under R. 66.1*bis*(c), 66.2, but objections by the EPO still exist. 9

If the applicant has requested a telephone consultation before the issuance of the IPRP, they will receive a transcript of the call with the invitation to submit amendments/counterarguments within the time limit. A second opinion is not issued. If the applicant has requested a telephone consultation and/or a second written opinion before the issuance of the IPRP, it is at the discretion of the EPO whether to consult the applicant by telephone or to issue a second written opinion. 10

If the request for a telephone consultation is made after the issuance of the second written opinion but before the date of the IPRP, the applicant only receives the transcript without an invitation to submit a further statement. 11

R. 66.2(d)	Time limit for reply
R. 69.2(i)–(iii)	Time limit for drawing up the IPRP: usually 28 months from the priority date or later

(b) On the request of the applicant, the International Preliminary Examining Authority may give him one or more additional opportunities to submit amendments or arguments.

66.4*bis* Consideration of Amendments, Arguments and Rectifications of Obvious Mistakes

Amendments, arguments and rectifications of obvious mistakes need not be taken into account by the International Preliminary Examining Authority for the purposes of a written opinion or the international preliminary examination report if they are received by, authorized by or notified to that Authority, as applicable, after it has begun to draw up that opinion or report.

66.5 Amendment

Any change, other than the rectification of an obvious mistake, in the claims, the description, or the drawings, including cancellation of claims, omission of passages in the description, or omission of certain drawings, shall be considered an amendment.

Description and drawings can only be amended under Art. 34, whereas claims can also be amended under Art. 19 (PCT Applicant's Guide 11.045). Additionally, correction under R. 91 and R. 26, submission of missing parts under R. 20.5, and correct parts or components under R. 20.5*bis* are not considered as amendments, according to PCT EPO Guidelines H-I 1. 12

66.6 Informal Communications with the Applicant

The International Preliminary Examining Authority may, at any time, communicate informally, over the telephone, in writing, or through personal interviews, with the applicant. The said Authority shall, at its discretion, decide whether it wishes to grant more than one personal interview if so requested by the applicant, or whether it wishes to reply to any informal written communication from the applicant.

Art. 34(2)(a)	Right to communicate orally and in writing with the IPEA.
W 4/93	The right under Art. 34(2)(a) to communicate orally with the IPEA does not include a right to an oral hearing. An informal hearing under R. 66.6 is usually not expedient in protest proceedings under R. 68.3(c) PCT (Reasons, 9).

66.7 Copy and Translation of Earlier Application Whose Priority Is Claimed

(a) If the International Preliminary Examining Authority needs a copy of the earlier application whose priority is claimed in the international application, the International Bureau shall, on request, promptly furnish such copy. If that copy is not furnished to the International Preliminary Examining Authority because the applicant failed to comply with the requirements of Rule 17.1, and if that earlier application was not filed with that Authority in its capacity as a national Office or the priority document is not available to that Authority from a digital library in accordance with the Administrative Instructions, the international preliminary examination report may be established as if the priority had not been claimed.

AIs 421	Request for a copy of the priority document
AIs 715	Provision of priority documents in digital libraries
AIs 716	Request to retrieve a priority document from a digital library

(b) If the application whose priority is claimed in the international application is in a language other than the language or one of the languages of the International Preliminary Examining Authority, that Authority may, where the validity of the priority claim is relevant for the formulation of the opinion referred to in Article 33(1), invite the applicant to furnish a translation in the said language or one of the said languages within two months from the date of the invitation. If the translation is not furnished within that time limit, the international preliminary examination report may be established as if the priority had not been claimed.

66.8 Form of Amendments

(a) Subject to paragraph (b), when amending the description or the drawings, the applicant shall be required to submit a replacement sheet for every sheet of the international application which, on account of an amendment, differs from the sheet previously filed. The replacement sheet or sheets shall be accompanied by a letter which shall draw attention to the differences between the replaced sheets and the replacement sheets, shall indicate the basis for the amendment in the application as filed and shall preferably also explain the reasons for the amendment.

R. 70.2(c-*bis*)	Ignoring amendment if the basis is not indicated
R. 66.1*ter*	Ignoring amendments not filed in due form in the top-up search
AIs 205	Numbering and designation of amended claims
AIs 602	Processing of amendments by the IPEA

(b) Where the amendment consists in the deletion of passages or in minor alterations or additions, the replacement sheet referred to in paragraph (a) may be a copy of the relevant sheet of the international application containing the alterations or additions, provided that the clarity and direct reproducibility of that sheet are not adversely affected. To the extent that any amendment results in the cancellation of an entire sheet, that amendment shall be communicated in a letter which shall preferably also explain the reasons for the amendment.

(c) When amending the claims, Rule 46.5 *(form of amendments)* shall apply *mutatis mutandis.* The set of claims submitted under Rule 46.5 as applicable by virtue of this paragraph shall replace all the claims originally filed or previously amended under Articles 19 or 34, as the case may be.

Rule 67
Subject Matter under Article 34(4)(a)(i)

67.1 Definition

No International Preliminary Examining Authority shall be required to carry out an international preliminary examination on an international application if, and to the extent to which, its subject matter is any of the following:

(i) scientific and mathematical theories,

(ii) plant or animal varieties or essentially biological processes for the production of plants and animals, other than microbiological processes and the products of such processes,

(iii) schemes, rules or methods of doing business, performing purely mental acts or playing games,

(iv) methods for treatment of the human or animal body by surgery or therapy, as well as diagnostic methods,

(v) mere presentations of information,

(vi) computer programs to the extent that the International Preliminary Examining Authority is not equipped to carry out an international preliminary examination concerning such programs.

Art. 34(4)(a)(i)	Examination of novelty, obviousness, and industrial applicability under Art. 33(1) by the IPEA is not mandatory for certain subject matter
R. 39	Corresponding regulation for the ISA
R. 39.1(iii)	The EPO does not conduct a search regarding business methods if the subject matter of the application has no obvious technical character. In this case, a statement under Art. 17(2) is made. R. 39.1 allows for some discretion. The EPO as ISA exercises this discretion according to the same standards that apply under the EPC (EPO Notice of October 1, 2007, OJ EPO 2007 p. 592 continues to apply according to Notice of October 27, 2014 OJ EPO 2014 A117; Euro-PCT Guide 3.3.005). See also annotations to Art. 16(2).

R. 66.1(e)	During the IPE, the IPEA is not obliged to take into consideration unsearched subject matter.
R. 66.1*ter*	In the case of R. 66.1(e), no top-up search is conducted.

Rule 68
Lack of Unity of Invention (International Preliminary Examination)

68.1 No Invitation to Restrict or Pay

Where the International Preliminary Examining Authority finds that the requirement of unity of invention is not complied with and chooses not to invite the applicant to restrict the claims or to pay additional fees, it shall proceed with the international preliminary examination, subject to Article 34(4)(b) and Rule 66.1(e), in respect of the entire international application, but shall indicate, in any written opinion and in the international preliminary examination report, that it considers that the requirement of unity of invention is not fulfilled and it shall specify the reasons therefor.

1 Art. 17, Art. 34(4), R. 40, and the annotations thereto provide a detailed overview of the procedure in cases of lack of unity.

Art. 64, 27, R. 51*bis*	There are no reservations to R. 13, meaning the question of unity is governed in all regional and national phases by R. 13
R. 13.2	Common special technical features
Art. 17, R. 40	Lack of unity in international search
R. 45*bis*.5(e), 45*bis*.6	Lack of unity in supplementary international search
R. 66.1*ter*	Lack of unity in top-up search.
Art. 34(3), R. 68	Lack of unity in IPE.
AIs 206	Unity of invention. AIs Annex B provides detailed examples of unity of invention. Further examples can be found in AIs 206. Among other things, the Markush practice is explained in AIs Annex B Part 2 III.

68.2 Invitation to Restrict or Pay

Where the International Preliminary Examining Authority finds that the requirement of unity of invention is not complied with and chooses to invite

the applicant, at his option, to restrict the claims or to pay additional fees, the invitation shall:

(i) specify at least one possibility of restriction which, in the opinion of the International Preliminary Examining Authority, would be in compliance with the applicable requirement;

(ii) specify the reasons for which the international application is not considered as complying with the requirement of unity of invention;

(iii) invite the applicant to comply with the invitation within one month from the date of the invitation;

(iv) indicate the amount of the required additional fees to be paid in case the applicant so chooses; and

(v) invite the applicant to pay, where applicable, the protest fee referred to in Rule 68.3(e) within one month from the date of the invitation, and indicate the amount to be paid.

Established jurisprudence (e.g., W 8/87): a request under Art. 34(3)(a) for the payment of additional fees is only legally effective if the lack of unity is sufficiently justified. Since April 1, 2005, the requirement to check whether the request for payment of additional fees was justified before requesting the payment of a protest fee has been abolished. 2

W 8/87	Under R. 13.1 PCT, the lack of unity of an invention can be determined *a posteriori*. The relevant notification under R. 40.1 must include, in addition to the listing of the inventions defined in the new independent claims (which result from the combination of the fallen main or subsidiary claim) and the request for payment of further search fees under Art. 17(3)(a), also the reasons for the determination of the lack of unity. A payment request that does not contain these reasons is not legally binding in view of the lack of unity determined *a posteriori* as mentioned above.

68.3 Additional Fees

(a) The amount of the additional fees due for international preliminary examination under Article 34(3)(a) shall be determined by the competent International Preliminary Examining Authority.

AG-IP Annex E	Additional fee for IPE
R. 158(2) EPC, Art. 2(1) No. 19 RFees:	Additional fee for lack of unity. Generally, the amount of the international examination fee that was applicable at the time of filing the examination request is charged. Subsequent fee increases are not considered.

(b) The additional fees due for international preliminary examination under Article 34(3)(a) shall be payable direct to the International Preliminary Examining Authority.

(c) Any applicant may pay the additional fees under protest, that is, accompanied by a reasoned statement to the effect that the international application complies with the requirement of unity of invention or that the amount of the required additional fees is excessive. Such protest shall be examined by a review body constituted in the framework of the International Preliminary Examining Authority which, to the extent that it finds the protest justified, shall order the total or partial reimbursement to the applicant of the additional fees. On the request of the applicant, the text of both the protest and the decision thereon shall be notified to the elected Offices as an annex to the international preliminary examination report.

(d) The membership of the review body referred to in paragraph (c) may include, but shall not be limited to, the person who made the decision which is the subject of the protest.

(e) The examination of a protest referred to in paragraph (c) may be subjected by the International Preliminary Examining Authority to the payment to it, for its own benefit, of a protest fee. Where the applicant has not, within the time limit under Rule 68.2(v), paid any required protest fee, the protest shall be considered not to have been made and the International Preliminary Examining Authority shall so declare. The protest fee shall be refunded to the applicant where the review body referred to in paragraph (c) finds that the protest was entirely justified.

3 Regarding the amount of the fee, see the Schedule of Fees.

AIs 403 and 603	Transmission of the protest against the payment of an additional fee and decision on this matter in case of lack of unity of the invention of the international application
W 4/93	1. The review, required under R. 68.3(e), of the justification for the invitation to pay an additional fee for the IPE must be based exclusively on the reasons contained in the invitation to pay, having regard to the facts and arguments submitted by the applicants in the grounds given for their protest. This rules out the subsequent submission of new reasons and evidence in the notification of the result of the review (Reasons, 2.1 and 2.2). 2. The notification of the result of the review of the invitation to pay under R. 68.3(e) should address the grounds given for the protest (Reasons, 2.3).

68.4 Procedure in the Case of Insufficient Restriction of the Claims

If the applicant restricts the claims but not sufficiently to comply with the requirement of unity of invention, the International Preliminary Examining Authority shall proceed as provided in Article 34(3)(c).

Regarding the procedure, see Euro-PCT Guide para. 4.2.037 et seq. and the annotations to Art. 34(3)(c). 4

68.5 Main Invention

In case of doubt which invention is the main invention for the purposes of Article 34(3)(c), the invention first mentioned in the claims shall be considered the main invention.

Rule 69
Start of and Time Limit for International Preliminary Examination

69.1 Start of International Preliminary Examination

(a) Subject to paragraphs (b) to (e), the International Preliminary Examining Authority shall start the international preliminary examination when it is in possession of all of the following:

(i) the demand;

(ii) the amount due (in full) for the handling fee and the preliminary examination fee, including, where applicable, the late payment fee under Rule 58*bis*.2; and

(iii) either the international search report or the declaration by the International Searching Authority under Article 17(2)(a) that no international search report will be established, and the written opinion established under Rule 43*bis*.1;

unless the applicant expressly requests to postpone the start of the international preliminary examination until the expiration of the applicable time limit under Rule 54*bis*.1(a).

R. 54*bis*	governs the timing of the demand while R. 69 regulates the start of the examination. Since July 1, 2019, the expiration of the time limit according to R. 54*bis*.1, as per R. 69.1(a), is only an exception and no longer the norm as a prerequisite for the start of the examination. The request for postponement of the start of the examination can be made using Form PCT/IPEA/401. The start of the IPE is also delayed if the demand is submitted late or if the fees are paid late, leaving less time for the IPE.
R. 60.1(g)	The applicant will be invited to submit amendments within a time limit if the applicant indicated he intends to file amendments
R. 66.4*bis*	No consideration of amendments filed after the commencement of the drafting of the written opinion or report

(b) If the national Office or intergovernmental organization that acts as International Searching Authority also acts as International Preliminary Examining Authority, the international preliminary examination may, if that national Office or intergovernmental organization so wishes and subject to paragraphs (d) and (e), start at the same time as the international search *(so-called telescopic procedure)*.

EPO as IPEA	does not apply paras (b) and (b-*bis*), meaning it does not start the IPE simultaneously with the search, unless the applicant expressly requests this, as per PCT EPO Guidelines C-VI 1

(b-*bis*) Where, in accordance with paragraph (b), the national Office or intergovernmental organization that acts as both International Searching Authority and International Preliminary Examining Authority wishes to start the international preliminary examination at the same time as the international search and considers that all of the conditions referred to in Article 34(2)(c)(i) to (iii) are fulfilled, that national Office or intergovernmental organization need not, in its capacity as International Searching Authority, establish a written opinion under Rule 43*bis*.1.

EPO as IPEA	does not apply paras (b) and (b-*bis*), meaning it does not start the IPE simultaneously with the search, unless the applicant expressly requests this, as per PCT EPO Guidelines C-VI 1

(c) Where the statement concerning amendments contains an indication that amendments under Article 19 are to be taken into account (Rule 53.9(a)(i)), the International Preliminary Examining Authority shall not start the international preliminary examination before it has received a copy of the amendments concerned.

(d) Where the statement concerning amendments *(Art. 19(1) sentence 2)* contains an indication that the start of the international preliminary examination is to be postponed (Rule 53.9(b)), the International Preliminary Examining Authority shall not start the international preliminary examination before whichever of the following occurs first:

(i) it has received a copy of any amendments made under Article 19;

(ii) it has received a notice from the applicant that he does not wish to make amendments under Article 19; or

(iii) the expiration of the applicable time limit under Rule 46.1.

R. 46.1	Time limit for amendments under Art. 19

(e) Where the statement concerning amendments contains an indication that amendments under Article 34 are submitted with the demand (Rule 53.9(c)) but no such amendments are, in fact, submitted, the International Preliminary Examining Authority shall not start the international preliminary examination

before it has received the amendments or before the time limit fixed in the invitation referred to in Rule 60.1(g) *(invitation to submit amendments)* has expired, whichever occurs first.

69.2 Time Limit for International Preliminary Examination

The time limit for establishing the international preliminary examination report shall be whichever of the following periods expires last:

(i) 28 months from the priority date; or

(ii) six months from the time provided under Rule 69.1 for the start of the international preliminary examination; or

(iii) six months from the date of receipt by the International Preliminary Examining Authority of the translation furnished under Rule 55.2.

1 The time limit for the preparation of the IPRP I is 30 months (see annotations to R. 44*bis*.1 and R. 44*bis*.2(a)).

Rule 70
International Preliminary Report on Patentability by the International Preliminary Examining Authority (International Preliminary Examination Report)

70.1 Definition

For the purposes of this Rule, "report" shall mean international preliminary examination report.

Art. 33	Preparation of examiner opinion as the subject of the IPE
Art. 35	Requirements
R. 70.15	Title of the report

70.2 Basis of the Report

(a) If the claims have been amended, the report shall issue on the claims as amended.

(b) If, pursuant to Rule 66.7(a) or (b), the report is established as if the priority had not been claimed, the report shall so indicate.

(c) If the International Preliminary Examining Authority considers that any amendment goes beyond the disclosure in the international application as filed, the report shall be established as if such amendment had not been made, and the report shall so indicate. It shall also indicate the reasons why it considers that the amendment goes beyond the said disclosure.

Art. 19(2)	In amendments under Art. 19
Art. 34(2)(b)2	During IPE
Art. 28(2)	Before designated Office
Art. 41(2)	Before elected Office

Art. 46 In translation of PCTa

(c-*bis*) If the claims, description or drawings have been amended but the replacement sheet or sheets were not accompanied by a letter indicating the basis for the amendment in the application as filed, as required under Rule 46.5(b)(iii), Rule 46.5(b)(iii) being applicable by virtue of Rule 66.8(c), or Rule 66.8(a), as applicable, the report may be established as if the amendment had not been made, in which case the report shall so indicate.

1 The requirements of R. 46.5(b)(iii) also apply to para. (a) of R. 66.8, i.e. to amendments under Art. 19. This should be clarified by the latest amendment (PCT/WG/3/8 Annex, p. 12). The above paragraph also applies to amendments under Art. 19 (R. 66.1(c)).

(d) Where claims relate to inventions in respect of which no international search report has been established and have therefore not been the subject of international preliminary examination, the international preliminary examination report shall so indicate.

Art. 34(4) Non-searchable subject matter in IPE

(e) If a rectification of an obvious mistake is taken into account under Rule 66.1, the report shall so indicate. If a rectification of an obvious mistake is not taken into account pursuant to Rule 66.4*bis*, the report shall, if possible, so indicate, failing which the International Preliminary Examining Authority shall notify the International Bureau accordingly and the International Bureau shall proceed as provided for in the Administrative Instructions.

AIs 413(d) Notification of non-consideration of a correction to the elected Office

(f) The report shall indicate the date on which a top-up search under Rule 66.1*ter* was made, or else state that no top-up search was made.

2 'The effect of amendments of Rules 66 and 70 would be to require International Preliminary Examining Authorities to conduct a "top-up" search during international preliminary examination subject to various exceptions, such as subject matter which is not examined by the Office, cases which have not been searched by the International Searching Authority and other cases where it is considered that such a search would serve no useful purpose.' www.wipo.int/edocs/mdocs/govbody/en/pct_a_44/pct_a_44_3.pdf.

R. 66.1*ter* Implementation of top-up search by the IPEA

70.3 Identifications

The report shall identify the International Preliminary Examining Authority which established it by indicating the name of such Authority, and the international application by indicating the international application number, the name of the applicant, and the international filing date.

70.4 Dates

The report shall indicate:

(i) the date on which the demand was submitted, and

(ii) the date of the report; that date shall be the date on which the report is completed.

70.5 Classification

(a) The report shall repeat the classification given under Rule 43.3 if the International Preliminary Examining Authority agrees with such classification.

(b) Otherwise, the International Preliminary Examining Authority shall indicate in the report the classification, at least according to the International Patent Classification, which it considers correct.

70.6 Statement under Article 35(2)

(a) The statement referred to in Article 35(2) *(novelty, inventive step (non-obviousness), industrial applicability)* shall consist of the words "YES" or "NO," or their equivalent in the language of the report, or some appropriate sign provided for in the Administrative Instructions, and shall be accompanied by the citations, explanations and observations, if any, referred to in the last sentence of Article 35(2).

(b) If any of the three criteria referred to in Article 35(2) (that is, novelty, inventive step (non-obviousness), industrial applicability) is not satisfied, the statement shall be negative. If, in such a case, any of the criteria, taken separately, is satisfied, the report shall specify the criterion or criteria so satisfied.

70.7 Citations under Article 35(2)

(a) The report shall cite the documents considered to be relevant for supporting the statements made under Article 35(2), whether or not such documents are cited in the international search report. Documents cited in the international search report need only be cited in the report when they are considered by the International Preliminary Examining Authority to be relevant.

(b) The provisions of Rule 43.5(b) and (e) shall apply also to the report.

70.8 Explanations under Article 35(2)

The Administrative Instructions shall contain guidelines for cases in which the explanations referred to in Article 35(2) should or should not be given and the form of such explanations. Such guidelines shall be based on the following principles:

(i) explanations shall be given whenever the statement in relation to any claim is negative;

(ii) explanations shall be given whenever the statement is positive unless the reason for citing any document is easy to imagine on the basis of consultation of the cited document;

(iii) generally, explanations shall be given if the case provided for in the last sentence of Rule 70.6(b) obtains.

AIs 604 Provisions for explanatory notes in the IPER

70.9 Non-Written Disclosures

Any non-written disclosure referred to in the report by virtue of Rule 64.2 shall be mentioned by indicating its kind, the date on which the written disclosure referring to the non-written disclosure was made available to the public, and the date on which the non-written disclosure occurred in public.

70.10 Certain Published Documents

Any published application or any patent referred to in the report by virtue of Rule 64.3 shall be mentioned as such and shall be accompanied by an indication of its date of publication, of its filing date, and its claimed priority date (if any). In respect of the priority date of any such document, the report may indicate that, in the opinion of the International Preliminary Examining Authority, such date has not been validly claimed.

70.11 Mention of Amendments

If, before the International Preliminary Examining Authority, amendments have been made, this fact shall be indicated in the report. Where any amendment has resulted in the cancellation of an entire sheet, this fact shall also be specified in the report.

70.12 Mention of Certain Defects and Other Matters

If the International Preliminary Examining Authority considers that, at the time it prepares the report:

(i) the international application contains any of the defects referred to in Rule 66.2(a)(iii) *(form, content)*, it shall include this opinion and the reasons therefor in the report;

(ii) the international application calls for any of the observations referred to in Rule 66.2(a)(v) *(clarity of claims, etc.)*, it may include this opinion in the report and, if it does, it shall also indicate in the report the reasons for such opinion;

(iii) any of the situations referred to in Article 34(4) *(lack of technicity, non-obviousness)* exists, it shall state this opinion and the reasons therefor in the report;

(iv) a nucleotide and/or amino acid sequence listing is not available to it in such a form that a meaningful international preliminary examination can be carried out, it shall so state in the report.

70.13 Remarks Concerning Unity of Invention

If the applicant paid additional fees for the international preliminary examination, or if the international application or the international preliminary examination was restricted under Article 34(3), the report shall so indicate. Furthermore, where the international preliminary examination was carried out on restricted claims (Article 34(3)(a)), or on the main invention only (Article 34(3)(c)), the report shall indicate what parts of the international application were and what parts were not the subject of international preliminary examination. The report shall contain the indications provided for in Rule 68.1, where the International Preliminary Examining Authority chose not to invite the applicant to restrict the claims or to pay additional fees.

Art. 34(3)(c)	75% reduction of the examination fee at the EPO under Art. 14(2) RFees if examination is to be carried out for the subject matter dealt with in the IPRP (OJ 2023 A28 p.6)

70.14 Authorized Officer

The report shall indicate the name of the officer of the International Preliminary Examining Authority responsible for that report.

AIs 612	Authorized officer, responsible staff member
EPO	as IPEA: one of the three examiners is entrusted with the examination (GL Exam E-IX, 4.3 and C-VIII 1)

70.15 Form; Title

(a) The physical requirements as to the form of the report shall be prescribed by the Administrative Instructions.

(b) The report shall bear the title "international preliminary report on patentability (Chapter II of the Patent Cooperation Treaty)" together with an indication that it is the international preliminary examination report established by the International Preliminary Examining Authority.

Therefore, the correct abbreviation for the report would be IPRP II. However, the EPO continues to use the abbreviation IPER (Euro-PCT Guide 4.1.004), in accordance with Art. 35 and the subheading: International Preliminary Examination Report. 3

70.16 Annexes to the Report

(a) The following replacement sheets and letters shall be annexed to the report:

(i) each replacement sheet under Rule 66.8 containing amendments under Article 34 and each letter under Rule 66.8(a), Rule 66.8(b) and Rule 46.5(b) as applicable by virtue of Rule 66.8(c);

Art. 34(2)(b)	Amendment of the claims, description and drawings before the IPEA

(ii) each replacement sheet under Rule 46.5 containing amendments under Article 19 and each letter under Rule 46.5; and

Art. 19	Amendment of claims in proceedings before the International Bureau

(iii) each replacement sheet under Rule 26.4 as applicable by virtue of Rule 91.2 containing a rectification of an obvious mistake authorized by that Authority under Rule 91.1(b)(iii) and each letter under Rule 26.4 as applicable by virtue of Rule 91.2; unless any such replacement sheet has been superseded or considered reversed by a later replacement sheet or an amendment resulting in the cancellation of an entire sheet under Rule 66.8(b); and

R. 91.2	Request for correction of obvious mistakes in the international application and other documents: contents, time limit and form
R. 26.4	Manner of correction

(iv) where the report contains an indication referred to in Rule 70.2(e) *(rectification of obvious mistakes)*, any sheet and letter relating to a rectification of an obvious mistake which is not taken into account pursuant to Rule 66.4*bis*.

R. 70.2(e)	Indication of whether or not the correction of obvious mistakes has been taken into account as a basis for the report
R. 66.1(d-*bis*)	Consideration by IPEA
R. 66.4*bis*	Disregard by IPEA after commencement of the preparation of the notice or report

(b) Notwithstanding paragraph (a), each superseded or reversed replacement sheet referred to in that paragraph and any letter referred to in that paragraph relating to such superseded or reversed sheet shall also be annexed to the report where:

(i) the International Preliminary Examining Authority considers that the relevant superseding or reversing amendment goes beyond the disclosure in the international application as filed and the report contains an indication referred to in Rule 70.2(c);

R. 70.2(c)	Reference to preparation of the report without consideration of amendments due to added matter

(ii) the relevant superseding or reversing amendment was not accompanied by a letter indicating the basis for the amendment in the application as filed and the report is established as if the amendment had not been made and contains an indication referred to in Rule 70.2(c-*bis*). In such a case, the superseded or reversed replacement sheet shall be marked as provided by the Administrative Instructions.

R. 70.2(c-*bis*)	Preparation of the report without consideration of amendments due to missing cover letter
AIs 602	Treatment of amendments by IPEA

70.17 Languages of the Report and the Annexes

The report and any annex shall be in the language in which the international application to which they relate is published, or, if the international preliminary examination is carried out, pursuant to Rule 55.2, on the basis of a translation of the international application, in the language of that translation.

Rule 71 Transmittal of the International Preliminary Examination Report and Related Documents

71.1 Recipients

(a) The International Preliminary Examining Authority shall, on the same day, transmit one copy of the international preliminary examination report and its annexes, if any, to the International Bureau, and one copy to the applicant.

(b) The International Preliminary Examining Authority shall transmit copies of other documents from the file of the international preliminary examination to the International Bureau in accordance with the Administrative Instructions.

1 This version applies to all documents created or received by the IPEA on or after July 1, 2020 (PCT/A/51/2 p. 3). By referring to the AIs and the regulation in R. 94.1(c), a legal basis for more transparency is initially created, with the goal that IPEAs will optionally, and later mandatorily, send IPE documents to the International Bureau, which the International Bureau then makes available on behalf of the elected Office to third parties (PCT/WG/12/12 Annex I p. 2), as soon as the technical requirements are met at the elected Office (PCT Newsletter 9/2020, p. 11).

2 Offices that have authorized the International Bureau to make other documents available under para. (b) are listed at https://www.wipo.int/pct/en/texts/access_iper.html. This includes the EPO.

AIs 420*bis*	The International Bureau sends documents received from the IPEA to each elected Office simultaneously with the transmission according to Art. 36(3)(a), R. 73.2, (i.e., according to AG-IP 10.080 with the IPRP II). In practice, an order from the elected Office is required, and thereafter the documents are generally made available through PATENTSCOPE, with transmission only upon the Office's request, WIPO PCT Circular C.PCT 1586 (2020), p. 2.
AIs 602*bis*	The following documents are transmitted by the IPEA to the International Bureau: Decision of the IPEA, replacement sheets and cover letters in case of amendments under Art. 34, cover letters

	according to R. 66.8 or response to the decision under R. 66.3, request to limit the claims or request for payment of additional fees, protest against this under R. 68.3(c). Other documents can be sent by the IPEA to the International Bureau. The applicant should not be obliged to submit translations for this, PCT/WG/12/24, Nos. 111–116, PCT/WG/12/12 Annex I, p. 2. Timing: as soon as available, but no later than with the transmission of the IPRP II to the International Bureau, R. 71.1(a).
AIs 610	Sequence protocol
R. 94.1(c)	Inspection of files at the International Bureau regarding IPE, making the transmitted documents available
R. 66.2	Written opinion of the IPEA
R. 66.3	Response of the applicant to the opinion

71.2 Copies of Cited Documents

(a) The request under Article 36(4) *(transmittal of documents cited in IPRP II)* may be presented any time during seven years from the international filing date of the international application to which the report relates.

(b) The International Preliminary Examining Authority may require that the party (applicant or elected Office) presenting the request pay to it the cost of preparing and mailing the copies. The level of the cost of preparing copies shall be provided for in the agreements referred to in Article 32(2) between the International Preliminary Examining Authorities and the International Bureau.

Art. 3(1) RFees OJ 2019, A15	Abolition of administrative fee for copies as they are now available online, except for certified copies. Certified copies are only available on reasoned request.

(c) [Deleted]

(d) Any International Preliminary Examining Authority may perform the obligations referred to in paragraphs (a) and (b) through another agency responsible to it.

Rule 72
Translation of the International Preliminary Examination Report and of the Written Opinion of the International Searching Authority

72.1 Languages

(a) Any elected State may require that the international preliminary examination report, established in any language other than the official language, or one of the official languages, of its national Office, be translated into English.

(b) Any such requirement shall be notified to the International Bureau, which shall promptly publish it in the Gazette.

R. 43*bis*	Written opinion of the ISA
R. 70.15	IPRP II

72.2 Copy of Translation for the Applicant

The International Bureau shall transmit a copy of the translation referred to in Rule 72.1(a) of the international preliminary examination report to the applicant at the same time as it communicates such translation to the interested elected Office or Offices.

72.2*bis* Translation of the Written Opinion of the International Searching Authority Established under Rule 43*bis*.1

In the case referred to in Rule 73.2(b)(ii), the written opinion established by the International Searching Authority under Rule 43*bis*.1 shall, upon request of the elected Office concerned, be translated into English by or under the responsibility of the International Bureau. The International Bureau shall transmit a copy of the translation to the elected Office concerned within two months from the date of receipt of the request for translation, and shall at the same time transmit a copy to the applicant.

72.3 Observations on the Translation

The applicant may make written observations as to the correctness of the translation of the international preliminary examination report or of the written opinion established by the International Searching Authority under Rule 43*bis*.1 and shall send a copy of the observations to each of the interested elected Offices and to the International Bureau.

Rule 73
Communication of the International Preliminary Examination Report or the Written Opinion of the International Searching Authority

73.1 Preparation of Copies

The International Bureau shall prepare the copies of the documents to be communicated under Article 36(3)(a).

73.2 Communication to Elected Offices

(a) The International Bureau shall effect the communication provided for in Article 36(3)(a) to each elected Office in accordance with Rule 93*bis*.1 but not before the expiration of 30 months from the priority date.

(b) Where the applicant makes an express request to an elected Office under Article 40(2), the International Bureau shall, upon the request of that Office or of the applicant,

(i) if the international preliminary examination report has already been transmitted to the International Bureau under Rule 71.1, promptly effect the communication provided for in Article 36(3)(a) to that Office;

(ii) if the international preliminary examination report has not been transmitted to the International Bureau under Rule 71.1, promptly communicate a copy of the written opinion established by the International Searching Authority under Rule 43*bis*.1 to that Office.

Art. 36	Communication of IPRP II (AG-IP 10.080)
Art. 40(2)	Request for early processing by elected Office

(c) Where the applicant has withdrawn the demand or any or all elections, the communication provided for in paragraph (a) shall nevertheless be effected, if the International Bureau has received the international preliminary examination report, to the elected Office or Offices affected by the withdrawal.

Rule 74
Translations of Annexes of the International Preliminary Examination Report and Transmittal Thereof

74.1 Contents of Translation and Time Limit for Transmittal Thereof

(a) Where the furnishing of a translation of the international application is required by the elected Office under Article 39(1), the applicant shall, within the time limit applicable under Article 39(1) *(30/31 months)*, transmit a translation of any replacement sheet referred to in Rule 70.16 *(amendments)* which is annexed to the international preliminary examination report, unless such sheet is in the language of the required translation of the international application. The same time limit shall apply where the furnishing of a translation of the international application to the elected Office must, because of a declaration made under Article 64(2)(a)(i), be effected within the time limit applicable under Article 22.

(b) Where the furnishing under Article 39(1) of a translation of the international application is not required by the elected Office, that Office may require the applicant to furnish, within the time limit applicable under that Article, a translation into the language in which the international application was published of any replacement sheet referred to in Rule 70.16 which is annexed to the international preliminary examination report and is not in that language.

AG-IP 10.078 Language of the IPER

Rule 75
[Deleted]

Rule 76
Translation of Priority Document; Application of Certain Rules to Procedures before Elected Offices

76.1, 76.2 and 76.3 [Deleted]

76.4 Time Limit for Translation of Priority Document

The applicant shall not be required to furnish to any elected Office a translation of the priority document before the expiration of the applicable time limit under Article 39.

For statements of WIPO concerning R. 76.4, see PCT/A/XXIV/10, p.7, para. 30 (https://www.wipo.int/edocs/mdocs/govbody/en/pct_a_xxiv/pct_a_xxiv_10-main1.pdf). 1

§ 14 DE-PatV — Unlike under the PCT, under the German Patent Ordinance, certification of the translation is not only required in case of doubt., Subsequent certification is also possible after the expiry of the time limit for filing the translation (BGH X ZB 4/19).

76.5 Application of Certain Rules to Procedures before Elected Offices

Rules 13*ter*.3 *(standard sequence listing)*, 20.8(c) (filing date), 22.1(g) *(incorrect transmission of record copy)*, 47.1 *(copy of PCTa and search report to designated Offices)*, 49 *(copy and translation of PCTa, payment of fee)*, 49*bis (indications as to protection sought)*, 49*ter (effect of restoration of right of priority)* and 51*bis (national requirements allowed)* shall apply, provided that:

(i) any reference in the said Rules to the designated Office or to the designated State shall be construed as a reference to the elected Office or to the elected State, respectively;

(ii) any reference in the said Rules to Article 22, Article 23(2) or Article 24(2) shall be construed as a reference to Article 39(1), Article 40(2) or Article 39(3), respectively;

(iii) the words "international applications filed" in Rule 49.1(c) shall be replaced by the words "a demand submitted";
(iv) for the purposes of Article 39(1), where an international preliminary examination report has been established, a translation of any amendment under Article 19 shall only be required if that amendment is annexed to that report;
(v) the reference in Rule 47.1(a) to Rule 47.4 shall be construed as a reference to Rule 61.2(d).

2 An interpretation exists for R. 76.5 (Gazette January 18, 2007, p. 11): 'In connection with the adoption of amended Rules 20.8(c) and 76.5, the Assembly noted that: (a) where an element or part is considered to have been incorporated by reference in the international application by virtue of a finding of the receiving Office under Rule 20.6(b), but that incorporation by reference does not apply to the international application for the purposes of the procedure before a designated or elected Office because of the operation of Rule 20.8(b), the time limit for performing the acts referred to in Articles 22 and 39 before such designated or elected Office would be calculated on the basis of the priority date referred to in Article 2(xi) having due regard to the international filing date as accorded by the receiving Office; and (b) the same should apply where that incorporation by reference does not apply to the international application for the purposes of the procedure before a designated or elected Office because of the operation of Rule 82*ter*.1(b) as adopted by the Assembly in October 2005 with effect from April 1, 2007.'

3 For statements of WIPO concerning R. 76.5 see PCT/CAL/III/10, p. 8, para. 61 (https://www.wipo.int/edocs/mdocs/pct/en/pct_cal_iii_part_ii/pct_cal_iii_part_ii_10.pdf) and PCT/A/XVIII/9, p. 8, para. 60 (https://www.wipo.int/edocs/mdocs/govbody/en/pct_a_xviii/pct_a_xviii_9.pdf).

Rule 77
Faculty under Article 39(1)(b)

77.1 Exercise of Faculty

(a) Any Contracting State allowing a time limit expiring later than the time limit provided for in Article 39(1)(a) shall notify the International Bureau of the time limit so fixed.

See the List of Contracting States in the Annex to this book for the individual time limits. 1

(b) Any notification received by the International Bureau under paragraph (a) shall be promptly published by the International Bureau in the Gazette.

(c) Notifications concerning the shortening of the previously fixed time limit shall be effective in relation to demands submitted after the expiration of three months computed from the date on which the notification was published by the International Bureau.

(d) Notifications concerning the lengthening of the previously fixed time limit shall become effective upon publication by the International Bureau in the Gazette in respect of demands pending at the time or submitted after the date of such publication, or, if the Contracting State effecting the notification fixes some later date, as from the latter date.

Art. 39	Copy, translation and fee to elected Offices, 30 months or later from the priority date
Art. 22	See Introduction for the start of the national phase

Rule 78
Amendment of the Claims, the Description, and the Drawings, before Elected Offices

78.1 Time Limit

(a) The applicant shall, if he so wishes, exercise the right under Article 41 to amend the claims, the description and the drawings, before the elected Office concerned within one month from the fulfillment of the requirements under Article 39(1)(a), provided that, if the transmittal of the international preliminary examination report under Article 36(1) has not taken place by the expiration of the time limit applicable under Article 39, he shall exercise the said right not later than four months after such expiration date. In either case, the applicant may exercise the said right at any later time if so permitted by the national law of the said State.

(b) In any elected State in which the national law provides that examination starts only on special request, the national law may provide that the time limit within or the time at which the applicant may exercise the right under Article 41 shall be the same as that provided by the national law for the filing of amendments in the case of the examination, on special request, of national applications, provided that such time limit shall not expire prior to, or such time shall not come before, the expiration of the time limit applicable under paragraph (a).

Art. 41	Amendment of claims, description, drawings before elected Office
Art. 28, R. 52	Amendments before designated Office
Art. 19, Art. 34	Amendments in international phase
Art. 22	See Introduction related to the entry into national phase

78.2 [Deleted]

78.3 Utility Models

The provisions of Rules 6.5 and 13.5 shall apply, *mutatis mutandis*, before elected Offices. If the election was made before the expiration of the 19th month from

the priority date, the reference to the time limit applicable under Article 22 is replaced by a reference to the time limit applicable under Article 39.

R. 6.5	Treating of utility models in designated Office
R. 13.5	Application of national law for utility models concerning unity of invention in designated Offices

Part D: Rules Concerning Chapter III of the Treaty

Rule 79
Calendar

79.1 Expressing Dates

Applicants, national Offices, receiving Offices, International Searching and Preliminary Examining Authorities, and the International Bureau, shall, for the purposes of the Treaty and the Regulations, express any date in terms of the Christian era and the Gregorian calendar, or, if they use other eras and calendars, they shall also express any date in terms of the Christian era and the Gregorian calendar.

Art. 47 See general notes for the calculation of time limits

Rule 80
Computation of Time Limits

INTRODUCTION

The PCT frequently uses the term 'time limit' and sometimes 'period' for the same notion, i.e. a period of time with a well-defined start, duration and expiration in which an applicant has to perform a certain act before an Office. The computation of time limits is governed by Art. 47, R. 79 and R. 80 PCT. Time limits mentioned in the PCT have to be computed using the Rules of the PCT. This means that if the EPO acts as receiving Office, ISA or IPEA and dispatches a communication or invitation to correct a defect, R. 80 PCT has to be used to compute any time limit for responding to the communication, not the corresponding R. 131 EPC. 1

A period is triggered by a relevant event, for example, by the filing of an international application or a demand. The date of the event is the date which prevails in the locality where and at the time when this relevant event occurred; this takes into account the time difference between time zones (R. 80.4(a)). 2

The term 'date of the event' is not used in the PCT but has been introduced here to avoid the unclarity of the term 'starting day'. The latter could mean 'start of the computation' according to R. 80.1-3 or 'start of the period' according to R. 80.6, which is one day earlier; it could mean both according to R. 80.4. The unclarity dates back to Art. 4C of the Paris Convention. The paragraph in this book gives the interpretation of R. 80.1-4 as used by all Offices. 3

R 80.4 has been rewritten to remove the ambiguity of 'starting day': the context suggests that the Rule should define the starting date of the period and not the starting date of the computation, which is the following day. 4

The phrase 'computation shall start on the day following the day on which the relevant event occurred' in R. 80.1 and 80.2 has been included in the law to emphasize that the month and year periods expire on the same day of the month, not one day earlier had the day of the event been included in the computation. The phrase does not exclude the day of the event from the period, as corroborated by R. 80.4(a) and 80.6. Offices differ on whether or not the day of the event is included in the period, which is relevant for same day priority claims; the International Bureau includes the day, the EPO excludes it. 5

6 If, in the last two cases, the month does not have a day with the same number, the period will expire on the last day of that month (R. 80.1, 80.2). The date of expiration is the date which prevails in the locality in which the required act must be performed, for example, filing a document or paying a fee (R. 80.4(b)).

7 An Office may extend a period at any time before a decision is taken; see, for example, R. 26.2. An Office will accept many acts performed by an applicant after expiry of a period but before dispatching an invitation or declaring that the application is deemed withdrawn; see, for example, R. 16*bis*.1(d) and Art. 14(3).

8 Many time limits in the PCT are calculated from the priority date. A change of that date – for example, in case of withdrawal of the priority claim – has effect on the calculation of the time limit if the time limit has not yet expired (R. 90*bis*.3(d); annotations to Art. 8).

Art. 47 Time Limits

R. 79 Calendar

80.1 Periods Expressed in Years

When a period is expressed as one year or a certain number of years, computation shall start on the day following the day on which the relevant event occurred, and the period shall expire in the relevant subsequent year in the month having the same name and on the day having the same number as the month and the day on which the said event occurred, provided that if the relevant subsequent month has no day with the same number the period shall expire on the last day of that month.

80.2 Periods Expressed in Months

When a period is expressed as one month or a certain number of months, computation shall start on the day following the day on which the relevant event occurred, and the period shall expire in the relevant subsequent month on the day which has the same number as the day on which the said event occurred, provided that if the relevant subsequent month has no day with the same number the period shall expire on the last day of that month.

80.3 Periods Expressed in Days

When a period is expressed as a certain number of days, computation shall start on the day following the day on which the relevant event occurred, and the period shall expire on the day on which the last day of the count has been reached.

80.4 Local Dates

(a) The date which is taken into consideration as the starting date of the computation of any period shall be the date which prevails in the locality at the time when the relevant event occurred.

(b) The date on which any period expires shall be the date which prevails in the locality in which the required document must be filed or the required fee must be paid.

80.5 Expiration on a Non-Working Day or Official Holiday

If the expiration of any period during which any document or fee must reach a national Office or intergovernmental organization falls on a day:

(i) on which such Office or organization is not open to the public for the purposes of the transaction of official business;

(ii) on which ordinary mail is not delivered in the locality in which such Office or organization is situated;

(iii) which, where such Office or organization is situated in more than one locality, is an official holiday in at least one of the localities in which such Office or organization is situated, and in circumstances where the national law applicable by that Office or organization provides, in respect of national applications, that, in such a case, such period shall expire on a subsequent day; or

(iv) which, where such Office is the government authority of a Contracting State entrusted with the granting of patents, is an official holiday in part of that Contracting State, and in circumstances where the national law applicable by that Office provides, in respect of national applications, that, in such a case, such period shall expire on a subsequent day;

the period shall expire on the next subsequent day on which none of the said four circumstances exists.

The regulation applies to all time limits in the PCT, including those specified in Art. 22 and 39. Art. 4 (C) (3) Paris Convention applies to the priority period (PCT Newsletter 3/2020 p. 6). 9

It may be useful to file a PCTa at another eligible receiving Office (see R. 19.1) if there is otherwise a risk of missing the time limit. If, for example, the last day of the priority year has already expired in Japan, the PCTa could still be filed at the International Bureau in Geneva, where the day has not yet ended. It is also possible to take advantage of a public holiday in Switzerland to file with the International Bureau on time on the next day. 10

For further remedies in connection with the Covid-19 pandemic, see PCT Newsletter 3/2020, p. 6 and www.wipo.int/pct/de/covid_19/covid_update.html.The closed days are published periodically in the PCT Gazette (https://www.wipo.int/pct/en/official_notices/index.html), PCT Newsletter (https://www.wipo.int/pct/en/newslett/) and on the WIPO website (https://www.wipo.int/pct/dc/closeddates/faces/page/index.xhtml. Note that the closed dates for the EPO, which the EPO communicated to WIPO, on the web page as retrieved on April 15, 2021 incorrectly implies that Vienna is an EPO filing Office. See, e.g. OJ EPO 2020 A9, https://www.epo.org/law-practice/legal-texts/official-journal/2020/01/a9.html for correct information). 11

12 If an Office is situated in more than one locality and a period is extended for the Office in one locality under R. 80.5, the period is also extended for the Office in the other localities (R. 80.5(iii)). For example, a period set by the EPO filing Office in The Hague expires on May 5 (Liberation Day in NL), the period for both the EPO filing Offices in The Hague and Munich will be extended to the first day on which both Offices are open again, even if the Munich Office is open on May 5 (see, for example, OJ EPO 2014 A9 introduction to Art. 21).

80.6 Date of Documents

Where a period starts on the day of the date of a document or letter emanating from a national Office or intergovernmental organization, any interested party may prove that the said document or letter was mailed on a day later than the date it bears, in which case the date of actual mailing shall, for the purposes of computing the period, be considered to be the date on which the period starts. Irrespective of the date on which such a document or letter was mailed, if the applicant offers to the national Office or intergovernmental organization evidence which satisfies the national Office or intergovernmental organization that the document or letter was received more than seven days after the date it bears, the national Office or intergovernmental organization shall treat the period starting from the date of the document or letter as expiring later by an additional number of days which is equal to the number of days which the document or letter was received later than seven days after the date it bears.

13 The PCT uses the dispatch theory for communications from an Office to an applicant: a period starts on the day of the date stamp of a document or letter emanating from an Office (R. 80.6), not on the date of receipt by the applicant. If an applicant proves before the Office that he received the document or letter more than seven days after the date it bears, the period will be treated as expiring later by the number of days which the document or letter was received later than the seven days (R. 80.6). This is not an exception to the dispatch theory; the period does not start later but the period is extended, extra days should be added at the end of the period.

14 The PCT uses the receipt theory for communications from an applicant to an Office: a time limit is regarded as being met if the applicant's communication has been received by the Office within the time limit, i.e. before midnight at the end of the date of expiry of the time limit. Similarly, the filing date of the international application is the date an Office receives the application, not the date the applicant dispatches the application.

15 R 80 deals with the calculation of the duration of the time limit. In the PCT, the end of the time limit is postponed, but not the date of delivery as in R. 126(2) EPC (PCT Newsletter 4/2021 p. 10 with example).

16 Electronic notification in proceedings under the PCT is governed by the provisions of the PCT, electronic notification in proceedings at the EPO (MyPortfolio) under the EPC follows EPC Rules. In case of electronic notification no paper copies will be notified in parallel. The procedure also applies to communications not subject to notification (OJ EPO 2024 A20 replacing OJ EPO 2023 A89).

Applicants can receive electronic communications from the EPO as receiving Office via WIPO's ePCT system. WIPO's ePCT system is currently a voluntary service and does not replace paper service (Euro-PCT Guide 2.2.033). 17

For proceedings before the EPO as designated Office/elected Office see GL Exam E-VI, 2: all notifications by postal services must be by registered letter (R. 126 EPC, OJ EPO 2019 A57). The date it bears is decisive unless it failed to reach the addressee (GL Exam E-VI, 2.4, 2.3). If the EPO can prove that delivery occurred more than seven days after the date of the document the time limit is postponed under R. 126(2) EPC. If, for example, the document is received after eight days, the time limit for exceeding the time limit under the PCT is one day. Where the user agreed to receive electronic communications the date of the document is decisive (R. 127(2) EPC). E-mail alerts are not considered as notifications under R. 127 EPC and failure to send an alert will have no effect on the time limit (OJ EPO 2024 A21 point 23). 18

Since November 1, 2019, postal items relevant for time limits are sent by registered letter without acknowledgment or receipt by the EPO. Prior to February 1, 2024 the EPO enclosed acknowledgements of receipt to be returned by the addressee by fax, post or preferably by online service (OJ EPO 2023 A108). Mail not relevant to the time limit will continue to be sent by ordinary post (Euro-PCT Guide marginal 5.3.002, OJ EPO 2021 A5). 19

Due to the lack of Rules for the payment of fees in the PCT, the Rules of the IPEA or the ISA have to be taken into account in the question of the day of a payment. 20

R. 4.4	Names and addresses in PCTa
R. 26.2	The time limit for correction is an example of the application of this Rule.
R. 82*quater*	Excuse of delay in meeting time limits and extension of time limits
AIs 108	Correspondence intended for the applicant
R. 89*bis*	Processing in electronic form
R. 92	See notes for the calculation of time limits where the Office dispatches an e-mail

For further remedies in connection with the Covid-19 pandemic see PCT Newsletter 3/2020, p. 6 and www.wipo.int/pct/de/covid_19/covid_update.html. 21

80.7 End of Working Day

(a) A period expiring on a given day shall expire at the moment the national Office or intergovernmental organization with which the document must be filed or to which the fee must be paid closes for business on that day.

(b) Any Office or organization may depart from the provisions of paragraph (a) up to midnight on the relevant day.

R. 2, 35 EPC	For information about opening hours of sites, automated mailbox and fax numbers at the EPO see https://www.epo.org/applying/european/filing.html. Abolition of fax service with effect from July 1, 2024 (OJ EPO 2024 A41).

Rule 81
Modification of Time Limits Fixed in the Treaty

Art. 47(2)	Time limits, see general notes
Art. 60	Revision of the Treaty, see general notes

81.1 Proposal

(a) Any Contracting State or the Director General may propose a modification under Article 47(2).

(b) Proposals made by a Contracting State shall be presented to the Director General.

81.2 Decision by the Assembly

(a) When the proposal is made to the Assembly, its text shall be sent by the Director General to all Contracting States at least two months in advance of that session of the Assembly whose agenda includes the proposal.

(b) During the discussion of the proposal in the Assembly, the proposal may be amended or consequential amendments proposed.

(c) The proposal shall be considered adopted if none of the Contracting States present at the time of voting votes against the proposal.

81.3 Voting by Correspondence

(a) When voting by correspondence is chosen, the proposal shall be included in a written communication from the Director General to the Contracting States, inviting them to express their vote in writing.

(b) The invitation shall fix the time limit within which the reply containing the vote expressed in writing must reach the International Bureau. That time limit shall not be less than three months from the date of the invitation.

(c) Replies must be either positive or negative. Proposals for amendments or mere observations shall not be regarded as votes.

(d) The proposal shall be considered adopted if none of the Contracting States opposes the amendment and if at least one-half of the Contracting States express either approval or indifference or abstention.

Rule 82
Irregularities in the Mail Service

INTRODUCTION

AG-IP Annex B indicates for each Contracting State whether its national Office will apply the above excuse procedure for postal service providers other than postal authorities of the State, such as courier delivery (R. 82.1(d), (e)). The EPO applies the excuse procedure to postal service and courier delivery by recognized providers. Compare R. 133 EPC for the practice under the EPC. The delivery service providers accepted by the EPO as International Authority under R. 82.1 PCT are the same as the ones that the EPO accepts under R. 133 EPC (see AG Annex B (EP) and OJ EPO 2015 A29: Chronopost, flexpress, DHL, Federal Express, SkyNet, TNT, UPS, Transworld). 1

R. 82 does not apply to the priority period, i.e. to filing a priority-claiming application after expiry of the priority period. R. 82 is the implementation of Art. 48(1). Art. 48(1) refers to a time limit fixed in the PCT Treaty or the Regulation. The priority period is, however, fixed in the Paris Convention (see annotations to Art. 8). Then again, restoration of the right of priority may be requested according to R. 26*bis*.3 (OJ EPO 2012 p. 58). Note also the provision for *force majeure* and for the unavailability of electronic means of communication (R. 82*quater*). For further remedy options in connection with the Covid-19 pandemic, see PCT Newsletter 3/2020, p. 6 and www.wipo.int/pct/de/covid_19/covid_update.html. 2

Requirements for the excuse are: 3

1. the document must have been sent five days before the expiry of the time limit (R. 82.1(a));
2. in principle, it must be sent by registered mail (with the limitations (R. 82.1(d));
3. it must be sent by airmail or two-day post or, if airmail is not available, by another service (R. 82.1(a)) or other transport service (R. 82.1(d));
4. proof of conformity with the original (R. 82.1(b)) must also be provided;
5. the evidence must be submitted within one month from the date of knowledge (R. 82.1(c)), but in no case later than six months after the expiry of the time limit.

82.1 Delay or Loss in Mail

(a) Any interested party may offer evidence that he has mailed the document or letter five days prior to the expiration of the time limit. Except in cases where surface mail normally arrives at its destination within two days of mailing, or where no airmail service is available, such evidence may be offered only if the mailing was by airmail. In any case, evidence may be offered only if the mailing was by mail registered by the postal authorities.

(b) If the mailing, in accordance with paragraph (a), of a document or letter is proven to the satisfaction of the national Office or intergovernmental organization which is the addressee, delay in arrival shall be excused, or, if the document or letter is lost in the mail, substitution for it of a new copy shall be permitted, provided that the interested party proves to the satisfaction of the said Office or organization that the document or letter offered in substitution is identical with the document or letter lost.

(c) In the cases provided for in paragraph (b), evidence of mailing within the prescribed time limit, and, where the document or letter was lost, the substitute document or letter as well as the evidence concerning its identity with the document or letter lost shall be submitted within one month after the date on which the interested party noticed – or with due diligence should have noticed – the delay or the loss, and in no case later than six months after the expiration of the time limit applicable in the given case.

(d) Any national Office or intergovernmental organization which has notified the International Bureau that it will do so shall, where a delivery service other than the postal authorities is used to mail a document or letter, apply the provisions of paragraphs (a) to (c) as if the delivery service was a postal authority. In such a case, the last sentence of paragraph (a) shall not apply but evidence may be offered only if details of the mailing were recorded by the delivery service at the time of mailing. The notification may contain an indication that it applies only to mailings using specified delivery services or delivery services which satisfy specified criteria. The International Bureau shall publish the information so notified in the Gazette.

Art. 48	Delay in meeting certain time limits
R. 26*bis*.3	Basis for restoration of the right of priority if R. 82 is not applicable, e.g. on expiry of the priority period laid down in Art. 4 C. (3) Paris Convention (OJ EPO 2011 p. 272, Newsletter 4/2011, p. 8).
R. 133 EPC	Late receipt of documents
R. 134 EPC	Extension of time limits, in relation to the Covid-19 pandemic (OJ EPO 2020 A29, A43, A60, A74) and for details, see OJ EPO 2020, A38.

DPMA	accepts no other delivery service than the postal authorities (AG-IP Annex B (DE)). No extension of time limits due to the Covid-19 pandemic in the case of legal time limits; the only remedy is re-establishment of rights under Section 123 of the German Patent Act. However, time limits set by the DPMA can be extended. See https://www.dpma.de/english/our_office/publications/important_notices/archive/importantnotices2020/notice_18032020/index.html.

(e) Any national Office or intergovernmental organization may proceed under paragraph (d):

(i) even if, where applicable, the delivery service used was not one of those specified, or did not satisfy the criteria specified, in the relevant notification under paragraph (d), or

(ii) even if that Office or organization has not sent to the International Bureau a notification under paragraph (d).

Rule 82*bis*
Excuse by the Designated or Elected State of Delays in Meeting Certain Time Limits

82*bis*.1 Meaning of "Time Limit" in Article 48(2)

The reference to "any time limit" in Article 48(2) shall be construed as comprising a reference:

(i) to any time limit fixed in the Treaty or these Regulations;

(ii) to any time limit fixed by the receiving Office, the International Searching Authority, the International Preliminary Examining Authority or the International Bureau or applicable by the receiving Office under its national law;

(iii) to any time limit fixed by, or in the national law applicable by, the designated or elected Office, for the performance of any act by the applicant before that Office.

Art. 48(2)	Failure to observe time limits is excused in individual cases, provided that a national excuse is given
PCT/A/XI/9, p.13, para. 67	'[T]he excusing of the delay in meeting a time limit may take place, under Article 48(2), only during the national phase, independent of whether the delay to be excused concerned a time limit pertaining to the international phase or a time limit pertaining to the national phase. It was further understood that, for the purposes of Article 48(2), the provisions referred to in Rule 81*bis*.2 may be applied only under the conditions set forth by the national law. For example, if the applicant failed to pay a fee or to correct a defect within a certain time limit and if such failure could be excused under the national law of a Contracting State, it must be excused for international applications.' (https://www.wipo.int/edocs/mdocs/govbody/en/pct_a_xi/pct_a_xi_9.pdf).

82*bis*.2 Reinstatement of Rights and Other Provisions to Which Article 48(2) Applies

The provisions of the national law which is referred to in Article 48(2) concerning the excusing, by the designated or elected State, of any delay in meeting any time

limit are those provisions which provide for reinstatement of rights, restoration, *restitutio in integrum* or further processing in spite of non-compliance with a time limit, and any other provision providing for the extension of time limits or for excusing delays in meeting time limits.

Art. 122 EPC	Re-establishment of rights
Art. 121 EPC	Further processing: the national requirements must be met.

For further remedies in connection with the Covid-19 pandemic, see PCT Newsletter 3/2020, p. 6 and www.wipo.int/pct/de/covid_19/covid_update.html. 1

Rule 82*ter* Rectification of Errors Made by the Receiving Office or by the International Bureau

82*ter*.1 Errors Concerning the International Filing Date and the Priority Claim

(a) If the applicant proves to the satisfaction of any designated or elected Office that the international filing date is incorrect due to an error made by the receiving Office or that the priority claim has been erroneously considered void by the receiving Office or the International Bureau, and if the error is an error such that, had it been made by the designated or elected Office itself, that Office would rectify it under the national law or national practice, the said Office shall rectify the error and shall treat the international application as if it had been accorded the rectified international filing date or as if the priority claim had not been considered void.

Art. 14	Certain defects in the PCTa
R. 26*bis*.3	Restoration of right of priority by receiving Office
R. 26*bis*.2	Defects in priority claims

(b) Where the international filing date has been accorded by the receiving Office under Rule 20.3(b)(ii), 20.5(d) or 20.5*bis*(d) on the basis of the incorporation by reference under Rules 4.18 and 20.6 of an element or part but the designated or elected Office finds that:

(i) the applicant has not complied with Rule 17.1(a), (b) or (b-*bis*) in relation to the priority document;

(ii) a requirement under Rule 4.18, 20.6(a)(i) or 51*bis*.1(e)(ii) *(translation)* has not been complied with; or

(iii) the element or part is not completely contained in the priority document concerned;

the designated or elected Office may, subject to paragraph (c), treat the international application as if the international filing date had been accorded under Rule

20.3(b)(i), 20.5(b) or 20.5*bis*(b), or corrected under Rule 20.5(c) or 20.5*bis*(c), as applicable, provided that Rule 17.1(c) *(opportunity to furnish priority document)* shall apply *mutatis mutandis.*

With effect from July 1, 2020, the reference to R. 20.5*bis* was newly added. The consequence of this Rule is that the filing date is shifted. The EPO proceeds in accordance with GL Exam B-XI, 2.1. 1

R. 20.3(b)(ii)	Accordance of filing date, incorporation by reference of missing parts (complete description, complete claims)
R. 20.5(d)	Accordance of filing date, incorporation by reference of missing parts (part of the description or claims or drawings or the complete drawings)
R. 20.5*bis*(d)	Accordance of filing date, incorporation by reference of erroneously filed parts or elements
R. 17.1(a), (b), (b-*bis*)	Formalities for submitting a priority document
R. 4.18	Statement of incorporation by reference
R. 20.6(a)(i)	Confirmation of incorporation by reference of elements and parts
R. 51*bis*.1(e)(ii)	Certain national requirements allowed under Art. 27

(c) The designated or elected Office shall not treat the international application under paragraph (b) as if the international filing date had been accorded under Rule 20.3(b)(i), 20.5(b) or 20.5*bis*(b), or corrected under Rule 20.5(c) or 20.5*bis*(c), without giving the applicant the opportunity to make observations on the intended treatment, or to make a request under paragraph (d), within a time limit which shall be reasonable under the circumstances.

With effect from July 1, 2020, the reference to R. 20.5*bis* was newly added. The EPO proceeds in accordance with GL Exam B-XI, 2.1. 2

R. 20.5*bis*	Erroneously filed elements and parts

(d) Where the designated or elected Office, in accordance with paragraph (c), has notified the applicant that it intends to treat the international application as if the international filing date had been corrected under Rule 20.5(c) or 20.5*bis*(c),the applicant may, in a notice submitted to that Office within the time limit referred to in paragraph (c), request that the missing part concerned, or the correct element or part concerned, be disregarded for the purposes of national processing before that Office, in which case that missing part, or that correct element or part, shall be considered not to have been furnished and that Office shall not treat the international application as if the international filing date had been corrected.

3 With effect from July 1, 2020, the reference to R. 20.5*bis* was newly added. The consequence of this Rule is that the filing date is shifted.

R. 20.5(e)	Request that missing part be disregarded
20.5*bis*	Erroneously filed elements and parts
R. 51*bis*.1(a)(viii)	Translation of erroneously filed elements and parts

Rule 82*quater* Excuse of Delay and Extension of Time Limits

INTRODUCTION

R 82*quater* allows an Office to excuse a delay in meeting any time limit set in the PCT Regulations in case of *force majeure* (AG-IP 11.065; see, for example, OJ EPO 2015 A61 §4). Examples of *force majeure* are a general failure of electronic communication services in the area where the party resides, war, revolution, civil disorder, strike, natural calamity, or similar reasons in his residency (R. 82*quater*.1(a); see OJ EPO 2015 A62 for more examples). If a party can prove *force majeure*, the delay will be excused (R. 82*quater*.1). The evidence must be furnished within six months from the expiry of the failed time limit (R. 82*quater*.1(b)). 1

According to AG-IP 11.065, R. 82*quater*.1 is a general basis for the excuse of delays in meeting time limits set in the PCT Regulations. Hence, it should not only cover time limits for filing documents but also time limits for paying fees set in the PCT Regulations (https://www.epo.org/service-support/faq/procedure-law/covid-remedies-non-observance-periods.html). It should be noted that R. 82*quater* only applies to time limits that are regulated in the Regulations. R. 82*quater* does not apply to the priority period, as this period is set in the Paris Convention. Note that R. 2.4 does not define the priority period but Art. 4C of the Paris Convention does. R. 82*quater* does not apply to time limits set in PCT Art. 8, Art. 22(1), Art. 39(1) (www.wipo.int/edocs/mdocs/govbody/en/pct_a_43/pct_a_43_4.pdf; OJ EPO 2012, 618) or acts that have to be performed in the national phase (PCT Newsletter 5/2020, p. 12). 2

R 82*quater* also does not apply to any time limit fixed in the Articles of the PCT, such as the time limit for entering the national phase (Art. 22 [39]). It does, however, cover the two-month time limit for restoration of the right of priority (R. 26*bis*.3), which is set in the Regulations. In comparison with R. 82, the scope of R. 82*quater* is narrower. 3

It should be noted that the excuse of delays in R. 82*quater* exists independently of the excuse of delays under national law. The applicant may also use communications from the Office under R. 82*quater*.3 as evidence of the excuse under R. 82*quater*.1 (PCT/WG/14/11 No. 18). Note that R. 82*quater* PCT is modeled on R. 134(5) EPC. The EPO allows application of R. 82*quater* to correct a late payment caused by a delay in the banking system (see, for example, OJ EPO 2015 A61 §4). 4

5 According to R. 82*quater*.2 an applicant may request excuse of a delay in case of technical problems affecting official means of electronic communication irrespective of whether these are scheduled (maintenance) or unforeseen (outages) by the Office concerned, and it would not be required to submit evidence. This Rule refers to the same time limits as R. 82*quater*.1 and Offices are free to apply the Rule. The practice of the EPO since November 2020 is set out in OJ EPO 2020 A120 (https://www.epo.org/law-practice/legal-texts/official-journal/2020/11/a120.html).

6 An Office may apply either R. 82*quater*.1 or R. 82*quater*.3, not both Rules simultaneously. Only after the expiry of the period determined by the Office under R. 82*quater*.3 can R. 82*quater*.1 be applied before that Office (PCT/WG/14/11 No. 19).

82*quater*.1 Excuse of Delay in Meeting Time Limits

(a) Any interested party may offer evidence that a time limit fixed in the Regulations for performing an action before the receiving Office, the International Searching Authority, the Authority specified for supplementary search, the International Preliminary Examining Authority or the International Bureau was not met due to war, revolution, civil disorder, strike, natural calamity, epidemic, a general unavailability of electronic communications services or other like reason in the locality where the interested party resides, has his place of business or is staying, and that the relevant action was taken as soon as reasonably possible.

7 Amendments entered into force on July 1, 2022 and apply to all time limits regulated in the Regulations expiring on or after that date (PCT/A/53/3 p. 2). The term epidemic was added on July 1, 2022 for clarification as an event of *force majeure*. The term pandemic falls under the term epidemic (PCT/WG/14/11 No. 8). For the time limits that can be excused, see general notes above.

AIs 111(b)	The outage of electronic communications services must affect larger geographical areas or many people and not just a localized problem. It is also a prerequisite that the failure was unexpected or unforeseeable and that no other means of communication were available.

(b) Any such evidence shall be addressed to the Office, Authority or the International Bureau, as the case may be, not later than six months after the expiration of the time limit applicable in the given case. If such circumstances are proven to the satisfaction of the addressee, delay in meeting the time limit shall be excused.

(c) The excuse of a delay need not be taken into account by any designated or elected Office before which the applicant, at the time the decision to excuse the delay is taken, has already performed the acts referred to in Article 22 or Article 39.

(d) The need for evidence may be waived by the Office, Authority or the International Bureau under the conditions set and published by that Office, Authority or the International Bureau, as the case may be. In such case, the interested party must submit a statement that the failure to meet the time limit was due to the

reason for which the Office, Authority or the International Bureau waived the requirement concerning the submission of evidence. The Office or Authority shall notify the International Bureau accordingly.

Amendments entered into force on July 1, 2022 that apply to all time limits regulated in the Regulations expiring on or after that date (PCT/A/53/3 p. 2). 8

The aim of inserting para. (d) was to save the parties in the *force majeure* situation from costs and work by allowing Authorities and Offices to waive evidence (PCT/WG/14/11). The applicant may also use communications from the Office or authority under R. 82*quater*.3 as evidence for the excuse under R. 82*quater*.1 (PCT/WG/14/11 No. 18). 9

The receiving Office and ISPE Guidelines provide details regarding the requirements for excusing missed time limits (https://www.wipo.int/pct/en/texts/gdlines.html). 10

R. 82*quater*.3	An Office may apply either R. 82*quater*.1 or R. 82*quater*.3, not both Rules simultaneously. Only after the expiry of the period determined by the Office under R. 82*quater*.3 can R. 82*quater*.1 be applied before that Office (PCT/WG/14/11 No. 19).
Art. 8	Claiming priority, R. 2.4. See also Art. 4C Paris Convention below
Art. 22(1)	Time limit for transmitting the PCTa to designated Office (i.e. if IPE demand has not been filed) for entry into national phase, remedy in case of closure of Office under R. 80.5 or R. 49.6, PCT Newsletter 3/2020
Art. 39(1)	Time limit for transmitting the PCTa to the elected Office (i.e. when IPE demand has been filed) for entry into national phase, remedy in case of closure of the Office under R. 80.5 or R. 49.6, PCT Newsletter 3/2020
Art. 4 C.(3) Paris Convention	Priority period. Remedy in case of closure of the Office. Otherwise: restoration of priority right according to R. 26*bis*.3, R. 49*ter*. Calculation of time limit in case of closure R. 80.5, 2.4(b).
R. 80.6	Excuse in case of receipt of a letter received more than seven days after the date it bears
R. 82.1	Excuse for delay in filing a document in case of mailing five days before the time limit expires
R. 82*bis*	Delays in the national phase for actions to be taken before the designated Office or elected Office
AIs 111	Procedure of the Offices: notification of the decision and transmission of the request to International Bureau. Normally, newspaper advertisements, statements from national authorities, statements from the internet provider or the electricity supplier are accepted as evidence (AG-IP 11.065 and 11.065A)
R. 134(1) EPC	Excuse for disruptions of the EPO's technical systems due to maintenance work and examination of purported technical faults in electronic communications (OJ EPO 2020 A120)

R. 134(5) EPC	Excuse in case of disruption of transmission of mail due to a natural catastrophe. For details of applicability in the case of postal strike, see OJ EPO 2015 A62, in connection with Covid-19: OJ EPO 2020 A29, A38, A43, A60, A74.
R. 134(5) EPC	Applicability in case of late payment due to bank closure and the prohibition of cross-border payments (OJ EPO 2015 A61), in connection with Covid-19: OJ EPO 2020 A29, A38, A43, A60, A74.

82*quater*.2 Unavailability of Electronic Means of Communication at the Office

(a) Any national Office or intergovernmental organization may provide that, where a time limit fixed in the Regulations for performing an action before that Office or organization is not met due to the unavailability of any of the permitted electronic means of communication at that Office or organization, delay in meeting that time limit shall be excused, provided that the respective action was performed on the next working day on which the said electronic means of communication were available. The Office or organization concerned shall publish information on any such unavailability including the period of the unavailability, and notify the International Bureau accordingly.

(b) The excuse of a delay in meeting a time limit under paragraph (a) need not be taken into account by any designated or elected Office before which the applicant, at the time the information referred to in paragraph (a) is published, has already performed the acts referred to in Article 22 or Article 39.

11 See general notes above for the application to certain time limits and excuse of delay.

AIs 111	Offices acting as receiving Office, ISA, SISA, IPEA shall inform the International Bureau of the application of a reason for excuse and concrete non-availability. This information is published in the PCT Gazette and included in the PCT Applicants' Guide Annex B.
EPO	The EPO applies the Rule under the conditions specified in the Gazette of November 26, 2020, p. 254, i.e. planned unavailability of at least 4 hours. No application below four hours and prior notice of at least two working days in advance. If the unavailability of less than four hours was announced but lasts longer, R. 82*quater*.2 applies. With regard to unscheduled unavailability, the EPO recommends that if there is any doubt about the successful transmission, contact Customer Service and appeal if necessary. In the case of unscheduled unavailability, the EPO will take and publish a decision regardless of the number of hours. If WIPO's ePCT system fails, the International Bureau will inform the EPO, which will take a decision on the application of R. 82*quater*. For details also on the unavailability of fee payment systems see OJ EPO 2020 A120 (continuation of the online service MyEPO Portfolio according to OJ EPO 2023 A89 Art. 3 No. 10).

International Bureau	Publication of details on the application of R. 82*quater*.2 by the International Bureau as receiving Office in PCT Gazette November 16, 2023 p. 217, AG-IP Annex B (IB). Applicability to all time limits governed by the PCT Rules and AIs and to time limits set in invitations or communications to the applicant by the International Bureau, but not to the priority period fixed in Art. 4 of the Paris Convention. See also the introduction. Electronic means of communication in the sense of the above Rule is ePCT and PCT Business Continuity Service. In terms of time, unavailability means at least one hour. Should this occur, it will be published on the WIPO website. A request to be excused and to make up the action on the next working day on which the means of communication are available again is required.
Art. 4 C.(3) Paris Convention	No application to the calculation of the priority period defined in the Paris Convention. However, the restoration of the right of priority according to R. 26*bis*.3, R. 49*ter* can be requested.

82*quater*.3 Extension of Time Limits due to General Disruption

(a) Any receiving Office, International Searching Authority, Authority specified for supplementary search, International Preliminary Examining Authority or the International Bureau may establish a period of extension such that time limits fixed in the Regulations within which a party has to perform an action before that Office, Authority or International Bureau may be extended when the State in which it is located is experiencing a general disruption caused by an event listed in Rule 82*quater*.1(a) which affects the operations at the said Office, Authority or International Bureau thereby interfering with the ability of parties to perform actions before that Office, Authority or International Bureau within the time limits fixed in the Regulations. The Office, Authority or the International Bureau shall publish the commencement and the end date of any such period of extension. The period of extension shall not be longer than two months from the date of commencement. The Office or Authority shall notify the International Bureau accordingly.

(b) After establishing a period of extension under paragraph (a), the Office, Authority or the International Bureau concerned may establish additional periods of extension, if necessary under the circumstances. In that case, paragraph (a) applies *mutatis mutandis.*

(c) The extension of a time limit under paragraph (a) or (b) need not be taken into account by any designated or elected Office if, at the time the information referred to in paragraph (a) or (b) is published, national processing before that Office has started.

The purpose of R. 82*quater*.3 is to provide a clear uniform legal basis for Offices 12
to apply an extension of time for the international phase in the case of a general disruption due to *force majeure*. Since, in contrast to R. 82*quater*.1, the applicant does not have to file either a request or proof, this means an avoidance of costs and

effort, PCT/WG/13/10 p. 3. The reason for the amendment in 2022 and an example is a lockdown in a pandemic, PCT/WG/14/19 Prov. No. 21.

13 Para. (c) is intended to avoid any disadvantage to the applicant if acts to enter the national phase have been commenced but not all acts have yet been performed (PCT/WG/14/11 No. 20).

14 For the application to time limits see the introduction above.

R. 82*quater*.1	An Office may apply either R. 82*quater*.1 or R. 82*quater*.3, not both Rules simultaneously. Only after the expiry of the period determined by the Office under R. 82*quater*.3 can R. 82*quater*.1 be applied before that Office (PCT/WG/14/11 No. 19).
AIs 111 f	Details of the implementation, in particular time limit and publication of the period of disruption
R. 80.5	Time limit expiry on the next day on which the disruption no longer exists

15 See also No. 22.52 E – H ISPE Guidelines under https://www.wipo.int/pct/en/texts/ispe/index.html.

Rule 83
Right to Practice before International Authorities

INTRODUCTION

An agent may act before the International Bureau as receiving Office if he may practice before the national Office of the Contracting State of which the applicant is resident or national (R. 83.1*bis*(a)). If there are two or more applicants, at least one of them must be resident or national of that Contracting State (R. 83.1*bis*(a)). For example, a Swedish and Dutch applicant of an international application may choose a Swedish, Dutch, or European patent attorney to act before the International Bureau. An agent having the right to practice before the International Bureau as receiving Office may also practice before the competent ISA and IPEA (R. 83.1*bis*(b)). 1

The International Bureau, ISA and IPEA may require proof of the right to practice before the national Office (R. 83.1). That national Office submits, on request, to the International Bureau, ISA or IPEA conclusive evidence of the right (R. 83.2). 2

Art. 27(7) allows a designated Office and receiving Office to apply national law for representation once the national phase has started. Most designated Offices have done so and require non-resident applicants to be represented by an agent; other designated Offices require non-resident applicants to have an address for service in the country (AG-NP 5.006; R. 51*bis*.1(b)). AG-NP National Chapter indicates for each designated Office who can act as agent. The Rules for representation before designated and elected Offices are the same (R. 76.5(i)). 3

An agent appointed for the international phase will not automatically be regarded as an agent before a designated Office during the national phase; an agent for the national phase must be appointed separately. Usually different agents have to be appointed for the national phase before each of the various designated Offices, who fulfill the specific requirements of that Office (AG-IP 11.001). 4

Before the EPO as receiving Office and designated Office, only attorneys or persons listed as professional representative before the EPO are admitted as agents. The EPC also allows the appointment of an association of representatives or several registered representatives (Art. 134 EPC; R. 152 EPC; see OJ EPO 2013 p.535 for details of the authorization of an association). Therefore, if the EPO acts as receiving Office, ISA 5 or IPEA, an applicant can be represented by an association of representatives. Where an applicant wishes to appoint the professional representatives practicing within an association of representatives registered with the EPO under R. 152(11) EPC, the name of that association and its registration number are to be indicated in Box No. IV of the Request form (AG-IP Annex C).

Art. 49	Right to practice before international authorities
R. 90.4	Power of attorney
R. 83.2	National Office provides information on the right of an agent to practice before it on request by other International Authorities

83.1 Proof of Right

The International Bureau, the competent International Searching Authority, and the competent International Preliminary Examining Authority, may require the production of proof of the right to practice referred to in Article 49.

83.1*bis* Where the International Bureau Is the Receiving Office

(a) Any person *(applicant or representative)* **who has the right to practice before the national Office of, or acting for, a Contracting State of which the applicant or, if there are two or more applicants, any of the applicants is a resident or national shall be entitled to practice in respect of the international application before the International Bureau in its capacity as receiving Office under Rule 19.1(a)(iii).**

(b) Any person having the right to practice before the International Bureau in its capacity as receiving Office in respect of an international application *(paragraph (a))* **shall be entitled to practice in respect of that application before the International Bureau in any other capacity and before the competent International Searching Authority and competent International Preliminary Examining Authority.**

6 A national representative without the right to practice before the EPO may represent an applicant before the EPO as ISA or IPEA if he has filed the application with the national Office or the International Bureau. However, representation without EPO admission is not possible before the EPO as receiving Office or in the regional phase (reference to national law in Art. 27(7) refers only to certain PCT authorities; see also annotations to R. 90.1). Although being restricted in this way this does not prevent the representative without the right to practice from filing the PCTa on behalf of the client. In cases where an agent cannot be recorded as such, there is the option of being recorded as an 'address for correspondence' under R. 4.4(d) which allows to receive correspondence and to make payments on behalf of the applicant. The agent cannot, however, sign documents on behalf of the client. Any missing or invalid signature is a defect under Art. 14 but an international filing date will be accorded and the signature of the applicant must be submitted subsequently. For further information see Pract. Adv. NL 2/2024.

83.2 Information

(a) The national Office or the intergovernmental organization which the interested person is alleged to have a right to practice before shall, upon request, inform the International Bureau, the competent International Searching Authority, or the competent International Preliminary Examining Authority, whether such person has the right to practice before it.

(b) Such information shall be binding upon the International Bureau, the International Searching Authority, or the International Preliminary Examining Authority, as the case may be.

Part E: Rules Concerning Chapter V of the Treaty

Rule 84
Expenses of Delegations

84.1 Expenses Borne by Governments

The expenses of each Delegation participating in any organ established by or under the Treaty shall be borne by the Government which has appointed it.

Rule 85
Absence of Quorum in the Assembly

85.1 Voting by Correspondence

In the case provided for in Article 53(5)(b), the International Bureau shall communicate the decisions of the Assembly (other than those concerning the Assembly's own procedure) to the Contracting States which were not represented and shall invite them to express in writing their vote or abstention within a period of three months from the date of the communication. If, at the expiration of that period, the number of Contracting States having thus expressed their vote or abstention attains the number of Contracting States which was lacking for attaining the quorum in the session itself, such decisions shall take effect provided that at the same time the required majority still obtains.

Refer to Art. 53 and corresponding annotations. This provision is rarely applied in practice. 1

Rule 86
The Gazette

86.1 Contents

(a) The Gazette referred to in Article 55(4) shall contain:

(i) for each published international application, the data specified by the Administrative Instructions taken from the front page of the publication of the international application, the drawing (if any) appearing on the said front page, and the abstract;

Art. 55	The International Bureau publishes the Gazette and other publications
AIs 407	The Gazette in electronic form
AIs Annex D, 407(b)	gives references to the elements of the front page of the international publication to be included on that page in accordance with R. 86.1(i)

1 Since 2006, the international applications (formerly Section I to III of the PCT Gazette) are published electronically on the multilingual, searchable database PATENTSCOPE (refer to WIPO webpage, Electronic publication of PCT Applications from April 2006, https://www.wipo.int/patentscope/en/news/pctdb/2006/news_0001.html).

(ii) the schedule of all fees payable to the receiving Offices, the International Bureau, and the International Searching and Preliminary Examining Authorities;

2 The fees are published in the Official Notices (https://www.wipo.int/pct/en/official_notices/index.html) and made available in the PCT Applicant's Guide (https://www.wipo.int/pct/en/guide) and the Fee tables (https://www.wipo.int/export/sites/www/pct/en/docs/fees.pdf) contained on the fee webpage (https://www.wipo.int/pct/en/fees/).

(iii) notices the publication of which is required under the Treaty or these Regulations;

There are several instances in which the Treaty or the Regulations refer to the publication of certain information. This is either done in PATENTSCOPE or the Official Notices (PCT Gazette) (https://www.wipo.int/pct/en/official_notices/index.html). Please note that the reference to expressly requiring publication in the Treaty and the Regulations partly overlaps with what is published according to Annex E of the Administrative Instructions (https://www.wipo.int/pct/en/texts/ai/annex_e.html) with reference to para. (v). 3

(iv) information concerning events at the designated and elected Offices notified to the International Bureau under Rule 95.1 in relation to published international applications;

R. 95.1 Information concerning events at the designated and elected Offices are: the date of national phase entry and any national application number; the number and date of the national publication if any; the date of grant if any and the date and number of publication of grant if any.

In 2015, the Assembly decided the following: 'In adopting the amendments to Rule 86.1(iv), the Assembly noted that the information concerning national phase entry will be made available to the public not only by way of inclusion in the Gazette on the PATENTSCOPE website but also as part of the bulk PCT bibliographic data offered to Offices and other subscribers to the PATENTSCOPE subscription data services' (PCT/A/47/9). 4

(v) any other useful information prescribed by the Administrative Instructions, provided access to such information is not prohibited under the Treaty or these Regulations.

AIs Annex E contains a list of indications to be published in the Official Notices (PCT Gazette) (https://www.wipo.int/pct/en/official_notices/index.html) under R. 86.1(v).

Annex E Administrative Instructions contains the following list of indications to be published in the Official Notes: 5

1. The time limits applicable under Art. 22 and 39 in respect of each Contracting State.
2. The list of the non-patent literature agreed upon by the ISAs for inclusion in the minimum documentation.
3. The names of the national Offices which do not wish to receive copies under Art. 13(2)(c).
4. The provisions of the national laws of Contracting States concerning international-type search.
5. The text of the agreements entered into between the International Bureau and the ISAs or the IPEAs.

6. The names of the national Offices which entirely or in part waived their rights to any communication under Art. 20.
7. The names of the Contracting States which are bound by Chapter II of the PCT.
8. Index of concordance of international application numbers and international publication numbers, listed according to international application numbers.
9. Index of applicants' names giving, for each name, the corresponding international publication number(s).
10. Index of international publication numbers, grouped according to the International Patent Classification symbols.
11. Indication of any subject matter that will not be searched or examined by the various ISAs and IPEAs under R. 39 and 67.
12. Requirements of designated and elected Offices under R. 49.5 and 76.5 in relation to the furnishing of translations.
13. The dates defining the period referred to in R. 32.1(b) during which the international application, whose effects may be extended to a successor State under R. 32.1, must have been filed.
14. The criteria for restoration of the right of priority applied by receiving Offices under R. 26*bis*.3 or designated Offices under R. 49*ter*.2, and any subsequent changes in that respect.
15. Information about the receiving Offices, the International Bureau and the ISAs and IPEAs which provide for the excuse of delays in meeting time limits under R. 82*quater*.2.
16. Any period of extension or additional period of extension under R. 82*quater*.3.

86.2 Languages; Form and Means of Publication; Timing

(a) The Gazette shall be published in English and French at the same time. The translations shall be ensured by the International Bureau in English and French.

(b) The Assembly may order the publication of the Gazette in languages other than those referred to in paragraph (a).

(c) The form in which and the means by which the Gazette is published shall be governed by the Administrative Instructions.

(d) The International Bureau shall ensure that, for each published international application, the information referred to in Rule 86.1(i) is published in the Gazette on, or as soon as possible after, the date of publication of the international application.

6 Refer to Section 407 AIs for the electronic form of publication.

86.3 Frequency

The frequency of publication of the Gazette shall be determined by the Director General.

7 The Official Notices are published weekly. International applications are also published weekly on PATENTSCOPE (usually on a Thursday morning).

86.4 Sale

The subscription and other sale prices of the Gazette shall be determined by the Director General.

The electronic publication is now free of charge (unlike the Paper Gazette before 2006). 8

86.5 Title

The title of the Gazette shall be determined by the Director General.

Section IV of the PCT Gazette is now called Official Notices (PCT Gazette) (https:// 9
www.wipo.int/pct/en/official_notices/index.html). Section I to III are now included in the searchable database PATENTSCOPE (https://patentscope.wipo.int/search/en/search.jsf).

86.6 Further Details

Further details concerning the Gazette may be provided for in the Administrative Instructions.

AIs 407	The Gazette
AIs Annex D	Elements of front page
AIs Annex E	Indications contained in the Official Notices (PCT Gazette)

Rule 87
Communication of Publications

87.1 Communication of Publications on Request

The International Bureau shall communicate, free of charge, every published international application, the Gazette and any other publication of general interest published by the International Bureau in connection with the Treaty or these Regulations, to International Searching Authorities, International Preliminary Examining Authorities and national Offices upon request by the Authority or Office concerned. Further details concerning the form in which and the means by which publications are communicated shall be governed by the Administrative Instructions.

1 The international applications are published in the database PATENTSCOPE (https://patentscope.wipo.int/search/en/structuredSearch.jsf), formerly PCT Gazette. They are made available to any interested Office or Authority (https://pct.wipo.int/ePCTExternal/pages/landing_offices.xhtml), usually via Electronic Data Exchange (EDI) (https://www.wipo.int/patentscope/en/pct-edi/) (Sect. 435 AIs), directly via ePCT for Authorities and Offices (https://pct.wipo.int/ePCTExternal/pages/landing_offices.xhtml) or in exceptional cases still by CD-R or DVD-R. Offices can also download the information directly from PATENTSCOPE.

2 Refer also to R. 89*bis* and Annex F of the Administrative Instructions as a Standard for the Filing and Processing of international applications in electronic format and the related annotations. Further, refer to Art. 20 on communicating the published international applications to Designated Offices. For the manner of communication to the Offices, refer to R. 93*bis*. R. 86 refers to the Gazette and Section 435 Administrative Instructions. The current list of distribution of documents is published for each Office in the distribution list in the PCT reference data lookup (ePCT external) (https://pct.wipo.int/ePCTExternal/pages/home.xhtml) in the Office Profiles (https://pct.wipo.int/ePCTExternal/pages/OfficeProfile.xhtml). For the communication of PCT Forms and any other document by the International Bureau to Offices refer also to R. 93*bis*.

Rule 88
Amendment of the Regulations

88.1 Requirement of Unanimity

Amendment of the following provisions of these Regulations shall require that no State having the right to vote in the Assembly vote against the proposed amendment:

(i) Rule 14.1 (Transmittal Fee),

(ii) [deleted]

(iii) Rule 22.3 (Time Limit under Article 12(3)),

(iv) Rule 33 (Relevant Prior Art for International Search),

(v) Rule 64 (Prior Art for International Preliminary Examination),

(vi) Rule 81 (Modification of Time Limits Fixed in the Treaty),

(vii) the present paragraph (i.e., Rule 88.1).

88.2 [Deleted]

88.3 Requirement of Absence of Opposition by Certain States

Amendment of the following provisions of these Regulations shall require that no State referred to in Article 58(3)(a)(ii) *(States with ISA or IPEA)* and having the right to vote in the Assembly vote against the proposed amendment:

(i) Rule 34 (Minimum Documentation),

(ii) Rule 39 (Subject Matter under Article 17(2)(a)(i)),

(iii) Rule 67 (Subject Matter under Article 34(4)(a)(i)),

(iv) the present paragraph (i.e., Rule 88.3).

88.4 Procedure

Any proposal for amending a provision referred to in Rules 88.1 or 88.3 shall, if the proposal is to be decided upon in the Assembly, be communicated to all Contracting States at least two months prior to the opening of that session of the Assembly which is called upon to make a decision on the proposal.

Art. 58(2)	Competence of the Assembly for amendments to the Regulations
Art. 60	Revision of the Treaty

1 In general, Assembly documents should be published two months before the session. For proposal with regard to R. 88, this is here expressly specified.

Rule 89
Administrative Instructions

89.1 Scope

(a) The Administrative Instructions shall contain provisions:

(i) concerning matters in respect of which these Regulations expressly refer to such Instructions,

(ii) concerning any details in respect of the application of these Regulations.

(b) The Administrative Instructions shall not be in conflict with the provisions of the Treaty, these Regulations, or any agreement concluded by the International Bureau with an International Searching Authority, or an International Preliminary Examining Authority.

For such agreements refer to ISA and IPEA Agreements (https://www.wipo.int/pct/en/access/isa_ipea_agreements.html). 1

89.2 Source

(a) The Administrative Instructions shall be drawn up and promulgated by the Director General after consultation with the receiving Offices and the International Searching and Preliminary Examining Authorities.

(b) They may be modified by the Director General after consultation with the Offices or Authorities which have a direct interest in the proposed modification.

(c) The Assembly may invite the Director General to modify the Administrative Instructions, and the Director General shall proceed accordingly.

The consultations with Offices and Authorities on modifications of the AIs happens by Consultation Circulars, refer to PCT Circulars (electronic collection of PCT Circulars available going back to 2002) (https://www.wipo.int/pct/en/circulars/). Once finalized, the modifications are communicated to Offices by a Promulgation Circular and posted on the PCT website at: PCT Treaty, Regulations and Administrative Instructions (https://www.wipo.int/pct/en/texts/index.html) either as a new consolidated or (more rarely) as a separate version of the Administrative Instructions 2

89.3 Publication and Entry into Force

(a) The Administrative Instructions and any modification thereof shall be published in the Gazette.

(b) Each publication shall specify the date on which the published provisions come into effect. The dates may be different for different provisions, provided that no provision may be declared effective prior to its publication in the Gazette.

3 For changes of the AIs, refer to PCT Treaty, Regulations and Administrative Instructions.

Part F: Rules Concerning Several Chapters of the Treaty

INTRODUCTION: METHODS OF COMMUNICATION

1. Communication of Applicant to Office

The methods by which an applicant can send international applications and other documents to International Authorities are laid down in the annexes of the PCT Applicant's Guide. 'Other documents', or sometimes called 'post-filing documents', are documents submitted after the international application has been filed, such as a submission of amendments. The following methods are possible, although an International Authority may not permit the use of all of them. 1

1.1 Personal Deposition

Most Offices and International Authorities accept personal deposition of documents relating to international applications, either by deposition in a letter box of the Office or handing to a porter of the Office (AG-IP 6.003). AG-IP Annex B and C do not mention this possibility, but national law usually does; see, for example, for the EPO R. 2 EPC and OJ EPO 2017 A11 Art. 1(3). See also annotations under No. 5 of the Introduction to Art. 10. 2

1.2 Mail or Postal Service

All Offices and International Authorities currently still accept the filing of international applications and other documents on paper by mail or postal service (AG-IP 6.003). However, there is a recommendation to the PCT Assembly to amend the Regulations in order to enable Offices to only allow for electronic filing and post-filing submissions, or at the choice of the Office require an electronic confirmation copy of a paper submission, or to keep the current system of allowing both paper and electronic filing and submissions (refer to document PCT/A/56/2 (https://www.wipo.int/meetings/en/doc_details.jsp?doc_id = 629283)). The mailing address of each Office is given in AG-IP Annex B. The number of copies of an international application and accompanying documents to be filed on paper (R. 11.1), varying between one and three, is given in AG-IP Annex C for each receiving Office. Other paper documents can be filed in a single copy. 3

1.3 Facsimile Transmission

Some Offices still accept the filing of international applications and other documents by fax (R. 92.4); AG-IP Annex B states for each Office whether it accepts filing by fax and the requirements for confirmation of the transmission. An international application filed by fax must usually be confirmed by filing a paper copy within 14 days from the fax transmission (R. 92.4(d)). Any other document filed by fax need only be confirmed on request. Many Offices regard the filing of documents by fax as an outdated technology and will 4 discontinue its use in the near future, even as a fallback in case methods of electronic filing are temporarily unavailable. As of January 2020, the International Bureau does no longer send faxes and will only accept faxes in emergency situations upon prior contact to the authorized officer or a message on its answering machine (https://www.wipo.int/pct/en/infoline.html). The International Bureau has set up a web-based Business Continuity Service for filing and uploading PDF documents as a fallback if ePCT is unavailable, replacing fax transmission as fallback (Gazette November 16, 2023, https://pctcs.wipo.int/ePCTFiling/) if necessary, the applicant may also file physical media such as CD-R or DVD-R with the International Bureau or use another receiving Office if possible, PCT Gazette November 16, 2023, Annex C (IB) and B (IB).

5 The EPO does not accept submissions by fax as from July 1, 2024 (OJ EPO 2024 A41).

1.4 E-mail

6 E-mail is a 'like means' of communication mentioned under R. 92.4. An Office or International Authority will only accept submissions by e-mail if it has notified the International Bureau (R. 92.4(h); see AG-IP Annex B: for example, DK, and others have notified that they accept submissions by e-mail).

7 The International Bureau as receiving Office or International Authority does not consider a response by e-mail as a valid submission, even if the International Bureau itself has sent an advance copy of a communication by e-mail. The International Bureau will only accept e-mails with informal queries which are not related to the processing of a specific international application (refer to PCT Information Service (https://www.wipo.int/pct/en/infoline.html)). The International Bureau will on request record a change of e-mail address (R. 92*bis*; AG-IP 11.018D).

8 It is not possible to file a PCTa by e-mail before the EPO (Euro-PCT Guide 2.2.002). The use of e-mails is only admissible for subsequently filed documents in the case of consultations and oral procedures conducted by videoconference (GL Exam C-VII, 3; OJ EPO 2020 A71).Other procedural actions filed by e-mail have no legal effect before the EPO as International Authority (Euro-PCT Guide 2.2.030–2.2.031).

1.5 Electronic Filing

9 Most Offices prefer to receive international applications and other documents in electronic form as permitted by R. 89*bis* and in accordance with the Administrative Instructions (AIs Part 7, especially Sec 710 and 713). Each Office that accepts electronic filing sends to the International Bureau an electronic filing notification that gets published (together with subsequent updates) in the Official Notices. The accepted methods of electronic filing are also listed in AG-IP Annex C for the receiving Offices and AG-IP Annex E for IPEAs. ePCT is the most used method.

10 The International Bureau accepts electronic filing, such as the recommended ePCT. Other electronic filing options are EPO Online Filing, as well as filing on CD-R or DVD-R (AG-IP Annex C(IB)). Furthermore, the ePCT Business Continuity Service (https://pctcs.wipo.int/ePCTFiling/) (FAQs) (https://www.wipo.int/pct/en/faqs/

epct-continuity-service-faq.html) can be used if any of the conventional online filing systems fails (PCT Newsletter No. 10/2023, p. 2 (https://www.wipo.int/edocs/pctndocs/en/2023/pct_news_2023_13.pdf)).

At the EPO the applicant can use ePCT services or MyEPO Portfolio (which replaces My Files), legacy Mailbox and Administration services as from July 1, 2024 (https://www.epo.org/en/applying/myepo-services, OJ EPO 2024 A43, OJ EPO 2023 A90). 11

See annotations to R. 89*bis* for details. 12

2. Communication of Office to Applicant

R 92.3 regulates the mailing by the Office to the applicant if a time limit is triggered. For certain communication from the Office to the applicant, the applicant shall indicate an address for postal delivery and rapid communication. R. 4.4 mainly deals with the address for postal delivery and rapid communication. Annotations to R. 4.4. refer to notification of the Office to the applicant by e-mail. 13

See the Introduction to R. 92 for communication of the Office by post, e-mail, and fax. See annotations to R. 80.6 for the relevant date and electronic notification of the Office to the applicant. R. 89*bis* refers to electronic communication but not from the Office to the applicant. 14

The International Bureau as receiving Office will use all means available in case of failure of electronic systems such as e-mail or notifications on the WIPO website to inform about procedures to follow (Gazette November 16, 2023, AIs 710(a)(v)). 15

At the EPO the applicant can receive electronic communications via EPO Mailbox service (https://www.epo.org/en/applying/myepo-services/interact/mailbox, OJ EPO 2021 A5) or via WIPO's ePCT System (https://pct.wipo.int/ePCT/about-epct.xhtml?lang=en, Euro-PCT Guide 2.2.033), The EPO stopped sending outgoing faxes on March 1, 2023 (see annotations to R. 4.4 and OJ EPO 2023 A15). Electronic notification is used for decisions, summonses, notices and communications (OJ EPO 2024 A21). Mail not relevant to the time limit will continue to be sent by ordinary post (Euro-PCT Guide 5.3.002, OJ EPO 2021 A5). E-mail may be used for arranging a consultation (PCT EPO Guidelines C-VII, 3). For informal clarification, the telephone or Mailbox may be used (PCT EPO Guidelines A-VIII, 3.3.1- 3.3.2). 16

Rule 89*bis*
Filing, Processing and Communication of International Applications and Other Documents in Electronic Form or by Electronic Means

INTRODUCTION

The legal basis for electronic filing can be found in R. 89*bis*, together with the detailed part 7 and Annex F of the AIs. For other means of communication and the relation to other Rules see Introduction to Part F of the Regulations. 17

1. Electronic Filing at International Bureau

18 WIPO offers a number of online filing options.

1.1 ePCT

19 ePCT is an online service for electronic communication between International Authorities and applicants. It is the preferred method for applicants to communicate with the International Bureau (Pract. Adv. NL 5/2008 and 3/2017). ePCT can also be used for communicating with many receiving Offices (https://pct.wipo.int/ePCTExternal/pages/EFilingServers.xhtml).

20 An applicant can use ePCT to file an international application, submit a priority document, submit amendments, sequence listings, declarations of inventorship or withdrawal of the international application, effect payments, and consult the most up-to-date bibliographic data and documents contained in the file of the international application, even if not yet published. Certain documents that are not yet publicly available in PATENTSCOPE after publication, such as documents relating to Chapter II, are available via ePCT. ePCT has services that are publicly accessible and services for confidential information only accessible for applicants.

21 Even if many Offices started using ePCT in the various functions as receiving Office, ISA, IPEA, some and, in particular, the medium-sized and large Offices maintain their own files and only documents that have already been transferred to the International Bureau are available and visible in ePCT. Thus, depending on the concrete situation, the applicant might have to contact the relevant Office in its respective function separately. Please note that ePCT is not yet available for national phase entry and access to document at designated Offices/elected Offices – beyond some very limited pilot projects.

22 ePCT *without strong authentication* is available to all WIPO online account holders. The functionality currently available is the online upload of electronic documents (with subsequent online viewing) and submission of TPOs with regard to novelty and inventive step (see Art. 33 for TPO).

23 ePCT *with strong authentication* permits access to all international applications filed as of January 1, 2009 that are owned or managed by the account holder, and allows preparing and filing of international applications and other documents. Almost all of the documents held by the International Bureau in relation to the applicant's international application can be viewed, including documents which have not yet been fully processed. This includes documents issued and received by the International Bureau as receiving Office and documents issued and received by other receiving Offices and International Authorities to the extent that a copy is sent to the International Bureau.

24 An applicant can access ePCT by creating a WIPO online user account via the WIPO Accounts Service (https://pct.eservices.wipo.int/direct.aspx?T = EN&UG = 4&N = 690). If access to ePCT *with strong authentication* is required, it is recommended to set up at least two strong authentication methods. Further, it is recommended that at least two persons in a company or law firm have access with strong authentication

to international applicants, in case one of the persons leaves or is not available at a certain time, in particular, to manage new access rights. See Pract. Adv. NL 1/2024 for the best practices for managing the WIPO account.

ePCT is an online service (http://www.wipo.int/pct-safe/en/download/download_client.html) without the need for updating by the user. 25

Filing via ePCT is currently offered at 87 receiving Offices (May 2024); documents are mainly stored on the WIPO server or sometimes at a local server (refer to https://pct.wipo.int/ePCTExternal/pages/EFilingServers.xhtml), with the exception of US, IL, CA, at which a ZIP file has to be downloaded on ePCT and uploaded on the national server for national security reasons. 26

1.2 ePCT Business Continuity Service

The ePCT Business Continuity Service, a web-based application that provides for the secure electronic transmission of documents, including the filing of international applications, if the ePCT system is unavailable for technical reasons, or if it is not possible to login to ePCT using the WIPO Accounts system. The Service guarantees business continuity since it is hosted in an entirely separate environment that does not include dependencies on the internal systems of the International Bureau. It replaces the previous Contingency Upload Service. (https://www.wipo.int/pct/en/faqs/epct-continuity-service-faq.html). 27

2. Fee Reductions Depending on the Way of Electronic Filing

Some types of electronic filing of an international application give entitlement to a reduction of the international filing fee: 28

- The reduction of No. 4(a) of the Schedule of Fees, annexed to the Regulations, applies when the request is not in character-coded format using Web-filing or the Contingency Upload Service (www.wipo.int/pct/en/faqs/contingency_upload_faq.html).
- The reduction of No. 4(b) applies when the request is in character-coded format, using OLF, web filing and also ePCT and the ePCT Business Continuity Service (https://www.wipo.int/pct/en/faqs/epct-continuity-service-faq.html).
- The reduction of No. 4(c) applies when the request, description, claims and abstract are in character-coded format. When filing with the EPO, the XML format fulfills these conditions (https://www.epo.org/applying/online-services/online-filing/features.html) and is provided by OLF and ePCT (https://www.epo.org/applying/international/guide-for-applicants/html/e/ga_c2_2_3.html).

3. Electronic Filing at the EPO

The EPO as International Authority also permits electronic filing. This includes online filing and offline filing with an electronic data carrier (AG-IP Annex C(EP); Euro-PCT Guide 2.2.004–2.2.008 (online), 2.2.009–2.2.010 (offline)). Where a document is 29 infected with a computer virus or other form of malicious logic, the Office may deem the document not to have been received (AIs 708(b) https://www.wipo.int/pct/en/texts/ai/s708.html; OJ EPO 2023 A48). An overview of the existing possibilities for electronic filing of documents with the EPO can be found on the EPO website (https://www.epo.org/en/applying/myepo-services/file-with-us, OJ EPO 2023 A48. Information concerning the software to be used is published in OJ EPO 2023 A96).

30 The EPO currently offers the following online filing options:

- *By Online Filing 2.0* (https://filing.epo.org/) substituting the former web-based application called CMS (case management system) since April 1, 2021, which requires no updating by the user; To access Online Filing 2.0, Online Filing (eOLF) and Central Fee Payment, a user will need to sign in via EPO account using two-factor authentication. As of the beginning of 2025, EPO smart card login support ends.
- *By software* installed locally with the need for regular updating by the user; any uploaded documents are stored locally; this option is called OLF (online filing), it requires an EPO account and authentication and may be used for filing priority documents.
- *By features of the ePCT service* as offered by WIPO (Euro-PCT Guide 2.2.006) which have been integrated in Online Filing 2.0 (OJ EPO 2023 A48 Art. 9). Since July 1, 2020, the EPO does not accept international applications filed with the EPO as receiving Office using the PCT-Safe filing software (OJ EPO 2020 A59).
- *By EPO Contingency Upload Service*. This offers an alternative method for submitting documents to the EPO in the unlikely event that the other EPO filing tools are not available. It allows for the upload of PDF documents including new European patent applications, international applications and/or subsequently filed documents (OJ EPO 2023 A50). The service requires temporary sign-in and authentication. Filing of priority documents is not accepted. EPO Contingency Upload Service accepts only documents in PDF format. Documents in XML format cannot be filed using EPO Web-Form Filing and Contingency upload service, with the exception of sequence listings, for which XML or ZIP format is allowed (https://www.epo.org/applying/online-services/online-filing/features.html, https://link.epo.org/web/EPO_online_filing_options_comparison_table_en.pdf, Guide 4.2.010 https://www.epo.org/en/legal/guide-epc/2023/ga_c4_2_5_1.html).
- *Until December 2024, by a web-based application called Web-Form Filing*. This can be used only for uploading documents in PDF format. It does not require updating; the documents are neither stored nor retrievable locally. The user has to register and to login with user name and password to upload his PDFs (Euro-PCT Guide 2.2004). Priority documents (R. 17; Euro-PCT Guide 2.15, 2.2.031, 2.17.004) and sequence listing (R. 13*ter*; OJ EPO 2004 p. 562; OJ EPO 2021 A96, OJ EPO 2021 A97; OJ EPO 2021 A42) cannot be filed using Web-Form Filing. Web-Form Filing has additional restrictions applying to specific procedures before the EPO such as opposition, limitation, revocation, or review proceedings. As of December 2024, Web-Form Filing will be decommissioned.

Rule 89*bis*
Filing, Processing and Communication of International Applications and Other Documents in Electronic Form or by Electronic Means

89*bis*.1 International Applications

(a) International applications may, subject to paragraphs (b) to (e), be filed and processed in electronic form or by electronic means, in accordance with the Administrative Instructions, provided that any receiving Office shall permit the filing of international applications on paper.

This Rule was intended to cover all aspects of filing and subsequent processing of PCTa, including communications between Offices and authorities and between applicants and Offices and authorities (PCT/A/XXIV/10, p.6, para. 24,https://www.wipo.int/edocs/mdocs/govbody/en/pct_a_xxiv/pct_a_xxiv_10-main1.pdf). 31

Electronic filing refers to online filings and offline filings by data carrier (Euro-PCT Guide 2.2.003, 2.2.010). 32

AIs	Part 7 Instructions relating to the filing and processing in electronic form of the international application in particular AIs 710, AIs 713
R. 17.1(b-*bis*)	Request to obtain the priority document from a digital library

(b) These Regulations shall apply *mutatis mutandis* to international applications filed in electronic form or by electronic means, subject to any special provisions of the Administrative Instructions.

(c) The Administrative Instructions shall set out the provisions and requirements in relation to the filing and processing of international applications filed, in whole or in part, in electronic form or by electronic means, including but not limited to, provisions and requirements in relation to acknowledgment of receipt, procedures relating to the according of an international filing date, physical requirements and the consequences of non-compliance with those requirements, signature of documents, means of authentication of documents and of the identity of parties communicating with Offices and authorities, and the operation of Article 12 in relation to the home copy, the record copy and the search copy, and may contain different provisions and requirements in relation to international applications filed in different languages.

This is included in Part 7 of the Administrative Instructions, the handing of home copy, record copy and search copy in Section 705*bis*. 33

(d) No national Office or intergovernmental organization shall be obliged to receive or process international applications filed in electronic form or by electronic means unless it has notified the International Bureau that it is prepared to do so

in compliance with the applicable provisions of the Administrative Instructions. The International Bureau shall publish the information so notified in the Gazette.

34 All electronic filing notifications are published in the Official Notices (PCT Gazette) (https://www.wipo.int/pct/en/official_notices/index.html), to a certain extent they are currently also available for each Office in the Office Profiles (https://pct.wipo.int/ePCTExternal/pages/OfficeProfile.xhtml). Information on accepting pre-conversion files (Section 706 AIs) has been separately compiled on the webpage on 'Acceptance by receiving Offices of documents in pre-conversion format (Section 706)' (https://www.wipo.int/pct/en/texts/preconversion-format.html). For International Bureau and EPO see the introduction above.

35 At the DPMA, an electronic application can be filed online using the DPMAdirektPro software (https://www.dpma.de/english/services/efiling/dpmadirekt/index.html).

36 Amendments to R. 89*bis*.1 to enter into force on July 1, 2025 have been proposed in order to allow an Office to require submission in electronic form only (PCT/A/56/2; refer also to annotations above).

(e) No receiving Office which has given the International Bureau a notification under paragraph (d) may refuse to process an international application filed in electronic form or by electronic means which complies with the applicable requirements under the Administrative Instructions.

89*bis*.2 Other Documents

Rule 89*bis*.1 shall apply *mutatis mutandis* to other documents and correspondence relating to international applications.

37 At the EPO, electronic filing is generally possible for all documents relating to the PCTa, see general annotations to R. 89*bis*.1(a). Form 1200 or electronic equivalent for entry into the regional phase at the EPO can also be filed online (AG-NP EP.01).

38 Amendments to enter into force on July 1, 2025 have been proposed in order to allow an Office to require resubmission in electronic form (PCT/A/56/2).

89*bis*.3 Communication between Offices

Where the Treaty, these Regulations or the Administrative Instructions provide for the communication, notification or transmittal ("communication") of an international application, notification, communication, correspondence or other document by one national Office or intergovernmental organization to another, such communication may, where so agreed by both the sender and the receiver, be effected in electronic form or by electronic means.

39 See Information for each Office (Office Profiles) at https://pct.wipo.int/ePCTExternal/pages/OfficeProfile.xhtml

Rule 89*ter*
Copies in Electronic Form of Documents Filed on Paper

89*ter*.1 Copies in Electronic Form of Documents Filed on Paper

Any national Office or intergovernmental organization may provide that, where an international application or other document relating to an international application is filed on paper, a copy thereof in electronic form, in accordance with the Administrative Instructions, may be furnished by the applicant.

Rule 90
Agents and Common Representatives

INTRODUCTION

1. Agents and Representatives

1 Representation is used as a generic term in AG-IP 11.001 that includes agent (R. 2.2) and common representative (R. 2.2*bis*).

1.1 Appointment of Agents

2 An applicant may effect the appointment of an agent in several ways. He may enter the name and address of the agent in the request, in the demand or in a separate power of attorney and sign the request, demand, or power of attorney (R. 90.4(a)). The separate power of attorney (authorization), signed by the applicant, authorizes the agent to represent the applicant in relation to a specific international application.

3 An agent may also be appointed by a general power of attorney, allowing the agent to represent the applicant in relation to any international application filed by that applicant. In that case, the request, demand or a separate notice must refer to the general power of attorney (R. 90.5).

4 Any changes in an indication of the agent after the filing of the application can be recorded with the International Bureau under R. 92*bis*.1(a)(ii). The International Bureau will not record a change that is received after the expiration of 30 months from the priority date (R. 92*bis*.1(b). The time limit is independent of the time limit for entry into the national phase (AG-IP 11.021).

5 The appointment of a new agent has the effect of a revocation of the appointment of the former agent, unless otherwise indicated. The requirements for revocation must be observed (R. 91). If a new agent requests the International Bureau to record a change of agent, a power of attorney may be required, in spite of any waiver according to R. 90.4(d).

6 Whether and how the appointment of an agent has to be proven depends on the manner in which he was appointed. If the applicant appoints the agent by signing the request or demand, no separate document (power of attorney) has to be signed

and submitted. If the applicant appoints the agent in a separate power of attorney, this document has to be submitted (R. 90.4(b)). If the applicant appoints the agent in a general power of attorney, the applicant must refer to an already deposited general power of attorney and enclose a copy of it, which copy need not be signed (R. 90.5(a)). The original, signed power of attorney must have been submitted to the receiving Office or to the ISA or IPEA if the appointment is only for those Offices (R. 90.5(b); AG-IP 5.043, 11.009). The assignment of access rights in ePCT is not sufficient to prove an appointment as agent (AIs 433(b); Pract. Adv. NL 9/2014, https://www.wipo.int/pct/en/newslett/practical_advice/pa_092014.html).

An International Authority may waive the requirement to submit a separate or general power of attorney (R. 90.4(d); R. 90.5(c)). The EPO acting as receiving Office, ISA, IPEA or SISA has waived the requirement that a separate or general power of attorney be attached to the request, demand or separate notice; however, it may require the filing of the power of attorney if there is doubt as to the agent's right to act (for details of the waiver see OJ EPO 2010 p. 335 and AG-IP Annexes C, D, E and SISA). The situation is similar in the US and the International Bureau, the latter however only in its capacity as receiving Office. The waiver does not apply to any notice of withdrawal (R. 90.4(e), R. 90.5(a), (d)). An up-to-date list of Offices that have waived the requirement of submitting a power of attorney can be found on the WIPO website (https://www.wipo.int/pct/en/texts/waivers.html) and in AG-IP Annex C for each receiving Office. 7

An agent may appoint a sub-agent to represent the applicant as agent before one or more or all competent International Authorities, unless otherwise indicated in the document appointing the agent (R. 90.1(d)). Appointment of a sub-agent could be useful, for example, where the sub-agent is familiar with the practice of the IPEA and the agent is not. 8

The appointment of an agent is considered non-existent if the signature of the applicant is missing or if the name and address of the agent do not comply with R. 4.4 (R. 90.4(c)). The applicant will be invited to correct the defect under Art. 14(1)(b) and R. 26. The receiving Office may extend the period for correction (R. 26.2). 9

Preferably, a power of attorney mentions explicitly whether it refers to a national patent application or to an international patent application and whether it refers to the international or/and national phase of the PCT procedure. A separate or general authorization can empower a representative to act in both the international and national phase. 10

1.2 *Common Agent and Common Representative*

Where there are two or more applicants, they should appoint a common agent or a common representative to act for all applicants. A common agent is an agent representing all applicants. A common representative is one of the applicants representing all of them; such an applicant must be entitled to file an international application (R. 90.2(a)). 11

12 The appointment of the common agent or common representative is effected by each applicant signing the request, demand, or separate power of attorney (R. 90.4(a)). A common representative can only be appointed if no common agent has been appointed (a consequence of R. 90.2(a); AG-IP 11.006).

13 If no common agent or common representative is appointed, the first-named applicant entitled to file an international application with the receiving Office will be considered to be the (deemed) common representative of all the applicants (R. 90.2(b)). See Art. 9 and Art. 10 for who is allowed to file an international application in view of residency and nationality, and annotations to Art. 27(7) for who is allowed to file an international application with the EPO.

14 Despite the wording of R. 90.4(a) ('each applicant signing'), an agent can also be appointed by a (deemed) common representative alone (R. 90.3(c); AG-IP 11.006). It is possible to appoint more than one agent representing the same applicant or applicants (a consequence of R. 90.3(b)).

1.3 Acts by Agent or Representative

15 An act by an agent has the effect of an act by the applicant (R. 90.3(a)). If there are two or more agents representing the same applicant or applicants, an act by one of those agents has the effect of an act by the applicant or applicants (R. 90.3(b)).

16 An act by a common representative or his agent has the effect of an act by all applicants (R. 90.3(c)). However, the deemed common representative may not sign notices of withdrawals on behalf of the other applicants (R. 90*bis*.5). The same applies to any agent appointed by him (AG-IP 11.006). Note that according to R. 2.1, the term 'applicant' can also mean 'agent or other representative of the applicant', which allows an agent to act even where a provision of the law only specifies the 'applicant'.

1.4 Revocation and Renunciation

17 An appointment of an agent or common representative may be revoked by the persons who made the appointment or by their successors in title (R. 90.6(a)). The applicant may also revoke the appointment of a sub-agent (R. 90.6(a)). The appointment of a new agent under R. 90.1(a) or a common representative causes the revocation of any earlier appointment of an agent under that Rule or a common representative, unless otherwise indicated (R. 90.6(b), (c)).

18 An agent or common representative may renounce his appointment by a notification signed by him (R. 90.6(d)).

19 A revocation or renunciation must be submitted to the receiving Office or International Bureau. However, where the power of attorney relates to an appointment for a specific Office, the revocation or renunciation must be submitted to that Office (R. 90.6(e)).

Rule 90
Agents and Common Representatives

90.1 Appointment as Agent

(a) A person having the right to practice before the national Office with which the international application is filed or, where the international application is filed with the International Bureau, having the right to practice in respect of the international application before the International Bureau as receiving Office may be appointed by the applicant as his agent to represent him before the receiving Office, the International Bureau, the International Searching Authority, any Authority specified for supplementary search and the International Preliminary Examining Authority.

Art. 27(7)	National rules for national representatives remain applicable for representation before the receiving Office and the designated Office (information in AG-NP Annex C and the EPC provisions cited below). According to Art. 2(x) this also refers to regional law.
R. 51*bis*.1(b)	National law for representation before the designated Office
R. 76.5	National law for representation before the elected Office
Art. 49	The right to practice before the national Office as receiving Office entitles to practice before International Bureau, ISA, IPEA.
R. 83.1*bis*	Right to practice before national Office entitles to practice before the International Bureau
Art. 4(1)(iii)	Required information concerning the agent in PCTa
R. 4.1(a)(iii)	Required information concerning the agent in PCTa
R. 4.4(d)	Additional address for correspondence
R. 4.7	Name and address of the agent in PCTa
R. 83	Proof of the right to practice before international authorities
Art. 133(2) EPC	In principle, there is no requirement for representation, but there is a requirement for the appointment of a professional representative or agent in connection with a European direct application or PCTa in the European phase if the applicant does not have his residence or place of business in an EPC Contracting State. The filing of the application and the acts in connection therewith are excepted from this requirement. The provisions on representation of the EPC do not apply if the EPO acts as ISA or IPEA. In this case, the right of representation is governed by Art. 49 and R. 83 PCT. The entitlement of national representatives who have filed a PCTa with their national Office as receiving Office is extended to acts necessary before the EPO for entry into the regional phase. Any person entitled to represent before the EPO may act before the EPO as receiving Office (Haugg in Singer/Stauder, *EPC*, 7th ed., 2016, Art. 133 EPC margin 11, 14). At the EPO, an appointment for

	the international phase does not automatically apply to the European phase; an explicit declaration in the request or separately is required (Euro-PCT Guide 2.11.019).
Art. 134 EPC	Entitled persons: only EPO listed representatives, details of registration in OJ 2013, 535
R. 152(11) EPC	allows the authorization of an association of professional representatives (e.g. partnership). Representation is reserved for natural persons under Art. 134, but the authorization of the association is deemed to be an authorization of each individual representative who practices within the association and furnishes proof thereof. The EPO will send all documents to the registered address unless a different address for service is used (see OJ EPO 2013 p. 539 et seq. for details).
R. 152(10) EPC	The applicant may appoint several authorized representatives. They must be listed by name in the power of attorney. In the case of a partnership, one name followed by the words 'et al.' is sufficient (OJ EPO 2013 p. 540). It should be clearly expressed whether an association or an individual representative is appointed (EPO Guidelines A-VIII 1.3).

20 Art. 49 speaks of 'attorneys, patent agents or other persons', i.e. natural persons. R. 90 speaks of 'a person', i.e. a natural person or, where applicable, a legal person. These provisions do not mention partnerships, associations or other forms of patent attorney cooperation. According to AG-IP Annex C (IB), if the International Bureau acts as sole receiving Office under R. 19.1(b), it must be a natural or legal person. This concerns only a few smaller Offices listed in Annex C (IB). For all other cases, Annex C (IB) refers to the law applicable at the national Office. This corresponds to R. 83.1*bis*. The wording 'or a firm or partnership that is not a legal entity' in No. 117 of WIPO Guideline PCT/GL/RO/20 (https://www.wipo.int/export/sites/www/pct/en/texts/pdf/ro.pdf) shows that the International Bureau in principle accepts such associations. There is no provision in the International Bureau corresponding to R. 152(11) EPC.

21 Before the EPO, the situation is very clear. As explained above, a registered association may be authorized. According to Art. 49 and R. 90.1(a), this right to practice before the regional Office (Art. 2(xii)) also extends to the receiving Office and the competent International Authorities (ISA, IPEA). In any case, if the EPO has been chosen as receiving Office, any registered association may be appointed as representative.

22 This does not necessarily apply to other countries, see AG-IP Annex C and AG-NP.

DE: § 25 PatG	Only non-national applicants must be represented by an authorized legal practitioner or patent attorney. This applies to the DPMA as receiving Office and as designated or elected Office (AG-IP Annex C (DE) and AG-NP (DE) Summary DE.05). An association of representatives may be authorized by indicating the name of the association (p. 6 Patent Applicant Information Sheet

(2022 edition) at https://www.dpma.de/docs/formulare/patent/p2791.pdf).

However, the obligation to be represented does not apply to de facto acts, such as filing applications or requests. Authorized European attorneys or patent attorneys can also be appointed to represent before the DPMA (Rudloff-Schäffer in Schulte: *PatG mit EPÜ Kommentar*, 10th ed. 2017, Section 25 para. 17, 20, 25).

EU: EuPAG and EuRAG — regulate the right to practice in Member States of the EU, in the European Economic Area and in Switzerland. As of January 1, 2021, UK patent attorneys and attorneys-at-law are no longer entitled to represent before the DPMA, DPMA Notice No. 1/2021.

(b) A person having the right to practice before the national Office or intergovernmental organization which acts as the International Searching Authority may be appointed by the applicant as his agent to represent him specifically before that Authority.

(b-*bis*) A person having the right to practice before the national Office or intergovernmental organization which acts as the Authority specified for supplementary search may be appointed by the applicant as his agent to represent him specifically before that Authority.

(c) A person having the right to practice before the national Office or intergovernmental organization which acts as the International Preliminary Examining Authority may be appointed by the applicant as his agent to represent him specifically before that Authority.

(d) An agent appointed under paragraph (a) may, unless otherwise indicated in the document appointing him, appoint one or more sub-agents to represent the applicant as the applicant's agent:

(i) before the receiving Office, the International Bureau, the International Searching Authority, any Authority specified for supplementary search and the International Preliminary Examining Authority, provided that any person so appointed as sub-agent has the right to practice before the national Office with which the international application was filed or to practice in respect of the international application before the International Bureau as receiving Office, as the case may be;

(ii) specifically before the International Searching Authority, any Authority specified for supplementary search or the International Preliminary Examining Authority, provided that any person so appointed as sub-agent has the right to practice before the national Office or intergovernmental organization which acts as the International Searching Authority, the Authority specified for supplementary search or the International Preliminary Examining Authority, as the case may be.

Paras (b), (b-*bis*) and (c) mention an appointment only before a certain authority. 23
For details of appointment see Introduction to R. 90. For details referring to the right to practice see annotations to R. 90.1(a).

90.2 Common Representative

(a) Where there are two or more applicants and the applicants have not appointed an agent representing all of them (a "common agent") under Rule 90.1(a), one of the applicants who is entitled to file an international application according to Article 9 may be appointed by the other applicants as their common representative.

24 The provision also applies during the IPE procedure (AG-IP 10.022). Only applicants who are PCT nationals or have their residence/place of business in a PCT Contracting State may be designated as common representatives. Unlike in the procedures before the EPO, a 'non-PCT applicant' may be represented by a PCT applicant in the procedure under the PCT. In the procedure under the EPC, the applicant who is not a national or has a residence/place of business in one of the EPC Contracting States must be represented (Art. 133(2) EPC).

Art. 27(7)	Representation before the EPO as receiving Office by the applicant himself is only possible if the applicant is an EPC national or has his place of business in one of the EPC Contracting States. In all other cases, a representative must be appointed (Art. 133 EPC).
Art. 9	Resident or national of a PCT Contracting State
R. 90.4(a)	A common representative shall be entitled to appoint an agent. The latter may act only to the extent that the common representative is entitled to.
R. 2.2*bis*	Definition of 'common representative' refers to R. 90.2
AIs 106	Change of common representative

(b) Where there are two or more applicants and all the applicants have not appointed a common agent under Rule 90.1(a) or a common representative under paragraph (a), the applicant first named in the request who is entitled according to Rule 19.1 to file an international application with the receiving Office shall be considered to be the common representative of all the applicants.

25 The Rule also applies in the IPE procedure (AG-IP 10.022). A deemed common representative may in principle do everything that an appointed representative may do, except for certain declarations for withdrawals (AG-IP 11.006).

Art. 9	Only those who are entitled under Art. 9 (nationality or domicile/business place in a PCT Contracting State) can be deemed common representatives

90.3 Effects of Acts by or in Relation to Agents and Common Representatives

(a) Any act by or in relation to an agent shall have the effect of an act by or in relation to the applicant or applicants concerned.

(b) If there are two or more agents representing the same applicant or applicants, any act by or in relation to any of those agents shall have the effect of an act by or in relation to the said applicant or applicants.

(c) Subject to Rule 90*bis*.5, second sentence *(signature of notice of withdrawal)*, any act by or in relation to a common representative or his agent shall have the effect of an act by or in relation to all the applicants.

Namely, the common representative may appoint an agent in accordance with R. 90.1. **26**
The deemed common representative may also do so. However, the common agent appointed by a deemed common representative (R. 90.2(a)) cannot withdraw the application or perform certain other acts mentioned in R. 90*bis*.2 to R. 90*bis*.4 such as designation, priority claim, supplementary search request, demand, or election.

90.4 Manner of Appointment of Agent or Common Representative *(power of attorney)*

(a) The appointment of an agent shall be effected by the applicant signing the request, the demand or a separate power of attorney. Where there are two or more applicants, the appointment of a common agent or common representative shall be effected by each applicant signing, at his choice, the request, the demand or a separate power of attorney.

Art. 14(1)	Missing signature
R. 4.15	Signature of all applicants
R. 26.2*bis*(a)	No formal deficiency in case of signature of applicant or attorney having the power of attorney of an applicant. In the case of waiver by the Office pursuant to R. 90.4(d), the power of attorney need not be submitted.
R. 51*bis*.1(a)(vi)	Invitation by designated Office to furnish missing signature
R. 60.1(a-*ter*)	No deficiency if one of several applicants signs a demand under R. 85.8 (Chapter II) demand
R. 90.3(c)	The common representative (R. 90.2(a)) or deemed common representative (R. 90.2(b)) may appoint the agent without signature by each applicant

(b) Subject to Rule 90.5, a separate power of attorney shall be submitted to either the receiving Office or the International Bureau, provided that, where a power of attorney appoints an agent under Rule 90.1(b), (b-*bis*), (c) or (d)(ii), it shall be submitted to the International Searching Authority, the Authority specified for supplementary search or the International Preliminary Examining Authority, as the case may be.

(c) If the separate power of attorney is not signed, or if the required separate power of attorney is missing, or if the indication of the name or address of the

appointed person does not comply with Rule 4.4, the power of attorney shall be considered non-existent unless the defect is corrected.

(d) Subject to paragraph (e), any receiving Office, any International Searching Authority, any Authority competent to carry out supplementary searches, any International Preliminary Examining Authority and the International Bureau may waive the requirement under paragraph (b) that a separate power of attorney be submitted to it, in which case paragraph (c) shall not apply.

27 For a list of countries in which Offices (or Authorities) have notified the International Bureau that they waive the requirement for filing a power of attorney under R. 90.4(b), further requirements and details, see Annex C PCT Applicant's Guide and http://wipo.int/pct/en/texts/pdf/p_a_waivers.pdf.

28 Waived: AT, AU, BN, BY, CA, CH, CY, DE, DK, EA, EP, ES, FI, FR, GB, GR, International Bureau, IL, IS, IT, JP, LT, LV, MD, MT, NL, NZ, PH, PT, RU, SE, SG, TR, US, XN, XV.

29 For effective acts before the International Bureau (e.g. under Art. 19, R. 92*bis*, R. 26*bis*), there must be at least one power of attorney signed by the deemed common representative in the files (R. 90.2(b), PCT Newsletter 1/2004).

30 For the EPO, details and cases to which the waiver does not apply, see OJ EPO 2010 p. 335. Waiver also applies to EPO as SISA (PCT Gazette May 6, 2010, p. 88, AG-IP Annex SISA (EP)).

R. 90*bis*	No waiver when filing a declaration of withdrawal: declarations of withdrawal then have no effect under R. 90.4(e), 90.5(d); rights of access under ePCT do not change this (PCT Newsletter 9/2014, p. 14)

(e) Where the agent or the common representative submits any notice of withdrawal referred to in Rules 90*bis*.1 to 90*bis*.4, the requirement under paragraph (b) for a separate power of attorney shall not be waived under paragraph (d).

90.5 General Power of Attorney

(a) Appointment of an agent in relation to a particular international application may be effected by referring in the request, the demand or a separate notice to an existing separate power of attorney appointing that agent to represent the applicant in relation to any international application which may be filed by that applicant (i.e., a "general power of attorney"), provided that:

(i) the general power of attorney has been deposited in accordance with paragraph (b), and

(ii) a copy of it is attached to the request, the demand or the separate notice, as the case may be; that copy need not be signed.

R. 152(4), (5) EPC	Power of attorney, details in OJ EPO 535 p. 2013

AG-IP 5.045	The appointment of a new agent shall be deemed to be a revocation of any previous appointment, unless otherwise stated.
R. 90.5(c)	Possibility of waiving proof of general power of attorney

(b) The general power of attorney shall be deposited with the receiving Office, provided that, where it appoints an agent under Rule 90.1(b), (b-*bis*), (c) or (d)(ii), it shall be deposited with the International Searching Authority, the Authority specified for supplementary search or the International Preliminary Examining Authority, as the case may be.

(c) Any receiving Office, any International Searching Authority, any Authority competent to carry out supplementary searches and any International Preliminary Examining Authority may waive the requirement under paragraph (a)(ii) that a copy of the general power of attorney is attached to the request, the demand or the separate notice, as the case may be.

List of Offices (or authorities) which have notified the International Bureau that they waive the requirement under R. 90.5(a)(ii) (copy of general authorization): AT, AU, BN, BY, CA, CH, CY, DE, DK, EA, EP, ES, FI, FR, GB, GR, International Bureau (in capacity as receiving Office), IL, IS, IT, JP, KG, LT, LV, MD, MT, NL, NZ, PH, PT, RU SE, SG, TR, US, XN, XV. See also annotation to R. 90.4(d). 31

Waiver by the EPO (OJ EPO 5/2010 p. 335, also as SISA in PCT Gazette May 6, 2010, p. 88). For details see AG-IP and http://wipo.int/pct/en/texts/pdf/p_a_waivers.pdf respectively. 32

(d) Notwithstanding paragraph (c), where the agent submits any notice of withdrawal referred to in Rules 90*bis*.1 to 90*bis*.4 to the receiving Office, the Authority specified for supplementary search, the International Preliminary Examining Authority or the International Bureau, as the case may be, a copy of the general power of attorney shall be submitted to that Office, Authority or Bureau.

R. 152(5) EPC	The power of attorney must indicate to which procedure (EPC, PCT) it applies (Euro-PCT Guide 2.11.019). Authorization by all applicants is required for all types of declarations of withdrawal (Euro-PCT Guide 2.11.17).

90.6 Revocation and Renunciation

(a) Any appointment of an agent or common representative may be revoked by the persons who made the appointment or by their successors in title, in which case any appointment of a sub-agent under Rule 90.1(d) by that agent shall also be considered as revoked. Any appointment of a sub-agent under Rule 90.1(d) may also be revoked by the applicant concerned.

(b) The appointment of an agent under Rule 90.1(a) shall, unless otherwise indicated, have the effect of revoking any earlier appointment of an agent made under that Rule.

(c) The appointment of a common representative shall, unless otherwise indicated, have the effect of revoking any earlier appointment of a common representative.

(d) An agent or a common representative may renounce his appointment by a notification signed by him.

(e) Rule 90.4(b) and (c) shall apply, *mutatis mutandis*, to a document containing a revocation or renunciation under this Rule.

PCT/CAL/IV/10, p. 8, para. 55

The Rule does not 'affect the relationship between the applicant and his agent, but rather dealt with the recognition of agents by Offices and authorities under the PCT. In the latter connection, a renunciation would be effective at the time when it was received by the authority concerned'. (https://www.wipo.int/edocs/mdocs/pct/en/pct_cal_iv_part_ii/pct_cal_iv_part_ii_10.pdf).

Rule 90*bis* Withdrawals

INTRODUCTION

During the international phase the applicant may withdraw the application, designations, priority claims, the supplementary search request, the demand or elections before the expiration of 30 months from the priority date (Art. 37; R. 90*bis*.1(a), 2(a), 3(a), 3*bis*(a), 4(a); see also annotations to Art. 22). Note that the extended period of 31 months for entering the national phase under Art. 22(3) and Art. 39(1)(b) is not applicable here because R. 90*bis*.2(a), 3(a), 4(a) specifically mention only 30 months. Withdrawals after expiry of the 30 months must be made before the designated or elected Offices, the effect of which being governed by national law. See Introduction to Art. 37 for the effect of the withdrawal on the publication of the application. 1

The withdrawal of an application, designation, or priority claim must be submitted to the International Bureau, receiving Office or, when the IPE is carried out, the IPEA (R. 90*bis*.1(b), 2(d), 3(c)). In contrast, the withdrawal of the demand or an election must be submitted to the International Bureau (R. 90*bis*.4(b)). If submitted to the IPEA instead, the IPEA will transmit it to the International Bureau, which will consider it to have been received on the date of receipt by the IPEA (R. 90*bis*.4(c)). The withdrawal of a request for supplementary search should be submitted to the SISA or to the International Bureau (R. 90*bis*.3*bis*(b)). 2

Any notice of withdrawal must be signed by the applicant (R. 90*bis*.5) or his agent (R. 2.1). Where there are several applicants and no common agent or common representative has been appointed, the deemed common representative or any agent appointed by him (see general annotation to R. 90) may not sign a notice of withdrawal; the notice requires the signature of all applicants (R. 90*bis*.5). Where an agent has been appointed by a separate or general power of attorney and has not yet submitted it, he should do so before or simultaneously with a notice of withdrawal. If an agent does not submit the general power of attorney, the respective authority will ask for it; the act of withdrawal only being deemed complete when the power of attorney is received by the respective authority (R. 90.4(e) and 5(d)). 3

When the designation of the US is to be withdrawn, the assignee can be named as sole applicant and, hence, only the applicant's signature is required to withdraw the international application (R. 4.15(b); PCT Newsletter 7–8/2012, p. 1, http:// 4 www.wipo.int/edocs/pctndocs/en/2012/pct_news_2012_08.pdf). Also, the agent can withdraw an international application, provided he submits a power of attorney (R. 90.4(e); R. 90.5(d)).

5 ePCT may be used to upload a withdrawal request, see general annotations to R. 89*bis*.

6 See for the withdrawal of

- a designation, annotations to Art. 4;
- a priority claim, annotations to Art. 8; and
- the demand or an election, Art. 37.

7 All withdrawals are free of charge (AG-IP 11.048).

90*bis*.1 Withdrawal of the International Application

(a) The applicant may withdraw the international application at any time prior to the expiration of 30 months from the priority date.

Art. 24(1)(i)	Legal consequences of withdrawals
R. 90.4(e)	Submission of individual power of attorney required
R. 90.5(d)	Submission of general power of attorney required
R. 90*bis*.5	Signature of the notice of withdrawal
R. 90*bis*.6	The withdrawal of the PCTa has no effect if the national or regional Offices have already started processing (AG-IP 11.048–11.061)
AIs 326 and 609	Withdrawal by applicant under R. 90*bis*.1, R. 90*bis*.2 or R. 90*bis*.3
AIs 415:	Notification of withdrawal under R. 90*bis*.1, R. 90*bis*.2, R. 90*bis*.3, R. 90*bis*.3*bis* or 90*bis*.4

(b) Withdrawal shall be effective on receipt of a notice addressed by the applicant, at his option, to the International Bureau, to the receiving Office or, where Article 39(1) applies, to the International Preliminary Examining Authority.

(c) No international publication of the international application shall be effected if the notice of withdrawal sent by the applicant or transmitted by the receiving Office or the International Preliminary Examining Authority reaches the International Bureau before the technical preparations for international publication have been completed.

Art. 21(5)	Withdrawal of the application before completion of the technical preparations, usually 15 days before publication
R. 48.6(c)	Announcing of certain facts
AG-IP 11.049	The withdrawal can also be declared conditionally. It is recommended to declare the withdrawal under the condition that it reaches the International Bureau in time to prevent publication.

90*bis*.2 Withdrawal of Designations

(a) The applicant may withdraw the designation of any designated State at any time prior to the expiration of 30 months from the priority date. Withdrawal of the designation of a State which has been elected shall entail withdrawal of the corresponding election under Rule 90*bis*.4.

R. 90*bis*.6	The declaration of withdrawal has no effect if the national or regional Offices have already started processing.

(b) Where a State has been designated for the purpose of obtaining both a national patent and a regional patent, withdrawal of the designation of that State shall be taken to mean withdrawal of only the designation for the purpose of obtaining a national patent, except where otherwise indicated.

The regional designation thus remains in place. 8

(c) Withdrawal of the designations of all designated States shall be treated as withdrawal of the international application under Rule 90*bis*.1.

(d) Withdrawal shall be effective on receipt of a notice addressed by the applicant, at his option, to the International Bureau, to the receiving Office or, where Article 39(1) applies, to the International Preliminary Examining Authority.

(e) No international publication of the designation shall be effected if the notice of withdrawal sent by the applicant or transmitted by the receiving Office or the International Preliminary Examining Authority reaches the International Bureau before the technical preparations for international publication have been completed.

Art. 21(5)	Withdrawal of a designation before completion of the technical preparations, completion usually 15 days before publication
R. 48.6(c)	Publication of notice of withdrawal. The withdrawal may be made conditional on non-publication (https://www.wipo.int/pct/en/texts/ro/ro314_321.html).

90*bis*.3 Withdrawal of Priority Claims

(a) The applicant may withdraw a priority claim, made in the international application under Article 8(1), at any time prior to the expiration of 30 months from the priority date.

R. 90*bis*.6(a)	No effect of withdrawal of priority claim before Offices where processing has already begun. Since it is not possible to declare withdrawal of priority claim only for certain Contracting States or to exclude certain Contracting States, WIPO recommends first entering the national phase early at the desired Office, expressly

requesting early processing and declaring withdrawal of priority after processing has begun. According to R. 90*bis*.3(d), the priority date will be recalculated after withdrawal of a priority claim, which is relevant for numerous time limits. This effect can be used to postpone entry into the national phase in other States and to postpone related payments to a later date. However, it should be noted that this entails risks with regard to prior art (PCT Newsletter 3/2021, p. 12). In the case of a withdrawal of a priority claim in the 21st or 31st month, national law is generally applicable.

Art. 23(2)	Early entry into the national phase at the designated Office
Art. 40(1)	Early entry into the national phase at the elected Office

(b) Where the international application contains more than one priority claim, the applicant may exercise the right provided for in paragraph (a) in respect of one or more or all of the priority claims.

(c) Withdrawal shall be effective on receipt of a notice addressed by the applicant, at his option, to the International Bureau, to the receiving Office or, where Article 39(1) applies, to the International Preliminary Examining Authority.

(d) Where the withdrawal of a priority claim causes a change in the priority date, any time limit which is computed from the original priority date and which has not already expired shall, subject to paragraph (e), be computed from the priority date resulting from that change.

GL Exam A-III, 6	Information on corresponding regulations for the procedure under the EPC

9 The withdrawal usually has an effect on the calculation of the time limit

(e) In the case of the time limit referred to in Article 21(2)(a), the International Bureau may nevertheless proceed with the international publication on the basis of the said time limit as computed from the original priority date if the notice of withdrawal sent by the applicant or transmitted by the receiving Office or the International Preliminary Examining Authority reaches the International Bureau after the completion of the technical preparations for international publication.

Art. 21(5)	Completion of technical preparations usually 15 days before publication
PCT RO Guidelines	Although the reference relates to a conditional withdrawal of the international application, it is probably also applicable to a conditional withdrawal of a priority claim (https://www.wipo.int/pct/en/texts/ro/ro314_321.html)
GL Exam F-VI, 3.5	Describes a corresponding provision in the procedure under the EPC.

90*bis*.3*bis* Withdrawal of Supplementary Search Request

(a) The applicant may withdraw a supplementary search request at any time prior to the date of transmittal to the applicant and to the International Bureau, under Rule 45*bis*.8(a), of the supplementary international search report or the declaration that no such report will be established.

(b) Withdrawal shall be effective on receipt, within the time limit under paragraph (a), of a notice addressed by the applicant, at his option, to the Authority specified for supplementary search or to the International Bureau, provided that, where the notice does not reach the Authority specified for supplementary search in sufficient time to prevent the transmittal of the report or declaration referred to in paragraph (a), the communication of that report or declaration under Article 20(1), as applicable by virtue of Rule 45*bis*.8(b), shall nevertheless be effected.

R. 90*bis*.6	Effect of withdrawal

90*bis*.4 Withdrawal of the Demand, or of Elections

(a) The applicant may withdraw the demand or any or all elections at any time prior to the expiration of 30 months from the priority date.

Art. 37	Withdrawal of demand or election
R. 90*bis*.6(c)	Discontinuation of processing

(b) Withdrawal shall be effective upon receipt of a notice addressed by the applicant to the International Bureau.

(c) If the notice of withdrawal is submitted by the applicant to the International Preliminary Examining Authority, that Authority shall mark the date of receipt on the notice and transmit it promptly to the International Bureau. The notice shall be considered to have been submitted to the International Bureau on the date marked.

90*bis*.5 Signature

Any notice of withdrawal referred to in Rules 90*bis*.1 to 90*bis*.4 shall be signed by the applicant or, if there are two or more applicants, by all of them. An applicant who is considered to be the common representative under Rule 90.2(b) shall not be entitled to sign such a notice on behalf of the other applicants.

R. 2.2	Applicant means also agent or other representative
R. 2.3	Signature
R. 90.4(d), 90.5(c)	Even if a power of attorney does not have to be filed with the PCTa, obtaining signatures from the applicants is recommended to avoid delays (PCT Newsletter 10/2013, p. 12).

90*bis*.6 Effect of Withdrawal

(a) Withdrawal under Rule 90*bis* of the international application, any designation, any priority claim, the demand or any election shall have no effect in any designated or elected Office where the processing or examination of the international application has already started under Article 23(2) or Article 40(2).

EPO	From the effective date of a request for early processing, a subsequent withdrawal under R. 90*bis*.6 has no effect on the European phase (OJ EPO 2013 p. 156). See also comments on R. 90*bis*.3(a) (withdrawal of priority claims)

(b) Where the international application is withdrawn under Rule 90*bis*.1, the international processing of the international application shall be discontinued.

Art. 24(1)(i)	Loss of effect in designated States

(b-*bis*) Where a supplementary search request is withdrawn under Rule 90*bis*.3*bis*, the supplementary international search by the Authority concerned shall be discontinued.

(c) Where the demand or all elections are withdrawn under Rule 90*bis*.4, the processing of the international application by the International Preliminary Examining Authority shall be discontinued.

Art. 37(4)(a)	Withdrawal of a demand (IPE) or election
Art. 150 EPC	In connection with Art. 16(3)(b) WIPO-EPO Agreement, Annex D Part II (5). Possibilities of reimbursement of the examination fee by the EPO as IPEA.

90*bis*.7 Faculty under Article 37(4)(b)

(a) Any Contracting State whose national law provides for what is described in the second part of Article 37(4)(b) shall notify the International Bureau in writing.

(b) The notification referred to in paragraph (a) shall be promptly published by the International Bureau in the Gazette, and shall have effect in respect of international applications filed more than one month after the date of such publication.

Rule 91
Rectification of Obvious Mistakes in the International Application and Other Documents

INTRODUCTION

An applicant may request that obvious mistakes in an international application or any other document submitted by him be rectified (R. 91.1(a), AG-IP 11.033–11.044). A mistake will only be rectified if duly authorized by the competent Authority (R. 91.1(b)). The competent Authority will authorize a rectification if it is obvious to the competent Authority that something else was intended than what appears in the document concerned and that nothing else could have been intended than the proposed rectification (R. 91.1(c)). Rectification may be made of the applicant's own volition or on request of an authority that discovered the error (R. 91.1(h)). The rectification is effected free of charge (AG-IP 11.033). The possibility to request rectification is in addition to file amendments (AG-IP 11.045). 1

Omission of entire elements or sheets of the international application is not rectifiable under R. 91.1(g)(i) (although such an omission may be rectifiable for example, under R. 20 or R. 82), nor are mistakes in the abstract under R. 91.1(g)(ii) (although a mistake in the abstract may be corrected using R. 38.3). A mistake in an Art. 19 amendment is not rectifiable unless under certain circumstances before the IPEA (R. 91.1(g)(iii), R. 91.1(b)(iii)). A request for rectification of obvious mistakes in the claims is only recommended if the mistakes are liable to affect the international search; otherwise, the rectification should be made by an amendment of the claims after the search (AG-IP 5.126). 2

A mistake in a priority claim may be rectified using R. 91 as long as the rectification does not change the earliest priority date (R. 91.1(g)(iv)). Note that such a rectification of a priority claim is possible within 26 months from the priority date (R. 91.2), whereas a correction of a priority claim under R. 26*bis*.1 is only possible until about 16 months from the priority date (see annotations to Art. 8). 3

The relevant competent Authority is: 4

- the receiving Office if the mistake is in the request (R. 91.1(b)(i));

- the ISA if the mistake is in the description, claims, or drawings, or in a correction thereof, unless the IPEA is competent (R. 91.1(b)(ii));
- the IPEA if the mistake is in the description, claims, or drawings, or in a correction thereof, or in an Art. 19 or 34 amendment, where a demand for IPE has been made and not withdrawn before examination has started (R. 91.1(b)(iii); R. 69.1); or
- the relevant Office, Authority or Bureau (receiving Office, ISA, IPEA or International Bureau) if the mistake is in a document not referred to above that is submitted to that Office, Authority or Bureau (R. 91.1(b)(iv)).

5 The applicant must submit his request for rectification to the competent Authority (AG-IP 11.039) within 26 months of the priority date (R. 91.2). The rectification must be filed in the language in which the international application is filed (R. 12.2(b)), and additionally in the language of the translation if such has been filed (R. 12.2(b)(i) and (ii)). The request for rectification should specify the mistake to be rectified, the proposed rectification and, at the option of the applicant, a brief explanation (R. 91.2).

6 If authorization of a request for rectification is received by or given by the International Bureau after the technical preparations for the international publication are complete, a statement reflecting the rectification and rectified sheets, or the replacement sheets, the request for rectification and the front page of the international application will be republished (R. 48.2(i)).

7 If an obvious mistake is rectified, the rectification will be effective as from the international filing date if the mistake was in the international application as filed (R. 91.3(c)(i)), and from the date on which the document was submitted if in a document other than the international application as filed (R. 91.3(c)(ii)).

8 The ISA and the IPEA have to take the authorized rectification into account, unless the ISA or IPEA has begun to draw up the report (R. 43.6*bis*, R. 66.1(d)*bis*, R. 66.4*bis*).

9 If the authorization is refused, the applicant may request the International Bureau in writing within two months of the refusal to publish the refused request along with reasons for the refusal, subject to the payment of a special fee (R. 91.3(d); see AG-IP Annex B(IB) for the fee). Publication is relevant if the applicant wants to pursue the rectification in the national phase under national law (AG-IP 11.043).

10 A designated Office need not take a rectification into account if processing or examination of the international application has begun prior to it being notified of the authorization of the rectification (R. 91.3(e)), and may disregard a rectification if it would have refused authorization had it been the competent Authority (R. 91.3(f)).

Art. 19	Amendments before the International Bureau
Art. 34	Amendments before the IPEA

91.1 Rectification of Obvious Mistakes

(a) An obvious mistake in the international application or another document submitted by the applicant may be rectified in accordance with this Rule if the applicant so requests.

The possibility of rectification exists in principle in addition to the possibility of amendment under Art. 19 or Art. 34 (AG-IP 11.045). If an error in the claims is to be corrected, an amendment before carrying out the international search is recommended only if the error may affect the international search, otherwise an amendment after the international search is recommended (AG-IP P 11.045). 11

The correction under R. 91 is free of charge (AG-IP P 11.033). 12

R. 12.2(b)	Language of changes in the PCTa
R. 66.5	Distinction from the term change
AIs 325 and 413	Taking into account of defects under R. 26.4 and of obvious mistakes under R. 91
AIs 335	Procedures relating to sequence listings
AIs 217	Corrections concerning expressions under R. 9.2
AIs 413*bis*	Rectification of obvious mistakes under R. 91 (International Bureau)
AIs 511 and 607	Rectification of obvious mistakes under R. 91 (ISA)
AIs Annex C	Instructions relating to the presentation of sequence listings

(b) The rectification of a mistake shall be subject to authorization by the "competent authority", that is to say:

(i) in the case of a mistake in the request part of the international application or in a correction thereof – by the receiving Office;

(ii) in the case of a mistake in the description, claims or drawings or in a correction thereof, unless the International Preliminary Examining Authority is competent under item (iii) – by the International Searching Authority;

(iii) in the case of a mistake in the description, claims or drawings or in a correction thereof, or in an amendment under Article 19 or 34, where a demand for international preliminary examination has been made and has not been withdrawn and the date on which international preliminary examination shall start in accordance with Rule 69.1 has passed – by the International Preliminary Examining Authority;

R. 48.2(i)	This Rule does not apply to a consent by IPEA according to the Working Group's commentary on the amendment of R. 48.2 (PCT/WG/3/8 pp. 3, Annex, p. 4)
R. 70.16	Amendments may be provided as an annex to the report under R. 70.16 or, if not possible, to the elected Office via the International Bureau under R. 70.2(e) and AIs 413 (PCT/WG/3/8 p. 3, Annex p. 4)

(iv) in the case of a mistake in a document not referred to in items (i) to (iii) submitted to the receiving Office, the International Searching Authority,

the International Preliminary Examining Authority or the International Bureau, other than a mistake in the abstract or in an amendment under Article 19 – by that Office, Authority or Bureau, as the case may be.

(c) The competent authority shall authorize the rectification under this Rule of a mistake if, and only if, it is obvious to the competent authority that, as at the applicable date under paragraph (f), something else was intended than what appears in the document concerned and that nothing else could have been intended than the proposed rectification.

R. 20.3	Defects according to Art. 11(1), such as late receipt of documents
R. 20.5	Missing parts
R. 20.5*bis*	Erroneously filed elements and parts
R. 20.6	Confirmation of incorporation by reference of elements and parts
R. 20.7	Time limit

(d) In the case of a mistake in the description, claims or drawings or in a correction or amendment thereof, the competent authority shall, for the purposes of paragraph (c), only take into account the contents of the description, claims and drawings and, where applicable, the correction or amendment concerned.

(e) In the case of a mistake in the request part of the international application or a correction thereof, or in a document referred to in paragraph (b)(iv), the competent authority shall, for the purposes of paragraph (c), only take into account the contents of the international application itself and, where applicable, the correction concerned, or the document referred to in paragraph (b)(iv), together with any other document submitted with the request, correction or document, as the case may be, any priority document in respect of the international application that is available to the authority in accordance with the Administrative Instructions, and any other document contained in the authority's international application file at the applicable date under paragraph (f).

AIs 715	Availability of priority documents from digital libraries
AIs 716	Request that priority document be obtained from a digital library under R. 17.1(b-*bis*)

(f) The applicable date for the purposes of paragraphs (c) and (e) shall be:

(i) in the case of a mistake in a part of the international application as filed – the international filing date;

(ii) in the case of a mistake in a document other than the international application as filed, including a mistake in a correction or an amendment of the international application – the date on which the document was submitted.

(g) A mistake shall not be rectifiable under this Rule if:

(i) the mistake lies in the omission of one or more entire elements of the international application referred to in Article 3(2) or one or more entire sheets of the international application;

R. 20.5	Missing parts
R. 20.5*bis*	Erroneously filed elements and parts

(ii) the mistake is in the abstract;

R. 38.3	Modification of abstract is possible

(iii) the mistake is in an amendment under Article 19, unless the International Preliminary Examining Authority is competent to authorize the rectification of such mistake under paragraph (b)(iii); or

R. 53.9	Correction only possible if demand for examination has been filed. No regulation regarding Art. 34 is necessary, as amendment according to Art. 34 is only possible in case of demand for IPE anyway, cf. annotation to R. 53.9.

(iv) the mistake is in a priority claim or in a notice correcting or adding a priority claim under Rule 26*bis*.1(a), where the rectification of the mistake would cause a change in the priority date; provided that this paragraph shall not affect the operation of Rules 20.4, 20.5,26*bis* and 38.3.

R. 26*bis*.1	Correction or addition of priority claim

(h) Where the receiving Office, the International Searching Authority, the International Preliminary Examining Authority or the International Bureau discovers what appears to be a rectifiable obvious mistake in the international application or another document, it may invite the applicant to request rectification under this Rule.

91.2 Requests for Rectification

A request for rectification under Rule 91.1 shall be submitted to the competent authority within 26 months from the priority date. It shall specify the mistake to be rectified and the proposed rectification, and may, at the option of the applicant, contain a brief explanation. Rule 26.4 shall apply *mutatis mutandis* as to the manner in which the proposed rectification shall be indicated.

91.3 Authorization and Effect of Rectifications

(a) The competent authority shall promptly decide whether to authorize or refuse to authorize a rectification under Rule 91.1 and shall promptly notify the applicant and the International Bureau of the authorization or refusal and, in the case of refusal, of the reasons therefor. The International Bureau shall proceed as provided for in the Administrative Instructions, including, as required, notifying the receiving Office, the International Searching Authority, the International Preliminary Examining Authority and the designated and elected Offices of the authorization or refusal.

(b) Where the rectification of an obvious mistake has been authorized under Rule 91.1, the document concerned shall be rectified in accordance with the Administrative Instructions.

R. 48.2(a)(vii)	Publication if request for publication received before completion of the technical preparations
R. 48.2(i)	Re-publication if received after completion of technical preparations
AIs 325	Rectification at the receiving Office
AIs 413*bis*	Rectification at the International Bureau
AIs 511	Rectifications at the ISA
AIs 607	Rectification at the IPEA

(c) Where the rectification of an obvious mistake has been authorized, it shall be effective:

(i) in the case of a mistake in the international application as filed, from the international filing date;

(ii) in the case of a mistake in a document other than the international application as filed, including a mistake in a correction or an amendment of the international application, from the date on which that document was submitted.

R. 43.6*bis*	Consideration by ISA
R. 66.1(d-*bis*)	Consideration by IPEA

(d) Where the competent authority refuses to authorize a rectification under Rule 91.1, the International Bureau shall, upon request submitted to it by the applicant within two months from the date of the refusal, and subject to the payment of a special fee whose amount shall be fixed in the Administrative Instructions, publish the request for rectification, the reasons for refusal by the authority and any further brief comments that may be submitted by the applicant, if possible together with the international application. A copy of the request, reasons and comments (if any) shall if possible be included in the communication under

Article 20 where the international application is not published by virtue of Article 64(3).

If the request for publication of the rejection of an application for rectification according to R. 91.3(d) is filed before completion of the technical preparations, it will be published with the international publication (AG-IP 11.041). If the application is filed after completion of the technical preparations, the rejected application for rectification is published according to R. 48.2(k), the granted application for rectification according to R. 48.2(i). 13

The publication of a refused request for rectification does not relieve the applicant from the need to request authorization of the rectification during the national phase (PCT/A/XI/9, p.8, para. 47, https://www.wipo.int/edocs/mdocs/govbody/en/pct_a_xi/pct_a_xi_9.pdf). 14

R. 48.2(a)(vii)	International publication contains any request for rectification
AIs 113	Special fee (AG-IP Annex B (IB))
Art. 21(5)	Completion of the technical preparations

(e) The rectification of an obvious mistake need not be taken into account by any designated Office in which the processing or examination of the international application has already started prior to the date on which that Office is notified under Rule 91.3(a) of the authorization of the rectification by the competent authority.

R. 150 EPC	A rejected request for rectification in the international phase is not automatically taken into account before the EPO upon entry into the regional phase. Rather, a request under R. 150 EPC is required.

(f) A designated Office may disregard a rectification that was authorized under Rule 91.1 only if it finds that it would not have authorized the rectification under Rule 91.1 if it had been the competent authority, provided that no designated Office shall disregard any rectification that was authorized under Rule 91.1 without giving the applicant the opportunity to make observations, within a time limit which shall be reasonable under the circumstances, on the Office's intention to disregard the rectification.

Rule 92
Correspondence

INTRODUCTION

1. Formal Requirements for Correspondence of Applicant to Office

1.1 Form and Language

1 Any paper submitted by the applicant to an Office in the international phase other than the international application itself must be in the form of a letter or a paper accompanied by a letter identifying the international application (R. 92.1(a)). The letter must be signed as set out in the next section. Any letter to the receiving Office must be in the language of publication of the international application (AIs 104(a)). Any letter or document sent by the applicant to the ISA or IPEA must be in the same language as the international application (R. 92.2(a)). However, where a translation of the international application has been made for the ISA or IPEA, the language of the translation must be used (R. 92.2(a)). Other languages accepted by an Office acting as ISA or IPEA under R. 92.2(b) are specified in the ISA and IPEA Agreements, Annex A(ii) (http://www.wipo.int/pct/en/access/isa_ipea_agreements.html), between the International Bureau and the Office.

2 The official languages of the EPO are English, French and German (Art. 14; R. 3 EPC). When the EPO acts in its capacity under the PCT, the applicant must perform all procedural acts with the EPO; he cannot perform them with a national Office of a Contracting State. As an exception, an international application may or must be filed with a national Office if prior authorisation for filing abroad is required in the interest of national security (Art. 151; Art. 75(2) EPC; OJ EPO 2013 p.18 §5).

3 Any letter to the International Bureau must be either in English, French or the language of publication when sent by ePCT or only in English or French when sent by other means (R. 92.2(d) and AIs 104(c), https://www.wipo.int/pct/en/texts/ai/s104.html; see also explanation of amendment of R. 92.2(d) in WIPO presentation of 2016.03.11, https://www.wipo.int/pct/en/texts/ppt/2016changes.pptx. This paragraph represents WIPO's interpretation of the amended Rule and Administrative Instructions.)

1.2 *Signature*

An international application, a demand and a letter must be signed by the applicant (R. 4.15; R. 53.8; R. 92.1(a)). It is sufficient that one of several applicants has signed the application or the demand (R. 26.2*bis*(a); R. 60.1(a-*ter*)). However, a withdrawal must be signed by all applicants (annotations to Art. 4, 37 and R. 90*bis*). See annotations to R. 90 for the signature of the power of attorney (R. 90.4(b)). A signature of a non-entitled person is regarded as a missing signature (see, for example, AG-IP 5.089). 4

The applicant will be informed of any non-compliance and will be invited to remedy the omission within a period specified by the Office (R. 26.1; R. 60.1(a); R. 92.1(b)). If remedied in time, the omission will be disregarded. Otherwise, the applicant will be informed that the international application is considered withdrawn (Art. 14(1)(b); R. 29.4; see annotations to Art. 14), the demand considered as not received (R. 60.1(b)), or the paper has been disregarded (R. 92.1(b)). 5

In the case where not all of several applicants have signed the international application, the designated Office may request the applicant in the national phase to remedy the omission of signatures in a way prescribed by the relevant national law (R. 51*bis*.1(a)(vi)). 6

R 92.4 applies if the applicant uses faxes or other like means. The means mentioned in that Rule are not electronic means. See R. 89*bis* for electronic communication. 7

2. Communication of Office to Applicant

2.1 *Form and Means of Communication*

R. 92 provides that any document or letter from an International Authority the dispatch of which triggers a time limit, is sent in paper form to the applicant by postal delivery. The delivery will be by airmail; surface mail may be used instead if it reaches its destination within two days or if airmail is not available (R. 92.3). Irregularities in the mail are dealt with in annotations to Art. 48. 8

Due to the impact of the Covid-19 pandemic on postal delivery worldwide, on March 30, 2020 the International Bureau suspended the transmittal on paper of PCT documents and notifications and until further notice will only transmit documents and notifications electronically (https://www.wipo.int/pct/en/news/2020/news_0008.html and https://www.wipo.int/pct/en/covid_19/communication.html). Users are encouraged to provide their e-mail address when filing an international application. 9

2.2 *Correspondence of Office by E-mail*

The applicant may indicate an e-mail address for the first applicant and/or agent in the PCT request form and demand form. The International Authorities will use the e-mail for communications that would otherwise be made by telephone (R. 4.4). 10

If an e-mail address is indicated in the request form and if the Office provides such a service at all, the Office will use e-mail for sending notifications of any invitation or 11 notification to be sent on paper by postal delivery (see annotations to R. 4.4). AG-IP Annex B states whether an Office will send notifications by e-mail. The International Bureau does, the EPO does not.

12 An Office may choose to send a notification on paper in addition to an e-mail (AG-IP 5.029). Provided that an Office sends such an advance notification, the e-mail does not replace the paper notification, and the paper invitations or notifications remain the legal copies, also for triggering any time limit in the notification (RO Guidelines Ch. II No. 27, R. 80.6).

13 If the applicant did not indicate an e-mail address or chose to exclusively receive postal mail, or if the Office does not send notifications by e-mail, notifications will be sent exclusively on paper by postal mail (AG-IP 5.029). Where the notifications is sent exclusively by e-mail, the date of mailing indicated on the electronic copy will commence any time limit within the meaning of R. 80 (RO Guidelines Ch. II No. 27).

3. Communication of EPO

14 Fax was not an official notification method under the EPC, but had been used by the EPO as a courtesy service to convey advance urgent information. In view of digital transformation the EPO stopped sending faxes on March 1, 2023. Instead the EPO will send urgent information via the Mailbox or via e-mail. (See OJ EPO 2023 A15 and annotations to R. 4.4(c)). E-Mail may be used for arranging a consultation (PCT EPO Guidelines C-VII, 3). Electronic notification is used for decisions, summonses, notices, and communications (OJ EPO 2024 A21). For informal clarification the telephone or Mailbox may be used (PCT EPO Guidelines A-VIII, 3.3.1- 3.3.2).

Rule 92
Correspondence

92.1 Need for Letter and for Signature

(a) Any paper submitted by the applicant in the course of the international procedure provided for in the Treaty and these Regulations, other than the international application itself, shall, if not itself in the form of a letter, be accompanied by a letter identifying the international application to which it relates. The letter shall be signed by the applicant.

(b) If the requirements provided for in paragraph (a) are not complied with, the applicant shall be informed as to the non-compliance and invited to remedy the omission within a time limit fixed in the invitation. The time limit so fixed shall be reasonable in the circumstances; even where the time limit so fixed expires later than the time limit applying to the furnishing of the paper (or even if the latter time limit has already expired), it shall not be less than 10 days and not more than one month from the mailing of the invitation. If the omission is remedied within the time limit fixed in the invitation, the omission shall be disregarded; otherwise, the applicant shall be informed that the paper has been disregarded.

(c) Where non-compliance with the requirements provided for in paragraph (a) has been overlooked and the paper taken into account in the international procedure, the non-compliance shall be disregarded.

92.2 Languages

(a) Subject to Rules 55.1 and 55.3 and to paragraph (b) of this Rule, any letter or document submitted by the applicant to the International Searching Authority or the International Preliminary Examining Authority shall be in the same language as the international application to which it relates. However, where a translation of the international application has been transmitted under Rule 23.1(b) or furnished under Rule 55.2, the language of such translation shall be used.

R. 12	Language of the international application and of the translation for the purposes of the international search and international publication

(b) Any letter from the applicant to the International Searching Authority or the International Preliminary Examining Authority may be in a language other than that of the international application, provided the said Authority authorizes the use of such language.

R. 3 EPC	governs the choice of language for filing documents. It is not possible to change the language of the application in the procedure under the EPC, since a PCT application is an EPC application under Art. 150 EPC (OJ EPO 1993 pp. 97, 596, 540 et seq.). The EPO allows DE, GB, FR as procedural languages (Art. 14(1), (3) EPC).
AIs 104	Language of correspondence in cases not covered by R. 92.2

(c) [Deleted]

(d) Any letter from the applicant to the International Bureau shall be in English, French or any other language of publication as may be permitted by the Administrative Instructions.

R. 48.3	Languages of publication
AIs 104(c)	Communication from the applicant to the International Bureau via ePCT must be in English, French or the language of publication of the application.

(e) Any letter or notification from the International Bureau to the applicant or to any national Office shall be in English or French.

AIs 104(b)	Requirement for choice among the languages

15 Amendments to enter into force on July 1, 2025 have been proposed in order to enable the International Bureau to correspond in any of the ten languages of the international publication for certain communications to be determined (PCT/A/56/2).

92.3 Mailings by National Offices and Intergovernmental Organizations

Any document or letter emanating from or transmitted by a national Office or an intergovernmental organization and constituting an event from the date of which any time limit under the Treaty or these Regulations commences to run shall be sent by air mail, provided that surface mail may be used instead of air mail in cases where surface mail normally arrives at its destination within two days from mailing or where air mail service is not available.

16 R 92.3 only refers to documents sent by the Office/organization that trigger time limits. See R. 80.6 for the date of documents and communication that triggers a time limit, R. 4.4 for the address and e-mail communication sent by the Office to the applicant. As electronic communication in R. 89*bis* does not refer to communication from the Office to the applicant, electronic communication by the Office is mentioned in R. 80.6.

92.4 Use of Telegraph, Teleprinter, Facsimile Machine, Etc.

(a) A document making up the international application, and any later document or correspondence relating thereto, may, notwithstanding the provisions of Rules 11.14 ***(later documents)*** **and 92.1(a)** ***(signature)*****, but subject to paragraph (h)** ***(no obligation for national Offices to receive)*****, be transmitted, to the extent feasible, by telegraph, teleprinter, facsimile machine or other like means of communication resulting in the filing of a printed or written document.**

17 R 92.4, like R. 92.1 and R. 92.2, refers only to communications sent by the applicant and authorises the use of machines for transmission provided that the result is a printed written document. On the one hand, it is more specific as to the means of transmission and, on the other hand, it is broader because it refers to all types of documents or letters including PCTa in contrast to R. 92.1.

R. 4.4(c)	Form of address in the PCTa
R. 20.3	Defects under Art. 11(1), such as late receipt of documents of the PCTa
R. 82	Irregularities in the mail service
R. 82*quater*	Excuse or delay in meeting time limits and extension of time limits
AIs 331	Receipt of confirmation copy
R. 89*bis*	Filing in electronic form
AG-IP Annex B	indicates whether Offices accept the mentioned means, and similar means such as e-mail

EPO	Filing of PCTa by fax is possible until June 30, 2024, but not by telegraph, e-mail or teletext (OJ EPO 2024 A41).
International Bureau	Contrary to the International Bureau's announcement that it will no longer accept faxes from 2020 onwards for technical reasons, this will continue to be possible in exceptional situations. Applicants should primarily use ePCT Business Continuity Service submit physical media or use a different receiving Office (AG-IP Annex C and B (IB)). It is recommended to have the receipt of the fax confirmed by telephone or e-mail to be on the safe side. The contact details of the responsible case officer can be found at http://pct.wipo.int/ePCTExternal/pages/TeamLookup.xhtml (PCT Newsletter 1/2019, p. 1, 11/2019). Filing of PCTa by e-mail is not accepted.

(b) A signature appearing on a document transmitted by facsimile machine shall be recognized for the purposes of the Treaty and these Regulations as a proper signature.

(c) Where the applicant has attempted to transmit a document by any of the means referred to in paragraph (a) but part or all of the received document is illegible or part of the document is not received, the document shall be treated as not having been received to the extent that the received document is illegible or that the attempted transmission failed. The national Office or intergovernmental organization shall promptly notify the applicant accordingly.

At the EPO, electronically filed documents infected with viruses are deemed to be illegible (OJ EPO 2021 A20 Art. 13). 18

(d) Any national Office or intergovernmental organization may require that the original of any document transmitted by any of the means referred to in paragraph (a) and an accompanying letter identifying that earlier transmission be furnished within 14 days from the date of the transmission, provided that such requirement has been notified to the International Bureau and the International Bureau has published information thereon in the Gazette. The notification shall specify whether such requirement concerns all or only certain kinds of documents.

EPO	No original has to be submitted for the withdrawal of the PCTa (AG-IP Annex B (EP), PCT Gazette of September 27, 2018)

(e) Where the applicant fails to furnish the original of a document as required under paragraph (d), the national Office or intergovernmental organization concerned may, depending on the kind of document transmitted and having regard to Rules 11 *(physical requirements of the PCTa)* and 26.3 *(requirements under Art. 14(1)(a)(v))*,

(i) waive the requirement under paragraph (d), or

(ii) invite the applicant to furnish, within a time limit which shall be reasonable under the circumstances and shall be fixed in the invitation, the original of the document transmitted, provided that, where the document transmitted contains defects, or shows that the original contains defects, in respect of which the national Office or intergovernmental organization may issue an invitation to correct, that Office or organization may issue such an invitation in addition to, or instead of, proceeding under item (i) or (ii) *(Invitation to furnish the original or to refrain)*.

EPO

Filing by fax is possible until June 30, 2024 (OJ EPO 2024 A41). If the PCTa is filed by fax, it must be filed at the same time by post in due form (R. 2(1) EPC) and be accompanied by a confirmation letter. Thereafter, further documents may be faxed with the exception of powers of attorney and priority documents. Subsequently faxed documents must be accompanied by a confirmation letter only if requested (OJ EPO 2019 A18 until June 30, 2024).

If a letter of confirmation has not been sent in time, the applicant will be invited to correct the defect. If no letter of confirmation is received, the application is deemed to be withdrawn (Euro-PCT Guide 2.2.027).

(f) Where the furnishing of the original of a document is not required under paragraph (d) but the national Office or intergovernmental organization considers it necessary to receive the original of the said document, it may issue an invitation as provided for under paragraph (e)(ii).

19 At the EPO, documents included in the electronic file are deemed to be originals (R. 147(3) EPC). There is therefore no need to request the filing of an original.

(g) If the applicant fails to comply with an invitation under paragraph (e)(ii) or (f):

(i) where the document concerned is the international application, the latter shall be considered withdrawn and the receiving Office shall so declare;

(ii) where the document concerned is a document subsequent to the international application, the document shall be considered as not having been submitted.

20 Comparable to R. 92.4(g)(ii) is R. 50(3) EPC. A national further processing and if necessary, a re-establishment of rights is possible before the EPO.

(h) No national Office or intergovernmental organization shall be obliged to receive any document submitted by a means referred to in paragraph (a) unless it has notified the International Bureau that it is prepared to receive such a document by that means and the International Bureau has published information thereon in the Gazette.

Rule 92*bis* Recording of Changes in Certain Indications in the Request or the Demand

92*bis*.1 Recording of Changes by the International Bureau

(a) The International Bureau shall, on the request of the applicant or the receiving Office, record changes in the following indications appearing in the request or demand:

International Bureau	No fees are payable. There are no special formal requirements and it is recommended to send the request directly to the International Bureau via ePCT (AG-IP 11.018, 11.018A, 11.020). For amendments in ePCT when the amendment concerns several PCTa of one applicant, see Pract. Adv. NL 12/2021.
AIs 329	Correction of indications concerning the applicant's residence or nationality
AIs 416	Correction of request in record copy
AIs 422	Notifications concerning changes recorded under R. 92*bis*.1
R. 4.4(c)	Since July 1, 2008, there is a further possibility of e-mail communication by adapting the forms and AIs 706, 710. The e-mail address can also be added or changed according to R. 92*bis* (AG-IP 5.029, 11.018D). In the context of the Covid-19 pandemic and temporarily discontinued sending of paper documents by the International Bureau, it requested e-mail addresses (PCT Gazette April 23, 2020, p. 73). Using ePCT, the e-mail address should be indicated in the PCTa or subsequently by uploading a letter with the request under R. 92*bis* for the receipt of documents. As the International Bureau generally no longer sends forms in paper format, it is mandatory to provide such an e-mail address (PCT Newsletter 1/2023 p.1). In case of failure of electronic systems, the Business Continuity Service can be used or, as a last resort, faxes, Annex C(IB) and B(IB). See also annotation to R. 4.4 and R. 89*bis*.

(i) person, name, residence, nationality or address of the applicant,

	No evidence is required for a change in the person of the applicant, e.g. a transfer, at the international stage, provided that the transfer is notified to the International Bureau by the previous applicant or his representative (AG-IP. 11.018B)
	A transfer need not be made to a resident or national of a PCT Contracting State (AG-IP 11.018C).
	A request for transfer by a person not yet named in the application without the written consent of the applicant must be supported by an assignment or other evidence (AB-IP 11.018B).
	The filing of a new power of attorney is required whenever the registered representative represents a new applicant and communicates changes in the person of the applicant. This does not apply if the Office has waived the requirement under R. 90.4(d) (PCT Applicant's Guide int. P. No. 11.018B).
EPO	No proof of entitlement required in the international phase in case of a change of applicants (J 4/10). Third party rights (licenses, liens, etc.) generally cannot be registered in the international phase (AG-IP. 11.018D).
Art. 27(2)(ii), R. 51*bis*.1(a)(ii)	Determine the permissible national requirements. Thus, the proof of transfer may be subject to stricter rules at the national stage. However, no new certificate under R. 22(1) EPC has to be filed before the EPO if it has already been filed in the procedure under the PCT. The status of the file will be taken over.
R. 4.4(d)	Address for correspondence
R. 92.4	A signed letter notifying the changes can be sent as a fax, but not as an e-mail.
R. 92*bis*	Only the changes are communicated to the International Bureau in writing – preferably by ePCT (see also AG-IP 11.018–11.018A)

(ii) person, name or address of the agent, the common representative or the inventor.

1 The private or professional address indicated for the inventor is visible in PATENTSCOPE. The change of address under R. 92*bis* is also visible, but in non-searchable image format. Since the conditions for exclusion from inspection of files under R. 94.1(e) are strict, it is advisable to check whether or when the information is required at the respective Office (AG-IP Annex B) and which address is indicated before naming the inventor and private address (PCT Newsletter 10/2020 p. 14).

AIs 328	Notifications concerning representation (revocation, renunciation) before the receiving Office

AIs 425, 512, 608	Notifications concerning representation (revocation, renunciation) before the International Bureau, ISA, IPEA
R. 90*bis*.5	Signed notice of withdrawal. Recording of change of representative requires power of attorney of new agent (PCT Newsletter 9/2014, p. 14). Submitting a power of attorney is possible via ePCT without having access rights to the application in ePCT (PCT Newsletter 7–8/2022, p. 21). There is a new procedure for requesting access rights in ePCT (PCT Newsletter 1/2023, p. 3, PCT Newsletter 4/2024, p. 8).

(b) The International Bureau shall not record the requested change if the request for recording is received by it after the expiration of 30 months from the priority date.

After expiry of the time limit and entry into the national phase, the change must be requested directly before the designated or elected Office (AG-IP 11.021). 2

Rule 93
Keeping of Records and Files

93.1 The Receiving Office

Each receiving Office shall keep the records relating to each international application or purported international application, including the home copy, for at least 10 years from the international filing date or, where no international filing date is accorded, from the date of receipt.

93.2 The International Bureau

(a) The International Bureau shall keep the file, including the record copy, of any international application for at least 30 years from the date of receipt of the record copy.

(b) The basic records of the International Bureau shall be kept indefinitely.

93.3 The International Searching and Preliminary Examining Authorities

Each International Searching Authority and each International Preliminary Examining Authority shall keep the file of each international application it receives for at least 10 years from the international filing date.

93.4 Reproductions

For the purposes of this Rule, records, copies and files may be kept as photographic, electronic or other reproductions, provided that the reproductions are such that the obligations to keep records, copies and files under Rules 93.1 to 93.3 are met.

AIs 705, 705*ter*, 711	PCTa in electronic form
R. 147 EPC	Electronic file system and communication OJ EPO 2024 A31, OJ EPO 2024 A31

Rule 93*bis*
Manner of Communication of Documents

93*bis*.1 Communication on Request; Communication via Digital Library

(a) Where the Treaty, these Regulations or the Administrative Instructions provide for the communication, notification or transmittal ("communication") of an international application, notification, communication, correspondence or other document ("document") by the International Bureau to any designated or elected Office, such communication shall be effected only upon request by the Office concerned and at the time specified by that Office. Such request may be made in relation to individually specified documents or a specified class or classes of documents.

(b) A communication under paragraph (a) shall, where so agreed by the International Bureau and the designated or elected Office concerned, be considered to be effected at the time when the International Bureau makes the document available to that Office in electronic form in a digital library, in accordance with the Administrative Instructions, from which that Office is entitled to retrieve that document.

The ePCT profile of the Offices in 'Current Distribution' shows which PCT Forms and 1
other documents (e.g. Part 8 AIs, Third Party Observations) Offices have requested and received (https://pct.wipo.int/ePCTExternal/pages/OfficeProfile.xhtml).

Rule 94
Access to Files

INTRODUCTION

1 The table 'Access to Files' in the Annex to this book gives an overview of how and when third parties can obtain access to information in the files of the Offices depending on the nature of the information and presented in the order of the stage of the procedure.

Art. 30	Confidential nature of the PCTa, see overview in the Introduction to Art. 22
Art. 38	Confidential nature of the IPE, see overview in the Introduction to Art. 38
R. 48.2(l)	Omission from access

94.1 Access to the File Held by the International Bureau

(a) At the request of the applicant or any person authorized by the applicant, the International Bureau shall furnish, subject to reimbursement of the cost of the service, copies of any document contained in its file.

(b) The International Bureau shall, at the request of any person but not before the international publication of the international application and subject to Article 38 and paragraphs (d) to (g), furnish copies of any document contained in its file. The furnishing of copies may be subject to reimbursement of the cost of the service.

2 Para. (b) is related to the provision of the possibility in R. 9 and R. 48.2 to exclude sensitive personal information from the publication of the application due to lack of overriding public interest and to inform the applicant accordingly (PCT/WG8/12 Nos. 18–21).

3 According to WIPO, the exclusion of file inspection by the International Bureau is directed against anyone, i.e. also against the designated or elected Office. Information excluded in the international phase is not to be indirectly accessible. Divergent national provisions are inferior unless they would be more favorable to the applicant, Art. 27(4). See however annotations to R. 94.1(c) below.

Art. 38 Confidential character of the IPE

(c) The International Bureau shall, if so requested by an elected Office, but not before the international preliminary examination report has been established, furnish on behalf of that Office copies under paragraph (b) of any document transmitted to it under Rule 71.1(a) or (b) by the International Preliminary Examining Authority. The International Bureau shall promptly publish details of any such request in the Gazette.

The wording of para. (c) is somewhat cryptical. 4

- First, the copies are made available to third parties. This means that it is possible to inspect the files.
- Secondly, this concerns both the IPRP I and the IPRP II.
- Thirdly, such a request is made by an elected Office, e.g. the EPO, for all PCTa and not for individual PCTa (see below).
- Fourthly, it does not matter whether the national or regional phase has actually been opened before the Office makes the request (see R. 94.3 with footnote and OJ EPO 2003 p. 382).
- Fifthly, it is made available on the WIPO website (via http://patentscope.wipo.int/search/de/structuredSearch.jsf).

As a result, IPRP I and II are available on the WIPO website, but only after 30 months have elapsed (AG-IP No. 10.080 relating to IPRP II and related documents, AG-IP 7031 relating to IPRP I). The original meaning of Art. 38 is thus largely attenuated. 5

Until June 30, 2020, not all documents of the IPE could be inspected at the International Bureau, for example not all notices of the IPEA as well as statements and replies of the applicant. However, as these also serve the purpose of better understanding the file by the elected Office, since then all documents received have in principle been made available if requested by an elected Office (AG-IP 10.003, 11.074; commentary according to PCT/WG/12/12 p. 2 and Annex I, p. 3) as soon as it is technically possible for the elected Office to send the documents (annotation to R. 71.1(b)). 6

Para. (c) regulates details of the provision of copies to third parties in accordance with para. (b). This is necessary because of the reservation of Art. 38 with regard to files of the IPE. According to Art. 38, however, the reservation does not apply to elected Offices once the IPRP has been prepared (R. 69.2 time limit). Therefore, the requirements are also stated in R. 94.1(c). Art. 38 is interpreted as not being intended to restrict inspection at the International Bureau of documents which are available for inspection at the elected Office under national law (PCT/WG/12/12). The making available at the International Bureau is done on behalf of the elected Office, because Art. 38 allows an exception for the elected Office. 7

The reservation of Art. 38 (no inspection of files) only refers to the procedure under Chapter II. Inspection before the expiry of 30 months of documents drawn up in the Chapter I procedure (WO-ISA R. 44*bis*.1, 94.1) is therefore in line with Art. 38, even 8 if the documents subsequently become part of the Chapter II procedure (www.wipo.int/edocs/mdocs/pct/en/pct_wg_6/pct_wg_6_24.pdf, p. 57, no. 292).

9 Inspection of files at the International Bureau exists independently of the possibility of inspection of files at other Offices, see the overview 'Access to Files' in the Annex.

10 The international preliminary examination report mentioned in the Rule means the IPRP II according to R. 70 (see annotation to R. 70.15).

R. 44*bis*	IPRP I, issuance and transmittal of the report
R. 69.2	Time limit for establishing the IPRP II
R. 71.1	Subject of the access to files regarding the IPE, transmittal of IPRP II by IPEA to the International Bureau
R. 73.2(a)	Transmittal of IPRP II by the International Bureau to the elected Offices after 30 months.
R. 94.3	Access to the file held by the elected Office
Art. 30	Confidential nature of the international application
Art. 30(4)	Definition of the term 'access'
Art. 38	Access under para. (c) shall be possible only upon the request of an elected Office.
	States and organizations which have requested the International Bureau to furnish copies of the IPRP II under R. 94.1(c): AU, AT, BY, EA (EAPO), EE, EG, EP (EPO), GB, GE, IT, JM, JP, LT, MW, MX, NO, SY (see www.wipo.int/pct/en/texts/pdf/access_iper.pdf). The request was made on a general basis in respect of all PCTa. It was made by the EPO in PCT Gazette of January 15, 2004, p. 1742. Request by the EPO in respect of the version of R. 94.1(c) in force since July 1, 2021 see PCT Gazette August 12, 2021. States and organisations requesting the International Bureau to furnish copies of other documents referred to in R. 71.1(b) are: EP (EPO), IT, MX (list dated February 14, 2022)
R. 4.1	Licensing indications are neither part of the PCTa nor of the international publication (PCT Newsletter 12/2011, p. 1). The indication is, however, available as part of the file of the International Bureau under PATENTSCOPE, see above. (For details see AG-IP 11.102.)
AIs 801 et seq.	TPOs are made available. After examination by the International Bureau, the observations are made available without the cited prior art documents but together with any statement by the applicant under PATENTSCOPE, see also AG-IP 11.109 et seq., Euro-PCT Guide E-II. and the table 'Access to Files' in this book.
ePCT	WIPO's electronic file of the PCTa gives only the applicant access to the cited prior art documents
R. 17.1(b-*bis*)	AIs 715, 716, DAS for priority documents only provides access to one's own file or allows Offices to obtain documents from one's own file (OJ EPO 2019 A27). It is therefore not included in the overview of file inspection for third parties.

(d) The International Bureau shall not provide access to any information contained in its file which has been omitted from publication under Rule 48.2(l) *(sensitive personal data)* and to any document contained in its file relating to a request under that Rule

R. 48.2(l)	Decision of International Bureau on non-publication of data in PCTa

(e) Upon a reasoned request by the applicant, the International Bureau shall not provide access to any information contained in its file and to any document contained in its file relating to such a request, if it finds that:

(i) this information does not obviously serve the purpose of informing the public about the international application;

(ii) public access to such information would clearly prejudice the personal or economic interests of any person; and

(iii) there is no prevailing public interest to have access to that information.

Rule 26.4 shall apply *mutatis mutandis* as to the manner in which the applicant shall present the information which is the subject of a request made under this paragraph.

The private or professional address indicated for the inventor is visible in PATENT-SCOPE. The change of address under R. 92*bis* is also visible, but in non-searchable image format. Since the conditions for exclusion from inspection of files under R. 94.1(e) are strict, it is advisable to check whether and when the information is required at the respective Office (Annex B AG-IP) and which address is indicated before mentioning the inventor and private address (PCT Newsletter 10/2020 p. 14). 11

R. 48.2(l)	Decision of International Bureau on non-publication of data in PCTa
R. 26.4	Formal requirements for the correction of the request offered to the receiving Office
AIs 218	Processing of a request for omission of information from public availability referred to in R. 48.2(l) and R. 94.1(e)

(f) Where the International Bureau has omitted information from public access in accordance with paragraphs (d) or (e), and that information is also contained in the file of the international application held by the receiving Office, the International Searching Authority, the Authority specified for supplementary search or the International Preliminary Examining Authority, the International Bureau shall promptly notify that Office and Authority accordingly.

(g) The International Bureau shall not provide access to any document contained in its file which was prepared solely for internal use by the International Bureau.

94.1*bis* Access to the File Held by the Receiving Office

(a) At the request of the applicant or any person authorized by the applicant, the receiving Office may provide access to any document contained in its file. The furnishing of copies of documents may be subject to reimbursement of the cost of the service.

(b) The receiving Office may, at the request of any person, but not before the international publication of the international application and subject to paragraph (c), provide access to any document contained in its file. The furnishing of copies of documents may be subject to reimbursement of the cost of the service.

(c) The receiving Office shall not provide access under paragraph (b) to any information in respect of which it has been notified by the International Bureau that the information has been omitted from publication in accordance with Rule 48.2(l) *(sensitive personal data)* or from public access in accordance with Rule 94.1(d) or (e) *(sensitive personal data)*.

12 File access in the international phase by authorities in their capacity as International Authorities is governed by the PCT and not by national law. National rules may be applied in addition to fill gaps or if application is expressly provided for in the PCT Rule.

Art. 30(2)(a), (3)	Earliest date for file access at the national Office and the receiving Office
R. 23*bis*.2(a)	Transmittal of documents pertaining to an earlier search or classification for the purposes of R. 41.2
R. 48.2(l)	Decision by International Bureau on non-publication of data in PCTa
EPO	Free online file access to PCT files via the European Patent Register as per OJ EPO 2019 A17, OJ EPO 2019 A16.
Art. 150 EPC	Principle priority of the PCT and the Regulations in case of lack of conformity with the EPC; supplementary application of the EPC
Art. 128(4), R. 144 EPC	Exclusion from the access to the file
Art. 27(4)	Exception for more favorable rules

94.1*ter* Access to the File Held by the International Searching Authority

(a) At the request of the applicant or any person authorized by the applicant, the International Searching Authority may provide access to any document contained in its file. The furnishing of copies of documents may be subject to reimbursement of the cost of the service.

(b) The International Searching Authority may, at the request of any person, but not before the international publication of the international application and subject to paragraph (c), provide access to any document contained in its file. The furnishing of copies of documents may be subject to reimbursement of the cost of the service.

(c) The International Searching Authority shall not provide access under paragraph (b) to any information in respect of which it has been notified by the International Bureau that the information has been omitted from publication in accordance with Rule 48.2(l) *(sensitive personal data)* or from public access in accordance with Rule 94.1(d) or (e).

(d) Paragraphs (a) to (c) *(sensitive personal data)* shall apply *mutatis mutandis* to the Authority specified for supplementary search.

R. 45*bis*.9	Competent SISA

The provisions for the ISA correspond to those for the SISA and the receiving Office. 13
See also the annotations to R. 94.1*bis*.

EPO	Free online file access to PCT files via the European Patent Register as per OJ EPO 2015 A15, OJ EPO 2019 A17.

94.2 Access to the File Held by the International Preliminary Examining Authority

(a) At the request of the applicant or any person authorized by the applicant, the International Preliminary Examining Authority shall provide access to any document contained in its file. The furnishing of copies of documents may be subject to reimbursement of the cost of the service.

(b) At the request of any elected Office, but not before the establishment of the international preliminary examination report and subject to paragraph (c), the International Preliminary Examining Authority shall provide access to any document contained in its file. The furnishing of copies of documents may be subject to reimbursement of the cost of the service.

The requests of an elected Office are made for all PCTa at once, not for individual 14
PCTa. See annotation to R. 94.1(c).

(c) The International Preliminary Examining Authority shall not provide access under paragraph (b) to any information in respect of which it has been notified by the International Bureau that the information has been omitted from publication in accordance with Rule 48.2(l) *(sensitive personal data)* or from public access in accordance with Rule 94.1(d) or (e) *(sensitive personal data)*.

The exceptions to file access correspond to those for the ISA or the receiving Office, 15
see annotations to R. 94.1*bis*.

94.2*bis* Access to the File Held by the Designated Office

If the national law applicable by any designated Office allows access by third parties to the file of a national application, that Office may allow access to any documents relating to the international application, contained in its file, to the

same extent as provided by the national law for access to the file of a national application, but not before the earliest of the dates specified in Article 30(2)(a) *(international publication)*. The furnishing of copies of documents may be subject to reimbursement of the cost of the service.

16 Information excluded in the international phase shall not be indirectly accessible. Divergent national provisions are inferior unless they would be more favorable to the applicant, Art. 27(4). See, however, the annotations to R. 94.1(c).

Art. 30(2)(a)	National Office – i.e. in the sense of Art. 2 xii) et seq. – gives access at the earliest after international publication or receipt of the PCTa as designated Office under Art. 22
Art. 38	Confidential nature of the IPE
R. 17.2(b) and (c)	Restrictions on the publication of priority documents
R. 61.4	The demand for international examination is published
Art. 3(1) RFees No. 2.1.14;	Abolition of administrative fee for copies for granting file access in connection with online file access (OJ EPO 2019 A15).
Art. 128(4), R. 145 EPC	For access to the EPO file, see GL Exam E-IX, 2.10 and annotation to R. 94.3.

94.3 Access to the File Held by the Elected Office

If the national law applicable by any elected Office allows access by third parties to the file of a national application, that Office may allow access to any documents relating to the international application, including any document relating to the international preliminary examination, contained in its file, to the same extent as provided by the national law for access to the file of a national application, but not before the earliest of the dates specified in Article 30(2)(a) *(international publication)*. The furnishing of copies of documents may be subject to reimbursement of the cost of the service.

17 Information excluded in the international phase shall not be indirectly accessible. Divergent national provisions are inferior unless they would be more favorable to the applicant, Art. 27(4).

Art. 30(2)(a)	National Office allows access at the earliest after international publication or receipt of the PCTa as designated Office under Art. 22.
GL Exam E-IX, 2.10 OJ EPO 1999 p. 329	Pursuant to Art. 128(4) EPC, R. 145(2) EPC, the EPO allows file access for applications filed since July 1, 1998, provided international publication has taken place, and for documents relating to Chapter II, provided the IPER has been established and the documents are not clearly intended for internal use. The former requirement that the applicant must have performed at least one

act under R. 159 EPC has been dropped since February 1, 2003 (OJ EPO 2003 p. 382). As of April 1, 2019, access is in principle only provided online and free of charge via the European Patent Register, and only exceptionally upon reasoned request by production of paper copies, OJ EPO 2019 A15, OJ EPO 2019 A16, OJ EPO 2019 A17. Documents may be inspected via MyEPO Portfolio (OJ EPO 2023 A89 replaced by OJ EPO 2024 A21). See also overview on 'Access to Files' in the Annex to this book.

Rule 95
Information and Translations from Designated and Elected Offices

95.1 Information Concerning Events at the Designated and Elected Offices

Any designated or elected Office shall notify the International Bureau of the following information concerning an international application within two months, or as soon as reasonably possible thereafter, of the occurrence of any of the following events:

(i) following the performance by the applicant of the acts referred to in Article 22 or Article 39, the date of performance of those acts and any national application number which has been assigned to the international application;

(ii) where the designated or elected Office explicitly publishes the international application under its national law or practice, the number and date of that national publication;

(iii) where a patent is granted, the date of grant of the patent and, where the designated or elected Office explicitly publishes the international application in the form in which it is granted under its national law, the number and date of that national publication.

1 Designated and elected Offices must notify the International Bureau of the entry of a PCTa into the national/regional phase.

2 The Assembly decided the following: 'In adopting the amendments to Rule 86.1(iv), the Assembly noted that the information concerning national phase entry will be made available to the public not only by way of inclusion in the Gazette on the PATENTSCOPE website but also as part of the bulk PCT bibliographic data offered to Offices and other subscribers to the PATENTSCOPE subscription data services.' (PCT/A/47/9).

95.2 Furnishing of Copies of Translations

(a) At the request of the International Bureau, any designated or elected Office shall provide it with a copy of the translation of the international application furnished by the applicant to that Office.

(b) The International Bureau may, upon request and subject to reimbursement of the cost, furnish to any person copies of the translations received under paragraph (a).

Art. 22	Copy, translation, and fee to designated Offices
Art. 39	Copy, translation, and fee to elected Offices
R. 12.3	Translation for the purposes of international search
R. 12.4	Translation for the purposes of international translation
R. 23	Transmittal of the search copy, translation, and sequence listings
R. 23*bis*	Transmittal of documents relating to earlier search or classification
R. 55.2	Translation of international application
R. 86.1(iv)	Content of the publication in the Gazette regarding national phase
Art. 153(3)-(5) EPC	Publication of the international application and its transmittal to the EPO as designated or elected Office

Rule 96
The Schedule of Fees; Receipt and Transfer of Fees

INTRODUCTION

1 The Schedule of Fees establishes only fees for the benefit of the International Bureau. The amount of the fees is fixed by the International Bureau. Fees for the benefit of other Offices are fixed by the Offices and can be found in the AG-IP Annexes.

2 Some of the fees are for the benefit of the International Bureau but are collected by another Office. According to R. 15 the international filing fee is for the benefit of the International Bureau and has to be paid to the receiving Office. According to R. 57 the handling fee for IPE is for the benefit for the International Bureau but has to be paid to the IPEA.

3 Offices allow payments in various currencies (AG-IP Annexes). As the fees in the schedule of fee are fixed by the International Bureau in Swiss currency, the equivalent amounts in various currencies of the Offices apply (https://www.wipo.int/pct/en/fees/equivalent_amounts.html). They have been established in accordance with the directives adopted by the PCT Assembly (PCT Gazette July 1, 2010) and are amended on a yearly basis due to changes in the exchange rates. The amounts are published in the Gazette (November 9, 2023).

4 The Schedule of Fees contains also fees that have to be paid to the International Bureau directly (R. 45*bis*.2 supplementary search handling fee).

5 Fees that have to be paid to the International Bureau which are not mentioned in the Schedule of Fees but in the Rules are established in R. 48.4(a), R. 26*bis*.2(e), R. 91.3d and the AIs. The International Bureau is also collecting fees for other Offices (R. 45*bis*.3 supplementary search fee for the benefit of the ISA collected by the International Bureau). Note that the International Bureau may also act as receiving Office (R. 14 transmittal fee, R. 15 international filing fee).

6 For general aspects of fees see annotations to Art. 3, Introduction No. 4.

96.1 Schedule of Fees Annexed to Regulations

The amounts of the fees referred to in Rules 15, 45*bis*.2 and 57 shall be expressed in Swiss currency. They shall be specified in the Schedule of Fees which is annexed to these Regulations and forms an integral part thereof.

R. 15	International filing fee for the benefit of the International Bureau has to be paid to the receiving Office
R. 45*bis*.2	Supplementary search handling fee for the benefit of the International Bureau has to be paid to the International Bureau
R. 57	Handling fee for IPE is for the benefit of the International Bureau and has to be paid to the IPEA
EPO	For the specification of the equivalent amounts in relation to the EPO with effect from January 1, 2024, see PCT Gazette November 9, 2023, OJ EPO 2023 A112 (prior: A2023 A11, 2022 A65, https://www.wipo.int/export/sites/www/pct/en/fees.pdf). Currently, fees can be paid via MyEPO Portfolio, central fee payment, online filing (OLF) or online filing 2.0 (OJ EPO 2023 A50 p. 5; unaffected by new features OJ EPO 2024 A21 point 4).

96.2 Notification of Receipt of Fees; Transfer of Fees

(a) For the purposes of this Rule, "Office" shall mean the receiving Office (including the International Bureau acting as receiving Office), the International Searching Authority, an Authority specified for supplementary international search, the International Preliminary Examining Authority or the International Bureau.

(b) Where, in accordance with these Regulations or the Administrative Instructions, a fee is collected by one Office ("collecting Office") for the benefit of another Office ("beneficiary Office"), the collecting Office shall promptly notify the receipt of each such fee in accordance with the Administrative Instructions. Upon receipt of the notification, the beneficiary Office shall proceed as if it had received the fee on the date on which the fee was received by the collecting Office.

(c) The collecting Office shall transfer any fees collected for the benefit of a beneficiary Office to that Office in accordance with the Administrative Instructions.

R. 96.2	aims to simplify procedures and save costs in the transfer and settlement of payments between different Offices without the Offices being obliged to participate (PCT/WG/12/20). Accordingly, in R. 15.2, 16.1, 57.2, 45*bis*.3 in connection with 16.1, reference is made to R. 96.2. The purpose of the Rule is to ensure that the beneficiary Office does not wait until it receives the fee before taking procedural action, but acts as soon as it is informed of the receipt of payment by the collecting Office. The Rule does not apply to an Office

	which collects fees for its own benefit, whether it acts in the same or other capacities (Comments Nos. 1–3 according to PCT/WG/12/20 Annex I, p. 9–10).
AIs 114	Transfer of fees in accordance with Annex G of the AIs

Schedule of Fees

Fees	Amounts
1. International filing fee (Rule 15.2):	1,330 Swiss francs plus 15 Swiss francs for each sheet of the international application in excess of 30 sheets
2. Supplementary search handling fee (Rule 45*bis*.2):	200 Swiss francs
3. Handling fee (Rule 57.2) *(for IPE)*:	200 Swiss francs

Reductions

4. The international filing fee is reduced by the following amount if the international application is, as provided for in the Administrative Instructions, filed:

(a) in electronic form, the request not being in character coded format: 100 Swiss francs

Only No. 4(a) covered filing with WIPO by the backup solution ePCT Business Continuity Service where data are packaged in exactly the same format as ePCT Filing (PCT Newsletter 10/2023 p. 2). See No. 4(b) and 4(c)) and the Introduction to Part F of the Regulations. 1

(b) in electronic form, the request *(but not the text of the description, claims or abstract)* being in character coded format: 200 Swiss francs

No. 4(b) covers the PDF format, which is possible at the EPO for OLF, CMS (until December 31, 2021), web-form filing, online filing 2.0, EPO Contingency Upload Service (OJ EPO 2023 A48 Art. 10) and also for ePCT (Gazette May 8, 2014, p. 67, https://www.wipo.int/pct/en/faqs/epct-continuity-service-faq.html, https://link.epo.org/web/EPO_online_filing_options_comparison_table_en.pdf). See the Introduction to Part F of the Regulations. 2

(c) in electronic form, the request, description, claims and abstract being in character coded format: 300 Swiss francs

3 No. 4(c) applies to the XML format. This is not possible at the EPO for web-form filing, but is possible for OLF, CMS (until December 31, 2021), online filing 2.0 and ePCT (https://www.wipo.int/pct/en/faqs/epct-continuity-service-faq.html). See www.epo.org/applying/online-services/online-filing/features_de.html in conjunction with the summary table http://documents.epo.org/projects/babylon/eponet.nsf/0/CDC4538605037FD4C1257D9B00344B6E/$File/EPO_online_filing_options_comparison_table_en.pdf and the annotations to Part F of the Regulations.

4 The fees mentioned here are for the benefit of the International Bureau. Some of these fees (R. 15.3, R. 57.1) are not payable to the International Bureau but collected by another Office.

5 The DPMAdirektpro software allows fee reduction under Nos. 4(b) and (c) (see https://www.dpma.de/english/services/fees/patents/index.html, https://www.dpma.de/docs/english/broschueren_eng/dpmadirekt_engl.pdf).

5. The international filing fee under item 1 (where applicable, as reduced under item 4), the supplementary search handling fee under item 2 and the handling fee under item 3 are reduced by 90% if the international application is filed by:

(a) an applicant who is a natural person and who is a national of and resides in a State that is listed as being a State whose per capita gross domestic product is below US$ 25,000 (according to the most recent 10-year average per capita gross domestic product figures at constant 2005 US$ values published by the United Nations), and whose nationals and residents who are natural persons have filed less than 10 international applications per year (per million population) or less than 50 international applications per year (in absolute numbers) according to the most recent five-year average yearly filing figures published by the International Bureau; or

(b) an applicant, whether a natural person or not, who is a national of and resides in a State that is listed as being classified by the United Nations as a least developed country;

provided that, at the time of filing of the international application, there are no beneficial owners of the international application who would not satisfy the criteria in sub-item (a) or (b) and provided that, if there are several applicants, each must satisfy the criteria set out in either sub-item (a) or (b). The lists of States referred to in sub-items (a) and (b) shall be updated by the Director General at least every five years according to directives given by the Assembly. The criteria set out in sub-items (a) and (b) shall be reviewed by the Assembly at least every five years.

6 There are two reasons for reduction, the electronic form of filing (under No. 4) and the nationality or residence of the applicant (under No. 5). According to the wording they can be combined. For further possibilities of fee reductions see the Annexes of the AG-IP.

7 The list of States whose residents and nationals are entitled to fee reductions can be found in the Annex 'Fee reduction' in this book and under https://www.wipo.

int/export/sites/www/pct/en/docs/fee-reduction-january.pdf. In the case of the reduction in the international filing fee, this list applies to international applications received by the receiving Office on or after January 1, 2020. In the case of reductions in the supplementary search handling fee and the handling fee, this list applies to international applications in respect of which the respective fee is paid on or after January 1, 2020 (https://www.wipo.int/export/sites/www/pct/en/docs/fee-reduction-january.pdf footnote 2). For future updates see the Annex 'Fee reduction'.

If there are several applicants, each applicant must satisfy the criteria (this is the 8 reason why also Non-Contracting States are listed in the above-referenced tables) and at least one of them must be a national of and/or reside in a PCT Contracting State (https://www.wipo.int/export/sites/www/pct/en/docs/fee-reduction-january.pdf footnote 3).

The PCT Assembly adopted an Understanding, with effect from 11 October 2017, 9 which clarifies that the reduction in the fees (...) is intended to apply only in the case where the applicants indicated in the request are the sole and true owners of the application and under no obligation to assign, grant, convey or license the rights in the invention to another party which is not eligible for the fee reduction. (https://www.wipo.int/export/sites/www/pct/en/docs/fee-reduction-january.pdf footnote 4). On the significance of resolutions of the assembly on interpretation, see annotation to Art. 58.

Applicants from non PCT Contracting States must file the PCT application together 10 with an applicant who is a national of and/or resident in a PCT Contracting State, and in order to benefit from the 90% reduction, the Contracting State concerned must be a PCT Contracting State indicated in the list (https://www.wipo.int/export/sites/www/pct/en/docs/fee-reduction-january.pdf footnote 6)

The Editor's Note (WIPO) to the legal text 'See Gazettes dated February 12, 2015, p. 32 11 and March 5, 2020, p. 45 et seq. (available at: www.wipo.int/pct/en/official_notices/index.html).' refers to the publication of the applicable list of States mentioned in subitems (a) and (b).

Fee Reduction According to the Schedule of Fees

The list below refers to the reduction in certain PCT Fees according to No. 5 of the 1
Schedule of Fees which is part of the Regulations. These fees are reduced by 90% for nationals and residents of Contracting and non-Contracting States with a low per capita gross domestic product or which are classified by the United Nations as among the least developed countries. For details see notes to the Schedule of Fees. The information contained in the list below originates from the WIPO website as retrieved on January 4, 2024 (https://www.wipo.int/export/sites/www/pct/en/docs/fee-reduction-january.pdf). It is applicable on or after January 1, 2020. The fee reduction is reviewed every five years.

Updated List

An updated list will enter into force on January 1, 2025, the criteria for the reductions 2
remain unchanged (PCT/A/56/1) – https://www.wipo.int/export/sites/www/pct/en/docs/fee-reduction-2025.pdf. The proposed updates of the list of States according to PCT/WG/17/5 Rev. p. 4 No. 14 are that:

> '(a) nationals and residents of Bahamas and Kuwait will become eligible for the reduction under item 5(a);
>
> (b) nationals and residents, whether natural persons or not, of Vanuatu and Bhutan will cease to be eligible for the reduction under item 5(b), but nationals and residents of those States who are natural persons will continue to be eligible for the reduction under item 5(a).'

Applicability of 90% Reduction in Certain PCT Fees[1] (applicable on or after January 1, 2020[2])

1. Where the international application is filed by an applicant[3, 4] who is a natural person and who is a national of and resides in one of the following States:[5]

(a) States which are PCT Contracting States:

Albania
Algeria
Angola
Antigua and Barbuda
Armenia
Azerbaijan
Bahrain
Barbados
Belarus
Belize
Benin

Bosnia and Herzegovina
Botswana
Brazil
Bulgaria
Burkina Faso
Cabo Verde
Cambodia
Cameroon
Central African Republic
Chad
Chile
China
Colombia
Comoros
Congo
Costa Rica
Côte d'Ivoire
Croatia
Cuba
Czechia
Democratic People's Republic of Korea
Djibouti
Dominica
Dominican Republic
Ecuador
Egypt
El Salvador
Equatorial Guinea
Estonia
Eswatini
Gabon
Gambia
Georgia
Ghana
Greece
Grenada
Guatemala
Guinea
Guinea-Bissau
Honduras
Hungary
India
Indonesia
Iran (Islamic Republic of)
Iraq
Jamaica
Jordan
Kazakhstan
Kenya
Kyrgyzstan
Lao People's Democratic Republic
Latvia
Lesotho
Liberia
Libya
Lithuania
Madagascar
Malawi
Malaysia
Mali
Malta
Mauritania
Mauritius
Mexico
Mongolia
Montenegro
Morocco
Mozambique
Namibia
Nicaragua
Niger
Nigeria
North Macedonia
Oman
Panama
Papua New Guinea
Peru
Philippines
Poland
Portugal
Republic of Moldova
Romania
Russian Federation
Rwanda
Saint Kitts and Nevis
Saint Lucia
Saint Vincent and the Grenadines
Samoa
Sao Tome and Principe
Saudi Arabia
Senegal
Serbia
Seychelles
Sierra Leone
Slovakia
Slovenia
South Africa
Sri Lanka
Sudan
Syrian Arab Republic
Tajikistan
Thailand
Togo
Trinidad and Tobago
Tunisia
Turkey
Turkmenistan
Uganda
Ukraine
United Republic of Tanzania
Uzbekistan
Viet Nam
Zambia
Zimbabwe

(b) States which are not PCT Contracting States:[6]

Afghanistan
Argentina
Bangladesh
Bhutan
Bolivia (Plurinational State of)
Burundi
Democratic Republic of the Congo
Eritrea
Ethiopia
Fiji
Guyana
Haiti
Kiribati
Lebanon
Maldives
Marshall Islands
Micronesia (Federated States of)
Myanmar
Nauru
Nepal
Pakistan
Palau
Paraguay
Solomon Islands
Somalia
South Sudan
Suriname
Timor-Leste
Tonga
Tuvalu
Uruguay
Vanuatu
Venezuela (Bolivarian Republic of)
Yemen

2. Where the international application is filed by an applicant[3, 4], whether a natural person or not, who is a national of and resides in one of the following States that is listed as being classified by the United Nations as a least developed country:

(a) States which are PCT Contracting States:

Angola
Benin
Burkina Faso
Cambodia
Central African Republic
Chad
Comoros
Djibouti
Gambia
Guinea
Guinea-Bissau
Lao People's Democratic Republic
Lesotho
Liberia
Madagascar
Malawi
Mali
Mauritania
Mozambique
Niger
Rwanda
Sao Tome and Principe
Senegal
Sierra Leone
Sudan
Togo
Uganda
United Republic of Tanzania
Zambia

(b) States which are not PCT Contracting States:[6]

Afghanistan
Bangladesh
Bhutan
Burundi
Democratic Republic of the Congo
Eritrea
Ethiopia
Haiti
Kiribati
Myanmar
Nepal
Solomon Islands
Somalia
South Sudan
Timor-Leste
Tuvalu
Vanuatu
Yemen

Notes

1: The international filing fee (including the fee per sheet over 30), the supplementary search handling fee and the handling fee.

2: In the case of the reduction in the international filing fee, this list applies to international applications received by the receiving Office on or after January 1, 2020; in the case of reductions in the supplementary search handling fee and the handling fee, this list applies to international applications in respect of which the respective fee is paid on or after January 1, 2020.

3: If there are several applicants, each must satisfy the criteria set out in parts 1 or 2 of the list, and at least one of them must be a national of and/or reside in a PCT Contracting State.

4: The PCT Assembly adopted an Understanding, with effect from October 11, 2017, which clarifies that the reduction in the fees mentioned in footnote 1 is intended to apply only in the case where the applicants indicated in the request are the sole and true owners of the application and under no obligation to assign, grant, convey or license the rights in the invention to another party which is not eligible for the fee reduction.

5: That is, States whose per capita gross domestic product is below US$ 25,000 (according to the most recent 10-year average per capita gross domestic product figures at constant 2005 US$ values published by the United Nations), and whose nationals and residents who are natural persons have filed less than 10 international applications per year (per million population) or less than 50 international applications per year (in absolute numbers) according to the most recent five-year average yearly filing figures published by the International Bureau.

6: Applicants from these States must file the PCT application together with an applicant who is a national of and/or resides in a PCT Contracting State, and in order to benefit from the 90% reduction, the State concerned must be one of the States indicated under 1(a) (if the applicant concerned is a natural person) or 2(a) (whether the applicant is a natural person or not).

Annex 1
List of Territories

The purpose of the List of Territories is to provide pieces of information about the territories of States and the membership of States to international patent treaties. It is also a particular purpose of this table to provide information about how to achieve patent protection in territories where the applicable law is not easily determined. Such territories may be overseas territories of some States, islands associated to some States, areas contested between different States, and the like. 1

The below table shows the various patent treaties applicable in a certain territory (status on August 22, 2024). 2

The columns of the table show the following information: 3

Territory	Most territories are independent States, some territories are dependent on another territory as shown in the column 'Relation'. A territory with a special status or in a special geographical situation is mentioned separately if it is mentioned separately in documents referring to the application of treaties or if the territory or its relation to a State may not be clear. No entry in the column means that there is no information or that a treaty does not apply. If a territory is party to a treaty there is a √ in the column. If a treaty is extended to a dependent territory, the Country Code of the sovereign territory or detailed information is given in the column 'Note'. Information on territories of the PCT Contracting States can be found in the Notifications[1] on the WIPO website, referring to WIPO-Administered Treaties.
Code	Two-letter Country Code according to the WIPO Standard ST.3[2] aligned with ISO 3166-1.[3]
Relation	The laws or treaties of the territory mentioned in this column apply in the territory mentioned in the first column, where a re-registration, extension or mutual recognition of a patent may apply.

1. https://www.wipo.int/treaties/en/SearchForm.jsp?search_what=N
2. https://www.wipo.int/standards/en/pdf/03-03-01.pdf; https://www.wipo.int/pct/en/texts/ai/s115.html
3. Code for subdivisions according to ISO 3166-2 https://en.wikipedia.org/wiki/ISO_3166-2

PCT	Indicates whether the State is a PCT Contracting State.[4] For the applicability of the PCT to the territories of EPC Contracting States see OJ EPO 2014 A33.
Paris	Indicates whether the State is party to the Paris Convention. Territorial information, especially for CN, DK, FI, GB, FR, NL, NO, NZ and US, is given in the column 'Details' of the table WIPO-Administered Treaties[5] on the WIPO website.
WTO	Indicates whether the State is member of the WTO.[6]
Region	The regional patent treaty to which the State in the first column is party. The abbreviations are given in the next paragraph. If a regional patent treaty is mentioned in the column 'Region', a regional patent can be obtained in addition to or instead of a national patent via PCT in case of membership to the PCT (see Introduction to the PCT No. 4). For territories without full sovereignty, information is given in the column 'Note'. Regional patent treaties: ARIPO: African Regional Intellectual Property Organization (AP) EAPO: Eurasian Patent Office (EA) EPO: European Patent Office (EP) GCC: Gulf Cooperation Council (GCC)[7] is not party to the PCT (not a regional patent treaty in the sense of Art. 45 PCT) OAPI: Organisation africaine de la propriété intellectuelle (OA)
Note	This column lists the following information: – whether only a regional patent can be obtained via PCT;[8] – validation and extension States to which the validity of a European patent can be extended;[9] see; – whether the EPC applies to a special territory of a Contracting State according to OJ EPO 2024 A53, § II.1, footnotes and National Law relating to the EPC, Table X, column 2;[10]

4. https://www.wipo.int/pct/en/pct_contracting_states.html
5. https://www.wipo.int/treaties/en/ShowResults.jsp?lang=en&treaty_id=2
6. https://www.wipo.int/export/sites/www/pct/en/texts/pdf/pct_paris_wto.pdf and new accessions: https://www.wto.org/english/thewto_e/acc_e/completeacc_e.htm
7. GCC has stopped accepting new patent applications as from January 2021; see https://gccpo.org/AboutUsEn/ShowNews?id=66; https://www.murgitroyd.com/resources/legal-updates/gulf-cooperation-council-gcc-patent-office-ceases-accepting-new-patent-filings/
8. https://www.wipo.int/pct/en/texts/reg_des.html and for EPC Contracting States see https://www.epo.org/about-us/foundation/member-states/date.html
9. https://www.epo.org/en/legal/extension-validation-system
10. https://www.epo.org/en/legal/national-law/archive

- status as a member of the Commonwealth of Nations (CON) or as British Overseas Territory (BOT) is only mentioned if information about extension of GB or EP-GB patents is available.[11] The Outermost Regions (OMR) form part of the EU, the Overseas Countries and Territories of the European Union (OCT) do not form part of the EU.[12]

Territory	Code	Relation	PCT	Paris	WTO	Region	Note
Afghanistan	AF			√	√		
Åland Islands	AX	FI	FI				PCT-EP[13]
Albania	AL		√	√	√	EP	
Algeria	DZ		√	√			
American Samoa	AS	US	US	US			
American Virgin Islands	VI	US	US	US			
Andorra	AD			√			
Angola	AO		√	√	√		
Anguilla	AI	GB					BOT, GB or EP-GB re-registration within 3 years
Antigua and Barbuda	AG		√	√	√		
Argentina	AR			√	√		
Armenia	AM		√	√	√	EA	
Aruba	AW	NL	NL	NL			Not EP, PCT-EP or PCT-NL. Not covered by NL nat. patent.[14] Legal entities constituted in AW are not nationals of NL and cannot select EPO as receiving Office (OJ EPO 2014 A33)

11. https://www.gov.uk/government/publications/extension-of-uk-intellectual-property-rights-abroad; https://en.wikipedia.org/wiki/Member_states_of_the_Commonwealth_of_Nations#Current_members; http://www.commonwealthofnations.org/commonwealth/commonwealth-membership/withdrawals-and-suspension/; http://www.commonwealthofnations.org/commonwealth/commonwealth-membership/associated-and-overseas-territories/
12. https://en.wikipedia.org/wiki/Special_member_state_territories_and_the_European_Union
13. AX Territory of FI: OJ EPO 2014 A33. https://www.epo.org/law-practice/legal-texts/html/natlaw/en/x/fi.htm
14. http://www.opi-aruba.org/Answer.htm#P1; https://www.doingbusinessdutchcaribbean.com/aruba/intellectual-property/patents/

Territory	Code	Relation	PCT	Paris	WTO	Region	Note
Ashmore and Cartier Island	AU						
Australia	AU		√	√	√		Islands, part of AU: Lord-Howe, Macquarie, Torres-Strait[15]
Austria	AT		√	√	√	EP	
Azerbaijan	AZ		√	√		EA	
Bahamas	BS			√			
Bahrain	BH		√	√	√	GCC	
Baker Island	UM	US	US	US			
Bangladesh	BD			√	√		
Barbados	BB		√	√	√		
Belarus	BY		√	√		EA	
Belgium	BE		√	√	√	EP	PCT-EP. Not PCT-BE.
Belize	BZ	GB	√	√	√		CON.
Benin	BJ		√	√	√	OA	PCT-OA. Not PCT-BJ.
Bermuda	BM	GB					BOT. GB or EP-GB re-registration within 3 years
Bhutan	BT			√			
Bolivia	BO			√	√		
Bonaire, Sint Eustatius and Saba	BQ	NL	NL	NL			Part of NL in Europe. PCT-EP, Not PCT-NL. NL nat. patent[16]
Bosnia and Herzegovina	BA		√	√			EP extension
Botswana	BW		√	√	√	AP	
Bouvet Island	BV	NO	NO				PCT-EP[17]
Brazil	BR		√	√	√		

15. https://www.regional.gov.au/territories/ and https://www.iso.org/obp/ui/#iso:code:3166:AU
16. https://www.doingbusinessdutchcaribbean.com/bonaire/intellectual-property-bon/patents-bon/, third paragraph
17. BV territory of NO: OJ 2014, A33. https://www.epo.org/law-practice/legal-texts/html/natlaw/en/x/no.htm?sm=c

Territory	Code	Relation	PCT	Paris	WTO	Region	Note
British Indian Ocean Territory (Chargos Archipel/Diego Garcia)	IO	GB					Not mentioned in territory list OJ EPO 2014 A33 but GB or EP-GB[18]
British Virgin Islands	VG	GB					BOT. GB or EP-GB re-registration within 3 years
Brunei Darussalam	BN	GB	√	√	√		CON. GB or EP-GB re-registration prior to 2012.
Bulgaria	BG		√	√	√	EP	
Burkina Faso	BF		√	√	√	OA	PCT-OA; not PCT-BF
Burundi	BI			√	√		
Cabo Verde, Republic of	CV		√	√	√	AP	
Cambodia	KH		√	√	√		EP validation
Cameroon	CM		√	√	√	OA	PCT-OA; Not PCT-CM
Canada	CA		√	√	√		
Cayman Islands	KY	GB					BOT. GB or from jurisdictions in the EU
Central African Republic	CF		√	√	√	OA	PCT-OA. Not PCT-CF.
Chad	TD		√	√	√	OA	PCT-OA. Not PCT-TD.
Chile	CL		√	√	√		
China	CN		√	√	√		See also HK and MO
Christmas Island	CX	AU					
Clipperton Island	CP	FR					State property under direct authority of FR government
Cocos (Keeling) Islands	CC	AU					
Colombia	CO		√	√	√		
Comoros	KM		√	√	√	OA	PCT-OA. Not PCT-KM.

18. https://www.gov.uk/government/publications/extension-of-uk-intellectual-property-rights-abroad/extension-of-uk-ip-right-abroad-countries-a-to-b#british-indian-ocean-territory

Territory	Code	Relation	PCT	Paris	WTO	Region	Note
Congo, Republic	CG		√	√	√	OA	PCT-OA. Not PCT-CG.
Congo, the Democratic Republic of the (former Zaire)	CD			√	√		
Cook Islands	CK	NZ					NZ associated.[19] Extension of NZ patents granted until 12.9. 2014[20]
Coral Sea Islands	AU						
Costa Rica	CR		√	√	√		
Cote d'Ivoire	CI		√	√	√	OA	PCT-OA. Not PCT-CI.
Croatia	HR		√	√	√	EP	
Cuba	CU		√	√	√		
Curaçao	CW	NL	NL	NL			NL nat. patent.[21] PCT-EP, not PCT-NL
Cyprus	CY		√	√	√	EP	Not including: Akrotiri and Dhekelia (GB). Turkish Republic of Northern Cyprus is de facto TR.[22] CY: PCT-EP, not PCT-CY.
Czech Republic	CZ		√	√	√	EP	
Denmark	DK		√	√	√	EP	See also FO, GL
Djibouti	DJ		√	√	√		
Dominica	DM		√	√	√		
Dominican Republic	DO		√	√	√		
East Timor	TL						
Ecuador	EC		√	√	√		
Egypt	EG		√	√	√		
El Salvador	SV		√	√	√		

19. https://en.wikipedia.org/wiki/Political_status_of_the_Cook_Islands_and_Niue
20. Under the NZ Patent Act 1953 according to information from NZ IP-Office upon request in 2017, Cook Islands Act 1915 http://www.paclii.org/journals/fJSPL/vol07no1/8.shtml
21. https://www.doingbusinessdutchcaribbean.com/curacao/intellectual-property-cur/patents-cur/
22. https://en.wikipedia.org/wiki/Northern_Cyprus

Territory	Code	Relation	PCT	Paris	WTO	Region	Note
Equatorial Guinea	GQ		√	√		OA	PCT-OA. Not PCT-GQ.
Eritrea	ER						
Estonia	EE		√	√	√	EP	
Eswatini (Former Swaziland)	SZ		√	√	√	AP	PCT-AP. Not PCT-SZ.
Ethiopia	ET						
Falkland Islands (Malvinas)	FK	GB					BOT. GB or EP-GB re-registration within 3 years
Faroe Islands	FO	DK	DK	DK			Not EPC.[23] DK nat. or PCT-DK. Not EP or PCT-EP.
Fiji	FJ	GB		√	√		CON, GB or EP-GB re-registration within 3 years
Finland	FI		√	√	√	EP	See also Åland Islands
France[24]	FR		√	√	√	EP	PCT-EP. Not PCT-FR. See also BL, GF, GP, MF, MQ, NC, PF, PM, RE, TF, WF, YT
French Guiana	GF	FR	FR	FR			PCT-EP. OMR
French Polynesia	PF	FR	FR	FR			PCT-EP. OCT, extension of FR patents
French Southern and Antarctic Territories	TF	FR	FR	FR			PCT-EP. OCT, partly administered by FR-RE, partly not int. recognised
Gabon	GA		√	√	√	OA	CON. PCT-OA. Not PCT-GA.
Gambia	GM	GB	√	√	√	AP	CON. GB or EP-GB re-registration within 3 years
Georgia	GE		√	√	√		EP validation

23. OJ EPO 2024 A53 § II.1 footnote 3
24. According to OJ EPO 2015 A43 the EPC applies to all overseas territories of FR and also to overseas departments according to http://www.bgbl.de/xaver/bgbl/start.xav?startbk=Bundesanzeiger_BGBl&jumpTo=bgbl277s0792.pdf; so this is similar to the territories covered by PCT Notification No. 15; https://www.wipo.int/treaties/en/notifications/pct/treaty_pct_15.html.

Territory	Code	Relation	PCT	Paris	WTO	Region	Note
Germany	DE		√	√	√	EP	
Ghana	GH		√	√	√	AP	
Gibraltar	GI	GB	GB	GB			BOT, GB or EP-GB re-registration within 3 years
Greece	GR		√	√	√	EP	Including Athos. PCT-EP. Not PCT-GR.
Greenland	GL	DK	DK				DK nat. or PCT-DK. Not EP or PCT-EP.[25]
Grenada	GD	GB	√	√	√		CON. GB or EP-GB re-registration within 3 years
Guadeloupe	GP	FR	FR	FR			PCT-EP. OMR
Guam	GU	US	US	US			
Guatemala	GT		√	√	√		
Guernsey	GG	GB	GB	GB			Crown dependency, GB or EP-GB re-registration at any time
Guinea	GN		√	√	√	OA	PCT-OA. Not PCT-GN.
Guinea-Bissau	GW		√	√	√	OA	PCT-OA. Not PCT-GW.
Guyana	GY	GB		√	√		CON. GB or EP-GB re-registration within 3 years
Haiti	HT			√	√		
Heard Island and McDonald Islands	HM	AU					
Holy See, see Vatican City							
Honduras	HN		√	√	√		
Hong Kong	HK	CN	CN	CN	CN		Special Administration Region. Re-registration of PCT-CN, PCT-GB, PCT-EP.[26]

25. OJ EPO 2024 A53, § II.1 footnote 3
26. OJ EPO 2020 A61

Territory	Code	Relation	PCT	Paris	WTO	Region	Note
Howland Island	UM	US	US	US			
Hungary	HU		√	√	√	EP	
Iceland	IS		√	√	√	EP	
India	IN		√	√	√		
Indonesia	ID		√	√	√		No extension to East Timor since 2002
Iran, Islamic Republic of	IR		√	√			
Iraq	IQ		√	√			
Ireland	IE		√	√	√	EP	PCT-EP. Not PCT-IE.
Isle of Man	IM	GB	GB	GB		EP	Crown dependency. GB or EP-GB re-registration within 3 years. PCT-GB, PCT-EP.
Israel	IL		√	√	√		
Italy	IT		√	√	√	EP	PCT-EP. Possibility of PCT-IT for international filing date July 1, 2020 or later. IT includes Campione d'Italia and Livigno. PCT-EP. Mutual recognition of national patents with SM.[27]
Jamaica	JM		√	√	√		
Jarvis Island	UM	US	US	US			
Jersey	JE	GB		GB			Crown dependency. GB or EP-GB re-registration within 3 years
Jonston Atoll	UM	US	US	US			
Jordan	JO		√	√	√		
Kazakhstan	KZ		√	√	√	EA	
Kenya	KE		√	√	√	AP	
Kingman Reef	UM	US	US	US			

27. https://www.wipo.int/export/sites/www/patent_register_portal/en/docs/it.pdf

Territory	Code	Relation	PCT	Paris	WTO	Region	Note
Kiribati	KI	GB		√			CON. GB or EP-GB re-registration within 3 years
Korea, Democratic People's Republic of, (North)	KP		√	√			
Korea, Republic of (South)	KR		√	√	√		
Kuwait	KW		√	√	√	GCC	
Kyrgyzstan	KG		√	√	√	EA	
Lao People's Democratic Republic	LA		√	√	√		
Latvia	LV		√	√	√	EP	PCT-EP. Not PCT-LV.
Lebanon	LB			√			
Lesotho	LS		√	√	√	AP	
Liberia	LR		√	√	√	AP	
Libya	LY		√	√			
Liechtenstein	LI		√	√	√	EP	Unitary patent under the PCT. Unified territory of protection with CH[28]
Lithuania	LT		√	√	√	EP	PCT-EP. Not PCT-LT.
Luxembourg	LU		√	√	√	EP	
Macau	MO	CN		CN	CN		Special Administration Region. CN and EP re-registration.[29]
Macedonia, The Former Yugoslav Republic of, see North Macedonia							
Madagascar	MG		√	√	√		
Malawi	MW		√	√	√	AP	
Malaysia	MY		√	√	√		
Maldives	MV				√		CON

28. https://archive.epo.org/oj/issues/1980/11-12/1980-11-12-issue.pdf. AG-NP CH.01
29. https://www.economia.gov.mo/en_US/web/public/pg_ip_ap?slug=ps-1310, https://www.economia.gov.mo/public/docs/LR/legislation/en/DL97-99-e.pdf

Territory	Code	Relation	PCT	Paris	WTO	Region	Note
Mali	ML		√	√	√	OA	PCT-OA. Not PCT-ML.
Malta	MT		√	√	√	EP	PCT-EP. Not PCT-MT.
Marshall Islands	MH						US associated
Martinique	MQ	FR	FR	FR			PCT-EP. OMR
Mauritania	MR		√	√	√	OA	PCT-OA. Not PCT-MR.
Mauritius	MU		√	√	√		
Mayotte	YT	FR	FR	FR			PCT-EP. OMR
Mexico	MX		√	√	√		
Midway Islands	UM	US	US	US			
Mircronesia	FM						US associated
Moldova, Republic of	MD		√	√	√		EP validation. De facto not Transnistria[30]
Monaco	MC		√	√		EP	PCT-EP. Not PCT-MC
Mongolia	MN		√	√	√		
Montenegro	ME		√	√	√	EP	Not PCT-ME.
Montserrat	MS	GB					BOT, EP-GB re-registration within 3 years
Morocco	MA		√	√	√		EP validation in MA.
Mozambique	MZ		√	√	√	AP	CON
Myanmar	MM				√		
Namibia	NA		√	√	√	AP	
Nauru	NR	GB					CON. GB re-registration within 3 years
Navassa Island	UM	US	US	US			
Nepal	NP			√	√		
Netherlands	NL		√	√	√	EP	PCT-EP. Not PCT-NL

30. https://en.wikipedia.org/wiki/Political_status_of_Transnistria

Territory	Code	Relation	PCT	Paris	WTO	Region	Note
Netherlands Antilles	AN	NL					Existed until October 10, 2010, see Aruba; Bonaire, Sint Eustatius, Saba; Curaçao; Sint Maarten
New Caledonia	NC	FR	FR	FR			PCT-EP. OCT
New Zealand			√	√	√		See also CK, NU, TK
Nicaragua	NI		√	√	√		
Niger	NE		√	√	√	OA	PCT-OA. Not PCT-NE.
Nigeria	NG		√	√	√		
Niue	NU	NZ					NZ associated.[31] Extension of NZ patents granted until September 12, 2014[32]
Norfolk Island	NF	AU					
North Macedonia	MK		√	√	√	EP	
Northern Mariana Islands	MP	US	US	US			US associated
Norway	NO		√	√	√	EP	See also Bouvet Island; Svalbard and Jan Mayen
Norway	NO		√	√	√	EP	See also Bouvet Island; Svalbard and Jan Mayen
Oman	OM		√	√	√	GCC	
Pakistan	PK			√	√		
Palau	PW						US associated
Palmyra Island	UMS	US	US	US			
Panama	PA		√	√	√		
Papua New Guinea	PG		√	√	√		
Paraguay	PY			√	√		
Peru	PE		√	√	√		

31. https://en.wikipedia.org/wiki/Political_status_of_the_Cook_Islands_and_Niue
32. under the NZ Patent Act 1953 according to information from NZ IP-Office upon request in 2017, Niue Act 1966, http://www.paclii.org/journals/fJSPL/vol07no1/8.shtml

Territory	Code	Relation	PCT	Paris	WTO	Region	Note
Philippines	PH		√	√	√		
Pitcairn	PN	GB					BOT
Poland	PL		√	√	√	EP	
Portugal	PT		√	√	√	EP	Including Azores and Madeira
Puerto Rico	PR	US		US			US associated
Qatar	QA		√	√	√	GCC	
Réunion	RE	FR	FR	FR			PCT-EP. OMR
Romania	RO		√	√	√	EP	
Russian Federation	RU		√	√	√	EA	
Rwanda	RW		√	√	√	AP	CON
Saint Barthélemy	BL	FR	FR	FR			PCT-EP. OCT
Saint Helena, Ascension and Tristan Da Cunha	SH	GB					BOT. GB re-registration within 3 years. No info for EP-GB re-registration
Saint Kitts and Nevis	KN		√	√	√		
Saint Lucia	LC	GB	√	√	√		CON. No EP-GB re-registration but GB re-registration within 3 years
Saint Martin	MF	FR	FR	FR			PCT-EP. OMR
Saint Pierre and Miquelon	PM	FR	FR	FR			PCT-EP. OCT
Saint Vincent and The Grenadines	VC	GB	√	√	√		CON. No GB re-registration but EP-GB re-registration within 3 years
Samoa	WS		√	√	√		CON.
San Marino	SM		√	√		EP	PCT-EP. Not PCT-SM since January 1, 2020. Mutual recognition of national patents with IT.[33]
Sao Tome and Principe	ST		√	√		AP	
Saudi Arabia	SA		√	√	√	GCC	

33. https://www.wipo.int/export/sites/www/patent_register_portal/en/docs/sm.pdf

Territory	Code	Relation	PCT	Paris	WTO	Region	Note
Senegal	SN		√	√	√	OA	PCT-OA. Not PCT-SN.
Serbia	RS		√	√		EP	De facto no sovereignty over Kosovo[34]
Seychelles	SC	GB	√	√	√	AP	CON. No EP-GB re-registration but GB re-registration within 3 years
Sierra Leone	SL	GB	√	√	√	AP	CON. No EP-GB re-registration but GB re-registration within 3 years
Singapore	SG		√	√	√		
Sint Maarten	SX	NL	NL	NL			PCT-EP. Not PCT-NL. NL national[35]
Slovakia	SK		√	√	√	EP	
Slovenia	SI		√	√	√	EP	PCT-EP. Not PCT-SI
Solomon Islands	SB	GB			√		CON, GB or EP-GB re-registration within 3 years
Somalia	SO						
South Africa	ZA		√	√	√		
South Georgia and the South Sandwich Islands	GS	GB					BOT. Not GB or EP-GB.
Spain	ES		√	√	√	EP	Including Canary Islands, Ceuta and Melilla
Sri Lanka	LK		√	√	√		
Sudan	SD		√	√		AP	
Sudan, South	SS						
Suriname	SR			√	√		
Svalbard and Jan Mayen	SJ	NO	NO				PCT-EP[36]

34. https://en.wikipedia.org/wiki/Kosovo#Provisional_self-government
35. https://www.doingbusinessdutchcaribbean.com/st-maarten/intellectual-property-sxm/patents-sxm/
36. SJ: territory of NO: OJ EPO 2014 A33. https://www.epo.org/law-practice/legal-texts/html/natlaw/en/x/no.htm?sm = c

Territory	Code	Relation	PCT	Paris	WTO	Region	Note
Swaziland, see Eswatini							
Sweden	SE		√	√	√	EP	
Switzerland	CH	LI	√	√	√	EP	Unitary patent under the PCT. Unified territory of protection with LI[37]
Syrian Arab Republic	SY		√	√			
Taiwan	TW	CN			√		Also called Chinese Taipei or Separate Customs Territory of Taiwan, Penghu, Kinmen and Matsu. National application in TW possible[38]
Tajikistan	TJ		√	√	√	EA	
Tanzania, United Republic of	TZ		√	√	√	AP	CON. Separate jurisdiction Zanzibar[39]
Thailand	TH		√	√	√		
Togo	TG		√	√	√	OA	CON. PCT-OA. Not PCT-TG.
Tokelau	TK	NZ					NZ dependent.[40] Extension of NZ patents granted until September 12, 2014[41]
Tonga	TO			√	√		
Trinidad and Tobago	TT		√	√	√		
Tunisia	TN		√	√	√		EP validation
Türkiye	TR		√	√	√	EP	

37. https://archive.epo.org/oj/issues/1980/11-12/1980-11-12-issue.pdf. AG-NP CH.01 https://www.wipo.int/export/sites/www/pct/guide/en/gdvol2/annexes/ch.pdf
38. Independent state but regarded by China (and the United Nations) as one of its provinces. WIPO, being an agency of the United Nations, follows China in this matter. More information on TW: https://www.epo.org/searching-for-patents/helpful-resources/asian/chinese-taipei/faq.html#faq-548
39. https://www.gov.uk/government/publications/extension-of-uk-intellectual-property-rights-abroad/extension-of-uk-ip-right-abroad-countries-t-to-z
40. https://en.wikipedia.org/wiki/Tokelau
41. Under the NZ Patent Act 1953 according to information from NZ IP-Office upon request in 2017, http://www.paclii.org/journals/fJSPL/vol07no1/8.shtml

Territory	Code	Relation	PCT	Paris	WTO	Region	Note
Turkmenistan	TM		√	√		EA	
Turks and Caicos Islands	TC	GB					BOT, GB or EP-GB re-registration within five years
Tuvalu	TV	GB					CON, GB or EP-GB re-registration within 3 years
Uganda	UG		√	√	√	AP	CON
Ukraine	UA		√	√	√		
United Arab Emirates	AE		√	√	√	GCC	
United Kingdom[42]	GB		√	√	√	EP	EP: Great Britain, Northern Ireland, Isle of Man. See also BOT: AI, BM, FK, GG, GI, GS, IM, JE, KY, MS, PN, SH, TC, VG
United States of America[43]	US		√	√	√		
Uruguay	UY			√	√		Uruguay (UY) will become bound by the PCT on January 7, 2025 (Gazette October 17, 2024)
Uzbekistan	UZ		√	√			
Vanuatu	VU	GB			√		CON. GB and EP-GB re-registration within 3 years
Vatican City State	VA			√			
Venezuela	VE			√	√		

42. GB: EP-GB Territory: https://www.epo.org/law-practice/legal-texts/html/natlaw/en/x/uk.htm; EP-GB in BOT see OJ 2018, A97; Extension/re-registration: https://www.gov.uk/government/publications/extension-of-uk-intellectual-property-rights-abroad, status on January 1, 2021. GB: Commonwealth of Nations (CON): https://en.wikipedia.org/wiki/Member_states_of_the_Commonwealth_of_Nations#Current_members; http://www.commonwealthofnations.org/commonwealth/commonwealth-membership/withdrawals-and-suspension/; http://www.commonwealthofnations.org/commonwealth/commonwealth-membership/associated-and-overseas-territories/
43. US outlying areas are mentioned separately with their code according to: https://www.iso.org/obp/ui/#iso:code:3166:US https://en.wikipedia.org/wiki/United_States_Minor_Outlying_Islands; https://www.state.gov/dependencies-and-areas-of-special-sovereignty/; US associated: https://www.doi.gov/ocl/freely-associated-states

Territory	Code	Relation	PCT	Paris	WTO	Region	Note
Viet Nam	VN		√	√	√		
Virgin Islands, American, see American Virgin Islands							
Virgin Islands, British, see British Virgin Islands							
Wake Island	UM	US	US	US			
Wallis and Futuna	WF	FR	FR	FR			PCT-EP. OCT
Yemen	YE			√	√		
Zambia	ZM		√	√	√	AP	
Zanzibar		TZ, GB					Own patent law and registration.[44] GB re-registration[45]
Zimbabwe	ZW		√	√	√	AP	

44. https://www.wipo.int/edocs/mdocs/mdocs/en/wipo_ip_dar_19/wipo_ip_dar_19_t_7_r.pdf
45. https://www.gov.uk/government/publications/extension-of-uk-intellectual-property-rights-abroad/extension-of-uk-ip-right-abroad-countries-t-to-z#the-united-republic-of-tanzania

Annex 2
List of Contracting States with Time Limits for Entry into the National Phase[1]

The below table shows the time limits for entry into the national phase for each PCT Contracting State, both as designated and elected Office (see Introduction to Art. 22). 1

This list is based on the information on the WIPO website[2] (status on July 6, 2022, updated to August 2024). Details for each State are available in the AG-NP, National Chapter.[3] For a few States, information about the possibility of delayed entry or of remedying a loss of rights due to a delay has been added in the third column. Information about territories related to States is provided in the List of Territories. Uruguay (UY) will become bound by the PCT on January 7, 2025 (Gazette October 17, 2024). 2

Contracting State	Date on which State became bound	Time limit according to Art. 22 [39] (months)	Delayed entry/ remedy
A			
Albania[4] (AL)	4 October 1995	31/31	
Algeria (DZ)	8 March 2000	31/31	
Angola (AO)	27 December 2007	30/30	
Antigua and Barbuda (AG)	17 March 2000	30/30	
ARIPO[5] (AP)		31/31	

1. Originally published in Köllner, *PCT-Handbuch*, 17th edition, 2022, Wolters Kluwer Germany
2. https://www.wipo.int/pct/en/texts/time_limits.html and https://www.wipo.int/pct/en/pct_contracting_states.html
3. https://www.wipo.int/pct/en/guide/index.html
4. If designated/elected for a European patent, see https://www.wipo.int/pct/en/texts/time_limits.html under 'EP' as DO/EO for the applicable time limits.
5. This Office acts as DO/EO for the following State which does not act in the capacity of DO/EO: SZ

Contracting State	Date on which State became bound	Time limit according to Art. 22 [39] (months)	Delayed entry/ remedy
Armenia[6] (AM)	25 December 1991	31/31	
Australia (AU)	31 March 1980	31/31	
Austria[7] (AT)	23 April 1979	30/30	
Azerbaijan[8] (AZ)	25 December 1995	30/31	
B			
Bahrain (BH)	18 March 2007	30/30	
Barbados (BB)	12 March 1985	30/30	
Belarus[9] (BY)	25 December 1991	31/31	
Belgium (BE)	14 December 1981	only regional EPO	
Belize (BZ)	17 June 2000	30/30	extendable upon written request (AG-NP (BZ))
Benin (BJ)	26 February 1987	only regional OAPI	
Bosnia and Herzegovina (BA)	7 September 1996	34/34	
Botswana[10] (BW)	30 October 2003	31/31	
Brazil (BR)	9 April 1978	30/30	A translation of the claims and payment of fees is sufficient within the time limit. A translation of the description can be furnished later. (AG-NP (BR))
Brunei Darussalam (BN)	24 July 2012	30/30	
Bulgaria[11] (BG)	21 May 1984	31/31	
Burkina Faso (BF)	21 March 1989	only regional OAPI	

6. If designated/elected for a Eurasian patent, see EA as designated/elected Office (DO/EO) for the applicable time limits.
7. If designated/elected for a European patent, see EP as DO/EO for the applicable time limits.
8. If designated/elected for a Eurasian patent, see EA as designated/elected Office (DO/EO) for the applicable time limits.
9. If designated/elected for a Eurasian patent, see EA as designated/elected Office (DO/EO) for the applicable time limits.
10. If designated/elected for an ARIPO patent, see AP as DO/EO for the applicable time limits.
11. If designated/elected for a European patent, see EP as DO/EO for the applicable time limits.

Contracting State	Date on which State became bound	Time limit according to Art. 22 [39] (months)	Delayed entry/ remedy
C			
Cabo Verde (CV)	6 July 2022	30/30	
Cambodia (KH)	8 December 2016	30/30	
Cameroon (CM)	24 January 1978	only regional OAPI	
Canada (CA)	2 January 1990	30/30	both extendable up to 12 months from the time limit upon a request for reinstatement (AG-NP (CA))
Central African Republic (CF)	24 January 1978	only regional OAPI	
Chad (TD)	24 January 1978	only regional OAPI	
Chile (CL)	2 June 2009	30/30	
China (CN)	1 January 1994	30/30	both + 2 months on payment of a fee (AG-NP (CN))
Colombia (CO)	28 February 2001	31/31	
Comoros (KM)	3 April 2005	only regional OAPI	
Congo, Republic (CG)	24 January 1978	only regional OAPI	
Costa Rica (CR)	3 August 1999	31/31	
Cote d'Ivoire (CI)	30 April 1991	only regional OAPI	
Croatia (HR)	1 July 1998	31/31	
Cuba (CU)	16 July 1996	30/30	
Cyprus (CY)	1 April 1998	only regional EPO	
Czechia[12] (CZ)	1 January 1993	31/31	
D			
Denmark[13] (DK)	1 December 1978	31/31	
Djibouti (DJ)	23 September 2016	30/30	
Dominica[14] (DM)	7 August 1999	30/30	

12. If designated/elected for a European patent, see EP as DO/EO for the applicable time limits.
13. If designated/elected for a European patent, see EP as DO/EO for the applicable time limits.
14. In the absence of information from the Office concerned, the time limits shown are those which would normally apply under PCT Articles 22(1) and 39(1)(a). If the Office decides to apply longer time limits, that information will be published in the PCT Newsletter.

Contracting State	Date on which State became bound	Time limit according to Art. 22 [39] (months)	Delayed entry/ remedy
Dominican Republic (DO)	28 May 2007	30/30	
E			
EAPO (EA)		31/31	+ 2 months for translation on payment of a fee (AG-NP (EA))
Ecuador (EC)	7 May 2001	31/31	
Egypt (EG)	6 September 2003	30/30	
El Salvador (SV)	17 August 2006	30/30	
EPO[15] (EP)		31/31	see footnote
Equatorial Guinea (GQ)	17 July 2001	only regional OAPI	
Estonia[16] (EE)	24 August 1994	31/31	
Eswatini (SZ)	20 September 1994	only regional ARIPO	
F			
Finland[17] (FI)	1 October 1980	31/31	
France (FR)	25 February 1978	only regional EPO	
G			
Gabon (GA)	24 January 1978	only regional OAPI	
Gambia[18] (GM)	9 December 1997	30/31	
Georgia (GE)	25 December 1991	31/31	

15. Extension period: communications under R. 112, 126°(2), 127°(2) EPC + 2 months for further processing. Fee payment for designation, extension, validation or European examination within 31 months after priority date or within 6 months after publication of the ISR, whichever is later (PCT Gazette 07.02.2019, AG-NP EP.25). Reinstatement of rights in respect of acts under Art. 22 according to R. 49.6 if period for further processing has expired. This Office acts as DO/EO for the following States which do not act in the capacity of DO/EO: BE, CY, FR, GR, IE, LT, LV, MC, MT, NL, SI, SM.
16. If designated/elected for a European patent, see EP as DO/EO for the applicable time limits.
17. If designated/elected for a European patent, see EP as DO/EO for the applicable time limits.
18. If designated/elected for an ARIPO patent, see AP as DO/EO for the applicable time limits.

Contracting State	Date on which State became bound	Time limit according to Art. 22 [39] (months)	Delayed entry/ remedy
Germany[19] (DE)	24 January 1978	31/31 until 30.04.2022: 30/30	Reinstatement acc. to § 123 PatG (AG-NP DE.13) + 2 months to split off of a utility model acc. to § 5 GbrMG
Ghana[20] (GH)	26 February 1997	30/30	
Greece (GR)	9 October 1990	only regional EPO	
Grenada[21] (GD)	22 September 1998	30/30	
Guatemala (GT)	14 October 2006	30/30	
Guinea (GN)	27 May 1991	only regional OAPI	
Guinea-Bissau (GW)	12 December 1997	only regional OAPI	
H			
Honduras (HN)	20 June 2006	30/30	
Hungary[22] (HU)	27 June 1980	31/31	
I			
Iceland[23] (IS)	23 March 1995	31/31	
India (IN)	7 December 1998	31/31	
Indonesia (ID)	5 September 1997	31/31	both can be extended on payment of a fee (AG-NP (ID))
Iran, Islamic Republic of (IR)	4 October 2013	30/30	
Iraq (IQ)	30 April 2022	31/31	
Ireland (IE)	1 August 1992	only regional EPO	
Israel (IL)	1 June 1996	30/30	

19. If designated/elected for a European patent, see EP as DO/EO for the applicable time limits.
20. If designated/elected for an ARIPO patent, see AP as DO/EO for the applicable time limits.
21. In the absence of information from the Office concerned, the time limits shown are those which would normally apply under PCT Articles 22(1) and 39(1)(a). If the Office decides to apply longer time limits, that information will be published in the PCT Newsletter.
22. If designated/elected for a European patent, see EP as DO/EO for the applicable time limits
23. If designated/elected for a European patent, see EP as DO/EO for the applicable time limits.

Contracting State	Date on which State became bound	Time limit according to Art. 22 [39] (months)	Delayed entry/ remedy
Italy[24] (IT)	28 March 1985	30/30	
J			
Jamaica (JM)	10 February 2022	30/30	
Japan (JP)	1 October 1978	30/30	+ 2 months for the translation on payment of a fee (AG-NP (JP))
Jordan (JO)	9 June 2017	30/30	
K			
Kazakhstan[25] (KZ)	25 December 1991	31/31	
Kenya[26] (KE)	8 June 1994	30/30	
Korea, Democratic People's Republic of (KP)	8 July 1980	30/30	
Korea, Republic of (KR)	10 August 1984	31/31	+ 1 month for the translation on request acc. to Art. 202(1) of the Korean Patent Act. Request must be filed within 31 months[27].
Kuwait (KW)	9 September 2016	30/30	
Kyrgyzstan[28] (KG)	25 December 1991	31/31	
L			
Lao People's Democratic Republic (LA)	14 June 2006	30/30 applicable since March 30, 2023, Gazette 2024 p. 138	
Latvia (LV)	7 September 1993	only regional EPO	
Lesotho[29] (LS)	21 October 1995	30/31	
Liberia (LR)	27 August 1994	30/31	

24. For international applications filed on or after 01.07.2020. If designated/elected for a European patent, see EP as DO/EO for the applicable time limits.
25. If designated/elected for a Eurasian patent, see EA as designated/elected Office (DO/EO) for the applicable time limits.
26. If designated/elected for an ARIPO patent, see AP as DO/EO for the applicable time limits.
27. https://www.kimchang.com/newsletter/20140822/ip/en/img/IP_Newsletter_Summer_Fall_2014.pdf
28. If designated/elected for a Eurasian patent, see EA as designated/elected Office (DO/EO) for the applicable time limits.
29. If designated/elected for an ARIPO patent, see AP as DO/EO for the applicable time limits.

Contracting State	Date on which State became bound	Time limit according to Art. 22 [39] (months)	Delayed entry/ remedy
Libya[30] (LY)	15 September 2005	30/30	
Liechtenstein (LI)	19 March 1980	see Switzerland[31]	
Lithuania (LT)	5 July 1994	only regional EPO	
Luxembourg[32] (LU)	30 April 1978	20/30	
M			
Madagascar (MG)	24 January 1978	30/30	
Malawi[33] (MW)	24 January 1978	30/30	
Malaysia (MY)	16 August 2006	30/30	
Mali (ML)	19 October 1984	only regional OAPI	
Malta (MT)	1 March 2007	only regional EPO	
Mauritania (MR)	13 April 1983	only regional OAPI	
Mauritius[34] (MU)	15 March 2023	30/30	
Mexico (MX)	1 January 1995	30/30	+ 2 months for the translation (AG-NP (MX))
Moldova, Republic of (MD)	25 December 1991	31/31	
Monaco (MC)	22 June 1979	only regional EPO	
Mongolia (MN)	27 May 1991	31/31	
Montenegro (ME)	3 June 2006	only regional EPO	
Morocco (MA)	8 October 1999	31/31	
Mozambique[35] (MZ)	18 May 2000	31/31	
N			
Namibia[36] (NA)	1 January 2004	31/31	

30. In the absence of information from the Office concerned, the time limits shown are those which would normally apply under PCT Articles 22(1) and 39(1)(a). If the Office decides to apply longer time limits, that information will be published in the PCT Newsletter.
31. Common provision for (CH) and (LI), OJ 1980, 407
32. This Office has notified the International Bureau of the non-applicability of the 30-month time limit under PCT Article 22(1), as modified with effect from 01.04.2002 – it does not yet apply the 30-month time limit for entering the national phase LU as designated Office.
33. If designated/elected for an ARIPO patent, see AP as DO/EO for the applicable time limits.
34. In the absence of information from the Office concerned, the time limits shown are those which would normally apply under PCT Articles 22(1) and 39(1)(a). If the Office decides to apply longer time limits, that information will be published in the PCT Newsletter.
35. If designated/elected for an ARIPO patent, see AP as DO/EO for the applicable time limits.
36. If designated/elected for an ARIPO patent, see AP as DO/EO for the applicable time limits.

Contracting State	Date on which State became bound	Time limit according to Art. 22 [39] (months)	Delayed entry/ remedy
Netherlands (NL)	10 July 1979	only regional EPO	
New Zealand (NZ)	1 December 1992	31/31	
Nicaragua (NI)	6 March 2003	30/30	
Niger (NE)	21 March 1993	only regional OAPI	
Nigeria (NG)	8 May 2005	30/30	
North Macedonia[37] (MK)	10 August 1995	31/31	
Norway[38] (NO)	1 January 1980	31/31	
O			
OAPI[39] (OA)		30/30	
Oman (OM)	26 October 2001	30/30	
P			
Panama (PA)	7 September 2012	30/30	
Papua New Guinea (PG)	14 June 2003	31/31	
Peru (PE)	6 June 2009	30/30	
Philippines (PH)	17 August 2001	30/30	31/31 on payment of a fee (AG-NP (PH))
Poland (PL)	25 December 1990	30/30	
Portugal[40] (PT)	24 November 1992	30/30	
Q			
Qatar (QA)	3 August 2011	30/30	
R			
Romania[41] (RO)	23 July 1979	30/30	
Russian Federation[42] (RU)	29 March 1978	31/31	translation and fees can be furnished later (AG-NP (RU))

37. If designated/elected for a European patent, see EP as DO/EO for the applicable time limits.
38. If designated/elected for a European patent, see EP as DO/EO for the applicable time limits.
39. This Office acts as DO/EO for the following States which do not act in the capacity of DO/EO: BF, BJ, CF, CG, CI, CM, GA, GN, GQ, GW, KM, ML, MR, NE, SN, TD, TG.
40. If designated/elected for a European patent, see EP as DO/EO for the applicable time limits
41. If designated/elected for a European patent, see EP as DO/EO for the applicable time limits.
42. If designated/elected for a Eurasian patent, see EA as designated/elected Office (DO/EO) for the applicable time limits.

Contracting State	Date on which State became bound	Time limit according to Art. 22 [39] (months)	Delayed entry/ remedy
Rwanda[43] (RW)	31 August 2011	30/30	
S			
Saint Kitts and Nevis (KN)	27 October 2005	30/30	
Saint Lucia[44] (LC)	30 August 1996	30/30	
Saint Vincent and the Grenadines (VC)	6 August 2002	31/31	
Samoa (WS)	2 January 2020	31/31	
San Marino (SM)	14 December 2004	only regional EPO since 01.01.2020	
Sao Tome and Principe[45] (ST)	3 July 2008	30/30	
Saudi Arabia (SA)	3 August 2013	30/30	
Senegal (SN)	24 January 1978	only regional OAPI	
Sweden[46] (SE)	17 May 1978	31/31	
Serbia[47] (RS)	1 February 1997	30/30	+ 30 days for both on payment of a fee (AG-NP (RS))
Seychelles (SC)	7 November 2002	31/31	
Sierra Leone[48] (SL)	17 June 1997	31/31	
Singapore (SG)	23 February 1995	30/30	can be extended for up to 18 months on payment of a fee (AG-NP (SG))

43. In the absence of information from the Office concerned, the time limits shown are those which would normally apply under PCT Articles 22(1) and 39(1)(a). If the Office decides to apply longer time limits, that information will be published in the PCT Newsletter. If designated/elected for an ARIPO patent, see AP as DO/EO for the applicable time limits.
44. In the absence of information from the Office concerned, the time limits shown are those which would normally apply under PCT Articles 22(1) and 39(1)(a). If the Office decides to apply longer time limits, that information will be published in the PCT Newsletter.
45. In the absence of information from the Office concerned, the time limits shown are those which would normally apply under PCT Articles 22(1) and 39(1)(a). If the Office decides to apply longer time limits, that information will be published in the PCT Newsletter. If designated/elected for an ARIPO patent, see AP as DO/EO for the applicable time limits.
46. If designated/elected for a European patent, see EP as DO/EO for the applicable time limits.
47. If designated/elected for a European patent, see EP as DO/EO for the applicable time limits.
48. If designated/elected for an ARIPO patent, see AP as DO/EO for the applicable time limits.

Contracting State	Date on which State became bound	Time limit according to Art. 22 [39] (months)	Delayed entry/ remedy
Slovakia[49] (SK)	1 January 1993	31/31	
Slovenia (SI)	1 March 1994	only regional EPO	
South Africa (ZA)	16 March 1999	31/31	
Spain[50] (ES)	16 November 1989	30/30	
Sri Lanka (LK)	26 February 1982	30/30	
Sudan[51] (SD)	16 April 1984	30/30	
Sweden[52] (SE)	17 May 1978	31/31	
Switzerland[53] (CH)	24 January 1978	30/30	
Syrian Arab Republic (SY)	26 June 2003	31/31	
T			
Tajikistan[54] (TJ)	25 December 1991	30/31	
Tanzania, United Republic of[55] (TZ)	14 September 1999	21/31	
Thailand (TH)	24 December 2009	30/30	
Togo (TG)	24 January 1978	only regional OAPI	
Trinidad and Tobago (TT)	10 March 1994	30/31	
Tunisia (TN)	10 December 2001	30/30	
Türkiye[56] (TR)	1 January 1996	30/30	33/33 on payment of a fee (AG-NP (TR))
Turkmenistan[57] (TM)	25 December 1991	30/31	
U			

49. If designated/elected for a European patent, see EP as DO/EO for the applicable time limits
50. If designated/elected for a European patent, see EP as DO/EO for the applicable time limits
51. If designated/elected for an ARIPO patent, see AP as DO/EO for the applicable time limits.
52. If designated/elected for a European patent, see EP as DO/EO for the applicable time limits.
53. This Office acts as DO/EO for the following State which does not act in the capacity of DO/EO: LI. If designated/elected for a European patent, see EP as DO/EO for the applicable time limits.
54. If designated/elected for a Eurasian patent, see EA as designated/elected Office (DO/EO) for the applicable time limits.
55. If designated/elected for an ARIPO patent, see AP as DO/EO for the applicable time limits.
56. If designated/elected for a European patent, see EP as DO/EO for the applicable time limits.
57. If designated/elected for a Eurasian patent, see EA as DO/EO for the applicable time limits.

Contracting State	Date on which State became bound	Time limit according to Art. 22 [39] (months)	Delayed entry/ remedy
Uganda[58] (UG)	9 February 1995	30/31	
Ukraine (UA)	25 December 1991	31/31	
United Arab Emirates (AE)	10 March 1999	30/30	
United Kingdom[59] (GB)	24 January 1978	31/31	+ 2 months on request (AG-NP GB.17)
United States of America[60] (US)	24 January 1978	30/30	see footnote
Uzbekistan (UZ)	25 December 1991	31/31	
V			
Viet Nam (VN)	10 March 1993	31/31	
Z			
Zambia[61] (ZM)	15 November 2001	30/30	
Zimbabwe[62] (ZW)	11 June 1997	30/31	

58. If designated/elected for an ARIPO patent, see AP as DO/EO for the applicable time limits.
59. Grace period of two months upon request (AG-NP GB.17). If designated/elected for a European patent, see EP as DO/EO for the applicable time limits.
60. 1. Extension of time limit: Invitation to submit the translation of the international application against payment of fees within two months from the invitation or 32 months from the priority date, whichever is later (AG-NP US.12). Declaration of inventorship, search and examination fees can also be submitted subsequently (AG-NP US.15, US.16, US.26). However, the basic national fee must be paid within the period of 30 months (37 CFR 1,495 c) – e)AG-NP US.14). 2. Remedy possibilities by a 'petition to revive an abandoned application' according to 37 CFR § 1.137 in connection with MPEP § 711.03 (c)(C): 'Unintentional Delay' (AG-NP US.42).
61. If designated/elected for an ARIPO patent, see AP as DO/EO for the applicable time limits.
62. If designated/elected for an ARIPO patent, see AP as DO/EO for the applicable time limits.

Annex 3
Access to Files

Overview of the provisions for access by third parties to files for various documents 1
arranged by the time they become accessible.

Type of information and date of availability	Legal basis of availability and details of access
From the date of filing of the international application:	
Office of filing of the international application, applicant, date of filing, file number, designation of the invention	Art. 30(2)(b), published by the national Office, as defined in Art. 2. This is an optional provision which is hardly ever implemented by Offices.
From international publication by IB under Art. 21, i.e. 18 months after the priority date:	
All documents, unless related to documents concerning the international preliminary examination and except for sensitive personal information.	Inspection of files at the IB. Art. 38; R. 94.1(b), (c) exceptions (d)–(g), the documents are also accessible under PATENTSCOPE (AG-IP 9.021). All International Authorities and Offices have comparable rules.
Written notification R. 43*bis*.1 (WO-ISA), translation R. 44*bis*.3, comment on translation R. 44*bis*.4	Inspection possible for international application with a filing date after 01.07.2014,[1] 2014 p. 2. R. 44*ter* and reference in the AG-IP 9.026 have been deleted. For ISA, see R. 94.1*ter*.
Informal statement on the decision R. 43*bis*.1	AG-IP 7.030 ISA: R. 94.1*ter*. See note in Form PCT/ISA/220.

1. http://www.wipo.int/pct/de/texts/ppt/rule_changes_archive.html

Type of information and date of availability	Legal basis of availability and details of access
EPO as ISA preliminary opinion on patentability as an annex to the result of the partial search in case of lack of unity	Online file inspection at the EPO as ISA according to OJ EPO 2017 A20 since 01.04.2017, R. 94.1*ter*
Objections of third parties to the IB on the prior art with the exception of the documents on the prior art, which are made available to the corresponding Offices	AIs 803, 801(b) via PATENTSCOPE at the IB
PCT Direct letter from the applicant to the EPO as RO/ISA with arguments on patentability claiming priority of an earlier application searched by the EPO	At the IB via PATENTSCOPE based on EPO Communication OJ EPO 2017 p. A21
Sequence listing furnished under R. 13*ter*	AIs 513(e) at the IB viaPATENTSCOPE https://www.wipo.int/standards/en/sequence/faq.html)
Where can the international application be inspected?	Art. 30(3) at the RO Art. 30(2)(a)(i) at the national Office Art. 30(1)(a) at IB or ISA
Content of publication of international application	Art. 21(1), R. 48, AIs 407 Publication by IB (see introduction to Art. 21) Publication takes place in electronic form (AG-IP 9.015) and is available at PATENTSCOPE. Sensitive data contained in the international application can be omitted from publication under R. 48.2(l).
Title page, description, claims, drawings	R. 48.2(a)(i), (ii), (iii), (iv), at PATENTSCOPE (AG-IP 9.016)
Erroneously filed elements or part if incorporated by reference (in contrast to documents that were furnished)	R. 20.5*bis*(c), (d); AIs 309(b)(iv); AG-IP 6.029A; PCT Newsletter 7–8/2020, p. 16
Search report Declaration under Art. 17(2) a) as alternative to ISR	R. 48.2(a)(v), (c), (g) at IB via PATENTSCOPE. If the search report is not available at the time of international publication of the international application, it is published separately. (AG-IP 7.028)

Type of information and date of availability	Legal basis of availability and details of access
Information sheet preceding the search report on details of the search	At IB via PATENTSCOPE (OJ EPO 2017 A106)
Amendment under Art. 19 and declaration thereto	At IB via PATENTSCOPE, R. 48.2(a)(vi), (f), (h)
Request for correction of obvious mistake in international application or other document under R. 91 and authorised by the elected Office, ISA or IB, not IPEA	At IB via PATENTSCOPE provided that the request is received before the completion of technical preparation (Art. 21) under R. 48.2(a)(vii), thereafter under R. 48.2(i)
Rejected request for correction, justification, comment according to R. 91.3(d)	R. 48.2(a)(vii), published at the IB via PATENTSCOPE if received before completion of technical preparations for international publication; thereafter according to R. 48.2(k)
Information on biol. material R. 13*bis*	At the IB via PATENTSCOPE, Rule48.2(a)(viii)
Corrected/added priority claim Rule26*bis*	At the IB via PATENTSCOPE, Rule48.2(a)(ix)
Information concerning restoration of priority right Rule26*bis*.3	At the IB via PATENTSCOPE, Rule48.2(a)(xi)
Inventor information according to R. 4.17 and correction according to Rule26*ter*	At the IB via PATENTSCOPE, Rule48.2(a)(x)
Notification of fictitious withdrawal of international application under R. 29.1(ii) Withdrawal of designations R. 90*bis*.2 or of priority claims R. 90*bis*.3 after completion of technical preparations of publication	At the IB via PATENTSCOPE R. 48.6(a) Publication if received after international publication, otherwise R. 29.1(v) R. 48.6(c) Publication if received after completion of technical preparations, otherwise R. 90*bis*.2(e), 90*bis*.3(e)
Priority document	IB provides copies to third parties on request according to R. 17.2(b), (c); R. 94.1

Type of information and date of availability	Legal basis of availability and details of access
Supplementary international search report R. 45*bis*.7	Art. 20(3), R. 44.3 analogous to R. 45*bis*.7(c), sent by SISA to DO upon request, no publication (Euro-PCT Guide 5.9.005), but file inspection at the IB under R. 94.1(b) via PATENTSCOPE (AG-IP 8.053), at SISA R. 94.1*ter*(d) as soon as it is available

From receipt of international application according to Art. 20 or 22 (transmission to DO):

Inspection of international application	Art. 30(2)(a)(ii), (iii) at the national designated Office (Art. 2); at DO R. 94.2*bis*; for example, GL Exam EPO E-IX, 2.10

As soon as demand for examination has been filed, but not before international publication:

Information on filing of the demand for examination	Publication by IB under R. 61.4, AIs 431

As soon as IPRP II is available (approximately 28 months from priority date):

Inspection of all documents relating to Chapter II (there may be more documents available at national Offices than at the IB, which are already available for inspection under PCT rules at that time).	Elected Office acc. to national law: Art. 38(1), R. 94.3 PCT/GL/ISPE/12 No. 3.26, Art. 128(4) EPC; GL Exam EPO E-IX, 2.10; Euro-PCT Guide 4.2.048 (IB on behalf of EPO) 4.2.049 (EPO as EO); AG-IP 10.003, 10.080, 10.081, 11.074.

Without demand for examination and after expiry of 30 months from priority date:

IPRP I (is only prepared by IB after 30 months and its contents correspond to that of the WO/ISA) R. 44*bis*.1, translation R. 44*bis*.3, statement on translation R. 44*bis*.4	Inspection at IB acc. to R. 94.1 via PATENTSCOPE, AG-IP 7.031; in the WO/ISA with the same content at ISA: R. 94.1*ter*

Type of information and date of availability	Legal basis of availability and details of access
After expiry of 30 months from the priority date and submission of the demand for examination (irrespective of the initiation of the national/regional phase):	
IPRP II, R. 70	Publication by IB on behalf of an EO Art. 38(1) last sentence, R. 94.1(c) via PATENTSCOPE. At the elected Office according to Art. 38(1) last sentence, R. 94.3 (AG-IP 10.080, 11.074). IB transmits the report and annexes according to Art. 36(1), 36(3)(a), R. 71.1, 73.2, R. 93*bis* to the elected Office upon request
Other documents relating to IPE	Publication by IB acc. to Art. 38(1) last sentence, R. 94.1(c), AG-IP 9.027, PCT/GL/ISPE/12 No.3.27, R. 71.1(b), AIs 602*bis* At the elected Office under Art. 38(1) last sentence, R. 94.3

From receipt of international application according to Art. 39 (transmission to elected Office):

The complete file except for those parts previously excluded under international law	At the elected Office under national law; R. 94.3

Entry into the national phase:

Data concerning the national phase entry	At IB (forwarded by designated and elected Office acc. to R. 95, R. 86.1(iv)))) via PATENTSCOPE and in the file of the EO

Index

The following Index is based on the PCT Legal Text Index of WIPO (https://www.wipo.int/export/sites/www/pct/en/docs/texts/legal-index.pdf, applicable to legal texts in force as of July 1, 2022), but has been complemented and amended where deemed necessary. For Acronyms/Terms used in the Index and their meaning see the part "Notations" in this book.

www.ingramcontent.com/pod-product-compliance
Lightning Source LLC
LaVergne TN
LVHW020956300926
849160LV00007B/165
* 9 7 8 9 4 0 3 5 0 3 8 8 2 *